Physics Galaxy

22 Years'

NEET
Chapterwise & Topicwise Solutions
(2001-2022)

Physics

Ashish Arora

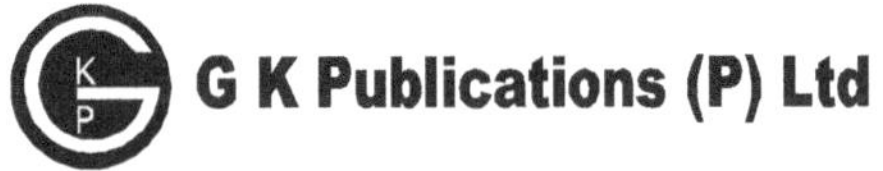

G K Publications (P) Ltd

First Edition : July, 2021

Revised Edition : November, 2022

Title   : Physics Galaxy : NEET Physics (UG) - 22 years'
                 Chapter-wise & Topic-Wise Solutions (2001-2022)

Language   : English

Author's Name : Ashish Arora

Copyright ©   : 2022 Ashish Arora

Typeset & Published by :

Career Launcher Infrastructure (P) Ltd.

A-45, Mohan Cooperative Industrial Area, Near Mohan Estate Metro Station, New Delhi - 110044

Marketed by :

G.K. Publications (P) Ltd.

Plot No. 9A, Sector-27A, Mathura Road, Faridabad, Haryana-121003

ISBN   : 978-93-5681-076-1

Printer's Details : Made in India, New Delhi.

For product information :

Visit *www.gkpublications.com* or email to *gkp@gkpublications.com*

Dedicated

to

My Parents, Son, Daughter

and

My beloved wife

In his teaching career since 1992 Ashish Arora personally mentored more than 10000 IITians and students who reached global heights in various career and profession chosen. It is his helping attitude toward students with which all his students remember him in life for his contribution in their success and keep connections with him live. Below is the list of some of the successful students in International Olympiad personally mentored by him.

NAVNEET LOIWAL	International GOLD Medal in IPhO-2000 at LONDON, Also secured AIR-4 in IIT JEE 2000
	PROUD FOR INDIA : Navneet Loiwal was the first Indian Student who won first International GOLD Medal for our country in International Physics Olympiad.
DUNGRA RAM CHOUDHARY	AIR-1 in IIT JEE 2002
HARSHIT CHOPRA	National Gold Medal in INPhO-2002 and got AIR-2 in IIT JEE-2002
KUNTAL LOYA	A Girl Student got position AIR-8 in IIT JEE 2002
LUV KUMAR	National Gold Medal in INPhO-2003 and got AIR-3 in IIT JEE-2003
RAJHANS SAMDANI	National Gold Medal in INPhO-2003 and got AIR-5 in IIT JEE-2003
SHANTANU BHARDWAJ	International SILVER Medal in IPhO-2002 at INDONESIA
SHALEEN HARLALKA	International GOLD Medal in IPhO-2003 at CHINA and got AIR-46 in IIT JEE-2003
TARUN GUPTA	National GOLD Medal in INPhO-2005
APEKSHA KHANDELWAL	National GOLD Medal in INPhO-2005
ABHINAV SINHA	Hon'ble Mension Award in APhO-2006 at KAZAKHSTAN
RAMAN SHARMA	International GOLD Medal in IPhO-2007 at IRAN and got AIR-20 in IIT JEE-2007
PRATYUSH PANDEY	International SILVER Medal in IPhO-2007 at IRAN and got AIR-85 in IIT JEE-2007
GARVIT JUNIWAL	International GOLD Medal in IPhO-2008 at VIETNAM and got AIR-10 in IIT JEE-2008
ANKIT PARASHAR	National GOLD Medal in INPhO-2008
HEMANT NOVAL	National GOLD Medal in INPhO-2008 and got AIR-25 in IIT JEE-2008
ABHISHEK MITRUKA	National GOLD Medal in INPhO-2009
SARTHAK KALANI	National GOLD Medal in INPhO-2009
ASTHA AGARWAL	International SILVER Medal in IJSO-2009 at AZERBAIJAN
RAHUL GURNANI	International SILVER Medal in IJSO-2009 at AZERBAIJAN
AYUSH SINGHAL	International SILVER Medal in IJSO-2009 at AZERBAIJAN
MEHUL KUMAR	International SILVER Medal in IPhO-2010 at CROATIA and got AIR-19 in IIT JEE-2010
ABHIROOP BHATNAGAR	National GOLD Medal in INPhO-2010
AYUSH SHARMA	International Double GOLD Medal in IJSO-2010 at NIGERIA
AASTHA AGRAWAL	Hon'ble Mension Award in APhO-2011 at ISRAEL and got AIR-93 in IIT JEE 2011
ABHISHEK BANSAL	National GOLD Medal in INPhO-2011
SAMYAK DAGA	National GOLD Medal in INPhO-2011
SHREY GOYAL	National GOLD Medal in INPhO-2012 and secured AIR-24 in IIT JEE 2012
RAHUL GURNANI	National GOLD Medal in INPhO-2012
JASPREET SINGH JHEETA	National GOLD Medal in INPhO-2012
DIVYANSHU MUND	National GOLD Medal in INPhO-2012
SHESHANSH AGARWAL	International SILVER Medal in IAO-2012 at KOREA
SWATI GUPTA	International SILVER Medal in IJSO-2012 at IRAN
PRATYUSH RAJPUT	International SILVER Medal in IJSO-2012 at IRAN
SHESHANSH AGARWAL	International BRONZE Medal in IOAA-2013 at GREECE
SHESHANSH AGARWAL	International GOLD Medal in IOAA-2014 at ROMANIA
SHESHANSH AGARWAL	International SILVER Medal in IPhO-2015 at INDIA and secured AIR-58 in JEE(Advanced)-2015
VIDUSHI VARSHNEY	International SILVER Medal in IJSO-2015 at SOUTH KOREA
AMAN BANSAL	AIR-1 in JEE Advanced 2016
KUNAL GOYAL	AIR-3 in JEE Advanced 2016
GOURAV DIDWANIA	AIR-9 in JEE Advanced 2016
DIVYANSH GARG	International SILVER Medal in IPhO-2016 at SWITZERLAND
NALIN KHANDELWAL	AIR-1 in NEET 2019
MRIDUL AGARWAL	AIR-1 in JEE Advanced 2021

ABOUT THE AUTHOR

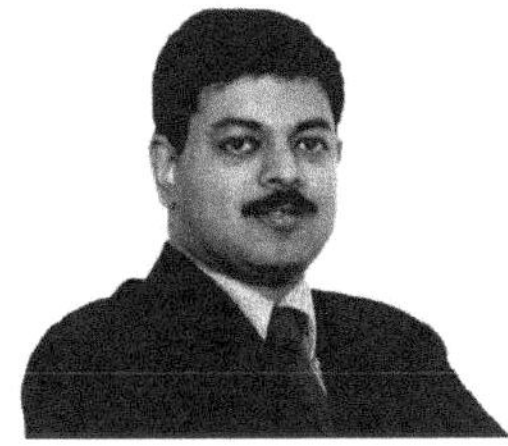

The complexities of Physics have given nightmares to many, but the homegrown genius of Jaipur-Ashish Arora has helped several students to live their dreams by decoding it.

Newton Law of Gravitation and Faraday's Magnetic force of attraction apply perfectly well with this unassuming genius. A Pied Piper of students, his webportal https://www.physicsgalaxy.com, The world's largest encyclopedia of video lectures on high school Physics possesses strong gravitational pull and magnetic attraction for students who want to make it big in life.

Ashish Arora, gifted with rare ability to train masterminds, has mentored over 10,000 IITians in his past 24 years of teaching sojourn including lots of students made it to Top 100 in IIT-JEE/JEE(Advance) including AIR-1 and many in Top-10. Apart from that, he has also groomed hundreds of students for cracking International Physics Olympiad. No wonder his student Navneet Loiwal brought laurel to the country by becoming the first Indian to win a Gold medal at the 2000 - International Physics Olympiad in London (UK).

His special ability to simplify the toughest of the Physics theorems and applications rates him as one among the best Physics teachers in the world. With this, Arora simply defies the logic that perfection comes with age. Even at 18 when he started teaching Physics while pursuing engineering, he was as engaging as he is now. Experience, besides graying his hair, has just widened his horizon.

Now after encountering all tribes of students - some brilliant and some not-so-intelligent - this celebrated teacher has embarked upon a noble mission to make the entire galaxy of Physics inform of his webportal PHYSICSGALAXY.COM to serve and help global students in the subject. Today students from 183 countries are connected with this webportal. On any topic of physics students can post their queries in comment section in Physics Galaxy Youtube channel on which many Physics experts with Ashish Arora reply to several queries posted online by students.

Dedicated to global students of middle and high school level, his website *www.physicsgalaxy.com* also has teaching sessions dubbed in American accent and subtitles in 87 languages. For students in India preparing for JEE & NEET, his online courses will be available soon on PHYSICSGALAXY.COM.

In 2011 he started authoring Physics Galaxy Youtube Channel which has now become World's Largest Youtube Channel for online physics lectures on high school physics and preparation of JEE & NEET. Daily about 4.0 lakh+ video lectures are being watched on the channel by students preparing for JEE, NEET & High school Physics.

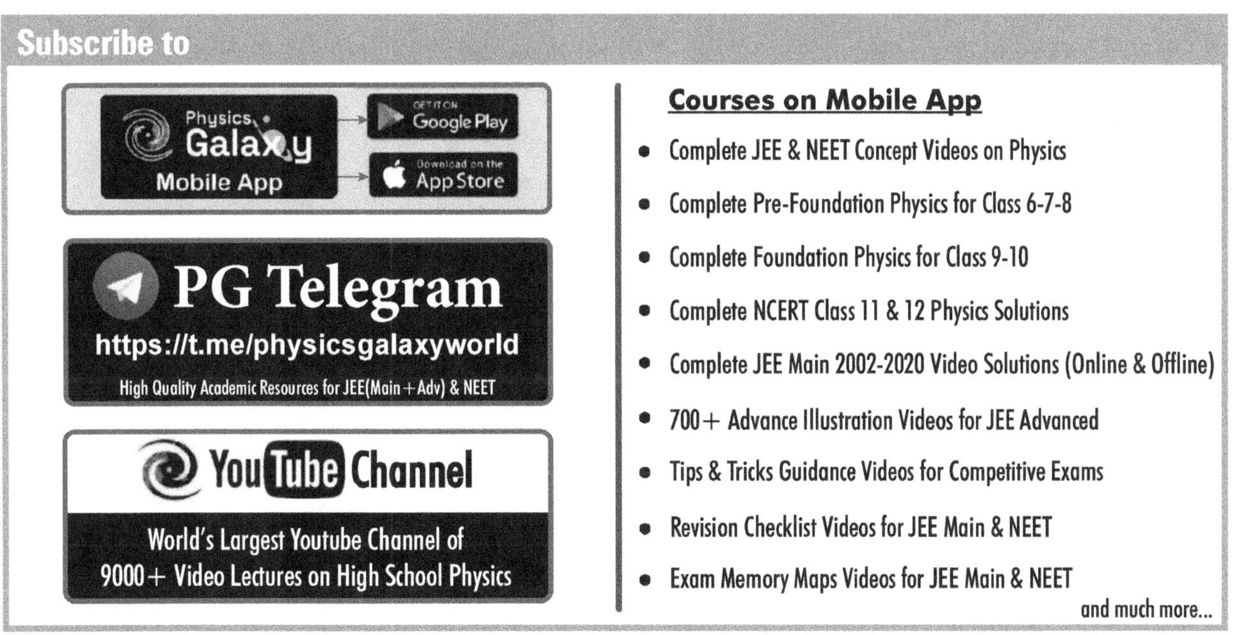

FOREWORD

I am extremely happy to share my views about this book written by Mr. Ashish Arora. He has contributed immensely to the teaching-learning of Physics though many innovative ways. His approach has always been student centric and this contribution is yet another example of the same.

As the title states "Physics Galaxy NEET Solutions" the book provides valuable information and covers the necessary components by offering solution to all questions asked in old NEET/AIPMT (2001-2022) with detailed explanations. All questions are categorized into check topics based on weightage of questions asked in the past 22 years. In every topic for quick revision of concepts one-shot revision videos are linked which students can watch by scanning the QR Code given at the start of book. All solutions of the questions are based on the conceptual analysis covered in the popular Physics Galaxy book series (5 volumes) so that aspirants following the book series will be able to relate and recall all the explanations already done.

I am sure the book promotes the concept of deeper learning in the domain of Physics. My best wishes to the many aspirants who will certainly find this book a very valuable tool to enhance thorough understanding of the subject.

November, 2022

Prof. Sandeep Sancheti
Ph. D. (U.K.), B.Tech. FIETE, MIEEE
VC, SRMIST, Chennai &
President, AIU, New Delhi

PREFACE

For a science student, preparing for JEE Main or NEET, Physics is the most important subject, unlike to other subjects it requires logical reasoning and high imagination of brain. Without improving the level of physics it is very difficult to achieve a goal in the present age of competitions. To score better, one does not require hard working at least in physics. It just requires a simple understanding and approach to think a physical situation. Actually physics is the surrounding of our everyday life. If you wish to make the concepts of physics strong, you should try to understand core concepts of physics in practical approach rather than theoretical.

This book *"PHYSICS GALAXY NEET Paper Solutions"* of past 22 years is designed in a totally different and friendly approach to develop the physics concepts psychologically. The book covers detailed solutions to all the questions previously asked in NEET/AIPMT papers from 2001 to 2022. Every year more than 65% questions are based on concepts asked in previous 10 to 15 years which were matching in style with the questions of these old papers.

All the questions of these past 22 years papers are divided in NEET/AIPMT Papers (check) topics for topic level understanding of questions asked in previous years. In my classroom teaching also I found that topic level understanding of previous year papers of exam helps students a lot in concept visualization from the point of view of preparation of final exam as well as for the purpose of last moment revision of all topics.

For every question asked in these old all concepts of all chapters are explained and recorded in form of one shot revision checklist videos which students can watch on Physics Galaxy You Tube channel or these videos are also accessible from Physics Galaxy website and mobile apps available on iOS app store and android play store. These quick revision checklist videos students can also watch by scanning the QR codes given in this book for all chapters at start of book.

I don't have words for my best friend my wife Anuja for always being together with me to complete this book in the unique style and format along with the whole series of Physics Galaxy book series and lecture notes series.

I would like to pay my gratitude to Sh. Dayashankar Prajapati in assisting me to complete the task in Design Labs of PHYSICSGALAXY.COM and presenting the book in totally new format of second edition.

At last but the most important person, my father who has devoted his valuable time to finally present the book in such a format and a simple language, thanks is a very small word for his dedication in this book.

In this first edition of book I have tried my best to make this book error free but owing to the nature of work, inadvertently, there is possibility of errors left untouched. I shall be grateful to the readers, if they point out me regarding errors and oblige me by giving their valuable and constructive suggestions via emails for further improvement of the book.

Date : November, 2022

Ashish Arora

PHYSICSGALAXY.COM
B-80, Model Town, Malviya Nagar, Jaipur-302017
e-mails: ashisharora@physicsgalaxy.com

30 Days Revision Plan using Revision Checklist Videos

NEET Aspirants can revise whole Physics within 30 days or less using Physics Galaxy Revision Checklist Videos which are one-shot videos to revise every chapter of Physics for NEET (or JEE Main) preparation. Below is the day-wise plane given for students to be followed along with coverage of all PYQs given in the book. In case students have less time then they can accelerate their preparation and cover everything in less days and for students preparing yearlong can follow the checklist videos as they complete chapters one by one and attempt PYQs.

Day-01

Checklist 01 Motion in One Dimension

Duration - 00:36:33

Checklist 02 Motion in Two Dimension

Duration - 00:23:03

Checklist 03 Relative Motion

Duration - 00:23:51

Day-02

Checklist 04 Newton's Law of Motion

Duration - 01:07:49

Checklist 05 Friction

Duration - 00:33:48

Day-03

Checklist 06 Work Energy Power

Duration - 00:51:02

Day-04

Checklist 07 Circular Motion

Duration - 00:55:13

Checklist 08 Banking Of Tracks

Duration - 00:27:37

Day-05

Checklist 09 Centre of Mass

Duration - 00:34:56

Checklist 10 Conservation of Momentum

Duration - 00:46:49

Day-06

Checklist 11 Rigid Body Dynamics P1

Duration - 00:38:28

Checklist 12 Rigid Body Dynamics P2

Duration - 00:54:26

Checklist 13 Fluid Statics

Duration - 00:30:42

Checklist 14 Fluid Dynamics

Duration - 00:27:46

Checklist 15 Surface Tension

Duration - 00:32:40

Checklist 16 Viscosity

Duration - 00:20:50

Checklist 17 Elasticity

Duration - 00:26:46

Checklist 18 Gravitational Field

Duration - 01:01:34

Checklist 19 Satellite Motion

Duration - 00:40:52

Checklist 20 Simple Harmonic Motion P1

Duration - 01:06:15

Checklist 21 Simple Harmonic Motion P2

Duration - 00:50:15

Checklist 22 Kinetic Theory of Gases

Duration - 00:51:15

Checklist 23 Law of Thermodynamics

Duration - 01:10:06

Checklist 24 Calorimetry

Duration - 00:38:13

Checklist 25 Heat Transfer

Duration - 00:51:43

Checklist 26 Wave Motion

Duration - 00:53:35

Day-15

Checklist 27 Stationary Waves and Beats
Duration - 01:20:45

Checklist 28 Doppler's Effect
Duration - 00:39:29

Day-16

Checklist 29 Electric Force & Electric Field
Duration - 01:22:26

Checklist 30 Electric Potential, Dipole & Conductors
Duration - 01:26:06

Day-17

Checklist 31 Capacitance
Duration - 01:36:21

Day-18

Checklist 32 Current Electricity
Duration - 01:23:05

Checklist 33 Thermal Effect of Current
Duration - 01:26:17

Day-19

Checklist 34 Magnetic Effect of Current
Duration - 01:17:57

Day-20

Checklist 35 Moving Charges and Magnetism
Duration - 01:25:53

Day-21

Checklist 36 Classical and Terrestrial Magnetism
Duration - 01:12:05

Day-22

Checklist 37 Electromagnetic Induction
Duration - 01:38:48

Day-23

Checklist 38 Alternating Current
Duration - 01:17:03

Checklist 39 Electromagnetic Waves
Duration - 00:20:53

Day-24

Checklist 40 Reflection of Light
Duration - 01:26:22

Checklist 41 Refraction of Light
Duration - 01:29:50

Checklist 42 Thin Lenses and Dispersion of Light
Duration - 01:17:05

Checklist 43 Optical Instruments
Duration - 00:52:07

Checklist 44 Interference of Light
Duration - 00:58:37

Checklist 45 Diffraction of Light
Duration - 00:31:49

Checklist 46 Polarization of Light
Duration - 00:31:10

Checklist 47 Atomic Structure
Duration - 01:11:38

Checklist 48 Photoelectric Effect
Duration - 00:42:24

Checklist 49 Dual Nature of Light
Duration - 00:42:47

Checklist 50 X Rays
Duration - 00:32:53

Checklist 51 Radioactivity
Duration - 00:38:11

Checklist 52 Nuclear Physics
Duration - 00:51:26

Checklist 53 Semiconductors
Duration - 00:48:08

Checklist 54 PN Junction and Diodes
Duration - 00:57:29

Checklist 55 Transistors
Duration - 00:41:50

CONTENTS

Ch-1 **Units & Measurements** **01-03**
1.1 Units 01-01
1.2 Dimensions 01-02
1.3 Measurements 02-02
1.4 Vectors 03-03

Ch-2 **Motion in a Straight line** **04-06**
2.1 Uniform Motion 04-04
2.2 Motion with Constant Acceleration 04-05
2.3 Variable Motion 05-06
2.4 Graphical Analysis 06-06

Ch-3 **Motion in a Plane** **07-08**
3.1 Motion in Two Dimensions 07-07
3.2 Projectile Motion 07-08

Ch-4 **Newton's Laws of Motion** **09-11**
4.1 Forces & Applications 09-10
4.2 Friction 11-11

Ch-5 **Work Energy Power & Applications** **12-16**
5.1 Kinetic & Potential Energy 12-13
5.2 Work 13-14
5.3 Power 14-14
5.4 Circular Motion 14-16
5.5 Non Uniform Circular Motion 16-16

Ch-6 **System of Particles & Rotational Motion** **17-24**
6.1 Centre of Mass 17-17
6.2 Impulse & Conservation of Momentum 17-19
6.3 Moment of Inertia 19-20
6.4 Torque & Angular Acceleration 20-22
6.5 Angular Momentum & Conservation 22-23
6.6 Rolling 23-24

Ch-7 **Gravitation** **25-28**
7.1 Gravitational Field & Force 25-26
7.2 Gravitational Energy & Gravitational Potential 26-27
7.3 Satellite & Planetary Motion 27-28

Ch-8	**Mechanical Properties of Solids**	**29-29**
	8.1 Elasticity	29-29
Ch-9	**Mechanical Properties of Fluids**	**30-31**
	9.1 Fluid Statics	30-30
	9.2 Fluid Dynamics	30-30
	9.3 Surface Tension	30-31
	9.4 Viscosity	31-31
Ch-10	**Thermal Properties of Matter**	**32-34**
	10.1 Thermal Expansion	32-32
	10.2 Calorimetry	32-32
	10.3 Conduction of Heat	32-33
	10.4 Radiation of Heat	33-34
Ch-11	**Thermodynamics**	**35-38**
	11.1 First Law of Thermodynamics	35-37
	11.2 Cyclic Process, Heat Engine and Refrigerator	37-38
	11.3 Thermocouple	38-38
Ch-12	**Kinetic Theory**	**39-40**
	12.1 Kinetic Theory of Gases	39-40
Ch-13	**Oscillations**	**41-43**
	13.1 Simple Harmonic Motion	41-43
Ch-14	**Waves**	**44-47**
	14.1 Wave Motion	44-45
	14.2 Stationary Waves	45-46
	14.3 Beats	46-46
	14.4 Doppler's Effect	46-47
Ch-15	**Electric Charges and Fields**	**48-50**
	15.1 Electric Force and Electric Field	48-49
	15.2 Electric Flux and Gauss Law	49-50
Ch-16	**Electric Potential and Capacitance**	**51-56**
	16.1 Electric Potential and Energy	51-53
	16.2 Electric Dipole	53-54
	16.3 Capacitance	54-56
Ch-17	**Current Electricity**	**57-65**
	17.1 Resistance and Ohm's Law	57-58
	17.2 Kirchhoff's Law & Electric Circuits	58-60

17.3 Thermal Effects of Current — 60-62
17.4 Electrical Measurements — 62-65

Ch-18 Moving Charges & Magnetism — 66-70
18.1 Magnetic Effects of Current — 66-67
18.2 Magnetic Force on Moving Charges — 67-69
18.3 Magnetic Force on Current — 69-70

Ch-19 Magnetism and Matter — 71-73
19.1 Magnetism of a Bar Magnet — 71-71
19.2 Earth's Magnetism — 71-72
19.3 Magnetic Properties of Materials — 72-73

Ch-20 Electromagnetic Induction — 74-77
20.1 Faraday's Law of EMI — 74-75
20.2 Self & Mutual Induction — 75-77

Ch-21 Alternating Current — 78-80
21.1 AC emf, Current, Impedance and Power — 78-78
21.2 RLC Circuit and Resonance — 78-80

Ch-22 Electromagnetic Waves — 81-82
22.1 Electromagnetic Spectrum — 81-81
22.2 $\vec{E}$, $\vec{B}$ and $\vec{C}$ of Electromagnetic Wave — 81-82

Ch-23 Ray Optics and Optical Instruments — 83-88
23.1 Geometrical Optics I - Reflection of Light — 83-83
23.2 Geometrical Optics II - Refraction of Light — 83-85
23.3 Geometrical Optics III - Thin Lenses — 85-86
23.4 Dispersion of Light — 86-87
23.5 Optical Instruments — 87-88

Ch-24 Wave Optics — 89-90
24.1 Interference — 89-89
24.2 Diffraction — 89-90
24.3 Polarization of Light — 90-90

Ch-25 Dual Nature of Radiation, Matter & X-Ray — 91-95
25.1 Photoelectric Effect — 91-93
25.2 Matter Waves and X-Rays — 93-95

Ch-26 Atoms — 96-97
26.1 Properties of Electron in Bohr Model — 96-96
26.2 Electron Transition & Hydrogen Spectrum — 96-97

Ch-27 Nuclei **98-102**
    27.1 Radioactivity 98-99
    27.2 Nuclear Physics 99-102

Ch-28 Semiconductors Electronics **103-110**
    28.1 Semiconductor 103-104
    28.2 PN Junction and Diodes 104-106
    28.3 Transistors 106-108
    28.4 Logic Gates 108-110

ANSWER KEY *111-115*
SOLUTIONS *116-242*

* * * * *

1 UNITS & MEASUREMENTS

1.1 Units

1. The dimensions of Planck's constant equals to that of :

[NEET (UG) 2001]

(A) Energy   (B) Momentum

(C) Angular momentum   (D) Power

2. Unit of Stefan's constant is :   **[NEET (UG) 2002]**

(A) watt $m^2 K^4$ (B) watt m^2/K^4

(C) watt/$m^2 K$ (D) watt/$m^2 K^4$

3. The unit of permittivity of free space, ε_0, is :

[NEET (UG) 2004]

(A) Coulomb/newton-metre   (B) Newton-metre^2/coulomb^2

(C) Coulomb^2/newton-metre^2 (D) Coulomb^2/(newton-metre)^2

4. The ratio of the dimension of Planck's constant and that of the moment of inertia is the dimension of : **[NEET (UG) 2005]**

(A) Velocity   (B) Angular momentum

(C) Time   (D) Frequency

5. The unit of thermal conductivity is :   **[NEET (UG) 2019]**

(A) $J m K^{-1}$ (B) $J m^{-1} K^{-1}$

(C) $W m K^{-1}$ (D) $W m^{-1} K^{-1}$

1.2 Dimensions

1. The dimensions of universal gravitational constant are :

[NEET (UG) 2004]

(A) ML^2T^{-1} (B) $M^{-2}L^3T^{-2}$

(C) $M^{-2}L^2T^{-1}$ (D) $M^{-1}L^3T^{-2}$

2. The velocity v of a particle at time t is given by $v = at + \dfrac{b}{t+c}$, where a, b and c are constants. The dimensions of a, b and c are respectively : **[NEET (UG) 2006]**

(A) LT^{-2}, L and T   (B) L^2, T and LT^2

(C) LT^2, LT and L   (D) L, LT and T^2

3. Dimensions of resistance in an electrical circuit, in terms of dimension of mass M, of length L, of time T and of current I, would be : **[NEET (UG) 2007]**

(A) ML^2T^{-2} (B) $ML^2T^{-1}I^{-1}$

(C) $ML^2T^{-3}I^{-2}$ (D) $ML^2T^{-3}I^{-1}$

4. If the dimensions of a physical quantity are given by $[M^a L^b T^c]$, then the physical quantity will be : **[NEET (UG) 2009]**

(A) Force if $a = 0$, $b = -1$, $c = -2$

(B) Pressure if $a = 1$, $b = -1$, $c = -2$

(C) Velocity if $a = 1$, $b = 0$, $c = -1$

(D) Acceleration if $a = 1$, $b = 1$, $c = -2$

5. The dimension of $\dfrac{1}{2}\varepsilon_0 E^2$, where ε_0 is permittivity of free space and E is electric field, is : **[NEET (UG) 2010]**

(A) MLT^{-1} (B) $ML^{-2}T^{-2}$

(C) $ML^{-1}T^{-2}$ (D) ML^2T^{-1}

6. The dimensions of $(\mu_0\varepsilon_0)^{-1/2}$ are :   **[NEET (UG) 2011, 12]**

(A) $[L^{1/2} T^{-1/2}]$ (B) $[L^{-1} T]$

(C) $[LT^{-1}]$ (D) $[L^{-1/2}T^{1/2}]$

7. If force (F), velocity (V) and time (T) are taken as fundamental units, then the dimensions of mass are : **[NEET (UG) 2014]**

(A) $[F V T^{-1}]$ (B) $[F V T^{-2}]$

(C) $[F V^{-1} T^{-1}]$ (D) $[F V^{-1} T]$

8. If dimensions of critical velocity v_c of a liquid flowing through a tube are expressed as $[\eta^x \rho^y r^x]$, where η, ρ and r are the coefficient of viscosity of liquid, density of liquid and radius of the tube respectively, then the values of x, y and z are given by : **[NEET (UG) 2015]**

(A) 1, 1, 1   (B) 1, -1, -1

(C) -1, -1, 1   (D) -1, -1, -1

9. Planck's constant (h), speed of light in vacuum (c) and Newton's gravitational constant (G) are three fundamental constants. Which of the following combinations of these has the dimension of length ? **[NEET (UG) 2016 Ph. II]**

(A) $\dfrac{\sqrt{hG}}{c^{3/2}}$ (B) $\dfrac{\sqrt{hG}}{c^{5/2}}$

(C) $\sqrt{\dfrac{hc}{G}}$ (D) $\sqrt{\dfrac{Gc}{h^{3/2}}}$

10. A physical quantity of the dimensions of length that can be formed out of c, G and $\dfrac{e^2}{4\pi\varepsilon_0}$ is [c is velocity of light, G is universal constant of gravitation and e is charge] :

[NEET (UG) 2017]

(A) $\dfrac{1}{c^2}\left[G\dfrac{e^2}{4\pi\varepsilon_0}\right]^{\frac{1}{2}}$ (B) $c^2\left[G\dfrac{e^2}{4\pi\varepsilon_0}\right]^{\frac{1}{2}}$

(C) $\dfrac{1}{c^2}\left[\dfrac{e^2}{G4\pi\varepsilon_0}\right]^{\frac{1}{2}}$ (D) $\dfrac{1}{c}G\dfrac{e^2}{4\pi\varepsilon_0}$

11. Dimensions of stress are :   **[NEET (UG) 2020]**
(A) $[M\,L^{-1}\,T^{-2}]$ (B) $[M\,L\,T^{-2}]$
(C) $[M\,L^2\,T^{-2}]$ (D) $[M\,L^0\,T^{-2}]$

12. If force [F], acceleration [A] and time [T] are chosen as the fundamental physical quantities. Find the dimensions of energy :   **[NEET (UG) 2021]**
(A) $[F]\,[A]\,[T]$ (B) $[F]\,[A]\,[T^2]$
(C) $[F]\,[A]\,[T^{-1}]$ (D) $[F]\,[A^{-1}]\,[T]$

13. If E and G respectively denote energy and gravitational constant, then $\dfrac{E}{G}$ has the dimensions of :   **[NEET (UG) 2021]**
(A) $[M^2]\,[L^{-1}]\,[T^0]$ (B) $[M]\,[L^{-1}]\,[T^{-1}]$
(C) $[M]\,[L^0]\,[T^0]$ (D) $[M^2]\,[L^{-2}]\,[T^{-1}]$

14. Plane angle and solid angle have :   **[NEET (UG) 2022]**
(A) Dimensions but no units
(B) No units and no dimensions
(C) Both units and dimensions
(D) Units but no dimensions

15. The dimensions $[MLT^{-2}\,A^{-2}]$ belong to the :   **[NEET (UG) 2022]**
(A) Self inductance   (B) Magnetic permeability
(C) Electric permittivity   (D) Magnetic flux

1.3 Measurements

1. If the error in the measurement of radius of a sphere is 2%, then the error in the determination of volume of the sphere will be :   **[NEET (UG) 2008]**
(A) 8%   (B) 2%
(C) 4%   (D) 6%

2. A student measures the terminal potential difference V of a cell of *emf* ε and internal resistance r as a function of the current I flowing through it. The slope and intercept of the graph between V and I, then respectively equal to :   **[NEET (UG) 2009]**
(A) $-\varepsilon$ and r (B) ε and $-r$
(C) $-r$ and ε (D) r and $-\varepsilon$

3. In an experiment four quantities a, b, c and d are measured with percentage error 1%, 2%, 3% and 4% respectively. Quantity P is calculated as follows : $P = \dfrac{a^3 b^2}{cd}$. % error in P is :   **[NEET (UG) 2013]**
(A) 14%   (B) 10%
(C) 7%   (D) 4%

4. A student measured the diameter of a small steel ball using a screw gauge of least count 0.001 cm. The main scale reading is 5 mm and zero of circular scale division coincides with 25 divisions above the reference level. If screw gauge has a zero error of -0.004 cm, the correct diameter of the ball is :   **[NEET (UG) 2018]**
(A) 0.053 cm   (B) 0.525 cm
(C) 0.521 cm   (D) 0.529 cm

5. In an experiment, the percentage of error occurred in the measurement of physical quantities A, B, C and D are 1%, 2%, 3% and 4% respectively. Then the maximum percentage of error in the measurement X, where $X = \dfrac{A^2 B^{1/2}}{C^{1/3} D^3}$, will be :   **[NEET (UG) 2019]**
(A) $\left(\dfrac{3}{13}\right)\%$ (B) 16%
(C) -10% (D) 10%

6. A screw gauge has least count of 0.01 mm and there are 50 divisions in its circular scale. The pitch of the screw gauge is :   **[NEET (UG) 2020]**
(A) 1.0 mm   (B) 0.01 mm
(C) 0.25 mm   (D) 0.5 mm

7. Taking into account of the significant figures, what is the value of 9.99 m $-$ 0.0099 m ?   **[NEET (UG) 2020]**
(A) 9.9 m   (B) 9.9801 m
(C) 9.98 m   (D) 9.980 m

8. A screw gauge gives the following readings when used to measure the diameter of a wire
    Main scale reading : 0 mm
    Circular scale reading : 52 divisions
Given that 1 mm on main scale corresponds to 100 divisions on the circular scale. The diameter of the wire from the above data is :   **[NEET (UG) 2021]**
(A) 0.52 cm   (B) 0.026 cm
(C) 0.26 cm   (D) 0.052 cm

9. The area of a rectangular field (in m^2) of length 55.3 m and breadth 25 m after rounding off the value for correct significant digits is :   **[NEET (UG) 2022]**
(A) 1382   (B) 1382.5
(C) 14×10^2 (D) 138×10^1

1.4 Vectors

1. If $|\vec{A}+\vec{B}| = |\vec{A}|+|\vec{B}|$ then angle between A and B will be :

[NEET (UG) 2001]

(A) 90° (B) 120°

(C) 0° (D) 60°

2. The vector sum of two forces is perpendicular to their vector differences. In that case, the forces : **[NEET (UG) 2003]**
(A) are equal to each other
(B) are equal to each other in magnitude
(C) are not equal to each other in magnitude
(D) cannot be predicted

3. If $|\vec{A}\times\vec{B}| = \sqrt{3}(\vec{A}\cdot\vec{B})$ then the value of $|\vec{A}+\vec{B}|$ is :

[NEET (UG) 2004]

(A) $(A^2+B^2+AB)^{1/2}$ (B) $\left(A^2+B^2+\dfrac{AB}{\sqrt{3}}\right)^{1/2}$

(C) $A+B$ (D) $(A^2+B^2+\sqrt{3})^{1/2}$

4. If a vector $2\hat{i}+3\hat{j}+8\hat{k}$ is perpendicular to the vector $4\hat{j}-4\hat{i}+\alpha\hat{k}$, then the value of α : **[NEET (UG) 2005]**

(A) -1 (B) $-\dfrac{1}{2}$

(C) $\dfrac{1}{2}$ (D) 1

5. If the angle between the vector $\vec{A}$ and $\vec{B}$ is θ, the value of the product $(\vec{B}\times\vec{A})\cdot\vec{A}$ is equal to : **[NEET (UG) 2005]**
(A) Zero (B) $BA^2\sin\theta\cos\theta$
(C) $BA^2\cos\theta$ (D) $BA^2\sin\theta$

6. The vectors $\vec{A}$ and $\vec{B}$ are such that $|\vec{A}+\vec{B}| = |\vec{A}-\vec{B}|$. The angle between the two vectors is : **[NEET (UG) 2006]**
(A) 90° (B) 60°
(C) 75° (D) 45°

7. $\vec{A}$ and $\vec{B}$ are two vectors and θ is the angle between them, if $|\vec{A}\times\vec{B}| = \sqrt{3}(\vec{A}\cdot\vec{B})$, the value of θ is : **[NEET (UG) 2007]**
(A) 45° (B) 30°
(C) 90° (D) 60°

8. Six vectors, $\vec{a}$ through $\vec{f}$ have the magnitude and directions indicated in the figure. Which of the following statements is true ? **[NEET (UG) 2010]**

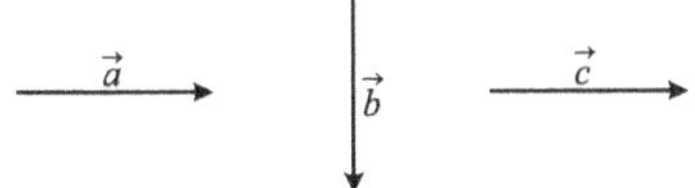
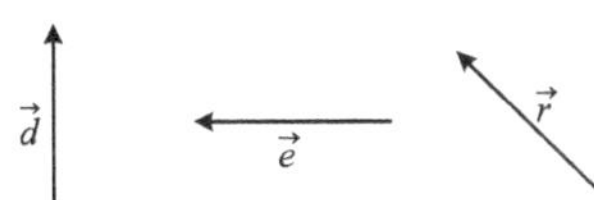

(A) $\vec{b}+\vec{c} = \vec{f}$ (B) $\vec{d}+\vec{c} = \vec{f}$

(C) $\vec{d}+\vec{e} = \vec{f}$ (D) $\vec{b}+\vec{e} = \vec{f}$

9. If vectors $\vec{A} = \cos\omega t\,\hat{i} + \sin\omega t\,\hat{j}$ and $\vec{B} = \cos\dfrac{\omega t}{2}\hat{i} + \sin\dfrac{\omega t}{2}\hat{j}$ are functions of time, then the value of t at which they are orthogonal to each other is : **[NEET (UG) 2015]**

(A) $t=0$ (B) $t=\dfrac{\pi}{4\omega}$

(C) $t=\dfrac{\pi}{2\omega}$ (D) $t=\dfrac{\pi}{\omega}$

10. Two particles A and B, move with constant velocities $\vec{v}_1$ and $\vec{v}_2$. At the initial moment their position vectors are $\vec{r}_1$ and $\vec{r}_2$ respectively. The condition for particles A and B for their collision is : **[NEET (UG) 2015]**

(A) $\vec{r}_1 - \vec{r}_2 = \vec{v}_1 - \vec{v}_2$ (B) $\dfrac{\vec{r}_1-\vec{r}_2}{|\vec{r}_1-\vec{r}_2|} = \dfrac{\vec{v}_2-\vec{v}_1}{|\vec{v}_2-\vec{v}_1|}$

(C) $\vec{r}_1\cdot\vec{v}_1 = \vec{r}_2\cdot\vec{v}_2$ (D) $\vec{r}_1\times\vec{v}_1 = \vec{r}_2\times\vec{v}_2$

11. If the magnitude of sum of two vectors is equal to the magnitude of difference of the two vectors, the angle between these vectors is : **[NEET (UG) 2016]**
(A) 0° (B) 90°
(C) 45° (D) 180°

* * * * *

2 MOTION IN A STRAIGHT LINE

2.1 Uniform Motion

1. Two boys are standing at the ends A and B of a ground where $AB = a$. The boy at B starts. Running in a direction perpendicular to AB with velocity v_1. The boy at A starts running simultaneously with velocity v and catches the other boy in a time t, where t is : **[NEET (UG) 2005]**

(A) $\dfrac{a}{\sqrt{v^2 + v_1^2}}$

(B) $\sqrt{\dfrac{a^2}{(v^2 - v_1^2)}}$

(C) $\dfrac{a}{(v - v_1)}$

(D) $\dfrac{a}{(v + v_1)}$

2. A car moves from X to Y with a uniform speed v_u and returns to Y with a uniform speed v_d. The average speed for this round trip is : **[NEET (UG) 2007]**

(A) $\sqrt{v_u v_d}$

(B) $\dfrac{v_d v_u}{v_d + v_u}$

(C) $\dfrac{v_u + v_d}{2}$

(D) $\dfrac{2 v_d v_u}{v_d + v_u}$

3. A bus is moving with a speed of $10\ \text{ms}^{-1}$ on a straight road. A scooterist wishes to overtake the bus in 100 s. If the bus is at a distance of 1 km from the scooterist, with what speed should the scooterist chase the bus ? **[NEET (UG) 2009]**

(A) $10\ \text{ms}^{-1}$

(B) $20\ \text{ms}^{-1}$

(C) $40\ \text{ms}^{-1}$

(D) $25\ \text{ms}^{-1}$

4. Preeti reached the metro station and found that the escalator was not working. She walked up the stationary escalator in time t_1. On other days, if she remains stationary on the moving escalator, then the escalator takes her up in time t_2. The time taken by her to walk up on the moving escalator will be : **[NEET (UG) 2017]**

(A) $\dfrac{t_1 + t_2}{2}$

(B) $\dfrac{t_1 t_2}{t_2 - t_1}$

(C) $\dfrac{t_1 t_2}{t_2 + t_1}$

(D) $t_1 - t_2$

2.2 Motion with Constant Acceleration

1. A particle is thrown vertically upward. Its velocity at half of the height is 10 m/s, then the maximum height attained by it $(g = 10\ \text{m/s}^2)$: **[NEET (UG) 2001]**

(A) $8\,\text{m}$

(B) $20\,\text{m}$

(C) $10\,\text{m}$

(D) $16\,\text{m}$

2. A man throws balls with the same speed vertically upwards one after the other at an interval of 2 seconds. What should be the speed of the throw so that more than two balls are in the sky at any time ? (Given $g = 9.8$ m/s^2) **[NEET (UG) 2003]**

(A) More than 19.6 m/s

(B) At least 9.8 m/s

(C) Any speed less than 19.6 m/s

(D) Only with speed 19.6 m/s

3. If a ball is thrown vertically upwards with speed u, the distance covered during the last t seconds of its ascent is : **[NEET (UG) 2003]**

(A) ut

(B) $\dfrac{1}{2} gt^2$

(C) $ut - \dfrac{1}{2} gt^2$

(D) $(u + gt)t$

4. A ball is thrown vertically upward. It has a speed of 10 m/s when it has reached one half of its maximum height. How high does the ball rise ? Take $g = 10$ m/s^2 : **[NEET (UG) 2005]**

(A) $5\,\text{m}$

(B) $15\,\text{m}$

(C) $10\,\text{m}$

(D) $20\,\text{m}$

5. Two bodies, A (of mass 1 kg) and B (of mass 3 kg), are dropped from heights of 16 m and 25 m respectively. The ratio of the time taken by them to reach the ground is : **[NEET (UG) 2006]**

(A) $\dfrac{5}{4}$

(B) $\dfrac{12}{5}$

(C) $\dfrac{5}{12}$

(D) $\dfrac{4}{5}$

6. The distance travelled by a particle starting from rest and moving with an acceleration $4/3\ \text{ms}^{-2}$, in the third second is : **[NEET (UG) 2008]**

(A) $\dfrac{10}{3}\,\text{m}$

(B) $\dfrac{19}{3}\,\text{m}$

(C) $6\,\text{m}$

(D) $4\,\text{m}$

7. A particle moves in a straight line with a constant acceleration. It changes its velocity from $10\ \text{ms}^{-1}$ to $20\ \text{ms}^{-1}$ while passing through a distance 135 m in t second. The value of t is : **[NEET (UG) 2008]**

(A) 12

(B) 9

(C) 10

(D) 1.8

8. A particle starts its motion from rest under the action of a constant force. If the distance covered in first 10 seconds is s_1 and that covered in the first 20 seconds is s_2 then :

[NEET (UG) 2009]

(A) $s_2 = s_1$ 　　　　　　(B) $s_2 = 2s_1$
(C) $s_2 = 3s_1$ 　　　　　　(D) $s_2 = 4s_1$

9. A body of mass 1 kg of thrown upwards with a velocity 20 m/s. It momentarily comes to rest after attaining a height of 18 m. How much energy is lost due to air friction ? $(g = 10\,\text{m/s}^2)$:　**[NEET (UG) 2009]**

(A) 10 J 　　　　　　(B) 20 J
(C) 30 J 　　　　　　(D) 40 J

10. A particle has initial velocity $(3\hat{i} + 4\hat{j})$ and has acceleration $(0.4\hat{i} + 0.3\hat{j})$. It's speed after 10 s is :　**[NEET (UG) 2010]**

(A) 10 units 　　　　　　(B) 7 units
(C) $7\sqrt{2}$ units 　　　　　　(D) 8.5 units

11. A ball is dropped from a high rise platform at $t = 0$ starting from rest. After 6 seconds another ball is thrown downwards from the same platform with a speed v. The two balls meet at $t = 18$ s. What is the value of v ? (take $g = 10\,\text{m/s}^2$) :

[NEET (UG) 2010]

(A) 60 m/s 　　　　　　(B) 75 m/s
(C) 55 m/s 　　　　　　(D) 40 m/s

12. A boy standing at the top of a tower of 20 m height drops a stone. Assuming $g = 10\,\text{ms}^{-2}$, the velocity with which it hits the ground is :　**[NEET (UG) 2011]**

(A) 10.0 m/s 　　　　　　(B) 20.0 m/s
(C) 40.0 m/s 　　　　　　(D) 5.0 m/s

13. A body is moving with a velocity 30 m/s towards east. After 10 seconds its velocity becomes 40 m/s towards north. The average acceleration of the body is :　**[NEET (UG) 2011]**

(A) 1 m/s² 　　　　　　(B) 7 m/s²
(C) $\sqrt{7}$ m/s² 　　　　　　(D) 5 m/s²

14. A particle has initial velocity $(3\hat{i} + 3\hat{j})$ and acceleration $(0.3\hat{i} + 0.2\hat{j})$. The magnitude of velocity after 10 seconds will be :　**[NEET (UG) 2012]**

(A) $9\sqrt{2}$ units 　　　　　　(B) $5\sqrt{2}$ units
(C) 5 units 　　　　　　(D) 9 units

15. A stone falls freely under gravity. It covers distances h_1, h_2 and h_3 in the first 5 seconds, the next 5 seconds and the next 5 seconds respectively. The relation between h_1, h_2 and h_3 is :

[NEET (UG) 2013]

(A) $h_1 = 2h_2 = 3h_3$ 　　　　　　(B) $h_1 = \dfrac{h_2}{3} = \dfrac{h_3}{5}$
(C) $h_2 = 3h_1$ and $h_3 = 3h_2$ 　　　　(D) $h_1 = h_2 = h_3$

16. When an object is shot from the bottom of a long smooth inclined plane kept at an angle 60° with horizontal, it can travel a distance x_1 along the plane. But when the inclination is decreased to 30° and the same object is shot with the same velocity, it can travel x_2 distance. Then $x_1 : x_2$ will be :

[NEET (UG) 2019]

(A) $1 : \sqrt{2}$ 　　　　　　(B) $\sqrt{2} : 1$
(C) $1 : \sqrt{3}$ 　　　　　　(D) $1 : 2\sqrt{3}$

17. A ball is thrown vertically downward with a velocity of 20 m/s from the top of a tower. It hits the ground after some time with a velocity of 80 m/s. The height of the tower is : $(g = 10\,\text{m/s}^2)$

[NEET (UG) 2020]

(A) 300 m 　　　　　　(B) 360 m
(C) 340 m 　　　　　　(D) 320 m

18. A small block slides down on a smooth inclined plane, starting from rest at time $t = 0$. Let S_n be the distance travelled by the block in the interval $t = n - 1$ to $t = n$. Then, the ratio $\dfrac{S_n}{S_{n+1}}$ is :　**[NEET (UG) 2021]**

(A) $\dfrac{2n-1}{2n}$ 　　　　　　(B) $\dfrac{2n-1}{2n+1}$
(C) $\dfrac{2n+1}{2n-1}$ 　　　　　　(D) $\dfrac{2n}{2n-1}$

19. The ratio of the distances travelled by a freely falling body in the 1ˢᵗ, 2ⁿᵈ, 3ʳᵈ and 4ᵗʰ second :　**[NEET (UG) 2022]**

(A) $1 : 4 : 9 : 16$ 　　　　　　(B) $1 : 3 : 5 : 7$
(C) $1 : 1 : 1 : 1$ 　　　　　　(D) $1 : 2 : 3 : 4$

2.3 Variable Motion

1. The displacement x of a particle varies with time t as $x = ae^{-\alpha t} + be^{\beta t}$, where a, b, α and β are positive constants. The velocity of the particle will :　**[NEET (UG) 2005]**

(A) Be independent of α and β
(B) Go on increasing with time
(C) Drop to zero when $\alpha = \beta$
(D) Go on decreasing with time

2. A particle moves along a straight line OX. At a time t (in seconds) the distance x (in metres) of the particle from O is given by $x = 40 + 12t - t^3$. How long would the particle travel before coming to rest : **[NEET (UG) 2006]**

(A) 24 m
(B) 40 m
(C) 56 m
(D) 16 m

3. The position x of a particle with respect to time t along x-axis is given by $x = 9t^2 - t^3$ where x is in metres and t in second. What will be the position of this particle when it achieves maximum speed along the $+ve\,x$ direction ? **[NEET (UG) 2007]**

(A) 54 m
(B) 81 m
(C) 24 m
(D) 32 m

4. A particle moving along x-axis has acceleration f, at time t, given by $f = f_0\left(1 - \dfrac{t}{T}\right)$, where f_0 and T are constants. The particle at $t = 0$ has zero velocity. In the time interval between $t = 0$ and the instant when $f = 0$, the particle's velocity (v_x) is : **[NEET (UG) 2007]**

(A) $\dfrac{1}{2} f_0 T^2$
(B) $f_0 T^2$
(C) $\dfrac{1}{2} f_0 T$
(D) $f_0 T$

5. A particle moves a distance x in time t according to equation $x = (t+5)^{-1}$. The acceleration of particle is proportional to : **[NEET (UG) 2010]**

(A) (Velocity)$^{2/3}$
(B) (Velocity)$^{3/2}$
(C) (Distance)^2
(D) (Distance)$^{-2}$

6. The motion of a particle along a straight line is described by equation :

$$x = 8 + 12t - t^3$$

where x is in metre and t in second. The retardation of the particle when its velocity becomes zero, is : **[NEET (UG) 2012]**

(A) 24 ms^{-2}
(B) Zero
(C) 6 ms^{-2}
(D) 12 ms^{-2}

7. If the velocity of a particle is $v = At + Bt^2$, where A and B are constants, then the distance travelled by it between 1 s and 2 s is : **[NEET (UG) 2016]**

(A) $\dfrac{3}{2}A + 4B$
(B) $3A + 7B$
(C) $\dfrac{3}{2}A + \dfrac{7}{3}B$
(D) $\dfrac{A}{2} + \dfrac{B}{3}$

8. Two cars P and Q start from a point at the same time in a straight line and their positions are represented by $x_P(t) = at + bt^2$ and $x_Q(t) = ft - t^2$. At what time do the cars have the same velocity ? **[NEET (UG) 2016 Ph. II]**

(A) $\dfrac{a - f}{1 + b}$
(B) $\dfrac{a + f}{2(b - 1)}$
(C) $\dfrac{a + f}{2(1 + b)}$
(D) $\dfrac{f - a}{2(1 + b)}$

2.4 Graphical Analysis

1. A particle shows distance-time curve as given in this figure. The maximum instantaneous velocity of the particle is around the point : **[NEET (UG) 2008]**

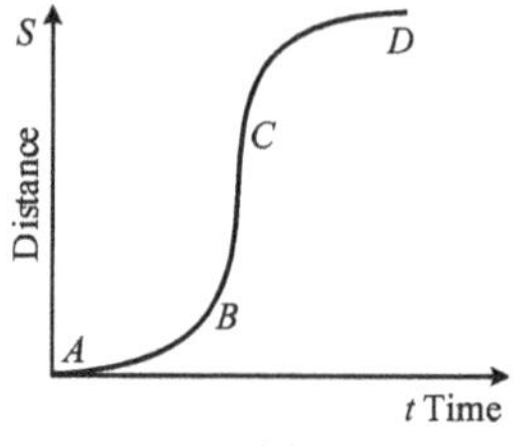

(A) D
(B) A
(C) B
(D) C

2. The displacement-time graphs of two moving particles make angles of 30° and 45° with the x-axis as shown in the figure. The ratio of their respective velocity is : **[NEET (UG) 2022]**

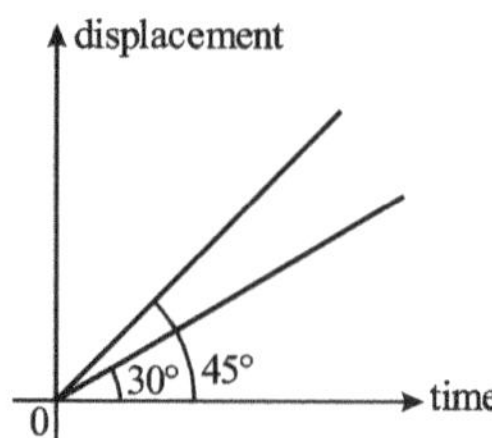

(A) $1 : 1$
(B) $1 : 2$
(C) $1 : \sqrt{3}$
(D) $\sqrt{3} : 1$

* * * * *

3 MOTION IN A PLANE

3.1 Motion in Two Dimensions

1. A particle starting from the origin (0, 0) moves in a straight line in the (x, y) plane. Its coordinates at a later time are $(\sqrt{3}, 3)$. The path of the particle makes with the x-axis an angle of :

[NEET (UG) 2007]

(A) 45° (B) 60°
(C) 0° (D) 30°

2. A particle of mass m is released from rest and follows a parabolic path as shown. Assuming that the displacement of the mass from the origin is small, which graph correctly depicts the position of the particle as a function of time :

[NEET (UG) 2011]

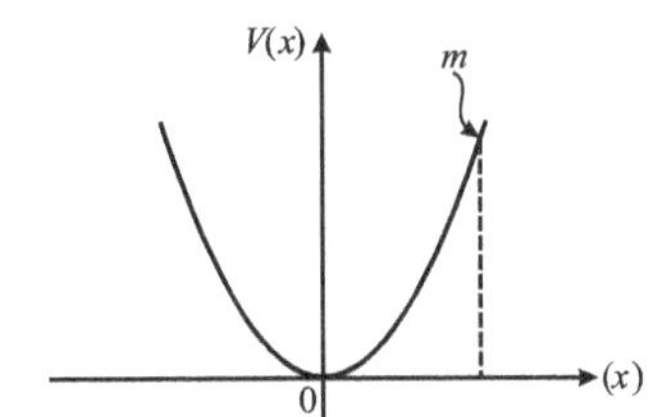

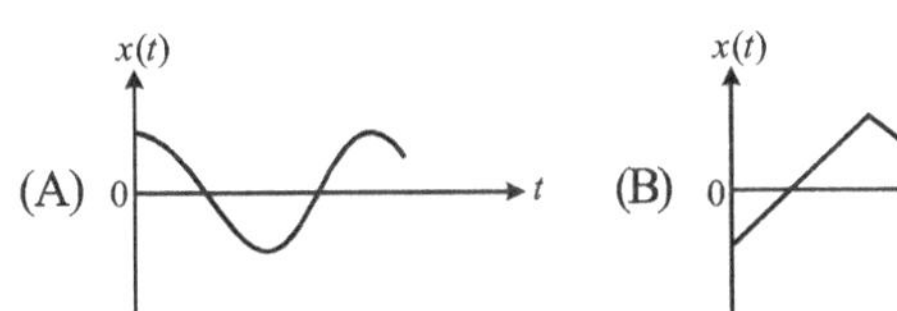

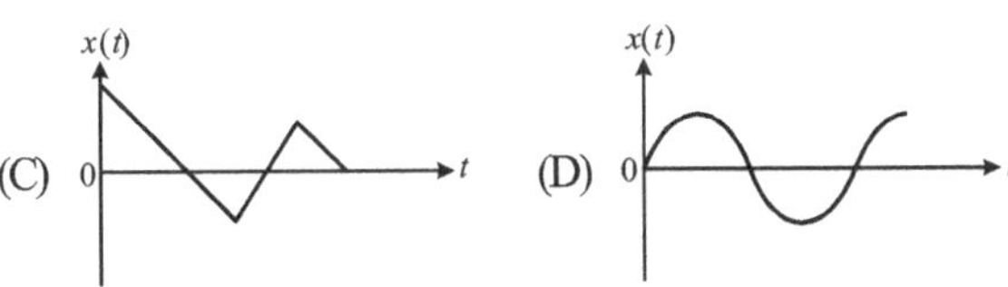

3. A particle is moving such that its position coordinates (x, y) are $(2\,m, 3\,m)$ at time $t = 0$, $(6\,m, 7\,m)$ at time $t = 2$ s and $(13\,m, 14\,m)$ at time $t = 5$ s. Average velocity vector $(\vec{V}_{av})$ from $t = 0$ to $t = 5$ s is :

[NEET (UG) 2014]

(A) $\frac{1}{5}(13\hat{i} + 14\hat{j})$ (B) $\frac{7}{3}(\hat{i} + \hat{j})$

(C) $2(\hat{i} + \hat{j})$ (D) $\frac{11}{5}(\hat{i} + \hat{j})$

4. The x and y coordinates of the particle at any time are $x = 5t - 2t^2$ and $y = 10t$ respectively, where x and y are in meters and t in seconds. The acceleration of the particle at $t = 2$ s is :

[NEET (UG) 2017]

(A) 0 (B) $5\ m/s^2$
(C) $-4\ m/s^2$ (D) $-8\ m/s^2$

5. The speed of a swimmer in still water is 20 m/s. The speed of river water is 10 m/s and is flowing due east. If he is standing on the south bank and wishes to cross the river along the shortest path the angle at which he should make his strokes w.r.t. north is given by : **[NEET (UG) 2019]**

(A) 30° west (B) 0°
(C) 60° west (D) 45° west

3.2 Projectile Motion

1. A particle A is dropped from a height and another particle B is projected in horizontal direction with speed of 5 m/s from the same height then correct statement is : **[NEET (UG) 2002]**

(A) Particle A will reach at ground first with respect to particle B
(B) Particle B will reach at ground first with respect to particle A
(C) Both particles will reach at ground simultaneously
(D) Both particles will reach at ground with same speed

2. For angles of projection of a projectile at angles $(45° - \theta)$ and $(45° + \theta)$, the horizontal ranges described by the projectile are in the ratio of : **[NEET (UG) 2006]**

(A) $1:1$ (B) $2:3$
(C) $1:2$ (D) $2:1$

3. A missile is fired for maximum range with an initial velocity of 20 m/s. If $g = 10\ m/s^2$, the range of the missile is :

[NEET (UG) 2011]

(A) 40 m (B) 50 m
(C) 60 m (D) 20 m

4. The horizontal range and the maximum height of a projectile are equal. The angle of projection of the projectiles is :

[NEET (UG) 2012]

(A) $\theta = \tan^{-1}\left(\frac{1}{4}\right)$ (B) $\theta = \tan^{-1}(4)$

(C) $\theta = \tan^{-1}(2)$ (D) $\theta = 45°$

5. The velocity of a projectile at the initial point A is $(2\hat{i} + 3\hat{j})$ m/s. It's velocity (in m/s) at point B is :

[NEET (UG) 2013]

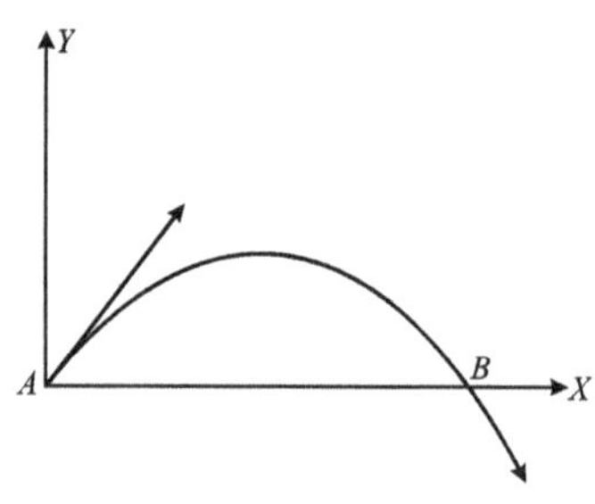

(A) $-2\hat{i}-3\hat{j}$

(B) $-2\hat{i}+3\hat{j}$

(C) $2\hat{i}-3\hat{j}$

(D) $2\hat{i}+3\hat{j}$

6. A projectile is fired from the surface of the earth with a velocity of 5 ms^{-1} and angle θ with the horizontal. Another projectile fired from another planet with a velocity of 3 ms^{-1} at the same angle follows a trajectory which is identical with the trajectory of the projectile fired from the earth. The value of the acceleration due to gravity on the planet is (in ms^{-2}) is : (Given $g = 9.8$ ms^{-2}) :   **[NEET (UG) 2014]**

(A) 3.5

(B) 5.9

(C) 16.3

(D) 110.8

7. A car starts from rest and accelerations at 5 m/s^2. At $t = 4$ s, a ball is dropped out of a window by a person sitting in the car. What is the velocity and acceleration of the ball at $t = 6$ s ? (Take $g = 10$ m/s^2)   **[NEET (UG) 2021]**

(A) 20 m/s, 5 m/s^2

(B) 20 m/s, 0

(C) $20\sqrt{2}$ m/s, 0

(D) $20\sqrt{2}$ m/s, 10 m/s^2

8. A ball is projected with a velocity, 10 ms^{-1}, at an angle of 60° with the vertical direction. Its speed at the highest point of its trajectory will be :   **[NEET (UG) 2022]**

(A) $5\sqrt{3}$ ms^{-1}

(B) 5 ms^{-1}

(C) 10 ms^{-1}

(D) Zero

* * * * *

4 NEWTON'S LAWS OF MOTION

4.1 Forces & Applications

1. A cricketer catches a ball of mass 150 gm in 0.1 s moving with speed 20 m/s, then he experiences force of :

[NEET (UG) 2001]

(A) 300 N   (B) 30 N

(C) 3 N   (D) 0.3 N

2. An object of mass 3 kg is at rest. Now a force of $\vec{F} = 6t^2\hat{i} + 4t\hat{j}$ is applied on the object then velocity of object at $t = 3$ s is : **[NEET (UG) 2002]**

(A) $18\hat{i} + 3\hat{j}$ (B) $18\hat{i} + 6\hat{j}$

(C) $3\hat{i} + 18\hat{j}$ (D) $18\hat{i} + 4\hat{j}$

3. A lift of mass 1000 kg which is moving with acceleration of 1 m/s² in upward direction, then the tension developed in string which is connected to lift is : **[NEET (UG) 2002]**

(A) 9800 N   (B) 10,800 N

(C) 11,000 N   (D) 10,000 N

4. A man weighs 80 kg. He stands on a weighing scale in a lift which is moving upwards with a uniform acceleration of 5 m/s². What would be the reading on the scale ? ($g = 10$ m/s²)

[NEET (UG) 2003]

(A) Zero   (B) 400 N

(C) 800 N   (D) 1200 N

5. A monkey of mass 20 kg is holding a vertical rope. The rope will not break when a mass of 25 kg is suspended from it but will break if the mass exceeds 25 kg. What is the maximum acceleration with which the monkey can climb up along the rope ? ($g = 10$ m/s²) **[NEET (UG) 2003]**

(A) 5 m/s²   (B) 10 m/s²

(C) 25 m/s²   (D) 2.5 m/s²

6. A block of mass m is placed on a smooth wedge of inclination θ. The whole system is accelerated horizontally so that the block does not slip on the wedge. The force exerted by the wedge on the block will be (g is acceleration due to gravity): **[NEET (UG) 2004]**

(A) $mg \cos\theta$ (B) $mg \sin\theta$

(C) mg (D) $mg/\cos\theta$

7. Three forces acting on a body are shown in the figure. To have the resultant force only along the y-direction, the magnitude of the minimum additional force needed is : **[NEET (UG) 2008]**

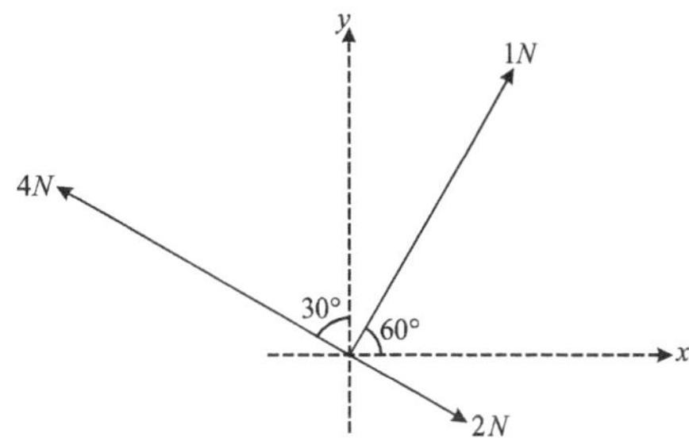

(A) $\dfrac{\sqrt{3}}{4} N$ (B) $\sqrt{3}N$

(C) $0.5 N$ (D) $1.5 N$

8. The mass of lift is 2000 kg. When the tension in the supporting cable is 28000 N, then its acceleration is : **[NEET (UG) 2009]**

(A) 14 ms⁻² upwards   (B) 30 ms⁻² downwards

(C) 4 ms⁻² upwards   (D) 4 ms⁻² downwards

9. A body, under the action of a force $\vec{F} = 6\hat{i} - 8\hat{j} + 10\hat{k}$, acquires an acceleration of 1 m/s². The mass of this body must be : **[NEET (UG) 2009]**

(A) $10\sqrt{2}$ kg   (B) $2\sqrt{10}$ kg

(C) 10 kg   (D) 20 kg

10. A person of mass 60 kg is inside a lift of mass 940 kg and presses the button on control panel. The lift starts moving upwards with an acceleration 1.0 m/s². If $g = 10$ ms⁻², then tension in the supporting cable is : **[NEET (UG) 2011]**

(A) 8600 N   (B) 9680 N

(C) 11000 N   (D) 1200 N

11. A stone is dropped from a height h. It hits the ground with a certain momentum P. If the same stone is dropped from a height 100% more than the previous height, the momentum when it hits the ground will change by : **[NEET (UG) 2012]**

(A) 41 %   (B) 200 %

(C) 100 %   (D) 68 %

12. Three blocks with masses m, $2\,m$ and $3\,m$ are connected by strings, as shown in the figure. After an upward force F is applied on block m, the masses move upward at constant speed v. What is the net force on the block of mass $2\,m$? (g is the acceleration due to gravity) : **[NEET (UG) 2013]**

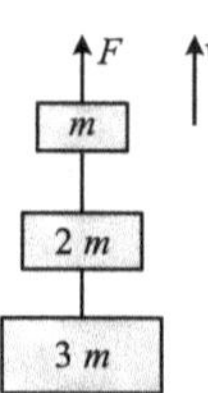

(A) Zero

(B) 2 mg

(C) 3 mg

(D) 6 mg

13. The force F acting on a particle of mass m is indicated by the force-time graph shown below. The change in momentum of the particle over the time interval from zero to 8 s is :

[NEET (UG) 2014]

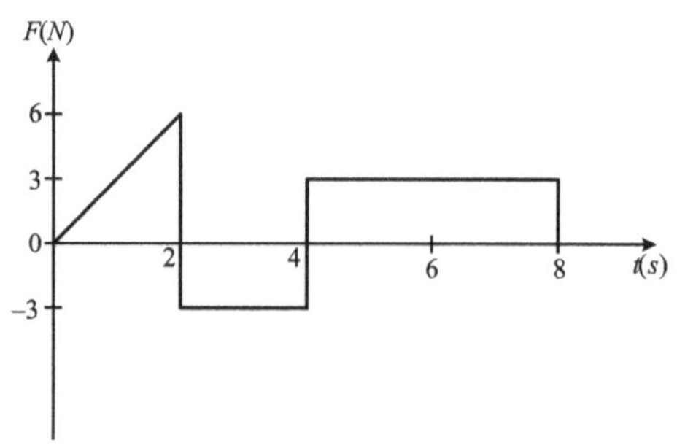

(A) 24 Ns

(B) 20 Ns

(C) 12 Ns

(D) 6 Ns

14. A balloon with mass m is descending down with an acceleration a (where $a < g$). How much mass should be removed from it so that it starts moving up with an acceleration a ?

[NEET (UG) 2014]

(A) $\dfrac{2ma}{g+a}$

(B) $\dfrac{2ma}{g-a}$

(C) $\dfrac{ma}{g+a}$

(D) $\dfrac{ma}{g-a}$

15. Two blocks A and B of masses $3\,m$ and m respectively are connected by a massless and inextensible string. The whole system is suspended by a massless spring as shown in figure. The magnitudes of acceleration of A and B immediately after the string is cut, are respectively :

[NEET (UG) 2017]

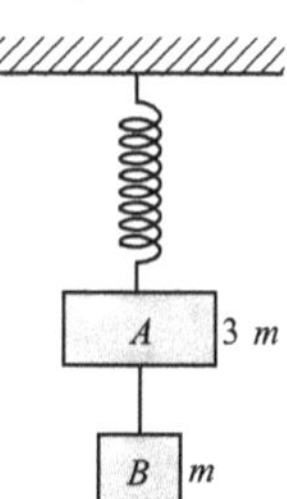

(A) $g, \dfrac{g}{3}$

(B) $\dfrac{g}{3}, g$

(C) g, g

(D) $\dfrac{g}{3}, \dfrac{g}{3}$

16. A block of mass m is placed on a smooth inclined wedge ABC of inclination θ as shown in the figure. The wedge is given an acceleration 'a' towards the right. The relation between a and θ for the block to remain stationary on the wedge is :

[NEET (UG) 2018]

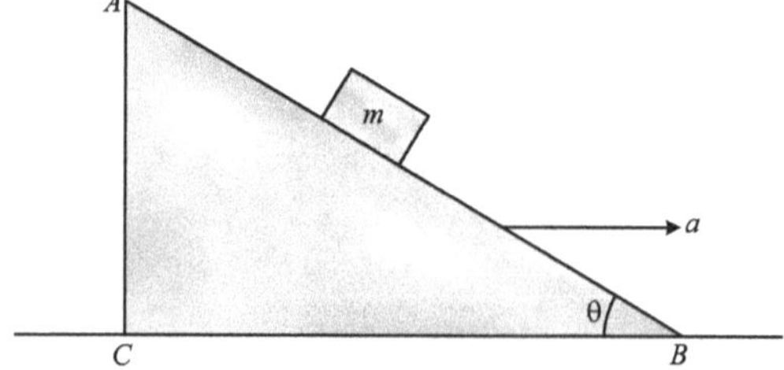

(A) $a = g \cos\theta$

(B) $a = \dfrac{g}{\sin\theta}$

(C) $a = \dfrac{g}{\mathrm{cosec}\,\theta}$

(D) $a = g \tan\theta$

17. A particle moving with velocity $\vec{V}$ is acted by three forces shown by the vector triangle PQR. The velocity of the particle will : **[NEET (UG) 2019]**

(A) Increase

(B) Decrease

(C) Remain constant

(D) Change according to the smallest force

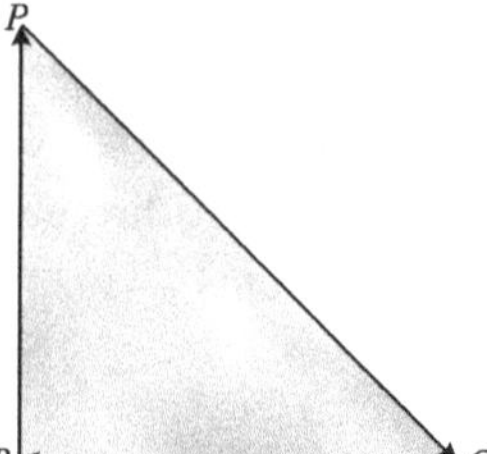

18. Two bodies of mass 4 kg and 6 kg are tied to the ends of a massless string. The string passes over a pulley which is frictionless (see figure). The acceleration of the system in terms of acceleration due to gravity (g) is : **[NEET (UG) 2020]**

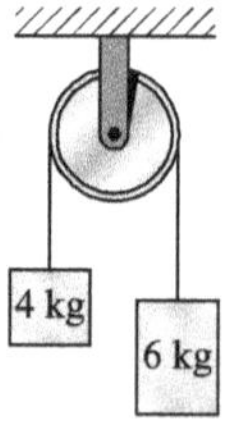

(A) $g/10$

(B) g

(C) $g/2$

(D) $g/5$

19. An electric lift with a maximum load of 2000 kg (lift + passengers) is moving up with a constant speed of 1.5 ms^{-1}. The frictional force opposing the motion is 3000 N. The minimum power delivered by the motor to the lift in watts is :

($g = 10$ ms^{-2}) **[NEET (UG) 2022]**

(A) 20000

(B) 34500

(C) 23500

(D) 23000

4.2 Friction

1. On the horizontal surface of a truck a block of mass 1 kg is placed ($\mu = 0.6$) and truck is moving with acceleration 5 m/s² then the frictional force on the block will be : **[NEET (UG) 2001]**

(A) 5 N
(B) 6 N
(C) 5.88 N
(D) 8 N

2. A block of mass 10 kg placed on rough horizontal surface having coefficient of friction $\mu = 0.5$, if a horizontal force of 100 N acting on it then acceleration of the block will be : **[NEET (UG) 2002]**

(A) 10 m/s²
(B) 5 m/s²
(C) 15 m/s²
(D) 0.5 m/s²

3. The coefficient of static friction, μ_s, between block A of mass 2 kg and the table as shown in the figure, is 0.2. What would be the maximum mass value of block B so that the two blocks do not move ? The string and the pulley are assumed to be smooth and massless. ($g = 10$ m/s²) : **[NEET (UG) 2004]**

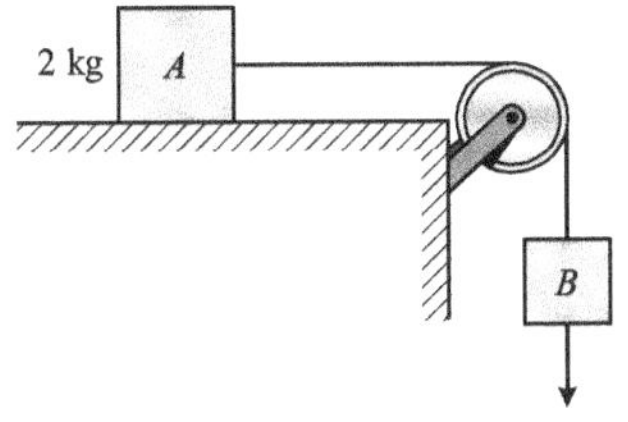

(A) 2.0 kg
(B) 4.0 kg
(C) 0.2 kg
(D) 0.4 kg

4. A block B is pushed momentarily along a horizontal surface with an initial velocity V. If μ is the coefficient of sliding friction between B and the surface, block B will come to rest after a time : **[NEET (UG) 2007]**

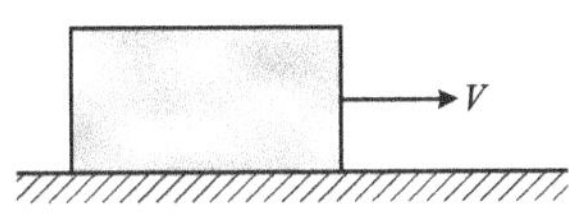

(A) $g\mu/V$
(B) g/V
(C) V/g
(D) $V/(g\mu)$

5. A block of mass m is in contact with the cart C as shown in the Figure. The coefficient of static friction between the block and the cart is μ. The acceleration α of the cart that will prevent the block from falling satisfies : **[NEET (UG) 2010]**

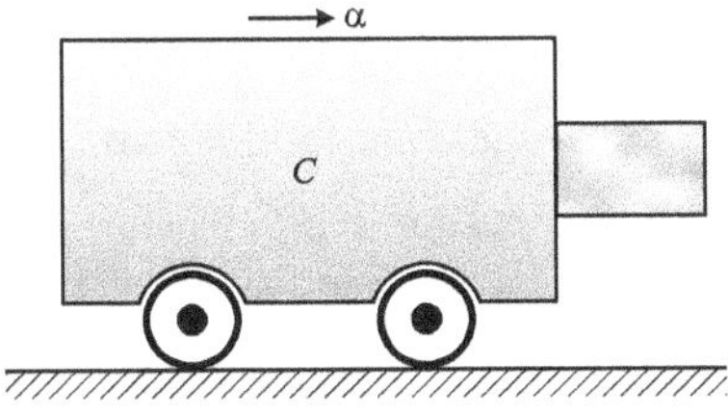

(A) $\alpha < \dfrac{g}{\mu}$
(B) $\alpha > \dfrac{g}{\mu m}$
(C) $\alpha > \dfrac{mg}{\mu}$
(D) $\alpha \geq \dfrac{g}{\mu}$

6. The upper half of an inclined plane of inclination θ is perfectly smooth while lower half is rough. A block starting from rest at the top of the plane will again come to rest at the bottom, if the coefficient of friction between the block and lower half of the plane is given by : **[NEET (UG) 2013]**

(A) $\mu = \dfrac{1}{\tan\theta}$
(B) $\mu = \dfrac{2}{\tan\theta}$
(C) $\mu = 2\tan\theta$
(D) $\mu = \tan\theta$

7. A system consists of three masses m_1, m_2 and m_3 connected by a string passing over a pulley P. The mass m_1 hangs freely and m_2 and m_3 are on a rough horizontal table (the coefficient of friction = μ). The pulley is frictionless and of negligible mass. The downward acceleration of mass m_1 is : (Assume $m_1 = m_2 = m_3 = m$) : **[NEET (UG) 2014]**

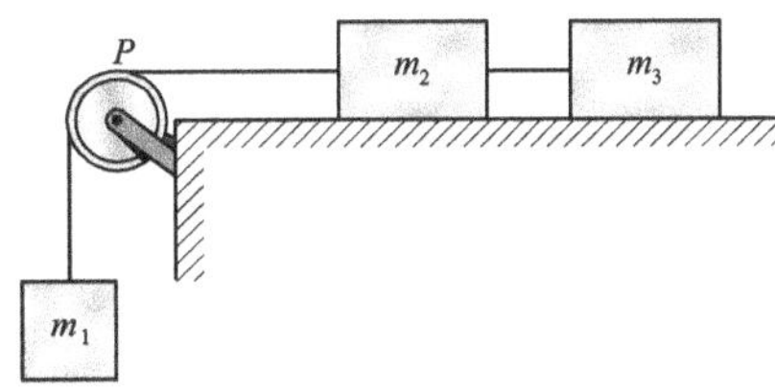

(A) $\dfrac{g(1 - g\mu)}{9}$
(B) $\dfrac{2g\mu}{3}$
(C) $\dfrac{g(1 - 2\mu)}{3}$
(D) $\dfrac{g(1 - 2\mu)}{2}$

8. A plank with a box on it at one end is gradually raised about the other end. As the angle of inclination with the horizontal reaches 30°, the box starts to slip and slides 4.0 m down the plank is 4.0 s. The coefficients of static and kinetic friction between the box and the plank will be, respectively : **[NEET (UG) 2015]**

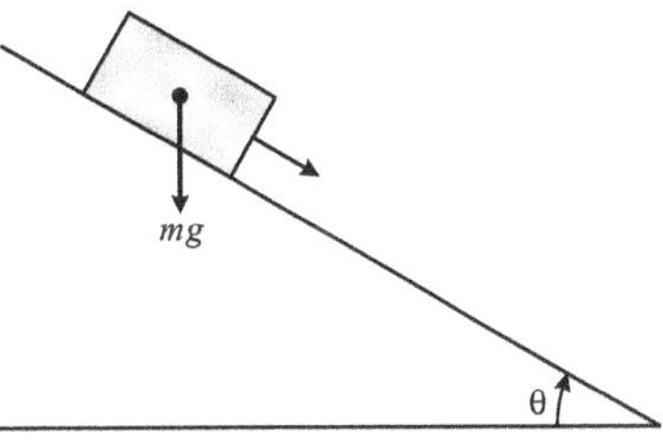

(A) 0.4 and 0.3
(B) 0.6 and 0.6
(C) 0.6 and 0.5
(D) 0.5 and 0.6

* * * * *

5.1 Kinetic & Potential Energy

1. A particle is projected making an angle of 45° with horizontal having kinetic energy K. The kinetic energy at highest point will be : **[NEET (UG) 2001]**

(A) $\dfrac{K}{\sqrt{2}}$

(B) $\dfrac{K}{2}$

(C) $2K$

(D) K

2. Two springs A and B having spring constant K_A and K_B ($K_A = 2K_B$) are stretched by applying force of equal magnitude. If energy stored in spring A is E_A then energy stored in B will be: **[NEET (UG) 2001]**

(A) $2E_A$

(B) $E_A/4$

(C) $E_A/2$

(D) $4E_A$

3. A child is sitting on a swing. Its minimum and maximum heights from the ground 0.75 m and 2 m respectively, its maximum speed will be : **[NEET (UG) 2001]**

(A) 10 m/s

(B) 5 m/s

(C) 8 m/s

(D) 15 m/s

4. If kinetic energy of a body is increased by 300% then percentage change in momentum will be : **[NEET (UG) 2002]**

(A) 100%

(B) 150%

(C) 265%

(D) 73.2%

5. When a long spring is stretched by 2 cm, its potential energy is U. If the spring is stretched by 10 cm, the potential energy stored in it will be : **[NEET (UG) 2003]**

(A) $U/5$

(B) $5U$

(C) $10U$

(D) $25U$

6. A particle of mass m_1 is moving with a velocity v_1 and another particle of mass m_2 is moving with a velocity v_2. Both of them have the same momentum but their different kinetic energies are E_1 and E_2 respectively. If $m_1 > m_2$ then : **[NEET (UG) 2004]**

(A) $E_1 < E_2$

(B) $\dfrac{E_1}{E_2} = \dfrac{m_1}{m_2}$

(C) $E_1 > E_2$

(D) $E_1 = E_2$

7. A ball of mass 2 kg and another of mass 4 kg are dropped together from a 60 feet tall building. After a fall of 30 feet each towards earth, their respective kinetic energies will be in the ratio of : **[NEET (UG) 2004]**

(A) $\sqrt{2} : 1$

(B) $1 : 4$

(C) $1 : 2$

(D) $1 : \sqrt{2}$

8. A mass of 0.5 kg moving with a speed of 1.5 m/s on a horizontal smooth surface, collides with a nearly weightless spring of force constant $k = 50$ N/m. The maximum compression of the spring would be : **[NEET (UG) 2004]**

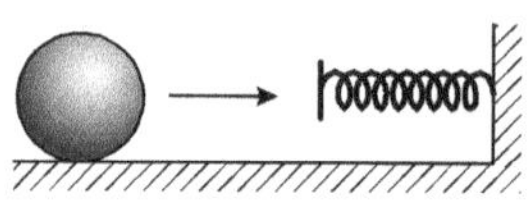

(A) 0.15 m

(B) 0.12 m

(C) 1.5 m

(D) 0.5 m

9. The potential energy of a long spring when stretched by 2 cm is U. If the spring is stretched by 8 cm the potential energy stored in it is : **[NEET (UG) 2006]**

(A) $4U$

(B) $8U$

(C) $16U$

(D) $\dfrac{U}{4}$

10. A block of mass M is attached to the lower end of a vertical spring. The spring is hung from a ceiling and has force constant value k. The mass is released from rest with the spring initially unstretched. The maximum extension produced in the length of the spring will be : **[NEET (UG) 2009]**

(A) $Mg/2k$

(B) Mg/k

(C) $2\,Mg/k$

(D) $4\,Mg/k$

11. The potential energy of a system increases if work is done : **[NEET (UG) 2011]**

(A) Upon the system by a non conservative force

(B) By the system against conservative force

(C) By the system against a non conservative force

(D) Upon the system by a conservative force

12. The potential energy of particle in a force field is $U = \dfrac{A}{r^2} - \dfrac{B}{r}$ where A and B are positive constants and r is the distance of particle from the centre of the field. For stable equilibrium, the distance of the particle is : **[NEET (UG) 2012]**

(A) $B/2A$

(B) $2A/B$

(C) A/B

(D) B/A

13. A particle is released from height S from the surface of the Earth. At a certain height its kinetic energy is three times its potential energy. The height from the surface of earth and the speed of the particle at that instant are respectively :

[NEET (UG) 2021]

(A) $\dfrac{S}{4}, \dfrac{3gS}{2}$

(B) $\dfrac{S}{4}, \dfrac{\sqrt{3gS}}{2}$

(C) $\dfrac{S}{2}, \dfrac{\sqrt{3gS}}{2}$

(D) $\dfrac{S}{4}, \sqrt{\dfrac{3gS}{2}}$

5.2 Work

1. 250 N force is required to raise 75 kg mass from a pulley. If rope is pulled 12 m then the load is lifted to 3 m, the efficiency of pulley system will be : **[NEET (UG) 2001]**

(A) 25%

(B) 33.3%

(C) 75%

(D) 90%

2. A force F acting on an object varies with distance x as shown here. The force is in newton and x in m. The work done by the force in moving the object from $x = 0$ to $x = 6$ m is :

[NEET (UG) 2005]

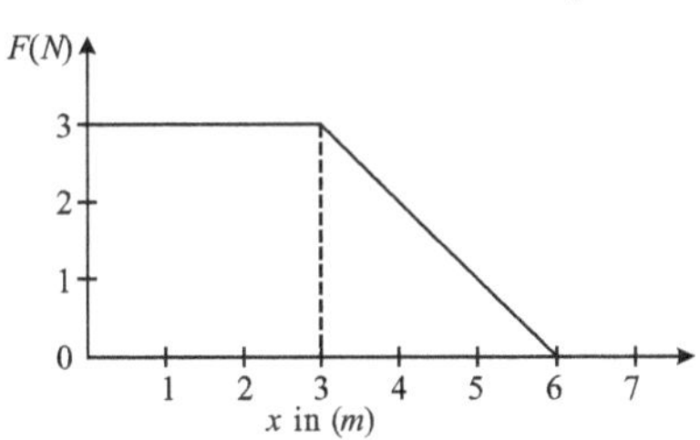

(A) 18.0 J

(B) 13.5 J

(C) 4.5 J

(D) 9.0 J

3. A body of mass 3 kg is under a constant force which causes a displacement s in metres in it, given by the relation $s = 1/3 t^2$, where t is in seconds. Work done by the force in 2 seconds is :

[NEET (UG) 2006]

(A) $\dfrac{5}{19} J$

(B) $\dfrac{3}{8} J$

(C) $\dfrac{8}{3} J$

(D) $\dfrac{19}{5} J$

4. 300 J of work is done in sliding a 2 kg block up an inclined plane of height 10 m. Taking $g = 10$ m/s^2, work done against friction is : **[NEET (UG) 2006]**

(A) 200 J

(B) 100 J

(C) Zero

(D) 1000 J

5. A vertical spring with force constant k is fixed on a table. A ball of mass m at a height h above the free upper end of the spring falls vertically on the spring so that the spring is compressed by a distance d. The net work done in the process is : **[NEET (UG) 2007]**

(A) $mg(h + d) - \dfrac{1}{2}kd^2$

(B) $mg(h - d) - \dfrac{1}{2}kd^2$

(C) $mg(h - d) + \dfrac{1}{2}kd^2$

(D) $mg(h + d) + \dfrac{1}{2}kd^2$

6. Force F on a particle moving in a straight line varies with distance d as shown in the figure. The work done on the particle during its displacement of 12 m is : **[NEET (UG) 2011]**

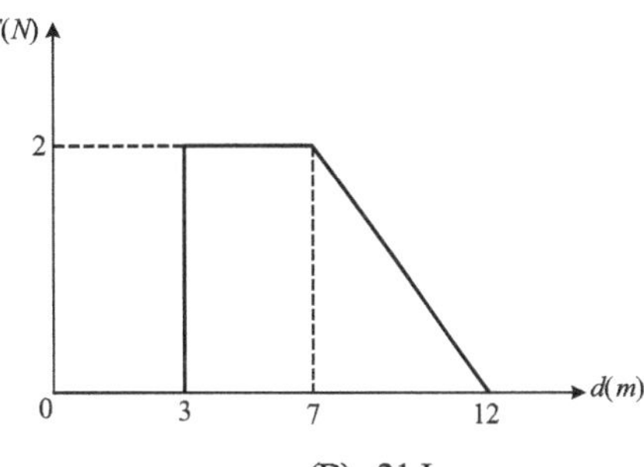

(A) 18 J

(B) 21 J

(C) 26 J

(D) 13 J

7. A uniform force of $(3\hat{i} + \hat{j})$ newton acts on a particle of mass 2 kg. Hence the particle is displaced from position $(2\hat{i} + \hat{k})$ meter to position $(4\hat{i} + 3\hat{j} - \hat{k})$ meter. The work done by the force on the particle is : **[NEET (UG) 2013]**

(A) 9 J

(B) 6 J

(C) 13 J

(D) 15 J

8. A particle moves from a point $(-2\hat{i} + 5\hat{j})$ to $(4\hat{j} + 3\hat{k})$ when a force of $(4\hat{i} + 3\hat{j})$ N is applied. How much work has been done by the force ? **[NEET (UG) 2016 Ph. II]**

(A) 8 J

(B) 11 J

(C) 5 J

(D) 2 J

9. A spring of force constant k is cut into lengths of ratio 1 : 2 : 3. They are connected in series and the new force constant is k'. Then they are connected in parallel and force constant is k''. Then $k' : k''$ is : **[NEET (UG) 2017]**

(A) 1 : 6

(B) 1 : 9

(C) 1 : 11

(D) 1 : 14

10. Consider a drop of rain water having mass 1 g falling from a height of 1 km. It hits the ground with a speed of 50 m/s. Take g constant with a value 10 m/s^2. The work done by the (i) gravitational force and the (ii) resistive force of air is :

[NEET (UG) 2017]

(A) (i) $- 10$ J   (ii) -8.25 J

(B) (i) 1.25 J   (ii) -8.25 J

(C) (i) 100 J   (ii) 8.75 J

(D) (i) 10 J   (ii) -8.75 J

11. A force $F = 20 + 10y$ acts on a particle in y-direction where F is in newton and y in meter. Work done by this force to move the particle from $y = 0$ to $y = 1$ m is : **[NEET (UG) 2019]**
(A) 30 J
(B) 5 J
(C) 25 J
(D) 20 J

5.3 Power

1. Water falls from a height of 60 m at the rate of 15 kg/s to operate a turbine. The losses due to frictional forces are 10% of energy. How much power is generated by the turbine ? $(g = 10 \text{ m/s}^2)$: **[NEET (UG) 2008]**
(A) 12.3 kW
(B) 7.0 kW
(C) 8.1 kW
(D) 10.2 kW

2. An engine pumps water continuously through a hose. Water leaves the hose with a velocity v and m is the mass per unit length of the water jet. What is the rate which kinetic energy is imparted to water ? **[NEET (UG) 2009]**
(A) $\frac{1}{2}m^2v^2$
(B) $\frac{1}{2}mv^3$
(C) mv^3
(D) $\frac{1}{2}mv^2$

3. An engine pumps water through a hose pipe. Water passes through the pipe and leaves it with a velocity of 2 m/s. The mass per unit length of water in the pipe is 100 kg/m. What is the power of the engine ? **[NEET (UG) 2010]**
(A) 800 W
(B) 400 W
(C) 200 W
(D) 100 W

4. A car of mass m starts from rest and accelerates so that the instantaneous power delivered to the car has a constant magnitude P_0. The instantaneous velocity of this car is proportional to : **[NEET (UG) 2012]**
(A) $t^{1/2}$
(B) $t^{-1/2}$
(C) $t / \sqrt{m}$
(D) $t^2 P_0$

5. The heart of a man pumps 5 litres of blood through the arteries per minute at a pressure of 150 mm of mercury. If the density of mercury be 13.6×10^3 kg/m^3 and $g = 10$ m/s^2 then the power of heart in watt is : **[NEET (UG) 2015]**
(A) 1.50
(B) 1.70
(C) 2.35
(D) 3.0

6. A body of mass 1 kg begins to move under the action of a time dependent force $F = (2t\,\hat{i} + 3t^2\,\hat{j})\,N$, where $\hat{i}$ and $\hat{j}$ are unit vectors along x and y-axis. What power will be developed by the force at the time t ? **[NEET (UG) 2016]**
(A) $(2t^2 + 3t^2)\,W$
(B) $(2t^2 + 4t^4)\,W$
(C) $(2t^3 + 3t^4)\,W$
(D) $(2t^3 + 3t^5)\,W$

7. Water falls from a height of 60 m at the rate of 15 kg/s to operate a turbine. The losses due to frictional force are 10% of the input energy. How much power is generated by the turbine ? $(g = 10 \text{ m/s}^2)$ **[NEET (UG) 2021]**
(A) 10.2 kW
(B) 8.1 kW
(C) 12.3 kW
(D) 7.0 kW

8. The energy that will be ideally radiated by a 100 kW transmitter in 1 hour is : **[NEET (UG) 2022]**
(A) 36×10^4 J
(B) 36×10^5 J
(C) 1×10^5 J
(D) 36×10^7 J

5.4 Circular Motion

1. Two particles having mass M and m are moving in a circular path having radius R and r. If their time period are same then the ratio of angular velocity will be : **[NEET (UG) 2001]**
(A) $\frac{r}{R}$
(B) $\frac{R}{r}$
(C) 1
(D) $\sqrt{R / r}$

2. A stone tied to the end of a string of 1 m long is whirled in a horizontal circle with a constant speed. If the stone makes 22 revolution in 44 seconds, what is the magnitude and direction of acceleration of the stone : **[NEET (UG) 2005]**
(A) $\pi^2 \text{ ms}^{-2}$ and direction along the tangent to the circle
(B) $\pi^2 \text{ ms}^{-2}$ and direction along the radius towards the centre
(C) $\pi^2/4 \text{ ms}^{-2}$ and direction along the radius towards the centre
(D) $\pi^2 \text{ ms}^{-2}$ and direction along the radius away from the centre

3. The circular motion of a particle with constant speed is : **[NEET (UG) 2005]**
(A) Periodic and simple harmonic
(B) Simple harmonic but not periodic
(C) Neither periodic nor simple harmonic
(D) Periodic but not simple harmonic

4. A car runs at a constant speed on a circular track of radius 100 m, taking 62.8 seconds for every circular lap. The average velocity and average speed for each circular lap respectively is : **[NEET (UG) 2006]**
(A) 0, 0
(B) 0, 10 m/s
(C) 10 m/s, 10 m/s
(D) 10 m/s, 0

5. A gramophone record is revolving with an angular velocity ω. A coin is placed at a distance r from the centre of the record. The static coefficient of friction is μ. The coin will revolve with the record if : **[NEET (UG) 2010]**
(A) $r \geq \dfrac{\mu g}{\omega^2}$
(B) $r = \mu g \omega^2$
(C) $r < \dfrac{\omega}{\mu g}$
(D) $r \leq \dfrac{\mu g}{\omega^2}$

6. A particle moves in a circle of radius 5 cm with constant speed and time period $0.2\pi\,s$. The acceleration of the particle is : **[NEET (UG) 2011]**

(A) $15\,\text{m/s}^2$ (B) $25\,\text{m/s}^2$

(C) $36\,\text{m/s}^2$ (D) $5\,\text{m/s}^2$

7. A car of mass 1000 kg negotiates a banked curve of radius 90 m on a frictionless road. If the banking angle is 45°, the speed of the car is : **[NEET (UG) 2012]**

(A) $20\,\text{ms}^{-1}$ (B) $30\,\text{ms}^{-1}$

(C) $5\,\text{ms}^{-1}$ (D) $10\,\text{ms}^{-1}$

8. A car of mass m is moving on a level circular track of radius R. If μ_s represents the static friction between the road and tyres of the car, the maximum speed of the car in circular motion is given by : **[NEET (UG) 2012]**

(A) $\sqrt{Rg\,/\,\mu_s}$ (B) $\sqrt{mRg\,/\,\mu_s}$

(C) $\sqrt{\mu_s Rg}$ (D) $\sqrt{\mu_s mRg}$

9. The position vector of a particle $\vec{R}$ as a function of time is given by :

$$\vec{R} = 4\sin(2\pi t)\,\hat{i} + 4\cos(2\pi t)\,\hat{j}$$

Where R is in meters, t is in seconds and $\hat{i}$ and $\hat{j}$ denote unit vectors along x and y-directions, respectively. Which one of the following statement is wrong for the motion of particle ? **[NEET (UG) 2015]**

(A) Path of the particle is a circle of radius 1 meter

(B) Acceleration vector is along $-\vec{R}$

(C) Magnitude of acceleration vector is v^2/R where v is the velocity of particle

(D) Magnitude of the velocity of particle is 8π m/s

10. Two stones of masses m and $2\,m$ are whirled in horizontal circles, the heavier one in radius $r/2$ and the lighter one in radius r. The tangential speed of lighter stone is n times that of the value of heavier stone when they experience same centripetal forces. The value of n is : **[NEET (UG) 2015]**

(A) 1   (B) 2

(C) 3   (D) 4

11. A particle moves so that its position vector is given by $\vec{r} = \cos\omega t\,\hat{x} + \sin\omega t\,\hat{y}$ where ω is a constant. Which of the following is true ? **[NEET (UG) 2016]**

(A) Velocity and acceleration both are perpendicular to $\vec{r}$

(B) Velocity and acceleration both are parallel to $\vec{r}$

(C) Velocity is perpendicular to $\vec{r}$ and acceleration is directed towards the origin

(D) Velocity is perpendicular to $\vec{r}$ and acceleration is directed away from the origin

12. A car is negotiating a curved road of radius R. The road is banked at an angle θ. The coefficient of friction between the tyres of the car and the road is μ_s. The maximum safe velocity on this road is : **[NEET (UG) 2016]**

(A) $\sqrt{gR^2\dfrac{\mu_s + \tan\theta}{1 - \mu_s\tan\theta}}$ (B) $\sqrt{gR\dfrac{\mu_s + \tan\theta}{1 - \mu_s\tan\theta}}$

(C) $\sqrt{\dfrac{g}{R}\dfrac{\mu_s + \tan\theta}{1 - \mu_s\tan\theta}}$ (D) $\sqrt{\dfrac{g}{R^2}\dfrac{\mu_s + \tan\theta}{1 - \mu_s\tan\theta}}$

13. One end of string of length l is connected to a particle of mass 'm' and the other end is connected to a small peg on a smooth horizontal table. If the particle moves in circle with speed 'v', the net force on the particle (directed towards center) will be (T represents the tension in the string) : **[NEET (UG) 2017]**

(A) T (B) $T + \dfrac{mv^2}{l}$

(C) $T - \dfrac{mv^2}{l}$ (D) Zero

14. Two particles A and B are moving in uniform circular motion in concentric circles of radii r_A and r_B with speed v_A and v_B respectively. Their time period of rotation is the same. The ratio of angular speed of A to that of B will be : **[NEET (UG) 2019]**

(A) $r_A : r_B$ (B) $v_A : v_B$

(C) $r_B : r_A$ (D) $1 : 1$

15. A block of mass 10 kg is in contact against the inner wall of a hollow cylindrical drum of radius 1 m. The coefficient of friction between the block and the inner wall of the cylinder is 0.1. The minimum angular velocity needed for the cylinder to keep the block stationary when the cylinder is vertical and rotating about its axis, will be : $(g = 10\,\text{m/s}^2)$: **[NEET (UG) 2019]**

(A) $\sqrt{10}$ rad/s   (B) $\dfrac{10}{2\pi}$ rad/s

(C) 10 rad/s   (D) 10π rad/s

16. The radius of circle, the period of revolution, initial position and sense of revolution are indicated in the figure y-projection of the radius vector of rotating particle P is : **[NEET (UG) 2019]**

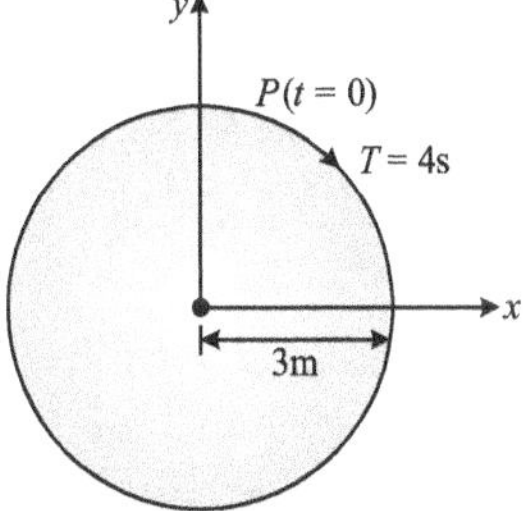

(A) $y(t) = -3\cos 2\pi t$, where y in m

(B) $y(t) = 4\sin\left(\dfrac{\pi t}{2}\right)$, where y in m

(C) $y(t) = 3 \cos\left(\dfrac{3\pi t}{2}\right)$, where y in m

(D) $y(t) = 3 \cos\left(\dfrac{\pi t}{2}\right)$, where y in m

17. A particle moving in a circle of radius R with a uniform speed takes a time T to complete one revolution. If this particle were projected with the same speed at an angle 'θ' to the horizontal, the maximum height attained by it equals $4R$. The angle of projection, θ, is then given by :   **[NEET (UG) 2021]**

(A) $\theta = \cos^{-1}\left(\dfrac{gT^2}{\pi^2 R}\right)^{1/2}$

(B) $\theta = \cos^{-1}\left(\dfrac{\pi^2 R}{gT^2}\right)^{1/2}$

(C) $\theta = \sin^{-1}\left(\dfrac{\pi^2 R}{gT^2}\right)^{1/2}$

(D) $\theta = \sin^{-1}\left(\dfrac{2gT^2}{\pi^2 R}\right)^{1/2}$

18. The angular speed on a fly wheel moving with uniform angular acceleration changes from 1200 rpm to 3120 rpm in 16 seconds. The angular acceleration in rad/s^2 is :

                                 [NEET (UG) 2022]

(A) 4π (B) 12π

(C) 104π (D) 2π

5.5 Non Uniform Circular Motion

1. A particle moves along a circle of radius $\left(\dfrac{20}{\pi}\right)$ m with constant tangential acceleration. If the velocity of the particle is 80 m/s at the end of the second revolution after motion has begun, the tangential acceleration is :   **[NEET (UG) 2003]**

(A) $40\ \text{m/s}^2$ (B) $640\ \pi\ \text{m/s}^2$

(C) $160\ \pi\ \text{m/s}^2$ (D) $40\ \pi\ \text{m/s}^2$

2. A stone is tied to a string of length l and is whirled in a vertical circle with the other end of the string as the centre. At a certain instant of time, the stone is at its lowest position and has a speed u. The magnitude of the change in velocity as it reaches a position where the string is horizontal (g being acceleration due to gravity) is :   **[NEET (UG) 2003]**

(A) $\sqrt{2(u^2 - gl)}$ (B) $\sqrt{u^2 - gl}$

(C) $u - \sqrt{u^2 - 2gl}$ (D) $\sqrt{2gl}$

3. A roller coaster is designed such that riders experience "weightlessness" as they go round the top of a hill whose radius of curvature is 20 m. The speed of the car at the top of the hill is between :   **[NEET (UG) 2008]**

(A) 16 m/s and 17 m/s   (B) 13 m/s and 14 m/s

(C) 14 m/s and 15 m/s   (D) 15 m/s and 16 m/s

4. A particle of mass 10 g moves along a circle of radius 6.4 cm with a constant tangential acceleration. What is the magnitude of this acceleration if the kinetic energy of the particle becomes equal to 8×10^{-4} J by the end of the second revolution after the beginning of the motion ?   **[NEET (UG) 2016]**

(A) $0.1\ \text{m/s}^2$ (B) $0.15\ \text{m/s}^2$

(C) $0.18\ \text{m/s}^2$ (D) $0.2\ \text{m/s}^2$

5. What is the minimum velocity with which a body of mass m must enter a vertical loop of radius R so that it can complete the loop ?   **[NEET (UG) 2016]**

(A) $\sqrt{gR}$ (B) $\sqrt{2gR}$

(C) $\sqrt{3gR}$ (D) $\sqrt{5gR}$

6. In the given figure, $a = 15$ m/s^2 represents the total acceleration of a particle moving in the clockwise direction in a circle of radius $R = 2.5$ m at a given instant of time. The speed of the particle is :   **[NEET (UG) 2016 Ph. II]**

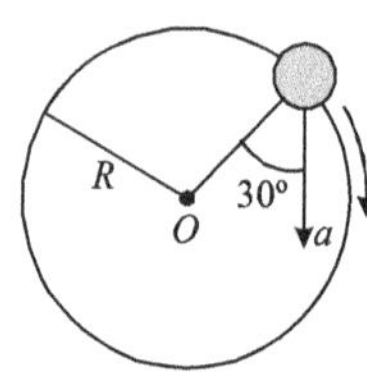

(A) 4.5 m/s   (B) 5.0 m/s

(C) 5.7 m/s   (D) 6.2 m/s

7. A body initially at rest and sliding along a frictionless track from a height h (as shown in the figure) just completes a vertical circle of diameter $AB = D$. The height h is equal to :

                                 [NEET (UG) 2018]

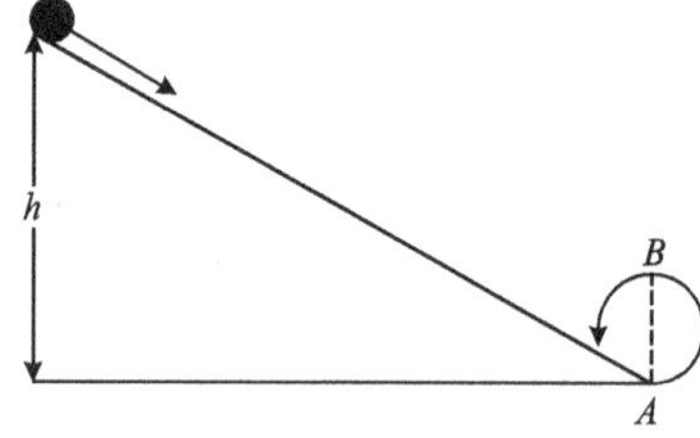

(A) $\dfrac{7}{5}D$ (B) D

(C) $\dfrac{3}{2}D$ (D) $\dfrac{5}{4}D$

8. A mass m is attached to a thin wire and whirled in a vertical circle. The wire is most likely to break when : **[NEET (UG) 2019]**

(A) The mass is at the highest point

(B) The wire is horizontal

(C) The mass is at the lowest point

(D) Inclined at an angle of 60° from vertical

*   *   *   *   *

SYSTEM OF PARTICLES & ROTATIONAL MOTION

6.1 Centre of Mass

1. A rod of length 3 m and its mass per unit length is directly proportional to distance x from one of its end then its centre of gravity from that end will be at : **[NEET (UG) 2002]**
(A) 1.5 m
(B) 2 m
(C) 2.5 m
(D) 3.0 m

2. Consider a system of two particles having masses m_1 and m_2. If the particle of mass m_1 is pushed towards the centre of mass of the particles through a distance d, by what distance would be particle of mass m_2 move so as to keep the centre of mass of the particles at the original position ?
[NEET (UG) 2004]
(A) $\dfrac{m_1}{m_1 + m_2} d$
(B) $\dfrac{m_1}{m_2} d$
(C) d
(D) $\dfrac{m_2}{m_1} d$

3. Two bodies of mass 1 kg and 3 kg have position vectors $\hat{i} + 2\hat{j} + \hat{k}$ and $-3\hat{i} - 2\hat{j} + \hat{k}$, respectively. The centre of mass of this system has a position vector : **[NEET (UG) 2009]**
(A) $-\hat{i} + \hat{j} + \hat{k}$
(B) $-2\hat{i} + 2\hat{k}$
(C) $-2\hat{i} - \hat{j} + \hat{k}$
(D) $2\hat{i} - \hat{j} - 2\hat{k}$

4. A man of 50 kg mass is standing in a gravity free space at a height of 10 m above the floor. He throws a stone of 0.5 kg mass downwards with a speed 2 m/s. When the stone reaches the floor, the distance of the man above the floor will be :
[NEET (UG) 2010]
(A) 20 m
(B) 9.9 m
(C) 10.1 m
(D) 10 m

5. Two persons of masses 55 kg and 65 kg respectively, are at the opposite ends of a boat. The length of the boat is 3.0 m and weighs 100 kg. The 55 kg man walks up to the 65 kg man and sits with him. If the boat is in still water the centre of mass of the system shifts by : **[NEET (UG) 2012]**
(A) 3.0 m
(B) 2.3 m
(C) Zero
(D) 0.75 m

6. Three masses are placed on the x-axis : 300 g at origin, 500 g at $x = 40$ cm and 400 g at $x = 70$ cm. The distance of the centre of mass from the origin is : **[NEET (UG) 2012]**
(A) 45 cm
(B) 50 cm
(C) 30 cm
(D) 40 cm

7. Which of the following statements are correct ?
[NEET (UG) 2017]
(a) Centre of mass of a body always coincides with the centre of gravity of the body
(b) Centre of mass of a body is the point at which the total gravitational torque on the body is zero
(c) A couple on a body produce both translational and rotational motion in a body
(d) Mechanical advantage greater than one means that small effort can be used to lift a large load
(A) (b) and (d)
(B) (a) and (b)
(C) (b) and (c)
(D) (c) and (d)

8. Two particles of mass 5 kg and 10 kg respectively are attached to the two ends of a rigid rod of length 1 m with negligible mass. The centre of mass of the system from the 5 kg particle is nearly at a distance of : **[NEET (UG) 2020]**
(A) 80 cm
(B) 33 cm
(C) 50 cm
(D) 67 cm

9. Two objects of mass 10 kg and 20 kg respectively are connected to the two ends of a rigid rod of length 10 m with negligible mass. The distance of the center of mass of the system from the 10 kg mass is : **[NEET (UG) 2022]**
(A) $\dfrac{20}{3}$ m
(B) 10 m
(C) 5 m
(D) $\dfrac{10}{3}$ m

6.2 Impulse & Conservation of Momentum

1. A stationary particle explodes into two particles of masses m_1 and m_2 which move in opposite directions with velocities v_1 and v_2. The ratio of their kinetic energies E_1/E_2 is :
[NEET (UG) 2003]
(A) m_2/m_1
(B) m_1/m_2
(C) 1
(D) $m_1 v_2 / m_2 v_1$

2. A bomb of mass 30 kg at rest explodes into two pieces of masses 18 kg and 12 kg. The velocity of 18 kg mass is 6 ms^{-1}. The kinetic energy of the other mass is : **[NEET (UG) 2005]**
(A) 524 J
(B) 256 J
(C) 486 J
(D) 324 J

3. A 0.5 kg ball moving with a speed of 12 m/s strikes a hard wall at an angle of 30° with the wall. It is reflected with the same speed and at the same angle. If the ball is in contact with the wall for 0.25 seconds, the average force acting on the wall is :

[NEET (UG) 2006]

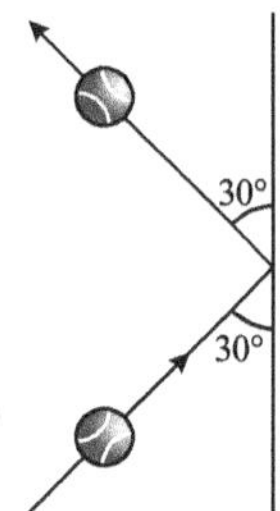

(A) 48 N

(B) 24 N

(C) 12 N

(D) 96 N

4. Sand is being dropped on a conveyor belt at the rate of M kg/s. The force necessary to keep the belt moving with a constant velocity of v m/s will be : **[NEET (UG) 2008]**

(A) $\dfrac{Mv}{2}$ newton

(B) Zero

(C) Mv newton

(D) $2\,Mv$ newton

5. A shell of mass 200 g is ejected from a gun of mass 4 kg by an explosion that generates 1.05 kJ of energy. The initial velocity of the shell is : **[NEET (UG) 2008]**

(A) $40\,ms^{-1}$

(B) $120\,ms^{-1}$

(C) $100\,ms^{-1}$

(D) $80\,ms^{-1}$

6. A particle of mass m is projected with velocity v making an angle of 45° with the horizontal from level ground. When the particle lands on the level ground the magnitude of the change in its momentum will be : **[NEET (UG) 2008]**

(A) $mv\sqrt{2}$

(B) Zero

(C) $2mv$

(D) $mv/\sqrt{2}$

7. A ball moving with velocity 2 m/s collides head on with another stationary ball of double the mass. If the coefficient of restitution is 0.5, then their velocities (in m/s) after collision will be : **[NEET (UG) 2010]**

(A) 0, 2

(B) 0, 1

(C) 1, 1

(D) 1, 05

8. Two particles which are initially at rest, move towards each other under the action of their internal attraction. If their speeds are v and $2v$ at any instant, then the speed of centre of mass of the system will be : **[NEET (UG) 2010]**

(A) v

(B) $2v$

(C) Zero

(D) $1.5\,v$

9. A body of mass M hits normally a rigid wall with velocity V and bounces back with the same velocity. The impulse experienced by the body is : **[NEET (UG) 2011]**

(A) MV

(B) $1.5\,MV$

(C) $2\,MV$

(D) Zero

10. An explosion blows a rock into three parts. Two parts go off at right angles to each other. These two are, 1 kg first part moving with a velocity of 12 ms^{-1} and 2 kg second part moving with a velocity of 8 ms^{-1}. If the thirds part files off with a velocity of 4 ms^{-1}, its mass would be : **[NEET (UG) 2009]**

(A) 3 kg

(B) 5 kg

(C) 7 kg

(D) 17 kg

11. A body of mass $(4\,m)$ is lying in x-y plane at rest. It suddenly explodes into three pieces. Two pieces each of mass (m) move perpendicular to each other with equal speeds (v). The total kinetic energy generated due to explosion is : **[NEET (UG) 2014]**

(A) mv^2

(B) $\dfrac{3}{2}mv^2$

(C) $2\,mv^2$

(D) $4\,mv^2$

12. A ball is thrown vertically downwards from a height of 20 m with an initial velocity v_0. It collides with the ground loses 50 percent of its energy in collision and rebounds to the same height. The initial velocity v_0 is : (Take $g = 10ms^{-2}$)

[NEET (UG) 2015]

(A) $10\,ms^{-1}$

(B) $14\,ms^{-1}$

(C) $20\,ms^{-1}$

(D) $28\,ms^{-1}$

13. On a frictionless surface a block of M moving at speed v collides elastically with another block of same mass M which is initially at rest. After collision the first block moves at an angle θ to its initial direction and has a speed $\dfrac{v}{3}$. The second block's speed after the collision is : **[NEET (UG) 2015]**

(A) $\dfrac{\sqrt{3}}{2}v$

(B) $\dfrac{2\sqrt{2}}{3}v$

(C) $\dfrac{3}{4}v$

(D) $\dfrac{3}{\sqrt{2}}v$

14. A bullet of mass 10 g moving horizontally with a velocity of 400 ms^{-1} strikes a wooden block of mass 2 kg which is suspended by a light inextensible string of length 5 m. As a result, the centre of gravity of the block is found to rise a vertical distance of 10 cm. The speed of the bullet after it emerges out horizontally from the block will be : **[NEET (UG) 2016 Ph. II]**

(A) $100\,ms^{-1}$

(B) $80\,ms^{-1}$

(C) $120\,ms^{-1}$

(D) $160\,ms^{-1}$

15. Two identical balls A and B having velocities of 0.5 m/s and -0.3 m/s respectively collide elastically in one dimension. The velocities of B and A after the collision respectively will be :

[NEET (UG) 2016 Ph. II]

(A) -0.5 m/s and 0.3 m/s   (B) 0.5 m/s and -0.3 m/s
(C) -0.3 m/s and 0.5 m/s   (D) 0.3 m/s and 0.5 m/s

16. A moving block having mass m, collides with another stationary block having mass 4 m. The lighter block comes to rest after collision. When the initial velocity of the lighter block is v, then the value of coefficient of restitution (e) will be :

[NEET (UG) 2018]

(A) 0.8   (B) 0.25
(C) 0.5   (D) 0.4

17. Body A of mass 4 m moving with speed u collides with another body B of mass 2 m, at rest. The collision is head on and elastic in nature. After the collision the fraction of energy lost by the colliding body A is : **[NEET (UG) 2019]**

(A) $\dfrac{1}{9}$ (B) $\dfrac{8}{9}$

(C) $\dfrac{4}{9}$ (D) $\dfrac{5}{9}$

18. A ball of mass 0.15 kg is dropped from a height 10 m, strikes the ground and rebounds to the same height. The magnitude of impulse imparted to the ball is ($g = 10$ m/s^2) nearly :

[NEET (UG) 2021]

(A) 0 kg m/s   (B) 4.2 kg m/s
(C) 2.1 kg m/s   (D) 1.4 kg m/s

19. A shell of mass m is at rest initially. It explodes into three fragments having mass in the ratio 2 : 2 : 1. If the fragments having equal mass fly off along mutually perpendicular directions with speed v, the speed of the third (lighter) fragment is : **[NEET (UG) 2022]**

(A) $\sqrt{2}v$ (B) $2\sqrt{2}v$
(C) $3\sqrt{2}v$ (D) v

6.3 Moment of Inertia

1. A circular disc is to be made by using iron and aluminium so that it acquires maximum moment of inertia about geometrical axis. It is possible with : **[NEET (UG) 2002]**
(A) Aluminium at interior and iron surrounding it
(B) Iron at interior and aluminium surrounding it
(C) Using iron and aluminium layers in alternate order
(D) Sheet of iron is used at both external surface and aluminium sheet as internal layers

2. The ratio of the radii of gyration of a circular disc about a tangential axis in the plane of the disc and of a circular ring of the same radius and mass about a tangential axis in the plane of the ring is : **[NEET (UG) 2004]**
(A) 2 : 3   (B) 2 : 1
(C) $\sqrt{5} : \sqrt{6}$ (D) $1 : \sqrt{2}$

3. Three particles, each of mass m gram, are situated at the vertices of an equilateral triangle ABC of side l cm (as shown in the figure). The moment of inertia of the system about a line AX perpendicular to AB and in the plane of ABC, in gram-cm^2 units will be : **[NEET (UG) 2004]**

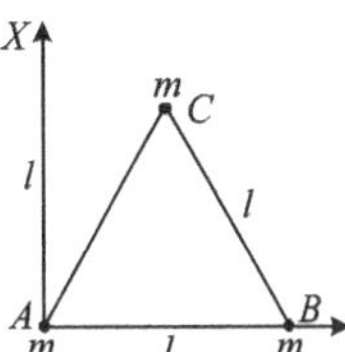

(A) $\dfrac{3}{4}ml^2$ (B) $2ml^2$

(C) $\dfrac{5}{4}ml^2$ (D) $\dfrac{3}{2}ml^2$

4. The moment of inertia of a uniform circular disc of radius 'R' and mass 'M' about an axis passing from the edge of the disc and normal to the disc is : **[NEET (UG) 2005]**

(A) $\dfrac{1}{2}MR^2$ (B) $\dfrac{7}{2}MR^2$

(C) $\dfrac{3}{2}MR^2$ (D) MR^2

5. Two bodies have their moments of inertia I and $2I$ respectively about their axis of rotation. If their kinetic energies of rotation are equal, their angular momentum will be in the ratio : **[NEET (UG) 2005]**

(A) 1 : 2   (B) $\sqrt{2} : 1$
(C) $1 : \sqrt{2}$ (D) 2 : 1

6. The moment of inertia of a uniform circular disc of radius 'R' and mass 'M' about an axis touching the disc at its diameter and normal to the disc is : **[NEET (UG) 2006]**

(A) MR^2 (B) $\dfrac{2}{5}MR^2$

(C) $\dfrac{3}{2}MR^2$ (D) $\dfrac{1}{2}MR^2$

7. A thin rod of length L and mass M is bent at its midpoint into two halves so that the angle between them is 90°. The moment of inertia of the bent rod about an axis passing through the bending point and perpendicular to the plane defined by the two halves of the rod is : **[NEET (UG) 2008]**

(A) $\dfrac{ML^2}{6}$

(B) $\dfrac{\sqrt{2}\,ML^2}{24}$

(C) $\dfrac{ML^2}{24}$

(D) $\dfrac{ML^2}{12}$

8. The ratio of the radii of gyration of a circular disc to that of a circular ring, each of same mass and radius around their respective axes is : **[NEET (UG) 2008]**

(A) $\sqrt{2}:1$

(B) $\sqrt{2}:\sqrt{3}$

(C) $\sqrt{3}:\sqrt{2}$

(D) $1:\sqrt{2}$

9. Four identical thin rods each of mass M and length l, form a square frame. Moment of inertia of this frame about an axis through the centre of the square and perpendicular to its plane is : **[NEET (UG) 2009]**

(A) $\dfrac{1}{2}Ml^2$

(B) $\dfrac{4}{3}Ml^2$

(C) $\dfrac{2}{3}Ml^2$

(D) $\dfrac{13}{3}Ml^2$

10. The moment of inertia of a thin uniform rod of mass M and length L about an axis passing through its midpoint and perpendicular to its length is I_0. Its moment of inertia about an axis passing through one of its ends and perpendicular to its length is : **[NEET (UG) 2011]**

(A) $I_0 + ML^2/2$

(B) $I_0 + ML^2/4$

(C) $I_0 + 2ML^2$

(D) $I_0 + ML^2$

11. The moment of inertia of a uniform circular disc is maximum about an axis perpendicular to the disc and passing through : **[NEET (UG) 2012]**

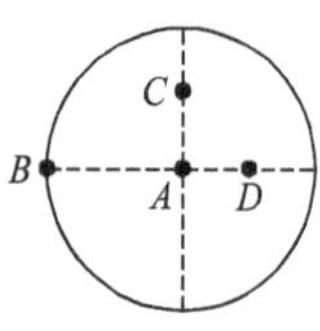

(A) C

(B) D

(C) A

(D) B

12. From a disc of radius R and mass M, a circular hole of diameter R, whose rim passes through the centre is cut. What is the moment of inertia of the remaining part of the disc about a perpendicular axis, passing through the centre ? **[NEET (UG) 2016]**

(A) $15MR^2/32$

(B) $13MR^2/32$

(C) $11MR^2/32$

(D) $9MR^2/32$

13. A light rod of length l has two masses m_1 and m_2 attached to its two ends. The moment of inertia of the system about an axis perpendicular to the rod and passing through the centre of mass is : **[NEET (UG) 2016 Ph. II]**

(A) $\dfrac{m_1 m_2}{m_1 + m_2}l^2$

(B) $\dfrac{m_1 + m_2}{m_1 m_2}l^2$

(C) $(m_1 + m_2)\, l^2$

(D) $\sqrt{m_1 m_2}\, l^2$

14. From a circular ring of mass 'M' and radius 'R' an arc corresponding to a 90° sector is removed. The moment of inertia of the remaining part of the ring about an axis passing through the centre of the ring and perpendicular to the plane of the ring is 'K' times 'MR^2'. Then the value of 'K' is : **[NEET (UG) 2021]**

(A) $\dfrac{3}{4}$

(B) $\dfrac{7}{8}$

(C) $\dfrac{1}{4}$

(D) $\dfrac{1}{8}$

15. The ratio of the radius of gyration of a thin uniform disc about an axis passing through its centre and normal to its plane to the radius of gyration of the disc about its diameter is : **[NEET (UG) 2022]**

(A) $\sqrt{2}:1$

(B) $4:1$

(C) $1:\sqrt{2}$

(D) $2:1$

6.4 Torque & Angular Acceleration

1. A wheel having moment of inertia 2 kg m^2 about its vertical axis, rotates at the rate of 60 rpm about this axis. The torque which can stop the wheel's rotation in one minute would be : **[NEET (UG) 2004]**

(A) $\dfrac{2\pi}{15}$ Nm

(B) $\dfrac{\pi}{12}$ Nm

(C) $\dfrac{\pi}{15}$ Nm

(D) $\dfrac{\pi}{18}$ Nm

2. A uniform rod of length l and mass m is free to rotate in a vertical plane about A. The rod initially in horizontal position is released. The initial angular acceleration of the rod is (Moment of inertia of rod about A is $\dfrac{ml^2}{3}$) : **[NEET (UG) 2006]**

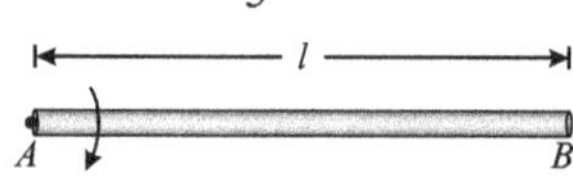

(A) $\dfrac{3g}{2l}$

(B) $\dfrac{2l}{3g}$

(C) $\dfrac{3g}{2l^2}$

(D) $mg\dfrac{l}{2}$

3. A wheel has angular acceleration of 3.0 rad/sec^2 and an

initial angular speed of 2.00 rad/s. In a time of 2 s it has rotated through an angle (in radian) of : **[NEET (UG) 2007]**
(A) 10
(B) 12
(C) 4
(D) 6

4. A uniform rod AB of length l, and mass m is free to rotate about point A. The rod is released from rest in the horizontal position. Given that the moment of inertia of the rod about A is $ml^2/3$, the initial angular acceleration of the rod will be : **[NEET (UG) 2007]**

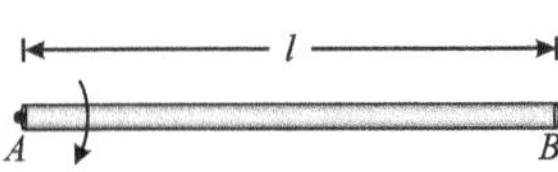

(A) $\dfrac{mgl}{2}$
(B) $\dfrac{3}{2}gl$

(C) $\dfrac{3g}{2l}$
(D) $\dfrac{2g}{3l}$

5. If $\vec{F}$ is the force acting on a particle having position vector $\vec{r}$ and $\vec{\tau}$ be the torque of this force about the origin, then : **[NEET (UG) 2009]**
(A) $\vec{r}\cdot\vec{\tau}=0$ and $\vec{F}\cdot\vec{\tau}\neq 0$
(B) $\vec{r}\cdot\vec{\tau}\neq 0$ and $\vec{F}\cdot\vec{\tau}=0$
(C) $\vec{r}\cdot\vec{\tau}>0$ and $\vec{F}\cdot\vec{\tau}<0$
(D) $\vec{r}\cdot\vec{\tau}=0$ and $\vec{F}\cdot\vec{\tau}=0$

6. The instantaneous angular position of a point on a rotating wheel is given by the equation $\theta(t)=2t^3-6t^2$. The torque on the wheel becomes zero at : **[NEET (UG) 2011]**
(A) $t=1$ s
(B) $t=0.5$ s
(C) $t=0.25$ s
(D) $t=2$ s

7. ABC is an equilateral triangle with O as its centre. $\vec{F}_1,\vec{F}_2$ and $\vec{F}_3$ represent three forces acting along the sides AB, BC and AC respectively. If the total torque about O is zero the magnitude of $\vec{F}_3$ is : **[NEET (UG) 2012]**

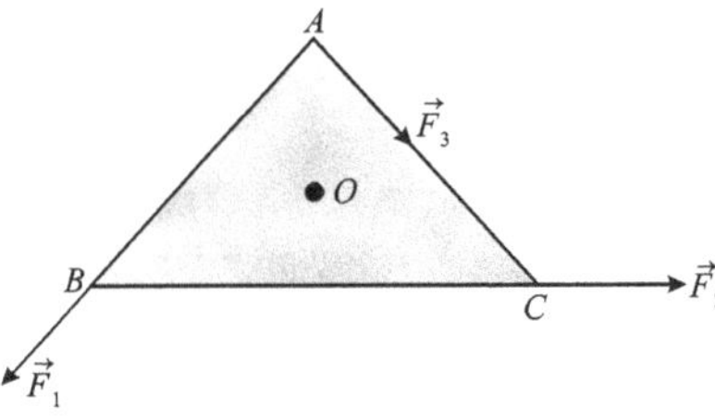

(A) F_1+F_2
(B) F_1-F_2
(C) $\dfrac{F_1+F_2}{2}$
(D) $2(F_1+F_2)$

8. A rod PQ of mass M and length L is hinged at end P. The rod is kept horizontal by a massless string tied to point Q as shown in figure. When string is cut, the initial angular acceleration of the rod is : **[NEET (UG) 2013]**

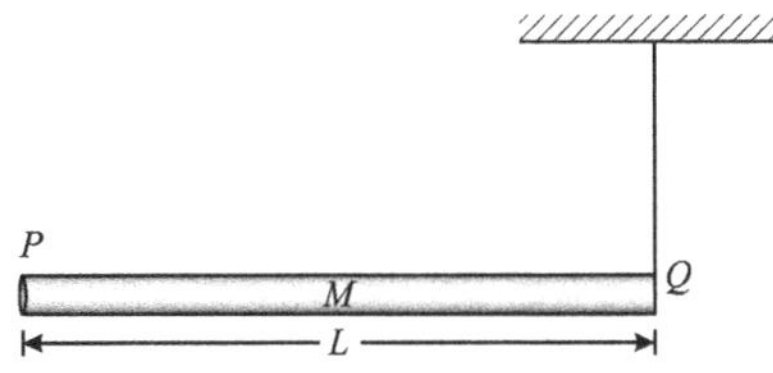

(A) $\dfrac{3g}{2L}$
(B) $\dfrac{g}{L}$
(C) $\dfrac{2g}{L}$
(D) $\dfrac{2g}{3L}$

9. A solid cylinder of mass 50 kg and radius 0.5 m is free to rotate about the horizontal axis. A massless string is wound round the cylinder with one end attached to it and other hanging freely. Tension in the string required to produce an angular acceleration of 2 revolutions s^{-2} is : **[NEET (UG) 2014]**
(A) 25 N
(B) 50 N
(C) 78.5 N
(D) 157 N

10. An automobile moves on a road with a speed of 54 kmh^{-1}. The radius of its wheels is 0.45 m and the moment of inertia of the wheel about its axis of rotation is 3 kgm^2. If the vehicle is brought to rest in 15 s, the magnitude of average torque transmitted by its brakes to the wheel is : **[NEET (UG) 2015]**
(A) 2.86 kgm^{2}s^{-2}
(B) 6.66 kgm^{2}s^{-2}
(C) 8.58 kgm^{2}s^{-2}
(D) 10.86 kgm^{2}s^{-2}

11. Point masses m_1 and m_2 are placed at the opposite ends of a rigid rod of length L, and negligible mass. The rod is to be set rotating about an axis perpendicular to it. The position of point P on this rod through which the axis should pass so that the work required to set the rod rotating with angular velocity ω_0 is minimum, is given by : **[NEET (UG) 2015]**

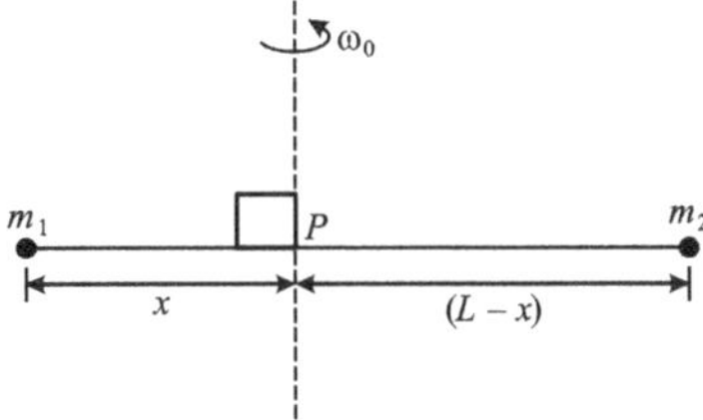

(A) $x=\dfrac{m_1 L}{m_1+m_2}$
(B) $x=\dfrac{m_2 L}{m_1+m_2}$
(C) $x=\dfrac{m_1}{m_2}L$
(D) $x=\dfrac{m_2}{m_1}L$

12. A force $\vec{F}=\alpha\hat{i}+3\hat{j}+6\hat{k}$ is acting at a point $\vec{r}=2\hat{i}-6\hat{j}-12\hat{k}$. The value of α for which angular momentum

about origin is conserved is : **[NEET (UG) 2015]**
(A) 1
(B) – 1
(C) 2
(D) Zero

13. A uniform circular disc of radius 50 cm at rest is free to turn about an axis which is perpendicular to its plane and passes through its centre. It is subjected to a torque which produces a constant angular acceleration of 2.0 rad s^{-2}. Net acceleration of a point on circumference of disc in ms^{-2} at the end of 2.0 s is approximately : **[NEET (UG) 2016]**
(A) 8.0
(B) 7.0
(C) 6.0
(D) 3.0

14. A rope is wound around a hollow cylinder of mass 3 kg and radius 40 cm. What is the angular acceleration of the cylinder if the rope is pulled with a force of 30 N ? **[NEET (UG) 2017]**
(A) 25 m/s^2
(B) 0.25 rad/s^2
(C) 25 rad/s^2
(D) 5 m/s^2

15. The moment of the force, $\vec{F} = 4i + 5j - 6\hat{k}$. at $(2, 0, -3)$, about the point $(2, -2, -2)$, is given by : **[NEET (UG) 2018]**

(A) $-7\hat{i} - 8\hat{j} - 4\hat{k}$
(B) $-4\hat{i} - \hat{j} - 8\hat{k}$

(C) $-8\hat{i} - 4\hat{j} - 7\hat{k}$
(D) $-7\hat{i} - 4\hat{j} - 8\hat{k}$

16. A disc of radius 2 m and mass 100 kg rolls on a horizontal floor. Its centre of mass has speed of 20 cm/s. How much work is needed to stop it ? **[NEET (UG) 2019]**
(A) 3 J
(B) 30 kJ
(C) 2 J
(D) 1 J

17. A solid cylinder of mass 2 kg and radius 4 cm rotating about its axis at the rate of 3 rpm. The torque required to stop after 2π revolutions is : **[NEET (UG) 2019]**
(A) 2×10^{-6} N m
(B) 2×10^{-3} N m
(C) 12×10^{-4} N m
(D) 2×10^{6} N m

18. Find the torque about the origin when a force of $3\hat{j}N$ acts on a particle whose position vector is $2\hat{k}$ m : **[NEET (UG) 2020]**

(A) $6\hat{k}$ Nm
(B) $6\hat{i}$ Nm

(C) $6\hat{j}$ Nm
(D) $-6\hat{i}$ Nm

19. A uniform rod of length 200 cm and mass 500 g is balanced on a wedge placed at 40 cm mark. A mass of 2 kg is suspended from the rod at 20 cm and another unknown mass 'm' is suspended from the rod at 160 cm mark as shown in the figure. Find the value of 'm' such that the rod is in equilibrium : ($g = 10$ m/s^2) **[NEET (UG) 2021]**

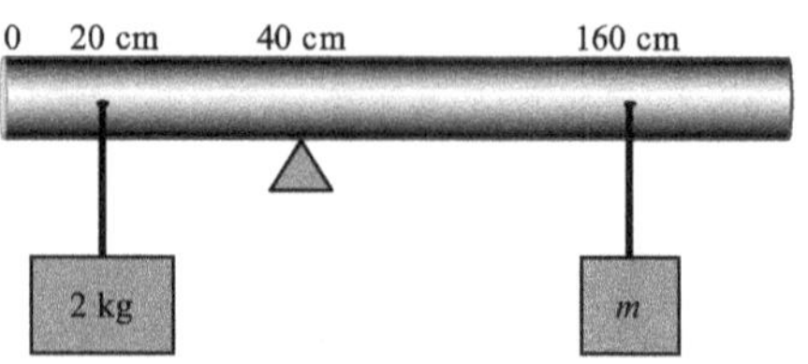

(A) $\dfrac{1}{2}$ kg
(B) $\dfrac{1}{3}$ kg

(C) $\dfrac{1}{6}$ kg
(D) $\dfrac{1}{12}$ kg

6.5 Angular Momentum & Conservation

1. A disc is rotating with angular speed ω. If a child sits on it, what is conserved ? **[NEET (UG) 2002]**
(A) Linear momentum
(B) Angular momentum
(C) Kinetic energy
(D) Potential energy

2. A thin circular ring of mass M and radius r is rotating about its axis with a constant angular velocity ω. Four objects each of mass m, are kept gently to the opposite ends of two perpendicular diameters of the ring. The angular velocity of the ring will be : **[NEET (UG) 2003]**

(A) $\dfrac{M\omega}{4m}$
(B) $\dfrac{M\omega}{M + 4m}$

(C) $\dfrac{(M + 4m)\omega}{M}$
(D) $\dfrac{(M - 4m)\omega}{M + 4m}$

3. A round disc of moment of inertia I_2 about its axis perpendicular to its plane and passing through its centre is placed over another disc of moment of inertia I_1 rotating with an angular velocity ω about the same axis. The final angular velocity of the combination of discs is : **[NEET (UG) 2004]**

(A) $\dfrac{I_2\omega}{I_1 + I_2}$
(B) ω

(C) $\dfrac{I_1\omega}{I_1 + I_2}$
(D) $\dfrac{(I_1 + I_2)\omega}{I_1}$

4. A particle of mass m moves in the XY plane with a velocity v along the straight line AB. If the angular momentum of the particle with respect to origin O is L_A when it is at A and L_B when it is at B, then : **[NEET (UG) 2007]**

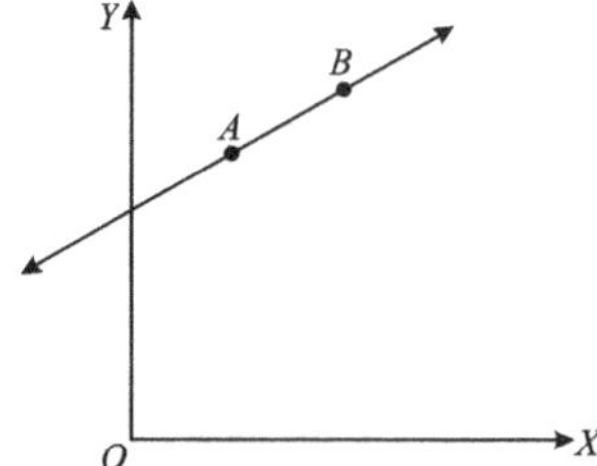

(A) $L_A = L_B$
(B) The relationship between L_A and L_B depends upon the slope of the line AB
(C) $L_A < L_B$
(D) $L_A > L_B$

5. A thin circular ring of mass M and radius R is rotating in a horizontal plane about an axis vertical to its plane with a constant angular velocity ω. If two objects each mass m be attached gently to the opposite ends of a diameter of the ring, the ring, will then rotate with an angular velocity: **[NEET (UG) 2009]**

(A) $\dfrac{\omega M}{M+m}$ (B) $\dfrac{\omega(M-2m)}{M+2m}$

(C) $\dfrac{\omega M}{M+2m}$ (D) $\dfrac{\omega(M+2m)}{M}$

6. A circular disc of moment of inertia I_t is rotating in a horizontal plane, its symmetry axis, with a constant angular speed ω_i. Another disc of moment of inertia I_b is dropped coaxially onto the rotating disk. Initially the second disc has zero angular speed Eventually both the disks rotate with a constant angular speed ω_f. The energy lost by the initially rotating disk to friction is: **[NEET (UG) 2010]**

(A) $\dfrac{1}{2}\dfrac{I_b I_t}{(I_t + I_b)}\omega_i^2$ (B) $\dfrac{1}{2}\dfrac{I_b^2}{(I_t + I_b)}\omega_i^2$

(C) $\dfrac{1}{2}\dfrac{I_t^2}{(I_t + I_b)}\omega_i^2$ (D) $\dfrac{I_b - I_t}{(I_t + I_b)}\omega_i^2$

7. When a mass is rotating in a plane about a fixed point, its angular momentum is directed along: **[NEET (UG) 2012]**
(A) A line perpendicular to the plane of rotation
(B) The line making an angle of $45°$ to the plane of rotation
(C) The radius
(D) The tangent to the orbit

8. A circular platform is mounted on a frictionless vertical axle. Its radius $R = 2$ m and its moment of inertia about the axle is $200\ kg\ m^2$. It is initially at rest. A 50 kg man stands on the edge of the platform and begins to walk along the edge at the speed of $1\ ms^{-1}$ relative to the ground. Time taken by the man to complete one revolution on the disc is: **[NEET (UG) 2012]**
(A) $3\pi/2$ s   (B) 2π s
(C) $\pi/2$ s   (D) π s

9. A solid sphere of mass m and radius R is rotating about its diameter. A solid cylinder of the same mass and same radius is also rotating about its geometrical axis with an angular speed twice that of the sphere. The ratio of their kinetic energies of rotation ($E_{sphere} / E_{cylinder}$) will be: **[NEET (UG) 2016 Ph. II]**
(A) $2:3$ (B) $1:5$
(C) $1:4$ (D) $3:1$

10. Two rotating bodies A and B of masses m and $2m$ with momenta of inertia I_A and I_B ($I_B > I_A$) have equal kinetic energy of rotation. If L_A and L_B be their angular momenta respectively, then: **[NEET (UG) 2016 Ph. II]**

(A) $L_A = \dfrac{L_B}{2}$ (B) $L_A = 2L_B$

(C) $L_B > L_A$ (D) $L_A > L_B$

11. Two discs of same moment of inertia rotating about their regular axis passing through centre and perpendicular to the plane of disc with angular velocities ω_1 and ω_2. They are brought into contact face to face coinciding the axis of rotation. The expression for loss of energy during this process is: **[NEET (UG) 2017]**

(A) $\dfrac{1}{2}I(\omega_1 + \omega_2)^2$ (B) $\dfrac{1}{4}I(\omega_1 - \omega_2)^2$

(C) $I(\omega_1 - \omega_2)^2$ (D) $\dfrac{I}{8}(\omega_1 - \omega_2)^2$

12. Three objects, A : (a solid sphere), B : (a thin circular disc) and C : (a circular ring), each have the same mass M and radius R. They all spin with the same angular speed ω about their own symmetry axes. The amounts of work (W) required to bring them to rest, would satisfy the relation: **[NEET (UG) 2018]**
(A) $W_B > W_A > W_C$ (B) $W_A > W_B > W_C$
(C) $W_C > W_B > W_A$ (D) $W_A > W_C > W_B$

13. A solid sphere is rotating freely about its symmetry axis in free space. The radius of the sphere is increased keeping its mass same. Which of the following physical quantities would remain constant for the sphere? **[NEET (UG) 2018]**
(A) Angular velocity   (B) Moment of inertia
(C) Rotational kinetic energy (D) Angular momentum

6.6 Rolling

1. A disc is rolling, the velocity of its centre of mass is v_{cm}. Which one will be correct? **[NEET (UG) 2001]**
(A) The velocity of highest point is $2v_{cm}$ and at point of contact is zero
(B) The velocity of highest point is v_{cm} and at point of contact is v_{cm}
(C) The velocity of highest point is $2v_{cm}$ and point of contact is v_{cm}
(D) The velocity of highest point is $2v_{cm}$ and point of contact is $2v_{cm}$

2. Consider a contact point P of a wheel on ground which rolls on ground without slipping. Then value of displacement of point P when wheel completes half of rotation (If radius of wheel is 1 m): **[NEET (UG) 2002]**

(A) 2m

(B) $\sqrt{\pi^2 + 4}$ m

(C) πm

(D) $\sqrt{\pi^2 + 2}$ m

3. A solid sphere of radius R is placed on a smooth horizontal surface. A horizontal force F is applied at height h from the lowest point. For the maximum acceleration of centre of mass, which is correct ? **[NEET (UG) 2002]**

(A) $h = R$

(B) $h = 2R$

(C) $h = 0$

(D) No relation between h and R

4. A solid cylinder of mass M and radius R rolls without slipping down an inclined plane of length L and height h. What is the speed of its centre of mass when the cylinder reaches its bottom : **[NEET (UG) 2003]**

(A) $\sqrt{2gh}$

(B) $\sqrt{\dfrac{3}{4}gh}$

(C) $\sqrt{\dfrac{4}{3}gh}$

(D) $\sqrt{4gh}$

5. A ball rolls without slipping. The radius of gyration of the ball about an axis passing through its centre of mass is K. If radius of the ball be R, then the fraction of total energy associated with its rotational energy will be : **[NEET (UG) 2003]**

(A) $\dfrac{K^2 + R^2}{R^2}$

(B) $\dfrac{K^2}{R^2}$

(C) $\dfrac{K^2}{K^2 + R^2}$

(D) $\dfrac{R^2}{K^2 + R^2}$

6. A drum of radius R and mass M, rolls down without slipping along an inclined plane of angle θ. The frictional force : **[NEET (UG) 2005]**

(A) Decreases the rotational and translational motion

(B) Dissipates energy as heat

(C) Decreases the rotational motion

(D) Converts translational energy to rotational energy

7. A solid cylinder of mass 3 kg is rolling on a horizontal surface with velocity 4 ms^{-1}. It collides with a horizontal spring of force constant 200 Nm^{-1}. The maximum compression produced in the spring will be : **[NEET (UG) 2012]**

(A) 0.5 m

(B) 0.6 m

(C) 0.7 m

(D) 0.2 m

8. A small object of uniform density rolls up a curved surface with an initially velocity 'v'. It reaches upto a maximum height of $\dfrac{3v^2}{4g}$ with respect to the initial position. The object is :

[NEET (UG) 2013]

(A) Ring

(B) Solid sphere

(C) Hollow sphere

(D) Disc

9. The ratio of the accelerations for a solid sphere (mass m and radius R) rolling down an incline of angle 'θ' without slipping and slipping down the incline without rolling is :

[NEET (UG) 2014]

(A) 5 : 7

(B) 2 : 3

(C) 2 : 5

(D) 7 : 5

10. A disc and a sphere of same radius but different masses roll off on two inclined planes of the same altitude and length. Which one of the two objects gets to the bottom of the plane first ? **[NEET (UG) 2016]**

(A) Disk

(B) Sphere

(C) Both reach at the same time

(D) Depends on their masses

11. Which one of the following statements is incorrect ?

[NEET (UG) 2018]

(A) Frictional force opposes the relative motion

(B) Limiting value of static friction is directly proportional to normal reaction

(C) Rolling friction is smaller than sliding friction

(D) Coefficient of sliding friction has dimensions of length

12. A solid sphere is in rolling motion. In rolling motion a body possesses translational kinetic energy (K_t) as well as rotational kinetic energy (K_r) simultaneously. The ratio $K_t : (K_t + K_r)$ for the sphere is : **[NEET (UG) 2018]**

(A) 10 : 7

(B) 5 : 7

(C) 7 : 10

(D) 2 : 5

* * * * *

7 GRAVITATION

7.1 Gravitational Field & Force

1. Two spheres of masses m and M are situated in air and the gravitational force between them is F. The space around the masses is now filled with a liquid of specific gravity 3. The gravitational force will now be : **[NEET (UG) 2003]**

(A) $3F$ (B) F

(C) $F/3$ (D) $F/9$

2. The acceleration due to gravity on the planet A is 9 times the acceleration due to gravity on planet B. A man jumps to a height of 2 m on the surface of A. What is the height of jump by the same person on the planet B ? **[NEET (UG) 2003]**

(A) $(2/9)$ m   (B) 18 m

(C) 6 m   (D) $(2/3)$ m

3. The density of a newly discovered planet is twice that of earth. The acceleration due to gravity at the surface of the planet is equal to that at the surface of the earth. If the radius of the earth is R, the radius of the planet would be :

[NEET (UG) 2004]

(A) $2R$ (B) $4R$

(C) $1/4R$ (D) $1/2R$

4. Imagine a new planet having the same density as that of earth but it is 3 times bigger than the earth in size. If the acceleration due to gravity on the surface of earth is g and that on the surface of the new planet is g', then : **[NEET (UG) 2005]**

(A) $g' = 3g$ (B) $g' = 9g$

(C) $g' = g/9$ (D) $g' = 27g$

5. The height at which the weight of a body becomes $1/16^{th}$, its weight on the surface of earth (radius R), is :

[NEET (UG) 2012]

(A) $5R$ (B) $15R$

(C) $3R$ (D) $4R$

6. A spherical planet has a mass M_p and diameter D_p. A particle of mass m falling freely near the surface of this planet will experience an acceleration due to gravity, equal to :

[NEET (UG) 2012]

(A) $4\,GM_p/D_p^2$ (B) $GM_p\,m/D_p^2$

(C) GM_p/D_p^2 (D) $4\,GM_p\,m/D_p^2$

7. Which one of the following plots represents the variation of gravitational field on a particle with distance r due to a thin spherical shell of radius R ? (r is measured from the centre of the spherical shell) : **[NEET (UG) 2012]**

(A) 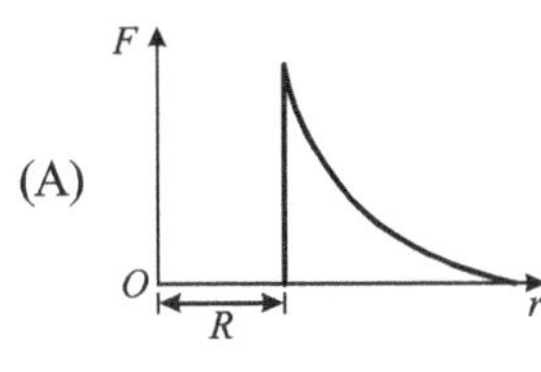   (B) 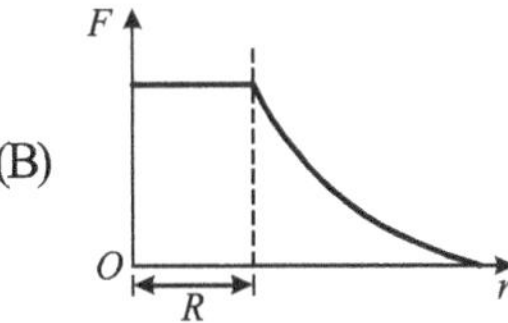

(C) 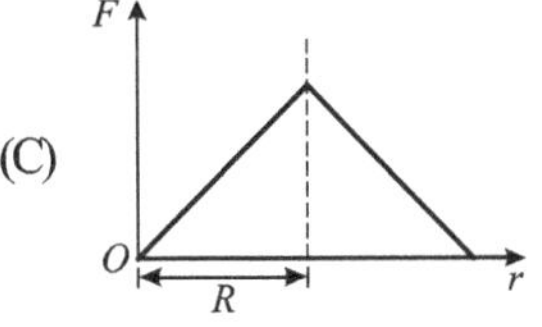   (D) 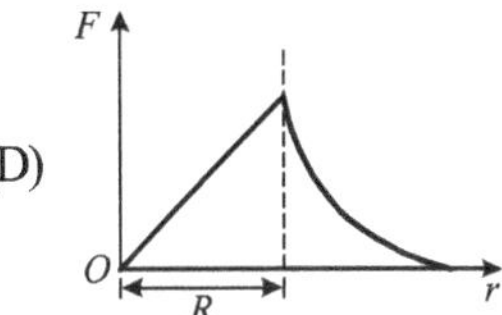

8. Dependence of intensity of gravitational field (E) of earth with distance (r) from centre of earth is correctly represented by : **[NEET (UG) 2014]**

(A) 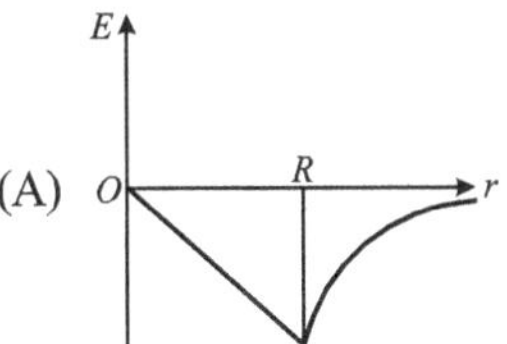   (B) 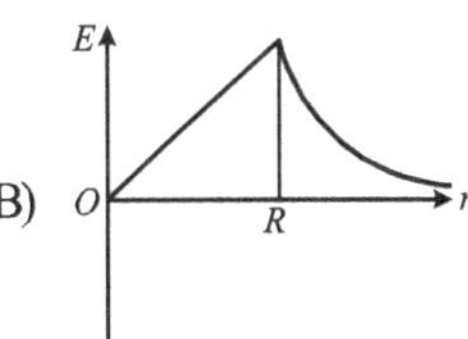

(C) 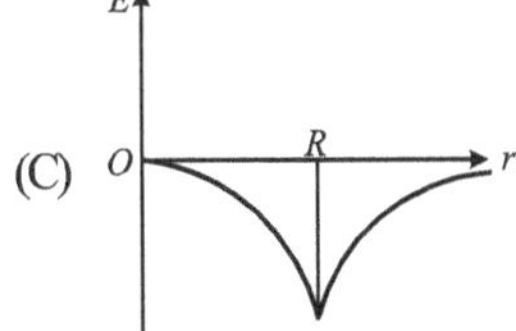   (D) 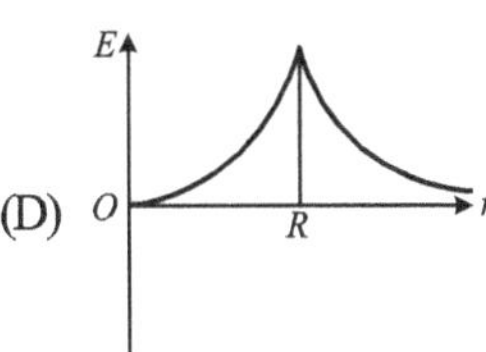

9. Starting from the centre of the earth having radius R, the variation of g (acceleration due to gravity) is shown by : **[NEET (UG) 2016 Ph. II]**

(A) 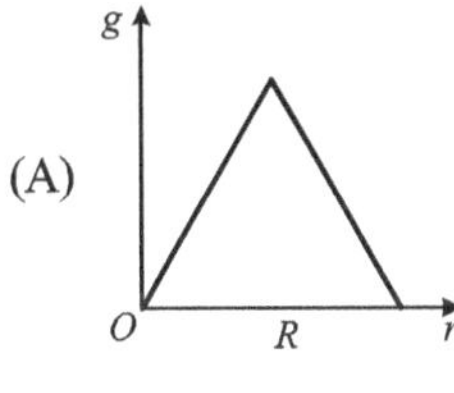   (B) 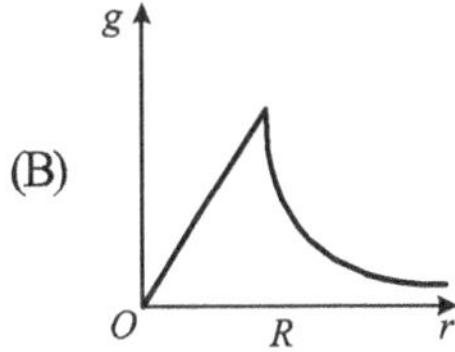

(C) 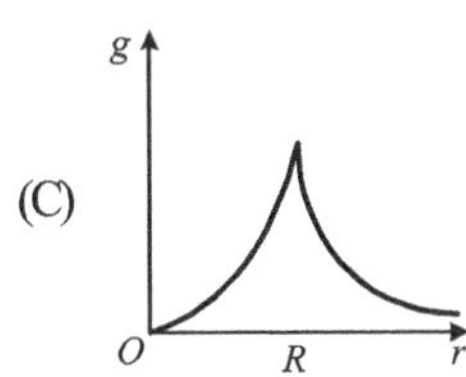   (D) 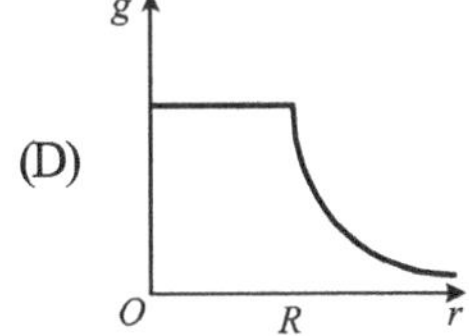

10. The acceleration due to gravity at a height 1 km above the earth is the same as at a depth d below the surface of earth. Then: **[NEET (UG) 2017]**

(A) $d = \dfrac{1}{2}$ km

(B) $d = 1$ km

(C) $d = \dfrac{3}{2}$ km

(D) $d = 2$ km

11. Two astronauts are floating in gravitational free space after having lost contact with their spaceship. The two will: **[NEET (UG) 2017]**

(A) Keep floating at the same distance between them
(B) Move towards each other
(C) Move away from each other
(D) Will become stationary

12. A body weighs 200 N on the surface of the earth. How much will it weigh half way down to the centre of the earth ? **[NEET (UG) 2019]**

(A) 150 N
(B) 200 N
(C) 250 N
(D) 100 N

13. A body weighs 72 N on the surface of the earth. What is the gravitational force on it, at a height equal to half the radius of the earth ? **[NEET (UG) 2020]**

(A) 24 N
(B) 48 N
(C) 32 N
(D) 30 N

14. A body of mass 60 g experiences a gravitational force of 3.0 N, when placed at a particular point. The magnitude of the gravitational field intensity at that point is : **[NEET (UG) 2022]**

(A) 50 N/kg
(B) 20 N/kg
(C) 180 N/kg
(D) 0.05 N/kg

7.2 Gravitational Energy & Gravitational Potential

1. With what velocity should a particle be projected so that its height becomes equal to radius of earth ? **[NEET (UG) 2001]**

(A) $\left(\dfrac{GM}{R}\right)^{1/2}$

(B) $\left(\dfrac{8GM}{R}\right)^{1/2}$

(C) $\left(\dfrac{2GM}{R}\right)^{1/2}$

(D) $\left(\dfrac{4GM}{R}\right)^{1/2}$

2. A body of mass m is placed on earth's surface which is taken from earth surface to a height of $h = 3R$, then change in gravitational potential energy is : **[NEET (UG) 2003]**

(A) $\dfrac{mgR}{4}$

(B) $\dfrac{2}{3} mgR$

(C) $\dfrac{3}{4} mgR$

(D) $\dfrac{mgR}{2}$

3. The Earth is assumed to be a sphere of radius R. A platform is arranged at a height R from the surface of the Earth. The escape velocity of a body from this platform is fv, where v is its escape velocity from the surface of the Earth. The value of f is : **[NEET (UG) 2006]**

(A) $\sqrt{2}$

(B) $\dfrac{1}{\sqrt{2}}$

(C) $\dfrac{1}{3}$

(D) $\dfrac{1}{2}$

4. A particle of mass M is situated at the centre of spherical shell of same mass and radius a. The gravitational potential at a point situated at $a/2$ distance from the centre will be : **[NEET (UG) 2010]**

(A) $-\dfrac{4GM}{a}$

(B) $-\dfrac{3GM}{a}$

(C) $-\dfrac{2GM}{a}$

(D) $-\dfrac{GM}{a}$

5. A body projected vertically from the earth reaches a height equal to earth's radius before returning to the earth. The power exerted by the gravitational force is greatest : **[NEET (UG) 2011]**

(A) At the highest position of the body
(B) At the instant just before the body hits the earth
(C) It remains constant all through
(D) At the instant just after the body is projected

6. If v_e is escape velocity and v_0 is orbital velocity of a satellite for orbit close to the earth's surface, then these are related by : **[NEET (UG) 2012]**

(A) $v_0 = v_e$

(B) $v_e = \sqrt{2}v_0$

(C) $v_e = \sqrt{2}\, v_0$

(D) $v_0 = \sqrt{2}\, v_e$

7. A body of mass 'm' is taken from the earth's surface to the height equal to twice the radius (R) of the earth. The change in potential energy of body will be : **[NEET (UG) 2013]**

(A) $mg\,2R$

(B) $\dfrac{2}{3} mgR$

(C) $3\,mgR$

(D) $\dfrac{1}{3} mgR$

8. Infinite number of bodies, each of mass 2 kg are situated on x-axis at distances 1 m, 2 m, 4 m, 8 m, ..., respectively, from the origin. The resulting gravitational potential due to this system at the origin will be : **[NEET (UG) 2013]**

(A) $-G$

(B) $-\dfrac{8}{3}G$

(C) $-\dfrac{4}{3}G$

(D) $-4G$

9. A black hole is an object whose gravitational field is so strong that even light cannot escape from it. To what approximate radius would earth (mass $= 5.98 \times 10^{24}$ kg) have to be compressed to be a black hole ? **[NEET (UG) 2014]**

(A) 10^{-9} m

(B) 10^{-6} m

(C) 10^{-2} m

(D) 100 m

10. At what height from the surface of earth the gravitation potential and the value of g are -5.4×10^{7} J kg^{-2} and 6.0 ms^{-2} respectively? Take the radius of earth as 6400 km : **[NEET (UG) 2016]**

(A) 2600 km

(B) 1600 km

(C) 1400 km

(D) 2000 km

11. The ratio of escape velocity at earth (v_e) to the escape velocity at a planet (v_p) whose radius and mean density are twice as that of earth is : **[NEET (UG) 2016]**

(A) $1:2$

(B) $1:2\sqrt{2}$

(C) $1:4$

(D) $1:\sqrt{2}$

12. The work done to raise a mass m from the surface of the earth to a height h, which is equal to the radius of the earth, is : **[NEET (UG) 2019]**

(A) mgR

(B) $2\,mgR$

(C) $\dfrac{1}{2}mgR$

(D) $\dfrac{3}{2}mgR$

13. The escape velocity from the Earth's surface is v. The escape velocity from the surface of another planet having a radius, four times that of Earth and same mass density is : **[NEET (UG) 2021]**

(A) v

(B) $2v$

(C) $3v$

(D) $4v$

14. A particle of mass 'm' is projected with a velocity $v = kV_e$ $(k < 1)$ from the surface of the earth.
(V_e = escape velocity)
The maximum height above the surface reached by the particle is : **[NEET (UG) 2021]**

(A) $R\left(\dfrac{k}{1-k}\right)^{2}$

(B) $R\left(\dfrac{k}{1+k}\right)^{2}$

(C) $\dfrac{R^{2}k}{1+k}$

(D) $\dfrac{Rk^{2}}{1-k^{2}}$

7.3 Satellite & Planetary Motion

1. For a satellite moving in an orbit around the earth, the ratio of kinetic energy to potential energy is : **[NEET (UG) 2005]**

(A) $\dfrac{1}{\sqrt{2}}$

(B) 2

(C) $\sqrt{2}$

(D) $\dfrac{1}{2}$

2. Two satellites of earth, S_1 and S_2 are moving in the same orbit. The mass of S_1 is four times the mass of S_2. Which one of the following statements is true ? **[NEET (UG) 2007]**
(A) The potential energies of earth satellites in the two cases are equal
(B) S_1 and S_2 are moving with the same speed
(C) The kinetic energies of the two satellites are equal
(D) The time period of S_1 is four times that of S_2

3. The figure shows elliptical orbit of a planet m about the sun S. The shaded area SCD is twice the shaded area SAB. If t_1 is the time for the planet to move from C to D and t_2 is the time to move from A to B then : **[NEET (UG) 2009]**

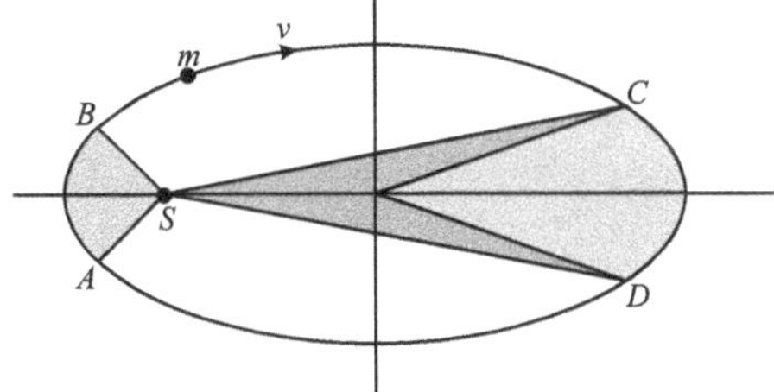

(A) $t_1 = t_2$

(B) $t_1 > t_2$

(C) $t_1 = 4t_2$

(D) $t_1 = 2t_2$

4. The radii of circular orbits of two satellites A and B of the earth, are $4R$ and R, respectively. If the speed of satellite A is $3V$, then the speed of satellite B will be : **[NEET (UG) 2010]**
(A) $3V/2$

(B) $3V/4$

(C) $6V$

(D) $12V$

5. A planet moving along an elliptical orbit is closest to the sun at a distance r_1 and farthest away at a distance of r_2. If v_1 and v_2 are the linear velocities at these points respectively, then the ratio $\dfrac{v_1}{v_2}$ is : **[NEET (UG) 2011]**

(A) $(r_1/r_2)^2$

(B) r_2/r_1

(C) $(r_2/r_1)^2$

(D) r_1/r_2

6. A geostationary satellite is orbiting the earth at a height of $5R$ above that surface of the earth, R being the radius of the earth. The time period of another satellite in hours at a height of $2R$ from the surface of the earth is : **[NEET (UG) 2012]**

(A) 5 (B) 10

(C) $6\sqrt{2}$ (D) $\dfrac{6}{\sqrt{2}}$

7. A satellite S is moving in an elliptical orbit around the earth. The mass of the satellite is very small compared to the mass of the earth. Then : **[NEET (UG) 2015]**

(A) The acceleration of S is always directed towards the centre of the earth

(B) The angular momentum of S about the centre of the earth changes in direction, but its magnitude remains constant

(C) The total mechanical energy of S varies periodically with time

(D) The linear momentum of S remains constant in magnitude

8. A remote-sensing satellite of earth revolves in a circular orbit at a height of 0.25×10^6 m above the surface of earth. If earth's radius is 6.38×10^6 m and $g = 9.8$ ms^{-2}, then the orbital speed of the satellite is : **[NEET (UG) 2015]**

(A) 6.67 km s^{-1} (B) 7.76 km s^{-1}

(C) 8.56 km s^{-1} (D) 9.13 km s^{-1}

9. A satellite of mass m is orbiting the earth (of radius R) at a height h from its surface. The total energy of the satellite in terms of g_0, the value of acceleration due to gravity at the earth's surface, is : **[NEET (UG) 2016 Ph. II]**

(A) $\dfrac{mg_0R^2}{2(R+h)}$ (B) $-\dfrac{mg_0R^2}{2(R+h)}$

(C) $\dfrac{2mg_0R^2}{R+h}$ (D) $-\dfrac{2mg_0R^2}{R+h}$

10. The kinetic energies of a planet in an elliptical orbit about the Sun, at positions A, B and C are K_A, K_B and K_C, respectively. AC is the major axis and SB is perpendicular to AC at the position of the Sun S as shown in the figure. Then : **[NEET (UG) 2018]**

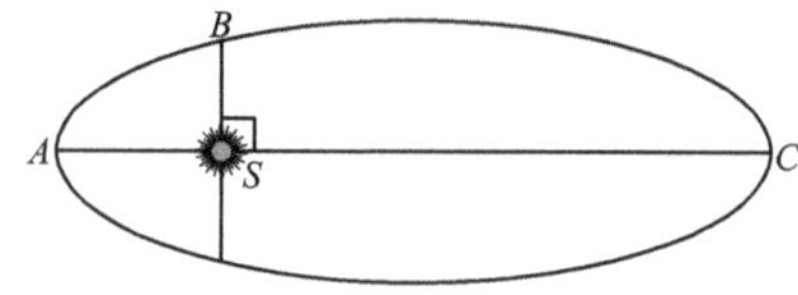

(A) $K_B < K_A < K_C$ (B) $K_A > K_B > K_C$

(C) $K_A < K_B < K_C$ (D) $K_B > K_A > K_C$

11. If the mass of the Sun were ten times smaller and the universal gravitational constant were ten times larger in magnitude, which of the following is not correct ?

[NEET (UG) 2018]

(A) Time period of a simple pendulum on the Earth would decrease

(B) Walking on the ground would become more difficult

(C) Raindrops will fall faster

(D) 'g' on the Earth will not change

12. Match List-I with List-II : **[NEET (UG) 2022]**

List-I	List-II
(a) Gravitational constant (G)	(i) $[L^2 T^{-2}]$
(b) Gravitational potential energy	(ii) $[M^{-1} L^3 T^{-2}]$
(c) Gravitational potential	(iii) $[LT^{-2}]$
(d) Gravitational intensity	(iv) $[ML^2 T^{-2}]$

Choose the **correct answer** from the options given below :

(A) (a) → (ii), (b) → (iv), (c) → (i), (d) → (iii)

(B) (a) → (ii), (b) → (iv), (c) → (iii), (d) → (i)

(C) (a) → (iv), (b) → (ii), (c) → (i), (d) → (iii)

(D) (a) → (ii), (b) → (i), (c) → (iv), (d) → (iii)

* * * * *

8 MECHANICAL PROPERTIES OF SOLIDS

8.1 Elasticity

1. The following four wires are made of the same material. Which of these will have the largest extension when the same tension is applied ? **[NEET (UG) 2013]**
(A) Length = 50 cm, diameter = 0.5 mm
(B) Length = 100 cm, diameter = 1 mm
(C) Length = 200 cm, diameter = 2 mm
(D) Length = 300 cm, diameter = 3 mm

2. Copper of fixed volume V is drawn into wire of length l. When this wire is subjected to a constant force F, the extension produced in the wire is Δl. Which of the following graphs is a straight line ? **[NEET (UG) 2014]**

(A) Δl versus $\dfrac{1}{l}$

(B) Δl versus l^2

(C) Δl versus $\dfrac{1}{l^2}$

(D) Δl versus l

3. The Young's modulus of steel is twice that of brass. Two wires of same length and of same area of cross section, one of steel and another of brass are suspended from the same roof. If we want the lower ends of the wires to be at the same level, then the weights added to the steel and brass wires must be in the ratio of : **[NEET (UG) 2015]**
(A) 1 : 1
(B) 1 : 2
(C) 2 : 1
(D) 4 : 2

4. The bulk modulus of a spherical object is 'B'. If it is subjected to uniform pressure 'p', the fractional decrease in radius is : **[NEET (UG) 2017]**

(A) $\dfrac{p}{B}$

(B) $\dfrac{B}{3p}$

(C) $\dfrac{3p}{B}$

(D) $\dfrac{p}{3B}$

5. Two wires are made of the same material and have the same volume. The first wire has cross-sectional area A and the second wire has cross-sectional area $3A$. If the length of the first wire is increased by Δl on applying a force F, how much force is needed to stretch the second wire by the same amount ? **[NEET (UG) 2018]**
(A) $4F$
(B) $6F$
(C) $9F$
(D) F

6. When a block of mass M is suspended by a long wire of length L, the length of the wire becomes $(L + l)$. The elastic potential energy stored in the extended wire is : **[NEET (UG) 2019]**

(A) Mgl

(B) MgL

(C) $\dfrac{1}{2}Mgl$

(D) $\dfrac{1}{2}MgL$

7. A wire of length L, area of cross section A is hanging from a fixed support. The length of the wire changes to L_1 when mass M is suspended from its free end. The expression for Young's modulus is : **[NEET (UG) 2020]**

(A) $\dfrac{MgL}{A(L_1 - L)}$

(B) $\dfrac{MgL_1}{AL}$

(C) $\dfrac{Mg(L_1 - L)}{AL}$

(D) $\dfrac{MgL}{AL_1}$

15. Given below are two statements: One is labelled as Assertion-(A) and the other is labelled as Reason-(R) : **[NEET (UG) 2022]**

Assertion-(A) : The stretching of a spring is determined by the shear modulus of the material of the spring

Reason-(R) : A coil spring of copper has more tensile strength than a steel spring of same dimensions

In the light of the above statements, choose the most appropriate answer from the options given below :
(A) Both (A) and (R) are true and (R) is not the correct explanation of (A)
(B) (A) is true but (R) is false
(C) (A) is false but (R) is true
(D) Both (A) and (R) are true and (R) is the correct explanation of (A)

* * * * *

9 MECHANICAL PROPERTIES OF FLUIDS

9.1 Fluid Statics

1. A tube of length L is filled completely with an incompressible liquid of mass M and closed at both the ends. The tube is then rotated in a horizontal plane about one of its ends with a uniform angular velocity ω. The force exerted by the liquid at the other ends is : **[NEET (UG) 2006]**

(A) $\dfrac{ML\omega^2}{2}$ (B) $\dfrac{ML^2\omega}{2}$

(C) $ML\omega^2$ (D) $\dfrac{ML^2\omega^2}{2}$

2. Two non-mixing liquids of densities ρ and $n\rho$ ($n > 1$) are put in a container. The height of each liquid is h. A solid cylinder of length L and density d is put in this container. The cylinder floats with its axis vertical and length pL ($p < 1$) in the denser liquid. The density d is equal to : **[NEET (UG) 2016]**

(A) $\{1 + (n + 1)p\}\rho$ (B) $\{2 + (n + 1)p\}\rho$

(C) $\{2 + (n - 1)p\}\rho$ (D) $\{1 + (n - 1)p\}\rho$

3. A U tube with both ends open to the atmosphere, is partially filled with water. Oil, which is immiscible with water, is poured into one side until it stands at a distance of 10 mm above the water level on the other side. Meanwhile the water rises by 65 mm from its original level (see diagram). The density of the oil is : **[NEET (UG) 2017]**

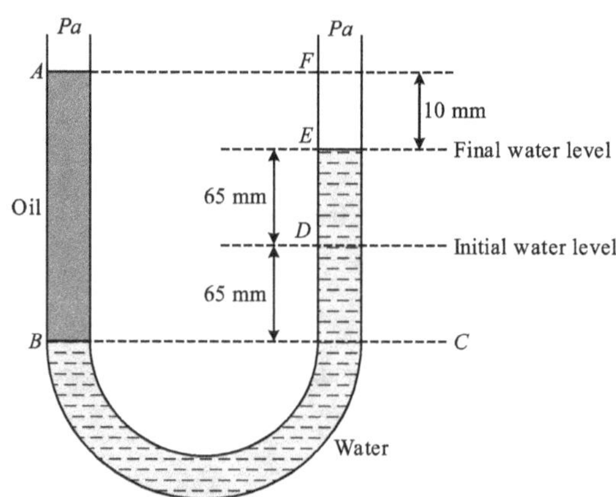

(A) $650\,\mathrm{kg\,m^{-3}}$ (B) $425\,\mathrm{kg\,m^{-3}}$
(C) $800\,\mathrm{kg\,m^{-3}}$ (D) $928\,\mathrm{kg\,m^{-3}}$

9.2 Fluid Dynamics

1. The cylindrical tube of a spray pump has radius R, one end of which has n fine holes, each of radius r. If the speed of the liquid in the tube is V, the speed of the ejection of the liquid through the holes is : **[NEET (UG) 2015]**

(A) $\dfrac{V^2 R}{nr}$ (B) $\dfrac{VR^2}{n^3 r^2}$

(C) $\dfrac{VR^2}{nr^2}$ (D) $\dfrac{VR^2}{n^2 r^2}$

2. A small hole of area of cross-section 2 mm^2 is present near the bottom of a fully filled open tank of height 2 m. Taking $g = 10$ m/s^2, the rate of flow of water through the open hole would be nearly : **[NEET (UG) 2019]**
(A) $12.6 \times 10^{-6}\,\mathrm{m^3/s}$ (B) $8.9 \times 10^{-6}\,\mathrm{m^3/s}$
(C) $2.23 \times 10^{-6}\,\mathrm{m^3/s}$ (D) $6.4 \times 10^{-6}\,\mathrm{m^3/s}$

9.3 Surface Tension

1. The wettability of a surface by a liquid depends primarily on : **[NEET (UG) 2013]**
(A) Viscosity
(B) Surface tension
(C) Density
(D) Angle of contact between the surface and the liquid

2. A certain number of spherical drops of a liquid of radius r coalesce to form a single drop of radius R and volume V. If T is the surface tension of the liquid, then : **[NEET (UG) 2014]**

(A) Energy $= 4VT\left(\dfrac{1}{r} - \dfrac{1}{R}\right)$ is released

(B) Energy $= 3VT\left(\dfrac{1}{r} + \dfrac{1}{R}\right)$ is absorbed

(C) Energy $= 3VT\left(\dfrac{1}{r} - \dfrac{1}{R}\right)$ is released

(D) Energy is neither released nor absorbed

3. Water rises to a height 'h' in a capillary tube. If the length of capillary tube above the surface of water is made less than 'h' then : **[NEET (UG) 2015]**
(A) Water does not rise at all
(B) Water rises upto the tip of capillary tube and then starts overflowing like fountain

(C) Water rises upto the top of capillary tube and stays there without overflowing

(D) Water rises upto a point a little below the top and stays there

4. A rectangular film of liquid is extended from $(4\,cm \times 2\,cm)$ to $(5\,cm \times 4\,cm)$. If the work done is $3 \times 10^{-4}\,J$, the value of the surface tension of the liquid is :　　**[NEET (UG) 2016 Ph. II]**

(A) $0.250\,Nm^{-1}$

(B) $0.125\,Nm^{-1}$

(C) $0.2\,Nm^{-1}$

(D) $8.0\,Nm^{-1}$

5. Three liquids of different densities in order $\rho_1 > \rho_2 > \rho_3$ with same value of surface tension T, rise to the same height in three identical capillaries. The angles of contact θ_1, θ_2 and θ_3 obey :　　**[NEET (UG) 2016 Ph. II]**

(A) $\dfrac{\pi}{2} > \theta_1 > \theta_2 > \theta_3 \geq 0$

(B) $0 \leq \theta_1 < \theta_2 < \theta_3 < \dfrac{\pi}{2}$

(C) $\dfrac{\pi}{2} < \theta_1 < \theta_2 < \theta_3 < \pi$

(D) $\pi > \theta_1 > \theta_2 > \theta_3 > \dfrac{\pi}{2}$

6. A soap bubble, having radius of 1 mm, is blown from a detergent solution having a surface tension of $2.5 \times 10^{-2}\,N/m$. The pressure inside the bubble equals at a point Z_0 below the free surface of water in a container. Taking $g = 10\,m/s^2$, density of water $= 10^3\,kg/m^3$, the value of Z_0 is :　　**[NEET (UG) 2019]**

(A) $100\,cm$

(B) $10\,cm$

(C) $1\,cm$

(D) $0.5\,cm$

7. A capillary tube of radius r is immersed in water and water rises in it to a height h. The mass of the water in the capillary is 5 g. Another capillary tube of radius $2\,r$ is immersed in water. The mass of water that will rise in this tube is :　　**[NEET (UG) 2020]**

(A) $20.0\,g$

(B) $2.5\,g$

(C) $5.0\,g$

(D) $10.0\,g$

8. If a soap bubble expands, the pressure inside the bubble :　　**[NEET (UG) 2022]**

(A) Increases

(B) Remains the same

(C) Is equal to the atmospheric pressure

(D) Decreases

9.4 Viscosity

1. A small sphere of radius r falls from rest in a viscous liquid. As a result, heat is produced due to viscous force. The rate of production of heat when the sphere attains its terminal velocity, is proportional to :　　**[NEET (UG) 2018]**

(A) r^5

(B) r^2

(C) r^3

(D) r^4

2. The velocity of a small ball of mass M and density d, when dropped in a container filled with glycerine becomes constant after some time. If the density of glycerine is $\dfrac{d}{2}$, then the viscous force acting on the ball will be :　　**[NEET (UG) 2021]**

(A) $\dfrac{Mg}{2}$

(B) Mg

(C) $\dfrac{3}{2}Mg$

(D) $2Mg$

3. A spherical ball is dropped in a long column of a highly viscous liquid. The curve in the graph shown, which represents the speed of the ball (v) as a function of time (t) is :　　**[NEET (UG) 2022]**

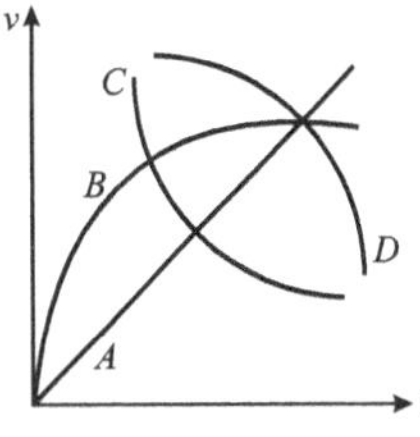

(A) B

(B) C

(C) D

(D) A

* * * * *

CHAPTER 10: THERMAL PROPERTIES OF MATTER

10.1 Thermal Expansion

1. On a new scale of temperature (which is linear) and called the W scale, the freezing and boiling points of water are 39°W and 239°W respectively. What will be the temperature on the new scale, corresponding to a temperature of 39°C on the Celsius scale ? **[NEET (UG) 2008]**
(A) 200°W
(B) 139°W
(C) 78°W
(D) 117°W

2. The value of coefficient of volume expansion of glycerine is $5 \times 10^{-4}\ K^{-1}$. The fractional change in the density of glycerine for a rise of 40°C in its temperature, is : **[NEET (UG) 2015]**
(A) 0.010
(B) 0.015
(C) 0.020
(D) 0.025

3. Coefficient of linear expansion of brass and steel rods are α_1 and α_2. Lengths of brass and steel rods are l_1 and l_2 respectively. If $(l_2 - l_1)$ is maintained same at all temperatures, which one of the following relations holds good ? **[NEET (UG) 2016]**
(A) $\alpha_1 l_2 = \alpha_2 l_1$
(B) $\alpha_1 l_2^2 = \alpha_2 l_1^2$
(C) $\alpha_1^2 l_2 = \alpha_2^2 l_1$
(D) $\alpha_1 l_1 = \alpha_2 l_2$

4. A copper rod of 88 cm and an aluminium rod of unknown length have their increase in length independent of increase in temperature. The length of aluminium rod is :
$(\alpha_{Cu} = 1.7 \times 10^{-5}\ K^{-1}$ and $\alpha_{Al} = 2.2 \times 10^{-5}\ K^{-1})$: **[NEET (UG) 2019]**
(A) 6.8 cm
(B) 113.9 cm
(C) 88 cm
(D) 68 cm

10.2 Calorimetry

1. An electric kettle takes 4 A current at 220 V. How much time will it take to boil 1 kg of water from temperature 20°C ? The temperature of boiling water is 100°C : **[NEET (UG) 2008]**
(A) 12.6 min
(B) 4.2 min
(C) 6.3 min
(D) 8.4 min

2. Steam at 100°C is passed into 20 g of water at 10°C. When water acquires a temperature of 80°C, the mass of water present will be :
[Take specific heat of water = 1 cal g^{-1} °C^{-1} and latent heat of steam = 540 cal g^{-1}] : **[NEET (UG) 2014]**
(A) 24 g
(B) 31.5 g
(C) 42.5 g
(D) 22.5 g

3. A piece of ice falls from a height h so that it melts completely. Only one-quarter of the heat produced is absorbed by the ice and all energy of ice gets converted into heat during its fall. The value of h is : **[NEET (UG) 2016]**
[Latent heat of ice is 3.4×10^5 J/kg and $g = 10$ N/kg]
(A) 34 km
(B) 544 km
(C) 136 km
(D) 68 km

4. Two identical bodies are made of a material for which the heat capacity increases with temperature. One of these is at 100°C, while the other one is at 0°C. If the two bodies are brought into contact, then, assuming no heat loss, the final common temperature is : **[NEET (UG) 2016 Ph. II]**
(A) 50°C
(B) More than 50°C
(C) Less than 50°C but greater than 0°C
(D) 0°C

5. The quantities of heat required to raise the temperature of two solid copper spheres of radii r_1 and r_2 $(r_1 = 1.5\ r_2)$ through 1 K are in the ratio : **[NEET (UG) 2020]**
(A) $\dfrac{5}{3}$
(B) $\dfrac{27}{8}$
(C) $\dfrac{9}{4}$
(D) $\dfrac{3}{2}$

10.3 Conduction of Heat

1. A cylindrical rod having temperature T_1 and T_2 at its end. The rate of flow of heat Q_1 cal/sec. If all the linear dimension are doubled keeping temperature constant, then rate of flow of heat Q_2 will be : **[NEET (UG) 2001]**
(A) $4Q_1$
(B) $2Q_1$
(C) $Q_1/4$
(D) $Q_1/2$

2. Consider two rods of same length and different specific heats (S_1, S_2), conductivities (K_1, K_2) and area of cross-sections (A_1, A_2) and both having temperatures T_1 and T_2 at their ends. If rate of loss of heat due to conduction is equal, then : **[NEET (UG) 2002]**
(A) $K_1 A_1 = K_2 A_2$
(B) $\dfrac{K_1 A_1}{S_1} = \dfrac{K_2 A_2}{S_2}$
(C) $K_2 A_1 = K_1 A_2$
(D) $\dfrac{K_2 A_1}{S_2} = \dfrac{K_1 A_2}{S_1}$

3. Consider a compound slab consisting of two different materials having equal thicknesses and thermal conductivities K and $2K$, respectively. The equivalent thermal conductivity of the slab is : **[NEET (UG) 2003]**

(A) $\dfrac{2}{3}K$

(B) $\sqrt{2}\,K$

(C) $3K$

(D) $\dfrac{4}{3}K$

4. Which of the following circular rods, (given radius r and length l) each made of the same energy material and whose ends are maintained at the same temperature will conduct most heat : **[NEET (UG) 2005]**

(A) $r = 2r_0;\, l = 2l_0$ (B) $r = 2r_0;\, l = l_0$

(C) $r = r_0;\, l = 2l_0$ (D) $r = r_0;\, l = l_0$

5. The two ends of a rod of length L and a uniform cross-sectional area A are kept at two temperatures T_1 and T_2 $(T_1 > T_2)$. The rate of heat transfer, $\dfrac{dQ}{dt}$, through the rod in a steady state is given by : **[NEET (UG) 2009]**

(A) $\dfrac{dQ}{dt} = \dfrac{kA(T_1 - T_2)}{L}$

(B) $\dfrac{dQ}{dt} = \dfrac{kL(T_1 - T_2)}{A}$

(C) $\dfrac{dQ}{dt} = \dfrac{k(T_1 - T_2)}{LA}$

(D) $\dfrac{dQ}{dt} = kLA(T_1 - T_2)$

6. A cylindrical metallic rod in thermal contact with two reservoirs of heat at its two ends conducts an amount of heat Q in time t. The metallic rod is melted and the material is formed into a rod of half the radius of the original rod. What is the amount of heat conducted by the new rod, when placed in thermal contact with the two reservoirs in time t ? **[NEET (UG) 2010]**

(A) $Q/2$ (B) $Q/4$

(C) $Q/16$ (D) $2Q$

7. A slab of stone of area $0.36\ m^2$ and thickness 0.1 is exposed on the lower surface to steam at 100°C. A block of ice at 0°C rests on the upper surface of the slab. In one hour 4.8 kg of ice is melted. The thermal conductivity of slab is : (Given latent heat of fusion of ice $= 3.36 \times 10^5\ J\ kg^{-1}$) **[NEET (UG) 2012]**

(A) 1.29 J/m/s/°C   (B) 2.05 J/m/s/°C

(C) 1.02 J/m/s/°C   (D) 1.24 J/m/s/°C

8. Two rods A and B of different materials are welded together as shown in figure. Their thermal conductivities are K_1 and K_2. The thermal conductivity of the composite rod will be : **[NEET (UG) 2017]**

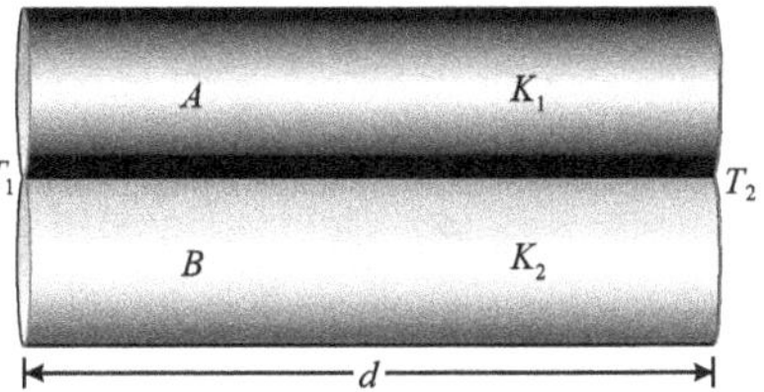

(A) $\dfrac{K_1 + K_2}{2}$

(B) $\dfrac{3(K_1 + K_2)}{2}$

(C) $K_1 + K_2$

(D) $2(K_1 + K_2)$

10.4 Radiation of Heat

1. A black body has wavelength λ_m corresponding to maximum energy at 2000 K. Its wavelength corresponding to maximum energy at 3000 K will be : **[NEET (UG) 2001]**

(A) $\dfrac{3}{2}\lambda_m$

(B) $\dfrac{2}{3}\lambda_m$

(C) $\dfrac{16}{81}\lambda_m$

(D) $\dfrac{81}{16}\lambda_m$

2. Which is having minimum wavelength : **[NEET (UG) 2002]**

(A) X-rays   (B) Ultra violet rays

(C) γ-rays   (D) Cosmic rays

3. For a black body at temperature 727°C, its radiating power is 60 watt and temperature of surrounding is 227°C. If temperature of black body is changed to 1227°C then its radiating power will be : **[NEET (UG) 2002]**

(A) 304 W   (B) 320 W

(C) 240 W   (D) 120 W

4. Which of the following is best close to an ideal black body ? **[NEET (UG) 2002]**

(A) Black lamp

(B) Cavity maintained at constant temperature

(C) Platinum black

(D) A lump of charcoal heated to high temperature

5. The Wien's displacement law express relation between : **[NEET (UG) 2002]**

(A) Wavelength corresponding to maximum energy and temperature

(B) Radiation energy and wavelength

(C) Temperature and wavelength

(D) Colour of light and temperature

6. If λ_m denotes the wavelength at which the radiative emission from a black body at a temperature T K is maximum, then : **[NEET (UG) 2004]**

(A) $\lambda_m \propto T^4$ (B) λ_m is independent of T

(C) $\lambda_m \propto T$ (D) $\lambda_m \propto T^{-1}$

7. A black body at 1227°C emits radiations with maximum intensity at a wavelength of 5000Å. The temperature of the body is increased by 1000°C, the maximum intensity will be observe at : **[NEET (UG) 2006]**

(A) 4000 Å   (B) 5000 Å

(C) 6000 Å   (D) 3000 Å

8. A black body is at 727°C. It emits energy at a rate which is proportional to : **[NEET (UG) 2007]**

(A) $(1000)^4$ (B) $(1000)^2$

(C) $(727)^4$ (D) $(727)^2$

9. Assuming the sun to have a spherical outer surface of radius r, radiating like a black body at temperature t°C, the power received by a unit surface, (normal to the incident rays) at a distance R from the centre of the sun is : **[NEET (UG) 2007]**

(A) $\dfrac{r^2\sigma(t+273)^4}{4\pi R^2}$ (B) $\dfrac{16\pi^2 r^2\sigma t^4}{R^2}$

(C) $\dfrac{r^2\sigma(t+273)^4}{R^2}$ (D) $\dfrac{4\pi r^2\sigma t^4}{R^2}$

Where σ is the Stefan's constant :

10. A black body at 227°C radiates heat at the rate of 7 cals/cm²-s. At a temperature of 727°C, the rate of heat radiated in the same units will be : **[NEET (UG) 2009]**

(A) 80   (B) 60

(C) 50   (D) 112

11. The total radiant energy per unit area, normal to the direction of incidence, received at a distance R from the centre of a star of radius r, whose outer surface radiates as a black body at a temperature T K is given by : (where σ is Stefan's constant) : **[NEET (UG) 2010]**

(A) $\dfrac{4\pi\sigma r^2 T^4}{R^2}$ (B) $\dfrac{\sigma r^2 T^4}{R^2}$

(C) $\dfrac{\sigma r^2 T^4}{r^2}$ (D) $\dfrac{\sigma r^4 T^4}{R^4}$

12. If the radius of a star is R and it acts as a black body, what would be the temperature of the star, in which the rate of energy production is Q ? **[NEET (UG) 2012]**

(A) $Q/4\pi R^2\sigma$ (B) $(Q/4\pi R^2\sigma)^{-1/2}$

(C) $(4\pi R^2 Q/\sigma)^{1/4}$ (D) $(Q/4\pi R^2\sigma)^{1/4}$

(σ stands for Stefan's constant)

13. A piece of iron is heated in a flame. It first becomes dull red then becomes reddish yellow and finally turns to white hot. The correct explanation for the above observation is possible by using : **[NEET (UG) 2013]**

(A) Stefan's law   (B) Wien's displacement law

(C) Kirchoff's law   (D) Newton's law of cooling

14. Certain quantity of water cools from 70°C to 60°C in the first 5 minutes and to 54°C in the next 5 minutes. The temperature of the surroundings is : **[NEET (UG) 2014]**

(A) 45°C   (B) 20°C

(C) 42°C   (D) 10°C

15. A black body is at a temperature of 5760 K. The energy of radiation emitted by the body at wavelength 250 nm is U_1, at wavelength 500 nm is U_2 and that at 1000 nm is U_3. Wien's constant, $b = 2.88 \times 10^6$ nmK. Which of the following is correct ? **[NEET (UG) 2016]**

(A) $U_1 = 0$ (B) $U_3 = 0$

(C) $U_1 > U_2$ (D) $U_2 > U_1$

16. A body cools from a temperature $3T$ to $2T$ in 10 minutes. The room temperature is T. Assume that Newton's law of cooling is applicable. The temperature of the body at the end of next 10 minutes will be : **[NEET (UG) 2016 Ph. II]**

(A) $7/4\,T$ (B) $3/2\,T$

(C) $4/3\,T$ (D) T

17. A spherical black body with a radius of 12 cm radiates 450 W power at 500 K. If the radius is halved and the temperature is doubled, the power radiated in watt would be : **[NEET (UG) 2017]**

(A) 225   (B) 450

(C) 1000   (D) 1800

18. The power radiated by a black body is P and it radiates maximum energy at wavelength, λ_0. If the temperature of the black body is now changed so that it radiates maximum energy at wavelength $\dfrac{3}{4}\lambda_0$, the power radiated by it becomes nP. The value of n is : **[NEET (UG) 2018]**

(A) $\dfrac{256}{81}$ (B) $\dfrac{4}{3}$

(C) $\dfrac{3}{4}$ (D) $\dfrac{81}{256}$

19. A cup of coffee cools from 90°C to 80°C in minutes, when the room temperature is 20°C. The time taken by a similar cup of coffee to cool from 80°C to 60°C at a room temperature same at 20°C is : **[NEET (UG) 2021]**

(A) $\dfrac{13}{10}t$ (B) $\dfrac{13}{5}t$

(C) $\dfrac{10}{13}t$ (D) $\dfrac{5}{13}t$

* * * * *

11 THERMODYNAMICS

11.1 First Law of Thermodynamics

1. One mole of an ideal gas at an initial temperature of T K does $6R$ joule of work adiabatically. If the ratio of specific heats of this gas at constant pressure and at constant volume is 5/3, the final temperature of gas will be : **[NEET (UG) 2004]**
(A) $(T+2.4)$ K
(B) $(T-2.4)$ K
(C) $(T+4)$ K
(D) $(T-4)$ K

2. Which of the following processes is reversible : **[NEET (UG) 2005]**
(A) Transfer of heat by radiation
(B) Transfer of heat by conduction
(C) Isothermal compression
(D) Electrical heating of a nichrome wire

3. The molar specific heat at constant pressure of an ideal gas is $\left(\dfrac{7}{2}\right)R$. The ratio of specific heat at constant pressure to that at constant volume is : **[NEET (UG) 2006]**

(A) $\dfrac{7}{5}$
(B) $\dfrac{8}{7}$

(C) $\dfrac{5}{7}$
(D) $\dfrac{9}{7}$

4. In thermodynamic processes which of the following statements is not true ? **[NEET (UG) 2009]**
(A) In an adiabatic process $PV^\gamma =$ constant
(B) In an adiabatic process the system is insulated from the surroundings
(C) In an isochoric process pressure remains constant
(D) In an isothermal process the temperature remains constant

5. The internal energy change in a system that has absorbed 2 kcal of heat and done 500 J of work is : **[NEET (UG) 2009]**
(A) 7900 J
(B) 8900 J
(C) 6400 J
(D) 5400 J

6. If ΔU and ΔW represent the increase in internal energy and work done by the system respectively in a thermodynamical process, which of the following is true ? **[NEET (UG) 2010]**
(A) $\Delta U = -\Delta W$, in a isothermal process
(B) $\Delta U = -\Delta W$, in a adiabatic process
(C) $\Delta U = \Delta W$, in an isothermal process
(D) $\Delta U = \Delta W$, in an isothermal process

7. During an isothermal expansion, a confined ideal gas does -150 J of work against its surroundings. This implies that : **[NEET (UG) 2011]**
(A) 150 J heat has been removed from the gas
(B) 300 J of heat has been added to the gas
(C) No heat is transferred because the process is isothermal
(D) 150 J of heat has been added to the gas

8. When 1 kg of ice at 0°C melts to water at 0°C, the resulting change in its entropy, taking latent heat of ice to be 80 cal/°K, is : **[NEET (UG) 2011]**
(A) 273 cal/K
(B) 8×10^4 cal/K
(C) 80 cal/K
(D) 293 cal/K

9. One mole of an ideal gas goes from an initial state A to final state B via two processes : It first undergoes isothermal expansion from volume V to $3V$ and then its volume is reduced from $3V$ to V at constant pressure. The correct P-V diagram representing the two processes is : **[NEET (UG) 2012]**

(A) 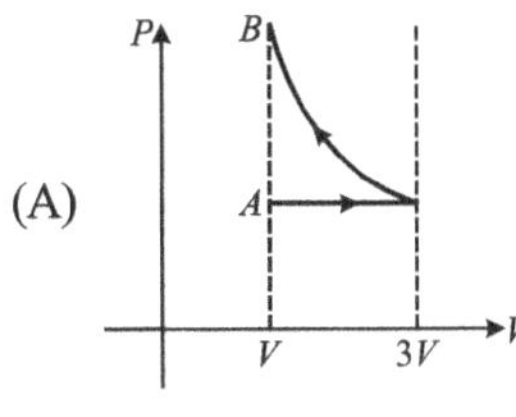
(B) 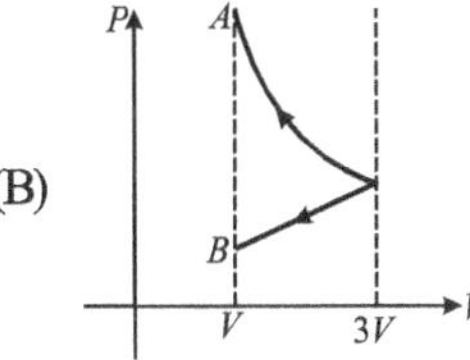

(C) 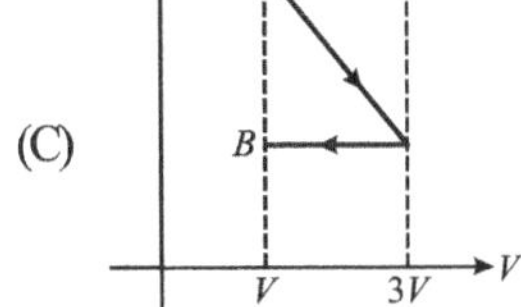
(D) 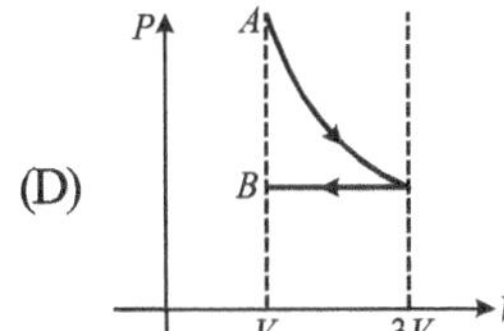

10. An ideal gas goes from state A to state B via three different processes as indicated in the P-V diagram. If Q_1, Q_2, Q_3 indicate the heat absorbed by the gas along the three processes and $\Delta U_1, \Delta U_2, \Delta U_3$ indicate the change in internal energy along the three processes respectively, then : **[NEET (UG) 2012]**

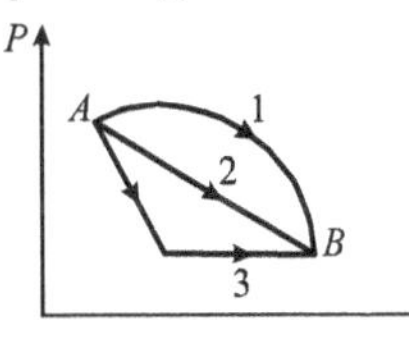

(A) $Q_3 > Q_2 > Q_1$ and $\Delta U_1 = \Delta U_2 = \Delta U_3$
(B) $Q_1 = Q_2 = Q_3$ and $\Delta U_1 > \Delta U_2 > \Delta U_3$
(C) $Q_3 > Q_2 > Q_1$ and $\Delta U_1 > \Delta U_2 > \Delta U_3$
(D) $Q_1 > Q_2 > Q_3$ and $\Delta U_1 = \Delta U_2 = \Delta U_3$

11. The molar specific heats of an ideal gas at constant pressure and volume are denoted by C_p and C_v, respectively. If $\gamma = \dfrac{C_p}{C_v}$ and R is the universal gas constant, then C_v is equal to :

[NEET (UG) 2013]

(A) $\dfrac{1+\gamma}{1-\gamma}$

(B) $\dfrac{R}{(\gamma-1)}$

(C) $\dfrac{(\gamma-1)}{R}$

(D) γR

12. During an adiabatic process, the pressure of a gas is found to be proportional to the cube of its temperature. The ratio of $\dfrac{C_p}{C_v}$ for the gas is :

[NEET (UG) 2013]

(A) $\dfrac{4}{3}$

(B) 2

(C) $\dfrac{5}{3}$

(D) $\dfrac{3}{2}$

13. In the given $(V-T)$ diagram, what is the relation between pressures P_1 and P_2 ?

[NEET (UG) 2013]

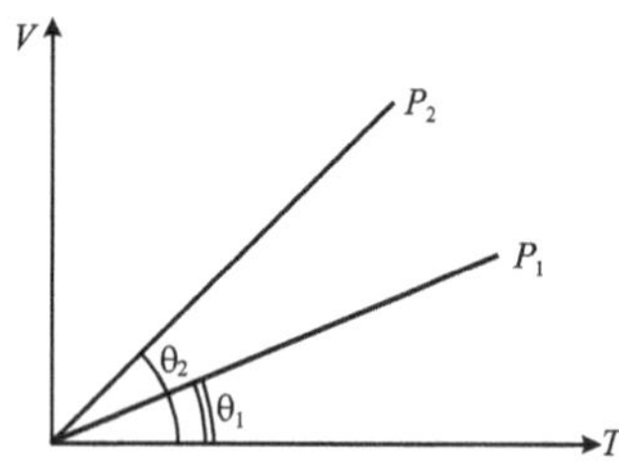

(A) $P_2 = P_1$

(B) $P_2 > P_1$

(C) $P_2 < P_1$

(D) Cannot be predicted

14. The amount of heat energy required to raise the temperature of 1 g of Helium at NTP, from T_1 K to T_2 K is :

[NEET (UG) 2013]

(A) $\dfrac{3}{8} N_a k_B (T_2 - T_1)$

(B) $\dfrac{3}{2} N_a k_B (T_2 - T_1)$

(C) $\dfrac{3}{4} N_a k_B (T_2 - T_1)$

(D) $\dfrac{3}{4} N_a k_B \left(\dfrac{T_2}{T_1}\right)$

15. A monoatomic gas at a pressure P, having a volume V expands isothermally to a volume $2V$ and then adiabatically to a volume $16V$. The final pressure of the gas is (take $\gamma = 5/3$) :

[NEET (UG) 2014]

(A) $64P$

(B) $32P$

(C) $\dfrac{P}{64}$

(D) $16P$

16. An ideal gas is compressed to half its initial volume by means of several processes. Which of the process results in the maximum work done on the gas ? **[NEET (UG) 2015]**

(A) Isothermal

(B) Adiabatic

(C) Isobaric

(D) Isochoric

17. A gas is compressed isothermally to half its initial volume. The same gas is compressed separately through an adiabatic process until its volume is again reduced to half. Then :

[NEET (UG) 2016]

(A) Compressing the gas isothermally will require more work to be done

(B) Compressing the gas through adiabatic process will require more work to be done

(C) Compressing the gas isothermally or adiabatically will require the same amount of work

(D) Which of the case (whether compression through isothermal or through adiabatic process) requires more work will depend upon the atomicity of the gas

18. One mole of an ideal monatomic gas undergoes a process described by the equation PV^3 = constant. The heat capacity of the gas during this process is : **[NEET (UG) 2016 Ph. II]**

(A) $3/2\,R$

(B) $5/2\,R$

(C) $2\,R$

(D) R

19. A gas mixture consists of 2 moles of O_2 and 4 moles of Ar at temperature T. Neglecting all vibrational modes, the total internal energy of the system is : **[NEET (UG) 2017]**

(A) $4\,RT$

(B) $15\,RT$

(C) $9\,RT$

(D) $11\,RT$

20. Thermodynamic processes are indicated in the following diagram : **[NEET (UG) 2017]**

Match the following :

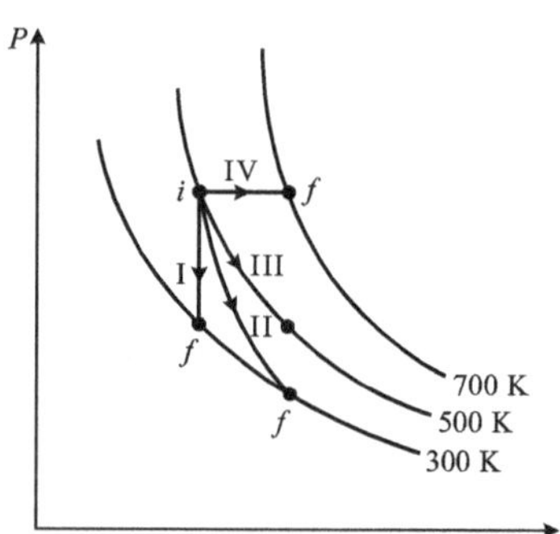

Column-1	Column-2
(P) Process-I	(a) Adiabatic
(Q) Process-II	(b) Isobaric
(R) Process-III	(c) Isochoric
(S) Process-IV	(d) Isothermal

(A) (P) → (a); (Q) → (c); (R) → (d); (S) → (b)
(B) (P) → (c); (Q) → (a); (R) → (d); (S) → (b)
(C) (P) → (c); (Q) → (d); (R) → (b); (S) → (a)
(D) (P) → (d); (Q) → (b); (R) → (a); (S) → (c)

21. The volume (V) of a monatomic gas varies with its temperature (T), as shown in the graph. The ratio of work done by the gas, to the heat absorbed by it, when it undergoes a change from state A to state B, is : **[NEET (UG) 2018]**

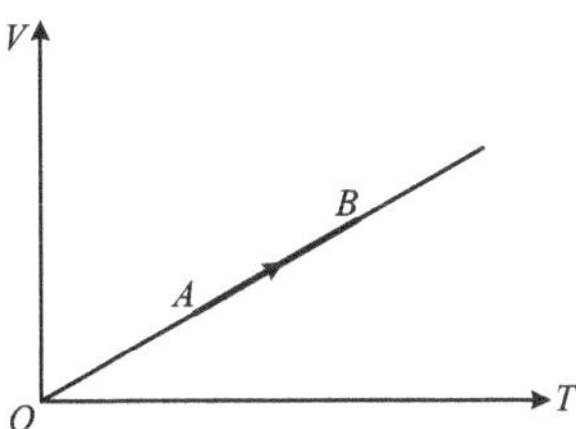

(A) $\dfrac{1}{3}$

(B) $\dfrac{2}{3}$

(C) $\dfrac{2}{5}$

(D) $\dfrac{2}{7}$

22. A sample of 0.1 g of water at 100°C and normal pressure (1.013×10^5 Nm^{-2}) requires 54 cal of heat energy to convert to steam at 100°C. If the volume of the steam produced is 167.1 cc, the change in internal energy of the sample, is : **[NEET (UG) 2018]**

(A) 42.2 J

(B) 208.7 J

(C) 104.3 J

(D) 84.5 J

23. Increase in temperature of a gas filled in a container would lead to : **[NEET (UG) 2019]**

(A) Increase in its mass

(B) Increase in its kinetic energy

(C) Decrease in its pressure

(D) Decrease in intermolecular distance

24. In which of the following processes, heat is neither absorbed nor released by a system ? **[NEET (UG) 2019]**

(A) Isothermal

(B) Adiabatic

(C) Isobaric

(D) Isochoric

25. Two cylinders A and B of equal capacity are connected to each other via a stop cock. A contains an ideal gas at standard temperature and pressure. B is completely evacuated. The entire system is thermally insulated. The stop cock is suddenly opened. The process is : **[NEET (UG) 2020]**

(A) isobaric

(B) isothermal

(C) adiabatic

(D) isochoric

26. An ideal gas undergoes four different processes from the same initial state as shown in the figure below. Those processes are adiabatic, isothermal, isobaric and isochoric. The curve which represents the adiabatic process among 1, 2, 3 and 4 is : **[NEET (UG) 2022]**

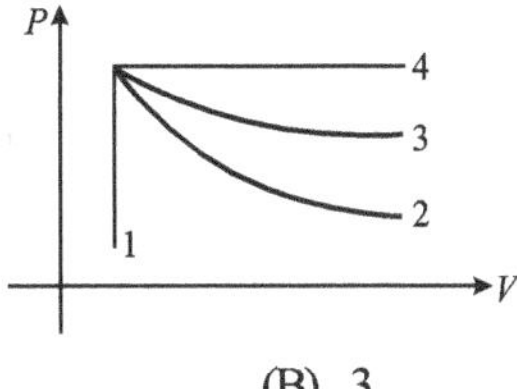

(A) 2

(B) 3

(C) 4

(D) 1

11.2 Cyclic Process, Heat Engine and Refrigerator

1. A scientist says that the efficiency of his heat engine which work at source temperature 127°C and sink temperature 27°C is 26 %, then : **[NEET (UG) 2001]**

(A) It is impossible

(B) It is possible but less probable

(C) It is quite probable

(D) Data are incomplete

2. The efficiency of Carnot engine is 50% and temperature of sink is 500 K. If temperature of source is kept constant and its efficiency raised to 60%, then the required temperature of sink will be : **[NEET (UG) 2002]**

(A) 100 K

(B) 600 K

(C) 400 K

(D) 500 K

3. An ideal gas heat engine operates in a Carnot cycle between 227°C and 127°C. It absorbs 6 kcal at the higher temperature. The amount of heat (in kcal) converted into work is equal to : **[NEET (UG) 2003]**

(A) 4.8

(B) 3.5

(C) 1.6

(D) 1.2

4. An ideal gas heat engine operates in Carnot cycle between 227°C and 127°C. It absorbs 6×10^4 cals of heat at higher temperature. Amount of heat converted to work is : **[NEET (UG) 2005]**

(A) 4.8×10^4 cals

(B) 2.4×10^4 cals

(C) 1.2×10^4 cals

(D) 6×10^4 cals

5. A Carnot engine whose sink is at 300 K has an efficiency of 40%. By how much should the temperature of source be increased so as to increase its efficiency by 50% of original efficiency : **[NEET (UG) 2006]**

(A) 275 K

(B) 325 K

(C) 250 K

(D) 380 K

6. A Carnot engine has an efficiency of 1/6. When the temperature of sink is reduced by 62°C, its efficiency is doubled. Temperature of the source is : **[NEET (UG) 2007]**

(A) 37°C

(B) 62°C

(C) 99°C

(D) 124°C

7. A thermodynamic system is taken through the cycle $ABCD$ as shown in figure. Heat rejected by the gas during the cycle is : **[NEET (UG) 2012]**

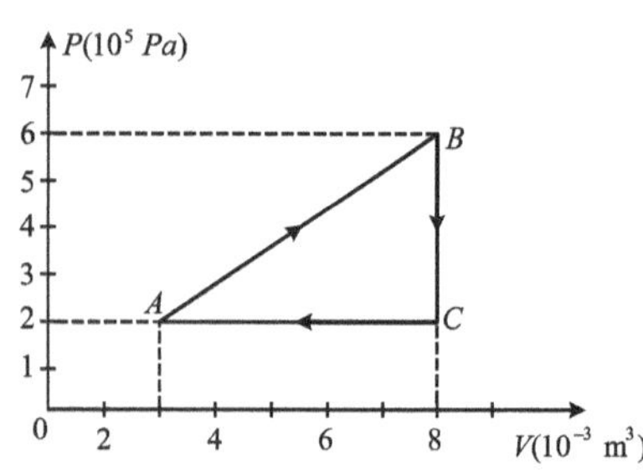

(A) $2PV$ (B) $4PV$
(C) $1/2 PV$ (D) PV

8. A gas is taken through the cycle $A \to B \to C \to A$, as shown. What is the net work done by the gas ? **[NEET (UG) 2013]**

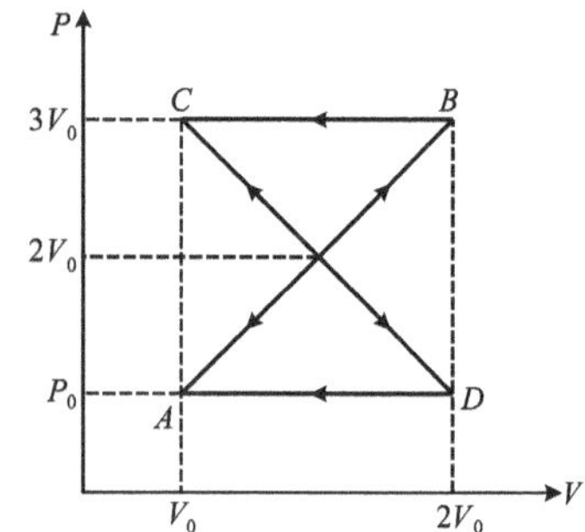

(A) $2000\,J$ (B) $1000\,J$
(C) Zero   (D) $-2000\,J$

9. A thermodynamic system undergoes cyclic process $ABCDA$ as shown in figure. The work done by the system in the cycle is : **[NEET (UG) 2014]**

(A) $P_0 V_0$ (B) $2\,P_0 V_0$
(C) $\dfrac{P_0 V_0}{2}$ (D) Zero

10. The coefficient of performance of a refrigerator is 5. If the temperature inside freezer is $-20°C$, the temperature of the surrounding to which is rejects heat is : **[NEET (UG) 2015]**
(A) $21°C$ (B) $31°C$
(C) $41°C$ (D) $11°C$

11. A refrigerator works between $4°C$ and $30°C$. It is required to remove 600 calories of heat every second in order to keep the temperature of the refrigerated space constant. The power required is [Take 1 cal = 4.2 joules] : **[NEET (UG) 2016]**
(A) $2.365\,W$ (B) $23.65\,W$
(C) $236.5\,W$ (D) $2365\,W$

12. A Carnot engine having an efficiency of $\dfrac{1}{10}$ as heat engine, is used as a refrigerator. If the work done on the system is 10 J, the amount of energy absorbed from the reservoir at lower temperature is : **[NEET (UG) 2017]**
(A) $1\,J$ (B) $90\,J$
(C) $99\,J$ (D) $100\,J$

13. The efficiency of an ideal heat engine working between the freezing point and boiling point of water, is : **[NEET (UG) 2018]**
(A) 6.25% (B) 20%
(C) 26.8% (D) 12.5%

11.3 Thermocouple

1. The temperature of inversion of a thermocouple is $620°C$ and the neutral temperature is $300°C$. What is the temperature of cold junction : **[NEET (UG) 2005]**
(A) $40°C$ (B) $20°C$
(C) $320°C$ (D) $-20°C$

* * * * *

12 KINETIC THEORY

12.1 Kinetic Theory of Gases

1. The equation of state for 5 g of oxygen at a pressure P and temperature T, when occupying a volume V, will be :
(where R is the gas constant) **[NEET (UG) 2004]**
(A) $PV = (5/32)RT$ (B) $PV = 5RT$
(C) $PV = (5/2)RT$ (D) $PV = (5/16)RT$

2. At 10°C the value of the density of a fixed mass of an ideal gas divided by its pressure is x. At 110°C this ratio is :
[NEET (UG) 2008]

(A) $\dfrac{10}{110}x$ (B) $\dfrac{283}{383}x$

(C) x (D) $\dfrac{383}{283}x$

3. Liquid oxygen at 50 K is heated to 300 K at constant pressure of 1 atm. The rate of heating is constant. Which one of the following graphs represents the variation of temperature with time ? **[NEET (UG) 2012]**

(A) 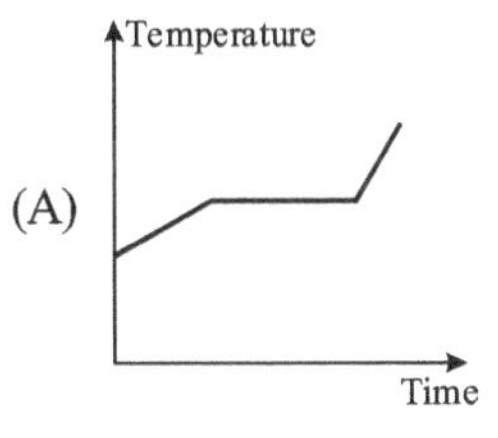

(B) 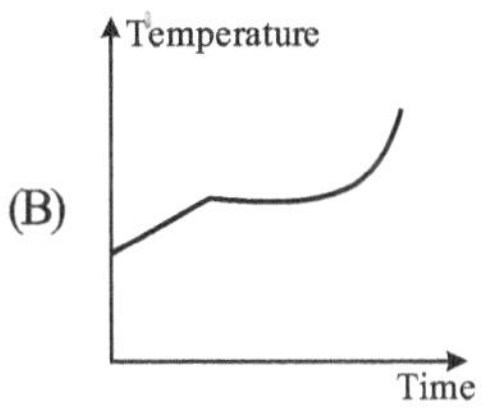

(C) 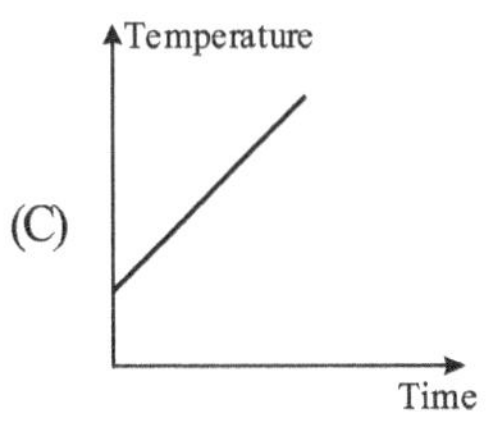

(D) 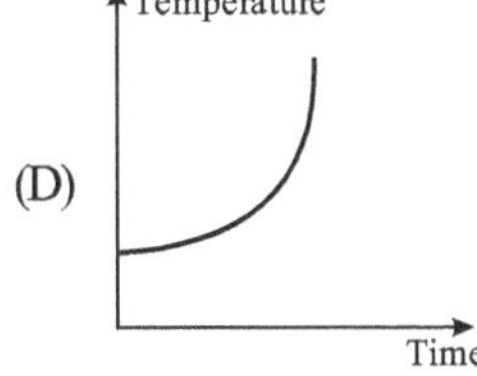

4. The mean free path of molecules of a gas, (radius r) is inversely proportional to : **[NEET (UG) 2014]**
(A) r^3 (B) r^2
(C) r (D) $\sqrt{r}$

5. Two vessels separately contain two ideal gases A and B at the same temperature. The pressure of A being twice that of B. Under such conditions, the density of A is found to be 1.5 times the density of B. The ratio of molecular weight of A and B is :
[NEET (UG) 2015]

(A) 1/2   (B) 2/3
(C) 3/4   (D) 2

6. 4.0 g of gas occupies 22.4 litres at NTP. The specific heat capacity of the gas at constant volume is 5.0 JK^{-1}. If the speed of sound in this gas at NTP is 952 ms^{-1}, then the heat capacity at constant pressure is (Take gas constant $R = 8.3$ JK^{-1} mol^{-1}) :
[NEET (UG) 2015]
(A) 8.5 JK^{-1} mol^{-1} (B) 8.0 JK^{-1} mol^{-1}
(C) 7.5 JK^{-1} mol^{-1} (D) 7.0 JK^{-1} mol^{-1}

7. The molecules of a given mass of a gas have rms velocity of 200 ms^{-1} at 27°C and 1.0×10^5 Nm^{-2} pressure. When the temperature and pressure of the gas are respectively, 127°C and 0.05×10^5 Nm^{-2}, the rms velocity of its molecules in ms^{-1} is :
[NEET (UG) 2016]

(A) $100\sqrt{2}$ (B) $\dfrac{400}{\sqrt{3}}$

(C) $\dfrac{100\sqrt{2}}{3}$ (D) $\dfrac{100}{3}$

8. A given sample of an ideal gas occupies a volume V at a pressure P and absolute temperature T. The mass of each molecule of the gas is m. Which of the following gives the density of the gas ? **[NEET (UG) 2016 Ph. II]**
(A) $P/(kT)$ (B) $Pm/(kT)$
(C) $P/(kTV)$ (D) mkT

9. The temperature inside a refrigerator is t_2°C and the room temperature is t_1°C. The amount of heat delivered to the room for each joule of electrical energy consumed ideally will be :
[NEET (UG) 2016 Ph. II]

(A) $\dfrac{t_1}{t_1 - t_2}$ (B) $\dfrac{t_1 + 273}{t_1 - t_2}$

(C) $\dfrac{t_2 + 273}{t_1 - t_2}$ (D) $\dfrac{t_1 + t_2}{t_1 + 273}$

10. At what temperature will the rms speed of oxygen molecules become just sufficient for escaping from the Earth's atmosphere?
[NEET (UG) 2018]
(Given : Mass of oxygen molecule (m) = 2.76×10^{-26} kg Boltzmann's constant $k_B = 1.38 \times 10^{-23}$ JK^{-1}) :
(A) 5.016×10^4 K   (B) 8.360×10^4 K
(C) 2.508×10^4 K   (D) 1.254×10^4 K

11. The mean free path for a gas, with molecular diameter d and number density n can be expressed as : **[NEET (UG) 2020]**

(A) $\dfrac{1}{\sqrt{2}\, n^2 \pi^2 d^2}$

(B) $\dfrac{1}{\sqrt{2}\, n\pi d}$

(C) $\dfrac{1}{\sqrt{2}\, n\pi d^2}$

(D) $\dfrac{1}{\sqrt{2}\, n^2 \pi d^2}$

12. The average thermal energy for a mono-atomic gas is : (k_B is Boltzmann constant and T, absolute temperature) :

[NEET (UG) 2020]

(A) $\dfrac{7}{2} k_B T$

(B) $\dfrac{1}{2} k_B T$

(C) $\dfrac{3}{2} k_B T$

(D) $\dfrac{5}{2} k_B T$

13. A cylinder contains hydrogen gas at pressure of 249 kPa and temperature 27°C. Its density is : ($R = 8.3$ J mol^{-1} K^{-1})

[NEET (UG) 2020]

(A) 0.02 kg/m^3

(B) 0.5 kg/m^3

(C) 0.2 kg/m^3

(D) 0.1 kg/m^3

14. Match Column-I and Column-II and choose the Correct match from the given choices : **[NEET (UG) 2021]**

	Column-I		Column-II
(a)	Root mean square speed of gas molecules	**(p)**	$\dfrac{1}{3} nmv^2$
(b)	Pressure exerted by ideal gas	**(q)**	$\sqrt{\dfrac{3RT}{M}}$
(c)	Average kinetic energy of a molecule	**(r)**	$\dfrac{5}{2} RT$
(d)	Total internal energy of 1 mole of a diatomic gas	**(s)**	$\dfrac{3}{2} k_B T$

(A) (a) $\rightarrow$ (r), (b) $\rightarrow$ (p), (c) $\rightarrow$ (s), (d) $\rightarrow$ (q)

(B) (a) $\rightarrow$ (q), (b) $\rightarrow$ (r), (c) $\rightarrow$ (s), (d) $\rightarrow$ (p)

(C) (a) $\rightarrow$ (q), (b) $\rightarrow$ (p), (c) $\rightarrow$ (s), (d) $\rightarrow$ (r)

(D) (a) $\rightarrow$ (r), (b) $\rightarrow$ (q), (c) $\rightarrow$ (p), (d) $\rightarrow$ (s)

19. The volume occupied by the molecules contained in 4.5 kg water at STP, if the intermolecular forces vanish away is :

[NEET (UG) 2022]

(A) 5.6×10^3 m^3

(B) 5.6×10^{-3} m^3

(C) 5.6 m^3

(D) 5.6×10^6 m^3

* * * * *

13.1 Simple Harmonic Motion

1. The total energy of particle performing SHM depends on : **[NEET (UG) 2001]**

(A) k, a, m (B) k, a

(C) k, a, x (D) k, x

2. Displacement between maximum potential energy position and maximum kinetic energy position for a particle executing simple harmonic motion is : **[NEET (UG) 2002]**

(A) $\pm a/2$ (B) $+a$

(C) $\pm a$ (D) -1

3. A mass is suspended separately by two different springs in successive order then time periods is t_1 and t_2 respectively. If it is connected by both spring as shown in figure then time period is t_0, the correct relation is : **[NEET (UG) 2002]**

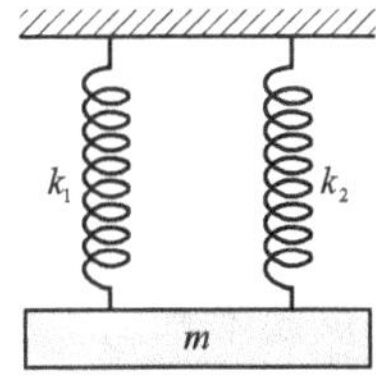

(A) $t_0^2 = t_1^2 + t_2^2$ (B) $t_0^{-2} = t_1^{-2} + t_2^{-2}$

(C) $t_0^{-1} = t_1^{-1} + t_2^{-1}$ (D) $t_0 = t_1 + t_2$

4. When an oscillator completes 100 oscillations, its amplitude is reduced to 1/3 of initial value. What will be its amplitude, when it completes 200 oscillations ? **[NEET (UG) 2002]**

(A) 1/8   (B) 2/3

(C) 1/6   (D) 1/9

5. Which one of the following statements is true for the speed v and the acceleration a of a particle executing simple harmonic motion ? **[NEET (UG) 2003]**

(A) When v is maximum, a is maximum

(B) Value of a is zero, whatever may be the value of v

(C) When v is zero, a is zero

(D) When v is maximum, a is zero

6. The potential energy of a simple harmonic oscillator when the particle is half way to its end point is : **[NEET (UG) 2003]**

(A) $2/3\,E$ (B) $1/8\,E$

(C) $1/4\,E$ (D) $1/2\,E$

7. A particle of mass m oscillates with simple harmonic motion between points x_1 and x_2, the equilibrium position being O. Its potential energy is plotted. It will be as given below in the graph : **[NEET (UG) 2003]**

(A) 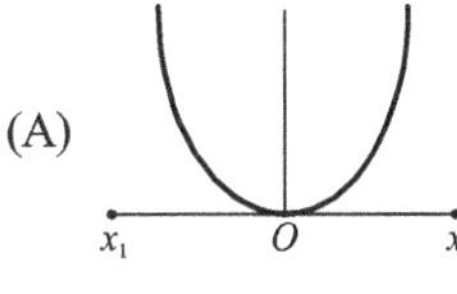   (B) 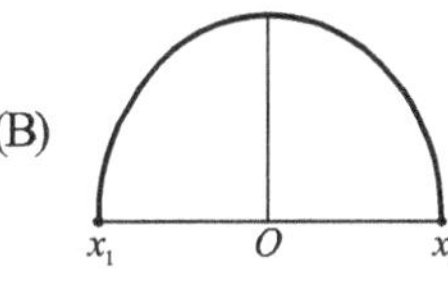

(C) 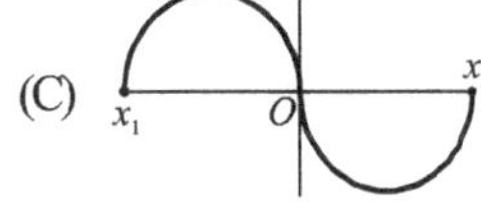   (D) 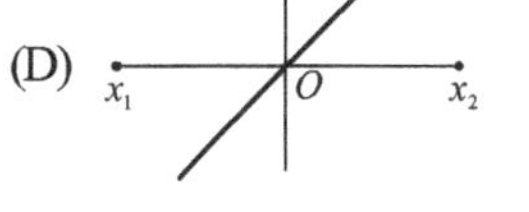

8. The time period of a mass suspended from a spring is T. If the spring is cut into four equal parts and the same mass is suspended from one of the parts, then the new time period will be : **[NEET (UG) 2003]**

(A) $T/4$ (B) T

(C) $T/2$ (D) $2T$

9. In case of a forced vibration, the resonance peak becomes very sharp when the : **[NEET (UG) 2003]**

(A) Damping force is small

(B) Restoring force is small

(C) Applied periodic force is small

(D) Quality factor is small

10. Two springs of spring constant k_1 and k_2 are joined in series. The effective spring constant of the combination is given by : **[NEET (UG) 2004]**

(A) $\sqrt{k_1 k_2}$ (B) $(k_1 + k_2)/2$

(C) $k_1 + k_2$ (D) $k_1 k_2/(k_1 + k_2)$

11. A particle executing simple harmonic motion of amplitude 5 cm has maximum speed of 31.4 cm/s. The frequency of its oscillation is : **[NEET (UG) 2005]**

(A) 1 Hz   (B) 3 Hz

(C) 2 Hz   (D) 4 Hz

12. A rectangular block of mass m and area of cross-section A floats in a liquid of density ρ. If it is given a small vertical displacement from equilibrium it undergoes oscillation with a time period T. Then : **[NEET (UG) 2006]**

(A) $T \propto \sqrt{\rho}$ (B) $T \propto \dfrac{1}{\sqrt{A}}$

(C) $T \propto \dfrac{1}{\rho}$ (D) $T \propto \dfrac{1}{\sqrt{m}}$

13. The phase difference between the instantaneous velocity and acceleration of a particle executing simple harmonic motion is : **[NEET (UG) 2007]**

(A) π

(B) $0.707\,\pi$

(C) Zero

(D) $0.5\,\pi$

14. The particle executing simple harmonic motion has a kinetic energy $K_0 \cos^2 \omega t$. The maximum values of the potential energy and the total energy are respectively : **[NEET (UG) 2007]**

(A) $K_0/2$ and K_0

(B) K_0 and $2K_0$

(C) K_0 and K_0

(D) 0 and $2K_0$

15. A particle executes simple harmonic oscillation with an amplitude a. The period of oscillation is T. The minimum time taken by the particle to travel half of the amplitude from the equilibrium position is : **[NEET (UG) 2007]**

(A) $T/8$

(B) $T/12$

(C) $T/2$

(D) $T/4$

16. A mass of 2.0 kg is put on a flat pan attached to a vertical spring fixed on the ground as shown in the figure. The mass of the spring and the pan is negligible. When pressed slightly and released the mass executes a simple harmonic motion. The spring constant is 200 N/m. What should be the minimum amplitude of the motion so that the mass gets detached from the pan (take $g = 10 \text{ m/s}^2$) ? **[NEET (UG) 2007]**

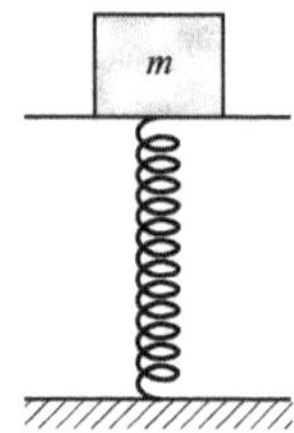

(A) 10.0 cm

(B) Any value less than 12.0 cm

(C) 4.0 cm

(D) 8.0 cm

17. Two simple Harmonic Motions of angular frequency 100 and 1000 rad s^{-1} have the same displacement amplitude. The ratio of their maximum accelerations is : **[NEET (UG) 2008]**

(A) $1 : 10^3$

(B) $1 : 10^4$

(C) $1 : 10$

(D) $1 : 10^2$

18. A point performs simple harmonic oscillation of period T and the equation of motion is given by $x = a \sin (\omega t + \pi/6)$. After the elapse of what fraction of the time period the velocity of the point will be equal to half of its maximum velocity ? **[NEET (UG) 2008]**

(A) $T/3$

(B) $T/12$

(C) $T/8$

(D) $T/6$

19. A simple pendulum performs simple harmonic motion about $x = 0$ with an amplitude a and time period T. The speed of the pendulum at $x = a/2$ will be : **[NEET (UG) 2009]**

(A) $\dfrac{\pi a \sqrt{3}}{T}$

(B) $\dfrac{\pi a \sqrt{3}}{2T}$

(C) $\dfrac{\pi a}{T}$

(D) $\dfrac{3\pi^2 a}{T}$

20. Which one of the following equations of motion represents simple harmonic motion ? **[NEET (UG) 2009]**

(A) Acceleration $= kx$

(B) Acceleration $= - k_0 x + k_1 x^2$

(C) Acceleration $= - k(x + a)$

(D) Acceleration $= k(x + a)$

Where k, k_0, k_1 and a are all positive

21. The displacement of a particle along the x-axis is given by $x = a \sin^2 \omega t$. The motion of the particle corresponds to : **[NEET (UG) 2010]**

(A) Simple harmonic motion of frequency $\dfrac{\omega}{2\pi}$

(B) Simple harmonic motion of frequency $\dfrac{\omega}{\pi}$

(C) Simple harmonic motion of frequency $\dfrac{3\omega}{2\pi}$

(D) Non simple harmonic motion

22. The period of oscillation of a mass M suspended from a spring of negligible mass is T. If along with it another mass M is also suspended, the period of oscillation will now be : **[NEET (UG) 2010]**

(A) $\sqrt{2}\,T$

(B) T

(C) $T/\sqrt{2}$

(D) $2T$

23. Out of the following functions, representing motion of a particle, which represents SHM ? **[NEET (UG) 2011]**

(a) $y = \sin \omega t - \cos \omega t$

(b) $y = \sin^3 \omega t$

(c) $y = 5\cos\left(\dfrac{3\pi}{4} - 3\omega t\right)$

(d) $y = 1 + \omega t + \omega^2 t^2$

(A) Only (a)

(B) Only (d) does not represent SHM

(C) Only (a) and (c)

(D) Only (a) and (b)

24. The damping force on an oscillator is directly proportional to the velocity. The units of the constant of proportionality are : **[NEET (UG) 2012]**

(A) kg ms^{-1}

(B) kg ms^{-2}

(C) kg s^{-1}

(D) kg s

25. The oscillation of a body on a smooth horizontal surface is represented by the equation,

$$x = A \cos(\omega t)$$

where x = displacement at time t

and ω = frequency of oscillation

Which one of the following graphs shows correctly the variation of a with t ?   **[NEET (UG) 2014]**

(A) 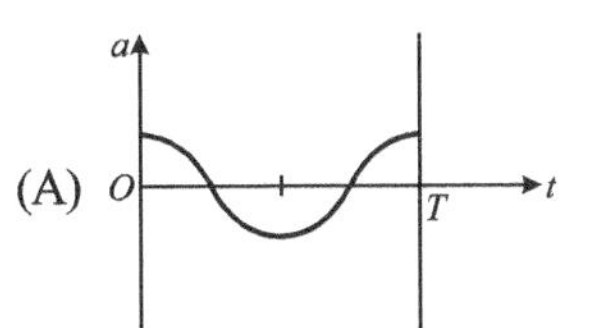   (B) 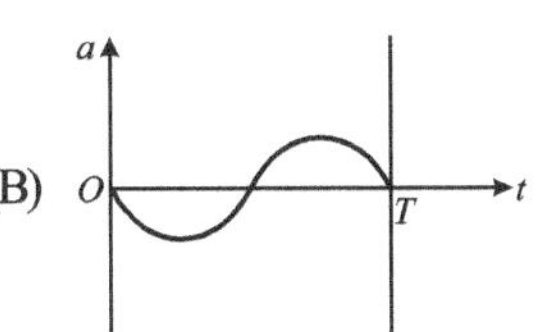

(C) 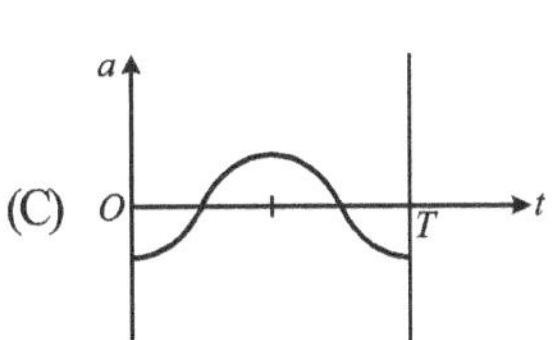   (D) 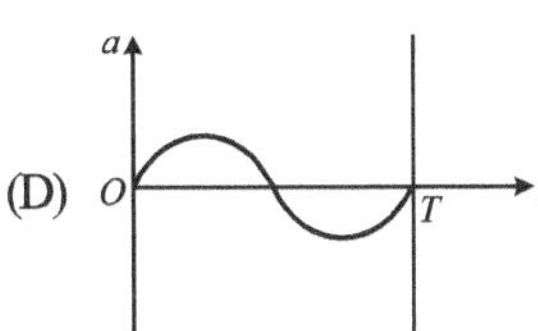

Here a = acceleration at time t

T = time period.

26. A particle is executing a simple harmonic motion. Its maximum acceleration is α and maximum velocity is β. Then its time period of vibration will be :   **[NEET (UG) 2015]**

(A) $\dfrac{2\pi\beta}{\alpha}$ (B) $\dfrac{\beta^2}{\alpha}$

(C) $\dfrac{\alpha}{\beta}$ (D) $\dfrac{\beta^2}{\alpha^2}$

27. A body of mass m is attached to the lower end of a spring whose upper end is fixed. The spring has negligible mass when the mass m is slightly pulled down and released, it oscillates with a time period of 3 s. When the mass m is increased by 1 kg, the time period of oscillations becomes 5 s. The value of m in kg is :   **[NEET (UG) 2016 Ph. II]**

(A) 3/4   (B) 4/3

(C) 16/9   (D) 9/16

28. A particle executes linear simple harmonic motion with an amplitude of 3 cm. When the particle is at 2 cm from the mean position, the magnitude of its velocity is equal to that of its acceleration. Then its time period in seconds is :   **[NEET (UG) 2017]**

(A) $\dfrac{\sqrt{5}}{\pi}$ (B) $\dfrac{\sqrt{5}}{2\pi}$

(C) $\dfrac{4\pi}{\sqrt{5}}$ (D) $\dfrac{2\pi}{\sqrt{3}}$

29. A pendulum is hung from the roof of a sufficiently high building and is moving freely to and fro like a simple harmonic oscillator. The acceleration of the bob of the pendulum is 20 m/s^2 at a distance of 5 m from the mean position. The time period of oscillation is :   **[NEET (UG) 2018]**

(A) 2 s   (B) π s

(C) 2π s   (D) 1 s

30. The displacement of a particle executing simple harmonic motion is given by   **[NEET (UG) 2019]**

$$y = A_0 + A \sin \omega t + B \cos \omega t$$

Then the amplitude of its oscillation is given by :

(A) $A_0 + \sqrt{A^2 + B^2}$ (B) $\sqrt{A^2 + B^2}$

(C) $\sqrt{A_0^2 + (A + B)^2}$ (D) $A + B$

31. Average velocity of a particle executing SHM in one complete vibration is :   **[NEET (UG) 2019]**

(A) $\dfrac{A\omega}{2}$ (B) $A\omega$

(C) $\dfrac{A\omega^2}{2}$ (D) Zero

32. The phase difference between displacement and acceleration of a particle in a simple harmonic motion is :   **[NEET (UG) 2020]**

(A) Zero   (B) π rad

(C) $\dfrac{3\pi}{2}$ rad   (D) $\dfrac{\pi}{2}$ rad

33. A body executing simple harmonic motion with frequency 'n', the frequency of its potential energy is : **[NEET (UG) 2021]**

(A) n (B) $2n$

(C) $3n$ (D) $4n$

34. A spring is stretched by 5 cm by a force 10 N. The time period of the oscillations when a mass of 2 kg is suspended by it is :   **[NEET (UG) 2021]**

(A) 0.0628 s   (B) 6.28 s

(C) 3.14 s   (D) 0.628 s

35. Two pendulums of length 121 cm and 100 cm start vibrating in phase. At some instant, the two are at their mean position in the same phase. The minimum number of vibrations of the shorter pendulum after which the two are again in phase at the mean position is :   **[NEET (UG) 2022]**

(A) 9   (B) 10

(C) 8   (D) 11

* * * * *

14 WAVES

14.1 Wave Motion

1. The equation of a wave is represented by $y = 10^{-4} \sin\left(100t - \dfrac{x}{10}\right)$ m, then the velocity of wave will be :

[NEET (UG) 2001]

(A) $100\,\text{m/s}$ (B) $4\,\text{m/s}$

(C) $1000\,\text{m/s}$ (D) $10\,\text{m/s}$

2. A wave travelling in positive x-direction with $a = 0.2$ m, velocity $= 360\,\text{m s}^{-1}$ and $\lambda = 60$ m, then correct expression for the wave is :

[NEET (UG) 2002]

(A) $y = 0.2 \sin\left[2\pi\left(6t + \dfrac{x}{60}\right)\right]$ (B) $y = 0.2 \sin\left[\pi\left(6t + \dfrac{x}{60}\right)\right]$

(C) $y = 0.2 \sin\left[2\pi\left(6t - \dfrac{x}{60}\right)\right]$ (D) $y = 0.2 \sin\left[\pi\left(6t - \dfrac{x}{60}\right)\right]$

3. The phase difference between two waves, represented by
$$y_1 = 10^{-6} \sin\left[100t + (x/50) + 0.5\right]\,\text{m}$$
$$y_2 = 10^{-6} \cos\left[100t + (x/50)\right]\,\text{m},$$
where x is expressed in metres and t is expressed in seconds, is approximately :

[NEET (UG) 2004]

(A) $1.07\,\text{radians}$ (B) $2.07\,\text{radians}$

(C) $0.5\,\text{radians}$ (D) $1.5\,\text{radians}$

4. A point source emits sound equally in all directions in a non-absorbing medium. Two points P and Q are at distance of 2 m and 3 m respectively from the source. The ratio of the intensities of the waves at P and Q is :

[NEET (UG) 2005]

(A) $3:2$ (B) $2:3$

(C) $9:4$ (D) $4:9$

5. A transverse wave propagating along x-axis is represented by $y(x, t) = 8.0 \sin\left(0.5\pi x - 4\pi t - \dfrac{\pi}{4}\right)$ where x is in metres and t is in seconds. The speed of the wave is :

[NEET (UG) 2006]

(A) $4\pi\,\text{m/s}$ (B) $0.5\pi\,\text{m/s}$

(C) $\dfrac{\pi}{4}\,\text{m/s}$ (D) $8\,\text{m/s}$

6. The time of reverberation of a room A is one second. What will be the time (in seconds) of reverberation of a room, having all the dimensions double of those of room A :

[NEET (UG) 2006]

(A) 2 (B) 4

(C) $1/2$ (D) 1

7. The wave described by $y = 0.25 \sin (10\pi x - 2\pi f)$, where x and y are in metres and t in seconds, is a wave travelling along the :

[NEET (UG) 2008]

(A) $+ve$ x direction with frequency 1 Hz and wavelength $\lambda = 0.2$ m

(B) $-ve$ x direction with amplitude 0.25 m and wavelength $\lambda = 0.2$ m

(C) $-ve$ x direction with frequency 1 Hz

(D) $+ve$ x direction with frequency π Hz and wavelength $\lambda = 0.2$ m

8. Two points are located at a distance of 10 m and 15 m from the source of oscillation. The period of oscillation is 0.05 sec and the velocity of the wave is 300 m/s. What is the phase difference between the oscillations of two points ?

[NEET (UG) 2008]

(A) π (B) $\pi/6$

(C) $\pi/3$ (D) $2\pi/3$

9. A wave in a string has an amplitude of 2 cm. The wave travels in the $+ve$ direction of x-axis with a speed of 128 m/s and it is noted that 5 complete waves fit in 4 m length of the string. The equation describing the wave is :

[NEET (UG) 2009]

(A) $y = (0.02)\,\text{m} \sin (7.58x - 1005t)$

(B) $y = (0.02)\,\text{m} \sin (7.85x + 1005t)$

(C) $y = (0.02)\,\text{m} \sin (15.7x - 2010t)$

(D) $y = (0.02)\,\text{m} \sin (15.7x + 2010t)$

10. A transverse wave is represented by $y = A \sin (\omega t - kx)$. For what value of the wavelength is the wave velocity equal to the maximum particle velocity ?

[NEET (UG) 2010]

(A) A (B) $\dfrac{\pi A}{2}$

(C) πA (D) $2\pi A$

11. Two waves are represented by the equations $y_1 = a \sin (\omega t + kx + 0.57)$ m and $y_2 = a \cos (\omega t + kx)$ m, where x in meter and t in sec. The phase difference between them is :

[NEET (UG) 2011]

(A) $1.0\,\text{radian}$ (B) $1.25\,\text{radian}$

(C) $1.57\,\text{radian}$ (D) $0.57\,\text{radian}$

12. Sound waves travel at 350 m/s through a warm air and at 3500 m/s through brass. The wavelength of a 700 Hz acoustic

wave as it enters brass from warm air : **[NEET (UG) 2011]**
(A) Decreases by a factor 10
(B) Increases by a factor 20
(C) Increases by a factor 10
(D) Decreases by a factor 20

13. The equation of a simple harmonic wave is given by

$$y = 3\sin\frac{\pi}{2}(50t - x)$$

Where x and y are in meters and t is in seconds. The ratio of maximum particle velocity to the wave velocity is :

[NEET (UG) 2012]

(A) $\frac{3}{2}\pi$

(B) 3π

(C) $\frac{2}{3}\pi$

(D) 2π

14. A wave travelling in the $+ve$ x-direction having maximum displacement along y-direction as 1 m, wavelength 2 πm and frequency of $\dfrac{1}{\pi}$ Hz is represented by : **[NEET (UG) 2013]**
(A) $y = \sin(x - 2t)$
(B) $y = \sin(2\pi x - 2\pi t)$
(C) $y = \sin(10\pi x - 20\pi t)$
(D) $y = \sin(2\pi x + 2\pi t)$

15. A uniform rope of length L and mass m_1 hangs vertically from a rigid support. A block of mass m_2 is attached to the free end of the rope. A transverse pulse of wavelength λ_1 is produced at the lower end of the rope. The wavelength of the pulse when it reaches the top of the rope is λ_2. The ratio λ_2/λ_1 is :

[NEET (UG) 2016]

(A) $\sqrt{\dfrac{m_1}{m_2}}$

(B) $\sqrt{\dfrac{m_1 + m_2}{m_2}}$

(C) $\sqrt{\dfrac{m_2}{m_1}}$

(D) $\sqrt{\dfrac{m_1 + m_2}{m_1}}$

14.2 Stationary Waves

1. Two waves having equation are given below are superposing
$x_1 = a\sin(\omega t - kx + \phi_1)$
$x_2 = a\sin(\omega t - kx + \phi_2)$
If in the resultant wave the frequency and amplitude remain equal to amplitude of superimposing waves, the phase difference between them is : **[NEET (UG) 2001]**
(A) $\pi/6$
(B) $2\pi/3$
(C) $\pi/4$
(D) $\pi/3$

2. If the tension and diameter of a sonometer wire of fundamental frequency n is doubled and density is halved then its fundamental frequency will become : **[NEET (UG) 2001]**
(A) $n/4$
(B) $\sqrt{2}n$
(C) n
(D) $n/\sqrt{2}$

3. When a string is divided into three segments of length l_1, l_2 and l_3 the fundamental frequencies of these three segments are v_1, v_2 and v_3 respectively. The original fundamental frequency (v) of the string is : **[NEET (UG) 2012]**

(A) $\sqrt{v} = \sqrt{v_1} + \sqrt{v_2} + \sqrt{v_3}$

(B) $v = v_1 + v_2 + v_3$

(C) $\dfrac{1}{v} = \dfrac{1}{v_1} + \dfrac{1}{v_2} + \dfrac{1}{v_3}$

(D) $\dfrac{1}{\sqrt{v}} = \dfrac{1}{\sqrt{v_1}} + \dfrac{1}{\sqrt{v_2}} + \dfrac{1}{\sqrt{v_3}}$

4. It we study the vibration of a pipe open at both ends, then the following statement is not true : **[NEET (UG) 2013]**
(A) Open end will be antinode
(B) Odd harmonics of the fundamental frequency will be generated
(C) All harmonics of the fundamental frequency will be generated
(D) Pressure change will be maximum at both ends

5. If n_1, n_2 and n_3 are the fundamental frequencies of three segments into which a string is divided, then the original fundamental frequency n of the string is given by : **[NEET (UG) 2014]**

(A) $\dfrac{1}{n} = \dfrac{1}{n_1} + \dfrac{1}{n_2} + \dfrac{1}{n_3}$

(B) $\dfrac{1}{\sqrt{n}} = \dfrac{1}{\sqrt{n_1}} + \dfrac{1}{\sqrt{n_2}} + \dfrac{1}{\sqrt{n_3}}$

(C) $\sqrt{n} = \sqrt{n_1} + \sqrt{n_2} + \sqrt{n_3}$

(D) $n = n_1 + n_2 + n_3$

6. The number of possible natural oscillations of air column in a pipe closed at one end of length 85 cm whose frequencies lie below 1250 Hz are (velocity of sound = 340 ms^{-1}) : **[NEET (UG) 2014]**
(A) 4
(B) 5
(C) 7
(D) 6

7. A string is stretched between fixed points separated by 75.0 cm. It is observed to have resonant frequencies of 420 Hz and 315 Hz. There are no other resonant frequencies between these two. The lowest resonant frequency for this string is : **[NEET (UG) 2015]**
(A) 105 Hz
(B) 155 Hz
(C) 205 Hz
(D) 10.5 Hz

8. An air column, closed at one end and open at the other, resonates with a tuning fork when the smallest length of the column is 50 cm. The next larger length of the column resonating

with the same tuning fork is : **[NEET (UG) 2016]**
(A) 66.7 cm
(B) 100 cm
(C) 150 cm
(D) 200 cm

9. The second overtone of an open organ pipe has the same frequency as the first overtone of a closed pipe L metre long. The length of the open pipe will be : **[NEET (UG) 2016 Ph. II]**
(A) L
(B) $2L$
(C) $L/2$
(D) $4L$

10. The two nearest harmonics of a tube closed at one end and open at other end are 220 Hz and 260 Hz. What is the fundamental frequency of the system ? **[NEET (UG) 2017]**
(A) 10 Hz
(B) 20 Hz
(C) 30 Hz
(D) 40 Hz

11. The fundamental frequency in an open organ pipe is equal to the third harmonic of a closed organ pipe. If the length of the closed organ pipe is 20 cm, the length of the open organ pipe is : **[NEET (UG) 2018]**
(A) 12.5 cm
(B) 8 cm
(C) 13.2 cm
(D) 16 cm

12. A tuning fork is used to produce resonance in a glass tube. The length of the air column in this tube can be adjusted by a variable piston. At room temperature of 27°C two successive resonances are produced at 20 cm and 73 cm of column length. If the frequency of the tuning fork is 320 Hz, the velocity of sound in air at 27°C is : **[NEET (UG) 2018]**
(A) 350 m/s
(B) 339 m/s
(C) 330 m/s
(D) 300 m/s

13. If the initial tension on a stretched string is doubled, then the ratio of the initial and final speeds of a transverse wave along the string is : **[NEET (UG) 2022]**
(A) $\sqrt{2}:1$
(B) $1:\sqrt{2}$
(C) $1:2$
(D) $1:1$

14.3 Beats

1. Two vibrating tuning forks produce progressive waves given by $Y_1 = 4 \sin 500\, \pi t$ and $Y_2 = 2 \sin 506\, \pi t$. Number of beats produced per minute is : **[NEET (UG) 2005]**
(A) 3
(B) 360
(C) 180
(D) 60

2. Two sound waves with wavelength 5.0 m and 5.5 m respectively, each propagate in a gas with velocity 330 m/s. We expect the following number of beats per second : **[NEET (UG) 2006]**
(A) 12
(B) 0
(C) 1
(D) 6

3. Each of the two strings of length 51.6 cm and 49.1 cm are tensioned separately by 20 N force. Mass per unit length of both the strings is same and equal to 1 g/m. When both the strings vibrate simultaneously the number of beats is : **[NEET (UG) 2009]**
(A) 3
(B) 5
(C) 7
(D) 8

4. A tuning fork of frequency 512 Hz makes 4 beats per second with the vibrating string of a piano. The beat frequency decreases to 2 beats per sec. When the tension in the piano string is slightly increased. The frequency of the piano string before increasing the tension was : **[NEET (UG) 2010]**
(A) 508 Hz
(B) 510 Hz
(C) 514 Hz
(D) 516 Hz

5. Two sources of sound placed close to each other are emitting progressive waves given by $y_1 = 4 \sin 600\, \pi t$ and $y_2 = 5 \sin 608\, \pi t$. An observer located near these two sources of sound will hear : **[NEET (UG) 2012]**
(A) 4 beats per second with intensity ratio 25 : 16 between waxing and waning
(B) 8 beats per second with intensity ratio 25 : 16 between waxing and waning
(C) 8 beats per second with intensity ratio 81 : 1 between waxing and waning
(D) 4 beats per second with intensity ratio 81 : 1 between waxing and waning

6. A source of unknown frequency gives 4 beats/s, when sounded with a source of known frequency 250 Hz. The second harmonic of the source of unknown frequency gives five beats per second, when sounded with a source of frequency 513 Hz. The unknown frequency is : **[NEET (UG) 2013]**
(A) 254 Hz
(B) 246 Hz
(C) 240 Hz
(D) 260 Hz

7. In a guitar, two strings A and B made of same material are slightly out of tune and produce beats of frequency 6 Hz. When tension in B is slightly decreased, the beat frequency increases to 7 Hz. If the frequency of A is 530 Hz, the original frequency of B will be : **[NEET (UG) 2020]**
(A) 537 Hz
(B) 523 Hz
(C) 524 Hz
(D) 536 Hz

14.4 Doppler's Effect

1. A whistle revolves in a circle with angular speed $\omega = 20$ rad/s using a string of length 50 cm. If the frequency of sound from the whistle is 385 Hz, then what is the minimum frequency heard by an observer which is far away from the centre (velocity of sound = 340 m/s) :   **[NEET (UG) 2002]**

(A) 385 Hz   (B) 374 Hz

(C) 394 Hz   (D) 333 Hz

2. An observer moves towards a stationary source of sound with a speed 1/5th of the speed of sound. The wavelength and frequency of the source emitted are λ and f respectively. The apparent frequency and wavelength recorded by the observer are respectively :   **[NEET (UG) 2003]**

(A) $1.2f, 1.2\lambda$ (B) $1.2f, \lambda$

(C) $f, 1.2\lambda$ (D) $0.8f, 0.8\lambda$

3. A car is moving towards a high cliff. The driver sounds a horn of frequency f. The reflected sound heard by the driver has frequency $2f$. If v is the velocity of sound, then the velocity of the car, in the same velocity units, will be : **[NEET (UG) 2004]**

(A) $v/\sqrt{2}$ (B) $v/3$

(C) $v/4$ (D) $v/2$

4. The driver of a car traveling with speed 30 m/s towards a hill sounds a horn of frequency 600 Hz. If the velocity of sound in air is 330 m/s, the frequency of reflected sound as heard by driver is :   **[NEET (UG) 2009]**

(A) 500 Hz   (B) 550 Hz

(C) 555.5 Hz   (D) 720 Hz

5. A train moving at a speed of 220 ms^{-1} towards a stationary object, emits a sound of frequency 1000 Hz. Some of the sound reaching the object gets reflected back to the train as echo. The frequency of the echo as detected by the driver of the train is : (speed of sound in air is 330 ms^{-1})   **[NEET (UG) 2012]**

(A) 4000 Hz   (B) 5000 Hz

(C) 3000 Hz   (D) 3500 Hz

6. A speeding motorcyclist sees traffic jam ahead of him. He slows down to 36 km/hour. He finds that traffic has eased and a car moving ahead of him at 18 km/hour is honking at a frequency of 1392 Hz. If the speed of sound is 343 m/s, the frequency of the honk as heard by him will be :   **[NEET (UG) 2014]**

(A) 1332 Hz   (B) 1372 Hz

(C) 1412 Hz   (D) 1454 Hz

7. A source of sound S emitting waves of frequency 100 Hz and an observer O are located at some distance from each other. The source is moving with a speed of 19.4 ms^{-1} at an angle of $60°$ with the source observer line as shown in the figure. The observer is at rest. The apparent frequency observed by the observer is (velocity of sound in air 330 ms^{-1}) :

[NEET (UG) 2015]

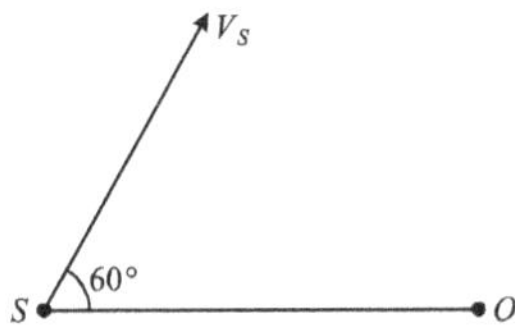

(A) 97 Hz   (B) 100 Hz

(C) 103 Hz   (D) 206 Hz

8. A siren emitting a sound of frequency 800 Hz moves away from an observer towards a cliff at a speed of 15 ms^{-1}. Then, the frequency of sound that the observer hears in the echo reflected from the cliff is :   **[NEET (UG) 2016]**

(Take velocity of sound in air $= 330 \text{ ms}^{-1}$) :

(A) 765 Hz   (B) 800 Hz

(C) 838 Hz   (D) 885 Hz

9. Two cars moving in opposite directions approach each other with speed of 22 m/s and 16.5 m/s respectively. The driver of the first car blows a horn having a frequency 400 Hz. The frequency heard by the driver of the second car is [velocity of sound 340 m/s] :   **[NEET (UG) 2017]**

(A) 350 Hz   (B) 361 Hz

(C) 411 Hz   (D) 448 Hz

*   *   *   *   *

15 ELECTRIC CHARGES AND FIELDS

15.1 Electric Force and Electric Field

1. A dipole of dipole moment $\vec{p}$ is placed in uniform electric field $\vec{E}$, then torque acting on it is given by : **[NEET (UG) 2001]**

(A) $\vec{\tau} = \vec{p} \cdot \vec{E}$

(B) $\vec{\tau} = \vec{p} \times \vec{E}$

(C) $\vec{\tau} = \vec{p} + \vec{E}$

(D) $\vec{\tau} = \vec{p} - \vec{E}$

2. A thin conducting ring of radius R is given a charge $+Q$. The electric field at the centre O of the ring due to the charge on the part AKB of the ring is E. The electric field at the centre due to the charge on the part $ACDB$ of the ring is :

[NEET (UG) 2008]

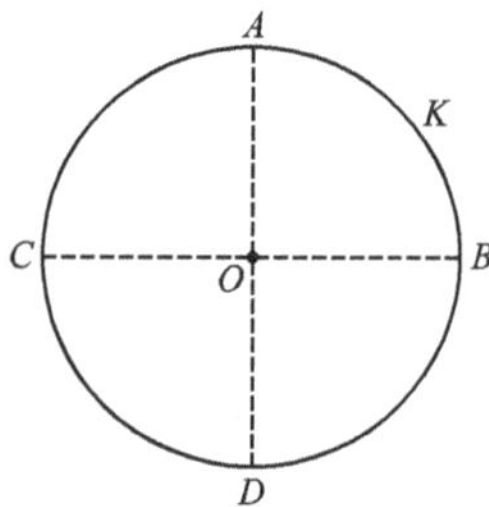

(A) E along KO

(B) $3E$ along OK

(C) $3E$ along KO

(D) E along OK

3. Two positive ions, each carrying a charge q, are separated by a distance d. If F is the force of repulsion between the ions, the number of electrons missing from each ion will be (e being the charge of an electron) : **[NEET (UG) 2010]**

(A) $\dfrac{4\pi\varepsilon_0 F d^2}{q^2}$

(B) $\dfrac{4\pi\varepsilon_0 F d^2}{e^2}$

(C) $\sqrt{\dfrac{4\pi\varepsilon_0 F e^2}{d^2}}$

(D) $\sqrt{\dfrac{4\pi\varepsilon_0 F d^2}{e^2}}$

4. Two pith balls carrying equal charges are suspended from a common point by strings of equal length, the equilibrium separation between them is r. Now the strings are rigidly clamped at half the height. The equilibrium separation between the balls now become : **[NEET (UG) 2013]**

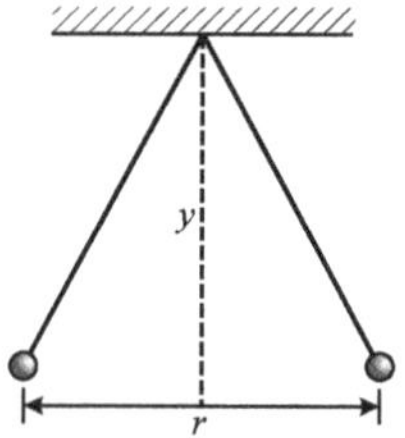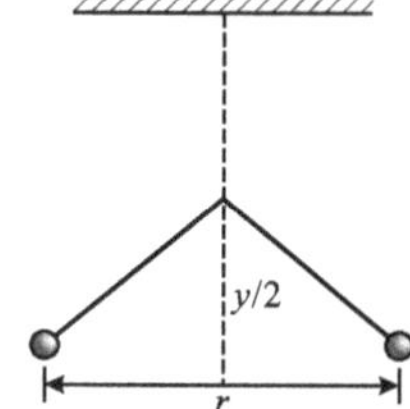

(A) $\left(\dfrac{1}{\sqrt{2}}\right)^2$

(B) $\left(\dfrac{r}{\sqrt[3]{2}}\right)$

(C) $\left(\dfrac{2r}{\sqrt{3}}\right)$

(D) $\left(\dfrac{2r}{3}\right)$

5. Two identical charged spheres suspended from a common point by two massless strings of lengths l, are initially at a distance $d(d \ll l)$ apart because of their mutual repulsion. The charges begin to leak from both the spheres at a constant rate. As a result, the spheres approach each other with a velocity v. Then v varies as a function of the distance x between the spheres, as : **[NEET (UG) 2016]**

(A) $v \propto x^{1/2}$

(B) $v \propto x$

(C) $v \propto x^{-1/2}$

(D) $v \propto x^{-1}$

6. Suppose the charge of a proton and an electron differ slightly. One of them is $-e$, the other is $(e + \Delta e)$. If the net of electrostatic force and gravitational force between two hydrogen atoms placed at a distance d (much greater than atomic size) apart is zero, then Δe is of the order of [Given mass of hydrogen $m_h = 1.67 \times 10^{-27}$ kg] : **[NEET (UG) 2017]**

(A) 10^{-20} C

(B) 10^{-23} C

(C) 10^{-37} C

(D) 10^{-47} C

7. An electron falls from rest through a vertical distance h in a uniform and vertically upward directed electric field E. The direction of electric field is now reversed, keeping its magnitude the same. A proton is allowed to fall from rest in it through the same vertical distance h. The time of fall of the electron, in comparison to the time of fall of the proton is :

[NEET (UG) 2018]

(A) 10 times greater

(B) 5 times greater

(C) Smaller

(D) Equal

8. A toy car with charge q moves on a frictionless horizontal plane surface under the influence of a uniform electric field $\vec{E}$. Due to the force $q\vec{E}$, its velocity increases from 0 to 6 m/s in one second duration. At that instant the direction of the field is reversed. The car continues to move for two more seconds under the influence of this field. The average velocity and the average speed of the toy car between 0 to 3 seconds are respectively : **[NEET (UG) 2018]**

(A) 1 m/s, 3.5 m/s   (B) 1 m/s, 3 m/s
(C) 2 m/s, 4 m/s   (D) 1.5 m/s, 3 m/s

9. A hollow metal sphere of radius R is uniformly charged. The electric field due to the sphere at a distance r from the centre : **[NEET (UG) 2019]**
(A) Increases as r increases for $r < R$ and for $r > R$
(B) Zero as r increases for $r < R$, decreases as r increases for $r > R$
(C) Zero as r increases for $r < R$, increases as r increases for $r > R$
(D) Decreases as r increases for $r < R$ and for $r > R$

10. Two parallel infinite line charges with linear charge densities $+\lambda$ C/m and $-\lambda$ C/m are placed at a distance of $2R$ in free space. What is the electric field mid-way between the two line charges ? **[NEET (UG) 2019]**

(A) Zero   (B) $\dfrac{2\lambda}{\pi\varepsilon_0 R}$ N/C

(C) $\dfrac{\lambda}{\pi\varepsilon_0 R}$ N/C   (D) $\dfrac{\lambda}{2\pi\varepsilon_0 R}$ N/C

11. Two point charges A and B, having charges $+Q$ and $-Q$ respectively, are placed at certain distance apart and force acting between them is F. If 25% charge of A is transferred to B, then force between the charges becomes : **[NEET (UG) 2019]**

(A) F (B) $\dfrac{9F}{16}$

(C) $\dfrac{16F}{9}$ (D) $\dfrac{4F}{3}$

12. A spherical conductor of radius 10 cm has a charge of 3.2×10^{-7} C distributed uniformly. What is the magnitude of electric field at a point 15 cm from the centre of the sphere ?

$\left(\dfrac{1}{4\pi\,\epsilon_0} = 9\times10^9 \text{ Nm}^2/\text{C}^2 \right)$ **[NEET (UG) 2020]**

(A) 1.28×10^7 N/C   (B) 1.28×10^4 N/C
(C) 1.28×10^5 N/C   (D) 1.28×10^6 N/C

15.2 Electric Flux and Gauss Law

1. A charge Q μC is placed at the centre of a cube, the flux coming out from each face will be : **[NEET (UG) 2001]**

(A) $\dfrac{Q}{6\varepsilon_0} \times 10^{-6}$ (B) $\dfrac{Q}{6\varepsilon_0} \times 10^{-3}$

(C) $\dfrac{Q}{24\varepsilon_0}$ (D) $\dfrac{Q}{8\varepsilon_0}$

2. A charge q is located at the centre of a cube. The electric flux through any face is : **[NEET (UG) 2003]**

(A) $\dfrac{2\pi q}{6(4\pi\varepsilon_0)}$ (B) $\dfrac{4\pi q}{6(4\pi\varepsilon_0)}$

(C) $\dfrac{\pi q}{6(4\pi\varepsilon_0)}$ (D) $\dfrac{q}{6(4\pi\varepsilon_0)}$

3. A square surface of side L metres is in the plane of the paper. A uniform electric field $\vec{E}$ (volt/m), also in the plane of the paper, is limited only to the lower half of the square surface, (see figure). The electric flux in SI units associated with the surface is : **[NEET (UG) 2006]**

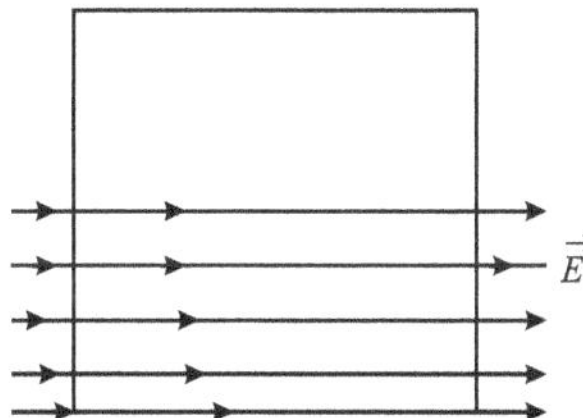

(A) $EL^2/(2\varepsilon_0)$ (B) $EL^2/2$
(C) Zero   (D) EL^2

4. A hollow cylinder has a charge q coulomb within i. If ϕ is the electric flux in units of volt-meter associated with the curved surface B, the flux linked with the plane surface A in units of volt-meter will be : **[NEET (UG) 2007]**

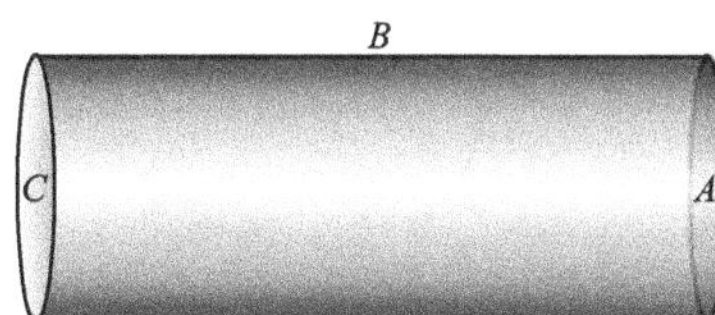

(A) $\dfrac{q}{2\varepsilon_0}$ (B) $\dfrac{\phi}{3}$

(C) $\dfrac{q}{\varepsilon_0} - \phi$ (D) $\dfrac{1}{2}\left(\dfrac{q}{\varepsilon_0} - \phi \right)$

5. A square surface of side L meter in the plane of the paper is placed in a uniform electric field E (volt/m) acting along the same plane at an angle θ with the horizontal side of the square as shown in figure. The electric flux linked to the surface, in units of volt-m, is : **[NEET (UG) 2010]**

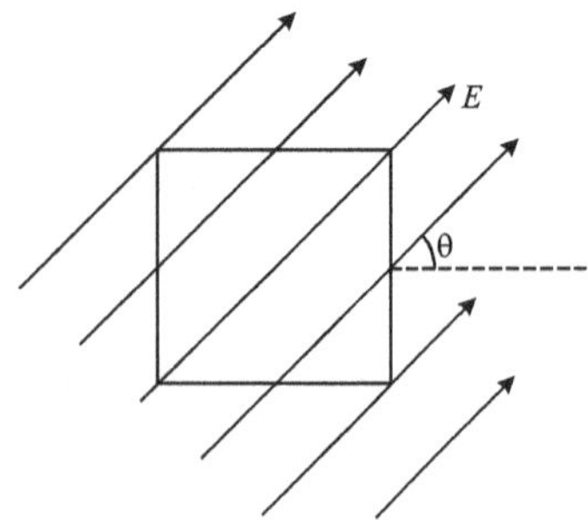

(A) Zero

(B) EL^2

(C) $EL^2 \cos\theta$

(D) $EL^2 \sin\theta$

6. A charge Q is enclosed by a Gaussian spherical surface of radius R. If the radius is doubled, then the outward electric flux will : **[NEET (UG) 2011]**

(A) Increase four times

(B) Be reduced to half

(C) Remain the same

(D) Be doubled

7. What is the flux through a cube of side 'a' if a point charge of q is at one of its corner : **[NEET (UG) 2012]**

(A) $\dfrac{2q}{\varepsilon_0}$

(B) $\dfrac{q}{8\varepsilon_0}$

(C) $\dfrac{q}{\varepsilon_0}$

(D) $\dfrac{q}{2\varepsilon_0} 6a^2$

8. The angle between the electric lines of force and the equipotential surface is : **[NEET (UG) 2022]**

(A) 45°

(B) 90°

(C) 180°

(D) 0°

* * * * *

16 ELECTRIC POTENTIAL AND CAPACITANCE

16.1 Electric Potential and Energy

1. Identical charges ($-q$) are placed at each corners of a cube of side b, then electrostatic potential energy of charge ($+q$) which is placed at centre of cube will be : **[NEET (UG) 2002]**

(A) $\dfrac{-4\sqrt{2}q^2}{\pi\varepsilon_0 b}$

(B) $\dfrac{-8\sqrt{2}q^2}{\pi\varepsilon_0 b}$

(C) $\dfrac{-4q^2}{\sqrt{3}\pi\varepsilon_0 b}$

(D) $\dfrac{8\sqrt{2}q^2}{4\pi\varepsilon_0 b}$

2. Some charge is being given to a conductor. Then its potential is : **[NEET (UG) 2002]**
(A) Maximum at surface
(B) Maximum at centre
(C) Remain same throughout the conductor
(D) Maximum somewhere between surface and centre

3. A bullet of mass 2 g is having a charge of 2 μC. Through what potential difference must it be accelerated, starting from rest, to acquire a speed of 10 m/s ? **[NEET (UG) 2004]**
(A) 5kV
(B) 50kV
(C) 5V
(D) 50V

4. As per this diagram a point charge $+q$ is placed at the origin O. Work done in taking another point charge $-Q$ from the point A coordinates $(0, a)$ to another point B coordinates $(a, 0)$ along the straight path AB is : **[NEET (UG) 2005]**

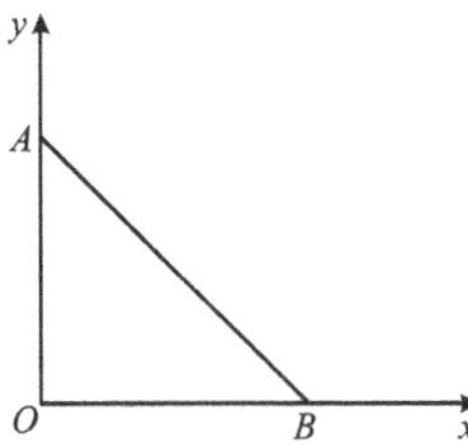

(A) $\left(\dfrac{-qQ}{4\pi\varepsilon_0}\dfrac{1}{a^2}\right)\sqrt{2}a$

(B) Zero

(C) $\left(\dfrac{qQ}{4\pi\varepsilon_0}\dfrac{1}{a^2}\right)\dfrac{1}{\sqrt{2}}$

(D) $\left(\dfrac{qQ}{4\pi\varepsilon_0}\dfrac{1}{a^2}\right)\sqrt{2}a$

5. Two charges q_1 and q_2 are placed 30 cm apart, as shown in the figure. A third charge q_3 is moved along the arc of a circle of radius 40 cm from C to D. The change in the potential energy of the system is $\dfrac{q_3}{4\pi\,\epsilon_0}k$, where k is : **[NEET (UG) 2005]**

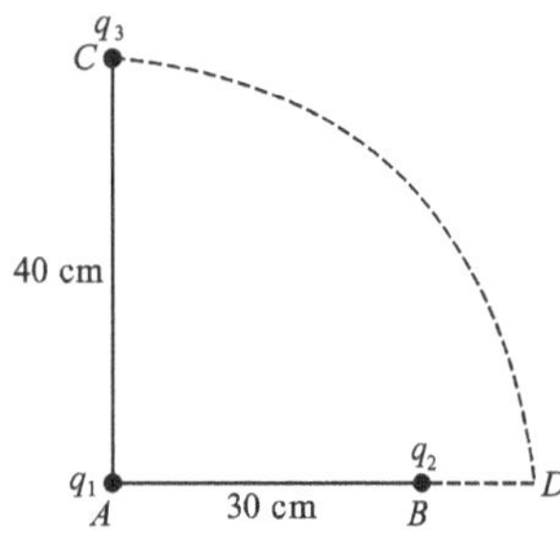

(A) $8q_2$
(B) $6q_2$
(C) $8q_1$
(D) $6q_1$

6. Charges $+q$ and $-q$ are placed at points A and B respectively which are a distance $2L$ apart, C is the midpoint between A and B. The work done in moving a charge $+Q$ along the semicircle CRD is : **[NEET (UG) 2007]**

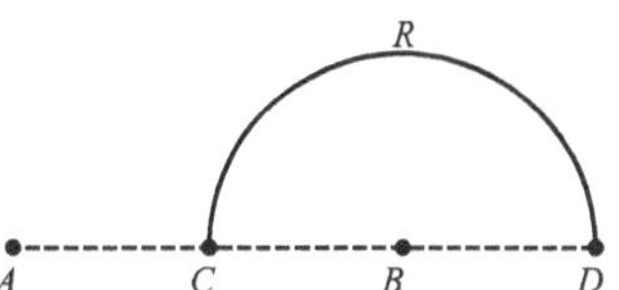

(A) $\dfrac{qQ}{2\pi\varepsilon_0 L}$

(B) $\dfrac{qQ}{6\pi\varepsilon_0 L}$

(C) $-\dfrac{qQ}{6\pi\varepsilon_0 L}$

(D) $\dfrac{qQ}{4\pi\varepsilon_0 L}$

7. The electric potential at a point in free space due to a charge Q coulomb is $Q \times 10^{11}$ volt. The electric field at that point is : **[NEET (UG) 2008]**
(A) $4\pi\varepsilon_0\,Q \times 10^{20}$ volt/m
(B) $12\pi\varepsilon_0\,Q \times 10^{22}$ volt/m
(C) $4\pi\varepsilon_0\,Q \times 10^{22}$ volt/m
(D) $12\pi\varepsilon_0\,Q \times 10^{20}$ volt/m

8. The electric potential at a point (x, y, z) is given by $V = -x^2y - xz^3 + 4$. The electric field $\vec{E}$ at that point is : **[NEET (UG) 2009]**

(A) $\vec{E} = \hat{i}\,(2xy - z^3) + \hat{j}\,xy^2 + \hat{k}\,3z^2x$

(B) $\vec{E} = \hat{i}\,(2xy + z^3) + \hat{j}\,x^2 + \hat{k}\,3xz^2$

(C) $\vec{E} = \hat{i}\,2xy + \hat{j}\,(x^2 + y^2) + \hat{k}\,(3xz - y^2)$

(D) $\vec{E} = \hat{i}\,z + \hat{j}\,xyz + \hat{k}\,z^2$

9. Three concentric spherical shells have radii a, b, and $c (a < b < c)$ and have surface charge densities σ, $-\sigma$ and σ respectively. If V_A, V_B and V_C denote the potentials of the three shells, then, for $c = a + b$, we have : **[NEET (UG) 2009]**

(A) $V_C = V_B = V_A$

(B) $V_C = V_A \neq V_B$

(C) $V_C = V_B \neq V_A$

(D) $V_C \neq V_B \neq V_A$

10. Four electric charges $+q$, $+q$, $-q$ and $-q$ are placed at the corners of a square of side $2L$ (see figure). The electric potential at point A, midway between the two charges $+q$ and $+q$, is : **[NEET (UG) 2011]**

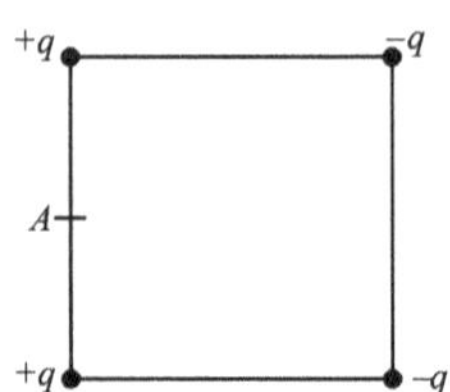

(A) $\dfrac{1}{4\pi\varepsilon_0}\dfrac{2q}{L}(1+\sqrt{5})$

(B) $\dfrac{1}{4\pi\varepsilon_0}\dfrac{2q}{L}\left(1+\dfrac{1}{\sqrt{5}}\right)$

(C) $\dfrac{1}{4\pi\varepsilon_0}\dfrac{2q}{L}\left(1-\dfrac{1}{\sqrt{5}}\right)$

(D) Zero

11. Four point charges $-Q$, $-q$, $2q$ and $2Q$ are placed, one at each corner of the square. The relation between Q and q for which the potential at the centre of the square is zero is : **[NEET (UG) 2012]**

(A) $Q = -q$

(B) $Q = -\dfrac{1}{q}$

(C) $Q = q$

(D) $Q = \dfrac{1}{q}$

12. A, B and C are three points in a uniform electric field. The electric potential is : **[NEET (UG) 2013]**

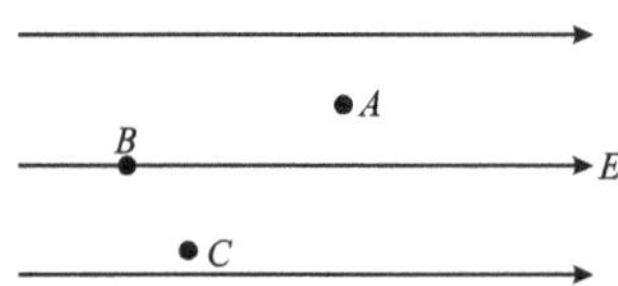

(A) Maximum at A

(B) Maximum at B

(C) Maximum at C

(D) Same at all the three points A, B and C

13. A conducting sphere of radius R is given a charge Q. The electric potential and the electric field at the centre of the sphere respectively are : **[NEET (UG) 2014]**

(A) Zero and $\dfrac{Q}{4\pi\varepsilon_0 R^2}$

(B) $\dfrac{Q}{4\pi\varepsilon_0 R}$ and zero

(C) $\dfrac{Q}{4\pi\varepsilon_0 R}$ and $\dfrac{Q}{4\pi\varepsilon_0 R^2}$

(D) Both are zero

14. In a region, the potential is represented by $V(x, y, z) = 6x - 8xy - 8y + 6yz$, where V is in volts and x, y, z are in metres. The electric force experienced by a charge of 2 coulomb situated at point $(1, 1, 1)$ is : **[NEET (UG) 2014]**

(A) $6\sqrt{5}$ N

(B) 30 N

(C) 24 N

(D) $4\sqrt{35}$ N

15. If potential (in volts) in a region is expressed as $V(x, y, z) = 6xy - y + 2yz$, the electric field (in N/C) at point $(1, 1, 0)$ is : **[NEET (UG) 2015]**

(A) $-(6\hat{i} + 9\hat{j} + \hat{k})$

(B) $-(3\hat{i} + 5\hat{j} + 3\hat{k})$

(C) $-(6\hat{i} + 5\hat{j} + 2\hat{k})$

(D) $-(2\hat{i} + 3\hat{j} + \hat{k})$

16. The diagrams below show regions of equipotential. A positive charge is moved from A to B in each diagram : **[NEET (UG) 2017]**

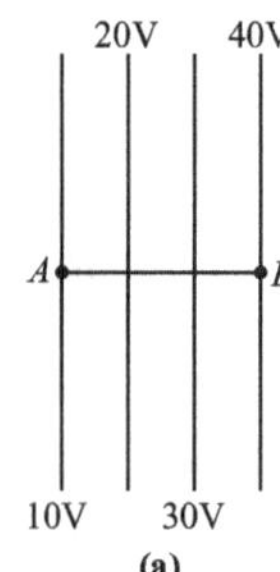
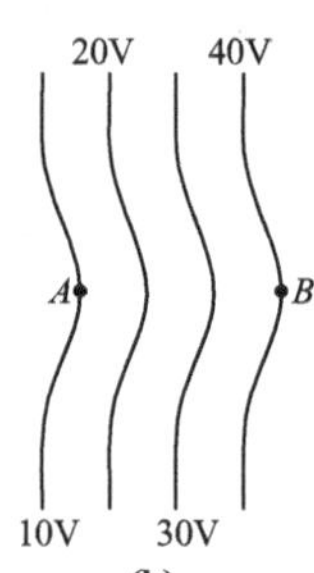
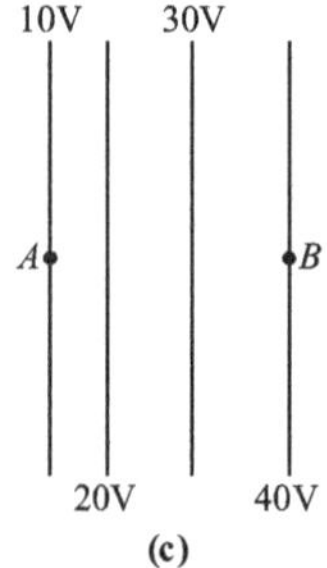
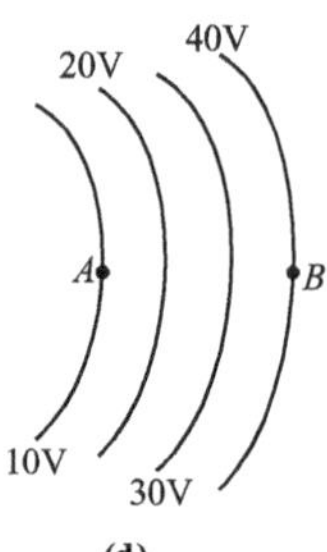

(A) Maximum work is required to move q in figure (c)

(B) In all the four cases the work done is the same

(C) Minimum work is required to move q in figure (a)

(D) Maximum work is required to move q in figure (b)

17. In a certain region of space with volume $0.2\ \text{m}^3$ the electric potential is found to be 5 V throughout. The magnitude of electric field in this region is : **[NEET (UG) 2020]**

(A) 5 N/C

(B) Zero

(C) 0.5 N/C

(D) 1 N/C

18. Two charged spherical conductors of radius R_1 and R_2 are connected by a wire. Then the ratio of surface charge densities of the spheres (σ_1/σ_2) is : **[NEET (UG) 2021]**

(A) $\dfrac{R_1}{R_2}$ (B) $\dfrac{R_2}{R_1}$

(C) $\sqrt{\left(\dfrac{R_1}{R_2}\right)}$ (D) $\dfrac{R_1^2}{R_2^2}$

19. Twenty seven drops of same size are charged at 220 V each. They combine to form a bigger drop. Calculate the potential of the bigger drop : **[NEET (UG) 2021]**

(A) 660 V   (B) 1320 V

(C) 1520 V   (D) 1980 V

20. Two hollow conducting spheres of radii R_1 and R_2 $(R_1 \gg R_2)$ have equal charges. The potential would be : **[NEET (UG) 2022]**

(A) More on smaller sphere

(B) Equal on both the spheres

(C) Dependent on the material property of the sphere

(D) More on bigger sphere

16.2 Electric Dipole

1. An electric dipole has the magnitude of its charge as q and its dipole moment is p. It is placed in a uniform electric field E. If its dipole moment is along the direction of the field, the force on it and its potential energy are respectively : **[NEET (UG) 2004]**

(A) $2q \cdot E$ and minimum   (B) $q \cdot E$ and $p \cdot E$

(C) Zero and minimum   (D) $q \cdot E$ and maximum

2. An electric dipole of moment $\vec{p}$ is lying along a uniform electric field $\vec{E}$. The work done in rotating the dipole by 90° is : **[NEET (UG) 2006]**

(A) $\sqrt{2}\,pE$ (B) $\dfrac{pE}{2}$

(C) $2pE$ (D) pE

3. Three point charges $+q$, $-q$ and $+q$ are placed at points $(x = 0, y = a, z = 0)$, $(x = 0, y = 0, z = 0)$ and $(x = a, y = 0, z = 0)$ respectively. The magnitude and direction of the electric dipole moment vector of this charge assembly are : **[NEET (UG) 2007]**

(A) $\sqrt{2}qa$ along the line joining points $(x = 0, y = 0, z = 0)$ and $(x = a, y = a, z = 0)$

(B) qa along the line joining points $(x = 0, y = 0, z = 0)$ and $(x = a, y = a, z = 0)$

(C) $\sqrt{2}qa$ along $+ve$ x-direction

(D) $\sqrt{2}qa$ along $+ve$ y-direction

4. An electric dipole of moment 'p' is placed in an electric field of intensity 'E'. The dipole acquires a position such that the axis of the dipole makes an angle θ with the direction of the field. Assuming that the potential energy of the dipole to be zero when $\theta = 90°$, the torque and the potential energy of the dipole will respectively be : **[NEET (UG) 2012]**

(A) $pE \sin\theta, -pE \cos\theta$ (B) $pE \sin\theta, -2pE \cos\theta$

(C) $pE \sin\theta, 2pE \cos\theta$ (D) $pE \cos\theta, -pE \cos\theta$

5. An electric dipole is placed at an angle of 30° with an electric field intensity 2×10^5 N/C. It experiences a torque equal to 4 Nm. The charge on the dipole, if the dipole length is 2 cm, is : **[NEET (UG) 2016 Ph. II]**

(A) 8 mC   (B) 2 mC

(C) 5 mC   (D) 7 μC

6. A short electric dipole has a dipole moment of 16×10^{-9} cm. The electric potential due to the dipole at a point at a distance of 0.6 m from the centre of the dipole, situated on a line making an angle of 60° with the dipole axis is :

$$\left(\frac{1}{4\pi\epsilon_0} = 9 \times 10^9 \, \text{Nm}^2/\text{C}^2\right)$$ **[NEET (UG) 2020]**

(A) Zero   (B) 50 V

(C) 200 V   (D) 400 V

7. A dipole is placed in an electric field as shown. In which direction will it move ? **[NEET (UG) 2021]**

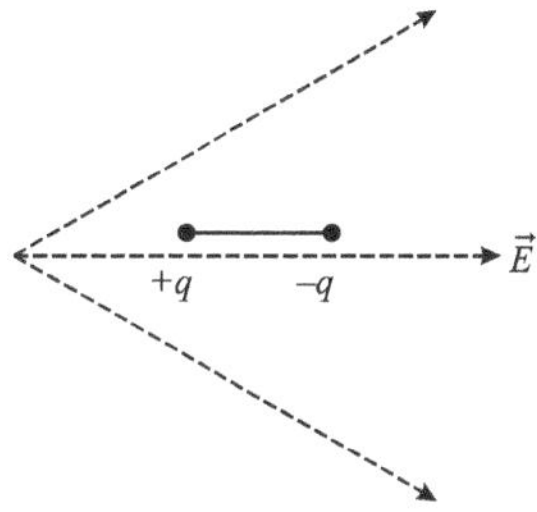

(A) Towards the left as its potential energy will increase

(B) Towards the right as its potential energy will decrease

(C) Towards the left as its potential energy will decrease

(D) Towards the right as its potential energy will increase

8. Polar molecules are the molecules : **[NEET (UG) 2021]**

(A) having zero dipole moment.

(B) acquire a dipole moment only in the presence of electric field due to displacement of charges.

(C) acquire a dipole moment only when magnetic field is absent.

(D) having a permanent electric dipole moment.

9. Two point charges $-q$ and $+q$ are placed at a distance of L, as shown in the figure.

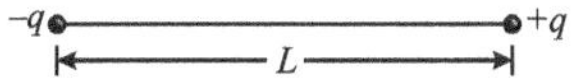

The magnitude of electric field intensity at a distance $R (R \gg L)$ varies as : **[NEET (UG) 2022]**

(A) $\dfrac{1}{R^3}$

(B) $\dfrac{1}{R^4}$

(C) $\dfrac{1}{R^6}$

(D) $\dfrac{1}{R^2}$

16.3 Capacitance

1. Energy per unit volume for a capacitor having area A and separation d kept at potential difference V is given by : **[NEET (UG) 2001]**

(A) $\dfrac{1}{2}\varepsilon_0 \dfrac{V^2}{d^2}$

(B) $\dfrac{1}{2\varepsilon_0} \dfrac{V^2}{d^2}$

(C) $\dfrac{1}{2}CV^2$

(D) $\dfrac{Q^2}{2C}$

2. A capacitor of capacity C_1 is charged upto V volt and then connected in parallel to an uncharged capacitor of capacity C_2. The final potential difference across each will be : **[NEET (UG) 2002]**

(A) $\dfrac{C_2 V}{C_1 + C_2}$

(B) $\dfrac{C_1 V}{C_1 + C_2}$

(C) $\left(1 + \dfrac{C_2}{C_1}\right)$

(D) $\left(1 - \dfrac{C_2}{C_1}\right)V$

3. Three capacitors each of capacity $4\ \mu F$ are to be connected in such a way that the effective capacitance is $6\ \mu F$. This can be done by : **[NEET (UG) 2003]**

(A) Connecting all of them in series

(B) Connecting them in parallel

(C) Connecting two in series and one in parallel

(D) Connecting two in parallel and one in series

4. A network of four capacitors of capacity equal to $C_1 = C$, $C_2 = 2C$, $C_3 = 3C$ and $C_4 = 4C$ are connected to a battery as shown in the figure. The ratio of the charges on C_2 and C_4 is : **[NEET (UG) 2005]**

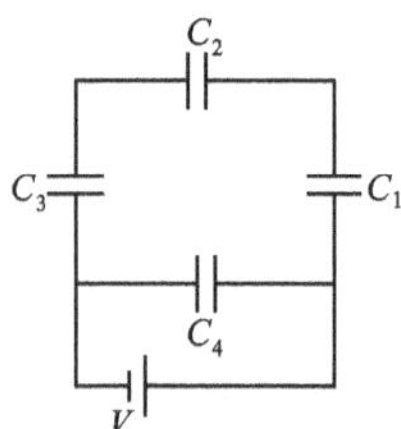

(A) $\dfrac{7}{4}$

(B) $\dfrac{22}{3}$

(C) $\dfrac{3}{22}$

(D) $\dfrac{4}{7}$

5. A parallel plate air capacitor is charged to a potential difference of V volts. After disconnecting the charging battery the distance between the plates of the capacitor is increased using an insulating handle. As a result the potential difference between the plates : **[NEET (UG) 2006]**

(A) Decreases

(B) Does not change

(C) Becomes zero

(D) Increases

6. Two condensers, one of capacity C and other of capacity $C/2$ are connected to a V-volt battery, as shown. The work done in charging fully both the condensers is : **[NEET (UG) 2007]**

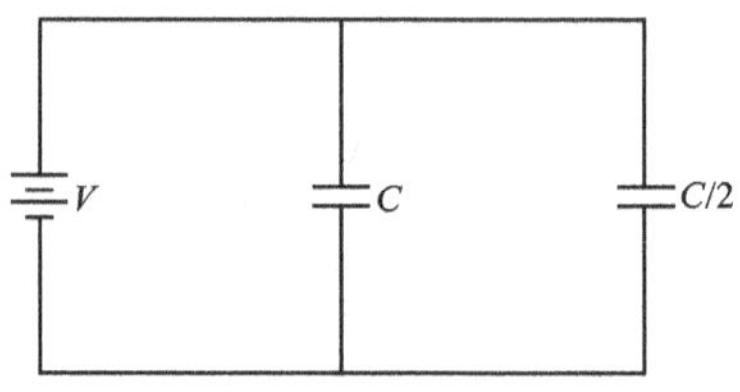

(A) $\dfrac{1}{4}CV^2$

(B) $\dfrac{3}{4}CV^2$

(C) $\dfrac{1}{2}CV^2$

(D) $2CV^2$

7. The energy required to charge a parallel plate condenser of plate separation d and plate area of cross-section A such that the uniform electric field between the plates is E, is : **[NEET (UG) 2008]**

(A) $\varepsilon_0 E^2 A d$

(B) $\dfrac{1}{2}\varepsilon_0 E^2 A d$

(C) $\dfrac{1}{2}\varepsilon_0 E^2 / A d$

(D) $\varepsilon_0 E^2 / A d$

8. Three capacitors each of capacitance C and of breakdown voltage V are joined in series. The capacitance and breakdown voltage of the combination will be : **[NEET (UG) 2009]**

(A) $3C, 3V$

(B) $\dfrac{C}{3}, \dfrac{V}{3}$

(C) $3C, \dfrac{V}{3}$

(D) $\dfrac{C}{3}, 3V$

9. A series combination of n_1 capacitors, each of value C_1, is charged by a source of potential difference $4V$. When another parallel combination of n_2 capacitors, each of value C_2, is charged by a source of potential difference V, it has the same (total) energy stored in it, as the first combination has. The value of C_2, in terms of C_1, is then : **[NEET (UG) 2010]**

(A) $\dfrac{16C_1}{n_1 n_2}$

(B) $\dfrac{2C_1}{n_1 n_2}$

(C) $16\dfrac{n_2}{n_1}C_1$

(D) $2\dfrac{n_2}{n_1}C_1$

10. A parallel plate condenser has a uniform electric field E V/m in the space between the plates. If the distance between the plates is d and area of each plate is A m^2 the energy in joule stored in the condenser is : **[NEET (UG) 2011]**

(A) $E^2 Ad/\varepsilon_0$

(B) $\dfrac{1}{2}\varepsilon_0 E^2$

(C) $\varepsilon_0 EAd$

(D) $\dfrac{1}{2}\varepsilon_0 E^2 Ad$

11. A parallel plate capacitor has a uniform electric field E in the space between the plates. If the distance between the plates is d and area of each plate is A, the energy stored in the capacitor is : **[NEET (UG) 2012]**

(A) $E^2 Ad/\varepsilon_0$

(B) $\dfrac{1}{2}\varepsilon_0 E^2 Ad$

(C) $\varepsilon_0 EAd$

(D) $\dfrac{1}{2}\varepsilon_0 E^2$

12. Two metallic spheres of radii 1 cm and 3 cm are given charges of -1×10^{-2} C and 5×10^{-2} C, respectively. If these are connected by a conducting wire, the final charge on the bigger sphere is : **[NEET (UG) 2012]**

(A) 3×10^{-2} C

(B) 4×10^{-2} C

(C) 1×10^{-2} C

(D) 2×10^{-2} C

13. Two thin dielectric slabs of dielectric constants K_1 and K_2 $(K_1 < K_2)$ are inserted between plates of a parallel plate capacitor, as shown in the figure. The variation of electric field E between the plates with distance d as measured from plate P is correctly shown by : **[NEET (UG) 2014]**

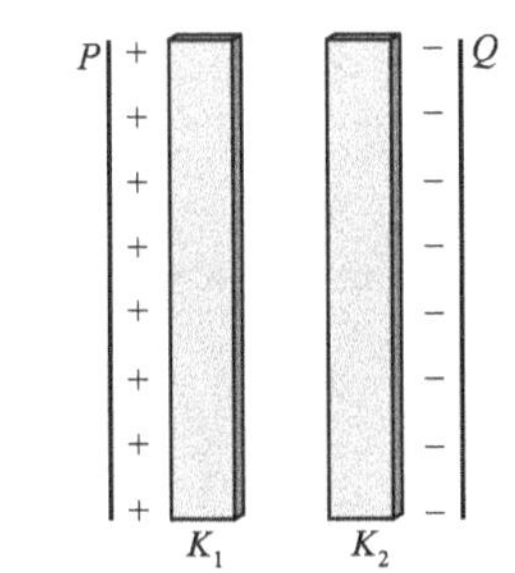

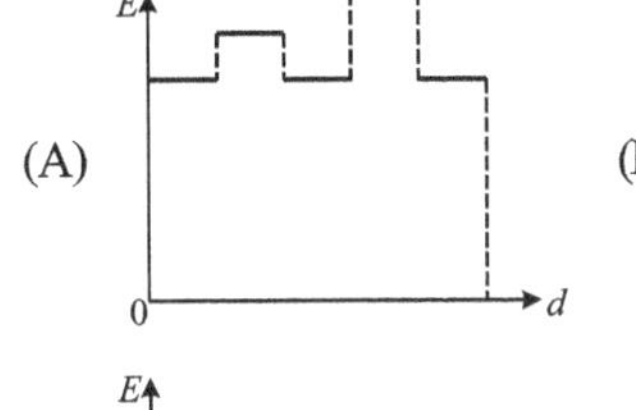
(A)

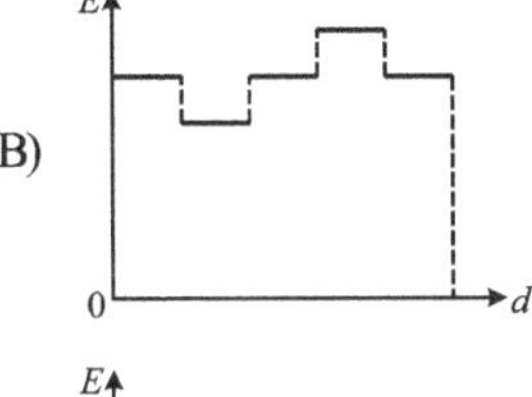
(B)

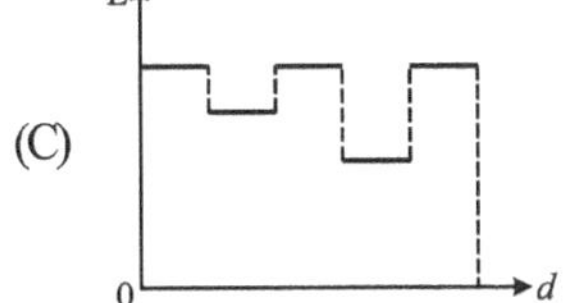
(C)

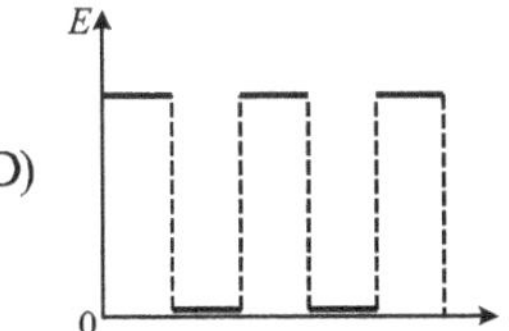
(D)

14. A parallel plate air capacitor has capacity C distance of separation between plates is d and potential difference V is applied between the plates. Force of attraction between the plates of the parallel plate air capacitor is : **[NEET (UG) 2015]**

(A) $\dfrac{C^2 V^2}{2d^2}$

(B) $\dfrac{C^2 V^2}{2d}$

(C) $\dfrac{CV^2}{2d}$

(D) $\dfrac{CV^2}{d}$

15. A capacitor of 2 μF is charged as shown in the diagram. When the switch S is turned to position 2, the percentage of its stored energy dissipated is : **[NEET (UG) 2016]**

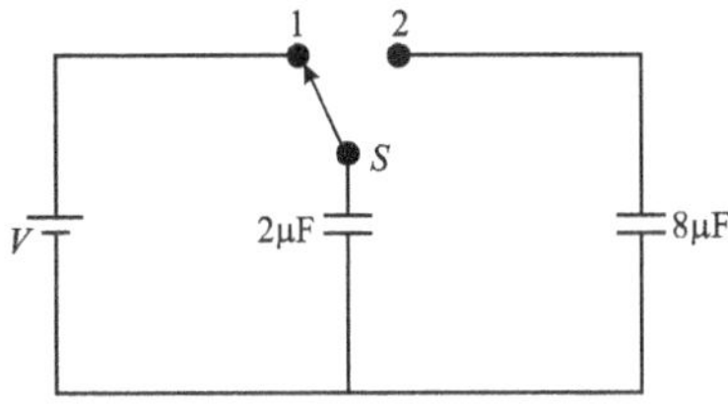

(A) 0%

(B) 20%

(C) 75%

(D) 80%

16. A parallel-plate capacitor of area A, plate separation d and capacitance C is filled with four dielectric materials having dielectric constants k_1, k_2, k_3 and k_4 as shown in the figure below. If a single dielectric material is to be used to have the same capacitance C in this capacitor, then its dielectric constant k is given by : **[NEET (UG) 2016 Ph. II]**

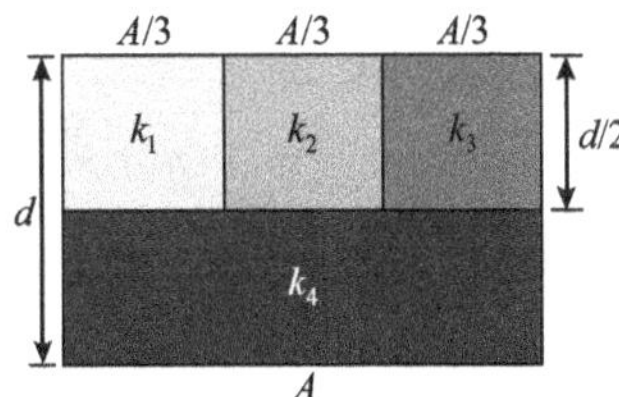

(A) $k = k_1 + k_2 + k_3 + 3k_4$

(B) $k = \dfrac{2}{3}(k_1 + k_2 + k_3) + 2k_4$

(C) $\dfrac{2}{k} = \dfrac{3}{k_1 + k_2 + k_3} + \dfrac{1}{k_4}$

(D) $\dfrac{1}{k} = \dfrac{1}{k_1} + \dfrac{1}{k_2} + \dfrac{1}{k_3} + \dfrac{3}{2k_4}$

17. A capacitor is charged by a battery. The battery is removed and another identical uncharged capacitor is connected in parallel. The total electrostatic energy of resulting system : **[NEET (UG) 2017]**

(A) Increases by a factor of 4

(B) Decreases by a factor of 2

(C) Remains the same

(D) Increases by a factor of 2

18. The electrostatic force between the metal plates of an isolated parallel plate capacitor C having a charge Q and area A, is : **[NEET (UG) 2018]**
(A) Proportional to the square root of the distance between the plates
(B) Linearly proportional to the distance between the plates
(C) Independent of the distance between the plates
(D) Inversely proportional to the distance between the plates

19. A parallel plate capacitor of capacitance 20 μF is being charged by a voltage source whose potential is changing at the rate of 3 V/s. The conduction current through the connecting wires, and the displacement current through the plates of the capacitor, would be, respectively : **[NEET (UG) 2019]**
(A) Zero, 60 μA (B) 60 μA, 60 μA
(C) 60 μA, zero   (D) Zero, zero

20. The capacitance of a parallel plate capacitor with air as medium is 6 μF. With the introduction of a dielectric medium, the capacitance becomes 30 μF. The permittivity of the medium is : $(\varepsilon_0 = 8.85 \times 10^{-12}\,C^2\,N^{-1}\,m^{-2})$ **[NEET (UG) 2020]**
(A) $5.00\,C^2\,N^{-1}\,m^{-2}$ (B) $0.44 \times 10^{-13}\,C^2\,N^{-1}\,m^{-2}$
(C) $1.77 \times 10^{-12}\,C^2\,N^{-1}\,m^{-2}$ (D) $0.44 \times 10^{-10}\,C^2\,N^{-1}\,m^{-2}$

21. The equivalent capacitance of the combination shown in the figure is : **[NEET (UG) 2021]**

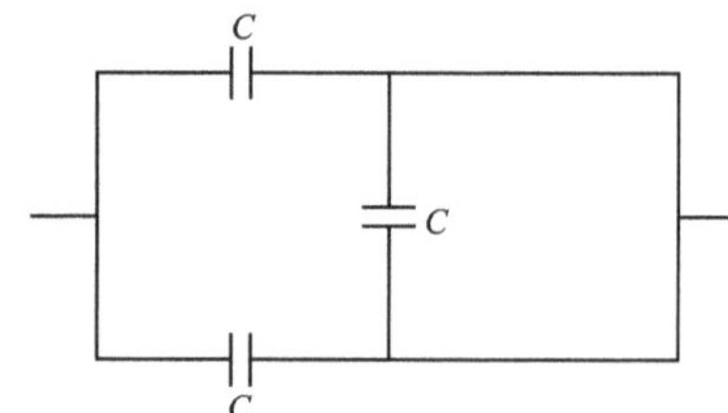

(A) $3C$ (B) $2C$
(C) $C/2$ (D) $3C/2$

22. A parallel plate capacitor has a uniform electric field ' $\vec{E}$ ' in the space between the plates. If the distance between the plates is ' d ' and the area of each plate is ' A ', the energy stored in the capacitor is : $(\varepsilon_0 = $ permittivity of free space) **[NEET (UG) 2021]**
(A) $\frac{1}{2}\varepsilon_0 E^2$ (B) $\varepsilon_0 EAd$
(C) $\frac{1}{2}\varepsilon_0 E^2 Ad$ (D) $\dfrac{E^2 Ad}{\varepsilon_0}$

23. A capacitor of capacitance $C = 900$ pF is charged fully by 100 V battery B as shown in figure (a). Then it is disconnected from the battery and connected to another uncharged capacitor of capacitance $C = 900$ pF as shown in figure (b). The electrostatic energy stored by the system (b) is : **[NEET (UG) 2022]**

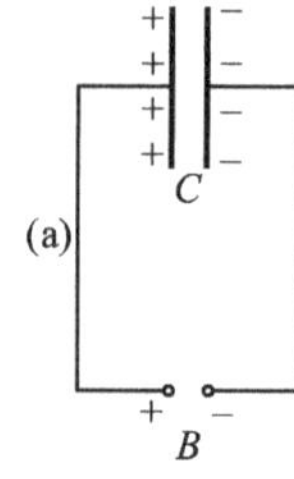
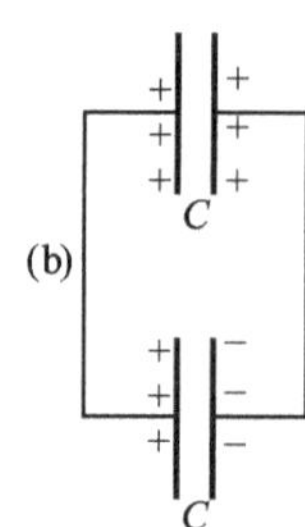

(A) $3.25 \times 10^{-6}\,J$ (B) $2.25 \times 10^{-6}\,J$
(C) $1.5 \times 10^{-6}\,J$ (D) $4.5 \times 10^{-6}\,J$

*   *   *   *   *

17 CURRENT ELECTRICITY

17.1 Resistance and Ohm's Law

1. The resistance of each arm of the Wheatstone's bridge is 10 ohm. A resistance of 10 ohm is connected in series with a galvanometer then the equivalent resistance across the battery will be : **[NEET (UG) 2001]**

(A) $10\,\Omega$ (B) $15\,\Omega$
(C) $20\,\Omega$ (D) $40\,\Omega$

2. Five equal resistances each of resistance R are connected as shown in the figure. A battery of V volt is connected between A and B. The current flowing in $AFCEB$ will be : **[NEET (UG) 2004]**

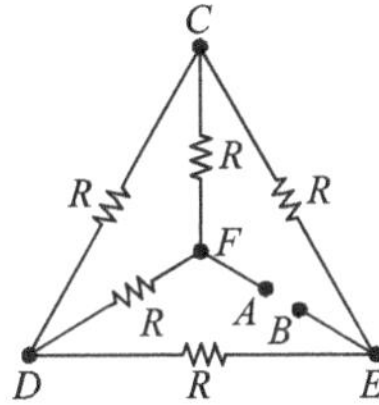

(A) $3V/R$ (B) V/R
(C) $V/2R$ (D) $2V/R$

3. Resistance n, each of r ohm, when connected in parallel give an equivalent resistance of R ohm. If these resistances were connected in series, the combination would have a resistance in ohms, equal to : **[NEET (UG) 2004]**

(A) n^2R (B) R/n^2
(C) R/n (D) nR

4. The electric resistance of a certain wire of iron is R. If its length and radius are both doubled, then : **[NEET (UG) 2004]**
(A) The resistance will be doubled and the specific resistance will be halved
(B) The resistance will be halved and the specific resistance will remain unchanged
(C) The resistance will be halved and the specific resistance will be doubled
(D) The resistance and the specific resistance, will both remain unchanged

5. A 6 volt battery is connected to the terminals of a three metre long wire of uniform thickness and resistance of 100 ohm. The difference of potential between two points on the wire separated by a distance of 50 cm will be : **[NEET (UG) 2004]**
(A) 2 volt   (B) 3 volt
(C) 1 volt   (D) 1.5 volt

6. Specific resistance of a conductor increases with : **[NEET (UG) 2002]**
(A) Increase in temperature
(B) Increase in cross-section area
(C) Increase in cross-section and decrease in length
(D) Decrease in cross-section area

7. Copper and silicon is cooled from 300 K to 60 K, the specific resistance : **[NEET (UG) 2001]**
(A) Decreases in copper but increases in silicon
(B) Increases in copper but decreases in silicon
(C) Increases in both
(D) Decreases in both

8. When a wire of uniform cross-section a, length l and resistance R is bent into a complete circle, resistance between any two of diametrically opposite points will be : **[NEET (UG) 2005]**

(A) $R/2$ (B) $R/4$
(C) $R/8$ (D) $4R$

9. A wire of a certain material is stretched slowly by ten percent. Its new resistance and specific resistance become respectively : **[NEET (UG) 2008]**
(A) Both remain the same   (B) 1.1 times, 1.1 times
(C) 1.2 times, 1.1 times   (D) 1.21 times, same

10. A student measures the terminal potential difference V of a cell of emf E and internal resistance r as a function of the current I flowing through it. The slope and intercept of the graph between V and I, then respectively equal to : **[NEET (UG) 2009]**
(A) $-\in$ and r (B) $\in$ and $-r$
(C) $-r$ and $\in$ (D) r and $-\in$

11. The mean free path of electrons in a metal is 4×10^{-8} m. The electric field which can give an average 2 eV energy to an electron in the metal will be in units of V/m : **[NEET (UG) 2009]**
(A) 5×10^7 (B) 8×10^7
(C) 5×10^{-11} (D) 8×10^{-11}

12. A wire of resistance 12 ohms per metre is bent to form a complete circle of radius 10 cm. The resistance between its two diametrically opposite points, A and B as shown in the figure, is : **[NEET (UG) 2009]**

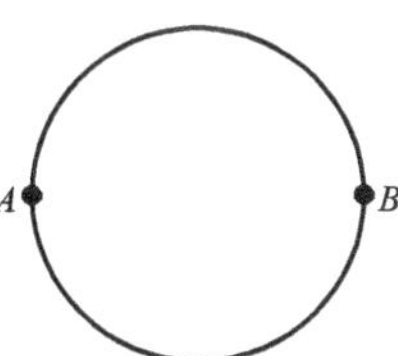

(A) $6\,\Omega$ (B) $0.6\,\pi\Omega$
(C) $3\,\Omega$ (D) $6\,\pi\Omega$

13. A wire of resistance $4\,\Omega$ is stretched to twice its original length. The resistance of stretched wire would be :

[NEET (UG) 2013]

(A) $2\,\Omega$ (B) $4\,\Omega$

(C) $8\,\Omega$ (D) $16\,\Omega$

14. Two metal wires of identical dimension are connected in series. If σ_1 and σ_2 are the conductivities of the metal wires respectively, the effective conductivity of the combination is :

[NEET (UG) 2015]

(A) $\dfrac{\sigma_1\sigma_2}{\sigma_1+\sigma_2}$ (B) $\dfrac{2\sigma_1\sigma_2}{\sigma_1+\sigma_2}$

(C) $\dfrac{\sigma_1+\sigma_2}{2\sigma_1\sigma_2}$ (D) $\dfrac{\sigma_1+\sigma_2}{\sigma_1\sigma_2}$

15. The resistance of a wire is R ohm. If it is melted and stretched to n times its original length, its new resistance will be :

[NEET (UG) 2017]

(A) nR (B) R/n

(C) n^2R (D) R/n^2

16. A carbon resistor of $(47 \pm 4.7)\,k\Omega$ is to be marked with rings of different colours for its identification. The colour code sequence will be :   [NEET (UG) 2018]

(A) Yellow – Green – Violet – Gold

(B) Yellow – Violet – Orange – Silver

(C) Violet – Yellow – Orange – Silver

(D) Green – Orange – Violet – Gold

17. A charged particle having drift velocity of $7.5 \times 10^{-4}\,\text{ms}^{-1}$ is an electric field of $3 \times 10^{-10}\,\text{Vm}^{-1}$, has a mobility in $\text{m}^2\,\text{V}^{-1}\text{s}^{-1}$ of :   [NEET (UG) 2020]

(A) 2.25×10^{-15} (B) 2.25×10^{15}

(C) 2.5×10^{6} (D) 2.5×10^{-6}

18. Which of the following graph represents the variation of resistivity (ρ) with temperature (T) for copper ?

[NEET (UG) 2020]

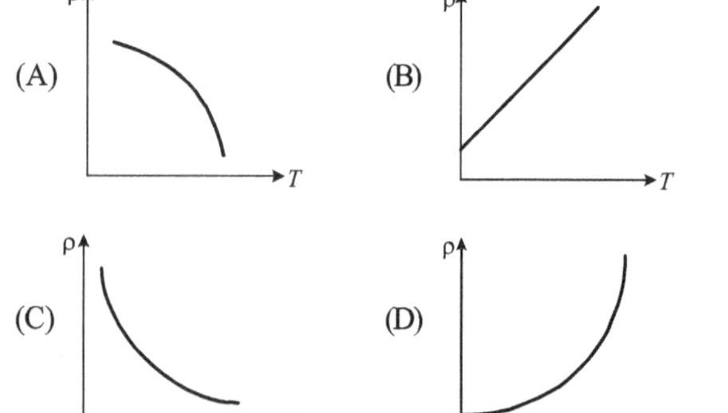

19. The color code of a resistance is given below. The values of resistance and tolerance, respectively, are :

[NEET (UG) 2020]

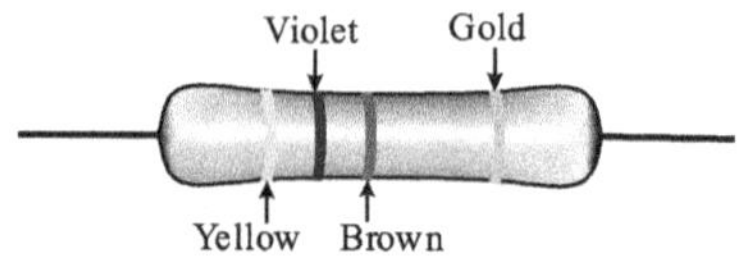

(A) $470\,\Omega,\,5\%$ (B) $470\,k\Omega,\,5\%$

(C) $47\,k\Omega,\,10\%$ (D) $4.7\,k\Omega,\,5\%$

20. Column-I gives certain physical terms associated with flow of current through a metallic conductor.

Column-II gives some mathematical relations involving electrical quantities. Match Column-I and Column-II with appropriate relations :   [NEET (UG) 2021]

	Column-I		Column-II
(a)	Drift Velocity	(p)	$\dfrac{m}{ne^2\rho}$
(b)	Electrical Resistivity	(q)	nev_d
(c)	Relaxation Period	(r)	$\dfrac{eE}{m}\tau$
(d)	Current Density	(s)	$\dfrac{E}{J}$

(A) (a) $\to$ (r), (b) $\to$ (s), (c) $\to$ (p), (d) $\to$ (q)

(B) (a) $\to$ (r), (b) $\to$ (s), (c) $\to$ (q), (d) $\to$ (p)

(C) (a) $\to$ (r), (b) $\to$ (p), (c) $\to$ (s), (d) $\to$ (q)

(D) (a) $\to$ (r), (b) $\to$ (q), (c) $\to$ (s), (d) $\to$ (p)

21. As the temperature increase, the electrical resistance :

[NEET (UG) 2022]

(A) Decreases for both conductors and semiconductors

(B) Increases for conductors but decreases for semiconductors

(C) Decreases for conductors but increase for semiconductors

(D) Increases for both conductors and semiconductors

22. A copper wire of length 10 m and radius $10^{-2}/\pi$ m has electrical resistance of $10\,\Omega$. The current density in the wire for an electric field strength of 10 V/m is :   [NEET (UG) 2022]

(A) $10^{6}\,\text{A/m}^2$ (B) $10^{-5}\,\text{A/m}^2$

(C) $10^{5}\,\text{A/m}^2$ (D) $10^{4}\,\text{A/m}^2$

17.2 Kirchhoff's Law & Electric Circuits

1. For a cell terminal potential difference is 2.2 V when circuit is open and reduces to 1.8 V when cell is connected to a resistance of $R = 5\,\Omega$. Determine internal resistance of cell (r) :

[NEET (UG) 2002]

(A) $10/9\,\Omega$ (B) $9/10\,\Omega$

(C) $11/9\,\Omega$ (D) $5/9\,\Omega$

2. For the network shown in the figure the value of the current i is : **[NEET (UG) 2005]**

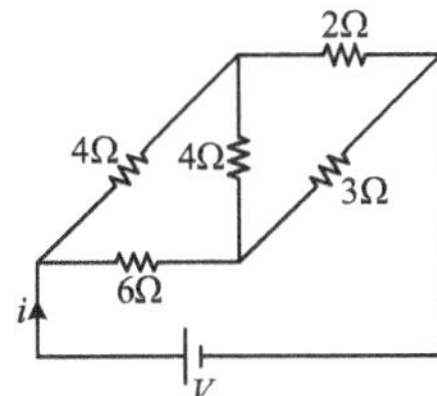

(A) $\dfrac{18V}{5}$ (B) $\dfrac{5V}{9}$

(C) $\dfrac{9V}{35}$ (D) $\dfrac{5V}{18}$

3. Two cells, having the same e.m.f., are connected in series through an external resistance R. Cell have internal resistances r_1 and r_2 ($r_1 > r_2$) respectively. When the circuit is closed, the potential difference across the first cell is zero. The value of R is : **[NEET (UG) 2006]**

(A) $r_1 - r_2$ (B) $\dfrac{r_1 + r_2}{2}$

(C) $\dfrac{r_1 - r_2}{2}$ (D) $r_1 + r_2$

4. In a discharge tube ionization of enclosed gas produced due to collisions between : **[NEET (UG) 2006]**
(A) Positive ions and neutral atoms/molecules
(B) Negative electrons and neutral atoms/molecules
(C) Photons and neutral atoms/molecules
(D) Neutral gas atoms/molecules

5. Kirchhoff's first and second laws for electrical circuits are consequences of : **[NEET (UG) 2006]**
(A) Conservation of energy
(B) Conservation of electric charge and energy respectively
(C) Conservation of electric charge
(D) Conservation of energy and electric charge respectively

6. In the circuit shown, the current through the 4 Ω resistor is 1 A when the points P and M are connected to a DC voltage source. The potential difference between the points M and N is : **[NEET (UG) 2008]**

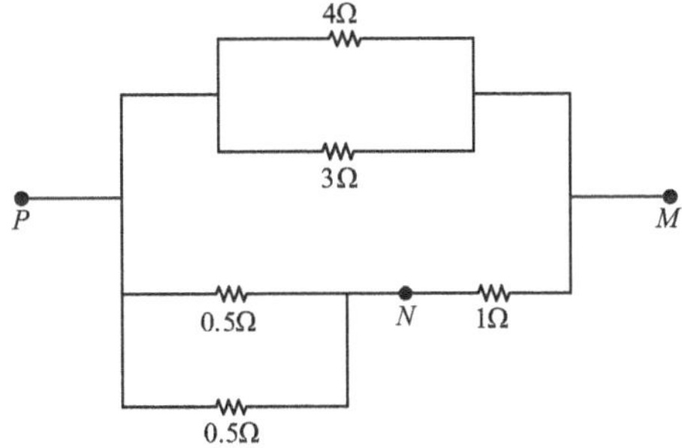

(A) 0.5 volt   (B) 3.2 volt
(C) 1.5 volt   (D) 1.0 volt

7. A current of 3 A flows through the 2 Ω resistor shown in the circuit. The power dissipated in the 5 Ω resistor is : **[NEET (UG) 2008]**

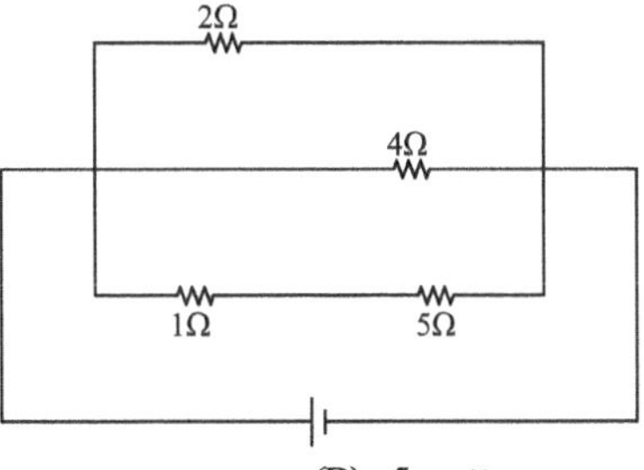

(A) 1 watt   (B) 5 watt
(C) 4 watt   (D) 2 watt

8. Consider the following two statements : **[NEET (UG) 2010]**
(a) Kirchhoff's junction law follows from the conservation of charge
(b) Kirchhoff's loop law follows from the conservation of energy
Which of the following is correct ?
(A) Both (a) and (b) are correct
(B) Both (a) and (b) are wrong
(C) (a) is correct and (b) is wrong
(D) (a) is wrong and (b) is correct

9. A current of 2 A flows through a 2 Ω resistor when connected across a battery. The same battery supplies a current of 0.5 A when connected across a 9 Ω resistor. The internal resistance of the battery is : **[NEET (UG) 2011]**
(A) 0.5 Ω   (B) 1/3 Ω
(C) 1/4 Ω   (D) 1 Ω

10. If power dissipated in the 9 Ω resistor in the circuit shown is 36 W, the potential difference across the 2 Ω resistor is : **[NEET (UG) 2011]**

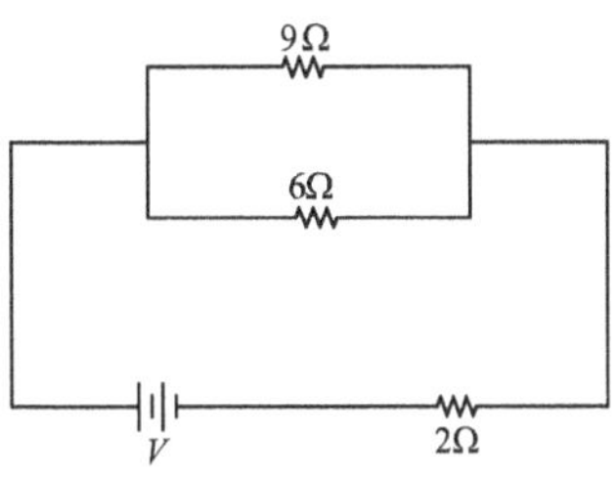

(A) 4 V   (B) 8 V
(C) 10 V   (D) 2 V

11. A ring is made of a wire having a resistance $R_0 = 12$ Ω. Find the points A and B as shown in the figure, at which a current carrying conductor should be connected so that the resistance R of the sub circuit between these points is equal to $8/3$ Ω : **[NEET (UG) 2012]**

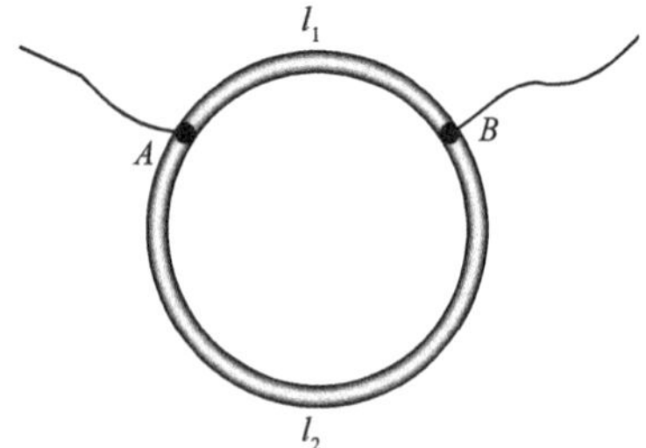

(A) $\dfrac{l_1}{l_2} = \dfrac{5}{8}$ (B) $\dfrac{l_1}{l_2} = \dfrac{1}{3}$

(C) $\dfrac{l_1}{l_2} = \dfrac{3}{8}$ (D) $\dfrac{l_1}{l_2} = \dfrac{1}{2}$

12. A cell having an emf E and internal resistance r is connected across a variable external resistance R. As the resistance R is increased, the plot of potential difference V across R is given by : **[NEET (UG) 2012]**

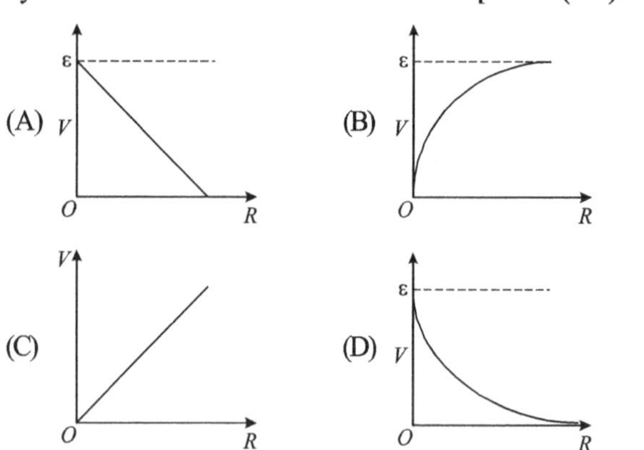

13. The internal resistance of a 2.1 V cell which gives a current of 0.2 A through a resistance of 10 Ω is : **[NEET (UG) 2013]**

(A) 0.2 Ω (B) 0.5 Ω

(C) 0.8 Ω (D) 1.0 Ω

14. The resistances of the four arms P, Q, R and S in a Wheatstone's bridge are 10 ohm, 30 ohm, 30 ohm and 90 ohm, respectively. The e.m.f. and internal resistance of the cell are 7 volt and 5 ohm respectively. If the galvanometer resistance is 50 ohm, the current drawn from the cell will be :

[NEET (UG) 2013]

(A) 1.0 A   (B) 0.2 A

(C) 0.1 A   (D) 2.0 A

15. The potential difference $(V_A - V_B)$ between the points A and B in the given figure is : **[NEET (UG) 2016 Ph. II]**

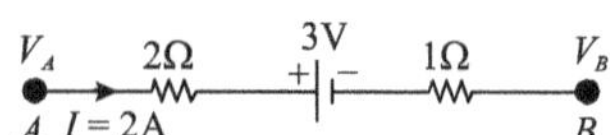

(A) -3 V   (B) $+3$ V

(C) $+6$ V   (D) $+9$ V

16. A set of n equal resistors, of value R each, are connected in series to a battery of emf E and internal resistance R. The current drawn is I. Now, the n resistors are connected in parallel to the same battery. Then the current drawn from battery becomes $10\,I$. The value of n is : **[NEET (UG) 2018]**

(A) 20   (B) 11

(C) 10   (D) 9

17. A battery consists of a variable number n of identical cells (having internal resistance r each) which are connected in series. The terminals of the battery are short-circuited and the current I is measured. Which of the graphs shows the correct relationship between I and n ? **[NEET (UG) 2018]**

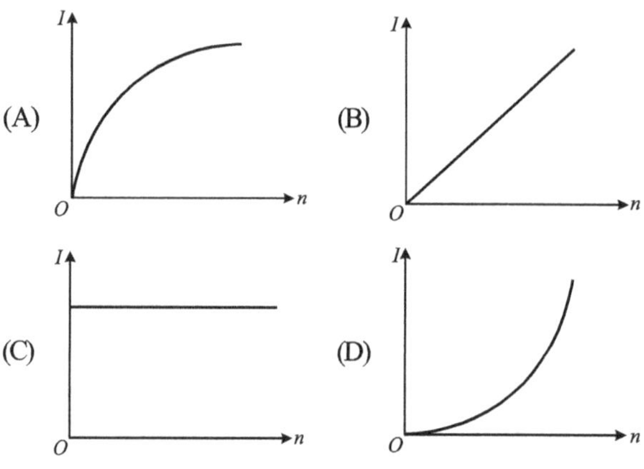

18. The effective resistance of a parallel connection that consists of four wires of equal length, equal area of cross-section and same material is $0.25\ \Omega$. What will be the effective resistance if they are connected in series ? **[NEET (UG) 2021]**

(A) $0.25\ \Omega$ (B) $0.5\ \Omega$

(C) $1\ \Omega$ (D) $4\ \Omega$

19. Three resistors having resistances r_1, r_2 and r_3 are connected as shown in the given circuit. The ratio $\dfrac{i_3}{i_1}$ of currents in terms of resistance used in the circuit is : **[NEET (UG) 2021]**

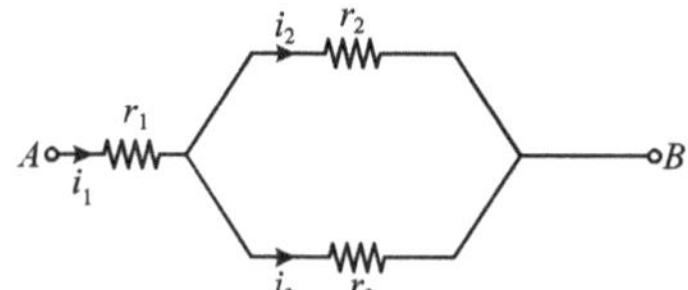

(A) $\dfrac{r_1}{r_2 + r_3}$ (B) $\dfrac{r_2}{r_2 + r_3}$

(C) $\dfrac{r_1}{r_1 + r_2}$ (D) $\dfrac{r_2}{r_1 + r_3}$

17.3 Thermal Effects of Current

1. Two 220 volt, 100 watt bulbs are connected first in series and then in parallel. Each time the combination is connected to

a 220 volt a.c. supply line. The power drawn by the combination in each case respectively will be :   **[NEET (UG) 2003]**
(A) 50 watt, 100 watt
(B) 100 watt, 50 watt
(C) 200 watt, 150 watt
(D) 50 watt, 200 watt

2. An electric kettle has two heating coils. When one of the coils is connected to an a.c. source, the water in the kettle boils in 10 minutes. When the other coil is used the water boils in 40 minutes. If both the coils are connected in parallel, the time taken by the same quantity of water to boil will be :
                                                                      [NEET (UG) 2003]
(A) 8 min
(B) 4 min
(C) 25 min
(D) 15 min

3. Fuse wire is a wire of :   **[NEET (UG) 2003]**
(A) High resistance and high melting point
(B) High resistance and low melting point
(C) Low resistance and low melting point
(D) Low resistance and high melting point

4. In India electricity is supplied for domestic use at 220 V. It is supplied at 110 V in USA. If the resistance of a 60 W bulb for use in India is R, the resistance of a 60 W bulb for use in USA will be :   **[NEET (UG) 2004]**
(A) R
(B) $2R$
(C) $R/4$
(D) $R/2$

5. A battery is charged at a potential of 15 V for 8 hours when the current flowing is 10 A. The battery on discharge supplies a current of 5 A for 15 hours. The mean terminal voltage during discharges is 14 V. The "Watt hour" efficiency of the battery is :
                                                                      [NEET (UG) 2004]
(A) 80 %
(B) 90 %
(C) 87.5 %
(D) 82.5 %

6. When three identical bulbs of 60 watt, 200 volt rating are connected in series to a 200 volt supply, the power drawn by them will be :   **[NEET (UG) 2004]**
(A) 60 watt
(B) 180 watt
(C) 10 watt
(D) 20 watt

7. A 5-ampere fuse wire can withstand a maximum power of 1 watt in the circuit. The resistance of the fuse wire is :
                                                                      [NEET (UG) 2005]
(A) 5 ohm
(B) 0.04 ohm
(C) 0.2 ohm
(D) 0.4 ohm

8. Power dissipated across the 8 Ω resistor in the circuit shown here is 2 watt. The power dissipated in watt units across the 3 Ω resistor is :   **[NEET (UG) 2006]**

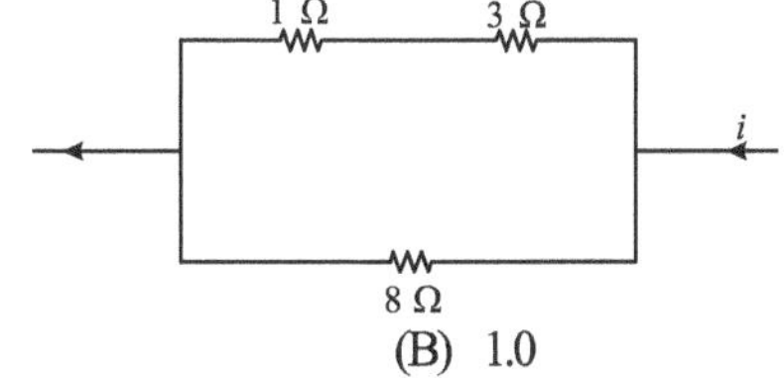

(A) 2.0
(B) 1.0
(C) 0.5
(D) 3.0

9. In producing chlorine through electrolysis 100 watt power at 125 V is being consumed. How much chlorine per minute is liberated ? E.C.E. of chlorine is 0.367×10^{-6} kg/coulomb :
                                                                      [NEET (UG) 2006]
(A) 17.6 mg
(B) 21.3 mg
(C) 24.3 mg
(D) 13.6 mg

10. The total power dissipated in watts in the circuit shown here is :   **[NEET (UG) 2007]**

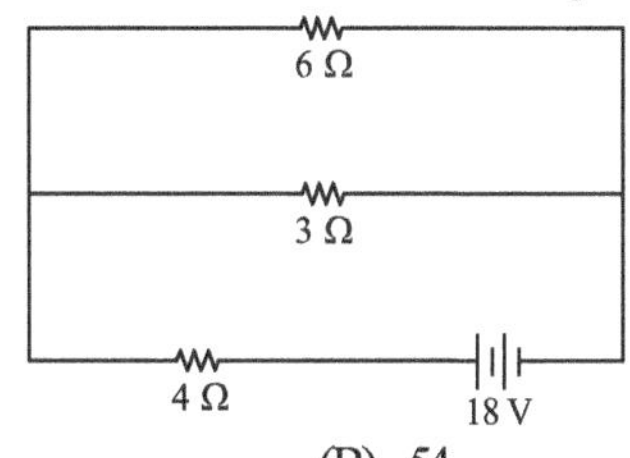

(A) 40
(B) 54
(C) 4
(D) 16

11. A steady current of 1.5 amp flows through a copper voltameter for 10 minutes. If the electrochemical equivalent of copper is 30×10^{-5} g coulomb^{-1}, the mass of copper deposited on the electrode will be :   **[NEET (UG) 2007]**
(A) 0.50 g
(B) 0.67 g
(C) 0.27 g
(D) 0.40 g

12. If the cold junction of a thermo-couple is kept at 0°C and the hot junction is kept at T°C then the relation between neutral temperature (T_n) and temperature of inversion (T_i) is :
                                                                      [NEET (UG) 2007]
(A) $T_n = 2T_i$
(B) $T_n = T_i - T$
(C) $T_n = T_i + T$
(D) $T_n = T_i/2$

13. See the electrical circuit shown in this figure. Which of the following equations is a correct equation for it ?
                                                                      [NEET (UG) 2009]

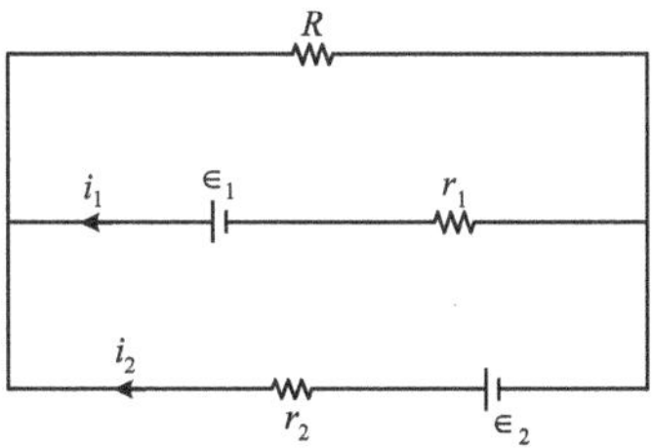

(A) $\in_1 - (i_1 + i_2)R + i_1 r_1 = 0$
(B) $\in_1 - (i_1 + i_2)R - i_1 r_1 = 0$
(C) $\in_1 - i_1 r_2 - \varepsilon_1 - i_1 r_1 = 0$
(D) $\in_1 - (i_1 + i_2)R + i_2 r_2 = 0$

14. The rate of increase of thermo-emf with temperature at the neutral temperature of a thermocouple :   **[NEET (UG) 2011]**
(A) Is positive
(B) Is zero
(C) Depends upon the choice of the two materials of the thermocouple
(D) Is negative

15. If voltage across a bulb rated 220 Volt – 100 Watt drops by 2.5% of its rated value, the percentage of the rated value by which the power would decrease is :   **[NEET (UG) 2012]**
(A) 20%   (B) 2.5%
(C) 5%   (D) 10%

16. The power dissipated in the circuit shown in the figure is 30 Watts. The value of R is :   **[NEET (UG) 2012]**

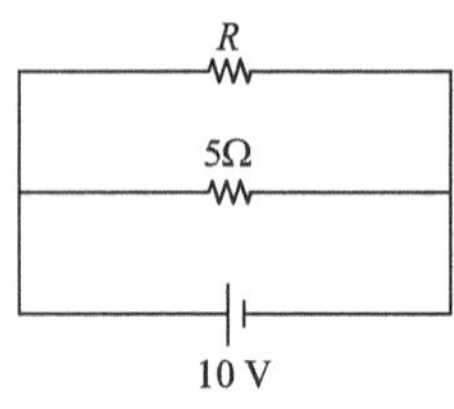

(A) $15\,\Omega$ (B) $10\,\Omega$
(C) $30\,\Omega$ (D) $20\,\Omega$

17. Two cities are 150 km apart. Electric power is sent from one city to another city through copper wires. The fall of potential per km is 8 volt and the average resistance per km is $0.5\,\Omega$. The power loss in the wire is :   **[NEET (UG) 2014]**
(A) 19.2 W   (B) 19.2 kW
(C) 19.2 J   (D) 12.2 kW

18. The charge flowing through a resistance R varies with time t as $Q = at - bt^2$, where a and b are positive constants. The total heat produced in R is :   **[NEET (UG) 2016]**
(A) $\dfrac{a^3 R}{6b}$ (B) $\dfrac{a^3 R}{3b}$
(C) $\dfrac{a^3 R}{2b}$ (D) $\dfrac{a^3 R}{b}$

19. A filament bulb (500 W, 100 V) is to be used in 230 V main supply. When a resistance R is connected in series, it works perfectly and the bulb consumes 500 W. The value of R is :
   [NEET (UG) 2016 Ph. II]
(A) $230\,\Omega$ (B) $46\,\Omega$
(C) $26\,\Omega$ (D) $13\,\Omega$

20. Six similar bulbs are connected as shown in the figure with a DC source of emf E and zero internal resistance. The ratio of power consumption by the bulbs when (i) all are glowing and (ii) in the situation when two from section A and one from section B are glowing, will be :   **[NEET (UG) 2019]**

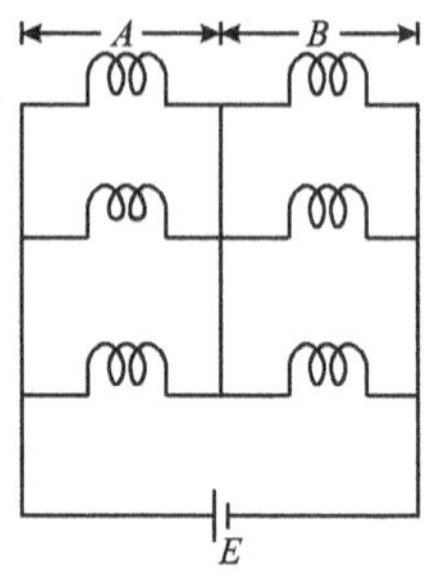

(A) $4:9$ (B) $9:4$
(C) $1:2$ (D) $2:1$

21. Which of the following acts as a circuit protecting device?
   [NEET (UG) 2019]
(A) Conductor   (B) Inductor
(C) Switch   (4) Fuse

22. Two resistors of resistance, $100\,\Omega$ and $200\,\Omega$ are connected in parallel in an electrical circuit. The ratio of the thermal energy developed in $100\,\Omega$ to that in $200\,\Omega$ in a given time is :   **[NEET (UG) 2022]**
(A) $2:1$ (B) $1:4$
(C) $4:1$ (D) $1:2$

17.4 Electrical Measurements

1. If specific resistance of a potentiometer wire is $10^{-7}\,\Omega$ m and current flow through it is 0.1 A, cross-sectional area of wire is $10^{-6}\,\mathrm{m^2}$ then potential gradient will be :   **[NEET (UG) 2001]**
(A) 10^{-2} volt/m   (B) 10^{-4} volt/m
(C) 10^{-6} volt/m   (D) 10^{-8} volt/m

2. To convert a galvanometer into a voltmeter one should connect a :   **[NEET (UG) 2002, 2004]**
(A) High resistance in series with galvanometer
(B) Low resistance in series with galvanometer
(C) High resistance in parallel with galvanometer
(D) Low resistance in parallel with galvanometer

3. In a Wheatstone's bridge all the four arms have equal resistance R. If the resistance of the galvanometer arm is also R, the equivalent resistance of the combination as seen by the battery is :   **[NEET (UG) 2003]**
(A) $R/4$ (B) $R/2$
(C) R (D) $2R$

4. A galvanometer of 50 ohm resistance has 25 divisions. A current of 4×10^{-4} ampere gives a deflection of one division. To convert this galvanometer into a voltmeter having a range of 25 volts, it should be connected with a resistance of :   **[NEET (UG) 2004]**
(A) $2500\,\Omega$ as a shunt   (B) $2450\,\Omega$ as a shunt
(C) $2550\,\Omega$ as a series   (D) $2450\,\Omega$ as a series

5. Two batteries, one of emf 18 volts and internal resistance 2 Ω and the other of emf 12 volt and internal resistance 1 Ω, are connected as shown. The voltmeter V will record a reading of :

[NEET (UG) 2005]

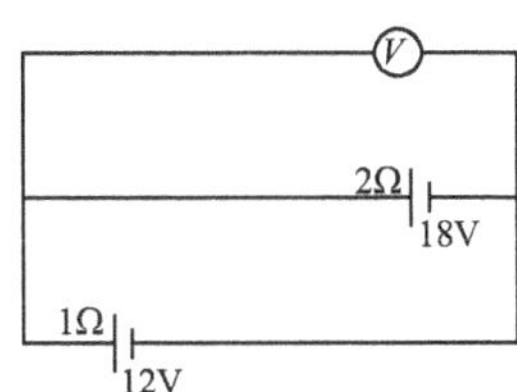

(A) 18 volt   (B) 30 volt

(C) 14 volt   (D) 15 volt

6. In the circuit shown, if a conducting wire is connected between points A and B, the current in this wire will :

[NEET (UG) 2006]

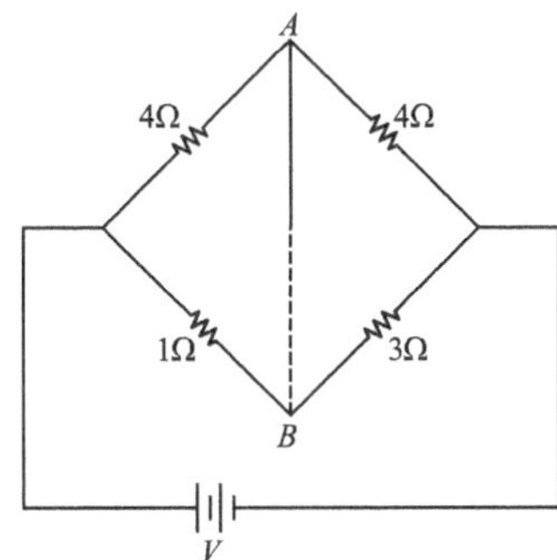

(A) Flow from A to B

(B) Flow in the direction which will be decided by the value of V

(C) Be zero

(D) Flow from B to A

7. Three resistances P, Q, R each of 2 Ω and an unknown resistance S form the four arms of a Wheatstone bridge circuit. When a resistance of 6 Ω is connected in parallel to S the bridge gets balanced. What is the value of S ?

[NEET (UG) 2007]

(A) 3 Ω   (B) 6 Ω

(C) 1 Ω   (D) 2 Ω

8. The resistance of an ammeter is 13 Ω and its scale is graduated for a current upto 100 A. After an additional shunt has been connected to this ammeter it becomes possible to measure currents upto 750 A by this meter. The value of shunt-resistance is : **[NEET (UG) 2007]**

(A) 2 Ω   (B) 0.2 Ω

(C) 2 $k\Omega$ (D) 20 Ω

9. A galvanometer of resistance 50 Ω is connected to a battery of 3 V along with a resistance of 2950 Ω in series. A full scale deflection of 30 divisions is obtained in the galvanometer. In order to reduce this deflection to 20 divisions, the resistance in series should be : **[NEET (UG) 2008]**

(A) 6050 Ω   (B) 4450 Ω

(C) 5050 Ω   (D) 5550 Ω

10. A cell can be balanced against 110 cm and 100 cm of potentiometer wire, respectively with and without being short circuited through a resistance of 10 Ω. Its internal resistance is :

[NEET (UG) 2008]

(A) 2.0 ohm   (B) Zero

(C) 1.0 ohm   (D) 0.5 ohm

11. A galvanometer having a coil resistance of 60 Ω shows full scale deflection when a current of 1.0 A passes through it. It can be converted into an ammeter to read currents upto 5.0 A by:

[NEET (UG) 2009]

(A) Putting in parallel a resistance of 15 Ω

(B) Putting in parallel a resistance of 240 Ω

(C) Putting in series a resistance of 15 Ω

(D) Putting in series a resistance of 240 Ω

12. A potentiometer circuit is set up as shown. The potential gradient, across the potentiometer wire, is k volt/cm and the ammeter, present in the circuit, reads 1.0 A when two way key is switched off. The balance points, when the key between the terminals (i) 1 and 2 (ii) 1 and 3, is plugged in, are found to be at lengths l_1 cm l_2 cm respectively. The magnitudes, of the resistors R and X, in ohms, are then, equal, respectively, to :

[NEET (UG) 2010]

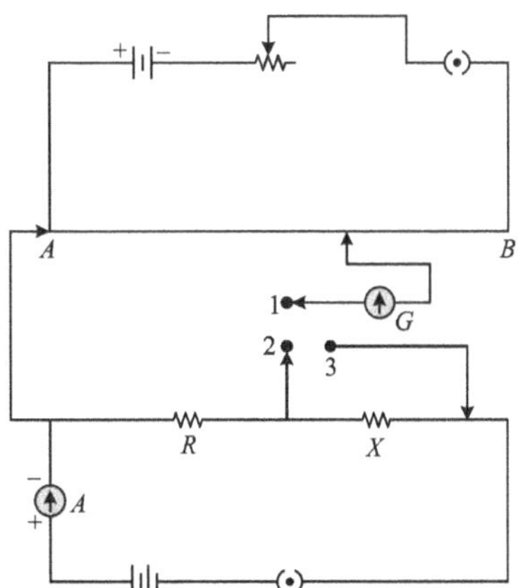

(A) kl_1 and kl_2 (B) $k(l_2 - l_1)$ and kl_2

(C) kl_1 and $k(l_2 - l_1)$ (D) $k(l_2 - l_1)$ and kl_1

13. A millivoltmeter of 25 millivolt range is to be converted into an ammeter of 25 ampere range. The value (in ohm) of necessary shunt will be : **[NEET (UG) 2012]**

(A) 0.001   (B) 0.01

(C) 1   (D) 0.05

14. In the circuit shown the cells A and B have negligible resistances. For $V_A = 12$ V, $R_1 = 5000\ \Omega$ and $R = 100\ \Omega$ the galvanometer (G) shows no deflection. The value of V_B is :

[NEET (UG) 2012]

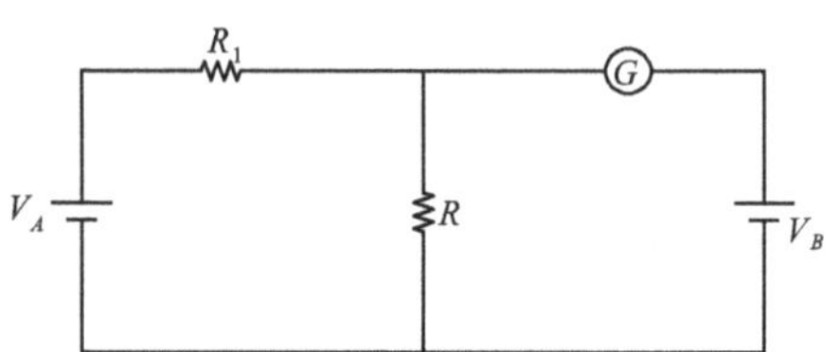

(A) $4\,V$ (B) $2\,V$

(C) $12\,V$ (D) $6\,V$

15. The resistances in the two arms of the meter bridge are 5 Ω and $R\ \Omega$, respectively. When the resistance R is shunted with an equal resistance, the new balance point is at $1.6\ l_1$. The resistance R, is :

[NEET (UG) 2014]

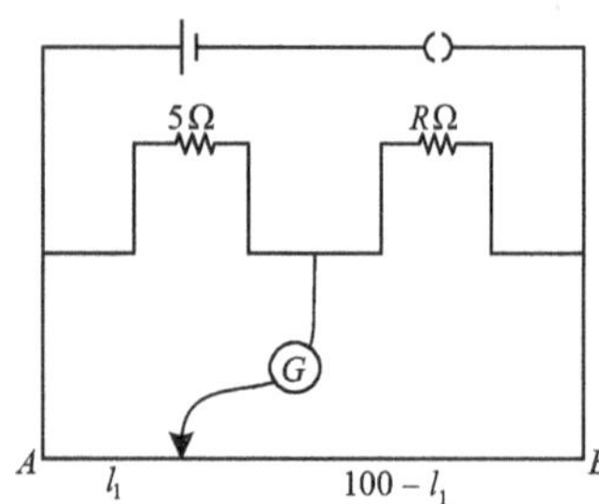

(A) $10\,\Omega$ (B) $15\,\Omega$

(C) $20\,\Omega$ (D) $25\,\Omega$

16. A potentiometer circuit has been set up for finding the internal resistance of a given cell. The main battery, used across the potentiometer wire, has an emf of 2.0 V and a negligible internal resistance. The potentiometer wire itself is 4 m long. When the resistance, R, connected across the given cell, has values of (i) Infinity (ii) 9.5 Ω, the 'balancing lengths', on the potentiometer wire are found to be 3 m and 2.85 m, respectively. The value of internal resistance of the cell is : **[NEET (UG) 2014]**

(A) $0.25\,\Omega$ (B) $0.95\,\Omega$

(C) $0.5\,\Omega$ (D) $0.75\,\Omega$

17. In an ammeter 0.2% of main current passes through the galvanometer. If resistance of galvanometer is G, the resistance of ammeter will be : **[NEET (UG) 2014]**

(A) $\dfrac{1}{499}G$ (B) $\dfrac{499}{500}G$

(C) $\dfrac{1}{500}G$ (D) $\dfrac{500}{499}G$

18. A potentiometer wire of length L and a resistance r are connected in series with a battery of e.m.f. E_0 and a resistance r_1. An unknown e.m.f. E is balanced at a length l of the potentiometer wire. The e.m.f. E will be given by :

[NEET (UG) 2015]

(A) $\dfrac{LE_0 r}{(r+r_1)l}$ (B) $\dfrac{LE_0 r}{lr_1}$

(C) $\dfrac{E_0 r}{(r+r_1)}\dfrac{l}{L}$ (D) $\dfrac{E_0 l}{L}$

19. A circuit contains an ammeter, a battery of 30 V and a resistance 40.8 Ω all connected in series. If the ammeter has a coil of resistance 480 Ω and a shunt of 20 Ω, the reading in the ammeter will be : **[NEET (UG) 2015]**

(A) $1\,A$ (B) $0.5\,A$

(C) $0.25\,A$ (D) $2\,A$

20. A potentiometer wire is 100 cm long and a constant potential difference is maintained across it. Two cells are connected in series first to support one another and then in opposite direction. The balance points are obtained at 50 cm and 10 cm from the positive end of the wire in the two cases. The ratio of emf's is : **[NEET (UG) 2016]**

(A) $5:1$ (B) $5:4$

(C) $3:4$ (D) $3:2$

21. A potentiometer is an accurate and versatile device to make electrical measurements of E.M.F, because the method involves : **[NEET (UG) 2017]**

(A) Cells

(B) Potential gradients

(C) A condition of no current flow through the galvanometer

(D) A combination of cells, galvanometer and resistances

22. Current sensitivity of a moving coil galvanometer is 5 div/mA and its voltage sensitivity (angular deflection per unit voltage applied) is 20 div/V. The resistance of the galvanometer is : **[NEET (UG) 2018]**

(A) $250\,\Omega$ (B) $25\,\Omega$

(C) $40\,\Omega$ (D) $500\,\Omega$

23. In the circuits shown below, the readings of voltmeters and the ammeters will be : **[NEET (UG) 2019]**

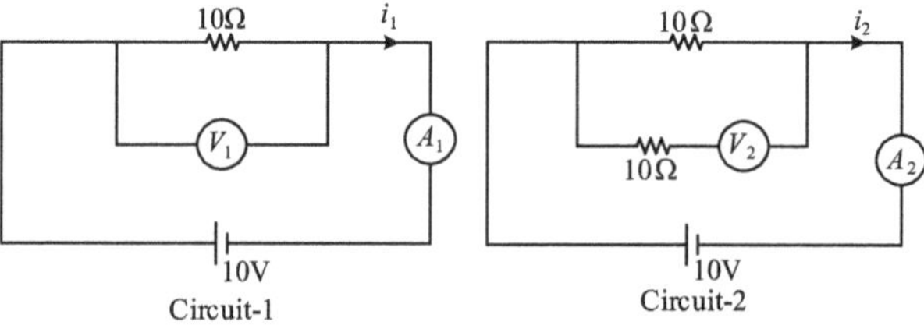

(A) $V_2 > V_1$ and $i_1 = i_2$ (B) $V_1 = V_2$ and $i_1 > i_2$

(C) $V_1 = V_2$ and $i_1 = i_2$ (D) $V_2 > V_1$ and $i_1 > i_2$

24. A resistance wire connected in the left gap of a metre bridge balances a 10 Ω resistance in the right gap at a point which divides the bridge wire in the ratio 3 : 2. If the length of the resistance wire is 1.5 m, then the length of 1 Ω of the resistance wire is : **[NEET (UG) 2020]**

(A) 1.5×10^{-2} m

(B) 1.0×10^{-2} m

(C) 1.0×10^{-1} m

(D) 1.5×10^{-1} m

25. In a potentiometer circuit a cell of EMF 1.5 V gives balance point at 36 cm length of wire. If another cell of EMF 2.5 V replaces the first cell, then at what length of the wire, the balance point occurs ? **[NEET (UG) 2021]**

(A) 60 cm

(B) 21.6 cm

(C) 64 cm

(D) 62 cm

26. A wheatstone bridge is used to determine the value of unknown resistance X by adjusting the variable resistance Y as shown in the figure. For the most precise measurement of X, the resistances P and Q : **[NEET (UG) 2022]**

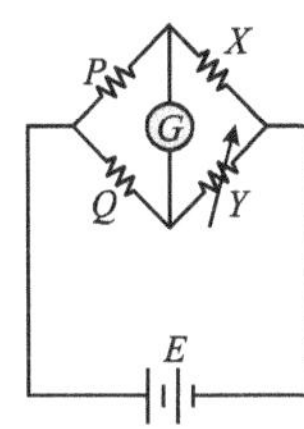

(A) Should be approximately equal and are small

(B) Should be very large and unequal

(C) Do not play any significant role

(D) Should be approximately equal to $2X$

* * * * *

18 MOVING CHARGES & MAGNETISM

18.1 Magnetic Effects of Current

1. The magnetic field of given length of wire for single turn coil at its centre is B then its value for two turns coil for the same wire is : **[NEET (UG) 2002]**
(A) $B/4$
(B) $B/2$
(C) $4B$
(D) $2B$

2. A long solenoid carrying a current produces a magnetic field B along its axis. If the current is doubled and the number of turns per cm is halved, the new value of the magnetic field is :
[NEET (UG) 2003]
(A) $B/2$
(B) B
(C) $2B$
(D) $4B$

3. Two circular coil 1 and 2 are made from the same wire but the radius of the 1st coil is twice that of the 2nd coil. What should be the ratio of potential differences in volts applied across these coils so that the magnetic field at their centres are them : **[NEET (UG) 2006]**
(A) 3
(B) 4
(C) 6
(D) 2

4. Which two of the following five physical parameters have the same dimensions ? **[NEET (UG) 2008]**
(a) Energy density
(b) Refractive index
(c) Dielectric constant
(d) Young's modulus
(e) Magnetic field
(A) (a) and (d)
(B) (a) and (e)
(C) (b) and (d)
(D) (c) and (e)

5. A thin ring of radius R meter has charge q coulomb uniformly spread on it. The ring rotates about its axis with a constant frequency of f rev/s. The value of magnetic induction in Wb/m^2 at the centre of the ring is : **[NEET (UG) 2010]**
(A) $\dfrac{\mu_0 qf}{2R}$
(B) $\dfrac{\mu_0 qf}{2\pi R}$
(C) $\dfrac{\mu_0 q}{2\pi fR}$
(D) $\dfrac{\mu_0 q}{2 fR}$

6. Two similar coils of radius R are lying concentrically with their planes at right angles to each other. The currents flowing in them are I an $2I$, respectively. The resultant magnetic field induction at the centre will be : **[NEET (UG) 2012]**
(A) $\dfrac{\sqrt{5}\mu_0 I}{2R}$
(B) $\dfrac{3\mu_0 I}{2R}$
(C) $\dfrac{\mu_0 I}{2R}$
(D) $\dfrac{\mu_0 I}{R}$

7. Two identical long conducting wires AOB and COD are placed at right angle to each other, with one above other such that O is their common point for the two. The wires carry I_1 and I_2 currents, respectively. Point P is lying at distance d from O along a direction perpendicular to the plane containing the wires. The magnetic field at the point P will be : **[NEET (UG) 2014]**
(A) $\dfrac{\mu_0}{2\pi d}\left(\dfrac{I_1}{I_2}\right)$
(B) $\dfrac{\mu_0}{2\pi d}(I_1 + I_2)$
(C) $\dfrac{\mu_0}{2\pi d}(I_1^2 + I_2^2)$
(D) $\dfrac{\mu_0}{2\pi d}(I_1^2 + I_2^2)^{1/2}$

8. A long straight wire of radius a carries a steady current I. The current is uniformly distributed over its cross-section. The ratio of the magnetic fields B and B' at radial distances $a/2$ and $2a$ respectively, from the axis of the wire is : **[NEET (UG) 2016]**
(A) $1/4$
(B) $1/2$
(C) 1
(D) 4

9. A long wire carrying a steady current is bent into a circular loop of one turn. The magnetic field at the centre of the loop is B. It is then bent into a circular coil of n turns. The magnetic field at the centre of this coil of n turns will be :
[NEET (UG) 2016 Ph. II]
(A) nB
(B) n^2B
(C) $2nB$
(D) $2n^2B$

10. A cylindrical conductor of radius R is carrying a constant current. The plot of the magnitude of the magnetic field. B with the distance d from the centre of the conductor, is correctly represented by the figure : **[NEET (UG) 2019]**

(A) 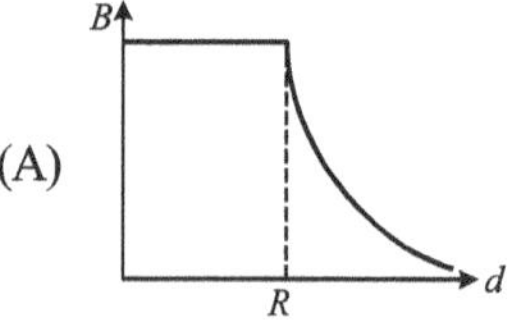
(B) 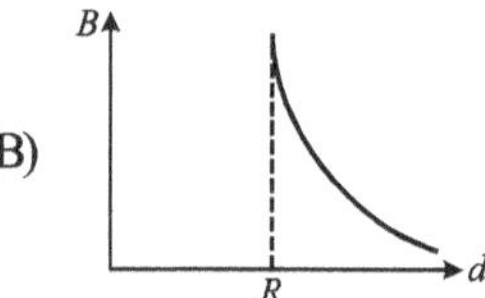
(C) 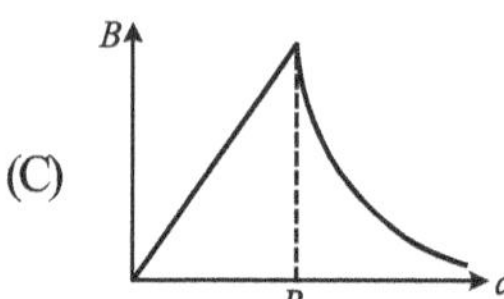
(D) 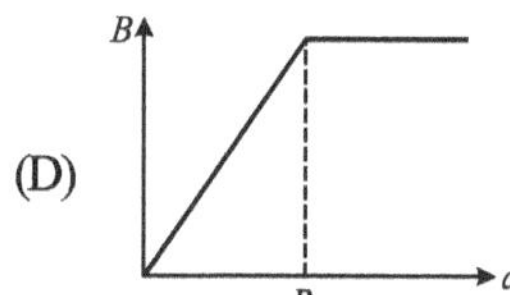

11. A long solenoid of 50 cm length having 100 turns carries a current of 2.5 A. The magnetic field at the centre of the solenoid

is : $(\mu_0 = 4\pi \times 10^{-7}\,\text{T m A}^{-1})$ **[NEET (UG) 2020]**
(A) $3.14 \times 10^{-5}\,\text{T}$ (B) $6.28 \times 10^{-4}\,\text{T}$
(C) $3.14 \times 10^{-4}\,\text{T}$ (D) $6.28 \times 10^{-5}\,\text{T}$

12. A thick current carrying cable of radius 'R' carries current 'I' uniformly distributed across its cross-section. The variation of magnetic field $B\,(r)$ due to the cable with the distance 'r' from the axis of the cable is represented by :   **[NEET (UG) 2021]**

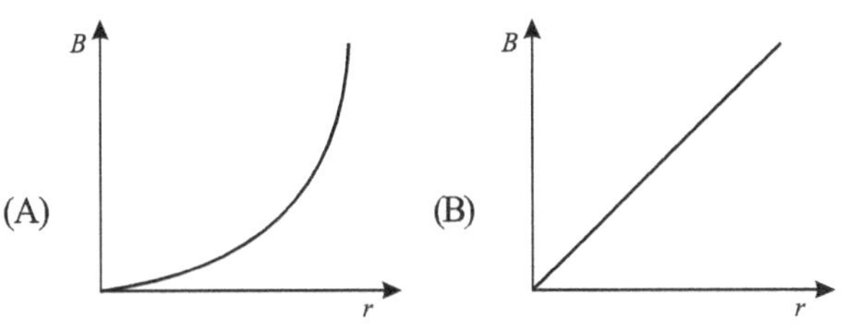

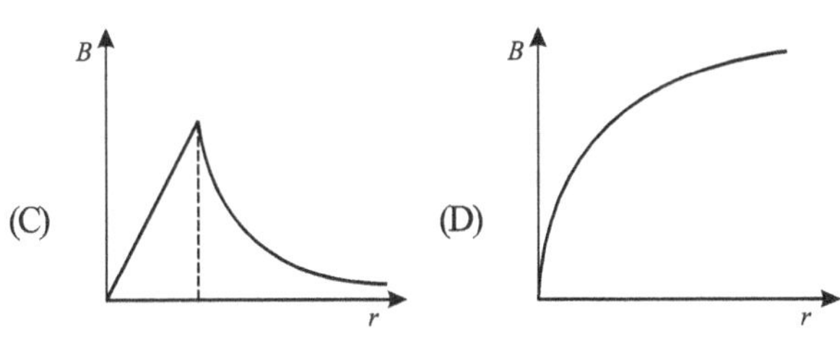

13. A long solenoid of radius 1 mm has 100 turns per mm. If 1 A current flows in the solenoid, the magnetic field strength at the centre of the solenoid is :   **[NEET (UG) 2022]**
(A) $12.56 \times 10^{-2}\,\text{T}$ (B) $12.56 \times 10^{-4}\,\text{T}$
(C) $6.28 \times 10^{-4}\,\text{T}$ (D) $6.28 \times 10^{-2}\,\text{T}$

14. Given blow are two statements :   **[NEET (UG) 2022]**
Statement-I : Biot-Savart's law gives us the expression for the magnetic field strength of an infinitesimal current element (Idl) of a current carrying conductor only.
Statement-II : Biot-Savart's law is analogous to Coulomb's inverse square law of change q, with the former being related to the field produced by a scalar source, Idl while the latter being produced by a vector source, q.

In light of above statement choose the most **appropriate** answer from the options given below :
(A) Both statement-I and Statement-II are incorrect
(B) Statement-I is correct and Statement-II is incorrect
(C) Statement-I is incorrect and Statement-II is correct
(D) Both statement-I and Statement-II are correct

15. From Ampere's circuital law for a long straight wire of circular cross-section carrying a steady current, the variation of magnetic field in the inside and outside region of the wire is :
                                                         [NEET (UG) 2022]
(A) A linearly increasing function of distance upto the boundary of the wire and then linearly decreasing for the outside region
(B) A linearly increasing function of distance r upto the boundary of the wire and then decreasing one with $1/r$ dependence for the outside region
(C) A linearly decreasing function of distance upto the boundary of the wire and then a linearly increasing one for the outside region
(D) Uniform and remains constant for both the regions

18.2 Magnetic Force on Moving Charges

1. An electron having mass m and kinetic energy E enter in uniform magnetic field B perpendicularly, then its frequency will be :   **[NEET (UG) 2001]**

(A) $\dfrac{eE}{qvB}$ (B) $\dfrac{2\pi m}{eB}$

(C) $\dfrac{eB}{2\pi m}$ (D) $\dfrac{2m}{eBE}$

2. In Thomson mass spectrograph $\vec{E} \perp \vec{B}$ then the velocity of electron beam will be :   **[NEET (UG) 2001]**

(A) $\dfrac{|\vec{E}|}{|\vec{B}|}$ (B) $\vec{E} \times \vec{B}$

(C) $\dfrac{|\vec{B}|}{|\vec{E}|}$ (D) $\dfrac{\vec{E}^2}{\vec{B}^2}$

3. A charge q moves in a region where electric field and magnetic field both exist, then force on it is : **[NEET (UG) 2002]**

(A) $q(\vec{v} \times \vec{B})$ (B) $q\vec{E} + q(\vec{v} \times \vec{B})$

(C) $q\vec{E} + \vec{q}(\vec{v} \times \vec{B})$ (D) $q\vec{B} + q(\vec{E} \times \vec{v})$

4. A charged particle moves through a magnetic field in a direction perpendicular to it. Then the :   **[NEET (UG) 2003]**
(A) Speed of the particle remains unchanged
(B) Direction of the particle remains unchanged
(C) Acceleration remains unchanged
(D) Velocity remains unchanged

5. An electron moves in a circular orbit with a uniform speed v. It produces a magnetic field B at the centre of the circle. The radius of the circle is proportional to :   **[NEET (UG) 2005]**

(A) $\sqrt{\dfrac{v}{B}}$ (B) $\dfrac{v}{B}$

(C) $\dfrac{B}{v}$ (D) $\sqrt{\dfrac{B}{v}}$

6. A very long straight wire carries a current I. At the instant when a charge $+Q$ at point P has velocity $\vec{V}$ as shown, the force on the charge is : **[NEET (UG) 2005]**

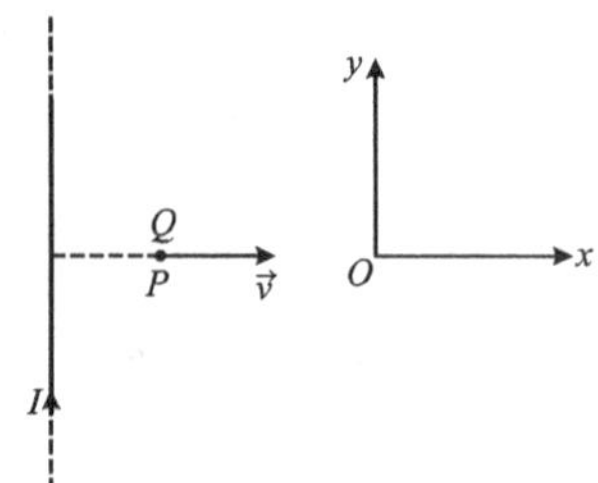

(A) Along ox (B) Opposite to oy
(C) Along oy (D) Opposite to ox

7. When a charged particle moving with velocity $\vec{V}$ is subjected to a magnetic field of induction $\vec{B}$, the force on it is non-zero. This implies the : **[NEET (UG) 2006]**

(A) Angle between $\vec{V}$ and $\vec{B}$ is necessary $90°$

(B) Angle between $\vec{V}$ and $\vec{B}$ can have at value other than $90°$

(C) Angle between $\vec{V}$ and $\vec{B}$ can have at value other than zero and $180°$

(D) Angle between $\vec{V}$ and $\vec{B}$ is either zero or $180°$

8. A beam of electron passes undeflected through mutually perpendicular electric and magnetic fields. If the electric field is switched off, and the same magnetic field is maintained, the electrons move : **[NEET (UG) 2007]**
(A) In a circular orbit   (B) Along a parabolic path
(C) Along a straight line   (D) In an elliptical orbit

9. In a mass spectrometer used for measuring the masses of ions, the ions are initially accelerated by an electric potential V and then made to describe semicircular path of radius R using a magnetic field B. If V and B are kept constant, the ratio $\left(\dfrac{\text{charge on the ion}}{\text{mass of the ion}}\right)$ will be proportional to : **[NEET (UG) 2007]**
(A) $1/R^2$ (B) R^2
(C) R (D) $1/R$

10. A charged particle with charge q is moving in a circle of radius R with uniform speed v. The associated magnetic moment μ is given by : **[NEET (UG) 2007]**
(A) qvR^2 (B) $qvR^2/2$
(C) qvR (D) $qvR/2$

11. Under the influence of a uniform magnetic field a charged particle is moving in a circle of radius R with constant speed v. The time period of the motion : **[NEET (UG) 2007, 2009]**
(A) Depends on both R and v

(B) Is independent of both R and v
(C) Depends on R and not on v
(D) Depends on v and not on R

12. A particle of mass m, charge Q and kinetic energy T enters a transverse uniform magnetic field of induction $\vec{B}$. After 3 seconds, the kinetic energy of the particle will be : **[NEET (UG) 2008]**
(A) T (B) $4T$
(C) $3T$ (D) $2T$

13. The magnetic force acting on a charged particle of charge $-2\mu c$ in a magnetic field of $2T$ acting in y direction, when the particle velocity is $(2\hat{i}+3\hat{j}) \times 10^6 \, \text{ms}^{-1}$, is : **[NEET (UG) 2009]**
(A) 8 N in z direction   (B) 8 N in $z-$direction
(C) 4 N in z direction   (D) 8 N in y direction

14. A beam of cathode rays is subjected to crossed Electric (E) and Magnetic field (B). The fields are adjusted such that the beam is not deflected. The specific charge of the cathode rays is given by (where V is the potential difference between cathode and anode) : **[NEET (UG) 2010]**

(A) $\dfrac{E^2}{2VB^2}$ (B) $\dfrac{B^2}{2VE^2}$

(C) $\dfrac{2VB^2}{E^2}$ (D) $\dfrac{2VE^2}{B^2}$

15. A uniform electric field and uniform magnetic field are acting along the same direction in a certain region. If an electron is projected in the region such that its velocity is pointed along the direction of fields, then the electron : **[NEET (UG) 2011]**
(A) Will turn towards right of direction of motion
(B) Speed will decrease
(C) Speed will increase
(D) Will turn towards left direction of motion

16. An alternating electric field of frequency ν, is applied across the dees (radius = R) of a cyclotron that is being used to accelerate protons (mass = m). The operating magnetic field (B) used in the cyclotron and the kinetic energy (K) of the proton beam, produced by it, are given by : **[NEET (UG) 2012]**

(A) $B = \dfrac{m\nu}{e}$ and $K = 2 \, m \, \pi^2\nu^2R^2$

(B) $B = \dfrac{2\pi m\nu}{e}$ and $K = m^2\pi\nu R^2$

(C) $B = \dfrac{2\pi m\nu}{e}$ and $K = 2 \, m \, \pi^2\nu^2R^2$

(D) $B = \dfrac{m\nu}{e}$ and $K = m^2\pi\nu R^2$

17. A proton carrying 1 MeV kinetic energy is moving in a circular path of radius R in uniform magnetic field. What should be the energy of an α-particle to describe a circle of same radius in the same field ?   **[NEET (UG) 2012]**
(A) 1 MeV
(B) 0.5 MeV
(C) 4 MeV
(D) 2 MeV

18. When a proton is released from rest in a room, it starts with an initial acceleration a_0 towards west. When it is projected towards north with a speed v_0 it moves with an initial acceleration $3a_0$ toward west. The electric and magnetic fields in the room are :   **[NEET (UG) 2013]**

(A) $\dfrac{ma_0}{e}$ west, $\dfrac{2ma_0}{ev_0}$ up
(B) $\dfrac{ma_0}{e}$ west, $\dfrac{2ma_0}{ev_0}$ down

(C) $\dfrac{ma_0}{e}$ east, $\dfrac{3ma_0}{ev_0}$ up
(D) $\dfrac{ma_0}{e}$ east, $\dfrac{3ma_0}{ev_0}$ down

19. A proton and an alpha particle both enter a region of uniform magnetic field B, moving at right angles to field B. If the radius of circular orbits for both the particles is equal and the kinetic energy acquired by proton is 1 MeV the energy acquired by the alpha particle will be :   **[NEET (UG) 2015]**
(A) 1 MeV
(B) 4 MeV
(C) 0.5 MeV
(D) 1.5 MeV

20. An electron is moving in a circular path under the influence of a transverse magnetic field of 3.57×10^{-2} T. If the value of e/m is 1.76×10^{11} C/kg, the frequency of revolution of the electron is :   **[NEET (UG) 2016 Ph. II]**
(A) 1 GHz
(B) 100 MHz
(C) 62.8 MHz
(D) 6.28 MHz

21. Ionized hydrogen atoms and α-particles with same momenta enters perpendicular to a constant magnetic field, B. The ratio of their radii of their paths $r_H : r_\alpha$ will be :   **[NEET (UG) 2019]**
(A) 2 : 1
(B) 1 : 2
(C) 4 : 1
(D) 1 : 4

22. An infinitely long straight conductor carries a current of 5A as shown. An electron is moving with a speed of 10^5 m/s parallel to the conductor. The perpendicular distance between the electron and the conductor is 20 cm at an instant. Calculate the magnitude of the force experienced by the electron at that instant :   **[NEET (UG) 2021]**

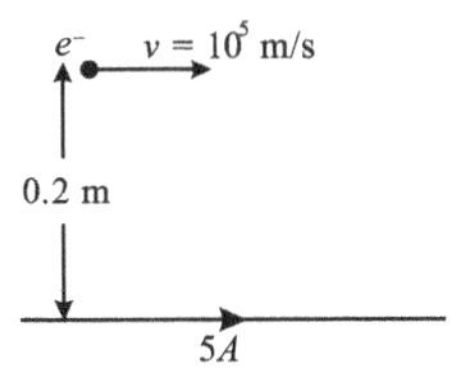

(A) 4×10^{-20} N
(B) $8\pi \times 10^{-20}$ N
(C) $4\pi \times 10^{-20}$ N
(D) 8×10^{-20} N

23. In the product

$$\vec{F} = q\,(\vec{v} \times \vec{B})$$

$$= q\,\vec{v} \times (B\hat{i} + B\hat{j} + B_0\hat{k})$$

For $q = 1$ and $\vec{v} = 2\hat{i} + 4\hat{j} + 6\hat{k}$ and

$$\vec{F} = 4\hat{i} - 20\hat{j} + 12\hat{k}$$

What will be the complete expression for $\vec{B}$? **[NEET (UG) 2021]**

(A) $-8\hat{i} - 8\hat{j} - 6\hat{k}$
(B) $-6\hat{i} - 6\hat{j} - 8\hat{k}$

(C) $8\hat{i} + 8\hat{j} - 6\hat{k}$
(D) $6\hat{i} + 6\hat{j} - 8\hat{k}$

18.3 Magnetic Force on Current

1. A coil in the shape of an equilateral triangle of side l is suspended between the pole pieces of a permanent magnet such that $\vec{B}$ is in plane of the coil. If due to a current i in the triangle a torque τ acts on it, the side l of the triangle is :
[NEET (UG) 2005]

(A) $\dfrac{2}{\sqrt{3}}\left(\dfrac{\tau}{Bi}\right)$
(B) $\dfrac{1}{\sqrt{3}}\dfrac{\tau}{Bi}$

(C) $2\left(\dfrac{\tau}{\sqrt{3}Bi}\right)^{\frac{1}{2}}$
(D) $\dfrac{2}{\sqrt{3}}\left(\dfrac{\tau}{Bi}\right)^{\frac{1}{2}}$

2. A closed loop $PQRS$ carrying a current is placed in a uniform magnetic field. If the magnetic forces on segments PS, SR and RQ are F_1, F_2 and F_3 respectively and are in the plane of the paper and along the directions shown, the force on the segment QP is :   **[NEET (UG) 2008]**

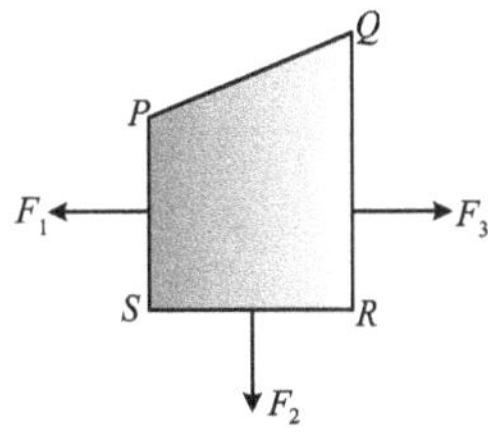

(A) $\sqrt{(F_3 - F_1)^2 - F_2^2}$
(B) $F_3 - F_1 - F_2$

(C) $F_3 - F_1 - F_2$
(D) $\sqrt{(F_3 - F_1)^2 + F_2^2}$

3. A square current carrying loop is suspended in a uniform magnetic field acting in the plane of the loop. If the force on one arm of the loop is $\vec{F}$, the net force on the remaining three arms of the loop is :   **[NEET (UG) 2010]**
(A) $\vec{F}$
(B) $3\vec{F}$
(C) $-\vec{F}$
(D) $-3\vec{F}$

4. A current carrying closed loop in the form of a right angle isosceles triangle ABC is placed in a uniform magnetic field acting along AB. If the magnetic force on the arm BC is $\vec{F}$, the force on the arm AC is : **[NEET (UG) 2011]**

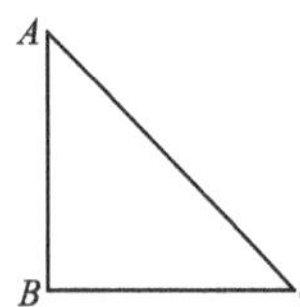

(A) $-\sqrt{2}\vec{F}$ (B) $-\vec{F}$

(C) $\vec{F}$ (D) $\sqrt{2}\vec{F}$

5. A current loop in a magnetic field : **[NEET (UG) 2013]**
(A) Experiences a torque whether the field is uniform or non-uniform in all orientations
(B) Can be in equilibrium in one orientation
(C) Can be in equilibrium in two orientations, both the equilibrium states are unstable
(D) Can be in equilibrium in two orientations, one stable while the other is unstable

6. A rectangular coil of length 0.12 m and width 0.1 m having 50 turns of wire is suspended vertically in a uniform magnetic field of strength 0.2 Wb/m². The coil carries a current of 2 A. If the plane of the coil is inclined at an angle of 30° with the direction of the field, the torque required to keep the coil in stable equilibrium will be : **[NEET (UG) 2015]**
(A) 0.12 Nm   (B) 0.15 Nm
(C) 0.20 Nm   (D) 0.24 Nm

7. A square loop $ABCD$ carrying a current i, is placed near and coplanar with a long straight conductor XY carrying a current I, the net force on the loop will be : **[NEET (UG) 2016]**

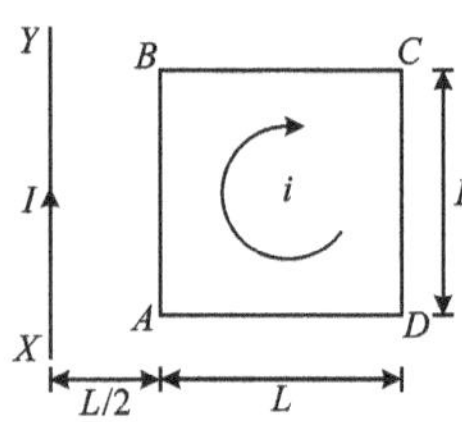

(A) $\dfrac{2\mu_0 Ii}{3\pi}$ (B) $\dfrac{\mu_0 Ii}{2\pi}$

(C) $\dfrac{2\mu_0 IiL}{3\pi}$ (D) $\dfrac{\mu_0 IiL}{2\pi}$

8. A 250-Turn rectangular coil of length 2.1 cm and width 1.25 cm carries a current of 85 μA and subjected to a magnetic field of strength 0.85 T. Work done for rotating the coil by 180° against the torque is : **[NEET (UG) 2017]**
(A) 9.1 μJ   (B) 4.55 μJ
(C) 2.3 μJ   (D) 1.15 μJ

9. An arrangement of three parallel straight wires placed perpendicular to plane of paper carrying same current 'I' along the same direction is shown in figure. Magnitude of force per unit length on the middle wire 'B' is given by : **[NEET (UG) 2017]**

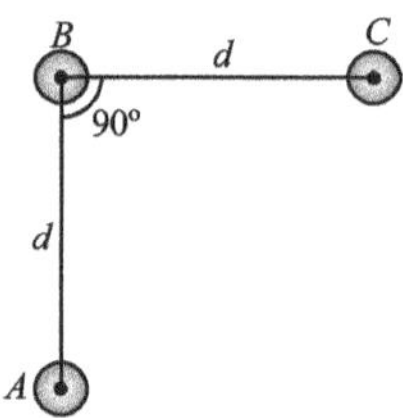

(A) $\dfrac{\mu_0 I^2}{2\pi d}$ (B) $\dfrac{2\mu_0 I^2}{\pi d}$

(C) $\dfrac{\sqrt{2}\mu_0 I^2}{\pi d}$ (D) $\dfrac{\mu_0 I^2}{\sqrt{2}\pi d}$

10. A metallic rod of mass per unit length 0.5 kg m⁻¹ is lying horizontally on a smooth inclined plane which makes an angle of 30° with the horizontal. The rod is not allowed to slide down by flowing a current through it when a magnetic field of induction 0.25 T is acting on it in the vertical direction. The current flowing in the rod to keep it stationary is : **[NEET (UG) 2018]**
(A) 14.76 A   (B) 5.98 A
(C) 7.14 A   (D) 11.32 A

* * * * *

MAGNETISM AND MATTER

19.1 Magnetism of a Bar Magnet

1. Two bar magnets having same geometry with magnetic moments M and $2M$, are firstly placed in such a way that their similar poles are in same side then its time period of oscillation is T_1. Now the polarity of one of the magnet is reversed then time period of oscillation is T_2, then :　　**[NEET (UG) 2002]**
(A) $T_1 < T_2$　　　　　　(B) $T_1 = T_2$
(C) $T_1 > T_2$　　　　　　(D) $T_2 = \infty$

2. A bar magnet is oscillating in the Earth's magnetic field with a period T. What happens to this period and motion if this mass is quadrupled :　　**[NEET (UG) 2003]**
(A) Motion remains S.H. with time period $= T/2$
(B) Motion remains S.H. with time period $= 2T$
(C) Motion remains S.H. with time period $= 4T$
(D) Motion remains S.H. with time and period remains nearly constant

3. If the magnetic dipole moment of an atom of diamagnetic material, paramagnetic material and ferromagnetic material are denoted by μ_d, μ_p and μ_f respectively, then : **[NEET (UG) 2005]**
(A) $\mu_p = 0$ and $\mu_f \neq 0$　　　(B) $\mu_d \neq 0$ and $\mu_p = 0$
(C) $\mu_d \neq 0$ and $\mu_f \neq 0$　　　(D) $\mu_d = 0$ and $\mu_p \neq 0$

4. A bar magnet having a magnetic movement of 2×10^4 JT^{-1} is free to rotate in a horizontal plane. A horizontal magnetic field $B = 6 \times 10^{-4}$ T exists in the space. The work done in taking the magnet slowly from a direction parallel to the field to a direction $60°$ from the field is :　　**[NEET (UG) 2009]**
(A) 2 J　　　　　　(B) 0.6 J
(C) 12 J　　　　　　(D) 6 J

5. A bar magnet of length l and magnetic dipole moment M is bent in the form of an arc as shown in figure. The new magnetic dipole moment will be :　　**[NEET (UG) 2013]**

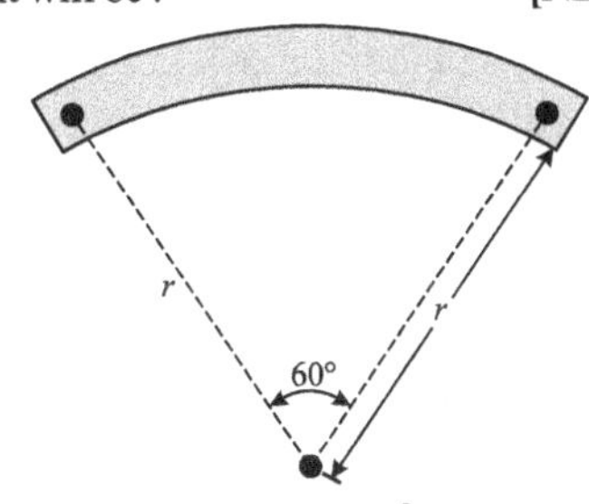

(A) M　　　　　　(B) $\dfrac{3}{\pi} M$
(C) $\dfrac{2}{\pi} M$　　　　　　(D) $\dfrac{M}{2}$

6. Following figures show the arrangement of bar magnets in different configurations. Each magnet has magnetic dipole moment $\vec{m}$. Which configuration has highest net magnetic dipole moment ?　　**[NEET (UG) 2014]**

(a) 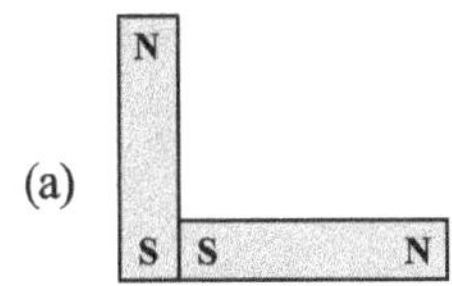

(b) 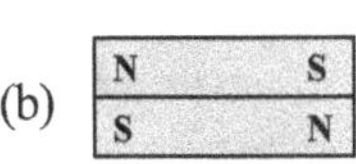

(c) 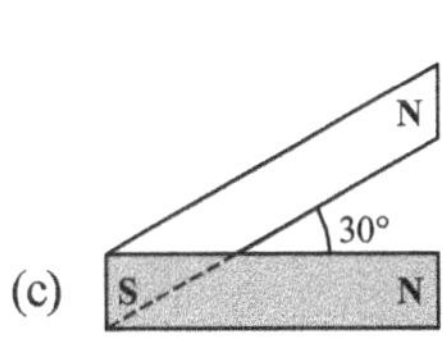

(d) 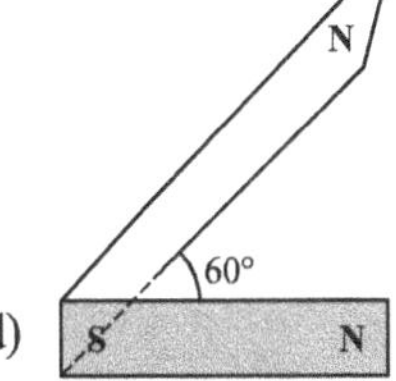

(A) a　　　　　　(B) b
(C) c　　　　　　(D) d

7. A bar magnet is hung by a thin cotton thread in a uniform horizontal magnetic field and is in equilibrium state. The energy required to rotate it by $60°$ is W. Now the torque required to keep the magnet in this new position is :　　**[NEET (UG) 2016 Ph. II]**
(A) $\dfrac{W}{\sqrt{3}}$　　　　　　(B) $\sqrt{3}W$
(C) $\dfrac{\sqrt{3}W}{2}$　　　　　　(D) $\dfrac{2W}{\sqrt{3}}$

8. A uniform conducting wire of length $12a$ and resistance 'R' is wound up as a current carrying coil in the shape of,
(i) an equilateral triangle of side 'a'.
(ii) a square of side 'a'.
The magnetic dipole moments of the coil in each case respectively are :　　**[NEET (UG) 2021]**
(A) $\sqrt{3}Ia^2$ and $3\,Ia^2$　　　(B) $3\,Ia^2$ and Ia^2
(C) $3\,Ia^2$ and $4\,Ia^2$　　　(D) $4\,Ia^2$ and $3\,Ia^2$

19.2 Earth's Magnetism

1. Tangent galvanometer is used to measure :
　　　　　　　　　　[NEET (UG) 2001]
(A) Potential difference　　　(B) Current
(C) Resistance　　　　　　(D) Charge

2. A vibration magnetometer placed in magnetic meridian has a small bar magnet. The magnet executes oscillations with a time period of 2 s in earth's horizontal magnetic field of 24 μT. When a horizontal field of 18 microtesla is produced opposite to the earth's field by placing a current carrying wire, the new time period of magnet will be : **[NEET (UG) 2010]**

(A) 4 s   (B) 1 s
(C) 2 s   (D) 3 s

3. A compass needle which is allowed to move in a horizontal plane is taken to a geomagnetic pole. It : **[NEET (UG) 2012]**
(A) Will become rigid showing no movement
(B) Will stay in any position
(C) Will stay in north-south direction only
(D) Will stay in east-west direction only

4. A magnetic needle suspended parallel to a magnetic field requires $\sqrt{3}$ J of work to turn it through 60°. The torque needed to maintain the needle in this position will be : **[NEET (UG) 2012]**

(A) 3 J   (B) $\sqrt{3}$ J
(C) $\dfrac{3}{2}$ J   (D) $2\sqrt{3}$ J

5. If θ_1 and θ_2 be the apparent angles of dip observed in two vertical planes at right angles to each other, then the true angle of dip θ is given by : **[NEET (UG) 2017]**
(A) $\cot^2\theta = \cot^2\theta_1 + \cot^2\theta_2$ (B) $\tan^2\theta = \tan^2\theta_1 + \tan^2\theta_2$
(C) $\cot^2\theta = \cot^2\theta_1 - \cot^2\theta_2$ (D) $\tan^2\theta = \tan^2\theta_1 - \tan^2\theta_2$

6. At a point A on the earth's surface the angle of dip, $\delta = +25°$. At a point B on the earth's surface the angle of dip, $\delta = -25°$. We can interpret that : **[NEET (UG) 2019]**
(A) A and B are both located in the northern hemisphere
(B) A is located in the southern hemisphere and B is located in the northern hemisphere
(C) A is located in the northern hemisphere and B is located in the southern hemisphere
(D) A and B are both located in the southern hemisphere

19.3 Magnetic Properties of Materials

1. Among which the magnetic susceptibility does not depend on the temperature ? **[NEET (UG) 2001]**
(A) Diamagnetism   (B) Paramagnetism
(C) Ferromagnetism   (D) Ferrite

2. If number of turns, area and current through a coil is given by n, A and i respectively then its magnetic moment will be : **[NEET (UG) 2001]**

(A) niA (B) n^2iA
(C) niA^2 (D) $\dfrac{ni}{\sqrt{A}}$

3. A diamagnetic material in a magnetic field moves : **[NEET (UG) 2003]**
(A) From stronger to the weaker parts of the field
(B) From weaker to the stronger parts of the field
(C) Perpendicular to the field
(D) In none of the above directions

4. According to Curie's law, the magnetic susceptibility of a substance at an absolute temperature T is proportional to : **[NEET (UG) 2003]**
(A) $1/T$ (B) T
(C) $1/T^2$ (D) T^2

5. Above Curie temperature : **[NEET (UG) 2006]**
(A) A ferromagnetic substance becomes paramagnetic
(B) A paramagnetic substance becomes diamagnetic
(C) A diamagnetic substance becomes paramagnetic
(D) A paramagnetic substance becomes ferromagnetic

6. Nickel shows ferromagnetic property at room temperature. If the temperature is increased beyond Curie temperature, then it will show : **[NEET (UG) 2007]**
(A) Anti ferromagnetism   (B) No magnetic property
(C) Diamagnetism   (D) Paramagnetism

7. Curie temperature is the temperature above which : **[NEET (UG) 2008]**
(A) Paramagnetic material becomes ferromagnetic material
(B) Ferromagnetic material becomes diamagnetic material
(C) Ferromagnetic material becomes paramagnetic material
(D) Paramagnetic material becomes diamagnetic material

8. If a diamagnetic substance is brought near the north or the south pole of a bar magnet, it is : **[NEET (UG) 2009]**
(A) Attracted by both the poles
(B) Repelled by both the poles
(C) Repelled by the north pole and attracted by the south pole
(D) Attracted by the north pole and repelled by the south pole

9. Electromagents are made of soft iron because soft iron has : **[NEET (UG) 2010]**
(A) Low retentivity and low coercive force
(B) Hight retentivity and high coercive force
(C) High retentivity and high coercive force
(D) Low retentivity and low coercive force

10. The magnetic susceptibility is negative for : **[NEET (UG) 2016]**
(A) Diamagnetic material only
(B) Paramagnetic material only
(C) Ferromagnetic material only
(D) Paramagnetic and ferromagnetic materials

11. There are four light-weight-rod samples A, B, C, D separately suspended by threads. A bar magnet is slowly brought near each sample and the following observations are noted : **[NEET (UG) 2011]**

(i) A is feebly repelled   (ii) B is feebly attracted

(iii) C is strongly attracted   (iv) D remains unaffected

Which one of the following is true ?

(A) B is of a paramagnetic material

(B) C is of a diamagnetic material

(C) D is of a ferromagnetic material

(D) A is of a non-magnetic material

12. A thin diamagnetic rod is placed vertically between the poles of an electromagnet. When the current in the electromagnet is switched on, then the diamagnetic rod is pushed up, out of the horizontal magnetic field. Hence the rod gains gravitational potential energy. The work required to do this comes from : **[NEET (UG) 2018]**

(A)   The lattice structure of the material of the rod

(B)   The magnetic field

(C)   The current source

(D)   The induced electric field due to the changing magnetic field

13. An iron rod of susceptibility 599 is subjected to a magnetising field of $1200\,\mathrm{A\,m^{-1}}$. The permeability of the material of the rod is : ($\mu_0 = 4\pi \times 10^{-7}\,\mathrm{T\,m\,A^{-1}}$) **[NEET (UG) 2020]**

(A) $2.4\pi \times 10^{-7}\,\mathrm{T\,m\,A^{-1}}$ (B) $2.4\pi \times 10^{-4}\,\mathrm{T\,m\,A^{-1}}$

(C) $8.0 \times 10^{-5}\,\mathrm{T\,m\,A^{-1}}$ (D) $2.4\pi \times 10^{-5}\,\mathrm{T\,m\,A^{-1}}$

*   *   *   *   *

20 ELECTROMAGNETIC INDUCTION

20.1 Faraday's Law of EMI

1. The magnetic flux through a circuit of resistance R changes by an amount $\Delta\phi$ in a time Δt. Then the total quantity of electric charge Q that passes any point in the circuit during the time Δt is represented by : **[NEET (UG) 2004]**

(A) $Q = \dfrac{1}{R} \cdot \dfrac{\Delta\phi}{\Delta t}$

(B) $Q = \dfrac{\Delta\phi}{R}$

(C) $Q = \dfrac{\Delta\phi}{\Delta t}$

(D) $Q = R \cdot \dfrac{\Delta\phi}{\Delta t}$

2. As a result of change in the magnetic flux linked to the closed loop shown in the figure, an *emf V* volt is induced in the loop. The work done (joules) in taking a charge Q coulomb once along the loop is : **[NEET (UG) 2005]**

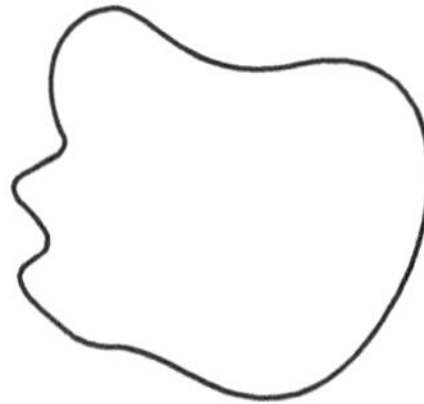

(A) QV
(B) $QV/2$
(C) $2QV$
(D) Zero

3. A circular disc of radius 0.2 metre is placed in a uniform magnetic field of induction $\dfrac{1}{\pi}\left(\dfrac{Wb}{m^2}\right)$ in such a way that its axis makes an angle of 60° with $\vec{B}$. The magnetic flux linked with the disc is : **[NEET (UG) 2008]**

(A) 0.08 Wb
(B) 0.01 Wb
(C) 0.02 Wb
(D) 0.06 Wb

4. A conducting circular loop is placed in a uniform magnetic field 0.04 T with its plane perpendicular to the magnetic field. The radius of the loop starts shrinking at 2 mm/s. The induced emf in the loop when the radius is 2 cm is : **[NEET (UG) 2009]**

(A) $1.6\,\pi\mu V$
(B) $3.2\,\pi\mu V$
(C) $4.8\,\pi\mu V$
(D) $0.8\,\pi\mu V$

5. A conducting circular loop is placed in a uniform magnetic field, $B = 0.025\ T$ with its plane perpendicular to the loop. The radius of the loop is made to shrink at a constant rate of 1 mm/s. The induced *emf* when the radius is 2 cm is : **[NEET (UG) 2010]**

(A) $2\,\mu V$
(B) $2\,\pi\mu V$
(C) $\pi\mu V$
(D) $\dfrac{\pi}{2}\,\mu V$

6. The current i in a coil varies with time as shown in the figure. The variation of induced emf with time would be : **[NEET (UG) 2011]**

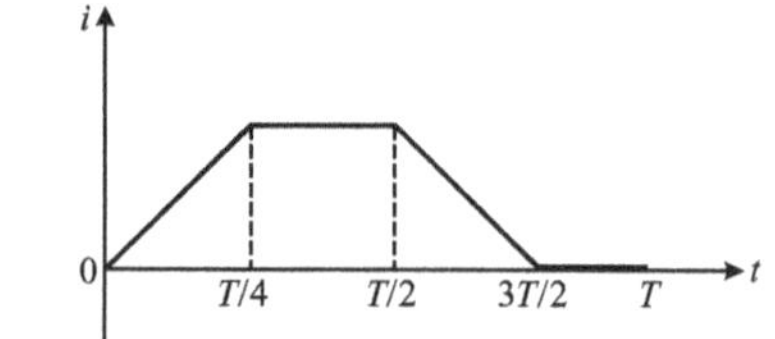

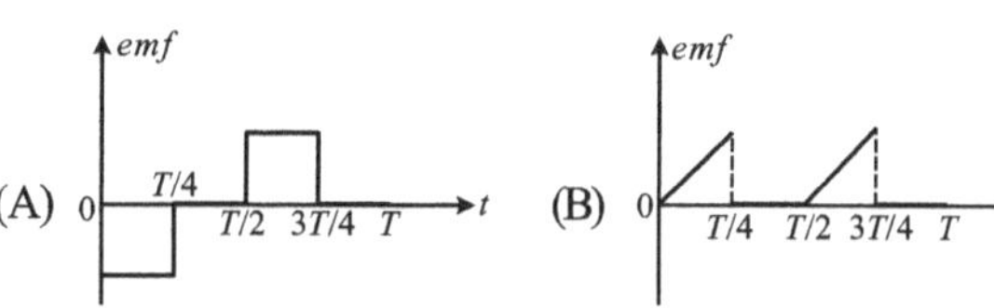

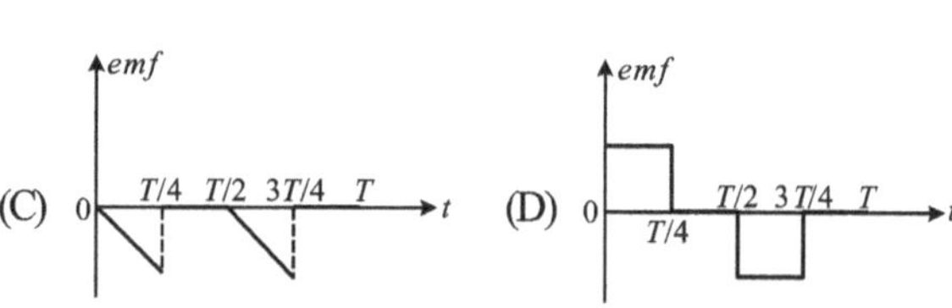

7. A coil of resistance 400 Ω is placed in a magnetic field. If the magnetic flux ϕ linked with the coil varies with timet as $\phi = 50t^2 + 4$. The current in the coil at $t = 2$ s is : **[NEET (UG) 2012]**

(A) 0.5 A
(B) 0.1 A
(C) 2 A
(D) 1 A

8. In a coil of resistance 10 Ω, the induced current developed by changing magnetic flux through it, is shown in figure as a function of time. The magnitude of change in flux through the coil in Weber is : **[NEET (UG) 2012]**

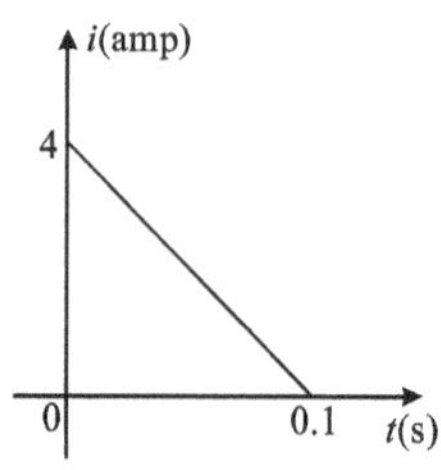

(A) 2
(B) 6
(C) 4
(D) 8

9. A wire loop is rotated in a magnetic field. The frequency of change of direction of the induced *emf* is : **[NEET (UG) 2013]**
(A) Once per revolution   (B) Twice per revolution
(C) Four times per revolution (D) Six times per revolution

10. A thin semicircular conducting ring (*PQR*) of radius *r* is falling with its plane vertical in a horizontal magnetic field *B*, as shown in figure. The potential difference developed across the ring when its speed is *v*, is :   **[NEET (UG) 2014]**

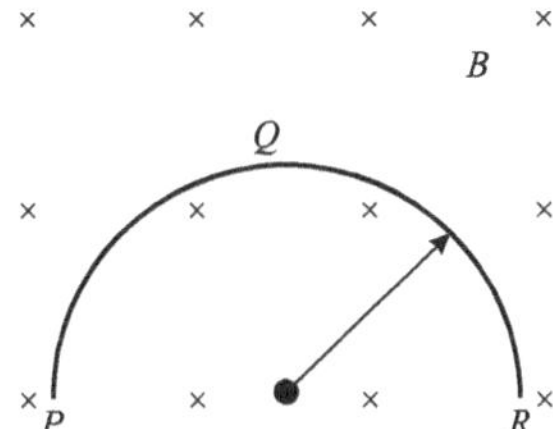

(A) Zero
(B) $Bv\pi r^2/2$ and *P* is at higher potential
(C) $\pi r B v$ and *R* is at higher potential
(D) $2rBv$ and *R* is at higher potential

11. An electron moves on a straight line path *XY* as shown. The *abcd* is a coil adjacent to the path of electron. What will be the direction of current if any, induced in the coil ?
                      [NEET (UG) 2015]

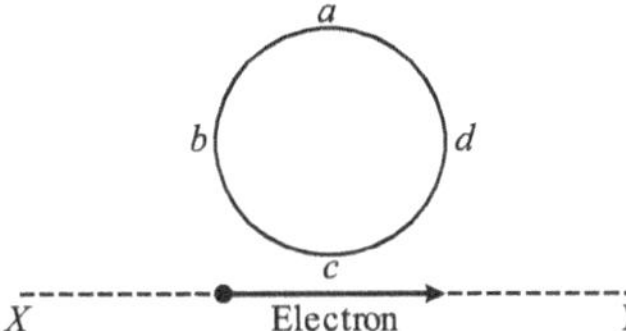

(A) No current induced
(B) *abcd*
(C) *adcb*
(D) The current will reverse its direction as the electron goes past the coil

12. A uniform magnetic field is restricted within a region of radius *r*. The magnetic field changes with time at a rate $\dfrac{d\vec{B}}{dt}$. Loop 1 of radius $R > r$ enclosed the region *r* and loop 2 of radius *R* is outside the region of magnetic field as shown in the figure below. Then the *emf* generated is : **[NEET (UG) 2016 Ph. II]**

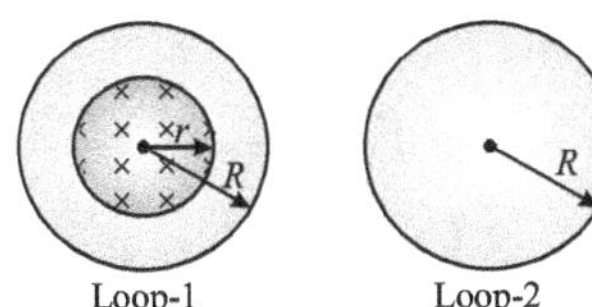

Loop-1   Loop-2

(A) Zero in loop 1 and zero in loop 2

(B) $-\dfrac{d\vec{B}}{dt}\,\pi r^2$ in loop 1 and $-\dfrac{d\vec{B}}{dt}\,\pi r^2$ in loop 2

(C) $-\dfrac{d\vec{B}}{dt}\,\pi R^2$ in loop 1 and zero in loop 2

(D) $-\dfrac{d\vec{B}}{dt}\,\pi r^2$ in loop 1 and zero in loop 2

13. A long solenoid of diameter 0.1 m has 2×10^4 turns per meter. At the centre of the solenoid, a coil of 100 turns and radius 0.01 m is placed with its axis coinciding with the solenoid axis. The current in the solenoid reduces at a constant rate to 0 A from 4 A in 0.05 s. If the resistance of the coil is $10\pi^2\,\Omega$, the total charge flowing through the coil during this time is : **[NEET (UG) 2017]**
(A) $32\pi\,\mu C$ (B) $16\,\mu C$
(C) $32\,\mu C$ (D) $16\pi\,\mu C$

14. A 800 turn coil of effective area $0.05\,m^2$ is kept perpendicular to a magnetic field 5×10^{-5} T. When the plane of the coil is rotated by 90° around any of its coplanar axis in 0.1 s, the emf induced in the coil will be : **[NEET (UG) 2019]**
(A) 2 V   (B) 0.2 V
(C) 2×10^{-3} V   (D) 0.02 V

15. A square loop of side 1 m and resistance 1 Ω is placed in a magnetic field of 0.5 T. If the plane of loop is perpendicular to the direction of magnetic field, the magnetic flux through the loop is : **[NEET (UG) 2022]**
(A) 0.5 weber   (B) 1 weber
(C) Zero weber   (D) 2 weber

16. A big circular coil of 1000 turns and average radius 10 m is rotating about its horizontal diameter at 2 rad s^{-1}. If the vertical component of earth's magnetic field at that place is 2×10^{-5} T and electrical resistance of the coil is 12.56 Ω, then the maximum induced current in the coil will be : **[NEET (UG) 2022]**
(A) 1.5 A   (B) 1 A
(C) 2 A   (D) 0.25 A

20.2 Self & Mutual Induction

1. For a coil having $L = 2$ mH, current flow through it is $I = t^2 e^{-t}$ then, the time at which emf becomes zero : **[NEET (UG) 2001]**
(A) 2 s   (B) 1 s
(C) 4 s   (D) 3 s

2. A coil of 40 H inductance is connected in series with a resistance of 8 Ω and the combination is joined to the terminals of a 2 V battery. The time constant of the circuit is : **[NEET (UG) 2004]**
(A) 5 s   (B) 1/5 s
(C) 40 s   (D) 20 s

3. The core of a transformer is laminated because : **[NEET (UG) 2006]**
(A) Energy losses due to eddy currents may be minimised
(B) The weight of the transformer may be reduced
(C) Rusting of the core may be prevented
(D) Ratio of voltage in primary and secondary may be increased

4. Two coils of self inductances 2 mH and 8 mH are placed so close together that the effective flux in one coil is completely linked with the other. The mutual inductance between these coils is : **[NEET (UG) 2006]**
(A) 10 mH (B) 6 mH
(C) 4 mH (D) 16 mH

5. The primary and secondary coil of a transformer have 50 and 1500 turns respectively. If the magnetic flux ϕ linked with the primary coil is given by $\phi = \phi_0 + 4t$, where ϕ is in webers, t is time in seconds and ϕ_0 is a constant, the output voltage across the secondary coil is : **[NEET (UG) 2007]**
(A) 120 volts (B) 220 volts
(C) 30 volts (D) 90 volts

6. A transformer is used to light a 100 W and 110 V lamp from a 220 V mains. If the main current is 0.5 A, the efficiency of the transformer is approximately : **[NEET (UG) 2007]**
(A) 50% (B) 90%
(C) 10% (D) 30%

7. A long solenoid has 500 turns. When a current of 2 ampere is passed through it, the resulting magnetic flux linked with each turn of the solenoid is 4×10^{-3} Wb. The self-inductance of the solenoid is : **[NEET (UG) 2008]**
(A) 1.0 henry (B) 4.0 henry
(C) 2.5 henry (D) 2.0 henry

8. A rectangular, a square, a circular and an elliptical loop, all in the $(x - y)$ plane, are moving out of a uniform magnetic field with a constant velocity, $\vec{V} = v \cdot \hat{j}$. The magnetic field is directed along the negative z-axis direction. The induced *emf*, during the time these loops come out of the field region, will not remain constant for : **[NEET (UG) 2009]**
(A) Any of the four loops
(B) The rectangular, circular and elliptical loops
(C) The circular and the elliptical loops
(D) Only the elliptical loop

9. A 220 volts input is supplied to a transformer. The output circuit draws a current of 2.0 ampere at 440 volts. If the efficiency of the transformer is 80%, the current drawn by the primary windings of the transformer is : **[NEET (UG) 2010]**
(A) 5.0 ampere (B) 3.6 ampere
(C) 2.8 ampere (D) 2.5 ampere

10. The current (I) in the inductance is varying with time according to the plot shown in figure. Which one of the following is the correct variation of voltage with time in the coil ? **[NEET (UG) 2012]**

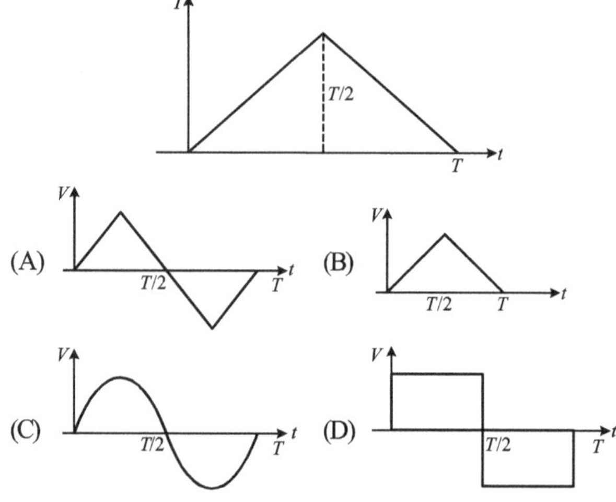

11. A transformer having efficiency of 90% is working on 200 V and 3 kW power supply. If the current in the secondary coil is 6 A, the voltage across the secondary coil and the current in the primary coil respectively are : **[NEET (UG) 2014]**
(A) 300 V, 15 A (B) 450 V, 15 A
(C) 450 V, 13.5 A (D) 600 V, 15 A

12. A long solenoid has 1000 turns. When a current of 4 A flows through it, the magnetic flux linked with each turn of the solenoid is 4×10^{-3} Wb. The self-inductance of the solenoid is : **[NEET (UG) 2016]**
(A) 4 H (B) 3 H
(C) 2 H (D) 1 H

13. Figure shows a circuit contains three identical resistors with resistance $R = 9.0\ \Omega$ each, two identical inductors with inductance $L = 2.0$ mH each, and an ideal battery with *emf* $\varepsilon = 18$ V. The current 'i' through the battery just after the switch closed is : **[NEET (UG) 2017]**

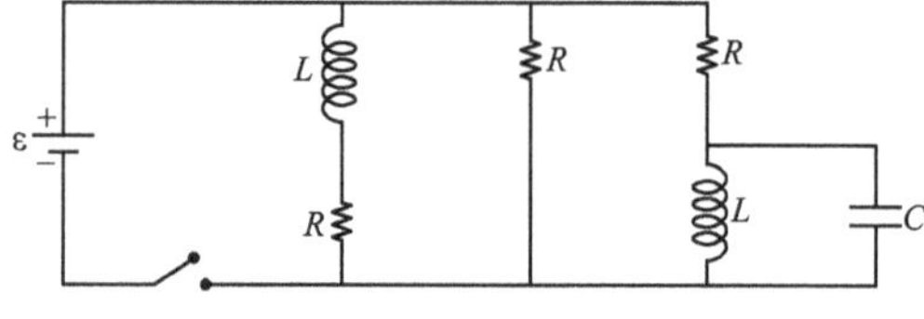

(A) 2 mA (B) 0.2 A
(C) 2 A (D) 0 ampere

14. The magnetic potential energy stored in a certain inductor is 25 mJ, when the current in the inductor is 60 mA. This inductor is of inductance : **[NEET (UG) 2018]**
(A) 1.389 H (B) 138.88 H
(C) 0.138 H (D) 13.89 H

15. In which of the following devices, the eddy current effect is not used ?   **[NEET (UG) 2019]**
(A) Induction furnace   (B) Magnetic braking in train
(C) Electromagnet   (D) Electric heater

16. An inductor of inductance L, a capacitor of capacitance C and resistor of resistance 'R' are connected in series to an ac source of potential difference 'V' volts as shown in figure. Potential difference across L, C and R is $40\ V$, $10\ V$ and $40\ V$, respectively. The amplitude of current flowing through LCR series circuit is $10\sqrt{2}$ A. The impedance of the circuit is :
[NEET (UG) 2021]

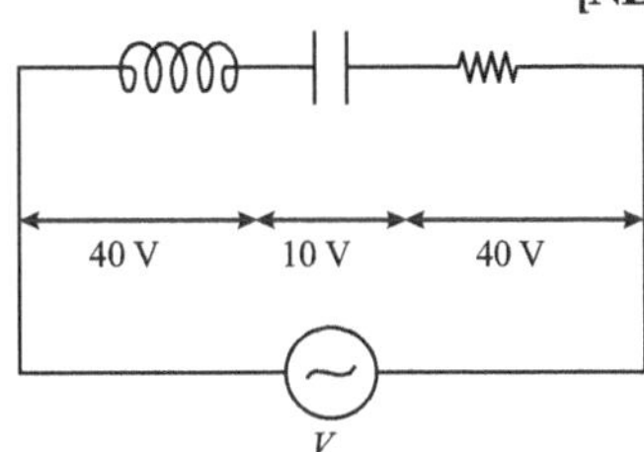

(A) $4\sqrt{2}\ \Omega$ (B) $5/\sqrt{2}\ \Omega$
(C) 4Ω (D) 5Ω

17. A step down transformer connected to an ac mains supply of 220 V is made to operate at 11 V, 44 W lamp. Ignoring power losses in the transformer, what is the current in the primary circuit ?   **[NEET (UG) 2021]**
(A) 0.2 A   (B) 0.4 A
(C) 2 A   (D) 4 A

18. Two conducting circular loops of radii R_1 and R_2 are placed in the same plane with their centres coinciding. If $R_1 \gg R_2$, the mutual inductance M between them will be directly proportional to :   **[NEET (UG) 2021]**

(A) $\dfrac{R_1}{R_2}$ (B) $\dfrac{R_2}{R_1}$

(C) $\dfrac{R_1^2}{R_2}$ (D) $\dfrac{R_2^2}{R_1}$

*   *   *   *   *

21 ALTERNATING CURRENT

21.1 AC emf, Current, Impedance and Power

1. A capacitor of capacity C has reactance X. If capacitance and frequency become double then reactance will be : **[NEET (UG) 2001]**

(A) $4X$ (B) $X/2$

(C) $X/4$ (D) $2X$

2. In an AC circuit the *emf* and the current at any instant are given respectively by : **[NEET (UG) 2008]**

$$e = E_0 \sin \omega t$$
$$i = I_0 \sin (\omega t - \phi)$$

The average power in the circuit over one cycle of AC is :

(A) $\dfrac{E_0 I_0}{2} \cos \phi$ (B) $E_0 I_0$

(C) $\dfrac{E_0 I_0}{2}$ (D) $\dfrac{E_0 I_0}{2} \sin \phi$

3. An AC voltage is applied to a resistance R and an inductor L in series. If R and the inductive reactance are both equal to $3\,\Omega$, the phase difference between the applied voltage and the current in the circuit is : **[NEET (UG) 2011]**

(A) $\pi/6$ (B) $\pi/4$

(C) $\pi/2$ (D) Zero

4. In an AC circuit an alternating voltage $e = 200\sqrt{2} \sin 100t$ volts is connected to a capacitor of capacity $1\,\mu F$. The *rms* value of the current in the circuit is : **[NEET (UG) 2011]**

(A) $10\,mA$ (B) $100\,mA$

(C) $200\,mA$ (D) $20\,mA$

5. The instantaneous values of alternating current and voltages in a circuit are given as

$$i = \frac{1}{\sqrt{2}} \sin(100\pi t)\ \text{ampere}$$

$$e = \frac{1}{\sqrt{2}} \sin(100\pi t + \pi/3)\ \text{volt}$$

The average power in watt consumed in the circuit is : **[NEET (UG) 2012]**

(A) $\sqrt{3}/4$ (B) $1/2$

(C) $1/8$ (D) $1/4$

6. A series R-C circuit is connected to an alternating voltage source. Consider two situations : **[NEET (UG) 2015]**

(a) When capacitor is air filled

(b) When capacitor is mica filled

Current through resistor is i and voltage across capacitor is V then :

(A) $V_a = V_b$ (B) $V_a < V_b$

(C) $V_a > V_b$ (D) $i_a > i_b$

7. A small signal voltage $V(t) = V_0 \sin \omega t$ is applied across an ideal capacitor C : **[NEET (UG) 2016]**

(A) Current $I(t)$ lags voltage $V(t)$ by $90°$

(B) Over a full cycle the capacitor C does not consume any energy from the voltage source

(C) Current $I(t)$ is in phase with voltage $V(t)$

(D) Current $I(t)$ leads voltage $V(t)$ by $180°$

8. A $100\,\Omega$ resistance and a capacitor of $100\,\Omega$ reactance are connected in series across a $220\,V$ source. When the capacitor is $50\,\%$ charged, the peak value of the displacement current is : **[NEET (UG) 2016 Ph. II]**

(A) $2.2\,A$ (B) $11\,A$

(C) $4.4\,A$ (D) $11\sqrt{2}\,A$

9. A $40\,\mu F$ capacitor is connected to a $200\,V$, $50\,Hz$ ac supply. The rms value of the current in the circuit is, nearly : **[NEET (UG) 2020]**

(A) $25.1\,A$ (B) $1.7\,A$

(C) $2.05\,A$ (D) $2.5\,A$

10. The peak voltage of the ac source is equal to : **[NEET (UG) 2022]**

(A) The *rms* value of the ac source

(B) 2 times the *rms* value of the ac source

(C) $1/\sqrt{2}$ time the *rms* value of the ac source

(D) The value of voltage supplied to the circuit

21.2 RLC Circuit and Resonance

1. For a series LCR circuit, the power loss at resonance is : **[NEET (UG) 2002]**

(A) $\dfrac{V^2}{\left[\omega L - \dfrac{1}{\omega C}\right]}$ (B) $I^2 L \omega$

(C) $I^2 R$ (D) $\dfrac{V^2}{C\omega}$

2. In a circuit L, C and R are connected in series with an alternating voltage source of frequency f. The current leads the voltage by 45°. The value of C is : **[NEET (UG) 2005]**

(A) $\dfrac{1}{2\pi f(2\pi fL - R)}$ (B) $\dfrac{1}{2\pi f(2\pi fL + R)}$

(C) $\dfrac{1}{\pi f(2\pi fL - R)}$ (D) $\dfrac{1}{\pi f(2\pi fL + R)}$

3. A coil of inductive reactance 31 Ω has a resistance of 8 Ω. It is placed in series with a condenser of capacitive reactance 25 Ω. The combination is connected to an AC source of 110 V. The power factor of the circuit is : **[NEET (UG) 2006]**

(A) 0.56   (B) 0.64

(C) 0.80   (D) 0.33

4. What is the value of inductance L for which the current is maximum in a series LCR circuit with $C = 10\ \mu F$ and $\omega = 1000\ \text{s}^{-1}$: **[NEET (UG) 2007]**

(A) 1 mH

(B) Cannot be calculated unless R is known

(C) 10 mH

(D) 100 mH

5. Power dissipated in an LCR series circuit connected to an AC source of emf ε is : **[NEET (UG) 2009]**

(A) $\varepsilon^2 R \Big/ \sqrt{R^2 + \left(L\omega - \dfrac{1}{C\omega}\right)^2}$

(B) $\varepsilon^2 R \Big/ \left[R^2 + \left(L\omega - \dfrac{1}{C\omega}\right)^2\right]$

(C) $\varepsilon^2 \sqrt{\left[R^2 + \left(L\omega - \dfrac{1}{C\omega}\right)\right]} \Big/ R$

(D) $\dfrac{\varepsilon^2 \left[R^2 + \left(L\omega - \dfrac{1}{C\omega}\right)^2\right]}{R}$

6. In the given circuit the reading of voltmeter V_1 and V_2 are 300 V each. The reading of the voltmeter V_3 and ammeter A are respectively : **[NEET (UG) 2010]**

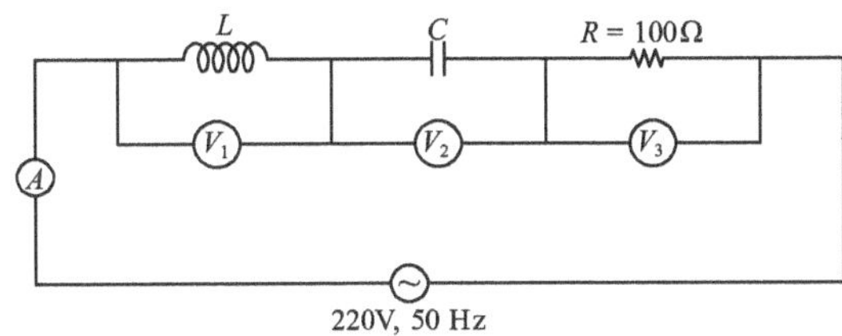

(A) 100 V, 2.0 A   (B) 150 V, 2.2 A

(C) 220 V, 2.2 A   (D) 220 V, 2.0 A

7. In an electrical circuit R, L, C and an AC voltage source are all connected in series. When L is removed from the circuit, the phase difference between the voltage and the current in the circuit is $\pi/3$. If instead, C is removed from the circuit, the phase difference is again $\pi/3$. The power factor of the circuit is : **[NEET (UG) 2012]**

(A) 1/2   (B) $1/\sqrt{2}$

(C) 1   (D) $\sqrt{3}/2$

8. A coil of self-inductance L is connected in series with a bulb B and an AC source. Brightness of the bulb decreases when : **[NEET (UG) 2013]**

(A) Frequency of the AC source is decreased

(B) Number of turns in the coil is reduced

(C) A capacitance of reactance $X_C = X_L$ is included in the same circuit

(D) An iron rod is inserted in the coil

9. An inductor 20 mH, a capacitor 50 μF and a resistor 40 Ω are connected in series across a source of emf $V = 10 \sin 340t$. The power loss in AC circuit is : **[NEET (UG) 2016]**

(A) 0.51 W   (B) 0.67 W

(C) 0.76 W   (D) 0.89 W

10. Which of the following combinations should be selected for better tuning of an L-C-R circuit used for communication ? **[NEET (UG) 2016 Ph. II]**

(A) $R = 20\ \Omega$, $L = 1.5\ H$, $C = 35\ \mu F$

(B) $R = 25\ \Omega$, $L = 2.5\ H$, $C = 45\ \mu F$

(C) $R = 15\ \Omega$, $L = 3.5\ H$, $C = 30\ \mu F$

(D) $R = 25\ \Omega$, $L = 1.5\ H$, $C = 45\ \mu F$

11. The potential differences across the resistance, capacitance and inductance are 80 V, 40 V and 100 V respectively in an L-C-R circuit. The power factor of this circuit is : **[NEET (UG) 2016 Ph. II]**

(A) 0.4   (B) 0.5

(C) 0.8   (D) 1.0

12. An inductor 20 mH, a capacitor 100 μF and a resistor 50 Ω are connected in series across a source of *emf*, $V = 10 \sin 314\,t$. The power loss in the circuit is : **[NEET (UG) 2018]**

(A) 2.74 W   (B) 0.43 W

(C) 0.79 W   (D) 1.13 W

13. A series LCR circuit is connected to an AC voltage source. When L is removed from the circuit, the phase difference between current and voltage is $\pi/3$. If instead C is removed from the circuit, the phase difference is again $\pi/3$ between current and voltage. The power factor of the circuit is : **[NEET (UG) 2020]**

(A) −1.0   (B) Zero

(C) 0.5   (D) 1.0

14. A series LCR circuit containing 5.0 H inductor, 80 μF capacitor and 40 Ω resistor is connected to 230V variable frequency ac source. The angular frequencies of the source at which power transferred to the circuit is half the power at the resonant angular frequency are likely to be : **[NEET (UG) 2021]**

(A) 25 rad/s and 75 rad/s   (B) 50 rad/s and 25 rad/s

(C) 46 rad/s and 54 rad/s   (D) 42 rad/s and 58 rad/s

15. A series LCR circuit with inductance 10 H, capacitance 10 μF, resistance 50 Ω is connected to an ac source of voltage, $V = 200 \sin (100t)$ volt. If the resonant frequency of the LCR circuit is ν_0 and the frequency of the ac source is ν, then :

[NEET (UG) 2022]

(A) $\nu_0 = \nu = \dfrac{50}{\pi}$ Hz   (B) $\nu_0 = \dfrac{50}{\pi}$ Hz, $\nu = 50$ Hz

(C) $\nu = 100$ Hz; $\nu_0 = \dfrac{100}{\pi}$ Hz   (D) $\nu_0 = \nu = 50$ Hz

$*$ $*$ $*$ $*$ $*$

CHAPTER 22: ELECTROMAGNETIC WAVES

22.1 Electromagnetic Spectrum

1. Biological importance of ozone layer is : **[NEET (UG) 2001]**
(A) It stops ultraviolet rays
(B) Ozone layer reduces green house effect
(C) Ozone layer reflects radio waves
(D) Ozone layer controls O_2/H_2 ratio in atmosphere

2. What is the cause of Green house effect ?
[NEET (UG) 2002]
(A) Infrared rays
(B) Ultra violet rays
(C) X-rays
(D) Radio waves

3. We consider the radiation emitted by the human body. Which one of the following statements is true ?
[NEET (UG) 2003]
(A) The radiation emitted is in the infrared region
(B) The radiation is emitted only during the day
(C) The radiation is emitted during the summers and absorbed during the winters
(D) The radiation emitted lies in the ultraviolet region and hence is not visible

4. Which of the following rays are not electromagnetic waves ?
[NEET (UG) 2003]
(A) X-rays
(B) γ-rays
(C) β-rays
(D) Heat rays

5. The condition under which a microwave oven heats up a food item containing water molecules most efficiently is :
[NEET (UG) 2013]
(A) The frequency of the microwaves must match the resonant frequency of water molecules
(B) The frequency of the microwaves has no relation with natural frequency of water molecules
(C) Microwaves are heat waves, so always produce heating
(D) Infrared waves produce heating in a microwave oven

6. The energy of the electromagnetic waves is of the order of 15 keV. To which part of the spectrum does it belong ?
[NEET (UG) 2015]
(A) γ-rays
(B) X-rays
(C) Infrared rays
(D) Ultraviolet rays

7. Out of the following options which one can be used to produce a propagating electromagnetic wave ?
[NEET (UG) 2016]
(A) A charge moving at constant velocity
(B) A stationary charge
(C) A chargeless particle
(D) An accelerating charge

8. Match List-I with List-II : **[NEET (UG) 2022]**

List-I		List-II	
(Electromagnetic waves)		**(Wavelength)**	
(a)	AM radio waves	(i)	$10^{-10}\,m$
(b)	Microwaves	(ii)	$10^2\,m$
(c)	Infrared radiations	(iii)	$10^{-2}\,m$
(d)	X-rays	(iv)	$10^{-4}\,m$

Choose the **correct** answer from the options given below :
(A) (a) $\to$ (iii), (b) $\to$ (ii), (c) $\to$ (i), (d) $\to$ (iv)
(B) (a) $\to$ (iii), (b) $\to$ (iv), (c) $\to$ (ii), (d) $\to$ (i)
(C) (a) $\to$ (ii), (b) $\to$ (iii), (c) $\to$ (iv), (d) $\to$ (i)
(D) (a) $\to$ (iv), (b) $\to$ (iii), (c) $\to$ (ii), (d) $\to$ (i)

22.2 $\vec{E}, \vec{B}$ and $\vec{C}$ of Electromagnetic Wave

1. The velocity of electromagnetic wave is parallel to :
[NEET (UG) 2002]
(A) $\vec{B} \times \vec{E}$
(B) $\vec{E} \times \vec{B}$
(C) $\vec{E}$
(D) $\vec{B}$

2. The electric and magnetic field of an electromagnetic wave are : **[NEET (UG) 2007]**
(A) In opposite phase and perpendicular to each other
(B) In opposite phase and parallel to each other
(C) In phase and perpendicular to each other
(D) In phase and parallel to each other

3. The velocity of electromagnetic radiation in a medium of permittivity ε_0 and permeability μ_0 is given by :
[NEET (UG) 2008]
(A) $\dfrac{1}{\sqrt{\mu_0 \varepsilon_0}}$
(B) $\sqrt{\dfrac{\mu_0}{\varepsilon_0}}$
(C) $\sqrt{\dfrac{\varepsilon_0}{\mu_0}}$
(D) $\sqrt{\mu_0 \varepsilon_0}$

4. The electric field part of an electromagnetic wave in a medium is represented by : **[NEET (UG) 2009]**

$E_x = 0$

$$E_y = 2.5 \frac{N}{C} \cos\left[\left(2\pi \times 10^6 \frac{rad}{m}\right)t - \left(\pi \times 10^{-2} \frac{rad}{s}\right)x\right]$$

$E_z = 0$

This electromagnetic wave is :

(A) Moving along $-x$-direction with frequency 10^6 Hz and wavelength 200 m

(B) Moving along y-direction with frequency $2\pi \times 10^6$ Hz and wavelength 200 m

(C) Moving along x-direction with frequency 10^6 Hz and wavelength 100 m

(D) Moving along x-direction with frequency 10^6 Hz and wavelength 200 m

5. The electric and the magnetic field, associated with an electromagnetic wave propagating along the $+z$-axis, can be represented by : **[NEET (UG) 2011]**

(A) $[\vec{E} = E_0\hat{i}, \vec{B} = B_0\hat{j}]$ (B) $[\vec{E} = E_0\hat{k}, \vec{B} = B_0\hat{i}]$

(C) $[\vec{E} = E_0\hat{j}, \vec{B} = B_0\hat{i}]$ (D) $[\vec{E} = E_0\hat{j}, \vec{B} = B_0\hat{k}]$

6. The electric field associated with an electromagnetic wave in vacuum is given by $\vec{E} = \hat{i}\, 40\cos(kz - 6 \times 10^8 t)$, where E, z and t are in V/m, meter and second respectively. The value of wave vector k is : **[NEET (UG) 2012]**

(A) $2\,m^{-1}$ (B) $0.5\,m^{-1}$

(C) $6\,m^{-1}$ (D) $3\,m^{-1}$

7. The ratio of amplitude of magnetic field to the amplitude of electric field for an electromagnetic wave propagating in vacuum is equal to : **[NEET (UG) 2012]**

(A) Reciprocal of speed of light in vacuum

(B) The ratio of magnetic permeability to the electric susceptibility of vacuum

(C) Unity

(D) The speed of light in vacuum

8. In an electromagnetic wave in free space the root mean square value of the electric field is $E_{rms} = 6$ V/m. The peak value of the magnetic field is : **[NEET (UG) 2017]**

(A) 1.41×10^{-8} T   (B) 2.83×10^{-8} T

(C) 0.70×10^{-8} T   (D) 4.23×10^{-8} T

9. An electromagnetic wave is propagating in a medium with a velocity $\vec{V} = V\hat{i}$. The instantaneous oscillating electric field of this em wave is along $+y$-axis. Then the direction of oscillating magnetic field of the electromangetic wave will be along : **[NEET (UG) 2018]**

(A) $-y$ direction   (B) $+z$ direction

(C) $-z$ direction   (D) $-x$ direction

10. The ratio of contributions made by the electric field and magnetic field components to the intensity of an electromagnetic wave is : (c = speed of electromagnetic waves) **[NEET (UG) 2020]**

(A) $1 : c^2$ (B) $c : 1$

(C) $1 : 1$ (D) $1 : c$

11. A capacitor of capacitance 'C', is connected across as ac source of voltage V given by

$$V = V_0 \sin \omega t$$

The displacement current between the plates of the capacitor, would then be given by : **[NEET (UG) 2021]**

(A) $I_d = V_0 \omega C \cos\omega t$ (B) $I_d = \dfrac{V_0}{\omega C} \cos\omega t$

(C) $I_d = \dfrac{V_0}{\omega C} \sin\omega t$ (D) $I_d = V_0 \omega C \sin\omega t$

12. For a plane electromagnetic wave propagating in x-direction, which one of the following combination gives the correct possible directions for electric field (E) and magnetic field (B) respectively ? **[NEET (UG) 2021]**

(A) $\hat{j} + \hat{k}, \hat{j} + \hat{k}$ (B) $-\hat{j} + \hat{k}, -\hat{j} - \hat{k}$

(C) $\hat{j} + \hat{k}, -\hat{j} - \hat{k}$ (D) $-\hat{j} + \hat{k}, -\hat{j} + \hat{k}$

13. When light propagates through a material medium of relative permittivity $\in_r$ and relative permeability μ_r, the velocity of light, v is given by : (c-velocity of light in vacuum) : **[NEET (UG) 2022]**

(A) $v = \sqrt{\dfrac{\mu_r}{\in_r}}$ (B) $v = \sqrt{\dfrac{\in_r}{\mu_r}}$

(C) $v = \dfrac{c}{\sqrt{\in_r \mu_r}}$ (D) $v = c$

*   *   *   *   *

23 RAY OPTICS AND OPTICAL INSTRUMENTS

23.1 Geometrical Optics I - Reflection of Light

1. A rod of length 10 cm lies along the principal axis of concave mirror of focal length 10 cm in such a way that its end closer to the pole is 20 cm away from the mirror. The length of the image is : **[NEET (UG) 2012]**
(A) 15 cm   (B) 2.5 cm
(C) 5 cm   (D) 10 cm

2. Match the corresponding entries of column-1 with column-2. [Where m is the magnification produced by the mirror] : **[NEET (UG) 2016]**

Column-1	Column-2
(i) $m = -2$	(a) Convex mirror
(ii) $m = -\dfrac{1}{2}$	(b) Concave mirror
(iii) $m = +2$	(c) Real image
(iv) $m = +\dfrac{1}{2}$	(d) Virtual image

(A) (i) → (b) and (c); (ii) → (b) and (c); (iii) → (b) and (d); (iv) → (a) and (d)
(B) (i) → (a) and (c); (ii) → (a) and (d); (iii) → (a) and (b); (iv) → (c) and (d)
(C) (i) → (a) and (d); (ii) → (b) and (c); (iii) → (b) and (d); (iv) → (b) and (c)
(D) (i) → (c) and (d); (ii) → (b) and (d); (iii) → (b) and (c); (iv) → (a) and (d)

3. A beam of light from a source L is incident normally on a plane mirror fixed at a certain distance x from the source. The beam is reflected back as a spot on a scale placed just above the source L. When the mirror is rotated through a small angle θ, the spot of the light is found to move through a distance y on the scale. The angle θ is given by : **[NEET (UG) 2017]**

(A) $\dfrac{y}{2x}$ (B) $\dfrac{y}{x}$

(C) $\dfrac{x}{2y}$ (D) $\dfrac{x}{y}$

4. An object is placed at a distance of 40 cm from a concave mirror of focal length 15 cm. If the object is displaced through a distance of 20 cm towards the mirror, the displacement of the image will be : **[NEET (UG) 2018]**

(A) 30 cm towards the mirror
(B) 36 cm away from the mirror
(C) 30 cm away from the mirror
(D) 36 cm towards the mirror

23.2 Geometrical Optics II - Refraction of Light

1. A ray of light travelling in air have wavelength λ, frequency n, velocity v and intensity I. If this ray enters into water then these parameters are λ', n', v' and I' respectively. Which relation is correct from following ? **[NEET (UG) 2001]**
(A) $\lambda = \lambda'$ (B) $n = n'$
(C) $v = v'$ (D) $I = I'$

2. Optical fibre are based on : **[NEET (UG) 2001]**
(A) Total internal reflection   (B) Less scattering
(C) Refraction   (D) Less absorption coefficient

3. A disc is placed on a surface of pond which has refractive index 5/3. A source of light is placed 4 m below the surface of liquid. The minimum radius of disc needed so that light is not coming out is : **[NEET (UG) 2001]**
(A) ∞   (B) 3m
(C) 6m   (D) 4m

4. For the given incident ray as shown in figure, the condition of total internal reflection of this ray, the required refractive index of prism will be : **[NEET (UG) 2002]**

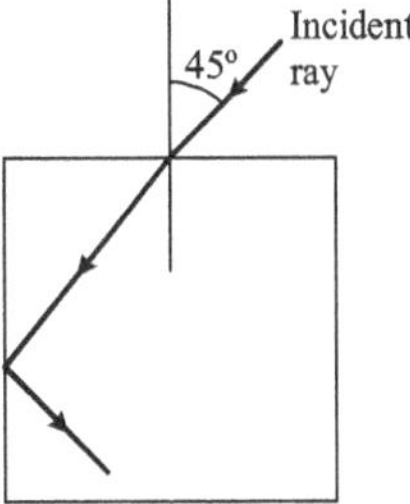

(A) $\dfrac{\sqrt{3}+1}{2}$ (B) $\dfrac{\sqrt{2}+1}{2}$

(C) $\sqrt{\dfrac{3}{2}}$ (D) $\sqrt{\dfrac{7}{6}}$

5. A bulb is located on a wall. Its image is to be obtained on a parallel wall with the help of convex lens. The lens is placed at a distance d ahead of second wall, then required focal length will be : **[NEET (UG) 2002]**

(A) Only $d/4$

(B) Only $d/2$

(C) More than $d/4$ but less than $d/2$

(D) Less than $d/4$

6. An equiconvex lens is cut into two halves along (i) XOX' and (ii) YOY' as shown in the figure. Let f, f', f'' be the focal lengths of the complete lens, of each half in case (i), and of each half in case (ii), respectively. Choose the correct statement from the following : **[NEET (UG) 2003]**

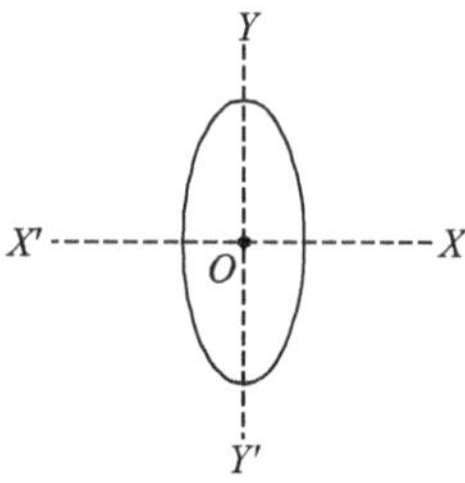

(A) $f'=f, f''=2f$

(B) $f'=2f, f''=f$

(C) $f'=f, f''=f$

(D) $f'=2f, f''=2f$

7. A convex lens is dipped in a liquid whose refractive index is equal to the refractive index of the lens. Then its focal length will : **[NEET (UG) 2003]**

(A) Become zero

(B) Become Infinite

(C) Become small, but non-zero

(D) Remain unchanged

8. The refractive index of the material of a prism is $\sqrt{2}$ and its refracting angle is 30°. One of the refracting surfaces of the prism is made a mirror inwards. A beam of monochromatic light entering the prism from the other face will retrace its path after reflection form the mirrored surface if its angle of incidence on the prism is : **[NEET (UG) 2004]**

(A) 60°

(B) 0°

(C) 30°

(D) 45°

9. The frequency of a light wave in a material is 2×10^{14} Hz and wavelength is 5000 Å. The refractive index of material will be : **[NEET (UG) 2007]**

(A) 1.50

(B) 3.00

(C) 1.33

(D) 1.40

10. A small coin is resting on the bottom of a beaker filled with a liquid. A specific ray of light shown in figure from the coin travels upto the surface of the liquid and moves along its surface. How fast is the light travelling in the liquid ? **[NEET (UG) 2007]**

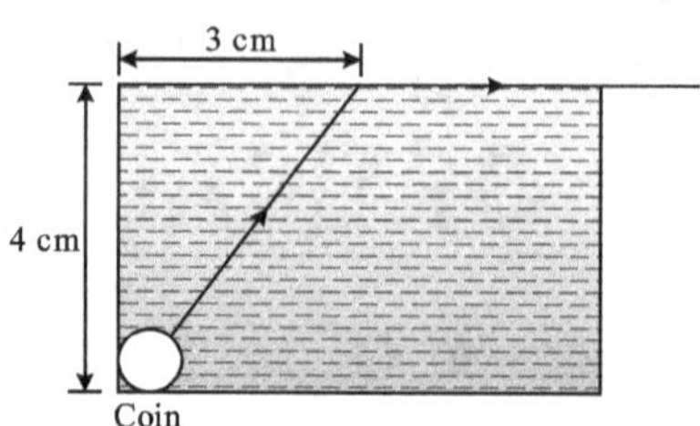

(A) 2.4×10^8 m/s

(B) 3.0×10^8 m/s

(C) 1.2×10^8 m/s

(D) 1.8×10^8 m/s

11. A ray of light travelling in a transparent medium of refractive index μ, falls on a surface separating the medium from air at an angle of incidence of 45°. For which of the following value of μ the ray can undergo total internal reflection ? **[NEET (UG) 2010]**

(A) $\mu = 1.25$

(B) $\mu = 1.33$

(C) $\mu = 1.40$

(D) $\mu = 1.50$

12. Which of the following is not due to total internal reflection ? **[NEET (UG) 2011]**

(A) Working of optical fibre

(B) Difference between apparent and real depth of pond

(C) Mirage on hot summer days

(D) Brilliance of diamond

13. A ray of light is incident at an angle of incidence i, on one face of prism of angle A (assumed to be small) and emerges normally from the opposite face. If the refractive index of the prism is μ, the angle of incidence i, is nearly equal to : **[NEET (UG) 2012]**

(A) μA

(B) $\mu A/2$

(C) A/μ

(D) $A/2\mu$

14. The angle of a prism is A. One of its refracting surfaces is silvered. Light rays falling at an angle of incidence $2A$ on the first surface returns back through the same path after suffering reflection at the silvered surface. The refractive index μ, of the prism is : **[NEET (UG) 2014]**

(A) $2 \sin A$

(B) $2 \cos A$

(C) $1/2 \cos A$

(D) $\tan A$

15. The angle of incidence for a ray of light at a refracting surface of a prism is 45°. The angle of prism is 60°. If the ray suffers minimum deviation through the prism, the angle of minimum deviation and refractive index of the material of the prism respectively, are : **[NEET (UG) 2016]**

(A) $45°; \dfrac{1}{\sqrt{2}}$

(B) $30°; \sqrt{2}$

(C) $45°; \sqrt{2}$

(D) $30°; \dfrac{1}{\sqrt{2}}$

16. An air bubble in a glass slab with refractive index 1.5 (near normal incidence) is 5 cm deep when viewed from one surface and 3 cm deep when viewed from the opposite face. The thickness (in cm) of the slab is :   **[NEET (UG) 2016 Ph. II]**
(A) 8   (B) 10
(C) 12   (D) 16

17. Two identical glass ($\mu_g = 3/2$) equiconvex lenses of focal length f each are kept in contact. The space between the two lenses is filled with water ($\mu_w = 4/3$). The focal length of the combination is :   **[NEET (UG) 2016 Ph. II]**

(A) $\dfrac{f}{3}$ (B) f

(C) $\dfrac{4f}{3}$ (D) $\dfrac{3f}{4}$

18. The refractive index of the material of a prism is $\sqrt{2}$ and the angle of the prism is 30°. One of the two refracting surfaces of the prism is made a mirror inwards, by silver coating. A beam of monochromatic light entering the prism from the other face will retrace its path (after reflection from the silvered surface) if its angle of incidence on the prism is :   **[NEET (UG) 2018]**
(A) 30°   (B) 45°
(C) 60°   (D) Zero

19. In total internal reflection when the angle of incidence is equal to the critical angle for the pair of media in contact, what will be angle of refraction ?   **[NEET (UG) 2019]**
(A) 180°
(B) 0°
(C) Equal to angle of incidence
(D) 90°

20. A ray is incident at an angle of incidence i on one surface of a small angle prism (with angle of prism A) and emerges normally from the opposite surface. If the refractive index of the material of the prism is μ, then the angle of incidence is nearly equal to :   **[NEET (UG) 2020]**
(A) $\mu A/2$ (B) $A/2\mu$
(C) $2A/\mu$ (D) μA

21. Find the value of the angle of emergence from the prism. Refractive index of the glass is $\sqrt{3}$.   **[NEET (UG) 2021]**
(A) 60°
(B) 30°
(C) 45°
(D) 90°

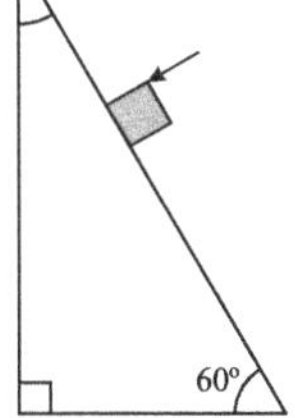

22. A light ray falls on a glass surface of refractive index $\sqrt{3}$, at an angle 60°. The angle between the refracted and reflected rays would be :   **[NEET (UG) 2022]**
(A) 60°   (B) 90°
(C) 120°   (D) 30°

23. Two transparent media A and B are separa ted by a plane boundary. The speed of light in those media are 1.5×10^8 m/s and 2.0×10^8 m/s, respectively. The critical angle for a ray of light for these two media is :   **[NEET (UG) 2022]**
(A) $\sin^{-1}(0.750)$ (B) $\tan^{-1}(0.500)$
(C) $\tan^{-1}(0.750)$ (D) $\sin^{-1}(0.500)$

23.3 Geometrical Optics III - Thin Lenses

1. A convex lens and a concave lens, each having same focal length of 25 cm, are put in contact to form a combination of lenses. The power in diopters of the combination is :
          [NEET (UG) 2006]
(A) 25   (B) 50
(C) Infinite   (D) Zero

2. A boy is trying to start a fire by focusing Sunlight on a piece of paper using an equiconvex lens of focal length 10 cm. The diameter of the Sun is 1.39×10^9 m and its mean distance from the earth is 1.5×10^{11} m. What is the diameter of the Sun's image on the paper ?   **[NEET (UG) 2008]**
(A) 6.5×10^{-5} m   (B) 12.4×10^{-4} m
(C) 9.2×10^{-4} m   (D) 6.5×10^{-4} m

3. Two thin lenses of focal lengths f_1 and f_2 are in contact and coaxial. The power of the combination is :   **[NEET (UG) 2008]**

(A) $\dfrac{f_1 + f_2}{2}$ (B) $\dfrac{f_1 + f_2}{f_1 f_2}$

(C) $\sqrt{\dfrac{f_1}{f_2}}$ (D) $\sqrt{\dfrac{f_2}{f_1}}$

4. A lens having focal length f and aperture of diameter d forms an image of intensity I. Aperture of diameter $d/2$ in central region of lens is covered by a black paper. Focal length of lens and intensity of image now will be respectively :
          [NEET (UG) 2010]

(A) $\dfrac{f}{2}$ and $\dfrac{I}{2}$ (B) f and $\dfrac{I}{4}$

(C) $\dfrac{3f}{4}$ and $\dfrac{I}{2}$ (D) f and $\dfrac{3I}{4}$

5. A biconvex lens has a radius of curvature of magnitude 20 cm. Which one of the following options best describe the image formed of an object of height 2 cm placed 30 cm from the lens ? **[NEET (UG) 2011]**

(A) Virtual, upright, height = 1 cm
(B) Virtual, upright, height = 0.5 cm
(C) Real, inverted, height = 4 cm
(D) Real, inverted, height = 1 cm

6. When a biconvex lens of glass having refractive index 1.47 is dipped in a liquid, it acts as a plane sheet of glass. This implies that the liquid must have refractive index : **[NEET (UG) 2012]**

(A) Equal to that of glass   (B) Less then one
(C) Greater than that of glass (D) Less then that of glass

7. A concave mirror of focal length 'f_1' is placed at a distance of 'd' from a convex lens of focal length 'f_2' A beam of light coming from infinity and falling on this convex lens-concave mirror combination returns to infinity. The distance 'd' must equal : **[NEET (UG) 2012]**

(A) $f_1 + f_2$ (B) $-f_1 + f_2$
(C) $2f_1 + f_2$ (D) $-2f_1 + f_2$

8. A plano convex lens fits exactly into a plano concave lens. Their plane surfaces are parallel to each other. If lenses are made of different materials of refractive indices μ_1 and μ_2 and R is the radius of curvature of the curved surface of the lenses, then the focal length of the combination is : **[NEET (UG) 2013]**

(A) $\dfrac{R}{2(\mu_1 + \mu_2)}$ (B) $\dfrac{R}{2(\mu_1 - \mu_2)}$

(C) $\dfrac{R}{(\mu_1 - \mu_2)}$ (D) $\dfrac{2R}{(\mu_2 - \mu_1)}$

9. Two similar thin equiconvex lenses, of focal length f each, are kept coaxially in contact with each other such that the focal length of the combination is F_1. When the space between the two lenses is filled with glycerine (which has the same refractive index ($\mu = 1.5$) as that of glass) then the equivalent focal length is F_2. The ratio $F_1 : F_2$ will be : **[NEET (UG) 2019]**

(A) 2 : 1   (B) 1 : 2
(C) 2 : 3   (D) 3 : 4

10. A convex lens 'A' of focal length 20 cm and a concave lens 'B' of focal 5 cm are kept along the same axis with a distance 'd' between them. If a parallel beam of light falling on 'A' leaves 'B' as a parallel beam, then the distance 'd' in cm will be : **[NEET (UG) 2021]**

(A) 25   (B) 15
(C) 50   (D) 30

11. A point object is placed at a distance of 60 cm from a convex lens of focal length 30 cm. If a plane mirror were put perpendicular

to the principal axis of the lens and at a distance of 40 cm from it, the final image would be formed at a distance of : **[NEET (UG) 2021]**

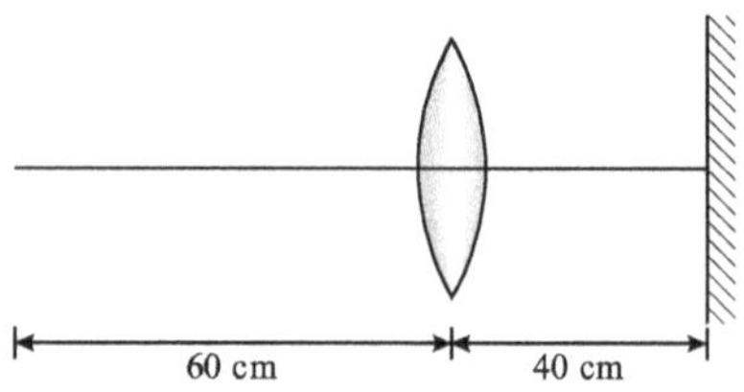

(A) 20 cm from the lens; it would be a real image
(B) 30 cm from the lens, it would be a real image
(C) 30 cm from the plane mirror, it would be a virtual image
(D) 20 cm from the plane mirror, it would be a virtual image

12. A biconvex lens has radii of curvature, 20 cm each. If the refractive index of the material of the lens is 1.5, the power of the lens is : **[NEET (UG) 2022]**

(A) +20 D   (B) +5 D
(C) Infinity   (D) +2 D

23.4 Dispersion of Light

1. A beam of light composed of red and green ray is incident obliquely at a point on the face of rectangular glass slab. When coming out on the opposite parallel face, the red and green ray emerge from : **[NEET (UG) 2004]**

(A) Two points propagating in two different non parallel directions
(B) Two points propagating in two different parallel directions
(C) One point propagating in two different directions
(D) One point propagating in the same directions

2. For the angle of minimum deviation of a prism to be equal to its refracting angle, the prism must be made of a material whose refractive index : **[NEET (UG) 2012]**

(A) lies between 2 and $\sqrt{2}$ (B) is less than 1

(C) is greater than 2   (D) lies between $\sqrt{2}$ and 1

3. A beam of light consisting of red, green and blue colours is incident on a right angled prism. The refractive index of the material of the prism for the above red, green and blue wavelengths are 1.39, 1.44 and 1.47, respectively. The prism will : **[NEET (UG) 2015]**

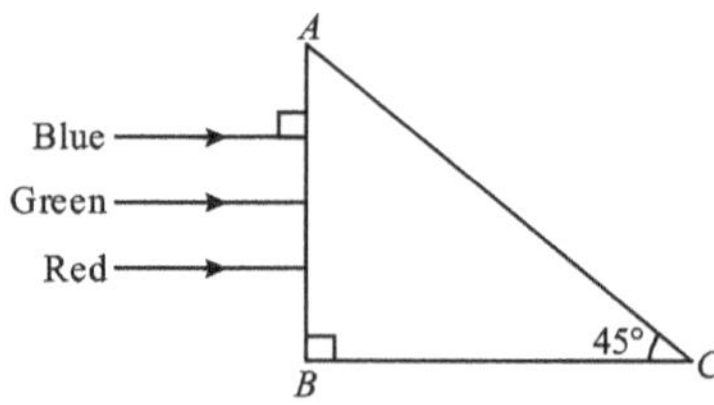

(A) Separate the red colour part from the green and blue colours

(B) Separate the blue colour part from the red and green colours
(C) Separate all three colours from one another
(D) Not separate the three colours at all

4. A thin prism having refracting angle $10°$ is made of glass of refractive index 1.42. This prism is combined with another thin prism of glass of refractive index 1.7. This combination produces dispersion without deviation. The refracting angle of second prism should be : **[NEET (UG) 2017]**

(A) $4°$ (B) $6°$
(C) $8°$ (D) $10°$

5. Which colour of the light has the longest wavelength ?
[NEET (UG) 2019]

(A) Red   (B) Blue
(C) Green   (D) Violet

6. Pick the wrong answer in the context with rainbow :
[NEET (UG) 2019]
(A) When the light rays undergo two internal reflections in a water drop, a secondary rainbow is formed
(B) The order of colours is reversed in the secondary rainbow
(C) An observer can see a rainbow when his front is towards the sun
(D) Rainbow is a combined effect of dispersion refraction and reflection of sunlight

23.5 Optical Instruments

1. Diameter of human eye lens is 2 mm. What will be the minimum distance between two points to resolve them, which are situated at a distance of 50 meter from eye ? (The wavelength of light is 5000 Å) : **[NEET (UG) 2002]**

(A) 2.32 m   (B) 4.28 mm
(C) 1.25 cm   (D) 12.48 cm

2. A telescope has an objective lens of 10 cm diameter and is situated at a distance of one kilometre from two objects. The minimum distance between these two objects, which can be resolved by the telescope, when the mean wavelength of light is 5000 Å, is of the order of : **[NEET (UG) 2004]**

(A) 0.5 cm   (B) 5 m
(C) 5 mm   (D) 5 cm

3. The angular resolution of a 10 cm diameter telescope at a wavelength of 5000 Å is of the order of : **[NEET (UG) 2005]**

(A) 10^{-4} rad   (B) 10^{-6} rad
(C) 10^{6} rad   (D) 10^{-2} rad

4. A microscope is focused on a mark on a piece of paper and then a slab of glass of thickness 3 cm and refractive index 1.5 is placed over the mark. How should the microscope be moved to get the mark in focus again : **[NEET (UG) 2006]**

(A) 1 cm upward   (B) 4.5 cm downward
(C) 1 cm downward   (D) 2 cm upward

5. The magnifying power of a telescope is 9. When it is adjusted for parallel rays the distance between the objective and eyepiece is 20 cm. The focal length of lenses are : **[NEET (UG) 2012]**

(A) 10 cm, 10 cm   (B) 15 cm, 5 cm
(C) 18 cm, 2 cm   (D) 11 cm, 9 cm

6. For a normal eye, the cornea of eye provides a converging power of 40 D and the least converging power of the eye lens behind the cornea is 20 D. Using this information, the distance between the retina and the cornea eye lens can be estimated to be : **[NEET (UG) 2013]**

(A) 5 cm   (B) 2.5 cm
(C) 1.67 cm   (D) 1.5 cm

7. If the focal length of objective lens is increased then magnifying power of : **[NEET (UG) 2014]**
(A) Microscope will increase but that of telescope decrease
(B) Microscope and telescope both will increase
(C) Microscope and telescope both will decrease
(D) Microscope will decrease but that of telescope will increase

8. In an astronomical telescope in normal adjustment a straight black line of length L is drawn on inside part of objective lens. The eyepiece forms a real image of this line. The length of this image is l. The magnification of the telescope is : **[NEET (UG) 2015]**

(A) $\dfrac{L}{l}$ (B) $\dfrac{L}{l} + 1$

(C) $\dfrac{L}{l} - 1$ (D) $\dfrac{L+l}{L-l}$

9. An astronomical telescope has objective and eyepiece of focal length 40 cm and 4 cm respectively. To view an object 200 cm away from the objective, the lenses must be separated by a distance : **[NEET (UG) 2016]**
(A) 37.3 cm   (B) 46.0 cm
(C) 50.0 cm   (D) 54.0 cm

10. A person can see clearly objects only when they lie between 50 cm and 400 cm from his eyes. In order to increase the maximum distance of distinct vision to infinity, the type and power of the correcting lens, the person has to use, will be : **[NEET (UG) 2016 Ph. II]**
(A) convex, + 2.25 diopter   (B) concave, – 0.25 diopter
(C) concave, – 0.2 diopter   (D) convex, + 0.15 diopter

11. The ratio of resolving powers of an optical microscope for two wavelengths $\lambda_1 = 4000$ Å and $\lambda_2 = 6000$ Å is : **[NEET (UG) 2017]**

(A) 8 : 27
(B) 9 : 4
(C) 3 : 2
(D) 16 : 81

12. An astronomical refracting telescope will have large angular magnification and high angular resolution, when it has an objective lens of :   **[NEET (UG) 2018]**
(A) Large focal length and large diameter
(B) Large focal length and small diameter
(C) Small focal length and large diameter
(D) Small focal length and small diameter

13. Assume that light of wavelength 600 nm is coming from a star. The limit of resolution of telescope whose objective has a diameter of 2 m is :   **[NEET (UG) 2020]**
(A) 6.00×10^{-7} rad
(B) 3.66×10^{-7} rad
(C) 1.83×10^{-7} rad
(D) 7.32×10^{-7} rad

14. A lens of large focal length and large aperture is best suited as an objective of an astronomical telescope since :   **[NEET (UG) 2021]**
(A) a large aperture contributes to the quality and visibility of the images
(B) a large area of the objective ensures better light gathering power
(C) a large aperture provides a better resolution
(D) all of the above

*   *   *   *   *

24 WAVE OPTICS

24.1 Interference

1. In Young's double slit experiment, the slits are 2 mm apart and are illuminated by photons of two wavelengths $\lambda_1 = 12000$ Å and $\lambda_2 = 10000$ Å. At what minimum distance from the common central bright fringe on the screen 2 m from the slit will a bright fringe from one interference pattern coincide with a bright fringe from the other ? **[NEET (UG) 2013]**

(A) 8mm   (B) 6mm

(C) 4mm   (D) 3mm

2. In the Young's double-slit experiment, the intensity of light at a point on the screen where the path difference is λ is K, (λ being the wavelength of light used). The intensity at a point where the path difference is $\lambda/4$, will be : **[NEET (UG) 2014]**

(A) K (B) $K/4$

(C) $K/2$ (D) Zero

3. Two slits in Young's experiment have widths in the ratio $1 : 25$. The ratio of intensity at the maxima and minima in the interference pattern, $\dfrac{I_{max}}{I_{min}}$ is : **[NEET (UG) 2015]**

(A) $\dfrac{4}{9}$ (B) $\dfrac{9}{4}$

(C) $\dfrac{121}{49}$ (D) $\dfrac{49}{121}$

4. The intensity at the maximum in a Young's double slit experiment is I_0. Distance between two slits is $d = 5\lambda$, where λ is the wavelength of light used in the experiment. What will be the intensity in front of one of the slits on the screen placed at a distance $D = 10\,d$? **[NEET (UG) 2016]**

(A) I_0 (B) $\dfrac{I_0}{4}$

(C) $\dfrac{3}{4}I_0$ (D) $\dfrac{I_0}{2}$

5. The interference pattern is obtained with two coherent light sources of intensity ratio n. In the interference pattern, the ratio $\dfrac{I_{max} - I_{min}}{I_{max} + I_{min}}$ will be : **[NEET (UG) 2016 Ph. II]**

(A) $\dfrac{\sqrt{n}}{n+1}$ (B) $\dfrac{2\sqrt{n}}{n+1}$

(C) $\dfrac{\sqrt{n}}{(n+1)^2}$ (D) $\dfrac{2\sqrt{n}}{(n+1)^2}$

6. Young's double slit experiment is first performed in air and then in a medium other than air. It is found that 8th bright fringe in the medium lies where 5th dark fringe lies in air. The refractive index of the medium is nearly : **[NEET (UG) 2017]**

(A) 1.25   (B) 1.59

(C) 1.69   (D) 1.78

7. In Young's double slit experiment the separation d between the slits is 2 mm, the wavelength λ of the light used is 5896 Å and distance D between the screen and slits is 100 cm. It is found that the angular width of the fringes is 0.20°. To increase the fringe angular width to 0.21° (with same λ and D) the separation between the slits needs to be changed to : **[NEET (UG) 2018]**

(A) 2.1 mm   (B) 1.9 mm

(C) 1.8 mm   (D) 1.7 mm

8. In a double slit experiment, when light of wavelength 400 nm was used, the angular width of the first minima formed on a screen placed 1 m away, was found to be 0.2°. What will be the angular width of the first minima, if the entire experimental apparatus is immersed in water? ($\mu_{water} = 4/3$) : **[NEET (UG) 2019]**

(A) 0.266°   (B) 0.15°

(C) 0.05°   (D) 0.1°

9. In Young's double slit experiment, if the separation between coherent sources is halved and the distance of the screen from the coherent sources is doubled, then the fringe width becomes : **[NEET (UG) 2020]**

(A) One-fourth   (B) Double

(C) Half   (D) Four times

10. In a Young's double slit experiment, a student observes 8 fringes in a certain segment of screen when a monochromatic light of 600 nm wavelength is used. If the wavelength of light is changed to 400 nm, then the number of fringes he would observe in the same region of the screen is : **[NEET (UG) 2022]**

(A) 8   (B) 9

(C) 12   (D) 6

24.2 Diffraction

1. A beam of light of $\lambda = 600$ nm from a distant source falls on a single slit 1 mm wide and the resulting diffraction pattern is observed on a screen 2 m away. The distance between first dark fringes on either side of the central bright fringe is :

[NEET (UG) 2014]

(A) 1.2 cm   (B) 1.2 mm

(C) 2.4 cm   (D) 2.4 mm

2. At the first minimum adjacent to the central maximum of a single-slit diffraction pattern, the phase difference between the Huygen's wavelet from the edge of the slit and the wavelet from the midpoint of the slit is : **[NEET (UG) 2015]**

(A) $\dfrac{\pi}{8}$ radian   (B) $\dfrac{\pi}{4}$ radian

(C) $\dfrac{\pi}{2}$ radian   (D) π radian

3. In a diffraction pattern due to a single slit of width a, the first minimum is observed at an angle 30° when light of wavelength 5000 Å is incident on the slit. The first secondary maximum is observed at an angle of : **[NEET (UG) 2016]**

(A) $\sin^{-1}\left(\dfrac{1}{4}\right)$ (B) $\sin^{-1}\left(\dfrac{2}{3}\right)$

(C) $\sin^{-1}\left(\dfrac{1}{2}\right)$ (D) $\sin^{-1}\left(\dfrac{3}{4}\right)$

4. A linear aperture whose width is 0.02 cm is placed immediately in front of a lens of focal length 60 cm. The aperture is illuminated normally by a parallel beam of wavelength 5×10^{-5} cm. The distance of the first dark band of the diffraction pattern from the centre of the screen is :

[NEET (UG) 2016 Ph. II]

(A) 0.10 cm   (B) 0.25 cm

(C) 0.20 cm   (D) 0.15 cm

24.3 Polarization of Light

1. Which one of the following statements is true :

[NEET (UG) 2006]

(A) Both light and sound waves in air are transverse

(B) The sound waves in air are longitudinal while the light waves are transverse

(C) Both light and sound waves in air are longitudinal

(D) Both light and sound waves can travel in vacuum

2. Two Polaroids P_1 and P_2 are placed with their axis perpendicular to each other. Unpolarised light I_0 is incident on P_1. A third polaroid P_3 is kept in between P_1 and P_2 such that its axis makes an angle 45° with that of P_1. The intensity of transmitted light through P_2 is : **[NEET (UG) 2017]**

(A) $\dfrac{I_0}{2}$ (B) $\dfrac{I_0}{4}$

(C) $\dfrac{I_0}{8}$ (D) $\dfrac{I_0}{16}$

3. Unpolarised light is incident from air on a plane surface of a material of refractive index μ. At a particular angle of incidence i, it is found that the reflected and refracted rays are perpendicular to each other. Which of the following options is correct for this situation ? **[NEET (UG) 2018]**

(A) $i = \sin^{-1}\left(\dfrac{1}{\mu}\right)$

(B) Reflected light is polarised with its electric vector perpendicular to the plane of incidence

(C) Reflected light is polarised with its electric vector parallel to the plane of incidence

(D) $i = \tan^{-1}\left(\dfrac{1}{\mu}\right)$

4. The Brewsters angle i_b for an interface should be : **[NEET (UG) 2020]**

(A) $i_b = 90°$ (B) $0° < i_b < 30°$

(C) $30° < i_b < 45°$ (D) $45° < i_b < 90°$

* * * * *

CHAPTER 25
DUAL NATURE OF RADIATION, MATTER & X-RAY

25.1 Photoelectric Effect

1. A photocell is illuminated by a source of light, which is placed at a distance d from the cell. If the distance become $d/2$, then number of electrons emitted per second will be :

[NEET (UG) 2001]

(A) Remain same   (B) Four times

(C) Two times   (D) One-fourth

2. Which one among the following shows particle nature of light ? **[NEET (UG) 2001]**

(A) Photoelectric effect   (B) Interference

(C) Refraction   (D) Polarization

3. When ultraviolet rays incident on metal plate then photoelectric effect does not occur, it occurs by incidence of :

[NEET (UG) 2002]

(A) Infrared rays   (B) X-rays

(C) Radio wave   (D) micro wave

4. The value of Planck's constant is : **[NEET (UG) 2002]**

(A) 6.63×10^{-34} J/s   (B) 6.63×10^{-34} kg m^2/s

(C) 6.63×10^{-34} kg m^2 (D) 6.63×10^{-34} J s

5. A photoelectric cell is illuminated by a point source of light 1 m away. When the source is shifted to 2 m then :

[NEET (UG) 2003]

(A) Each emitted electron carries one quarter of the initial energy

(B) Number of electrons emitted is half the initial number

(C) Each emitted electron carries half the initial energy

(D) Number of electrons emitted is a quarter of the initial number

6. According to Einstein's photoelectric equation, the graph between the kinetic energy of photoelectrons ejected and the frequency of incident radiation is : **[NEET (UG) 2004]**

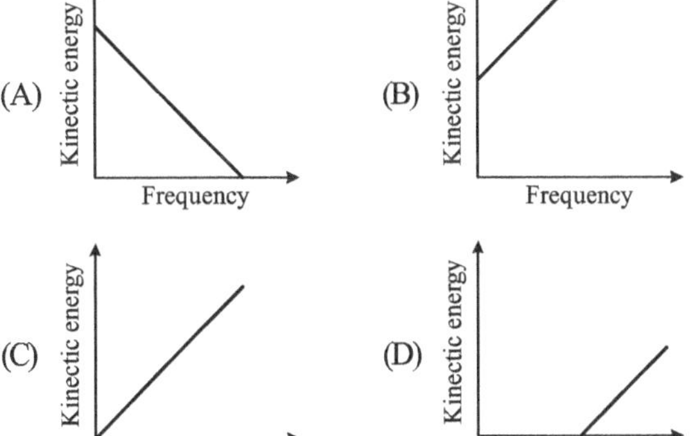

7. The work functions for metals A, B and C are respectively 1.92 eV, 2.0 eV and 5 eV. According to Einstein's equation, the metals which will emit photo electrons for a radiation of wavelength 4100 Å is/are : **[NEET (UG) 2005]**

(A) None   (B) A only

(C) A and B only   (D) All the three metals

8. A photosensitive metallic surface has work function, $h\nu_0$. If photons of energy $2\,h\nu_0$ fall on this surface, the electrons come out with a maximum velocity of 4×10^6 m/s. When the photon energy is increased to $5\,h\nu_0$, then maximum velocity of photo electrons will be : **[NEET (UG) 2005]**

(A) 2×10^7 m/s   (B) 2×10^6 m/s

(C) 8×10^5 m/s   (D) 8×10^6 m/s

9. A photo-cell employs photoelectric effect to convert : **[NEET (UG) 2006]**

(A) Change in the frequency of light into a change in electric voltage

(B) Change in the intensity of illumination into a change in photoelectric current

(C) Change in the intensity of illumination into a change in the work function of the photocathode

(D) Change in the frequency of light into a change in the electric current

10. When photons of energy $h\nu$ fall on an aluminium plate (of work function E_0), photoelectrons of maximum kinetic energy K are ejected. If the frequency of the radiation is doubled, the maximum kinetic energy of the ejected photoelectrons will be :

[NEET (UG) 2006]

(A) $K + E_0$ (B) $2\,K$

(C) K (D) $K + h\nu$

11. Monochromatic light of frequency 6.0×10^{14} Hz is produced by a laser. The power emitted is 2×10^{-3} W. The number of photons emitted, on the average, by the sources per second is : **[NEET (UG) 2007]**

(A) 5×10^{16} (B) 5×10^{17}

(C) 5×10^{14} (D) 5×10^{15}

12. A 5 W source emits monochromatic light of wavelength 5000 Å. When placed 0.5 m away, it liberates photoelectrons from a photosensitive metallic surface. When the source is moved to a distance of 1.0 m, the number of photoelectrons liberated will be reduced by a factor of : **[NEET (UG) 2007]**

(A) 8   (B) 16

(C) 2   (D) 4

13. In the phenomenon of electric discharge through gases at low pressure, the coloured glow in the tube appears as a result of : **[NEET (UG) 2008]**
(A) Collision between the charged particles emitted from the cathode and the atoms of the gas
(B) Collision between different electrons of the atoms of the
(C) Excitation of electrons in the atoms
(D) Collision between the atoms of the gas

14. The work function of a surface of photosensitive material is 6.2 eV. The wavelength of the incident radiation for which the stopping potential is 5 V lies in the : **[NEET (UG) 2008]**
(A) Infrared region
(B) X-ray region
(C) Ultraviolet region
(D) Visible region

15. The number of photoelectrons emitted for light of a frequency ν (higher than the threshold frequency ν_0) is proportional to : **[NEET (UG) 2009]**
(A) Frequency of light (ν)
(B) $\nu - \nu_0$
(C) Threshold frequency (ν_0)
(D) Intensity of light

16. The figure shows a plot of photo current versus anode potential for a photo sensitive surface for three different radiations. Which one of the following is a correct statement ? **[NEET (UG) 2009]**

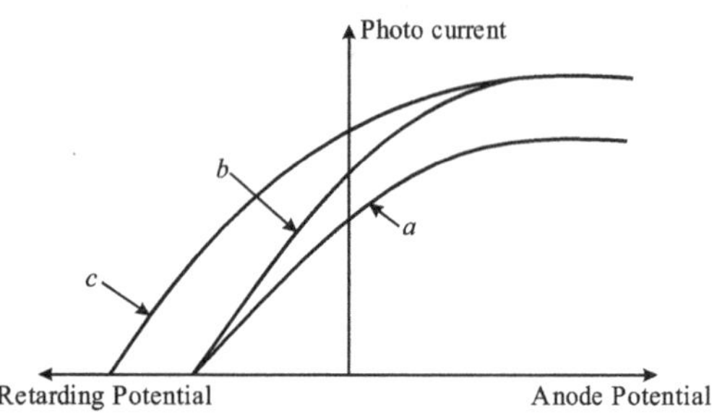

(A) Curves (b) and (c) represent incident radiations same frequencies having same intensity
(B) Curves (a) and (b) represent incident radiations of different frequencies and different intensities
(C) Curves (a) and (b) represent incident radiations of same frequencies but of different intensities
(D) Curves (b) and (c) represent incident radiations of different frequencies and different intensities

17. The potential difference that must be applied to stop the fastest photo electrons emitted by a nickel surface, having work function 5.01 eV, when ultraviolet light of 200 nm falls on it, must be : **[NEET (UG) 2010]**
(A) 1.2 V
(B) 2.4 V
(C) –1.2 V
(D) –2.4 V

18. Photoelectric emission occurs only when the incident light has more than a certain minimum : **[NEET (UG) 2011]**
(A) Power
(B) Wavelength
(C) Intensity
(D) Frequency

19. Light of two different frequencies whose photons have energies 1.0 eV and 2.5 eV respectively illuminate a metallic surface whose work function is 0.5 eV successively. Ratio of maximum speeds of emitted electrons will be : **[NEET (UG) 2011]**
(A) 1 : 4
(B) 1 : 2
(C) 1 : 1
(D) 1 : 5

20. In photoelectric emission process from a metal of work function 1.8 eV, the kinetic energy of most energetic electrons is 0.5 eV. The corresponding stopping potential is : **[NEET (UG) 2011]**
(A) 1.8 V
(B) 1.3 V
(C) 0.5 V
(D) 2.3 V

21. If the momentum of an electron is changed by P, then the de-Broglie wavelength associated with it changes by 0.5 %. The initial momentum of electron will be : **[NEET (UG) 2012]**
(A) 400 P
(B) $P/200$
(C) 100 P
(D) 200 P

22. Two radiations of photons energies 1 eV and 2.5 eV, successively illuminate a photosensitive metallic surface of work function 0.5 eV. The ratio of the maximum speeds of the emitted electrons is : **[NEET (UG) 2012]**
(A) 1 : 2
(B) 1 : 1
(C) 1 : 5
(D) 1 : 4

23. The value of Planck's constant is 6.63×10^{-34} Js. The speed of light is 3×10^{17} nm s^{-1}. Which value is closest to the wavelength in nanometer of a quantum of light with frequency of 6×10^{15} s^{-1} ? **[NEET (UG) 2013]**
(A) 10
(B) 25
(C) 50
(D) 75

24. When the energy of the incident radiation is increased by 20%, the kinetic energy of the photoelectrons emitted from a metal surface increased from 0.5 eV to 0.8 eV. The work function of the metal is : **[NEET (UG) 2014]**
(A) 0.65 eV
(B) 1.0 eV
(C) 1.3 eV
(D) 1.5 eV

25. A photoelectric surface is illuminated successively by monochromatic light of wavelength λ and $\lambda/2$. If the maximum kinetic energy of the emitted photoelectrons in the second case is 3 times that in the first case, the work function of the surface of the material is: (h = Planck's constant, c = speed of light) : **[NEET (UG) 2015]**
(A) $hc/3\lambda$
(B) $hc/2\lambda$
(C) hc/λ
(D) $2hc/\lambda$

26. When a metallic surface is illuminated with radiation of wavelength λ, the stopping potential is V. If the same surface is illuminated with radiation of wavelength 2λ, the stopping potential is $V/4$. The threshold wavelength for the metallic surface is : **[NEET (UG) 2016]**

(A) 4λ (B) 5λ

(C) $5/2\,\lambda$ (D) 3λ

27. Photons with energy 5 eV are incident on a cathode C in a photoelectric cell. The maximum energy of emitted photoelectrons is 2 eV. When photons of energy 6 eV are incident on C, no photoelectrons will reach the anode A, if the stopping potential of A relative to C is :

[NEET (UG) 2016 Ph. II]

(A) $+3\,V$ (B) $+4\,V$

(C) $-1\,V$ (D) $-3\,V$

28. The photoelectric threshold wavelength of silver is 3250×10^{-10} m. The velocity of the electron ejected from a silver surface by ultraviolet light of wavelength 2536×10^{-10} m is : (Given $h = 4.14 \times 10^{-15}$ eVs and $c = 3 \times 10^{8}$ ms^{-1}) :

[NEET (UG) 2017]

(A) $\approx 6 \times 10^{5}$ ms^{-1} (B) $\approx 0.6 \times 10^{6}$ ms^{-1}

(C) $\approx 61 \times 10^{3}$ ms^{-1} (D) $\approx 0.3 \times 10^{6}$ ms^{-1}

29. When the light of frequency $2\nu_0$ (where ν_0 is threshold frequency), is incident on a metal plate, the maximum velocity of electrons emitted is v_1. When the frequency of the incident radiation is increased to $5\nu_0$, the maximum velocity of electrons emitted from the same plate is v_2. The ratio of v_1 to v_2 is :

[NEET (UG) 2018]

(A) $4:1$ (B) $1:4$

(C) $1:2$ (D) $2:1$

30. Light of frequency 1.5 times the threshold frequency is incident on a photosensitive material. What will be the photoelectric current if the frequency is halved and intensity is doubled ? **[NEET (UG) 2020]**

(A) Zero   (B) Doubled

(C) Four times   (D) One-fourth

31. Light with an average flux of 20 W/cm^2 falls on a non-reflecting surface at normal incidence having surface area 20 cm^2. The energy received by the surface during time span of 1 minute is : **[NEET (UG) 2020]**

(A) 48×10^{3} J   (B) 10×10^{3} J

(C) 12×10^{3} J   (D) 24×10^{3} J

32. An electromagnetic wave of wavelength 'λ' is incident on a photosensitive surface of negligible work function. If 'm' mass is of photoelectron emitted from the surface has de-Broglie wavelength λ_d, then : **[NEET (UG) 2021]**

(A) $\lambda = \left(\dfrac{2m}{hc}\right)\lambda_d^2$ (B) $\lambda_d = \left(\dfrac{2mc}{h}\right)\lambda^2$

(C) $\lambda = \left(\dfrac{2mc}{h}\right)\lambda_d^2$ (D) $\lambda = \left(\dfrac{2h}{mc}\right)\lambda_d^2$

33. The number of photons per second on an average emitted by the source of monochromatic light of wavelength 600 nm, when it delivers the power of 3.3×10^{-3} watt will be : ($h = 6.6 \times 10^{-34}$ Js) **[NEET (UG) 2021]**

(A) 10^{18} (B) 10^{17}

(C) 10^{16} (D) 10^{15}

43. When two monochromatic lights of frequency, υ and $\dfrac{\upsilon}{2}$ are incident on a photoelectric metal, their stopping potential becomes $\dfrac{V_s}{2}$ and V_s respectively. The threshold frequency for this metal is : **[NEET (UG) 2022]**

(A) 3υ (B) $\dfrac{2}{3}\upsilon$

(C) $\dfrac{3}{2}\upsilon$ (D) 2υ

25.2 Matter Waves and X-Rays

1. The interplanar distance in a crystal is 2.8×10^{-8} m. The value of maximum wavelength which can be diffracted : **[NEET (UG) 2001]**

(A) 2.8×10^{-8} m   (B) 5.6×10^{-8} m

(C) 1.4×10^{-8} m   (D) 7.6×10^{-8} m

2. If particles are moving with same velocity, then which has maximum de-Broglie wavelength ? **[NEET (UG) 2002]**

(A) Proton   (B) α-particle

(C) Neutron   (D) β-particle

3. Which of the following is not the property of cathode rays ? **[NEET (UG) 2002]**

(A) It produces heating effect

(B) It does not deflect in electric field

(C) It casts shadow

(D) It produces fluorescence

4. J.J. Thomson's cathode-ray tube experiment demonstrated that : **[NEET (UG) 2003]**

(A) Cathode rays are streams of negatively charged ions

(B) All the mass of an atom is essentially in the nucleus

(C) The e/m of electrons is much greater than the e/m of protons

(D) The e/m ratio of the cathode-ray particles changes when a different gas is placed in the discharge tube

5. If λ_v, λ_x and λ_m represent the wavelengths of visible light, X-rays and microwaves respectively, then : **[NEET (UG) 2005]**
(A) $\lambda_m > \lambda_x > \lambda_v$
(B) $\lambda_v > \lambda_m > \lambda_x$
(C) $\lambda_v > \lambda_x > \lambda_m$
(D) $\lambda_m > \lambda_v > \lambda_x$

6. The momentum of a photon of energy 1 MeV in kg m/s, will be : **[NEET (UG) 2006]**
(A) 0.33×10^6
(B) 7×10^{-24}
(C) 10^{-22}
(D) 5×10^{-22}

7. A particle of mass 1 mg has the same wavelength as an electron moving with a velocity of 3×10^6 ms^{-1}. The velocity of the particle is : (mass of electron $= 9.1 \times 10^{-31}$ kg) : **[NEET (UG) 2008]**
(A) 3×10^{-31} ms^{-1}
(B) 2.7×10^{-21} ms^{-1}
(C) 2.7×10^{-18} ms^{-1}
(D) 9×10^{-2} ms^{-1}

8. Monochromatic light of wavelength 667 nm is produced by a helium neon laser. The power emitted is 9 mW. The number of photons arriving per second on the average at a target irradiated by this beam is : **[NEET (UG) 2009]**
(A) 3×10^{19}
(B) 9×10^{17}
(C) 3×10^{16}
(D) 9×10^{15}

9. A source S_1 is producing, 10^{15} photons per second of wavelength 5000 Å. Another source S_2 is producing 1.02×10^{15} photons per second of wavelength 5100 Å. Then ratio of power of source S_2 to power of source S_1 is equal to : **[NEET (UG) 2010]**
(A) 0.98
(B) 1.00
(C) 1.02
(D) 1.04

10. Electrons used in an electron microscope are accelerated by a voltage of 25 kV. If the voltage is increased to 100 kV then the de-Broglie wavelength associated with the electrons would : **[NEET (UG) 2011]**
(A) Increase by 2 times
(B) Decrease by 2 times
(C) Decrease by 4 times
(D) Increase by 4 times

11. In the Davisson and Germer experiment, the velocity of electrons emitted from the electron gun can be increased by : **[NEET (UG) 2011]**
(A) Increasing the potential difference between the anode and filament
(B) Increasing the filament current
(C) Decreasing the filament current
(D) Decreasing the potential difference between the anode and filament

12. The decreasing order of wavelength of infrared, microwave, ultraviolet and gamma rays is : **[NEET (UG) 2011]**
(A) Microwave, infrared, ultraviolet, gamma rays
(B) Gamma rays, ultraviolet, infrared, microwave
(C) Microwaves, gamma rays, infrared, ultraviolet
(D) Infrared, microwave, ultraviolet, gamma rays

13. A 200 W sodium street lamp emits yellow light of wavelength 0.6 μm. Assuming it to be 25% efficient in converting electrical energy to light, the number of photons of yellow light it emits per second is : **[NEET (UG) 2012]**
(A) 1.5×10^{20}
(B) 6×10^{18}
(C) 62×10^{20}
(D) 3×10^{19}

14. An α-particle moves in a circular path of radius 0.83 cm in the presence of a magnetic field of 0.25 Wb/m^2. The de-Broglie wavelength associated with the particle will be : **[NEET (UG) 2012]**
(A) 1 Å
(B) 0.1 Å
(C) 10 Å
(D) 0.01 Å

15. The wavelength λ_e of an electron and λ_p of a photon of same energy E are related by : **[NEET (UG) 2013]**
(A) $\lambda_p \propto \lambda_e^2$
(B) $\lambda_p \propto \lambda_e$
(C) $\lambda_p \propto \sqrt{\lambda_e}$
(D) $\lambda_p \propto \dfrac{1}{\sqrt{\lambda_e}}$

16. A parallel beam of fast moving electrons is incident normally on a narrow slit. A fluorescent screen is placed at a large distance from the slit. If the speed of the electrons is increased, which of the following statements is correct ? **[NEET (UG) 2013]**
(A) Diffraction pattern is not observed on the screen in the case of electrons
(B) The angular width of the central maximum of the diffraction pattern will increase
(C) The angular width of the central maximum will decrease
(D) The angular width of the central maximum will be unaffected

17. Light with an energy flux of 25×10^4 Wm^{-2} falls on a perfectly reflecting surface at normal incidence. If the surface area is 15 cm^2, the average force exerted on the surface is : **[NEET (UG) 2014]**
(A) 1.25×10^{-6} N
(B) 2.50×10^{-6} N
(C) 1.20×10^{-6} N
(D) 3.0×10^{-6} N

18. If the kinetic energy of the particle is increased to 16 times its previous value, the percentage change in the de-Broglie wavelength of the particle is : **[NEET (UG) 2014]**
(A) 25
(B) 75
(C) 60
(D) 50

19. Light of wavelength 500 nm is incident on a metal with work function 2.28 eV. The de-Broglie wavelength of the emitted electron is : **[NEET (UG) 2015]**
(A) $\leq 2.8 \times 10^{-12}$ m
(B) $< 2.8 \times 10^{-10}$ m
(C) $< 2.8 \times 10^{-9}$ m
(D) $\geq 2.8 \times 10^{-9}$ m

20. An electron of mass m and a photon have same energy E. The ratio of de-Broglie wavelengths associated with them is (c being velocity of light) : **[NEET (UG) 2016]**

(A) $\dfrac{1}{c}\left(\dfrac{E}{2m}\right)^{1/2}$

(B) $\left(\dfrac{E}{2m}\right)^{1/2}$

(C) $c(2mE)^{1/2}$

(D) $\dfrac{1}{c}\left(\dfrac{2m}{E}\right)^{1/2}$

21. Electrons of mass m with de-Broglie wavelength λ fall on the target in an X-ray tube. The cut off wavelength (λ_0) of the emitted X-ray is : **[NEET (UG) 2016 Ph. II]**

(A) $\lambda_0 = \dfrac{2mc\lambda^2}{h}$

(B) $\lambda_0 = \dfrac{2h}{mc}$

(C) $\lambda_0 = \dfrac{2m^2c^2\lambda^3}{h^2}$

(D) $\lambda_0 = \lambda$

22. The de-Broglie wavelength of a neutron in thermal equilibrium with heavy water at a temperature T (Kelvin) and mass m, is : **[NEET (UG) 2017]**

(A) $\dfrac{h}{\sqrt{mkT}}$

(B) $\dfrac{h}{\sqrt{3mkT}}$

(C) $\dfrac{2h}{\sqrt{3mkT}}$

(D) $\dfrac{2h}{\sqrt{mkT}}$

23. An electron of mass m with an initial velocity $\vec{V} = V_0\hat{i}$ ($V_0 > 0$) enters an electric field $\vec{E} = -E_0\hat{i}$ ($E_0 =$ constant > 0) at $t = 0$. If λ_0 is its de-Broglie wavelength initially, then its de-Broglie wavelength at time t is : **[NEET (UG) 2018]**

(A) $\lambda_0 t$

(B) $\lambda_0\left(1 + \dfrac{eE_0}{mV_0}t\right)$

(C) $\dfrac{\lambda_0}{\left(1 + \dfrac{eE_0}{mV_0}t\right)}$

(D) λ_0

24. An electron is accelerated through a potential difference of 10,000 V. Its de-Broglie wavelength is, (nearly) : ($m_e = 9 \times 10^{-31}$ kg) : **[NEET (UG) 2019]**

(A) 12.2×10^{-13} m

(B) 12.2×10^{-12} m

(C) 12.2×10^{-14} m

(D) 12.2 nm

25. An electron is accelerated from rest through a potential difference of V volt. If the de-Broglie wavelength of the electron is 1.227×10^{-2} nm, the potential difference is : **[NEET (UG) 2020]**

(A) 10^4 V

(B) 10 V

(C) 10^2 V

(D) 10^3 V

26. The graph which shows the variation of the de-Broglie wavelength (λ) of a particle and its associated momentum (p) is : **[NEET (UG) 2022]**

(A) 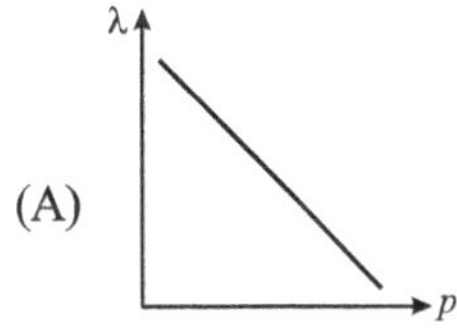

(B) 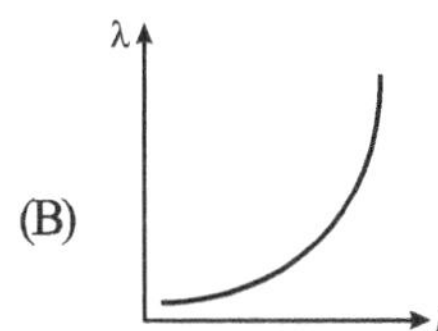

(C) 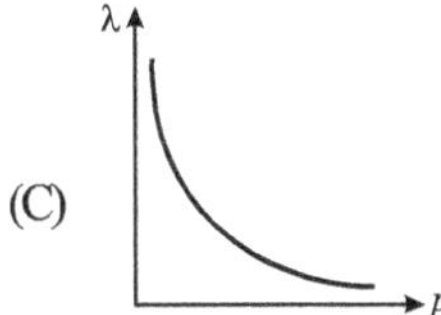

(D) 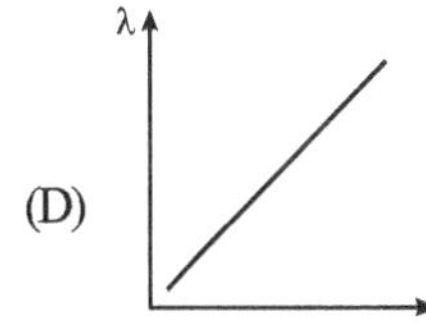

* * * * *

26 ATOMS

26.1 Properties of Electron in Bohr Model

1. The energy of hydrogen atom in n^{th} orbit is E_n then the energy in n^{th} orbit of singly ionised helium atom will be :

[NEET (UG) 2001]

(A) $4E_n$

(B) $E_n/4$

(C) $2E_n$

(D) $E_n/2$

2. In which of the following systems will the radius of the first orbit $(n=1)$ be minimum ? **[NEET (UG) 2003]**

(A) Doubly ionized lithium

(B) Singly ionized helium

(C) Deuterium atom

(D) Hydrogen atom

3. An electron is moving round the nucleus of a hydrogen atom in a circular orbit of radius r. The Coulomb force $\vec{F}$ between the two is : **[NEET (UG) 2003]**

(A) $K\dfrac{e^2}{r^2}\hat{r}$

(B) $-K\dfrac{e^2}{r^3}\hat{r}$

(C) $K\dfrac{e^2}{r^3}\vec{r}$

(D) $-K\dfrac{e^2}{r^3}\vec{r}$

4. The Bohr model of atoms : **[NEET (UG) 2004]**

(A) Assumes that the angular momentum of electrons is quantized

(B) Uses Einstein's photoelectric equation

(C) Predicts continuous emission spectra for atoms

(D) Predicts the same emission spectra for all types of atoms

5. The total energy of an electron in the first excited state of hydrogen atom is about -3.4 eV. Its kinetic energy in this state is : **[NEET (UG) 2005]**

(A) -6.8 eV

(B) 3.4 eV

(C) 6.8 eV

(D) -3.4 eV

6. The total energy of electron in the ground state of hydrogen atom is -13.6 eV. The kinetic energy of an electron in the first excited state is : **[NEET (UG) 2007]**

(A) 6.8 eV

(B) 13.6 eV

(C) 1.7 eV

(D) 3.4 eV

7. The ground state energy of hydrogen atom is -13.6 eV. When its electron is in the first excited state, its excitation energy is : **[NEET (UG) 2008]**

(A) 10.2 eV

(B) Zero

(C) 3.4 eV

(D) 6.8 eV

8. The energy of a hydrogen atom in the ground state is -13.6 eV. The energy of a He^+ ion in the first excited state will be : **[NEET (UG) 2010]**

(A) -6.8 eV

(B) -13.6 eV

(C) -27.2 eV

(D) -54.4 eV

9. What is the maximum numbers of electrons that can be associated with the following set of quantum numbers ? $n=3$, $l=1$ and $m=-1$ **[NEET (UG) 2013]**

(A) 10

(B) 6

(C) 4

(D) 2

10. The ratio of kinetic energy to the total energy of an electron in a Bohr orbit of the hydrogen atom, is : **[NEET (UG) 2018]**

(A) $2:-1$

(B) $1:-1$

(C) $1:1$

(D) $1:-2$

11. The total energy of an electron in an atom in an orbit is -3.4 eV. Its kinetic and potential energies are, respectively : **[NEET (UG) 2019]**

(A) -3.4 eV, -3.4 eV

(B) -3.4 eV, -6.8 eV

(C) 3.4 eV, -6.8 eV

(D) 3.4 eV, 3.4 eV

12. For which one of the following, Bohr model in not valid ? **[NEET (UG) 2020]**

(A) Singly ionised neon atom (Ne^+)

(B) Hydrogen atom

(C) Singly ionised helium atom (He^+)

(D) Deuteron atom

13. Let T_1 and T_2 be the energy of an electron in the first and second excited states of hydrogen atom, respectively. According to the Bohr's model of an atom, the ratio $T_1 : T_2$ is : **[NEET (UG) 2022]**

(A) $4:1$

(B) $4:9$

(C) $9:4$

(D) $1:4$

26.2 Electron Transition & Hydrogen Spectrum

1. Energy E of a hydrogen atom with principal quantum number n is given by $E = \dfrac{-13.6}{n^2}$ eV. The energy of a photon ejected when the electron jumps from $n=3$ state to $n=2$ state of hydrogen is approximately : **[NEET (UG) 2004]**

(A) 0.85 eV

(B) 3.4 eV

(C) 1.9 eV

(D) 1.5 eV

2. Energy levels A, B and C of a certain atom correspond to increasing values of energy i.e. $E_A < E_B < E_C$. If λ_1, λ_2 and λ_3 are wave lengths of radiations corresponding to transitions C to B, B to A and C to A respectively, which of the following relations is correct : **[NEET (UG) 2005]**
(A) $\lambda_3 = \lambda_1 + \lambda_2$
(B) $\lambda_1 + \lambda_2 + \lambda_3 = 0$
(C) $\lambda_3^2 = \lambda_1^2 + \lambda_2^2$
(D) $\lambda_3 = \dfrac{\lambda_1 \lambda_2}{\lambda_1 + \lambda_2}$

3. Ionization potential of hydrogen atom is 13.6 eV. Hydrogen atoms in the ground state are excited by monochromatic radiation of photon energy 12.1 eV. According to Bohr's theory, the spectral lines emitted by hydrogen will be : **[NEET (UG) 2006]**
(A) Two
(B) Three
(C) Four
(D) One

4. The ionization energy of the electron in the hydrogen atom in its grounds state is 13.6 eV. The atoms are excited to higher energy levels to emit radiations of 6 wavelengths. Maximum wavelength of emitted radiation corresponds to the transition between : **[NEET (UG) 2009]**
(A) $n = 4$ to $n = 3$ states
(B) $n = 3$ to $n = 2$ states
(C) $n = 3$ to $n = 1$ states
(D) $n = 2$ to $n = 1$ states

5. The wavelength of the first line of Lyman series for hydrogen atom is equal to that of the second line of Balmer series for a hydrogen like ion. The atomic number Z of hydrogen like ion is : **[NEET (UG) 2011]**
(A) 3
(B) 4
(C) 1
(D) 2

6. Electron in hydrogen atom first jumps from third excited state to second excited state and then from second excited to the first excited state. The ratio of the wavelength $\lambda_1 : \lambda_2$ emitted in the two cases is : **[NEET (UG) 2012]**
(A) 7/5
(B) 27/20
(C) 27/5
(D) 20/7

7. The transition from the state $n = 3$ to $n = 1$ in a hydrogen like atom results in ultraviolet radiation. Infrared radiation will be obtained in the transition from : **[NEET (UG) 2012]**
(A) $3 \to 2$
(B) $4 \to 2$
(C) $4 \to 3$
(D) $2 \to 1$

8. Monochromatic radiation emitted when electron on hydrogen atom jumps from first excited to the ground state irradiates a photosensitive material. The stopping potential is measured to be 3.57 V. The threshold frequency of the materials is : **[NEET (UG) 2012]**

(A) 4×10^{15} Hz
(B) 5×10^{15} Hz
(C) 1.6×10^{15} Hz
(D) 2.5×10^{15} Hz

9. An electron of a stationary hydrogen atom passes from the fifth energy level to the ground level. The velocity that the atom acquired as a result of photon emission will be : **[NEET (UG) 2012]**

(A) $\dfrac{24hR}{25m}$
(B) $\dfrac{25hR}{24m}$
(C) $\dfrac{25m}{24hR}$
(D) $\dfrac{24m}{25hR}$

(m is the mass of the electron, R Rybderg constant and h Planck's constant)

10. Ratio of longest wave lengths corresponding to Lyman and Balmer series in hydrogen spectrum is : **[NEET (UG) 2015]**
(A) $\dfrac{5}{27}$
(B) $\dfrac{3}{23}$
(C) $\dfrac{7}{29}$
(D) $\dfrac{9}{31}$

11. Hydrogen atom in ground state is excited by a monochromatic radiation of $\lambda = 975$ Å. Number of spectral lines in the resulting spectrum emitted will be : **[NEET (UG) 2014]**
(A) 3
(B) 2
(C) 6
(D) 10

12. Given the value of Rydberg constant is 10^7 m^{-1}, the wave number of the last line of the Balmer series in hydrogen spectrum will be : **[NEET (UG) 2016]**
(A) 0.025×10^4 m^{-1}
(B) 0.5×10^7 m^{-1}
(C) 0.25×10^7 m^{-1}
(D) 2.5×10^7 m^{-1}

13. If an electron in a hydrogen atom jumps from the 3rd orbit to the 2nd orbit, it emits a photon of wavelength λ. When it jumps from the 4th orbit to the 3rd orbit, the corresponding wavelength of the photon will be : **[NEET (UG) 2016 Ph. II]**
(A) $\dfrac{16}{25}\lambda$
(B) $\dfrac{9}{16}\lambda$
(C) $\dfrac{20}{7}\lambda$
(D) $\dfrac{20}{13}\lambda$

14. The ratio of wavelengths of the last line of Balmer series and the last line of Lyman series is : **[NEET (UG) 2017]**
(A) 2
(B) 1
(C) 4
(D) 0.5

$*$ $*$ $*$ $*$ $*$

27 NUCLEI

27.1 Radioactivity

1. Half life of a radioactive element is 12.5 hours and its quantity is 256 g. After how much time its quantity will remain 1g ? **[NEET (UG) 2001]**
(A) 50 hrs
(B) 100 hrs
(C) 150 hrs
(D) 200 hrs

2. A sample of radioactive element containing 4×10^{16} active nuclei. Half life of element is 10 days, then number of decayed nuclei after 30 days : **[NEET (UG) 2002]**
(A) 0.5×10^{16}
(B) 2×10^{16}
(C) 3.5×10^{16}
(D) 1×10^{16}

3. A sample of radioactive element has a mass of 10 g at an instant $t = 0$. The approximate mass of this element in the sample after two mean lives is : **[NEET (UG) 2003]**
(A) 1.35 g
(B) 2.50 g
(C) 3.70 g
(D) 6.30 g

4. The half life of radium is about 1600 years. If 100 g of radium existing now, 25 g will remain unchanged after : **[NEET (UG) 2004]**
(A) 4800 years
(B) 6400 years
(C) 2400 years
(D) 3200 years

5. In a radioactive material the activity at time t_1 is R_1 and at a later time t_2, it is R_2. If the decay constant of the material is λ, then : **[NEET (UG) 2006]**
(A) $R_1 = R_2 \, e^{-\lambda \, (t_1 - t_2)}$
(B) $R_1 = R_2 \, e^{\lambda \, (t_1 - t_2)}$
(C) $R_1 = R_2 \, (t_2/t_1)$
(D) $R_1 = R_2$

6. Two radioactive substances A and B have decay constants 5λ and λ respectively. At $t = 0$ they have the same number of nuclei. The ratio of number of nuclei of A to those of B will be $(1/e)^2$ after a time interval : **[NEET (UG) 2007]**
(A) 4λ
(B) 2λ
(C) $1/2\lambda$
(D) $1/4\lambda$

7. In a radioactive decay process, the negatively charged emitted β-particles are : **[NEET (UG) 2007]**
(A) The electrons produced as a result of the decay of neutrons inside the nucleus
(B) The electrons produced as a result of collisions between atoms
(C) The electrons orbiting around the nucleus
(D) The electrons present inside the nucleus

8. Two radioactive materials X_1 and X_2 have decay constants 5λ and λ respectively. If initially they have the same number of nuclei, then the ratio of the number of nuclei of X_1 to that of X_2 will be $1/e$ after a time : **[NEET (UG) 2008]**
(A) $\dfrac{1}{4\lambda}$
(B) $\dfrac{e}{\lambda}$
(C) λ
(D) $\dfrac{1}{2}\lambda$

9. The activity of a radioactive sample is measured as N_0 counts per minute at $t = 0$ and N_0/e counts per minute at $t = 5$ minutes. The time (in minutes) at which the activity reduces to half its value is : **[NEET (UG) 2010]**
(A) $5 \log_e 2$
(B) $\log_e \dfrac{2}{5}$
(C) $\dfrac{5}{\log_e 2}$
(D) $5 \log_{10} 5$

10. The half life of a radioactive isotope X is 50 years. It decays to another element Y which is stable. The two elements X and Y were found to be in the ratio of 1 : 15 in a sample of a given rock. The age of the rock was estimated to be : **[NEET (UG) 2011]**
(A) 150 years
(B) 200 years
(C) 250 years
(D) 100 years

11. A mixture consists of two radioactive materials A_1 and A_2 with half lives of 20 s and 10 s respectively. Initially the mixture has 40 g of A_1 and 160 g of A_2. The amount of the two in the mixture will become equal after : **[NEET (UG) 2012]**
(A) 60 s
(B) 80 s
(C) 20 s
(D) 40 s

12. The half life of a radioactive nucleus is 50 days. The time interval $(t_2 - t_1)$ between the time t_2 when two third of it has decayed and the time t_1 when one third of it had decayed is : **[NEET (UG) 2012]**
(A) 50 days
(B) 60 days
(C) 15 days
(D) 30 days

13. The half-life of a radioactive isotope X is 20 years. It decays to another element Y which is stable. The two elements X and Y were found to be in the ratio 1 : 7 in a sample of a given rock. The age of the rock is estimated to be : **[NEET (UG) 2013]**
(A) 40 years
(B) 60 years
(C) 80 years
(D) 100 years

14. A radio isotope X with a half life 1.4×10^9 years decays of Y which is stable. A sample of the rock from a cave was found to contain X and Y in the ratio $1 : 7$. The age of the rock is :

[NEET (UG) 2014]

(A) 1.96×10^9 years   (B) 3.92×10^9 years

(C) 4.20×10^9 years   (D) 8.40×10^9 years

15. The half-life of a radioactive substance is 30 minutes. The time (in minutes) taken between 40% decay and 85% decay of the same radioactive substance is : **[NEET (UG) 2016 Ph. II]**

(A) 15   (B) 30

(C) 45   (D) 60

16. Radioactive material 'A' has decay constant '8λ' and material 'B' has decay constant 'λ'. Initially they have same number of nuclei. After what time, the ratio of number of nuclei of material 'B' to that 'A' will be $1/e$? **[NEET (UG) 2017]**

(A) $\dfrac{1}{\lambda}$ (B) $\dfrac{1}{7\lambda}$

(C) $\dfrac{1}{8\lambda}$ (D) $\dfrac{1}{9\lambda}$

17. For a radioactive material, half-life is 10 minutes. If initially there are 600 number of nuclei, the time taken (in minutes) for the disintegration of 450 nuclei is : **[NEET (UG) 2018]**

(A) 30   (B) 10

(C) 20   (D) 15

18. A radioactive nucleus $^{A}_{Z}X$ undergoes spontaneous decay in the sequence

$^{A}_{Z}X \rightarrow {}_{Z-1}B \rightarrow {}_{Z-3}C \rightarrow {}_{Z-2}D$, where Z is the atomic number of element X. The possible decay particles in the sequence are : **[NEET (UG) 2021]**

(A) α, β^-, β^+ (B) α, β^+, β^-

(C) β^+, α, β^- (D) β^-, α, β^+

19. The half life of a radioactive nuclide is 100 hours. The fraction of original activity that will remain after 150 hours would be : **[NEET (UG) 2021]**

(A) $\dfrac{1}{2}$ (B) $\dfrac{1}{2\sqrt{2}}$

(C) $\dfrac{2}{3}$ (D) $\dfrac{2}{3\sqrt{2}}$

27.2 Nuclear Physics

1. Energy released in nuclear fission is due to :

[NEET (UG) 2001]

(A) Some mass is converted into energy

(B) Total binding energy of fragments is more than the binding energy of parental element

(C) Total binding energy of fragments is less than the binding energy of parental element

(D) Total binding energy of fragments is equal to the binding energy of parental element

2. M_n and M_p represent the mass of neutron and proton respectively. An element having mass M has N neutrons and Z protons, then the correct relation will be : **[NEET (UG) 2001]**

(A) $M < \{N \cdot M_n + Z \cdot M_p\}$ (B) $M > \{N \cdot M_n + Z \cdot M_p\}$

(C) $M = \{N \cdot M_n + Z \cdot M_p\}$ (D) $M = N \{M_n + M_p\}$

3. Which rays contain (positive) charged particles ?

[NEET (UG) 2001]

(A) α-rays   (B) β-rays

(C) γ-rays   (D) X-rays

4. $X(n, \alpha)\,{}^{7}_{3}Li$, then X will be : **[NEET (UG) 2001]**

(A) $^{10}_{5}B$ (B) $^{9}_{5}B$

(C) $^{11}_{4}Be$ (D) $^{4}_{2}He$

5. Which of the following are suitable for the fusion process ?

[NEET (UG) 2002]

(A) Light nuclei   (B) Heavy nuclei

(C) Element lying in the middle of the periodic table

(D) Middle elements, which are lying on binding energy curve

6. A deutron is bombarded on $_{8}O^{16}$ nucleus then α-particle is emitted. The product nucleus is : **[NEET (UG) 2002]**

(A) $_{7}N^{13}$ (B) $_{5}B^{10}$

(C) $_{4}Be^{9}$ (D) $_{7}N^{14}$

7. The mass of proton is $1.0073\,u$ and that of neutron is $1.0087\,u$ (u = atomic mass unit). The binding energy of $^{4}_{2}He$ is (Given helium nucleus mass $\approx 4.0015\,u$) : **[NEET (UG) 2003]**

(A) $0.0305\,J$ (B) $0.0305\,erg$

(C) $28.4\,MeV$ (D) $0.061\,u$

8. The mass number of a nucleus is : **[NEET (UG) 2003]**

(A) Always less than its atomic number

(B) Always more than its atomic number

(C) Sometimes equal to its atomic number

(D) Sometimes less than and sometimes more than its atomic number

9. The volume occupied by an atom is greater than the volume of the nucleus by a factor of about : **[NEET (UG) 2003]**

(A) 10^1 (B) 10^5

(C) 10^{10} (D) 10^{15}

10. Solar energy is mainly caused due to : **[NEET (UG) 2003]**

(A) Burning of hydrogen in the oxygen

(B) Fission of uranium present in the Sun

(C) Fusion of protons during synthesis of heavier elements

(D) Gravitational contraction

11. A nuclear reaction given by $_Z X^A \rightarrow Z + _1 Y^A + _{-1}e^0 + \bar{v}$ represents : **[NEET (UG) 2003]**

(A) β-decay   (B) γ-decay

(C) Fusion   (D) Fission

12. M_P denotes the mass of a proton and M_n that of a neutron. A given nucleus, of binding energy B, contains Z protons and N neutrons. The mass $M(N, Z)$ of the nucleus is given by (c is velocity of light) : **[NEET (UG) 2004]**

(A) $M(N, Z) = NM_n + ZM_P + Bc^2$

(B) $M(N, Z) = NM_n + ZM_P - B/c^2$

(C) $M(N, Z) = NM_n + ZM_P + B/c^2$

(D) $M(N, Z) = NM_n + ZM_P - Bc^2$

13. If in a nuclear fusion process the masses of the fusing nuclei be m_1 and m_2 and the mass of the resultant nucleus be m_3, then : **[NEET (UG) 2004]**

(A) $m_3 = m_1 + m_2$ (B) $m_3 = |m_1 - m_2|$

(C) $m_3 < (m_1 + m_2)$ (D) $m_3 > (m_1 + m_2)$

14. A nucleus represented by the symbol $_Z^A X$ has : **[NEET (UG) 2004]**

(A) Z neutrons and $A - Z$ protons

(B) Z protons and $A - Z$ neutrons

(C) Z protons and A neutrons

(D) A protons and $Z - A$ neutrons

15. In the reaction $_1^2 H + _1^3 H \rightarrow _2^4 He + _0^1 n$. If the binding energies of $_1^2 H$, $_1^3 H$ and $_2^4 He$ are respectively a, b and c (in MeV), then the energy (in MeV) released in this reaction is : **[NEET (UG) 2005]**

(A) $a + b + c$ (B) $c + a - b$

(C) $c - a - b$ (D) $a + b - c$

16. The nuclei of which one of the following pairs of nuclei are isotones : **[NEET (UG) 2005]**

(A) $_{34}Se^{74}$, $_{31}Ga^{71}$ (B) $_{38}Sr^{84}$, $_{38}Sr^{86}$

(C) $_{42}Mo^{92}$, $40Zr^{92}$ (D) $_{20}Ca^{40}$, $_{16}S^{32}$

17. In any fission process the ratio $\dfrac{\text{mass of fission products}}{\text{mass of parent nucleus}}$ is : **[NEET (UG) 2005]**

(A) Greater than 1

(B) Depends on the mass of the parent nucleus

(C) Equal to 1

(D) Less than 1

18. Fission of nuclei is possible because the binding energy per nucleon in them : **[NEET (UG) 2005]**

(A) Decreases with mass number at low mass numbers

(B) Increases with mass number at low mass numbers

(C) Decreases with mass number at high mass numbers

(D) Increases with mass number at high mass numbers

19. The binding energy of deuteron is 2.2 MeV and that of $_2^4 He$ is 28 MeV. If two deuterons are fused to form one $_2^4 He$ then the energy released is : **[NEET (UG) 2006]**

(A) 25.8 MeV   (B) 23.6 MeV

(C) 19.2 MeV   (D) 30.2 MeV

20. The radius of Germanium (Ge) nuclide is measured to be twice the radius of $_4^9 Be$. The number of nucleons in Ge are : **[NEET (UG) 2006]**

(A) 73   (B) 74

(C) 75   (D) 72

21. A nucleus $_Z^A X$ has mass represented by $M(A, Z)$. If M_p and M_n denote the mass of proton and neutron respectively and B.E. the binding energy in MeV, then : **[NEET (UG) 2007]**

(A) B.E. $= [ZM_p + (A - Z)M_p - M(A, Z)]c^2$

(B) B.E. $= [ZM_p + ZM_n - M(A, Z)]c^2$

(C) B.E. $= M(A, Z) - ZM_p - (A - Z)M_n$

(D) B.E. $= [M(A, Z) - ZM_p - (A - Z)M_n]c^2$

22. If the nucleus $_{13}^{27} Al$ has nuclear radius of about 3.6 fm, then $_{32}^{125} Te$ would have its radius approximately as : **[NEET (UG) 2007]**

(A) 9.6 fm   (B) 12.0 fm

(C) 4.8 fm   (D) 6.0 fm

23. Two nuclei have their mass numbers in the ratio of 1 : 3. The ratio of their nuclear densities would be : **[NEET (UG) 2008]**

(A) $(3)^{1/3} : 1$ (B) $1 : 1$

(C) $1 : 3$ (D) $3 : 1$

24. If $M(A, Z)$, M_p and M_n denote the masses of the nucleus $_Z^A X$, proton and neutron respectively in units of u ($1 u = 931.5$ MeV/c^2) and BE represents its bonding energy in MeV, then : **[NEET (UG) 2008]**

(A) $M(A, Z) = ZM_p + (A - Z)M_n - BE$

(B) $M(A, Z) = ZM_p + (A - Z)M_n + BE/C^2$

(C) $M(A, Z) = ZM_p + (A - Z)M_n - BE/C^2$

(D) $M(A, Z) = ZM_p + (A - Z)M_n + BE$

25. The number of beta particles emitted by a radioactive substance is twice the number of alpha particles emitted by it. The resulting daughter nucleus is an : **[NEET (UG) 2009]**

(A) Isotope of parent   (B) Isobar of parent

(C) Isomer of parent   (D) Isotone of parent

26. In the nuclear decay given below :

$$^A_Z X \longrightarrow ^A_{Z+1} Y \longrightarrow ^{A-4}_{Z-1} B^* \longrightarrow ^{A-4}_{Z-1} B$$

The particles emitted in the sequence are : **[NEET (UG) 2009]**
(A) α, β, γ (B) β, α, γ
(C) γ, β, α (D) β, γ, α

27. In a Rutherford scattering experiment when a projectile of charge Z_1 and mass M_1 approaches a target nucleus of charge Z_2 and mass M_2, the distance of closest approach is r_0. The energy of the projectile is : **[NEET (UG) 2009]**
(A) Directly proportional to mass M_1
(B) Directly proportional to $M_1 \times M_2$
(C) Directly proportional to $Z_1 Z_2$
(D) Inversely proportional to Z_1

28. The mass of a $^7_3$Li nucleus is 0.042 u less than the sum of the masses of all its nucleons. The binding energy per nucleon of $^7_3$Li nucleus is nearly : **[NEET (UG) 2010]**
(A) 23 MeV   (B) 46 MeV
(C) 5.6 MeV   (D) 3.9 MeV

29. An alpha nucleus of energy $1/2\ mv^2$ bombards a heavy nuclear target of charge Ze. Then the distance of closest approach for the alpha nucleus will be proportional to : **[NEET (UG) 2010]**

(A) $\dfrac{1}{v^4}$ (B) $\dfrac{1}{m}$

(C) v^2 (D) $\dfrac{1}{Ze}$

30. The power obtained in a reactor using U^{235} disintegration is 1000 kW. The mass decay of U^{235} per hour is (Energy produced per kg of U^{235} is 9×10^{16} J) : **[NEET (UG) 2011]**
(A) 10 microgram   (B) 20 microgram
(C) 40 microgram   (D) 1 microgram

31. A nucleus $^m_n X$ emits one α-particle and two β^- particles. The resulting nucleus is : **[NEET (UG) 2011]**

(A) $^{m-6}_{n-4} Z$ (B) $^{m-6}_n Z$

(C) $^{m-4}_n X$ (D) $^{m-4}_{n-2} Y$

32. Fusion reaction takes place at high temperature because : **[NEET (UG) 2011]**
(A) Nuclei break up at high temperature
(B) Atoms get ionised at high temperature
(C) Kinetic energy is high enough to overcome the coulomb repulsion between nuclei
(D) Molecules break up at high temperature

33. A radioactive nucleus of mass M emits a photon of frequency ν and the nucleus recoils. The recoil energy will be : **[NEET (UG) 2011]**
(A) $Mc^2 - h\nu$ (B) $h^2\nu^2/2Mc^2$
(C) Zero   (D) $h\nu$

34. If the nuclear radius of ^{27}Al is 3.6 Fermi, the approximate nuclear radius of ^{64}Cu in fermi is : **[NEET (UG) 2012]**
(A) 2.4   (B) 1.2
(C) 4.8   (D) 3.6

35. A certain mass of Hydrogen is changed to Helium by the process of fusion. The mass defect in fusion reaction is 0.02866 u. The energy liberated per nucleon is : **[NEET (UG) 2013]** (Given 1 u = 931 MeV) :
(A) 2.67 MeV   (B) 26.7 MeV
(C) 6.675 MeV   (D) 13.35 MeV

36. The binding energy per nucleon of $^7_3$Li and $^4_2$He nuclei are 5.60 MeV and 7.06 MeV, respectively. In the nuclear reaction $^7_3\text{Li} + ^1_1\text{H} \rightarrow ^4_2\text{He} + ^4_2\text{He} + Q$, the value of energy Q released is : **[NEET (UG) 2014]**
(A) 19.6 MeV   (B) -2.4 MeV
(C) 8.4 MeV   (D) 17.3 MeV

37. A nucleus of uranium decays at rest into nuclei of thorium and helium. Then : **[NEET (UG) 2015]**
(A) The helium nucleus has less kinetic energy than the thorium nucleus
(B) The helium nucleus has more kinetic energy than the thorium nucleus
(C) The helium nucleus has less momentum than the thorium nucleus
(D) The helium nucleus has more momentum than the thorium nucleus

38. When an α-particle of mass m moving with velocity v bombards on a heavy nucleus of charge 'Ze', its distance of closest approach from the nucleus depends on m as : **[NEET (UG) 2016]**

(A) $\dfrac{1}{m}$ (B) $\dfrac{1}{\sqrt{m}}$

(C) $\dfrac{1}{m^2}$ (D) m

39. α-particle consists of : **[NEET (UG) 2019]**
(A) 2 protons and 2 neutrons only
(B) 2 electrons, 2 protons and 2 neutrons
(C) 2 electrons and 4 protons only
(D) 2 protons only

40. The energy required to break one bond in *DNA* is 10^{-20} J. This value in eV is nearly :   **[NEET (UG) 2020]**
(A) 0.006
(B) 6
(C) 0.6
(D) 0.06

41. When a uranium isotope $^{235}_{92}$U is bombarded with a neutron, it generates $^{89}_{36}$Kr, three neutrons and :   **[NEET (UG) 2020]**

(A) $^{103}_{36}$Kr
(B) $^{144}_{56}$Ba

(C) $^{91}_{40}$Zr
(D) $^{101}_{36}$Kr

42. The energy equivalent of 0.5 g of a substance is :
                    [NEET (UG) 2020]
(A) 0.5×10^{13} J
(B) 4.5×10^{16} J
(C) 4.5×10^{13} J
(D) 1.5×10^{13} J

43. A nucleus with mass number 240 breaks into two fragments each of mass number 120, the binding energy per nucleon of unfragmented nuclei is 7.6 MeV while that of fragments is 8.5 MeV. The total gain in the Binding Energy in the process is :
                    [NEET (UG) 2021]
(A) 0.9 MeV
(B) 9.4 MeV
(C) 804 MeV
(D) 216 MeV

44. In the given nuclear reaction, the element X is :
$$^{22}_{11}\text{Na} \longrightarrow X + e^+ + \nu$$
                    [NEET (UG) 2022]
(A) $^{23}_{10}$Ne
(B) $^{22}_{10}$Ne
(C) $^{22}_{12}$Mg
(D) $^{23}_{11}$Ne

45. A nucleus of mass number 189 splits into two nuclei having mass number 125 and 64. The ratio of radius of two daughter nuclei respectively is :   **[NEET (UG) 2022]**
(A) $4 : 5$
(B) $5 : 4$
(C) $25 : 16$
(D) $1 : 1$

* * * * *

28 SEMICONDUCTORS ELECTRONICS

28.1 Semiconductor

1. In a *p-n* junction : **[NEET (UG) 2002]**
(A) High potential at *n* side and low potential at *p* side
(B) High potential at *p* side and low potential at *n* side
(C) *p* and *n* both are at same potential
(D) Undetermined

2. In semiconductors at a room temperature :
[NEET (UG) 2004]
(A) The valence band is partially empty and the conduction band is partially filled
(B) The valence band is completely filled and the conduction band is partially filled
(C) The valence band is completely filled
(D) The conduction band is completely empty

3. Choose the only false statement from the following :
[NEET (UG) 2005]
(A) The resistivity of a semiconductor increases with increase in temperature
(B) Substances with energy gap of the order of 10 *eV* are insulators
(C) In conductors the valence and conduction bands may over lap
(D) The conductivity of a semiconductor increases with increases in temperature

4. Carbon, Silicon and Germanium atoms have four valence electrons each. Their valence and conduction bands are separated by energy band gaps represented by $(E_g)_C$, $(E_g)_{Si}$ and $(E_g)_{Ge}$ respectively. Which one of the following relationships is true in their case : **[NEET (UG) 2005]**
(A) $(E_g)_C < (E_g)_{Ge}$ (B) $(E_g)_C > (E_g)_{Si}$
(C) $(E_g)_C = (E_g)_{Si}$ (D) $(E_g)_C < (E_g)_{Si}$

5. In the energy band diagram of a material shown below, the open circles and filled circles denote holes and electrons respectively. The material is : **[NEET (UG) 2007]**

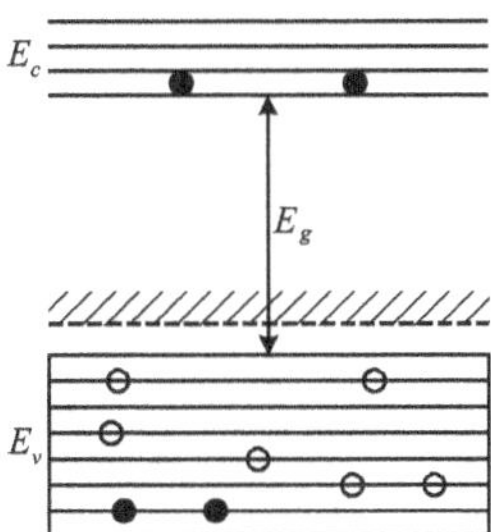

(A) An insulator
(B) A metal
(C) An *n*-type semiconductor
(D) A *p*-type semiconductor

6. Which of the following statement is False ?
[NEET (UG) 2010]
(A) The resistance of intrinsic semiconductor decreases with increase of temperature
(B) Pure *Si* doped with trivalent impurities gives a *p*-type semiconductor
(C) Majority carries in a *n*-type semiconductors are holes
(D) Minority carries in a *p*-type semiconductor are electrons

7. *C* and *Si* both have same lattice structure, having 4 bonding electrons in each. However, *C* is insulator where as *Si* is intrinsic semiconductor. This is because : **[NEET (UG) 2012]**
(A) In case of *C* the valence band is not completely filled at absolute zero temperature
(B) In case of *C* the conduction band is partly filled even at absolute zero temperature
(C) The four bonding electrons in the case of *C* lie in the second orbit, whereas in the case of *Si* they lie in the third
(D) The four bonding electrons in the case of *C* lie in the third orbit, whereas for *Si* they lie in the fourth orbit

8. For a *p*-type semiconductor, which of the following statements is true ? **[NEET (UG) 2019]**
(A) Electrons are the majority carriers and trivalent atoms are the dopants
(B) Holes are the majority carriers and trivalent atoms are the dopants
(C) Holes are the majority carriers and pentavalent atoms are the dopants
(D) Electrons are the majority carriers and pentavalent atoms are the dopants

9. The solids which have the negative temperature coefficient of resistance are : **[NEET (UG) 2020]**
(A) Insulators and semiconductors
(B) Metals
(C) Insulators only
(D) Semiconductors only

28.2 PN Junction and Diodes

1. The current in the circuit will be : **[NEET (UG) 2001]**

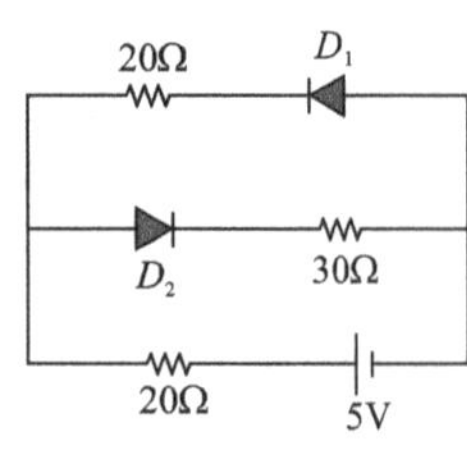

(A) 5/40 A
(C) 5/10 A
(B) 5/50 A
(D) 5/20 A

2. For the given circuit of p-n junction diode which is correct?

[NEET (UG) 2002]

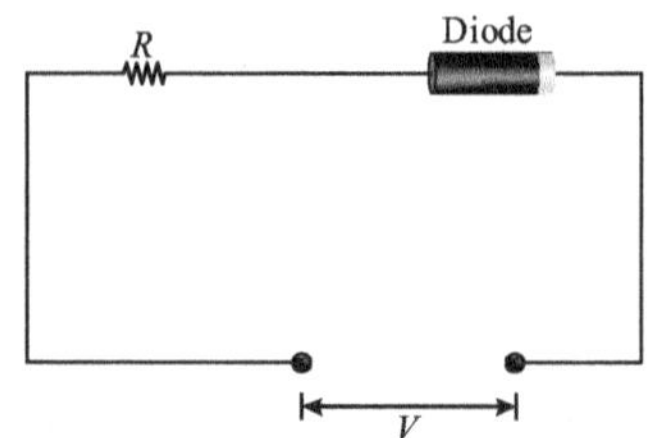

(A) In forward bias the voltage across R is V
(B) In reverse bias the voltage across R is V
(C) In forward bias the voltage across R is $2V$
(D) In reverse bias the voltage across R is $2V$

3. Reverse bias applied to a junction diode :

[NEET (UG) 2003]

(A) Lowers the potential barrier
(B) Raises the potential barrier
(C) Increases the majority carrier current
(D) Increases the minority carrier current

4. Barrier potential of a p-n junction diode does not depend on : **[NEET (UG) 2003]**

(A) Diode design
(C) Forward bias
(B) Temperature
(D) Doping density

5. If a full wave rectifier circuit is operating from 50 Hz mains, the fundamental frequency in the ripple will be :

[NEET (UG) 2003]

(A) 25 Hz
(C) 70.7 Hz
(B) 50 Hz
(D) 100 Hz

6. In a p-n junction photo cell, the value of the photo electromotive force produced by monochromatic light is proportional to : **[NEET (UG) 2004]**

(A) The intensity of the light falling on the cell
(B) The frequency of the light falling on the cell
(C) The voltage applied at the p-n junction
(D) The barrier voltage at the p-n junction

7. Of the diodes shown in the following diagrams, which one is reverse biased ? **[NEET (UG) 2004]**

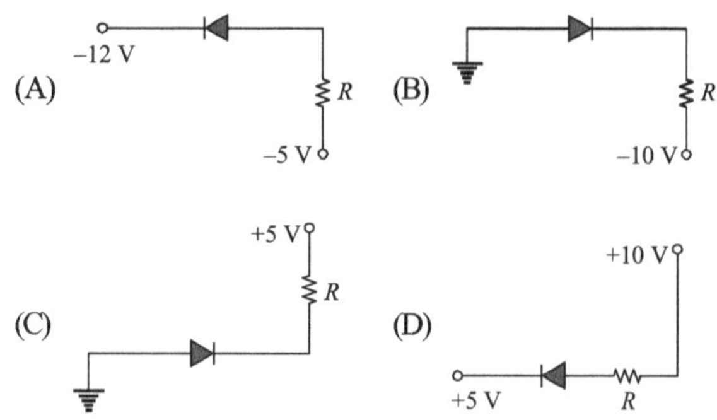

8. The peak voltage in the output of a half wave diode rectifier fed with a sinusoidal signal without filter is 10 V. The dc component of the output voltage is : **[NEET (UG) 2004]**

(A) $10 / \sqrt{2}$V
(C) 10V
(B) $10 / \pi$V
(D) $20 / \pi$V

9. Zener diode is used for : **[NEET (UG) 2005]**

(A) Rectification
(B) Stabilisation
(C) Amplification
(D) Producing oscillations in an oscillator

10. Application of a forward bias to a p-n junction :

[NEET (UG) 2005]

(A) Widens the depletion zone
(B) Increases the number of donors on the n side
(C) Increases the potential difference across the depletion zone
(D) Increases the electric field in the depletion zone

11. A forward biased diode is : **[NEET (UG) 2006]**

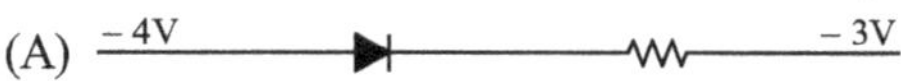

12. A p-n photodiode is made of a material with a band gap of 2.0 eV. The minimum frequency of the radiation that can be absorbed by the material is nearly : **[NEET (UG) 2008]**

(A) 1×10^{14} Hz
(C) 10×10^{14} Hz
(B) 20×10^{14} Hz
(D) 5×10^{14} Hz

13. A p-n photodiode is fabricated from a semiconductor with a band gap of 2.5 eV. It can detect a signal of wavelength :

[NEET (UG) 2009]

(A) 496 Å
(C) 4000 nm
(B) 6000 Å
(D) 6000 nm

14. The device that can act as a complete electronic circuit is :
[NEET (UG) 2010]
(A) Zener diode   (B) Junction diode
(C) Integrated circuit   (D) Junction transistor

15. In forward biasing of the p-n junction : **[NEET (UG) 2011]**
(A) The positive terminal of the battery is connected to p-side and the depletion region becomes thick
(B) The positive terminal of the battery is connected to n-side and the depletion region becomes thin
(C) The positive terminal of the battery is connected to n-side and the depletion region becomes thick
(D) The positive terminal of the battery is connected to p-side and the depletion region becomes thin

16. If a small amount of antimony is added to germanium crystal :
[NEET (UG) 2011]
(A) It becomes a p-type semiconductor
(B) The antimony becomes an acceptor atom
(C) There will be more free electrons than holes in the semiconductors
(D) Its resistance is increased

17. Two ideal diodes are connected to a battery as shown in the circuit. The current supplied by the battery is :
[NEET (UG) 2012]

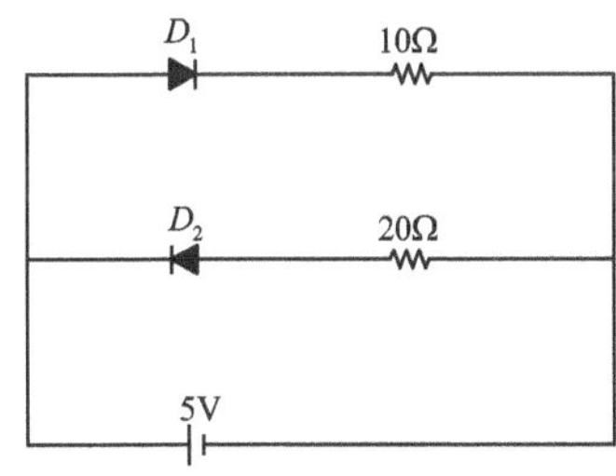

(A) 0.75 A   (B) Zero
(C) 0.25 A   (D) 0.5 A

18. In a n-type semiconductor, which of the following statements is true : **[NEET (UG) 2013]**
(A) Electrons are majority carriers and trivalent atoms are dopants
(B) Electrons are minority carriers and pentavalent atoms are dopants
(C) Holes are minority carriers and pentavalent atoms are dopants
(D) Holes are majority carriers and trivalent atoms are dopants

19. The given graph represents $V - I$ characteristic for a semiconductor device. Which of the following statement is correct ? **[NEET (UG) 2014]**

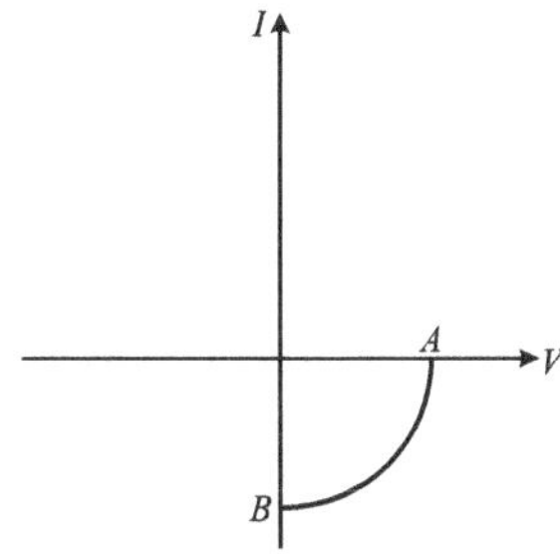

(A) It is $V - I$ characteristic for solar cell where point A represents open circuit voltage and point B short circuit current
(B) It is for a solar cell and points A and B represent open circuit voltage and current, respectively
(C) It is for a photodiode and points A and B represent open circuit voltage and current, respectively
(D) It is for a LED and points A and B represents open circuit voltage and short circuit current respectively

20. The barrier potential of a p-n junction depends on :
[NEET (UG) 2014]
a.   Type of semiconductor material
b.   Amount of doping
c.   Temperature
Which one of the following is correct ?
(A) a and b only   (B) b only
(C) b and c only   (D) a, b and c

21. In the given figure, a diode D is connected to an external resistance $R = 100\ \Omega$ and an *emf* of 3.5 V. If the barrier potential developed across the diode is 0.5 V, the current in the circuit will be : **[NEET (UG) 2015]**

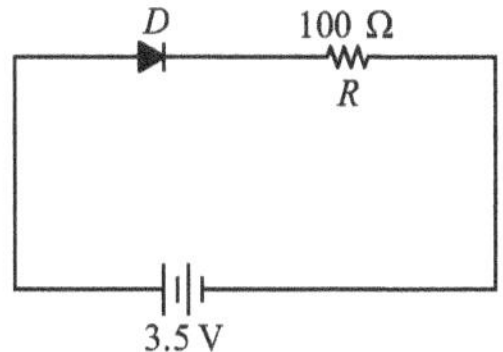

(A) 35 mA   (B) 30 mA
(C) 40 mA   (D) 20 mA

22. Consider the junction diode as ideal. The value of current flowing through AB is : **[NEET (UG) 2016]**

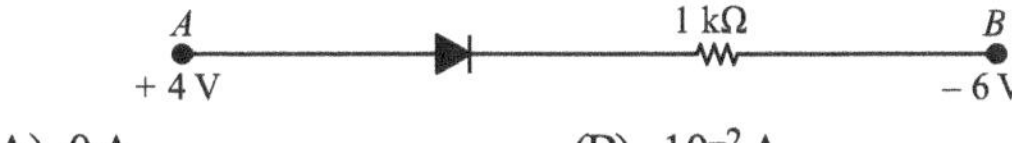

(A) 0 A   (B) 10^{-2} A
(C) 10^{-1} A   (D) 10^{-3} A

23. The given circuit has two ideal diodes connected as shown in the figure below. The current flowing through the resistance R_1 will be : **[NEET (UG) 2016 Ph. II]**

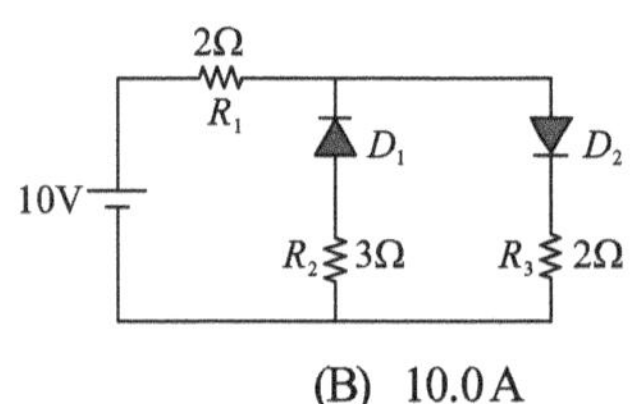

(A) 2.5 A (B) 10.0 A
(C) 1.43 A (D) 3.13 A

24. Which one of the following represents forward bias diode?
[NEET (UG) 2017]

(A) $\xrightarrow{0V}$ ▶| $\xrightarrow{R}$ $-2V$

(B) $\xrightarrow{-4V}$ ▶| $\xrightarrow{R}$ $-3V$

(C) $\xrightarrow{-2V}$ ▶| $\xrightarrow{R}$ $+2V$

(D) $\xrightarrow{3V}$ ▶| $\xrightarrow{R}$ $5V$

25. In a p-n junction diode, change in temperature due to heating : **[NEET (UG) 2018]**
(A) Does not affect resistance of p-n junction
(B) Affects only forward resistance
(C) Affects only reverse resistance
(D) Affects the overall V-I characteristics of p-n junction

26. The increase in the width of depletion region in a p-n junction diode is due to : **[NEET (UG) 2020]**
(A) Increase in forward current
(B) Forward bias only
(C) Reverse bias only
(D) Both forward bias and reverse bias

27. The electron concentration in an n-type semiconductor is the same as hole concentration in a p-type semiconductor. An external field (electric) is applied across each of them. Compare the currents in them : **[NEET (UG) 2021]**
(A) current in n-type = current in p-type
(B) current in p-type > current in n-type
(C) current in n-type > current in p-type
(D) No current will flow in p-type, current will only flow in n-type

28. Consider the following statements (A) and (B) and identify the correct answer.
(a) A zener diode is connected in reverse bias, when used as a voltage regulator.
(b) The potential barrier of p-n junction lies between 0.1 V to 0.3 V. **[NEET (UG) 2021]**
(A) (a) and (b) both are correct
(B) (a) and (b) both are incorrect
(C) (a) is correct and (b) is incorrect
(D) (a) is incorrect but (b) is correct

29. In the given circuits (a), (b) and (c), the potential drop across the two p-n junctions are equal in : **[NEET (UG) 2022]**

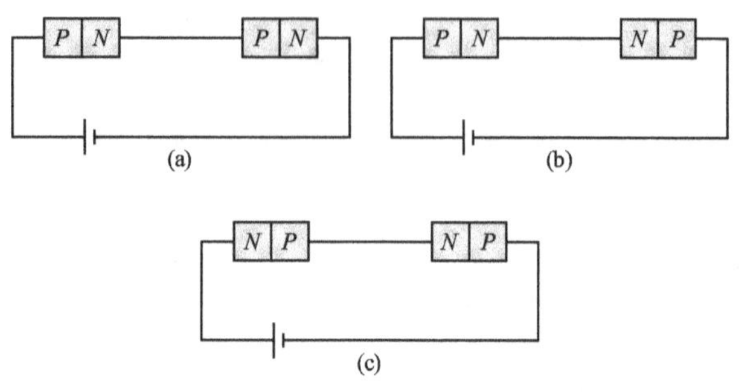

(A) Circuit (b) only (B) Circuit (c) only
(C) Both circuits (a) and (c) (D) Circuit (a) only

30. In half wave rectification, if the input frequency is 60 Hz, then the output frequency would be : **[NEET (UG) 2022]**
(A) 30 Hz (B) 60 Hz
(C) 120 Hz (D) Zero

28.3 Transistors

1. For a common base circuit if $\dfrac{I_C}{I_E} = 0.98$ then current gain for common emitter circuit will be : **[NEET (UG) 2001]**
(A) 49 (B) 98
(C) 4.9 (D) 25.5

2. For a transistor $\dfrac{I_C}{I_E} = 0.96$, then current gain for common emitter is : **[NEET (UG) 2002]**
(A) 12 (B) 6
(C) 48 (D) 24

3. A n-p-n transistor conducts when : **[NEET (UG) 2003]**
(A) Both collector and emitter are positive with respect to the base
(B) Collector is positive and emitter is negative with respect to the base
(C) Collector is positive and emitter is at same potential as the base
(D) Both collector and emitter are negative with respect to the base

4. A transistor-oscillator using a resonant circuit with an inductor L (of negligible resistance) and a capacitor C in series produce oscillations of frequency f. If L is doubled and C is changed to $4C$, the frequency will be : **[NEET (UG) 2006]**
(A) $\dfrac{f}{4}$ (B) $8f$
(C) $\dfrac{f}{2\sqrt{2}}$ (D) $\dfrac{f}{2}$

5. A transistor is operated in common emitter configuration at constant collector voltage $V_c = 1.5$ V such that a change in the base current from $100\ \mu A$ to $150\ \mu A$ produces a change in the collector current from 5 mA to 10 mA. The current gain (β) is : **[NEET (UG) 2006]**

(A) 67   (B) 75
(C) 100   (D) 50

6. A common emitter amplifier has a voltage gain of 50, an input impedance of $100\ \Omega$ and an output impedance of $200\ \Omega$. The power gain of the amplifier is : **[NEET (UG) 2007]**

(A) 1000   (B) 1250
(C) 100   (D) 500

7. The voltage gain of an amplifier with 9% negative feedback is 10. The voltage gain without feedback will be :

[NEET (UG) 2008]

(A) 1.25   (B) 100
(C) 90   (D) 10

8. A transistor is operated in common-emitter configuration at $V_C = 2$ V such that a change in the base current from $100\ \mu A$ to $200\ \mu A$ produces a change in the collector current from 5 mA to 10 mA. The current gain is : **[NEET (UG) 2009]**

(A) 50   (B) 75
(C) 100   (D) 150

9. A common emitter amplifier has a voltage gain of 50, an input impedance of $100\ \Omega$ and an output impedance of $200\ \Omega$. The power gain of the amplifier is : **[NEET (UG) 2010]**

(A) 50   (B) 500
(C) 1000   (D) 1250

10. A transistor is operated in common emitter configuration at $V_C = 2$ V such that a change in the base current from $100\ \mu A$ to $300\ \mu A$ produces a change in the collector current from 10 mA to 20 mA. The current gain is : **[NEET (UG) 2011]**

(A) 50   (B) 75
(C) 100   (D) 25

11. In a common emitter transistor amplifier, the audio signal voltage across the collector resistance of $2\ k\Omega$ is 2 V. If the base resistance is $1\ k\Omega$ and the current amplification of the transistor is 100, the input signal voltage is : **[NEET (UG) 2012]**

(A) 0.1 V   (B) 1.0 V
(C) 1mV   (D) 10mV

12. Transfer characteristics [output voltage (V_0) vs input voltage (V_i)] for a base biased transistor in common emitter configuration is as shown in the figure. For using transistor as a switch, it is used : **[NEET (UG) 2012]**

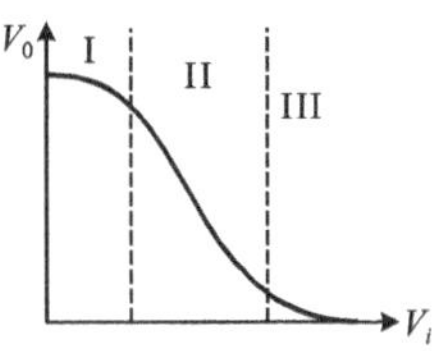

(A) In region III   (B) Both in region I and III
(C) In region II   (D) In region I

13. The input resistance of a silicon transistor is $100\ \Omega$. Base current is changed by $40\ \mu A$ which results in a change in collector current by 2 mA. This transistor is used as a common emitter amplifier with a load resistance of $4\ K\Omega$. The voltage gain of the amplifier is : **[NEET (UG) 2012]**

(A) 3000   (B) 4000
(C) 1000   (D) 2000

14. In a common emitter amplifier having a voltage gain G, the transistor used has transconductance 0.03 mho and current gain 25. If the above transistor is replaced with another one with transconductance 0.02 mho and current gain 20, the voltage gain will be : **[NEET (UG) 2013]**

(A) $\dfrac{2}{3}G$ (B) $1.5\,G$

(C) $\dfrac{1}{3}G$ (D) $\dfrac{5}{4}G$

15. The input signal given to a common emitter amplifier having a voltage gain of 150 is $V_1 = 2\cos\left(15t + \dfrac{\pi}{3}\right)$. The corresponding output signal will be : **[NEET (UG) 2015]**

(A) $300\cos\left(15t + \dfrac{4\pi}{3}\right)$ (B) $300\cos\left(15t + \dfrac{\pi}{3}\right)$

(C) $75\cos\left(15t + \dfrac{2\pi}{3}\right)$ (D) $2\cos\left(15t + \dfrac{5\pi}{6}\right)$

16. A *npn* transistor is connected in common emitter configuration in a given amplifier. A load resistance of $800\ \Omega$ is connected in the collector circuit and the voltage drop across it is 0.8 V. If the current amplification factor is 0.96 and the input resistance of the circuit is $192\ \Omega$, the voltage gain and the power gain of the amplifier will respectively be : **[NEET (UG) 2016]**

(A) 4, 3.84   (B) 3.69, 3.84
(C) 4, 4   (D) 4, 3.69

17. For common emitter transistor amplifier, the audio signal voltage across the collector resistance of $2\ k\Omega$ is 4 V. If the current amplification factor of the transistor is 100 and the base resistance is $1\ k\Omega$, then the input signal voltage is : **[NEET (UG) 2016 Ph. II]**

(A) 10mV   (B) 20mV
(C) 30mV   (D) 15mV

18. In a common emitter transistor amplifier the audio signal voltage across the collector is 3 V. The resistance of collector is 3 kΩ. If current gain is 100 and the base resistance is 2 kΩ, the voltage and power gain of the amplifier is : **[NEET (UG) 2017]**

(A) 200 and 1000
(B) 15 and 200
(C) 150 and 15000
(D) 20 and 2000

19. In the circuit shown in the figure, the input voltage V_i is 20 V, $V_{BE} = 0$ and $V_{CE} = 0$. The values of I_B, I_C and β are given by : **[NEET (UG) 2018]**

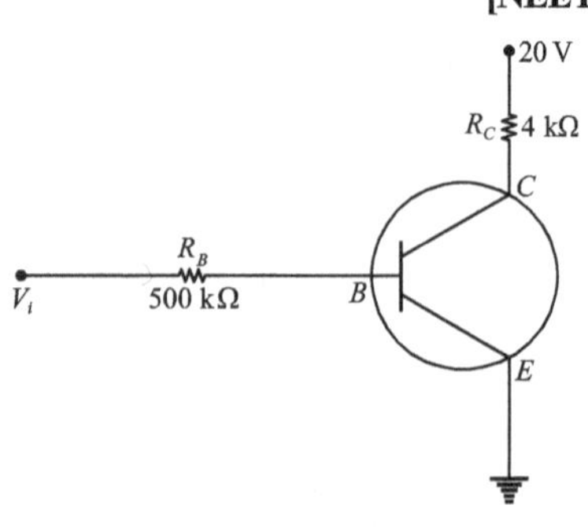

(A) $I_B = 20\,\mu A$, $I_C = 5\,mA$, β $= 250$
(B) $I_B = 25\,\mu A$, $I_C = 5\,mA$, β $= 200$
(C) $I_B = 40\,\mu A$, $I_C = 10\,mA$, β $= 250$
(D) $I_B = 40\,\mu A$, $I_C = 5\,mA$, β $= 125$

20. For transistor action, which of the following statements is correct ? **[NEET (UG) 2020]**
(A) The base region must be very thin and lightly doped
(B) Base, emitter and collector regions should have same doping concentrations
(C) Base, emitter and collector regions should have same size
(D) Both emitter junction as well as the collector junction are forward biased

28.4 Logic Gates

1. Following truth table represent which logic gate : **[NEET (UG) 2001]**

A	B	C
1	1	0
0	1	1
1	0	1
0	0	1

(A) XOR
(B) NOT
(C) NAND
(D) AND

2. Following diagram performs the logic function of : **[NEET (UG) 2003]**

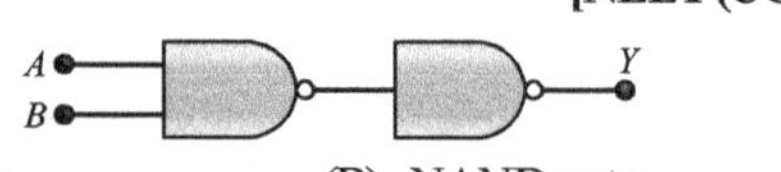

(A) AND gate
(B) NAND gate
(C) OR gate
(D) XOR gate

3. The output of OR gate is 1 : **[NEET (UG) 2004]**
(A) If both inputs are zero
(B) If either or both inputs are 1
(C) Only if both inputs are 1
(D) If either input is zero

4. The following figure shows a logic gate circuit with two inputs A and B and the output C. The voltage waveforms of A, B and C are as shown below : **[NEET (UG) 2006]**

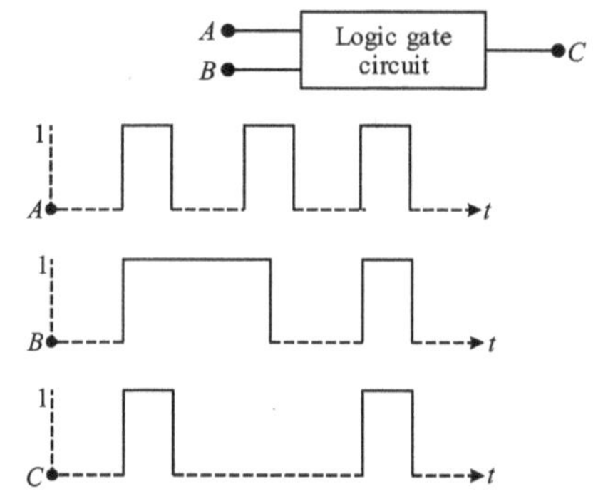

The logic circuit gate is :
(A) AND gate
(B) NAND gate
(C) NOR gate
(D) OR gate

5. In the following circuit, the output Y for all possible inputs A and B is expressed by the truth table : **[NEET (UG) 2007]**

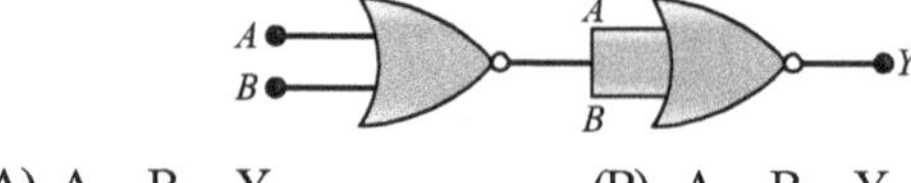

(A)

A	B	Y
0	1	1
0	1	1
0	0	1
1	1	0

(B)

A	B	Y
0	0	1
0	1	0
0	0	0
1	1	0

(C)

A	B	Y
0	0	0
0	1	1
1	0	1
1	1	1

(D)

A	B	Y
0	0	0
0	1	0
1	0	0
1	1	1

6. The below circuit is equivalent to : **[NEET (UG) 2008]**

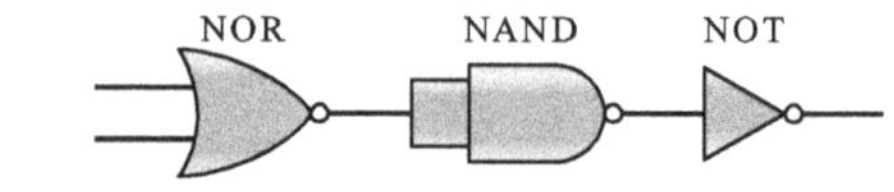

(A) NOR
(B) OR
(C) AND
(D) NAND

7. The symbolic representation of four logic gates are given below : **[NEET (UG) 2009]**

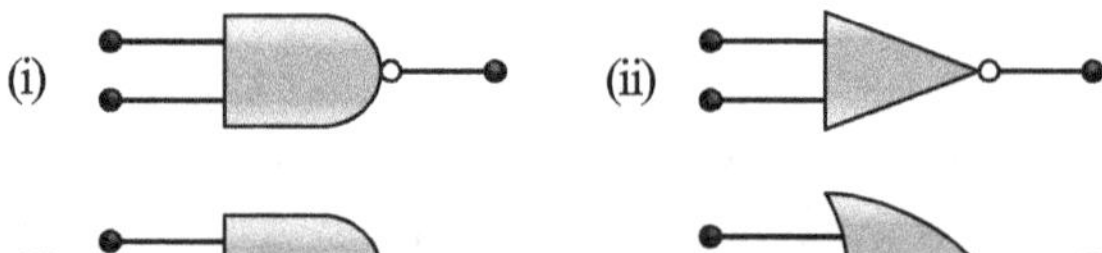

The logic symbols for OR, NOT and NAND gates are respectively :

(A) (i), (iii), (iv)
(B) (iii), (iv), (ii)
(C) (iv), (i), (iii)
(D) (iv), (ii), (i)

8. To get an output $Y = 1$ from the circuit shown below, the input must be : **[NEET (UG) 2010]**

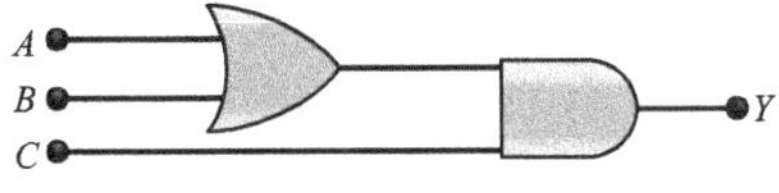

	A	**B**	**C**
(A)	1	0	0
(B)	0	1	0
(C)	0	0	1
(D)	1	0	1

9. Symbolic representation of four logic gate are shown as : **[NEET (UG) 2011]**

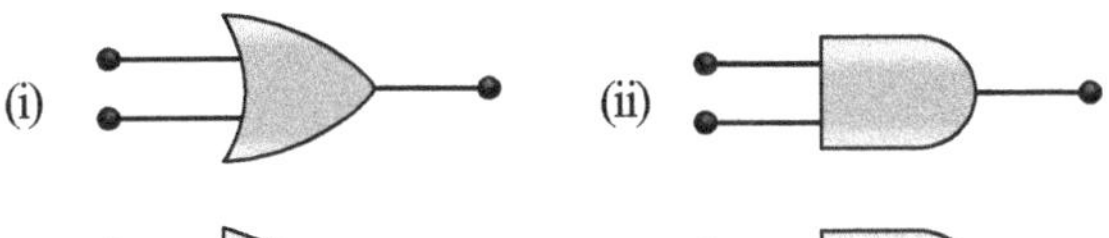

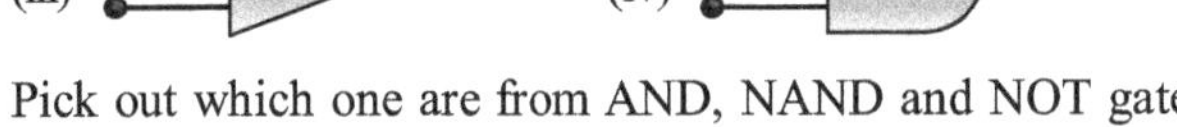

Pick out which one are from AND, NAND and NOT gates, respectively :

(A) (ii), (iii) and (iv)
(B) (iii), (ii) and (i)
(C) (iii), (ii) and (iv)
(D) (ii), (iv) and (iii)

10. The figure shows a logic circuit with two inputs A and B and the output C. The voltage wave forms across A, B and C are as given. The logic circuit gate is : **[NEET (UG) 2012]**

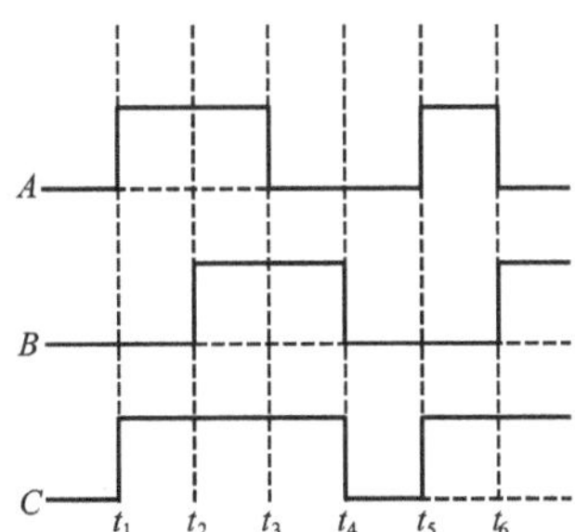

(A) OR gate
(B) NOR gate
(C) AND gate
(D) NAND gate

11. To get an output $Y = 0$ in given circuit which of the following input will be correct : **[NEET (UG) 2012]**

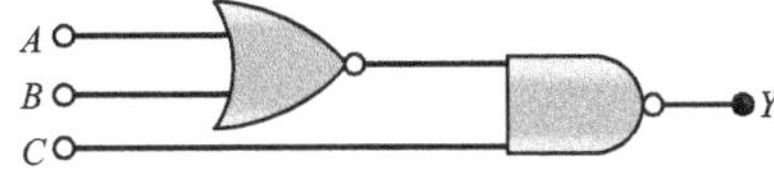

(A) $A \rightarrow 1, B \rightarrow 0, C \rightarrow 1$
(B) $A \rightarrow 1, B \rightarrow 1, C \rightarrow 0$
(C) $A \rightarrow 0, B \rightarrow 1, C \rightarrow 0$
(D) $A \rightarrow 1, B \rightarrow 0, C \rightarrow 0$

12. The output (X) of the logic circuit shown in figure will be : **[NEET (UG) 2013]**

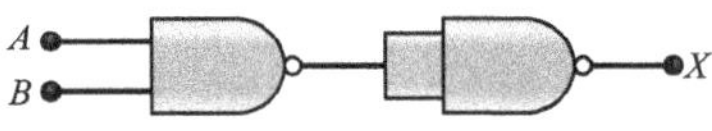

(A) $X = \overline{\overline{A} \cdot \overline{B}}$
(B) $X = \overline{A \cdot B}$
(C) $X = A \cdot B$
(D) $X = \overline{A + B}$

13. To get output 1 for the following circuit, the correct choice for the input is : **[NEET (UG) 2016]**

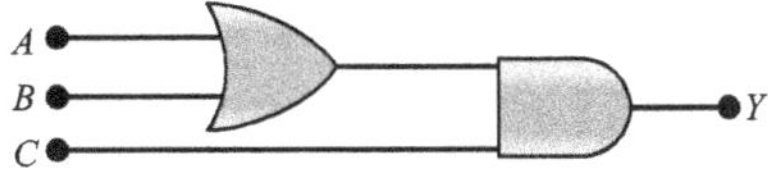

(A) $A = 0, B = 1, C = 0$
(B) $A = 1, B = 0, C = 0$
(C) $A = 1, B = 1, C = 0$
(D) $A = 1, B = 0, C = 1$

14. What is the output Y in the following circuit, when all the three inputs A, B, C are first 0 and then 1 ? **[NEET (UG) 2016 Ph. II]**

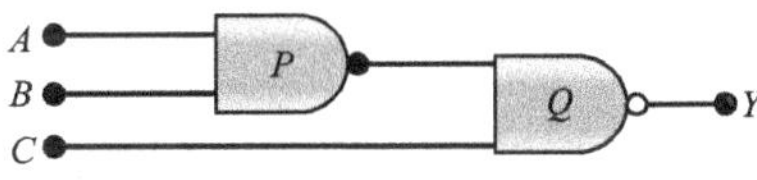

(A) 0, 1
(B) 0, 0
(C) 1, 0
(D) 1, 1

15. The given electrical network is equivalent to : **[NEET (UG) 2017]**

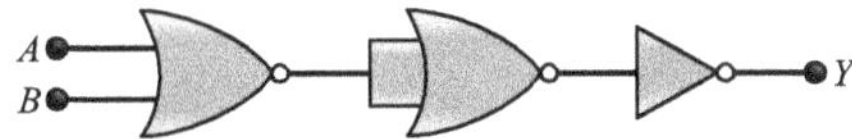

(A) AND gate
(B) OR gate
(C) NOR gate
(D) NOT gate

16. In the combination of the following gates the output Y can be written in terms of inputs A and B as : **[NEET (UG) 2018]**

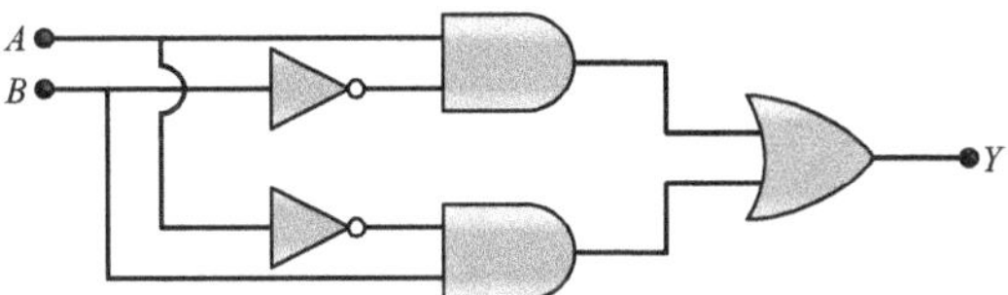

(A) $\overline{A \cdot B} + A \cdot B$
(B) $A \cdot \overline{B} + \overline{A} \cdot B$
(C) $\overline{A \cdot B}$
(D) $\overline{A + B}$

17. The correct Boolean operation represented by the circuit diagram drawn is : **[NEET (UG) 2019]**

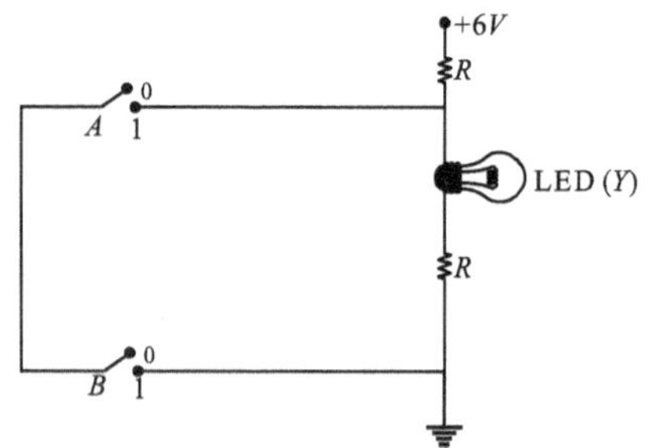

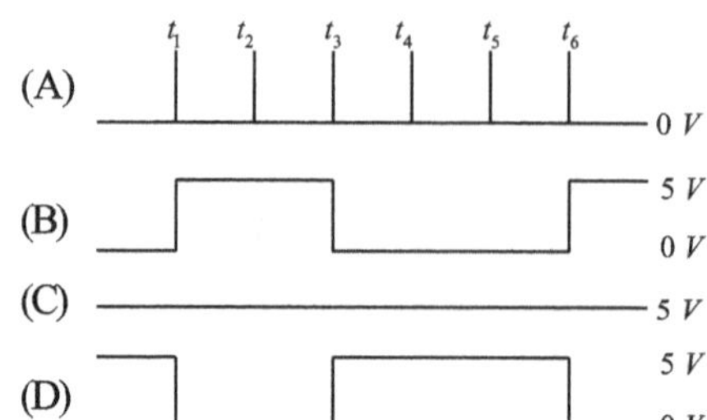

(A) AND   (B) OR
(C) NAND   (D) NOR

18. For the logic circuit shown, the truth table is :

[NEET (UG) 2020]

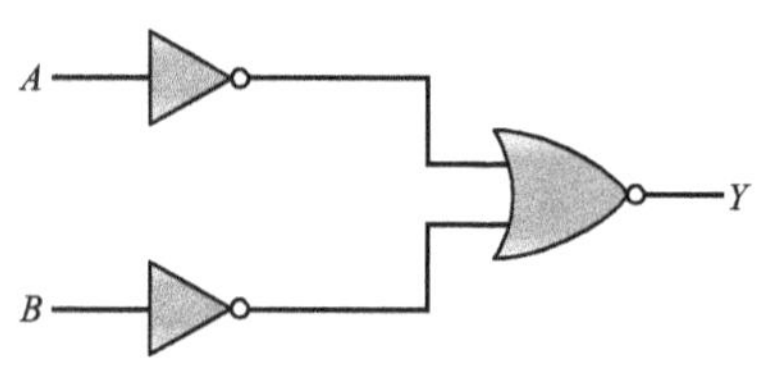

(A)

A	B	Y
0	0	1
0	1	0
1	0	0
1	1	0

(B)

A	B	Y
0	0	0
0	1	0
1	0	0
1	1	1

(C)

A	B	Y
0	0	0
0	1	1
1	0	1
1	1	1

(D)

A	B	Y
0	0	1
0	1	1
1	0	1
1	1	0

19. For the given circuit, the input digital signals are applied at the terminals a, b and c. What would be the output at the terminal y? **[NEET (UG) 2021]**

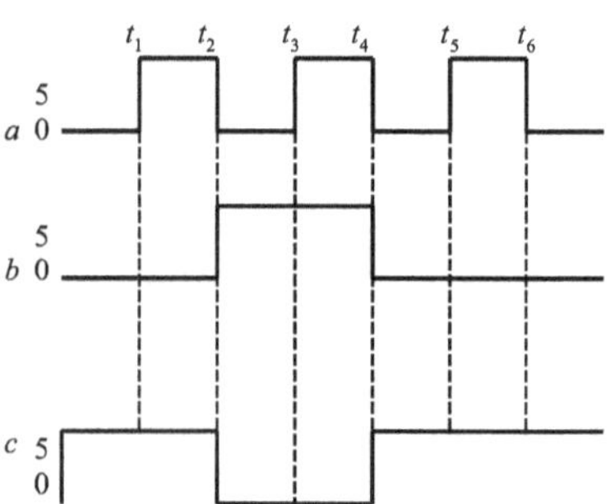

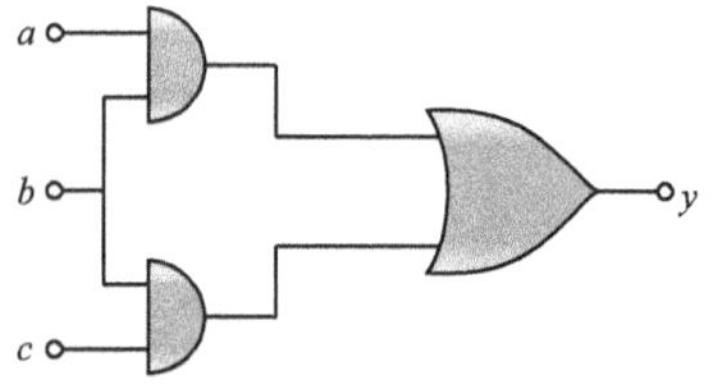

20.

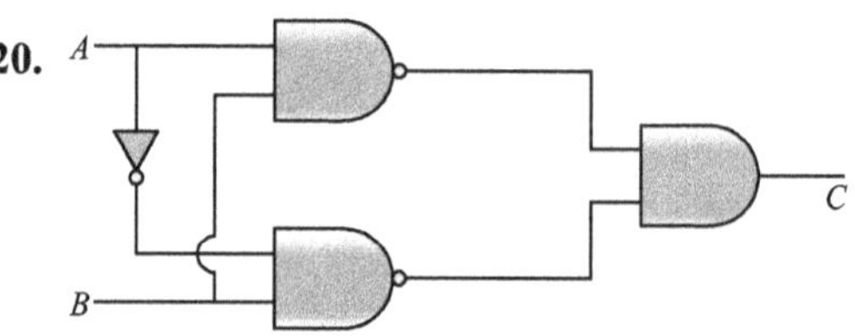

The truth table for the given logic circuit is :

[NEET (UG) 2022]

(A)

A	B	C
0	0	1
0	1	0
1	0	0
1	1	1

(B)

A	B	C
0	0	1
0	1	0
1	0	1
1	1	0

(C)

A	B	C
0	0	0
0	1	1
1	0	0
1	1	1

(D)

A	B	C
0	0	0
0	1	1
1	0	1
1	1	0

* * * * *

ANSWER KEY

Ch-1 Units & Measurements

1.1 Units

1. (C) 2. (D) 3. (C) 4. (D) 5. (D)

1.2 Dimensions

1. (D) 2. (A) 3. (C) 4. (B) 5. (C)
6. (C) 7. (D) 8. (B) 9. (A) 10. (A)
11. (A) 12. (B) 13. (A) 14. (D) 15. (B)

1.3 Measurements

1. (D) 2. (C) 3. (A) 4. (D) 5. (B)
6. (D) 7. (C) 8. (D) 9. (C)

1.4 Vectors

1. (C) 2. (B) 3. (A) 4. (B) 5. (A)
6. (A) 7. (D) 8. (C) 9. (D) 10. (B)
11. (B)

Ch-2 Motion in a Straight Line

2.1 Uniform Motion

1. (B) 2. (D) 3. (B) 4. (C)

2.2 Motion with Constant Acceleration

1. (C) 2. (A) 3. (B) 4. (C) 5. (D)
6. (A) 7. (B) 8. (D) 9. (B) 10. (C)
11. (B) 12. (B) 13. (D) 14. (B) 15. (B)
16. (C) 17. (A) 18. (B) 19. (B)

2.3 Variable Motion

1. (B) 2. (D) 3. (A) 4. (C) 5. (B)
6. (D) 7. (C) 8. (D)

2.4 Graphical Analysis

1. (D) 2. (C)

Ch-3 Motion in a Plane

3.1 Motion in Two Dimensions

1. (B) 2. (A) 3. (D) 4. (C) 5. (A)

3.2 Projectile Motion

1. (C) 2. (A) 3. (A) 4. (B) 5. (C)
6. (A) 7. (D) 8. (A)

Ch-4 Newton's Laws of Motion

4.1 Forces & Applications

1. (B) 2. (B) 3. (B) 4. (D) 5. (D)
6. (D) 7. (C) 8. (C) 9. (A) 10. (C)
11. (A) 12. (A) 13. (C) 14. (A) 15. (B)
16. (D) 17. (C) 18. (D) 19. (B)

4.2 Friction

1. (A) 2. (B) 3. (D) 4. (D) 5. (D)
6. (C) 7. (C) 8. (C)

Ch-5 Work Energy Power & Applications

5.1 Kinetic & Potential Energy

1. (B) 2. (A) 3. (B) 4. (A) 5. (D)
6. (A) 7. (C) 8. (A) 9. (C) 10. (C)
11. (B) 12. (B) 13. (D)

5.2 Work

1. (C) 2. (B) 3. (C) 4. (B) 5. (A)
6. (D) 7. (A) 8. (C) 9. (C) 10. (D)
11. (C)

5.3 Power

1. (C) 2. (B) 3. (B) 4. (A) 5. (B)
6. (D) 7. (B) 8. (D)

5.4 Circular Motion

1. (C) 2. (B) 3. (D) 4. (B) 5. (D)
6. (D) 7. (C) 8. (C) 9. (A) 10. (B)
11. (C) 12. (B) 13. (A) 14. (D) 15. (C)
16. (D) 17. (D) 18. (A)

5.5 Non Uniform Circular Motion

1. (A) 2. (A) 3. (C) 4. (A) 5. (D)
6. (C) 7. (D) 8. (C)

Ch-6 System of Particles & Rotational Motion

6.1 Centre of Mass

1. (B) 2. (B) 3. (C) 4. (C) 5. (C)
6. (D) 7. (A) 8. (D) 9. (A)

6.2 Impulse & Conservation of Momentum

1. (A) 2. (C) 3. (B) 4. (C) 5. (C)

6. (A)	**7.** (B)	**8.** (C)	**9.** (C)	**10.** (B)
11. (B)	**12.** (C)	**13.** (B)	**14.** (C)	**15.** (B)
16. (B)	**17.** (B)	**18.** (B)	**19.** (B)	

6.3 Moment of Inertia

1. (A)	**2.** (C)	**3.** (C)	**4.** (C)	**5.** (C)
6. (C)	**7.** (D)	**8.** (D)	**9.** (B)	**10.** (B)
11. (D)	**12.** (B)	**13.** (A)	**14.** (A)	**15.** (A)

6.4 Torque & Angular Acceleration

1. (C)	**2.** (A)	**3.** (A)	**4.** (C)	**5.** (D)
6. (A)	**7.** (A)	**8.** (A)	**9.** (D)	**10.** (B)
11. (B)	**12.** (B)	**13.** (A)	**14.** (C)	**15.** (D)
16. (A)	**17.** (A)	**18.** (D)	**19.** (D)	

6.5 Angular Momentum & Conservation

1. (B)	**2.** (B)	**3.** (C)	**4.** (A)	**5.** (C)
6. (A)	**7.** (A)	**8.** (B)	**9.** (B)	**10.** (C)
11. (B)	**12.** (C)	**13.** (D)		

6.6 Rolling

1. (A)	**2.** (B)	**3.** (D)	**4.** (C)	**5.** (C)
6. (D)	**7.** (B)	**8.** (D)	**9.** (A)	**10.** (B)
11. (D)	**12.** (B)			

Ch-7 Gravitation

7.1 Gravitational Field & Force

1. (B)	**2.** (B)	**3.** (D)	**4.** (A)	**5.** (C)
6. (A)	**7.** (A)	**8.** (A)	**9.** (B)	**10.** (D)
11. (B)	**12.** (D)	**13.** (C)	**14.** (A)	

7.2 Gravitational Energy & Gravitational Potential

1. (A)	**2.** (C)	**3.** (B)	**4.** (B)	**5.** (D)
6. (C)	**7.** (B)	**8.** (D)	**9.** (C)	**10.** (A)
11. (B)	**12.** (C)	**13.** (D)	**14.** (D)	

7.3 Satellite & Planetary Motion

1. (D)	**2.** (B)	**3.** (D)	**4.** (C)	**5.** (B)
6. (C)	**7.** (A)	**8.** (B)	**9.** (B)	**10.** (B)
11. (D)	**12.** (A)			

Ch-8 Mechanical Properties of Solids

8.1 Elasticity

1. (A)	**2.** (B)	**3.** (C)	**4.** (D)	**5.** (C)
6. (C)	**7.** (A)	**8.** (B)		

Ch-9 Mechanical Properties of Fluids

9.1 Fluid Statics

1. (A)	**2.** (D)	**3.** (D)

9.2 Fluid Dynamics

1. (C)	**2.** (A)

9.3 Surface Tension

1. (D)	**2.** (C)	**3.** (C)	**4.** (B)	**5.** (B)
6. (C)	**7.** (D)	**8.** (D)		

9.4 Viscosity

1. (A)	**2.** (A)	**3.** (B)

Ch-10 Thermal Properties of Matter

10.1 Thermal Expansion

1. (D)	**2.** (C)	**3.** (D)	**4.** (D)

10.2 Calorimetry

1. (C)	**2.** (D)	**3.** (C)	**4.** (B)	**5.** (B)

10.3 Conduction of Heat

1. (B)	**2.** (A)	**3.** (A)	**4.** (B)	**5.** (A)
6. (C)	**7.** (D)	**8.** (A)		

10.4 Radiation of Heat

1. (B)	**2.** (D)	**3.** (B)	**4.** (B)	**5.** (A)
6. (D)	**7.** (D)	**8.** (A)	**9.** (C)	**10.** (D)
11. (B)	**12.** (D)	**13.** (B)	**14.** (A)	**15.** (D)
16. (B)	**17.** (D)	**18.** (A)	**19.** (B)	

Ch-11 Thermodynamics

11.1 First Law of Thermodynamics

1. (D)	**2.** (C)	**3.** (A)	**4.** (C)	**5.** (A)
6. (B)	**7.** (A)	**8.** (D)	**9.** (D)	**10.** (D)
11. (B)	**12.** (D)	**13.** (C)	**14.** (A)	**15.** (C)
16. (B)	**17.** (B)	**18.** (D)	**19.** (D)	**20.** (B)
21. (C)	**22.** (B)	**23.** (B)	**24.** (B)	**25.** (C)
26. (A)				

11.2 Cyclic Process, Heat Engine and Refrigerator

1. (A)	**2.** (C)	**3.** (D)	**4.** (C)	**5.** (C)
6. (C)	**7.** (A)	**8.** (B)	**9.** (D)	**10.** (B)
11. (C)	**12.** (B)	**13.** (C)		

11.3 Thermocouple

1. (D)

Ch-12 Kinetic Theory

12.1 Kinetic Theory of Gases

1. (A)	2. (B)	3. (A)	4. (B)	5. (C)
6. (B)	7. (B)	8. (B)	9. (B)	10. (B)
11. (C)	12. (C)	13. (C)	14. (C)	15. (C)

Ch-13 Oscillations

13.1 Simple Harmonic Motion

1. (B)	2. (C)	3. (B)	4. (D)	5. (D)
6. (C)	7. (A)	8. (C)	9. (A)	10. (D)
11. (A)	12. (B)	13. (D)	14. (C)	15. (B)
16. (A)	17. (D)	18. (B)	19. (A)	20. (C)
21. (B)	22. (A)	23. (C)	24. (C)	25. (C)
26. (A)	27. (D)	28. (C)	29. (B)	30. (B)
31. (D)	32. (B)	33. (B)	34. (D)	35. (D)

Ch-14 Waves

14.1 Wave Motion

1. (C)	2. (C)	3. (A)	4. (C)	5. (D)
6. (A)	7. (A)	8. (D)	9. (A)	10. (D)
11. (A)	12. (C)	13. (A)	14. (A)	15. (B)

14.2 Stationary Waves

1. (B)	2. (C)	3. (C)	4. (D)	5. (A)
6. (D)	7. (A)	8. (C)	9. (B)	10. (B)
11. (C)	12. (B)	13. (B)		

14.3 Beats

1. (C)	2. (D)	3. (C)	4. (A)	5. (D)
6. (A)	7. (C)			

14.4 Doppler's Effect

1. (B)	2. (B)	3. (B)	4. (D)	5. (B)
6. (C)	7. (C)	8. (C)	9. (D)	

Ch-15 Electric Charges and Fields

15.1 Electric Force and Electric Field

1. (B)	2. (D)	3. (D)	4. (B)	5. (C)
6. (C)	7. (C)	8. (B)	9. (B)	10. (C)
11. (B)	12. (C)			

15.2 Electric Flux and Gauss Law

1. (A)	2. (B)	3. (C)	4. (D)	5. (A)
6. (C)	7. (B)	8. (B)		

Ch-16 Electric Potential and Capacitance

16.1 Electric Potential and Energy

1. (C)	2. (C)	3. (B)	4. (B)	5. (A)
6. (C)	7. (C)	8. (B)	9. (B)	10. (C)
11. (A)	12. (B)	13. (B)	14. (D)	15. (C)
16. (B)	17. (B)	18. (B)	19. (D)	20. (A)

16.2 Electric Dipole

1. (C)	2. (D)	3. (A)	4. (A)	5. (B)
6. (C)	7. (B)	8. (D)	9. (A)	

16.3 Capacitance

1. (A)	2. (B)	3. (C)	4. (C)	5. (D)
6. (B)	7. (A)	8. (D)	9. (A)	10. (D)
11. (B)	12. (A)	13. (C)	14. (C)	15. (D)
16. (None)	17. (B)	18. (C)	19. (B)	20. (D)
21. (B)	22. (C)	23. (B)		

Ch-17 Current Electricity

17.1 Resistance and Ohm's Law

1. (A)	2. (C)	3. (A)	4. (B)	5. (C)
6. (A)	7. (A)	8. (B)	9. (D)	10. (C)
11. (A)	12. (B)	13. (D)	14. (B)	15. (C)
16. (B)	17. (C)	18. (D)	19. (A)	20. (A)
21. (B)	22. (C)			

17.2 Kirchoff's Law & Electric Circuits

1. (A)	2. (D)	3. (A)	4. (B)	5. (B)
6. (B)	7. (B)	8. (A)	9. (B)	10. (C)
11. (D)	12. (B)	13. (B)	14. (B)	15. (D)
16. (C)	17. (C)	18. (D)	19. (B)	

17.3 Thermal Effects of Current

1. (D)	2. (A)	3. (B)	4. (C)	5. (C)
6. (D)	7. (B)	8. (D)	9. (A)	10. (B)
11. (C)	12. (D)	13. (B)	14. (B)	15. (C)
16. (B)	17. (B)	18. (A)	19. (C)	20. (B)
21. (D)	22. (A)			

17.4 Electrical Measurements

1. (A)	2. (A)	3. (C)	4. (D)	5. (C)
6. (D)	7. (A)	8. (A)	9. (B)	10. (C)
11. (A)	12. (C)	13. (A)	14. (B)	15. (B)
16. (C)	17. (C)	18. (C)	19. (B)	20. (D)
21. (C)	22. (A)	23. (C)	24. (C)	25. (A)
26. (A)				

Ch-18 Moving Charges & Magnetism

18.1 Magnetic Effects of Current

1. (C)	2. (B)	3. (B)	4. (A)	5. (A)
6. (A)	7. (D)	8. (C)	9. (B)	10. (C)
11. (B)	12. (C)	13. (A)	14. (B)	15. (B)

18.2 Magnetic Force on Moving Charges

1. (C)	2. (A)	3. (B)	4. (A)	5. (A)
6. (C)	7. (C)	8. (A)	9. (A)	10. (D)
11. (D)	12. (A)	13. (B)	14. (A)	15. (B)
16. (C)	17. (A)	18. (B)	19. (A)	20. (A)
21. (A)	22. (D)	23. (B)		

18.3 Magnetic Force on Current

1. (C)	2. (D)	3. (C)	4. (B)	5. (D)
6. (C)	7. (A)	8. (A)	9. (D)	10. (D)

Ch-19 Magnetism and Matter

19.1 Magnetism of a Bar Magnet

1. (A)	2. (B)	3. (D)	4. (D)	5. (B)
6. (C)	7. (B)	8. (A)		

19.2 Earth's Magnetism

1. (B)	2. (A)	3. (B)	4. (A)	5. (A)
6. (C)				

19.3 Magnetic Properties of Materials

1. (A)	2. (A)	3. (A)	4. (A)	5. (A)
6. (D)	7. (C)	8. (B)	9. (D)	10. (A)
11. (A)	12. (C)	13. (B)		

Ch-20 Electromagnetic Induction

20.1 Faraday's Law of EMI

1. (B)	2. (A)	3. (C)	4. (B)	5. (C)
6. (A)	7. (A)	8. (A)	9. (B)	10. (D)
11. (D)	12. (D)	13. (C)	14. (D)	15. (A)
16. (B)				

20.2 Self & Mutual Induction

1. (A)	2. (A)	3. (A)	4. (C)	5. (A)
6. (B)	7. (A)	8. (C)	9. (A)	10. (D)
11. (B)	12. (D)	13. (None)	14. (D)	15. (D)
16. (D)	17. (A)	18. (D)		

Ch-21 Alternating Current

21.1 AC emf, Current, Impedance and Power

1. (C)	2. (A)	3. (B)	4. (D)	5. (C)
6. (C)	7. (B)	8. (A)	9. (D)	10. (B)

21.2 RLC Circuit and Resonance

1. (C)	2. (B)	3. (C)	4. (D)	5. (B)
6. (C)	7. (C)	8. (D)	9. (A)	10. (C)
11. (C)	12. (C)	13. (D)	14. (C)	15. (A)

Ch-22 Electromagnetic Waves

22.1 Electromagnetic Spectrum

1. (A)	2. (A)	3. (A)	4. (C)	5. (A)
6. (B)	7. (D)	8. (C)		

22.2 $\vec{E}, \vec{B}$ and $\vec{C}$ of Electromagnetic Wave

1. (B)	2. (C)	3. (A)	4. (D)	5. (A)
6. (A)	7. (A)	8. (B)	9. (B)	10. (C)
11. (A)	12. (B)	13. (C)		

Ch-23 Ray Optics and Optical Instruments

23.1 Geometrical Optics I - Reflection of Light

1. (C)	2. (A)	3. (A)	4. (B)

23.2 Geometrical Optics II - Refraction of Light

1. (B)	2. (A)	3. (B)	4. (C)	5. (B)
6. (A)	7. (B)	8. (D)	9. (B)	10. (D)
11. (D)	12. (B)	13. (A)	14. (B)	15. (B)
16. (C)	17. (D)	18. (B)	19. (D)	20. (D)
21. (A)	22. (B)	23. (A)		

23.3 Geometrical Optics III - Thin Lenses

1. (D)	2. (C)	3. (B)	4. (D)	5. (C)
6. (A)	7. (C)	8. (C)	9. (B)	10. (B)
11. (D)	12. (B)			

23.4 Dispersion of Light

1. (B)	2. (A)	3. (A)	4. (B)	5. (A)
6. (C)				

23.5 Optical Instruments

1. (C)	2. (C)	3. (B)	4. (A)	5. (C)
6. (C)	7. (D)	8. (A)	9. (D)	10. (B)
11. (C)	12. (A)	13. (B)	14. (D)	

Ch-24 Wave Optics

24.1 Interference

1. (B)	2. (C)	3. (B)	4. (D)	5. (B)
6. (D)	7. (B)	8. (B)	9. (D)	10. (C)

24.2 Diffraction

1. (D)	2. (D)	3. (D)	4. (D)

24.3 Polarization of Light

1. (B)	2. (C)	3. (B)	4. (D)

Ch-25 Dual Nature of Radiation, Matter & X-Ray

25.1 Photoelectric Effect

1. (B)	2. (A)	3. (B)	4. (D)	5. (D)
6. (D)	7. (C)	8. (D)	9. (B)	10. (D)
11. (D)	12. (D)	13. (C)	14. (C)	15. (D)
16. (C)	17. (C)	18. (D)	19. (B)	20. (C)
21. (D)	22. (A)	23. (C)	24. (B)	25. (B)
26. (D)	27. (D)	28. (A & B)	29. (C)	30. (A)
31. (D)	32. (C)	33. (C)	34. (Bonus)	

25.2 Matter Waves and X-Rays

1. (B)	2. (D)	3. (B)	4. (C)	5. (D)
6. (D)	7. (B)	8. (C)	9. (B)	10. (B)
11. (A)	12. (A)	13. (A)	14. (D)	15. (A)
16. (C)	17. (B)	18. (B)	19. (D)	20. (A)
21. (A)	22. (B)	23. (C)	24. (B)	25. (A)
26. (C)				

Ch-26 Atoms

26.1 Properties of Electron in Bohr Model

1. (A)	2. (A)	3. (D)	4. (A)	5. (B)
6. (D)	7. (A)	8. (B)	9. (D)	10. (B)
11. (C)	12. (A)	13. (C)		

26.2 Electron Transition & Hydrogen Spectrum

1. (C)	2. (D)	3. (B)	4. (A)	5. (D)
6. (D)	7. (C)	8. (C)	9. (A)	10. (A)
11. (C)	12. (C)	13. (C)	14. (C)	

Ch-27 Nuclei

27.1 Radioactivity

1. (B)	2. (C)	3. (A)	4. (D)	5. (A)
6. (C)	7. (A)	8. (A)	9. (A)	10. (B)
11. (D)	12. (A)	13. (B)	14. (C)	15. (D)
16. (B)	17. (C)	18. (C)	19. (B)	

27.2 Nuclear Physics

1. (A)	2. (A)	3. (A)	4. (A)	5. (A)
6. (D)	7. (C)	8. (C)	9. (D)	10. (C)
11. (A)	12. (B)	13. (C)	14. (B)	15. (C)
16. (A)	17. (D)	18. (C)	19. (B)	20. (D)
21. (A)	22. (D)	23. (B)	24. (C)	25. (A)
26. (B)	27. (C)	28. (C)	29. (B)	30. (C)
31. (C)	32. (C)	33. (A)	34. (C)	35. (C)
36. (D)	37. (B)	38. (A)	39. (A)	40. (D)
41. (B)	42. (C)	43. (D)	44. (B)	45. (B)

Ch-28 Semiconductors Electronics

28.1 Semiconductor

1. (A)	2. (A)	3. (A)	4. (B)	5. (D)
6. (C)	7. (C)	8. (B)	9. (A)	

28.2 PN Junction and Diodes

1. (B)	2. (A)	3. (B)	4. (A)	5. (D)
6. (A)	7. (C)	8. (B)	9. (B)	10. (B)
11. (D)	12. (D)	13. (A)	14. (C)	15. (D)
16. (C)	17. (D)	18. (C)	19. (A)	20. (D)
21. (B)	22. (B)	23. (A)	24. (A)	25. (D)
26. (C)	27. (C)	28. (C)	29. (C)	30. (B)

28.3 Transistors

1. (A)	2. (D)	3. (B)	4. (C)	5. (C)
6. (B)	7. (B)	8. (A)	9. (D)	10. (A)
11. (D)	12. (B)	13. (D)	14. (A)	15. (A)
16. (A)	17. (B)	18. (C)	19. (D)	20. (A)

28.4 Logic Gates

1. (C)	2. (A)	3. (B)	4. (A)	5. (C)
6. (A)	7. (D)	8. (D)	9. (D)	10. (A)
11. (A)	12. (C)	13. (D)	14. (C)	15. (C)
16. (B)	17. (C)	18. (B)	19. (C)	20. (B)

* * * * *

Ch-1 Units & Measurements

1.1 Units

Sol. 1 Dimensions of Planck's constant can be given as

$$[h] = \frac{\text{Energy}}{\text{Frequency}} = \frac{[ML^2T^{-2}]}{[T^{-1}]}$$

$$= [ML^2T^{-1}]$$

This is the dimensional formula of angular momentum so option (C) is correct. **Ans. (C)**

Sol. 2 From Stefan's law $E = \sigma T^4$, the unit of Stefan's constant can be given as watt/m²K⁴. **Ans. (D)**

Sol. 3 Force between two charges is given by Coulomb's law as

$$F = \frac{1}{4\pi\varepsilon_0} \frac{q^2}{r^2}$$

$$\Rightarrow \qquad \varepsilon_0 = \frac{1}{4\pi} \frac{q^2}{Fr^2}$$

Thus unit of permittivity can be deduced from above formula, given as C²/N-m². **Ans. (C)**

Sol. 4 Unit of plank's constant is given as J-sec and that of moment of inertia is given as kg.m². Thus dimensional formula for the ratio of plank's constant to the moment of inertia is given as

$$[\frac{h}{I}] = [\frac{ML^2T^{-1}}{ML^2}] = [\frac{1}{T}]$$

Which is that of dimensions of frequency. **Ans. (D)**

Sol. 5 The flow rate of heat conduction in steady state is given as

$$\frac{dQ}{dt} = \frac{KA}{l}\Delta T$$

$$\Rightarrow \qquad K = \frac{l\,dQ}{A\,dt\,\Delta T}$$

From above expression unit of thermal conductivity can be given as Wm⁻¹ K⁻¹. **Ans. (D)**

1.2 Dimensions

Sol. 1 From Newton's law of gravitation, force between two masses m_1 and m_2 separated by a distance r is given as

$$F = \frac{Gm_1m_2}{r^2}$$

From above expression, dimensions of G can be calculated as

$$[G] = \left[\frac{Fr^2}{m^2}\right] \equiv \frac{MLT^{-2}L^2}{M^2}$$

$$\Rightarrow \qquad [G] = M^{-1}L^3T^{-2} \qquad\qquad \textbf{Ans. (D)}$$

Sol. 2 In the given question, velocity v as a function of time is given as

$$v = at + \frac{b}{t+c}$$

For the above equation by principle of homogeneity, we use

$$[c] = [t] = [T]$$

and

$$[v] = [at]$$

$$\Rightarrow \qquad [a] = \frac{[v]}{[t]} = [LT^{-2}]$$

$$\Rightarrow \qquad [\frac{b}{t+c}] = [v] = [LT^{-1}]$$

$$\Rightarrow \qquad [b] = [LT^{-1}][T] = [L] \qquad \textbf{Ans. (A)}$$

Sol. 3 Dimensions of resistance is given as

$$\Rightarrow \quad R = \frac{[V]}{[I]} = \frac{[ML^2T^{-3}I^{-1}]}{[I]} = [ML^2T^{-3}I^{-2}] \qquad \textbf{Ans. (C)}$$

Sol. 4 Dimensions of force, pressure, velocity & acceleration are given as

$$[F] = ma = m^1L^1T^{-2}$$
$$a = 1, b = 1, c = -2$$
$$[P] = \frac{F}{A} = \left[\frac{MLT^{-2}}{L^2}\right] = [ML^{-1}T^{-2}]$$
$$a = 1, b = -1, c = -2$$
$$[V] = L^{-1}T^{-1}$$
$$\Rightarrow \qquad a = 0, b = 1, c = -1$$
$$[a] = L^1T^{-2}$$
$$\Rightarrow \qquad a = 0, b = 1, c = -2$$

Thus dimensions of pressure are matching with the given options so option (B) is correct. **Ans. (B)**

Sol. 5 This expression is of energy density which has dimensions given as

$$[u_e] = \frac{M^1L^2T^{-2}}{L^3}$$

$$\Rightarrow \qquad [u_e] = M^1L^{-1}T^{-2} \qquad\qquad \textbf{Ans. (C)}$$

Sol. 6 Velocity of electromagnetic radiation is given as

$$C = \frac{1}{\sqrt{\mu_0 \varepsilon_0}}$$

$$(\mu_0 \varepsilon_0)^{-1/2} = \frac{1}{\sqrt{\mu_0 \varepsilon_0}}$$

Thus the given dimensions is that of velocity, given as $[LT^{-1}]$

Ans. (C)

Sol. 7 By newton's II law, we have

$$F = ma = \frac{m\Delta v}{\Delta t}$$

Thus dimensions of force in terms of M, V and T are given as

$$\Rightarrow \qquad [F] = [M\,V\,T^{-1}]$$

Rearranging terms to get dimensions of mass in terms of F, V and T, given as

$$\Rightarrow \qquad [M] = [F\,V^{-1}\,T]$$ **Ans. (D)**

Sol. 8 Dimensional formula of coefficient of viscosity and density are given as

$$[\eta] = [M^1 L^{-1} T^{-1}]$$

$$[\rho] = [M^1 L^{-3}]$$

Critical velocity of the flowing liquid is expressed as

$$V_c = \eta^x \rho^y r^z$$

Writing dimensional formula on both sides, we have

$$\Rightarrow \qquad [M^0 L^1 T^{-1}] = [M^1 L^{-1} T^{-1}]^x\,[M^1 L^{-3}]^y\,[L^1]^z$$

$$\Rightarrow \qquad M^0 L^1 T^{-1} = M^{x+y}\,L^{-x-3y+z}\,T^{-x}$$

Equating dimensions of LHS and RHS gives

$$-x = -1$$

$$\Rightarrow \qquad x = 1 \qquad\qquad \dots(1)$$

$$\text{and} \qquad x + y = 0 = 0$$

$$\Rightarrow \qquad y = -x = -1 \qquad\qquad \dots(2)$$

$$\text{and} \qquad -x - 3y + z = 1$$

$$\Rightarrow \qquad -1 - 3(-1) + z = 1$$

$$\Rightarrow \qquad z = -1 \qquad\qquad \textbf{Ans. (B)}$$

Sol. 9 If for a given situation length 'L' depends on h, c, G as

$$L \propto h^x\, c^y\, G^z$$

Now writing dimensional formula for all, we have

$$[M^0 L^1 T^0] = [ML^2 T^{-1}]^x\,[LT^{-1}]^y\,[M^{-1}L^3 T^{-2}]^z$$

$$\Rightarrow \qquad L^1 = M^{x-z}\,L^{2x+y+3z}\,T^{-x-y-2z}$$

Equating dimensions on both sides, we have

$$\left.\begin{array}{l} x - z = 0 \Rightarrow x = z \\[4pt] 2x + y + 3z + 1 \\[4pt] -x - y - 2z = 0 \end{array}\right\} \begin{array}{l} x = z = 1/2 \\[8pt] y = -3/2 \end{array} \qquad \textbf{Ans. (A)}$$

Sol. 10 By Coulomb's law, we have

$$F = \frac{kq_1 q_2}{r^2}$$

$$\Rightarrow \qquad k = \frac{Nm^2}{c^2}$$

Thus dimensions of electrostatic constant k are given as

$$\Rightarrow \qquad [k] = \frac{[M^1 L^1 T^{-2}] \times [L^2]}{[A^1 T^1]^2}$$

$$\Rightarrow \qquad [k] = [M^1 L^3 T^{-4} A^{-2}]$$

$$\Rightarrow \qquad [E] = [\frac{e^2}{4\pi\varepsilon_0}] = [A^2 T^2]\,[M^1 L^3 T^{-4} A^{-2}]$$

$$= [M^1 L^3 T^{-2}]$$

Let dimensions of length depends on c, G & $E = \dfrac{e^2}{4\pi\varepsilon_0}$ as given below

$$l = c^x G^y E^z$$

Writing dimensional formula for all terms and equating dimensions on LHS & RHS gives

$$[L] = [LT^{-1}]^x\,[M^{-1}L^3 T^{-2}]^y\,[ML^3 T^{-2}]^z$$

$$-y + z = 0$$

$$\Rightarrow \qquad y = z \qquad\qquad \dots(1)$$

$$\text{and} \qquad x + 3y + 3z = 1 \qquad\qquad \dots(2)$$

$$\text{and} \qquad -x - 4z = 0 \qquad\qquad \dots(3)$$

$$\Rightarrow \qquad z = y = \frac{1}{2},\ x = -2 \qquad \textbf{Ans. (A)}$$

Sol. 11 Dimensions of stress are given as

$$[\text{stress}] = \left[\frac{\text{Force}}{\text{Area}}\right]$$

$$= \left[\frac{M^1 L^1 T^{-2}}{L^2}\right]$$

$$= [M^1 L^{-1} T^{-2}] \qquad \textbf{Ans. (A)}$$

Sol. 12 Energy can be considered dependent upon the given fundamental physical quantities with dimensions a, b and c and can be expressed as

$$E \propto F^a A^b T^c$$

Substituting the dimensions in terms of M, L and T gives

$$[M^1 L^2 T^{-2}] \propto [M^1 L^1 T^{-2}]^a\,[LT^{-2}]^b\,[T]^c$$

Comparing LHS and RHS dimension gives

$$a = 1$$

$$\text{and} \qquad a + b = 2$$

$$\Rightarrow \qquad b = 1$$

$$\text{and} \quad -2a - 2b + c = -2$$

$$\Rightarrow \qquad c = 2$$

$$\Rightarrow \qquad a = 1 \quad b = 1 \quad c = 2$$

$$\Rightarrow \qquad E \propto [F]\,[A]\,[T^2] \qquad \textbf{Ans. (B)}$$

Sol. 13 Dimensions of energy and gravitational constant are given as

$$[E] = [ML^2T^{-2}]$$
$$[G] = [M^{-1}L^3T^{-2}]$$

$$\Rightarrow \quad \frac{[E]}{[G]} = \frac{ML^2T^{-2}}{M^{-1}L^3T^{-2}} = [M^2L^{-1}T^0] \qquad \textbf{Ans. (A)}$$

Sol. 14 Plane angle and solid angle are dimensionless but have units of radian and steradian. **Ans. (D)**

Sol. 15 The given dimensions is of magnetic permeability. **Ans. (B)**

1.3 Measurements

Sol. 1 Volume of a sphere of radius r is given as

$$V = \frac{4}{3}\pi r^3$$

Analyzing percentage error in volume with respect to radius is given as

$$\frac{\Delta V}{V} \times 100 = 3 \times \left(\frac{\Delta r}{r} \times 100 \right)$$

$$\Rightarrow \quad \frac{\Delta V}{V} \times 100 = 3 \times 2 = 6\% \qquad \textbf{Ans. (D)}$$

Sol. 2 For current supplied by the cell, the terminal potential difference across the cell is given as

$$V = \varepsilon - Ir$$

Comparing above relation with general equation of a straight line in *slope-intercept* form given as

$$y = mx + c$$

From above equations we get, slope of line is '$-r$' and intercept of graph on V axis is 'ε'. **Ans. (C)**

Sol. 3 For the given expression of quantity P, the percentage error is given as

$$P = \frac{a^3b^2}{cd}$$

$$\left(\frac{\Delta P}{P} \right) = 3\left(\frac{\Delta a}{a} \right) + 2\left(\frac{\Delta b}{b} \right) + \left(\frac{\Delta c}{c} \right) + \left(\frac{\Delta d}{d} \right)$$

$$\Rightarrow \quad \left(\frac{\Delta P}{P} \right) = 3\,(1\%) + 2\,(2\%) + 3\% + 4\% = 14\% \qquad \textbf{Ans. (A)}$$

Sol. 4 Measured diameter of the ball is given as

$$R = MSR + CSR \times (\text{Least count}) - \text{Zero error}$$

$$\Rightarrow \quad R = 0.5\,\text{cm} + 25 \times 0.001\,\text{cm} - (-0.004\,\text{cm})$$

$$\Rightarrow \quad R = 0.5 + 0.025 + 0.004 = 0.529\,\text{cm} \qquad \textbf{Ans. (D)}$$

Sol. 5 For the given expression of X, the percentage error is given as

$$\frac{\Delta x}{x} \times 100 = 2\frac{\Delta A}{A} \times 100 + \frac{1}{2}\frac{\Delta B}{B} \times 100 + \frac{1}{3}\frac{\Delta c}{c}$$
$$\times 100 + 3\frac{\Delta D}{D} \times 100$$

$$\Rightarrow \quad \frac{\Delta x}{x} \times 100 = 2 \times 1\% + \frac{1}{2} \times 2\% + \frac{1}{3} \times 3\% + 3 \times 4\%$$

$$\Rightarrow \quad \frac{\Delta x}{x} \times 100 = 2\% + 1\% + 1\% + 12\% = 16\% \qquad \textbf{Ans. (B)}$$

Sol. 6 Pitch of screw gauge is the displacement of screw during one rotation and least count of it is given as

$$\text{Least count} = \frac{\text{Pitch}}{\text{Number of division on circular scale}}$$

$$\Rightarrow \quad 0.01\,\text{mm} = \frac{\text{Pitch}}{50}$$

$$\Rightarrow \quad \text{Pitch} = 0.5\,\text{mm} \qquad \textbf{Ans. (D)}$$

Sol. 7 In subtraction the number of decimal places in the result should be equal to the number of decimal places of that term in the operation which contain lesser number of decimal places.

$$9.99 - 0.0099 = 9.98 \qquad \textbf{Ans. (C)}$$

Sol. 8 Least count of screw gauge is given as

$$LC = \frac{1\,\text{mm}}{100} = 0.01\,\text{mm}$$

Diameter of wire is given as

$$D = \text{main scale reading} + \text{circular scale reading}$$
$$D = 0 + 52 \times 0.01\,\text{mm}$$
$$= 0.52\,\text{mm} = 0.052\,\text{cm} \qquad \textbf{Ans. (D)}$$

Sol. 9 Area of a rectangular field is given as

$$A = \text{Length} \times \text{Breadth}$$

$$\Rightarrow \quad A = 55.3 \times 25$$

$$\Rightarrow \quad A = 1382.5$$

As breadth is given in two significant digits so rounding off the area value to two significant digits, we get

$$A = 14 \times 10^2 \qquad \textbf{Ans. (C)}$$

1.4 Vectors

Sol. 1 For the given condition, it is possible only if the given vectors are parallel to each other so angle between them must be 0°. **Ans. (C)**

Sol. 2 As per vector condition given in question, we have

$$(\vec{F}_1 + \vec{F}_2) \cdot (\vec{F}_1 - \vec{F}_2) = 0$$

$$\Rightarrow \quad F_1^2 - F_2^2 - \vec{F}_1 \cdot \vec{F}_2 + \vec{F}_2 \cdot \vec{F}_1 = 0$$

$\Rightarrow \quad F_1^2 = F_2^2$

$\Rightarrow \quad F_1 = F_2$ **Ans. (B)**

Sol. 3 The given vector condition is

$$|\vec{A} \times \vec{B}| = \sqrt{3}\,\vec{A} \cdot \vec{B}$$

$\Rightarrow \quad |\vec{A}\,\| \vec{B}\,|\sin\theta = \sqrt{3}\,|\vec{A}\,\| \vec{B}\,|\cos\theta$

$\Rightarrow \quad \tan\theta = \sqrt{3}$

$\Rightarrow \quad \theta = 60^\circ$

$\Rightarrow \quad |\vec{A} + \vec{B}| = \sqrt{|\vec{A}|^2 + |\vec{B}|^2 + 2\,|\vec{A}\,\| \vec{B}\,|\cos\theta}$

$\Rightarrow \qquad = (A^2 + B^2 + AB)^{1/2}$ **Ans. (A)**

Sol. 4 When two vectors $\vec{A}$ and $\vec{B}$ are despendicular then we can use their dot product to be zero, so we have

$$\vec{A} \cdot \vec{B} = 0$$

$\Rightarrow \quad (2\hat{i} + 3\hat{j} + 8\hat{k}) \cdot (4\hat{j} - 4\hat{i} + \alpha\hat{k}) = 0$

$\Rightarrow \quad 8 - 12 + 8\alpha = 0$

$\Rightarrow \quad \alpha = -1/2$ **Ans. (B)**

Sol. 5 The cross product in the given product $(\vec{B} \times \vec{A}) \cdot \vec{A}$ results a vector which is perpendicular to vector A so dot product with a perpendicular vector will be zero. **Ans. (A)**

Sol. 6 Given vector condition is

$$|\vec{A} + \vec{B}| = |\vec{A} - \vec{B}|$$

$\Rightarrow \qquad |\vec{A} + \vec{B}|^2 = |\vec{A} - \vec{B}|^2$

$\Rightarrow \quad A^2 + B^2 + 2AB \cos\theta = A^2 + B^2 - 2AB \cos\theta$

$\Rightarrow \qquad \cos\theta = 0$

$\Rightarrow \qquad \theta = 90^\circ$ **Ans. (A)**

Sol. 7 This question is same as that of Q. 3. Students can refer solution of Q. 3. **Ans. (D)**

Sol. 8 By triangle law of vector addition for the given figures, we have

$$\vec{d} + \vec{e} = \vec{f}$$ **Ans. (C)**

Sol. 9 For perpendicular vectors, we use

$$\vec{A} \cdot \vec{B} = 0$$

$\Rightarrow \quad [\cos\omega t\,\hat{i} + \sin\omega t\,\hat{j}] \times \left[\cos\dfrac{\omega t}{2}\hat{i} + \sin\dfrac{\omega t}{2}\hat{j}\right] = 0$

$\Rightarrow \quad \cos\omega t \cos\dfrac{\omega t}{2} + \sin\omega t \sin\dfrac{\omega t}{2} = 0$

$\Rightarrow \quad \cos\left(\omega t - \dfrac{\omega t}{2}\right) = 0$

$\Rightarrow \quad \cos\dfrac{\omega t}{2} = 0$

$\Rightarrow \quad \dfrac{\omega t}{2} = \dfrac{\pi}{2}$

$\Rightarrow \quad t = \dfrac{\pi}{\omega}$ **Ans. (D)**

Sol. 10 For collision the particles must move in such a way that after a specific time t both particle will be at same position vector as shown in figure below

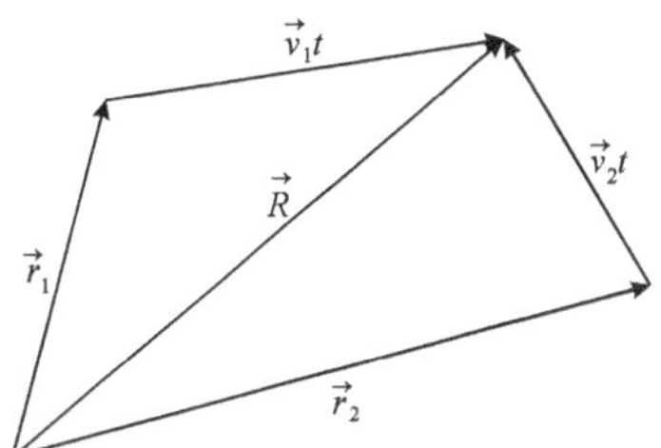

By triangle law of vector addition after time t, we use

$$\vec{R} = \vec{r}_1 + \vec{v}_1 t = \vec{r}_2 + \vec{v}_2 t$$

$\Rightarrow \quad \vec{r}_1 - \vec{r}_2 = (\vec{v}_2 - \vec{v}_1)t$

$\Rightarrow \quad \dfrac{\vec{r}_1 - \vec{r}_2}{|\vec{r}_1 - \vec{r}_2|} = \dfrac{(\vec{v}_2 - \vec{v}_1)t}{|\vec{v}_2 - \vec{v}_1|\,t}$

$\Rightarrow \quad \dfrac{\vec{r}_1 - \vec{r}_2}{|\vec{r}_1 - \vec{r}_2|} = \dfrac{\vec{v}_2 - \vec{v}_1}{|\vec{v}_2 - \vec{v}_1|}$ **Ans. (B)**

Sol. 11 Given condition for the vectors, we use

$$|\vec{A} + \vec{B}| = |\vec{A} - \vec{B}|$$

$\Rightarrow \qquad \cos\theta = 0$

$\Rightarrow \qquad \theta = 90^\circ$ **Ans. (B)**

Ch-2 Motion in a Straight Line

2.1 Uniform Motion

Sol. 1 Figure below shows the path of motion of boys A and B.

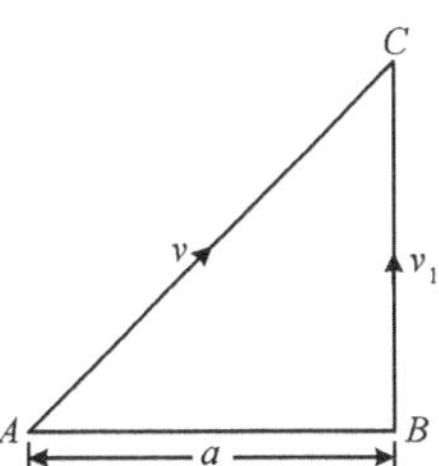

From above figure we can see that distance travelled by boy at A with velocity v in time t is given as

$$Ac = vt,$$

During the same time distance travelled by boy as B is given as

$$BC = v_1 t$$

$\Rightarrow \qquad AB = \sqrt{AC^2 - BC^2}$

$$\Rightarrow \qquad a = \sqrt{v^2 t^2 - v_1^2 t^2}$$

$$\Rightarrow \qquad a = t\sqrt{v^2 - v_1^2}$$

$$\Rightarrow \qquad t = \frac{a}{\sqrt{v^2 - v_1^2}} \qquad \textbf{Ans. (B)}$$

Sol. 2 For a given motion average speed is defined as

$$< v_{avg} > = \frac{\text{total distance travelled}}{\text{total time taken}}$$

If s is the total distance from point X to Y, average speed is given as

$$< v_{avg} > = \frac{s + s}{t_1 + t_2}$$

$$< v_{avg} > = \frac{2s}{\dfrac{s}{v_u} + \dfrac{s}{v_d}} = \frac{2v_u v_d}{v_d + v_u} \qquad \textbf{Ans. (D)}$$

Sol. 3

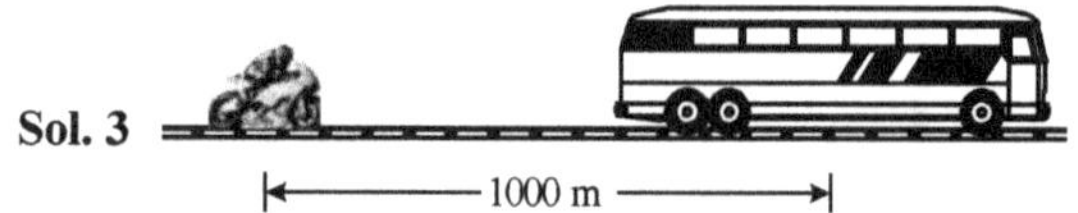

$$\longleftarrow \quad 1000\ \text{m} \quad \longrightarrow$$

To overtake the bus, the scooterist velocity can be taken as v, so the relative velocity of scooterist with respect to bus is taken as

$$v_{SB} = v - 10$$

Time taken to overtake the bus can be written as

$$t = \frac{s_{\text{relative}}}{v_{\text{relative}}} = \frac{1000}{v - 10} = 100\ \text{s}$$

$$\Rightarrow \qquad v - 10 = \frac{1000}{100} = 10$$

$$\Rightarrow \qquad v = 10 + 10 = 20\ \text{m/s} \qquad \textbf{Ans. (B)}$$

Sol. 4 Velocity of Preeti with respect to elevator is given as

$$V_{PE} = \frac{d}{t_1} = v_{ge}$$

Velocity of elevator w.r.t. ground is $v_{eG} = \dfrac{d}{t_2}$ then velocity of girls w.r.t. ground is given as

$$v_{gG} = v_{ge} + v_{eG}$$

$$\Rightarrow \qquad \frac{d}{t} = \frac{d}{t_1} + \frac{d}{t_2}$$

$$\Rightarrow \qquad \frac{1}{t} = \frac{1}{t_1} + \frac{1}{t_2}$$

$$\Rightarrow \qquad t = \frac{t_1 t_2}{(t_1 + t_2)} \qquad \textbf{Ans. (C)}$$

2.2 Motion with Constant Acceleration

Sol. 1 For half height, velocity of the particle is 10 m/s as shown in figure below

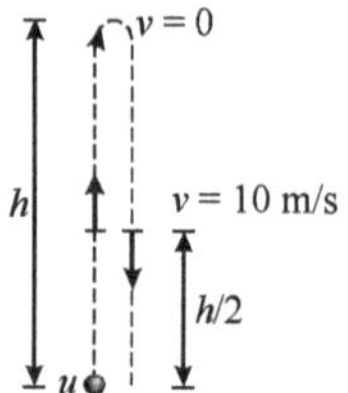

Using equation of motion for velocity at half height, we get

$$10^2 = u^2 - 2g\frac{h}{2} \qquad \ldots(1)$$

For maximum height velocity becomes zero, so we use

$$0 = u^2 - 2gh \qquad \ldots(2)$$

Form (1) and (2)

$$\Rightarrow \qquad 10^2 = \frac{2gh}{2}$$

$$\Rightarrow \qquad h = 10\ \text{m} \qquad \textbf{Ans. (C)}$$

Sol. 2 Interval between throw of the two balls is 2 s so if minimum three (more than two) balls to remain in air then time of flight of first ball must be greater than 4 s so we use

$$T > 4\ \text{s}$$

$$\Rightarrow \qquad \frac{2u}{g} > 4\ \text{s}$$

$$\Rightarrow \qquad u > 19.6\ \text{m/s} \qquad \textbf{Ans. (A)}$$

Sol. 3 If total time of ascent is T $(=u/g)$ and total height ascended is H, we use

$$H = uT - \frac{1}{2}gT^2$$

Distance covered by ball in time $(T - t)$ seconds from start is given as

$$y = u(T - t) - \frac{1}{2}g(T - t)^2$$

Thus distance covered by ball in last t seconds is given as

$$h = H - y$$

$$\Rightarrow \quad h = \left[uT - \frac{1}{2}gT^2\right] - \left[u(T - t) - \frac{1}{2}g(T - t)^2\right]$$

$$\Rightarrow \qquad h = \frac{1}{2}gt^2 \qquad \textbf{Ans. (B)}$$

Sol. 4 Ball will have same speed at half the height during return journey so for the motion of ball from top to half height, we can write

$$10^2 = 2(g)\left(\frac{h}{2}\right)$$

$$\Rightarrow \qquad h = \frac{100}{10} = 10\ \text{m} \qquad \textbf{Ans. (C)}$$

Sol. 5 For uniformly accelerated motion in downward direction, we use

$$h = ut + \frac{1}{2}gt^2$$

As $u = 0$, we have

$$h = \frac{1}{2}gt^2$$

$$\Rightarrow \qquad t \propto \sqrt{h}$$

$$\Rightarrow \qquad \frac{t_1}{t_2} = \sqrt{\frac{h_1}{h_2}} = \sqrt{\frac{16}{25}} = \frac{4}{5} \qquad \textbf{Ans. (D)}$$

Sol. 6 For uniformly accelerated motion distance covered particle in n^{th} second is given as

$$S_n = u + \frac{1}{2}a(2n-1);$$

$$\Rightarrow \qquad S_n = 0 + \frac{1}{2} \times \frac{4}{3}(2 \times 3 - 1)$$

$$\Rightarrow \qquad S_n = \frac{1}{2} \times \frac{4}{3} \times 5 = \frac{10}{3} \text{ m} \qquad \textbf{Ans. (A)}$$

Sol. 7 For uniformly accelerated motion, we use

$$v^2 = u^2 + 2as$$

$$\Rightarrow \qquad (20)^2 = (10)^2 + 2\,a(135)$$

$$\Rightarrow \qquad a = \frac{300}{270} \text{ m/s}^2$$

We also use

$$v = u + at$$

$$\Rightarrow \qquad 20 = 10 + at$$

$$\Rightarrow \qquad 10 = at$$

$$\Rightarrow \qquad 10 = \frac{300}{270} \times t$$

$$\Rightarrow \qquad t = 9 \text{ s} \qquad \textbf{Ans. (B)}$$

Sol. 8 As force applied is constant so acceleration is also constant and for uniformly accelerated motion, we use

$$s = ut + \frac{1}{2}at^2$$

At $u = 0$, we have

$$\Rightarrow \qquad s = \frac{1}{2}at^2$$

$$\Rightarrow \qquad \frac{s_2}{s_1} = \left(\frac{20}{10}\right)^2 = 4$$

$$\Rightarrow \qquad s_2 = 4s_1 \qquad \textbf{Ans. (D)}$$

Sol. 9 Loss of energy can be directly given as

$$U_{loss} = \frac{1}{2}mv^2 - mgh = 20 \text{ J} \qquad \textbf{Ans. (B)}$$

Sol. 10 For uniformly accelerated motion, we use

$$\vec{v} = \vec{u} + \vec{a}t$$

$$\Rightarrow \qquad \vec{v} = (3\hat{i} + 4\hat{j}) + 10(0.4\hat{i} + 0.3\hat{j})$$

$$\Rightarrow \qquad \vec{v} = 3\hat{i} + 4\hat{j} + 4\hat{i} + 3\hat{j}$$

$$\Rightarrow \qquad \vec{v} = 7\hat{i} + 7\hat{j}$$

$$\Rightarrow \qquad |\vec{v}| = 7\sqrt{2}$$

or $\qquad v = 7\sqrt{2} \qquad \textbf{Ans. (C)}$

Sol. 11 When both the balls meet, distance travelled by first ball in 18 s is equal to distance travelled by second ball in 12 s, so we use

$$\frac{1}{2}g\,(18)^2 = (v \times 12) + \frac{1}{2}\,g\,(12)^2$$

$$\Rightarrow \qquad 12v = \frac{1}{2}g\,[18^2 - 12^2]$$

$$\Rightarrow \qquad 12v = \frac{1}{2}\,(10)\,[(18+12)(18-12)]$$

$$\Rightarrow \qquad v = \frac{5 \times 30 \times 6}{12} = 75 \text{ m/s} \qquad \textbf{Ans. (B)}$$

Sol. 12 Stone is falling under uniformly accelerated motion under gravity so we use in given situation

$$v^2 - u^2 = 2as$$

For $\qquad u = 0, a = -g, s = -20 \text{ m}$

$$v^2 = 2gh$$

$$\Rightarrow \qquad v = \sqrt{2gh} = \sqrt{2 \times 10 \times 20} = \sqrt{400} = 20 \text{ m/s}$$

$$\textbf{Ans. (B)}$$

Sol. 13 Figure below shows the change in velocity of body from east to north.

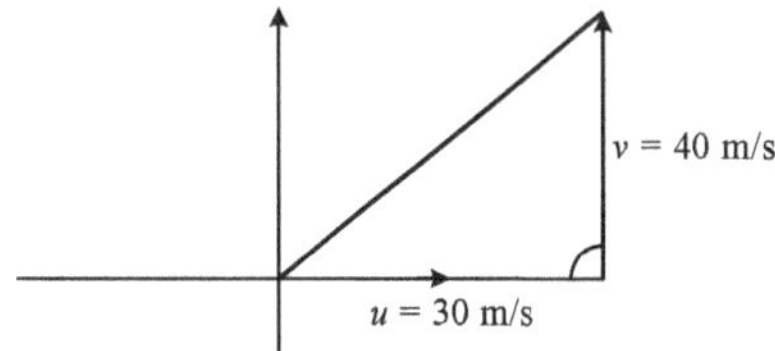

In above situation, average acceleration of body is given as

$$\text{Average Acceleration} = \frac{\text{Change in velocity}}{\text{Time taken}}$$

$$\text{Change in velocity} = v\hat{j} - u\hat{i}$$

$$|\text{Change in velocity}| = \sqrt{40^2 + 30^2}$$

$$= \sqrt{1600 + 900}$$

$$= 50 \text{ m/s}$$

$$\Rightarrow \quad \text{Acceleration} = \frac{50}{10} = 5 \text{ m/s}^2 \qquad \textbf{Ans. (D)}$$

Sol. 14 For uniformly accelerated motion, we use

$$\vec{v} = \vec{u} + \vec{a}t$$

$$\Rightarrow \quad v = (2\hat{i} + 3\hat{j}) + (0.3\hat{i} + 0.2\hat{j}) \times 10$$

$$\Rightarrow \quad v = 5\hat{i} + 5\hat{j}$$

$$\Rightarrow \quad |\vec{v}| = 5\sqrt{2}\ \text{units} \qquad \textbf{Ans. (B)}$$

Sol. 15 Distance covered in first 5 s of free fall motion of stone is given as

$$h_1 = 0 + \frac{1}{2}a(5)^2$$

$$\Rightarrow \quad h_1 = \frac{25a}{2} \qquad \ldots(1)$$

Distance covered in first 10 s

$$S_2 = 0 + \frac{1}{2}a(10)^2 = \frac{100a}{2}$$

So distance covered in second 5 s

$$h_2 = S_2 - h_1 = \frac{100a}{2} - \frac{25a}{2} = \frac{75a}{2} \qquad \ldots(2)$$

Distance covered in first 15 s

$$S_3 = 0 + \frac{1}{2}a(15)^2 = \frac{225a}{2}$$

So, distance covered in last 5 s

$$h_3 = S_3 - S_2 = \frac{225a}{2} - \frac{100a}{2} = \frac{125a}{2} \qquad \ldots(3)$$

Using (1), (2) and (3) equation

$$\frac{h_1}{\frac{25a}{2}} = \frac{h_2}{\frac{75a}{2}} = \frac{h_3}{\frac{125a}{2}}$$

$$h_1 = \frac{h_2}{3} = \frac{h_3}{5} \qquad \textbf{Ans. (B)}$$

Sol. 16 The two situations described in the question are shown below.

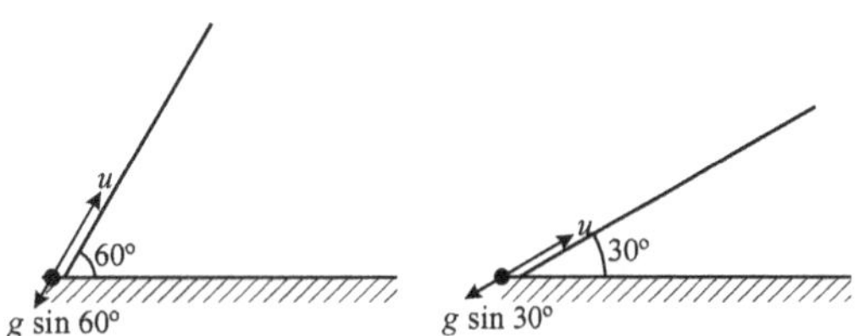

For motion of object in both cases, we use

Along the incline acceleration is given as

$$v^2 - u^2 = 2as$$

$$= 0 - u^2 = 2(-g\sin\theta)\cdot x_1$$

Taking $v = 0$ we get

$$\Rightarrow \quad \text{(Stopping distance)} \quad x_1 = \frac{u^2}{2g\sin 60°}$$

$$\Rightarrow \quad \text{(Stopping distance)} \quad x_2 = \frac{u^2}{2g\sin 30°}$$

$$\Rightarrow \quad \frac{x_1}{x_2} = \frac{\sin 30°}{\sin 60°} = \frac{1 \times 2}{2 \times \sqrt{3}} = 1 : \sqrt{3} \qquad \textbf{Ans. (C)}$$

Sol. 17

Using equation of motion for acceleration motion, we get

$$\Rightarrow \quad v^2 = u^2 + 2gh$$

$$\Rightarrow \quad 80^2 = 20^2 + 2 \times 10h$$

$$\Rightarrow \quad h = 300\ \text{m} \qquad \textbf{Ans. (A)}$$

Sol. 18 For a body starts from rest and travelling at acceleration a, the distance travelled in n^{th} second is given as

$$S_n = \frac{a}{2}(2n-1)$$

$$\Rightarrow \quad \frac{S_n}{S_{n+1}} = \frac{\frac{a}{2}(2n-1)}{\frac{a}{2}(2(n+1)-1)} = \frac{2n-1}{2n+1}$$

$$\Rightarrow \quad \frac{S_n}{S_{n+1}} = \frac{2n-1}{2n+1} \qquad \textbf{Ans. (B)}$$

Sol. 19 The distance travelled by the freely falling body in n^{th} second is given as

$$s_n = u + \frac{a}{2}(2n-1)$$

As body is starting from rest, we use $u = 0$, which gives

$$s_n = 0 + \frac{a}{2}(2n-1)$$

$$s_n \propto (2n-1)$$

$$\Rightarrow \quad s_1 : s_2 : s_3 : s_4 = 1 : 3 : 5 : 7 \qquad \textbf{Ans. (B)}$$

2.3 Variable Motion

Sol. 1 Displacement function with time is given as

$$x = ae^{-\alpha t} + be^{\beta t}$$

Velocity of particle is given as

$$v = \frac{dx}{dt} = -a\alpha e^{-\alpha t} + .b\beta e^{\beta t}$$

Acceleration of particle is given as

$$f = \frac{dv}{dt} = a\alpha^2 e^{-\alpha t} + b\beta^2 e^{\beta t}$$

Above expression of acceleration shows that it will always be positive. Thus v is continuously increasing function of t.

Ans. (B)

Sol. 2 Distance travelled by the particle as a function of time is given as

$$x = 40 + 12t - t^3$$

Thus velocity of particle is given as

$$v = \frac{dx}{dt} = 12 - 3t^2$$

When particle comes to rest, we use

$$v = 0$$

$$\Rightarrow \quad 12 - 3t^2 = 0$$

$$\Rightarrow \quad t = 2 \text{ s}$$

Thus distance travelled by particle before it comes to rest is given as

$$s = x_{t=2} - x_{t=0}$$

$$\Rightarrow \quad s = [40 + 12 \times 2 - 2^3] - [40] = 16 \text{ m} \qquad \textbf{Ans. (D)}$$

Sol. 3 Position of particle as function of time t is given as

$$x = 9t^2 - t^3$$

Particle's velocity is given as

$$v = \frac{dx}{dt} = \frac{d}{dt}(9t^2 - t^3) = 18t - 3t^2$$

For maximum speed, we use maxima & minima so we have

$$\frac{dv}{dt} = 0$$

$$\Rightarrow \quad 18 - 6t = 0$$

$$\Rightarrow \quad t = 3 \text{ s}$$

At $t = 3$ s, second derivative is negative hence speed is maximum and at this instant position of particle is given as

$$x_{\mathrm{m}} = 81 - 27 = 54 \text{ m} \qquad \textbf{Ans. (A)}$$

Sol. 4 Acceleration of particle f is given as

$$f = f_0\left(1 - \frac{t}{T}\right)$$

$$\Rightarrow \quad a = \frac{dv}{dt} = f_0\left(1 - \frac{t}{T}\right)$$

$$\Rightarrow \quad dv = f_0\left(1 - \frac{t}{T}\right)dt$$

To calculate particle's velocity we integrate above expression on both sides as

$$\int_0^v dv = \int_0^t \left[f_0\left(1 - \frac{t}{T}\right)\right]dt$$

$$\Rightarrow \quad v = f_0\left(t - \frac{t^2}{2T}\right)$$

When $f = 0$, we have

$$0 = f_0\left(1 - \frac{t}{T}\right)$$

$$\Rightarrow \quad t = T$$

Thus particle's velocity in the time interval $t = 0$ and $t = T$ is given as

$$v_x = \int_{t=0}^{t=T} dv = \int_{t=0}^{T}\left[f_0\left(1 - \frac{t}{T}\right)\right]dt$$

$$\Rightarrow \quad v_x = f_0\left[\left(t - \frac{t^2}{2t}\right)\right]_0^T$$

$$\Rightarrow \quad v_x = f_0\left(T - \frac{T^2}{2T}\right) = f_0\left(T - \frac{T}{2}\right)$$

$$\Rightarrow \quad v_x = \frac{1}{2} f_0 T \qquad \textbf{Ans. (C)}$$

Sol. 5 Position of particle as a function of time is given as

$$x = (t + 5)^{-1}$$

Velocity of particle can be given as

$$v = \frac{dx}{dt} \quad \Rightarrow \quad v = -(t + 5)^{-2}$$

Acceleration can be given as

$$a = \frac{dv}{dt} \quad \Rightarrow \quad a = 2(t + 5)^{-3}$$

$$\Rightarrow \quad a = 2v^{3/2} \qquad \textbf{Ans. (B)}$$

Sol. 6 Position as a function of time is given as

$$x = 8 + 12t - t^3$$

$$\Rightarrow \quad v = \frac{dx}{dt}$$

$$\Rightarrow \quad v = 0 + 12 - 3t^2 = 0$$

For velocity to be zero, we use

$$v = 0$$

$$\Rightarrow \quad 3t^2 = 12$$

$$\Rightarrow \quad t = 2 \text{ s}$$

$$\Rightarrow \quad a = \frac{dv}{dt} = 0 - 6t$$

at $\quad t = 2$ s $\qquad a = -12 \text{ m/s}^2$

$$\Rightarrow \quad \text{Retardation} = 12 \text{ m/s}^2 \qquad \textbf{Ans. (D)}$$

Sol. 7 Velocity as a function of time is given as

$$v = At + Bt^2$$

$$\Rightarrow \quad \frac{dx}{dt} = At + Bt^2$$

$$\Rightarrow \quad dx = (At + Bt^2)dt$$

By integrating both side from $t = 1$ to $t = 2$ s, we get

$$\Rightarrow \qquad x = \left[\frac{At^2}{2} + \frac{Bt^3}{3}\right]_1^2$$

$$\Rightarrow \qquad x = \frac{A}{2}(4-1) + \frac{B}{3}(8-1)$$

$$\Rightarrow \qquad x = \frac{3}{2}A + \frac{7}{3}B \qquad \textbf{Ans. (C)}$$

Sol. 8 Velocity of P and Q are given as

$$V_P = \frac{dx_P}{dt} = a + 2bt$$

$$V_Q = \frac{dx_Q}{dt} = f - 2t$$

As per given condition in question, we use

$$V_P = V_Q \quad \text{[Given]}$$

$$\Rightarrow \qquad a + 2bt = f - 2t$$

$$\Rightarrow \qquad t = \frac{f-a}{2(b+1)} \qquad \textbf{Ans. (D)}$$

2.4 Graphical Analysis

Sol. 1 In distance-time graph, the speed at an instant is given by the magnitude of slope of curve at that instant. In the question given graph the slope is maximum at C. **Ans. (D)**

Sol. 2 Velocity is slope of x-t graph

$$v = \frac{dx}{dt} = \tan\theta$$

$$\Rightarrow \qquad \frac{v_1}{v_2} = \frac{\tan\theta_1}{\tan\theta_2} = \frac{\tan 30°}{\tan 45°} = \frac{1}{\sqrt{3}} \qquad \textbf{Ans. (C)}$$

Ch-3 Motion in a Plane

3.1 Motion in Two Dimensions

Sol. 1 The motion of particle is shown in figure below

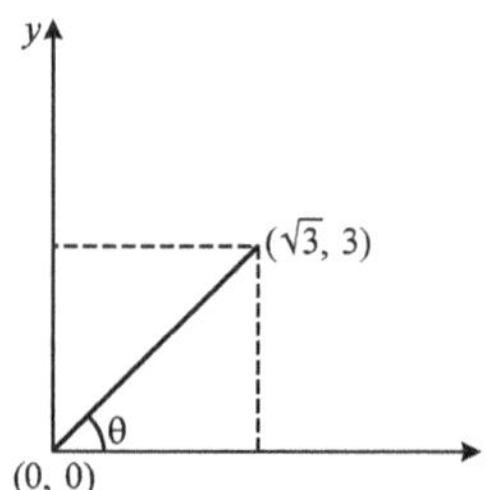

If θ be the angle which the particle makes with x-axis then from

figure we have

$$\tan\theta = \frac{3}{\sqrt{3}} = \sqrt{3}$$

$$\Rightarrow \qquad \theta = \tan^{-1}(\sqrt{3}) = 60° \qquad \textbf{Ans. (B)}$$

Sol. 2 From given situation it is clear that mass will be executing oscillations under the parabolic path shown in question. Since the mass is released at some value of x from rest at $t = 0$ which will be the amplitude of oscillations. From all the given options we can see that $x(t)$ is maximum at $t = 0$ only in option (A).

Ans. (A)

Sol. 3 Average velocity of any particle's motion can be given as

$$\vec{V}_{avg} = \frac{\text{Total displacement}}{\text{Time taken}}$$

$$\Rightarrow \qquad \vec{V}_{avg} = \frac{(x_2 - x_1)\hat{i} + (y_2 - y_1)\hat{j}}{t_2 - t_1}$$

$$\Rightarrow \qquad \vec{V}_{avg} = \frac{(13-2)\hat{i} + (14-3)\hat{j}}{5-0}$$

$$\Rightarrow \qquad \vec{V}_{avg} = \frac{11\hat{i} + 11\hat{j}}{5} = \frac{11}{5}(\hat{i} + \hat{j}) \qquad \textbf{Ans. (D)}$$

Sol. 4 The position coordinates of particle, velocity and acceleration at any time are given as

$$x = 5t - 2t^2 \qquad\qquad y = 10t$$

$$\Rightarrow \quad v_x = \frac{dx}{dt} = 5 - 4t \qquad\qquad \frac{dy}{dt} = 10$$

$$\Rightarrow \qquad v_x = 5 - 4t \qquad\qquad v_y = 10$$

$$a_x = \frac{dv}{dt} = -4 \qquad\qquad a = \frac{dv}{dt} = 10$$

$$\Rightarrow \qquad a_x = -4 \qquad\qquad a_y = 0$$

Thus acceleration of particle at $t = 2$ s is $= -4$ m/s^2. **Ans. (C)**

Sol. 5 Velocity of swimmer with respect to river is given as

$$V_{SR} = 20 \text{ m/s}$$

Flow velocity of river with respect to ground is given as

$$V_{RG} = 10 \text{ m/s}$$

Velocity of swimmer with respect to ground can be calculated as

$$\vec{V}_{SG} = \vec{V}_{SR} + \vec{V}_{RG}$$

The angle of resulting motion of swimmer with the bank as shown in figure is given as

$$\sin\theta = \frac{|\vec{V}_{RG}|}{|\vec{V}_{SR}|}$$

$$\Rightarrow \qquad \sin \theta = \frac{10}{20}$$

$$\Rightarrow \qquad \sin \theta = \frac{1}{2}$$

$$\Rightarrow \qquad \theta = 30° \text{ west} \qquad \textbf{Ans. (A)}$$

3.2 Projectile Motion

Sol. 1 When a body is projected from a point then time required to reach the ground depend on the initial vertical velocity of the particle. In this given situation, vertical motion of both the particles A and B are exactly same. As particle B has an initial velocity, but that is in horizontal direction and it has no component in vertical (component of a vector at a direction of $90° = 0$) direction. Hence they will reach the ground simultaneously. **Ans. (C)**

Sol. 2 In projectile motion for complementary angles of projection, ranges will be same as shown in figure below, so we use

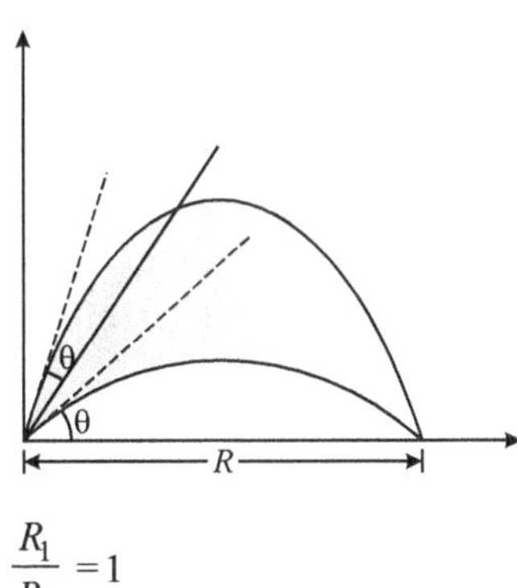

$$\frac{R_1}{R_2} = 1 \qquad \textbf{Ans. (A)}$$

Sol. 3 Maximum range of projectile is given as

$$R_{max} = \frac{u^2}{g} = \frac{20 \times 20}{10} = 40 \text{ m} \qquad \textbf{Ans. (A)}$$

Sol. 4 Horizontal range of projectile is given as

$$R = \frac{u^2 \sin 2\theta}{g} \qquad \qquad \dots(1)$$

Maximum height of projectile is given as

$$H = \frac{u^2 \sin^2 \theta}{2g} \qquad \qquad \dots(2)$$

As stated in question that $R = H$, we use

$$\frac{u^2 \sin 2\theta}{g} = \frac{u^2 \sin^2 \theta}{2g}$$

$$\Rightarrow \quad 2 \sin \theta \cos \theta = \frac{\sin^2 \theta}{2}$$

$$\Rightarrow \qquad \tan \theta = 4$$

$$\Rightarrow \qquad \theta = \tan^{-1}(4) \qquad \textbf{Ans. (B)}$$

Sol. 5 As the projectile strikes at B, only y component changes its direction, x-component remains same as shown in figure below, so final velocity vector of particle is given as

$$v_f = 2\hat{i} - 3\hat{j}$$

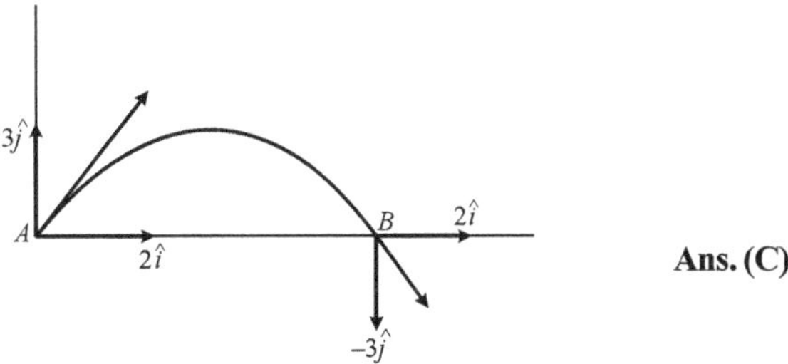

Ans. (C)

Sol. 6 Equation of trajectory is of a projectile motion is given as

$$y = x \tan \theta - \frac{gx^2}{2u^2 \cos^2 \theta}$$

For identical trajectories for same angle of projection, we should have

$$\frac{g}{u^2} = \text{constant for both planets}$$

$$\Rightarrow \qquad \frac{9.8}{5^2} = \frac{g'}{3^2}$$

$$\Rightarrow \qquad g' = \frac{9.8 \times 9}{25} = 3.528 \text{ m/s}^2$$

$$\Rightarrow \qquad g' = 3.5 \text{ m/s}^2 \qquad \textbf{Ans. (A)}$$

Sol. 7 Velocity of car at $t = 4$ s is given as

$$v = u + at$$

$$v = 0 + 5(4) = 20 \text{ m/s}$$

Thus the stone dropped from car has its velocity component in horizontal direction (X-direction) equal to 20 m/s and in downward direction (Y-direction) initial speed is zero and acceleration due to gravity 10 m/s².

At $t = 6$ s, X-direction velocity of stone remain same whereas Y-direction velocity of stone becomes

$$v_y = u + at$$

$$= 0 + g(2) = 20 \text{ m/s}$$

Thus net velocity of stone at $t = 6$ s is given as

$$v = \sqrt{v_x^2 + v_y^2} = \sqrt{20^2 + 20^2} = 20\sqrt{2} \text{ m/s}$$

Ans. (D)

Sol. 8 At highest point of trajectory, only horizontal component of velocity is there in the ball, given as

$$u_x = u \cos \theta$$

$$\Rightarrow \qquad u_x = u \cos \theta = 10 \cos 30°$$

$$\Rightarrow \qquad u_x = 5\sqrt{3} \text{ ms}^{-1} \qquad \qquad \textbf{Ans. (A)}$$

4 Newton's Laws of Motion

4.1 Forces & Applications

Sol. 1 Impulse during the process of catch is equal to Change in momentum. If F is the force applied by the cricketer during catch then we use

$$F \cdot \Delta t = m \cdot v$$

$$\Rightarrow \qquad F = \frac{mv}{\Delta t}$$

$$\Rightarrow \qquad F = \frac{150 \times 10^{-3} \times 20}{0.1}$$

$$\Rightarrow \qquad F = 30 \text{ N} \qquad \qquad \textbf{Ans. (B)}$$

Sol. 2 The acceleration of mass is given as

$$a = \frac{F}{m} = \frac{6t^2 \hat{i} + 4t\hat{j}}{3} = 2t^2 \hat{i} + \frac{4}{3} t\hat{j}$$

$$\Rightarrow \qquad a = \frac{dv}{dt} = 2t^2 \hat{i} + \frac{4}{3} t\hat{j}$$

$$\Rightarrow \qquad dv = \left(2t^2 \hat{i} + \frac{4}{3} t\hat{j} \right) dt$$

Integrating on both sides within proper limits, we get

$$v = \int_0^3 \left(2t^2 \hat{i} + \frac{4}{3} t\hat{j} \right) dt$$

$$\Rightarrow \qquad v = \frac{2}{3} t^3 \hat{i} + \frac{4}{6} t^2 \hat{j} \Big|_0^3$$

$$\Rightarrow \qquad v = 18\hat{i} + 6\hat{j} \qquad \qquad \textbf{Ans. (B)}$$

Sol. 3 As lift is moving in upward direction with an acceleration a, the tension T developed in the string connected to the lift is given as

$$T = m (g + a)$$

$$\Rightarrow \qquad T = 1000 (9.8 + 1)$$

$$\Rightarrow \qquad T = 10,800 \text{ N} \qquad \qquad \textbf{Ans. (B)}$$

Sol. 4 As lift is accelerating upwards with acceleration a, then reading on the scale is gives the normal reaction acting on the

man, given as

$$R = m (g + a)$$

$$\Rightarrow \qquad R = 80 (10 + 5) \text{ N}$$

$$\Rightarrow \qquad R = 1200 \text{ N} \qquad \qquad \textbf{Ans. (D)}$$

Sol. 5 If T is the tension in the rope when monkey climbs up with an acceleration a, then we use

$$T - mg = ma$$

$$\Rightarrow \qquad 25g - 20g = 20\, a$$

$$\Rightarrow \qquad a = \frac{5 \times 10}{20}$$

$$\Rightarrow \qquad a = 2.5 \text{ m/s}^2 \qquad \qquad \textbf{Ans. (D)}$$

Sol. 6 Figure below shows the forces acting on the block

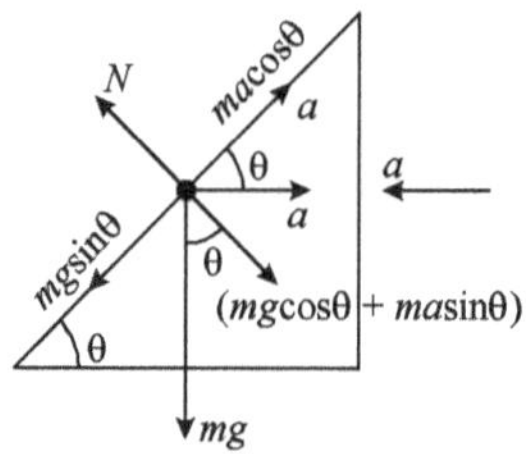

The wedge is given an acceleration to the left so we can consider a pseudo force on block with respect to wedge of magnitude 'ma' in rightward direction. For equilibrium of block on the surface of wedge, we use

$$mg\sin\theta = ma\cos\theta$$

$$\Rightarrow \qquad a = \frac{g \sin \theta}{\cos \theta}$$

Normal reaction of the wedge on the block is given as

$$N = mg\cos\theta + ma\sin\theta$$

$$\Rightarrow \qquad N = mg\cos\theta + \frac{mg \sin \theta \cdot \sin \theta}{\cos \theta}$$

$$\Rightarrow \qquad N = \frac{mg(\cos^2 \theta + \sin^2 \theta)}{\cos \theta}$$

$$\Rightarrow \qquad N = \frac{mg}{\cos \theta} \qquad \qquad \textbf{Ans. (D)}$$

Sol. 7 As 4 N and 2 N are opposite forces the resulting force diagram is shown below

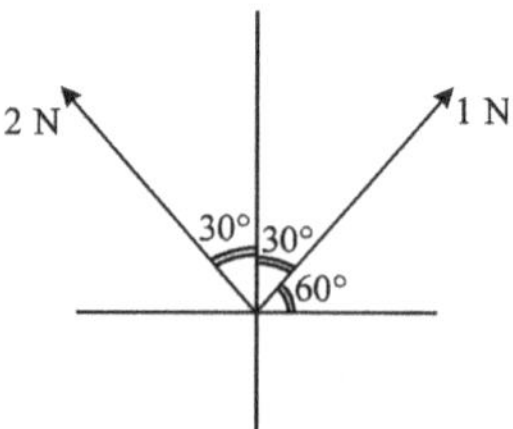

Horizontal component of 2 N along x-direction is given as

$$F_{x1} = 2 \sin 30° = 1 \text{ N (along -}x\text{ direction)}$$

Horizontal component of 1 N along x-direction is given as

$$x_2 = 1\cos 60° = \frac{1}{2} \text{ N (along } +x \text{ direction)}$$

So, net horizontal force is $\frac{1}{2}$ N along negative x-direction, hence

$\frac{1}{2}$ N is required in to be applied in positive x-direction so that net force along x-direction becomes zero and net force will be only along y-direction. **Ans. (C)**

Sol. 8 Figure below shows the free body diagram of the lift

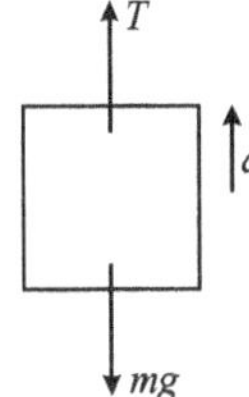

If lift is acceleration upward with acceleration a, we use

$$T - mg = ma$$

$$\Rightarrow \quad a = \frac{T - mg}{m} = 4 \text{ m/s}^2 \qquad \text{Ans. (C)}$$

Sol. 9 The magnitude of applied force is given as

$$|\vec{F}| = \sqrt{6^2 + 8^2 + 10^2} = 10\sqrt{2}\,\text{N}$$

Mass of body can be given as

$$m = \frac{|\vec{F}|}{a} = \frac{10\sqrt{2}}{1} = 10\sqrt{2}\,\text{kg} \qquad \text{Ans. (A)}$$

Sol. 10 Free body diagram of lift is shown in figure below

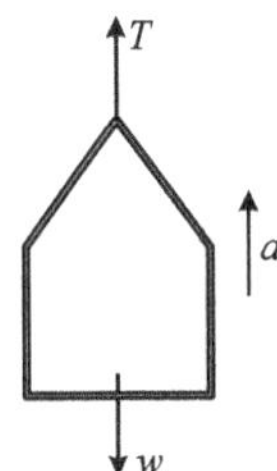

If acceleration of lift is 'a' in upward direction, we use

$$T - w = ma$$

$$\Rightarrow \quad T = (m_1 + m_2)\,g + 1000 \times 1$$

$$\Rightarrow \quad T = 10000 + 1000 = 11000\,\text{N} \qquad \text{Ans. (C)}$$

Sol. 11 Velocity when stone strikes the ground is given as

$$v = \sqrt{2gh}$$

Momentum of stone at the point of hit is given as

$$P = mv = m\sqrt{2gh}$$

$$P \propto \sqrt{h}$$

$$\Rightarrow \quad \frac{P_2}{P_1} = \sqrt{\frac{h_2}{h_1}} = \sqrt{\frac{2h}{h}} = \sqrt{2}$$

$$\Rightarrow \quad P_2 = 1.414\,P_1$$

$$\Rightarrow \quad \% \text{ change} = \frac{P_2 - P_1}{P_1} \times 100\,\% = 41.4\,\% \qquad \text{Ans. (A)}$$

Sol. 12 As blocks are moving with constant speed so net force on each block and their acceleration will be zero. **Ans. (A)**

Sol. 13 Change in momentum for a motion is given by the area under the F-t graph in a given interval of time. Thus for above graph, it is given as

$$\Delta J = \left(\frac{1}{2} \times 2 \times 6\right) - (2 \times 3) + (4 \times 3)$$

$$= 6 - 6 + 12 = 12\,\text{Ns} \qquad \text{Ans. (C)}$$

Sol. 14 Initially balloon is descending down with an acceleration 'a'. Its free body diagram is given as

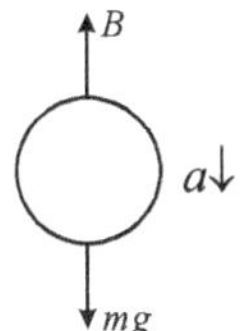

In above diagram B is the buoyant force acting on the balloon in upward direction, the equation of motion of balloon is written as

$$mg - B = ma \qquad \dots(1)$$

If we remove a mass m_0, balloon starts moving upward with same acceleration 'a' so now the equation of motion is written as

$$B - (m - m_0)g = (m - m_0)a \qquad \dots(2)$$

From above equations-(1) and (2), we have

$$mg - mg + m_0 g = ma + ma - m_0 a$$

$$\Rightarrow \quad m_0 = \frac{2ma}{g + a} \qquad \text{Ans. (A)}$$

Sol. 15 Free body diagram of block A and B are shown below

before cutting the string

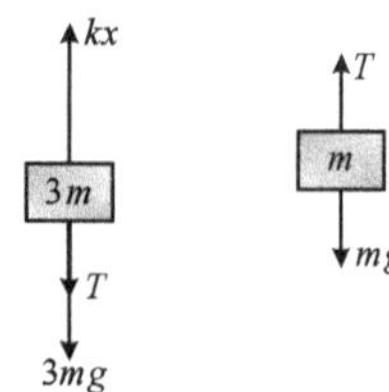

Before the string is cut as blocks were in equilibrium, we use

$$kx = T + 3\,mg \qquad \ldots(1)$$

$$T = mg \qquad \ldots(2)$$

$$\Rightarrow \qquad kx = 4\,mg$$

After the string is cut, $T = 0$ so block B will be in free fall and have acceleration g and acceleration of block A can be given as

$$a = \frac{kx - 3mg}{3m}$$

$$\Rightarrow \qquad a = \frac{4mg - 3mg}{3m}$$

$$\Rightarrow \qquad a = \frac{g}{3}\uparrow \qquad \textbf{Ans. (B)}$$

Sol. 16 Free body diagram of block is shown in figure below

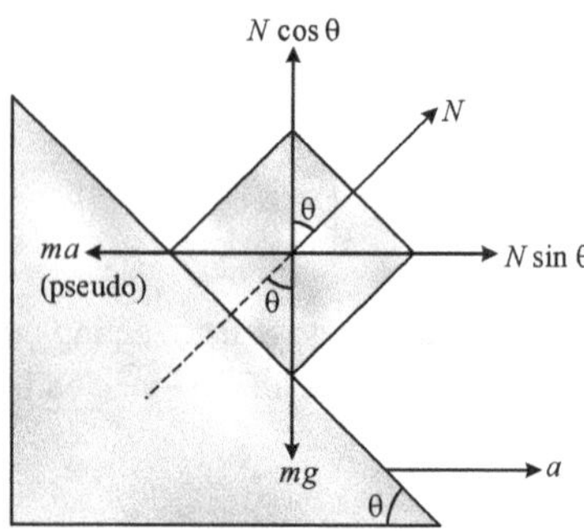

In non-inertial frame, as wedge is accelerated, for equilibrium of block, we use

$$N \sin\theta = ma \qquad \ldots(1)$$

$$N \cos\theta = mg \qquad \ldots(2)$$

$$\Rightarrow \qquad \tan\theta = \frac{a}{g}$$

$$\Rightarrow \qquad a = g\tan\theta \qquad \textbf{Ans. (D)}$$

Sol. 17 As forces are forming closed loop in sequential order so resultant of all these force is zero hence velocity of the particle remain constant. **Ans. (C)**

Sol. 18 Acceleration of system of Atwood's machine is given as

$$a = \frac{(m_2 - m_1)g}{m_1 + m_2} = \frac{(6-4)g}{6+4} = \frac{g}{5} \qquad \textbf{Ans. (D)}$$

Sol. 19 As lift is moving at constant velocity, its acceleration will be zero hence, we use

$$T = W + f$$

$$\Rightarrow \qquad T = 20000 + 3000 = 23000\,\text{N}$$

Power delivered by the motor is calculated as

$$P = Tv$$

$$\Rightarrow \qquad P = 23000 \times 1.5 = 34500\,\text{W} \qquad \textbf{Ans. (B)}$$

4.2 Friction

Sol. 1 Figure below shows the situation given in question.

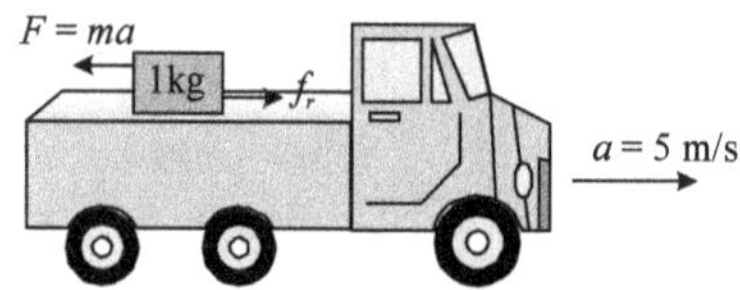

Limiting Friction force on block can be calculated as

$$f_{rL} = \mu_s N$$

$$\Rightarrow \qquad f_{rL} = \mu_s \times mg$$

$$\Rightarrow \qquad f_{rL} = 0.6 \times 1 \times 10 = 6\,\text{N}$$

Where f_{rL} is the force of limiting friction. Pseudo force acting on the block can be given as

$$\text{Pseudo force} = ma = 1 \times 5 = 5\,\text{N}$$

If pseudo force $F < f_{rL}$ block does not move. So static friction would be acting on the block to keep it at rest.

$$\Rightarrow \qquad f_r = 5\,\text{N} \qquad \textbf{Ans. (A)}$$

Sol. 2 Figure below shows the free body diagram of the block

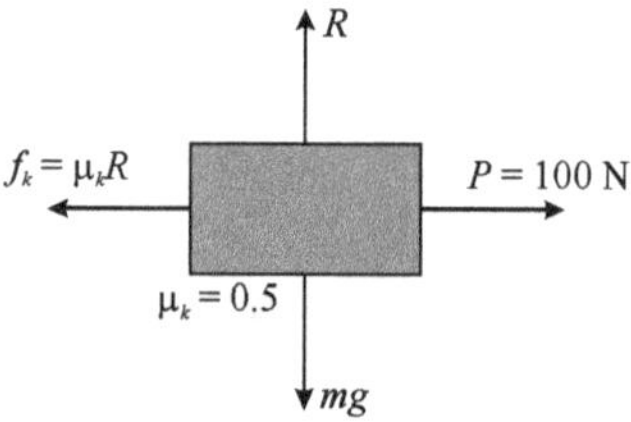

As block is in equilibrium in vertical direction, we use

$$R = mg$$

Frictional force on block is calculated as

$$f_k = \mu_k R = \mu_k mg$$

$$= 0.5 \times 10 \times 10 = 50\,\text{N}$$

Acceleration of the block is given as

$$a = (F - \mu_k mg)/m$$

$$= (100 - 50)/10 = 5\,\text{m/s}^2 \qquad \textbf{Ans. (B)}$$

Sol. 3 Free body diagram of two masses are shown in below figures

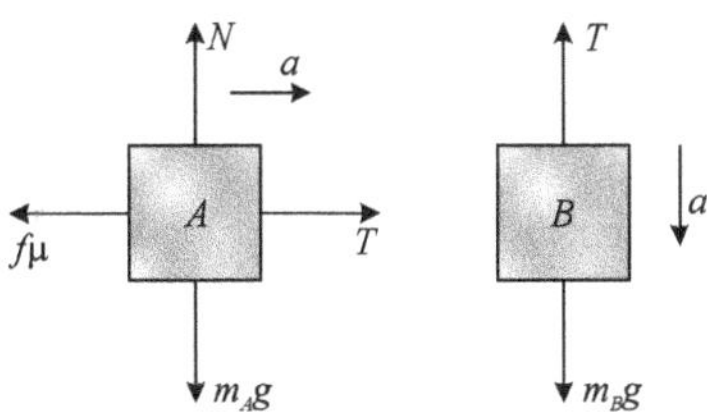

For equilibrium of blocks, as these are not moving, we use

For block A $T = f = \mu N_A$

For block B $T = m_B g$

$\Rightarrow$ $\mu N_A = m_B g$

$\Rightarrow$ $m_B = \mu m_A = 0.2 \times 2 = 0.4 \, \text{kg}$ **Ans. (D)**

Sol. 4 Friction is the only retarding force acting on the block so retardation of block is during motion is given as

$$a = \mu mg / m = \mu g$$

If after time t block will come to rest, we use

$$v = u - at$$

$$0 = V - \mu g t$$

$\Rightarrow$ $t = \dfrac{V}{\mu g}$ **Ans. (D)**

Sol. 5 As cart C is accelerated by 'α' then in frame of cart a pseudo force '$m\alpha$' acts on block in leftward direction. The free body diagrams are shown in figure below

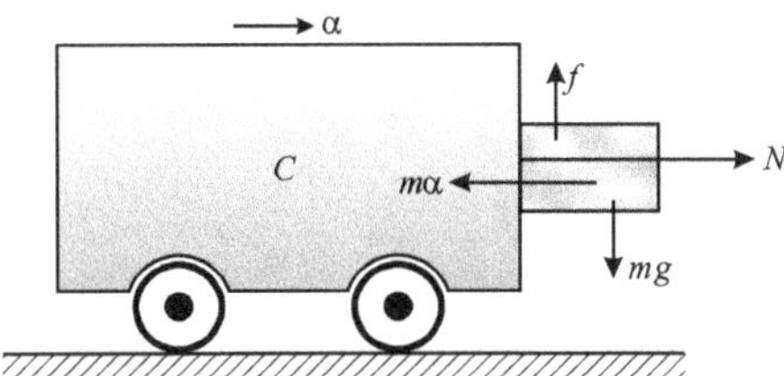

For preventing small block from sliding down, limiting friction on it must be more than or equal to the weight of block so we use

$$f \geq mg$$

$\Rightarrow$ $\mu m\alpha \geq mg$

$\Rightarrow$ $\alpha \geq \dfrac{g}{\mu}$ **Ans. (D)**

Sol. 6 For first half of incline plane acceleration of block is given as

$$a_1 = g \sin\theta$$

For second half of incline plane acceleration of block is given as

$$a_2 = g \sin\theta - \mu g \cos\theta$$

If the block is coming to rest at bottom we use

$$a_1 = a_2$$

$\Rightarrow$ $g \sin\theta = g \sin\theta - \mu g \cos\theta$

$\Rightarrow$ $\mu = 2 \tan\theta$ **Ans. (C)**

Sol. 7 Figure below shows the free body diagram of masses.

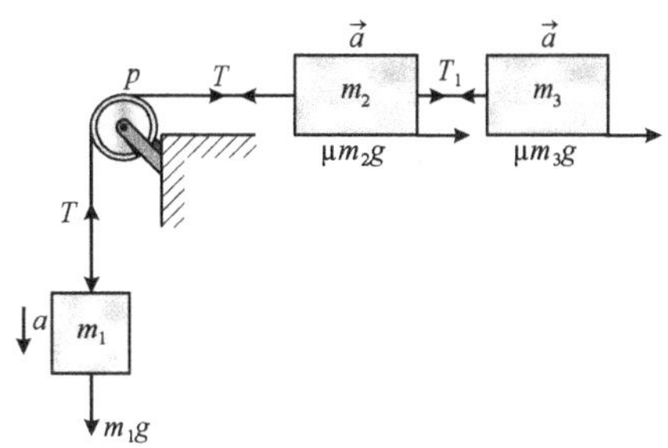

Writing equations of motion for m_1 m_2 and m_3

$$m_1 g - T = m_1 a \qquad \ldots(1)$$

$$T - T_1 - \mu m_2 g = m_2 a \qquad \ldots(2)$$

$$T_1 - \mu m_3 g = m_3 a \qquad \ldots(3)$$

$\Rightarrow$ $T = (m_2 + m_3)a + \mu g(m_2 + m_3) \qquad \ldots(4)$

By equation-(1) & (4), we get

$$m_1 g - m_1 a = (m_2 + m_3)a + \mu g(m_2 + m_3)$$

$\Rightarrow$ $a(m_1 + m_2 + m_3) = m_1 g - \mu g(m_2 + m_3)$

$\Rightarrow$ $a = \dfrac{m_1 g - \mu(m_2 + m_3)g}{m_1 + m_2 + m_3} = \dfrac{g}{3}(1 - 2\mu)$ **Ans. (C)**

Sol. 8 Figure below shows the free body diagram of the box on inclined plane

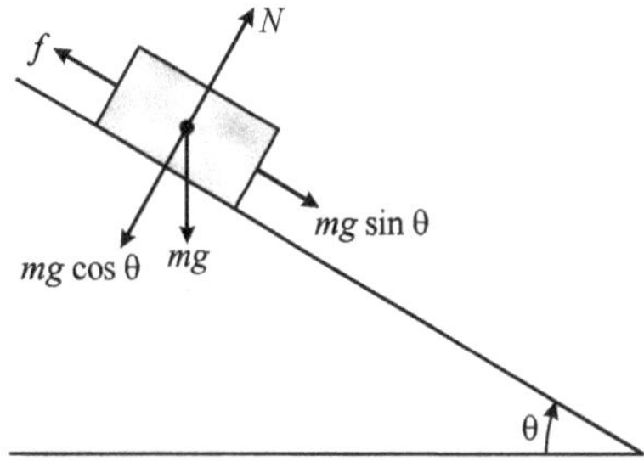

Angle of repose given in question is 30° so static friction coefficient is given as

$$\mu_s = \tan 30° = \frac{1}{\sqrt{3}} = 0.57 \approx 0.6$$

If kinetic friction coefficient is μ_k, the acceleration of box is given as

$$a = g(\sin 30° - \mu_k \cos 30°)$$

By speed equation for box, we have

$$S = ut + \frac{1}{2} at^2$$

$$\Rightarrow \qquad 4 = 0 + \frac{1}{2}(g \sin 30^\circ - \mu_k \cos 30^\circ)(4)^2$$

$$\Rightarrow \qquad 0.5 = (10)\left(\frac{1}{2}\right) - \mu_k(10)\left(\frac{\sqrt{3}}{2}\right)$$

$$\Rightarrow \qquad 5\sqrt{3}\,\mu_k = 4.5$$

$$\Rightarrow \qquad \mu_k = 0.51 \qquad\qquad \textbf{Ans. (C)}$$

Ch-5 Work Energy Power & Applications

5.1 Kinetic & Potential Energy

Sol. 1 Velocity of the ball at the highest point

$$v\cos\theta = v\cos 45^\circ = \frac{v}{\sqrt{2}}$$

Thus kinetic energy of the ball at the topmost point is given as

$$K = \frac{1}{2}m \times \left(\frac{v}{\sqrt{2}}\right)^2$$

$$K = \frac{1}{4}mv^2 = \frac{K}{2} \qquad\qquad \textbf{Ans. (B)}$$

Sol. 2 Energy stored in spring A is given as

$$E_A = \frac{1}{2}Kx^2 = \frac{1}{2}\frac{F^2}{K}$$

$$\Rightarrow \qquad \frac{K_A}{K_B} = 2$$

$$\Rightarrow \qquad \frac{E_A}{E_B} = \frac{1}{2}$$

$$\Rightarrow \qquad E_B = 2E_A \qquad\qquad \textbf{Ans. (A)}$$

Sol. 3 During oscillations of spring when it moves from maximum height to minimum height, potential energy changes to kinetic energy so we can use

Drop in Potential Energy = Gain in Kinetic Energy

$$\Rightarrow \quad mg(2-0.75) = \frac{1}{2}mv^2$$

$$\Rightarrow \qquad v = \sqrt{2g(1.25)}$$

$$\Rightarrow \qquad v = 5 \text{ m/s} \qquad\qquad \textbf{Ans. (B)}$$

Sol. 4 Momentum p of a body moving with kinetic energy K is given as

$$p = \sqrt{2mK}$$

If kinetic energy is increased by 300% then new kinetic energy becomes

$$K_{\text{new}} = K + 3K = 4K$$

Thus new momentum will be

$$P_{\text{new}} = \sqrt{2m(4K)} = 2\sqrt{2mK} = 2p$$

Thus momentum increased by 100%. **Ans. (A)**

Sol. 5 Potential energy stored in a spring is given as

$$U = -\frac{1}{2}kx^2$$

Where k is the spring constant of the spring used.

Ratio of potential energy stored in two states of same spring is given as

$$\frac{U_1}{U_2} = \frac{x_1^2}{x_2^2} = \frac{4}{100}$$

$$\Rightarrow \qquad U_2 = 25U_1 \qquad\qquad \textbf{Ans. (D)}$$

Sol. 6 Kinetic energy of a moving body is related to the momentum of body as

$$E = \frac{p^2}{2m}$$

$$\Rightarrow \qquad \frac{E_1}{E_2} = \frac{p_1^2/2m_1}{p_2^2/2m_2}$$

As momentum of the bodies is same, we use

$$\frac{E_1}{E_2} = \frac{m_1}{m_2}$$

$$\Rightarrow \qquad E_1 < E_2 \quad [\text{as } m_1 > m_2] \qquad \textbf{Ans. (A)}$$

Sol. 7 After fall of 30 ft the ratio of their kinetic energies of the two bodies is given as

$$\frac{KE_1}{KE_2} = \frac{(1/2)m_1v_1^2}{(1/2)m_2v_2^2} \qquad\qquad \ldots(1)$$

As balls are dropped (with zero initial velocities), velocity attained after falling through a distance h is given as

$$v^2 = 2gh$$

As for same distance of all both attains same speed, from equation-(1), we use

$$\Rightarrow \qquad \frac{KE_1}{KE_2} = \frac{m_1}{m_2} = \frac{2}{4} = \frac{1}{2} \qquad \textbf{Ans. (C)}$$

Sol. 8 The kinetic energy of the mass is converted into energy required to compress a spring which is given as

$$\frac{1}{2}mv^2 = \frac{1}{2}kx^2$$

$$\Rightarrow \qquad x = \sqrt{\frac{mv^2}{k}}$$

$$\Rightarrow \qquad x = \sqrt{\frac{0.5 \times (1.5)^2}{50}} = 0.15\,\text{m} \qquad \textbf{Ans. (A)}$$

Sol. 9 Potential energy stored in a spring is given as

$$U = \frac{1}{2} kx^2$$

Where k is the force constant of the spring. In two states of stretch of same spring the stored potential energies can be given in the ratio

$$\Rightarrow \qquad \frac{U'}{U} = \left(\frac{8}{2}\right)^2 = 16$$

$$\Rightarrow \qquad U' = 16U \qquad \textbf{Ans. (C)}$$

Sol. 10 If block falls by a distance x before coming to rest, we use work-energy theorem to determine the value of x. During fall the gravitational potential energy gets converted into spring potential energy in the spring.

$$\Rightarrow \qquad Mgx = \frac{1}{2} kx^2$$

$$\Rightarrow \qquad x = \frac{2Mg}{k} \qquad \textbf{Ans. (C)}$$

Sol. 11 Potential energy of a system changes by work done by the conservative forces only. In case of non-conservative forces we cannot define potential energy as work done by such forces is dissipated to surrounding and this energy cannot be recovered. When every negative work is done by a system (against external forces) by conservative forces, it increases potential energy of system. **Ans. (B)**

Sol. 12 For equilibrium, net force acting on the particle is zero, so we use

$$F = -\frac{dU}{dr} = 0$$

$$\Rightarrow \qquad \frac{-2A}{r^3} + \frac{B}{r^2} = 0$$

$$\Rightarrow \qquad r = \frac{2A}{B}$$

For stable equilibrium, potential energy should be minimum at equilibrium position so we can check second derivative $\dfrac{d^2U}{dr^2}$, which should be positive for the equilibrium value of r. This gives

$$\frac{d^2U}{dr^2} = \frac{6A}{r^4} - \frac{2B}{r^3} = +\,\text{ve for } r = \frac{2A}{B} \qquad \textbf{Ans. (B)}$$

Sol. 13 Total energy of the particle when released from a

height S is given as

$$E = KE + PE = mgS$$

$$\Rightarrow \qquad 4PE = mgS$$

If it happens at a height h above the surface of earth, we use

$$4\,mgh = mgS$$

$$\Rightarrow \qquad h = \frac{S}{4}$$

The speed of particle after falling by a distance S - $S/4$ is given as

$$V = \sqrt{2g\left(\frac{3S}{4}\right)} = \sqrt{\frac{3gS}{2}} \qquad \textbf{Ans. (D)}$$

5.2 Work

Sol. 1 Work done by agent in pulling the rope is given as

$$W_{\text{agent}} = 250 \times 12 = 3000\,\text{J}$$

Work done in lifting the mass by pulley system is given as

$$W_{\text{mass}} = 750 \times 3 = 2250\,\text{J}$$

Efficiency of a pulley system is given as

$$\eta = \frac{\text{Work done on mass}}{\text{Work done by agent}}$$

$$\eta = \frac{2250}{3000} = \left(\frac{3}{4}\right) \times 100 = 75\,\% \qquad \textbf{Ans. (C)}$$

Sol. 2 Work done by the force is given as

$$W = \int F \cdot dx = \text{Area under the curve}$$

$$\Rightarrow \qquad W = (3 \times 3) + \frac{1}{2} \times (3)(3) = 13.5\,\text{J} \qquad \textbf{Ans. (B)}$$

Sol. 3 By using work energy theorem, we have

$$W = \Delta KE = \frac{1}{2} mv_2^2 - \frac{1}{2} mv_1^2$$

Displacement and velocity of the body is given as

$$s = \frac{1}{3} t^2$$

$$\Rightarrow \qquad v = \frac{2}{3} t$$

$$\Rightarrow \quad \text{at } t = 0 \text{ s, velocity is given as}$$

$$v_1 = 0$$

and at $t = 2$ s, velocity is given as

$$v_2 = \frac{2}{3} \times 2 = \frac{4}{3}\,\text{ms}^{-1}$$

Work done by the force is gain in kinetic energy so it can be calculated as

$$W = \frac{1}{2} \times 3\left(\frac{4}{3}\right)^2 - \frac{1}{2} \times 3 \times (0)^2 = \frac{8}{3}\,\text{J} \quad \textbf{Ans. (C)}$$

Sol. 4 By using work energy theorem from initial point to the final point, we have

$$300 - W_{\text{gravity}} - W_{\text{friction}} = 0$$

$$\Rightarrow \qquad W_{\text{friction}} = 300 - mgh$$

$$= 300 - (2)(10)(10) = 100 \text{ J}$$

Ans. (B)

Sol. 5 During downward falling motion of ball gravity is doing positive work on ball and after striking the upper free end of the spring, spring force opposes the ball so it does negative work. After total fall by $(h + d)$ the total work done on ball can be given as

$$W = W_{\text{gravity}} - W_{\text{spring}}$$

$$\Rightarrow \qquad W = mg(h + d) - \frac{1}{2}kd^2$$

Ans. (A)

Sol. 6 Work done can be calculated by area under F-x curve, so it can be calculated as

$$\text{Work done} = \text{Area under } (F\text{-}x) \text{ graph}$$

$$\Rightarrow \quad \text{Work done} = 0 + 4 \times 2 + \frac{1}{2} \times 5 \times 2 = 8 + 5 = 13 \text{ J}$$

Ans. (D)

Sol. 7 During the motion explained in above situation, the displacement of particle is given as

$$\vec{d} = \vec{r_2} - \vec{r_1} = (4\hat{i} + 3\hat{j} - \hat{k}) - (2\hat{i} + \hat{k})$$

$$\Rightarrow \qquad \vec{d} = 2\hat{i} + 3\hat{j} - 2\hat{k}$$

Work done in above process is given as

$$W = \vec{F} \cdot \vec{d} = (3\hat{i} + \hat{j}) \cdot (2\hat{i} + 3\hat{j} - 2\hat{k})$$

$$\Rightarrow \qquad W = 6 + 3 = 9 \text{ J} \qquad \textbf{Ans. (A)}$$

Sol. 8 Workdone in above given process can be calculated as

$$W = \vec{F} \cdot \vec{d}$$

$$W = (4\hat{i} + 3\hat{j}) \cdot [(4\hat{j} + 3\hat{k}) - (-2\hat{i} + 5\hat{j})]$$

$$W = (4\hat{i} + 3\hat{j}) \cdot (2\hat{i} - \hat{j} + 3\hat{k})$$

$$W = 8 - 3 = 5 \text{ J} \qquad \textbf{Ans. (C)}$$

Sol. 9 Spring constant $\propto \dfrac{1}{\text{length}}$

$$k \propto \frac{1}{l}$$

i.e, $$k_1 = 6k$$

$$k_2 = 3k$$

$$k_3 = 2k$$

In series connection

$$\frac{1}{k'} = \frac{1}{6k} + \frac{1}{3k} + \frac{1}{2k}$$

$$\Rightarrow \qquad \frac{1}{k'} = \frac{6}{6k}$$

$$\Rightarrow \qquad k' = k$$

When connected in parallel

$$k'' = 6k + 3k + 2k = 11k$$

$$\Rightarrow \qquad \frac{k'}{k''} = \frac{1}{11}$$

$$\Rightarrow \qquad k' : k'' = 1 : 11 \qquad \textbf{Ans. (C)}$$

Sol. 10 During downward motion of drop, gravity does positive work and air friction does negative work. Work done by gravity can be directly given as

$$W_g = mgh = 10^{-3} \times 10 \times 1000 = 10 \text{ J}$$

The total work done by all the forces is given by work energy theorem, written as

$$K_i + W + W_f = K_f$$

$$mgh + w_{air} = \frac{1}{2}mv^2 - 0$$

$$10^{-3} \times 10 \times 10^3 + w_{air} = \frac{1}{2} \times 10^{-3} \times (50)^2$$

$$w_{air} = -8.75 \text{ J} \qquad \textbf{Ans. (D)}$$

Sol. 11 Work done by variable force is given as

$$W = \int_0^1 F\,dy$$

$$\Rightarrow \qquad W = \int_0^1 (20 + 10y)\,dy$$

$$\Rightarrow \qquad W = \left[20y + \frac{10y^2}{2}\right]_0^1 = 25 \text{ J} \qquad \textbf{Ans. (C)}$$

5.3 Power

Sol. 1 Energy used per second to operate turbine is given as

$$P = mgh = 15 \times 10 \times 60 \text{ J/s}$$

$$= 9000 \text{ J/s}$$

Power loss due to friction are 10% so it is given as

$$P_f = 900 \text{ J/s}$$

Power generated by turbine can be given as

$$P_g = (9000 - 900) \text{ J/s}$$

$$= 8100 \text{ J/s}$$

$$= 8.1 \text{ kW} \qquad \textbf{Ans. (C)}$$

Sol. 2 Kinetic energy imparted to water per second is equal to

$$K = \frac{1}{2} m_1 v^2$$

Here m_1 is the mass ejected from hose pipe in one second. As m is mass per unit length of water jet, in one second v meter length of water is ejected out so mass ejected in one second from hose pipe is given as

$$m_1 = m \times v$$

$$\Rightarrow \qquad K = \frac{1}{2}(m \times v)v^2 = \frac{1}{2} mv^3 \qquad \textbf{Ans. (B)}$$

Sol. 3 Engine power can be given by the energy imparted to the water per unit time. As in one second 200 kg water is being ejected out at a speed of 2 m/s, the engine power can be given as

$$P = \frac{1}{2} mv^2 = 0.5 \times 200 \times (2)^2 = 400 \text{ W} \qquad \textbf{Ans. (B)}$$

Sol. 4 If instantaneous velocity of this car is v, its acceleration is a, then its instantaneous power can be given as

$$P_0 = F. \, v = mav$$

$$\Rightarrow \qquad P_0 = mv \frac{dv}{dt}$$

Separating variables and integrating both side gives

$$\int mv \, dv = \int P_0 \, dt$$

$$\Rightarrow \qquad m \frac{v^2}{2} = P_0 t$$

$$\Rightarrow \qquad v \propto \sqrt{t} \qquad \textbf{Ans. (A)}$$

Sol. 5 Power of heart can be given as

$$P = \frac{W}{t} = \frac{mgh}{t} = \frac{V}{t} \rho g h$$

$$\Rightarrow \qquad P = \frac{5 \times 10^{-3}}{60} \times 13.6 \times 10^3 \times 10 \times 150 \times 10^{-3}$$

$$\Rightarrow \qquad P = \frac{5 \times 13.6 \times 150}{6} \times 10^{-3} = 1700 \times 10^{-3} = 1.7 \text{ W} \qquad \textbf{Ans. (B)}$$

Sol. 6 Acceleration of mass is given as

$$\vec{a} = 2t\hat{i} + 3t^2 \hat{j}$$

Instantaneous velocity of the body can be given as

$$a = \frac{dv}{dt}$$

$$\Rightarrow \qquad \int dv = \int a \, dt$$

$$\Rightarrow \qquad v = \int_0^t a \, dt = t^2 \hat{i} + t^3 \hat{j}$$

Instantaneous power developed by the external force can be given as

$$P = \vec{F} \cdot \vec{v} = 2t \cdot t^2 + 3t^2 \cdot t^3$$

$$\Rightarrow \qquad P = 2t^3 + 3t^5 \text{ W} \qquad \textbf{Ans. (D)}$$

Sol. 7 Average power produced by the turbine is given as

$$P_{in} = \frac{mgh}{t} = \frac{15 \times 10 \times 60}{1} = 9000 \text{ W}$$

At 90% efficiency, power generated is given as

$$P_{out} = 90\% \text{ of } P_{in} = 8.1 \text{ kW} \qquad \textbf{Ans. (B)}$$

Sol. 8 The energy radiated by the radiator in time t is given as

$$E = P \times t = 100 \times 10^3 \times 3600$$

$$\Rightarrow \qquad E = 36 \times 10^7 \text{ J} \qquad \textbf{Ans. (D)}$$

5.4 Circular Motion

Sol. 1 Angular velocity of circular motion is given as

$$\omega = \frac{2\pi}{t}$$

As time period of both particles is same

$$\Rightarrow \qquad \frac{\omega_1}{\omega_2} = 1 \qquad \textbf{Ans. (C)}$$

Sol. 2 For uniform circular motion, acceleration of stone is only centripetal acceleration which acts toward center and it can be given as

$$a_r = \omega^2 r = (2\pi n)^2 r = \left(2\pi \times \frac{1}{2}\right)^2 (1) = \pi^2 \text{ m/s}^2 \qquad \textbf{Ans. (B)}$$

Sol. 3 The circular motion of a particle with constant speed is periodic motion because particle repeats its motion after a regular interval of time but as particle is not oscillating about a fixed point, so motion of particle is not simple harmonic. **Ans. (D)**

Sol. 4 For a circular lap average velocity is always zero because in one round displacement of car is zero, so we use

$$\text{Average velocity} = \frac{\text{Displacement}}{\text{Time taken}}$$

$$= \frac{0}{62.8} = 0$$

Average speed of car in one round is given as

$$\text{Average speed} = \frac{\text{Distance}}{\text{Time taken}} = \frac{2\pi r}{T}$$

$$= \frac{(2\pi)(100)}{(62.8)} = 10 \text{ m/s} \qquad \textbf{Ans. (B)}$$

Sol. 5 For circular motion of coin the centripetal force is provided due to friction so we use

$$f \geq \frac{mv^2}{r}$$

$$\Rightarrow \quad \mu mg \geq mr\omega^2$$

$$\Rightarrow \quad r \leq \frac{\mu g}{\omega^2} \qquad \textbf{Ans. (D)}$$

Sol. 6 In uniform circular motion, acceleration of particle is given as

$$\text{Acceleration} = r\omega^2 = 5 \times 10^{-2} \times \left(\frac{2\pi}{0.2\pi}\right)^2$$

$$= 5 \times 10^{-2} \times 100 = 5 \text{ m/s}^{-2} \qquad \textbf{Ans. (D)}$$

Sol. 7 For banked road, banking angle for a speed v is given as

$$\tan\theta = \frac{V^2}{Rg}$$

$$\Rightarrow \quad \tan 45 = \frac{V^2}{90 \times 10} = 1$$

$$\Rightarrow \quad V = 30 \text{ m/s}^2 \qquad \textbf{Ans. (C)}$$

Sol. 8 For maximum safe speed on level road, the limiting friction on car tyres toward the center of circle must be more than or equal to the centripetal force for safe turning, so we use

$$\mu\, mg \geq \frac{mv^2}{R}$$

$$\Rightarrow \quad v \leq \sqrt{\mu Rg}$$

$$\Rightarrow \quad v_{\text{max}} = \sqrt{\mu Rg} \qquad \textbf{Ans. (C)}$$

Sol. 9 Position vector $\vec{R}$ as a function of time is given as

$$\vec{R} = 4\sin(2\pi t)\,\hat{i} + 4\cos(2\pi t)\,\hat{j}$$

x and y positions of particle are given as

$$x = 4\sin 2\pi t \qquad \qquad \ldots(1)$$

$$y = 4\cos 2\pi t \qquad \qquad \ldots(2)$$

From equation-(1) and (2), eliminating t, we have

$$x^2 + y^2 = 4^2$$

This is an equation of circle and radius 4 m. Thus option (A) is wrong.

Given motion is a uniform circular motion in which net acceleration of particle is centripetal acceleration v^2/R which will act toward its center hence along the direction $-\vec{R}$ hence option (B) and (C) are correct.

Particle's velocity is given by differentiating equations-(1) and (2), given as

$$V_x = +4(\cos 2\pi t)(2\pi)$$

and

$$V_y = -4(\sin 2\pi t)(2\pi)$$

$$\Rightarrow \quad V = \sqrt{V_x^2 + V_x^2}$$

$$\Rightarrow \quad V = \sqrt{(8\pi)^2(\cos^2 2\pi t + \sin^2 2\pi t)}$$

$$\Rightarrow \quad V = 8\pi \text{ m/s}$$

Thus option (D) is correct. $\qquad \textbf{Ans. (A)}$

Sol. 10 Figure below shows the situation described in question.

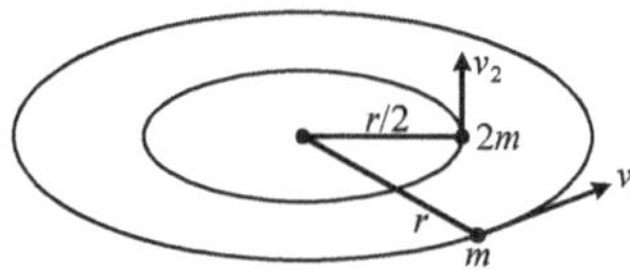

As equal centripetal forces are experienced by the two masses, we have

$$\frac{mv_1^2}{r} = \frac{(2m)v_2^2}{r/2}$$

$$\Rightarrow \quad v_1^2 = 4v_2^2$$

$$\Rightarrow \quad v_1 = 2v_2 \qquad \textbf{Ans. (B)}$$

Sol. 11 Velocity vector of particle is given as

$$\vec{v} = \frac{d\vec{r}}{dt} = -\omega \sin\omega t\,\hat{x} + \omega \cos\omega t\,\hat{y}$$

Acceleration vector of particle is given as

$$\vec{a} = \frac{d\vec{v}}{dt} = -\omega^2 \cos\omega t\,\hat{x} - \omega^2 \sin\omega t\,\hat{y} = -\omega^2 \vec{r}$$

As $\vec{v}\cdot\vec{r} = 0$ thus velocity vector is perpendicular to position vector and acceleration directed towards origin. $\qquad \textbf{Ans. (C)}$

Sol. 12 Free body diagram of car while taking the turn on banked road is shown in figure.

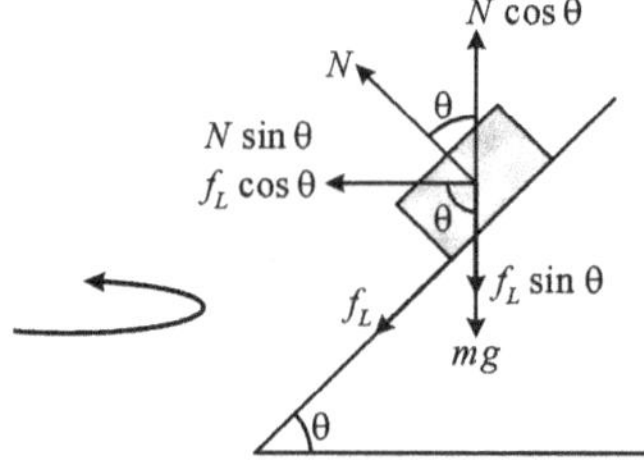

As car is in equilibrium in vertical direction, we use

$$N\cos\theta = mg + f_L\sin\theta$$

$$\Rightarrow \quad mg = N\cos\theta - f_L\sin\theta \qquad \ldots(1)$$

Along horizontal direction, for maximum safe speed car has a tendency to slide in upward direction so friction is taken in downward direction as shown. Total centripetal force on car is given as

$$N \sin\theta + f_L \cos\theta = \frac{mv^2}{R} \qquad \ldots(2)$$

From equations-(1) and (2), we have

$$\frac{v^2}{Rg} = \frac{\sin\theta + \mu_S \cos\theta}{\cos\theta - \mu_S \sin\theta}$$

$$\Rightarrow \qquad v = \sqrt{Rg\,\frac{\sin\theta + \mu_S \cos\theta}{\cos\theta - \mu_S \sin\theta}}$$

$$\Rightarrow \qquad v = \sqrt{Rg\,\frac{\tan\theta + \mu_S}{1 - \mu_S \tan\theta}} \qquad \textbf{Ans. (B)}$$

Sol. 13 Figure below shows the situation described in the question.

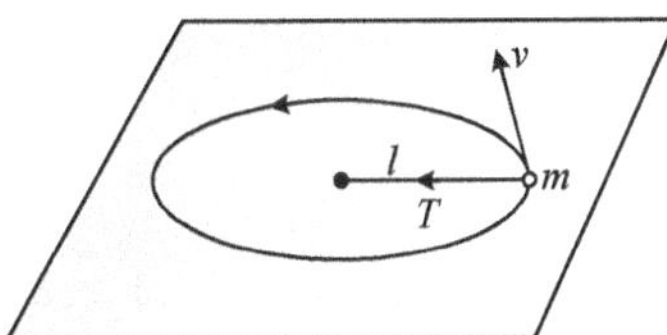

In this case the centripetal force $\left(\dfrac{mv^2}{l}\right)$ required for circular motion of particle is provided by tension so net force acting on particle will be only tension T. **Ans. (A)**

Sol. 14 Angular speed of circular motion is given as

$$\omega = \frac{2\pi}{T} \qquad \ldots(1)$$

As time period of both the circular motions is same so angular speed must also be same for both hence the ratio of angular speed of these two circular motions will be 1 : 1. **Ans. (D)**

Sol. 15 Figure below shows the situation described in the question.

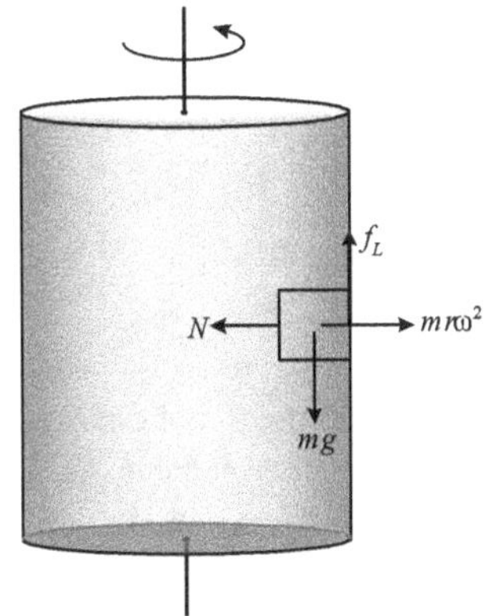

For equilibrium of the block, limiting friction must balance the weight of the block so we use

$$f_L \ge mg$$

$$\Rightarrow \qquad \mu N \ge mg$$

$$\Rightarrow \qquad \mu m r \omega^2 \ge mg$$

$$\Rightarrow \qquad \omega \ge \sqrt{\frac{g}{r\mu}}$$

$$\Rightarrow \qquad \omega_{\min} = \sqrt{\frac{g}{r\mu}} = \sqrt{\frac{10}{0.1 \times 1}} = 10\,\text{rad/s} \qquad \textbf{Ans. (C)}$$

Sol. 16 At $t = 0$, y displacement is maximum, so in equation of motion y-coordinate will be taken as a cosine function

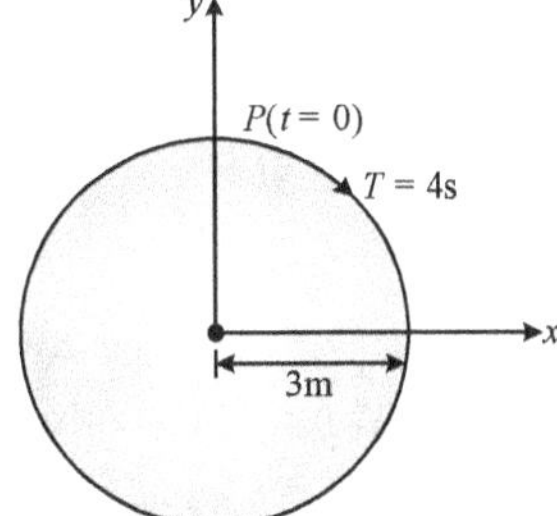

Angular speed of circular motion is given as

$$\omega = \frac{2\pi}{T} = \frac{2\pi}{4} = \frac{\pi}{2}\,\text{rad/s}$$

y-position of particle can be given as

$$y = a \cos\omega t$$

$$\Rightarrow \qquad y = 3\cos\frac{\pi}{2}t \qquad \textbf{Ans. (D)}$$

Sol. 17 The speed of revolving particle is given as

$$v = \frac{2\pi R}{T} \qquad \ldots(1)$$

At the speed, for a projectile the maximum height attained is given as

$$H_{\max} = \frac{v^2 \sin^2\theta}{2g} = \frac{2\pi^2 R^2 \sin^2\theta}{gT^2} = 4R$$

$$\Rightarrow \qquad \sin\theta = \left(\frac{2gT^2}{\pi^2 R}\right)^{1/2}$$

$$\Rightarrow \qquad \theta = \sin^{-1}\left[\frac{2gT^2}{\pi^2 R}\right]^{1/2} \qquad \textbf{Ans. (D)}$$

Sol. 18 Using speed equation for angular motion, we have

$$\omega = \omega_0 + \alpha t$$

$$\Rightarrow \qquad \alpha = \frac{\omega - \omega_0}{t}$$

$$\Rightarrow \qquad \alpha = \frac{(3120 - 1200)}{16\,\text{s}}\,\text{rpm}$$

$$\Rightarrow \qquad \alpha = \frac{1920}{16} \times \frac{2\pi}{60}\,\text{rad/s}^3$$

$$\Rightarrow \qquad \alpha = 4\pi\,\text{rad/s}^2 \qquad \textbf{Ans. (A)}$$

5.5 Non Uniform Circular Motion

Sol. 1 For constant tangential acceleration in circular motion, we can use speed equations for circular motion

$$\omega^2 = \omega_0^2 + 2\alpha\theta$$

$$\omega^2 = 2\alpha\theta\ (\text{As } \omega_0 = 0)$$

We use $\left(\omega = \dfrac{v}{r} \text{ and } a = r\alpha \right)$, gives

$$a = \frac{v^2}{2r\theta} = 40\,\text{m/s}^2 \qquad \textbf{Ans. (A)}$$

Sol. 2 During motion of particle from lowest position to horizontal position of string, final velocity is given by conservation of energy as

$$\frac{1}{2}mu^2 = \frac{1}{2}mv^2 + mgl$$

$$\Rightarrow \qquad v = \sqrt{u^2 - 2gl}$$

Change in magnitude of velocity is given as

$$\Delta v = \sqrt{u^2 + v^2} = \sqrt{2(u^2 - gl)} \qquad \textbf{Ans. (A)}$$

Sol. 3 Net force acting towards centre is centripetal force

$$mg - N = \frac{mv^2}{r}$$

When $N = 0$, for weightlessness, we use

$$\Rightarrow \qquad \frac{mv^2}{r} = mg$$

$$\Rightarrow \qquad v^2 = rg = 20 \times 10 = 200$$

$$v = 14.14\,\text{m/s} \qquad \textbf{Ans. (C)}$$

Sol. 4 After end of second revolution, kinetic energy of particle

becomes

$$\frac{1}{2}mv^2 = 8 \times 10^{-4}\,\text{J}$$

$$\Rightarrow \qquad v^2 = \frac{16 \times 10^{-4}}{0.01} = 16 \times 10^{-2}$$

Speed after two revolution in uniformly accelerated circular motion is given as

$$v^2 = 2a_t s$$

$$\Rightarrow \qquad v^2 = 2a_t(4\pi r)$$

$$\Rightarrow \qquad a_t = \frac{v^2}{8\pi r} = \frac{16 \times 10^{-2}}{8 \times 3.14 \times 6.4 \times 10^{-2}} = 0.1\,\text{m/s}^2$$

$$\textbf{Ans. (A)}$$

Sol. 5 To complete the vertical circular motion at bottommost point the minimum speed required is given as

$$v_{\text{bottom}} = \sqrt{5gR}$$

This is calculated by work energy theorem between top and bottom point and considering tension in string zero at the topmost point. Complete derivation is covered in theory of Circular Motion. **Ans. (D)**

Sol. 6 Figure in question shows that total acceleration is at an angle 30° from the radial direction, so normal acceleration is given as

$$a_N = a \cos 30°$$

$$\Rightarrow \qquad \frac{V^2}{R} = 15 \times \frac{\sqrt{3}}{2}$$

$$\Rightarrow \qquad V^2 = \frac{15 \times \sqrt{3} \times 2.5}{2}$$

$$\Rightarrow \qquad V = \sqrt{32.476} = 5.7\,\text{m/s} \qquad \textbf{Ans. (C)}$$

Sol. 7 To complete the vertical circular motion the velocity of body at A is given as

$$v_A \geq \sqrt{5gR}$$

As track is frictionless, so total mechanical energy will remain conserved so during sliding on incline plane, we use

$$0 + mgh = \frac{1}{2}mv_A^2 + 0$$

$$\Rightarrow \qquad h = \frac{v_A^2}{2g}$$

$$\Rightarrow \qquad h = \frac{5gR}{2g} = \frac{5}{2}R = \frac{5}{4}D \qquad \textbf{Ans. (D)}$$

Sol. 8 In case of vertical circular motion of a mass attached to a string, the tension is maximum at the lowest position of mass, so the chance of breaking is maximum at the lowest position only. **Ans. (C)**

Ch-6 System of Particles & Rotational Motion

6.1 Centre of Mass

Sol. 1 Figure below shows the situation described in this question. To calculate center of mass of this system, let us consider an elementary length dx at a distance x from one end which has a mass $kx\,dx$.

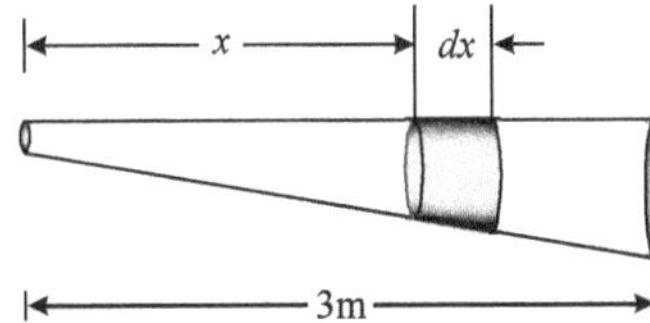

Then centre of gravity of the rod x_c is given as

$$x_c = \frac{\displaystyle\int_0^3 kx\,dx\,x}{\displaystyle\int_0^3 kx\,dx} = \frac{\displaystyle\int_0^3 x^2\,dx}{\displaystyle\int_0^3 x\,dx} = \frac{\left.\dfrac{x^3}{3}\right|_0^3}{\left.\dfrac{x^2}{3}\right|_0^3}$$

or $\qquad x_c = \dfrac{27/3}{9/2} = 2\,\text{m}$

Thus centre of gravity of the rod will be located at a distance of 2 m from one end. **Ans. (B)**

Sol. 2 Center of mass of a multi particle system is given as

$$x_{com} = \frac{m_1 x_1 + m_2 x_2}{m_1 + m_2} \qquad \ldots(1)$$

After changing position of m_1 and to keep the position of center of mass same, we use displacement of center of mass as

$$\Delta x = \frac{m_1(-d) + m_2(d_2)}{m_1 + m_2}$$

$\Rightarrow \qquad 0 = \dfrac{-m_1 d + m_2 d_2}{m_1 + m_2}$

$\Rightarrow \qquad d_2 = \dfrac{m_1}{m_2} d \qquad\qquad$ **Ans. (B)**

Sol. 3 Position vector of centre of mass is given as

$$\vec{R}_{cm} = \frac{m_1 \vec{r}_1 + m_2 \vec{r}_2}{m_1 + m_2} = -2\hat{i} - \hat{j} + \hat{k} \qquad \text{Ans. (C)}$$

Sol. 4 If we consider the speed of the man in upward direction as v and using conservation of linear momentum for man and stone, we get

$$m_{\text{man}} v = m_{\text{stone}}\, v_{\text{stone}}$$

$\Rightarrow \qquad 50v = 0.5 \times 2 = 1$

$\Rightarrow \qquad v = \dfrac{1}{50} = 0.02\,\text{m/s}$

Time taken by stone to reach the ground can be given as

$$t = \frac{10}{2} = 5\,\text{s}$$

The distance covered by man in 5 s in upward direction can be given as

$$d = vt = 0.02 \times 5 = 0.1\,\text{m}$$

Thus distance of man above the floor is given as

$$h = 10 + 0.1 = 10.1\,\text{m} \qquad \text{Ans. (C)}$$

Sol. 5 Figure below shows the situation described in the question.

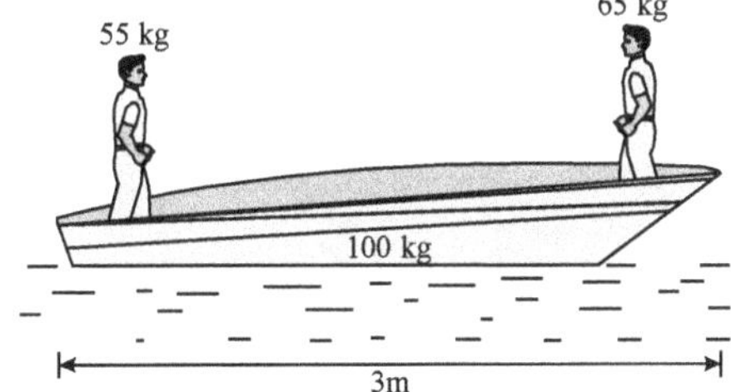

As there is no external force acting on system so centre of mass will not shift. **Ans. (C)**

Sol. 6 Position of centre of mass from origin is given as

$$x_{\text{cm}} = \frac{m_1 x_1 + m_2 x_2 + m_3 x_3}{m_1 + m_2 + m_3}$$

$$= \frac{300 \times 0 + 500 \times 40 + 400 \times 70}{300 + 500 + 400} = \frac{48000}{1200} = 40\,\text{cm}$$

Ans. (D)

Sol. 7 Centre of mass may or may not coincide with centre of gravity. Only for small sized objects on earth surface it is true. Hence option (a) is not correct.

Centre of mass of a body is the point at which the total mass is concentrated. If external force is applied on COM, torque will be zero. Thus option (b) is correct.

Torque due to couple forces only produces rotational motion in body not the translational motion because net force is zero due to equal and opposite forces acting on body. Hence option (c) is not correct.

If a small if front lift the heavy object the efficiency of machine is high

$$\text{Mechanical Advantage} = \frac{\text{output force}}{\text{input force}}$$

Mechanical advantage $> 1 \Rightarrow$ Output force $>$ Input force. Hence option (d) is correct. **Ans. (A)**

Sol. 8 The situation described is shown in below figure

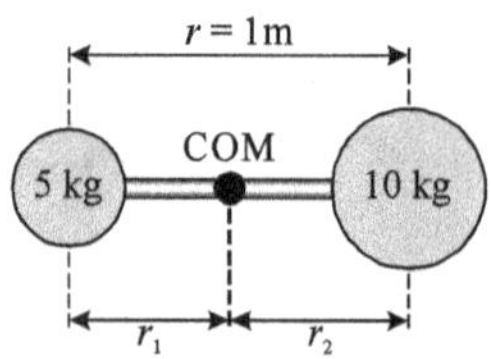

Center of mass of a two body system is given as

$$r_1 = \frac{m_2 r}{m_1 + m_2} = \frac{10(1)}{5 + 10} = \frac{2}{3}\,\text{m} = 67\,\text{cm} \qquad \textbf{Ans. (D)}$$

Sol. 9 Figure below shows the situation described in the question

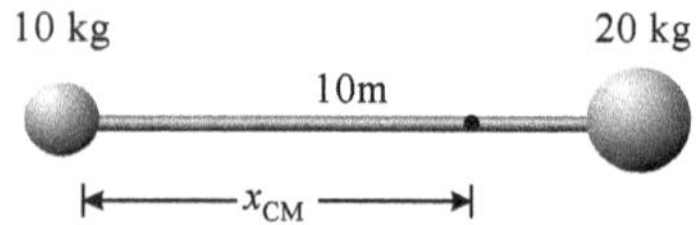

The centre of mass of the given system from 10 kg mass is given as

$$x_{CM} = \frac{20 \times 10}{20 + 10} = \frac{20}{3}\,\text{m} \qquad \textbf{Ans. (A)}$$

6.2 Impulse & Conservation of Momentum

Sol. 1 By conservation of linear momentum, we use

$$m_1 v_1 = m_2 v_2$$

$$\Rightarrow \qquad \frac{E_1}{E_2} = \frac{(1/2) m_1 v_1^2}{(1/2) m_2 v_2^2}$$

$$\Rightarrow \qquad \frac{E_1}{E_2} = \frac{m_1^2 v_1^2}{m_2^2 v_2^2} \cdot \frac{m_2}{m_1} = \frac{m_2}{m_1} \qquad \textbf{Ans. (A)}$$

Sol. 2 If momentum is P, mass 'm' then kinetic energy

$$KE = \frac{P^2}{2m} = \frac{(18 \times 6)^2}{2 \times 12} = 486\,\text{J} \qquad \textbf{Ans. (C)}$$

Sol. 3 By Newton's II law, average force acting is given by rate of change of momentum, same is done here.

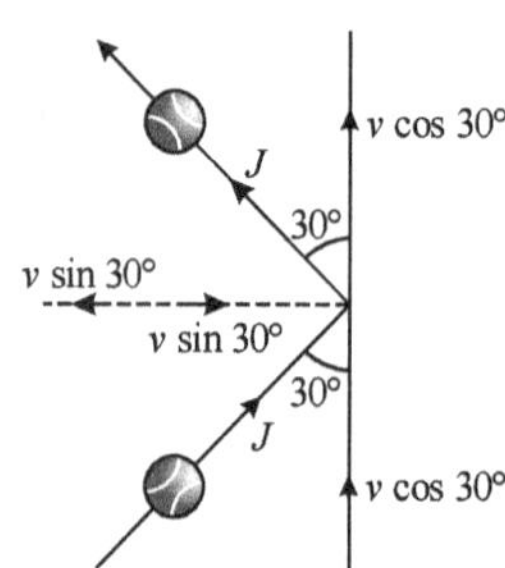

$$F = \frac{\Delta p}{\Delta t} = \frac{2mv \sin 30°}{0.25} = 24\,\text{N} \qquad \textbf{Ans. (B)}$$

Sol. 4 By Newton's II law, we use

$$F_{ext.} = \frac{dp}{dt} = \frac{d(mv)}{dt}$$

m = mass of system as conveyor belt with sand drops at time t

$$F_{ext.} = m\frac{dv}{dt} + v\frac{dm}{dt}$$

but $v \rightarrow$ constant,

so, $$\frac{dv}{dt} = 0$$

$$\Rightarrow \qquad F_{ext.} = v\frac{dm}{dt} = Mv$$

$F_{ext.}$ is in direction of $\vec{v}$ of belt. Consider belt as a system with variable mass, so we use

$$F_{reaction} = v_{rec} \cdot \frac{dm}{dt} = -v\frac{dm}{dt} \qquad \ldots(2)$$

$$\Rightarrow \qquad F_{ext.} = v \cdot \frac{dm}{dt} = Mv$$

$\vec{F}_{ext}$ is in direction of $\vec{v}$ to keep belt moving with constant velocity. **Ans. (C)**

Sol. 5 By conservation of momentum, we use

$$P_{gun} = P_{shell}$$

$$\Rightarrow \qquad m_1 v_1 = m_2 v_2$$

$$\Rightarrow \qquad 4 \times v_1 = \frac{200}{1000} \times v_2$$

$$\Rightarrow \qquad \frac{v_2}{v_1} = 20 \qquad \ldots(1)$$

By energy conservation, we have

$$\frac{1}{2} m_1 v_1^2 + \frac{1}{2} m_2 v_2^2 = 1.05 \times 10^3$$

$$\Rightarrow \qquad 2v_1^2 + \frac{1}{10} v_2^2 = 1.05 \times 10^3 \qquad \ldots(2)$$

By equation-(1) and (2)

$$v_2 = 100\,\text{m/s} \qquad \textbf{Ans. (C)}$$

Sol. 6 From starting to end point in a projectile motion on level ground, only vertical component of velocity changes during projectile motion so, change in momentum is there in vertical direction only, which is given as

$$\Delta \vec{P} = -mv \sin 45° - (mv \sin 45°)$$

$$= -2mv \sin 45°$$

$$= -\sqrt{2}mv$$

In above expression negative sign shows the direction of change in momentum in negative y-direction. **Ans. (A)**

Sol. 7 By momentum conservation, we use

$$m \times 2 = m \times v_1 + 2mv_2$$

$$\Rightarrow \qquad 2 = v_1 + 2v_2 \qquad \ldots(1)$$

$\Rightarrow \qquad 0.5 \times 2 = v_2 - v_1 \qquad \qquad \ldots(2)$

Adding $(1) + (2) \qquad v_2 = 1, v_1 = 0 \qquad$ **Ans. (B)**

Sol. 8 Initially both particles are in rest so velocity centre of mass is zero when the net external force is zero speed of centre of mass remains constant mass so it should remain zero only.

$$v_{cm} = 0 \qquad \textbf{Ans. (C)}$$

Sol. 9 In case of straight rebound, change in momentum will be double that of one sided momentum of body i.e. $2MV$.

Ans. (C)

Sol. 10 During explosion as the net external force is zero, total momentum of system of objects remain conserved. So we use

$$\vec{P_1} + \vec{P_2} + \vec{P_3} = 0$$

$$\Rightarrow \qquad |\vec{P_3}| = |\vec{P_1} + \vec{P_2}|$$

$$\Rightarrow \qquad m \times 4 = \sqrt{P_1^2 + P_2^2}$$

$$\Rightarrow \qquad 4m = \sqrt{12^2 + 16^2}$$

$$\Rightarrow \qquad m = 5 \text{ kg} \qquad \textbf{Ans. (B)}$$

Sol. 11 In explosion no external force is acting so total momentum of system will remain conserved. So we use

Initial momentum $P_i = 0$

Final momentum $P_f = 0 = mv\,\hat{i} + mv\,\hat{j} + \vec{P_3}$

$$\Rightarrow \qquad P_3 = mv\sqrt{2}$$

Thus total kinetic energy generated during explosion is given as

$$K = \frac{P_3^2}{2 \times 2m} + \frac{1}{2}mv^2 + \frac{1}{2}mv^2$$

$$\Rightarrow \qquad K = \frac{2m^2v^2}{4m} + mv^2 = \frac{3mv^2}{2} \qquad \textbf{Ans. (B)}$$

Sol. 12 By energy conservation after collision at the ground after 50% energy is lost and then during upward motion

$$0.5\left(mgh + \frac{1}{2}mv^2\right) = mgh$$

$$\Rightarrow \qquad 0.25mv^2 = 0.5mgh$$

$$\Rightarrow \qquad v = \sqrt{2gh} = \sqrt{2 \times 10 \times 20}$$
$$= 20 \text{ m/s} \qquad \textbf{Ans. (C)}$$

Sol. 13 Figure below shows the process of collision as described in question

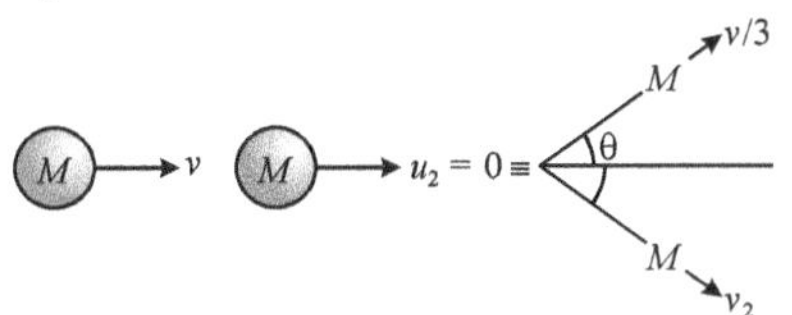

For elastic collision, kinetic energy before and after collision remain conserved, so we use

$$\frac{1}{2}Mv^2 + 0 = \frac{1}{2}M\left(\frac{v}{3}\right)^2 + \frac{1}{2}Mv_2^2$$

$$\Rightarrow \qquad v^2 = \frac{v^2}{9} + v_2^2$$

$$\Rightarrow \qquad v_2^2 = \frac{8v^2}{9}$$

$$\Rightarrow \qquad v_2 = \frac{2\sqrt{2}v}{3} \qquad \textbf{Ans. (B)}$$

Sol. 14

Velocity of block $= \sqrt{2gh}$

$$= \sqrt{2 \times g \times 0.1} = \sqrt{2} \text{ m/s}$$

$$P_i = P_f \qquad \text{(By momentum conservation)}$$

$$(10 \times 10^{-3}) \times 400 + 0 = 2 \times \sqrt{2} + (10 \times 10^{-3})V$$

$$\Rightarrow \qquad V = \frac{(4 - 2\sqrt{2})}{10 \times 10^{-3}}$$

$$= 120 \text{ m/s} \qquad \textbf{Ans. (C)}$$

Sol. 15 For identical balls if collision is inelastic head-on then their velocities will interchange thus final velocities are given as

$$V_B = 0.5 \text{ m/s}$$

$$V_A = -0.3 \text{ m/s} \qquad \textbf{Ans. (B)}$$

Sol. 16 Using the law of conservation of linear momentum in above described collision, we have

$$mv + 4m \times 0 = 4mv' + 0$$

$$\Rightarrow \qquad v' = \frac{v}{4}$$

Coefficient of restitution in a collision is given as

$$e = \frac{\text{Relative velocity of separation}}{\text{Relative velocity of approach}} = \frac{\frac{v}{4}}{v}$$

$$\Rightarrow \qquad e = \frac{1}{4} = 0.25 \qquad \textbf{Ans. (B)}$$

Sol. 17 As collision is head-on elastic the velocity of body B is given as

$$v_B = \left(\frac{m_2 - m_1}{m_1 + m_2}\right)u_2 + \left(\frac{2m_1}{m_1 + m_2}\right)u_1$$

$$\Rightarrow \qquad v_B = \frac{2(4m)u}{6m} = \frac{4}{3}u$$

Fraction of energy lost by body A in the collision is given as

$$f = \frac{KE_f}{KE_i}$$

$$\Rightarrow \qquad f = \frac{\frac{1}{2}m_2 v_B^2}{\frac{1}{2}m_1 u_1^2} = \frac{\frac{1}{2} \times 2m \times \left(\frac{4}{3}u\right)^2}{\frac{1}{2} \times 4m \times u^2} = \frac{8}{9} \qquad \textbf{Ans. (B)}$$

Sol. 18 Velocity of ball just before striking the ground is given as

$$v_1 = \sqrt{2gh} = \sqrt{2(10)(10)} = 10\sqrt{2}\ \text{m/s}$$

Taking upward direction positive, vectorially just before collision vectorially is given as

$$\overline{v}_1 = -10\sqrt{2}\ \text{m/s}$$

If it reaches the same height, speed remains same after collision only the direction changes so after collision, velocity of ball is given as

$$\overline{v}_2 = 10\sqrt{2}\,\hat{j}$$

Impulse imparted to the ball due to contact force is given as

$$J = m\,|\Delta \vec{v}|$$

$$\Rightarrow \qquad J = m\,|\,10\sqrt{2}\text{j} - (10\sqrt{2}\text{j})\,|$$

$$\Rightarrow \qquad J = 0.15\,[2(10\sqrt{2})] = 3\sqrt{2}\ \text{kg m/s} = 4.2\ \text{kg m/s}$$
$$\textbf{Ans. (B)}$$

Sol. 19 Figure below shows the situation of explosion as described in the question.

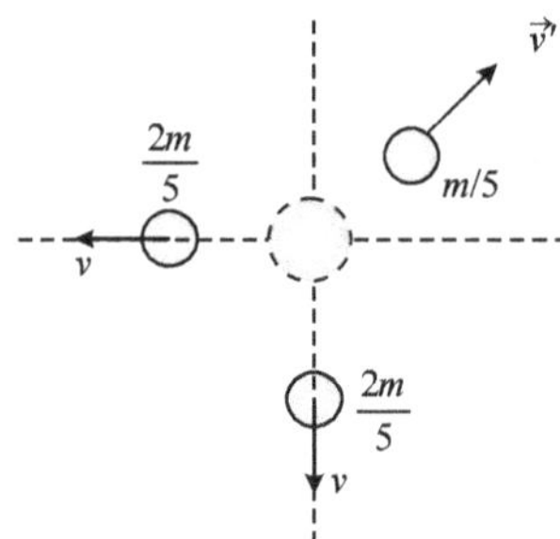

By conservation of momentum of shell before and after explosion, we have

$$m(0) = \frac{2m}{5}(-v\hat{i}) + \frac{2m}{5}(-v\hat{j}) + \frac{m}{5}\vec{v}'$$

$$\Rightarrow \qquad \vec{v}' = 2v\hat{i} + 2v\hat{j}$$

$$\Rightarrow \qquad v' = \sqrt{(2v)^2 + (2v)^2}$$

$$\Rightarrow \qquad v' = 2\sqrt{2}v \qquad \textbf{Ans. (B)}$$

6.3 Moment of Inertia

Sol. 1 As the moment of inertia of a body increases if distance of mass distribution from axis of rotation increases like for a circular ring about its geometrical axis moment of inertia is MR^2. Since the density (mass per unit volume) for iron is more than that of aluminium, the proposed disc is to be made in such a way that iron should be placed at a higher radius to get more value of moment of inertia because iron is heavier than aluminium. Hence to get maximum moment of inertia for the circular disc, aluminium should be placed at interior and iron at the exterior position. **Ans. (A)**

Sol. 2 Radius of gyration of disc about a tangential axis in the plane of disc is given as

$$K_1 = \frac{\sqrt{5}}{2}R$$

Radius of gyration of circular ring of same radius about tangential axis in the plane of circular ring is

$$K_2 = \frac{\sqrt{3}}{2}R$$

$$\Rightarrow \qquad \frac{K_1}{K_2} = \frac{\sqrt{5}}{\sqrt{6}} \qquad \textbf{Ans. (C)}$$

Sol. 3 All the distances in situation described in question are mentioned in figure below.

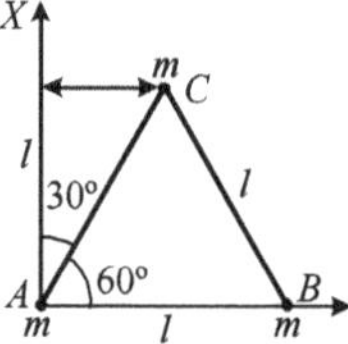

The moment of inertia of the system about axis AX is given as

$$I = m_A r_A^2 + m_B r_B^2 + m_C r_C^2$$
$$= m_A(0)^2 + m(l)^2 + m(l\sin 30°)^2$$
$$= ml^2 + ml^2 \times (1/4) = (5/4)\,ml^2 \qquad \textbf{Ans. (C)}$$

Sol. 4 By parallel axis theorem it can be calculated directly as given below.

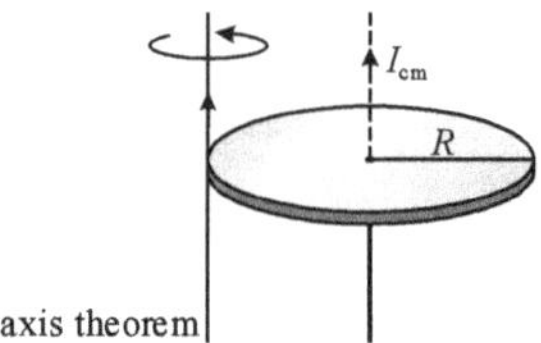

$$I = I_{cm} + Md^2 = \frac{MR^2}{2} + MR^2 = \frac{3}{2}MR^2 \qquad \textbf{Ans. (C)}$$

Sol. 5 Kinetic energy of rotational motion is given as

$$K = \frac{1}{2}I\omega^2 = \frac{L^2}{2I}$$

For the two bodies as kinetic energies of rotation are same, we use

$$\frac{L_1^2}{2I_1} = \frac{L_2^2}{2I_1}$$

$$\Rightarrow \qquad \frac{L_1^2}{2(I)} = \frac{L_2^2}{2(2I)}$$

$$\Rightarrow \qquad \frac{L_1}{L_2} = \frac{1}{\sqrt{2}} \qquad\qquad \textbf{Ans. (C)}$$

Sol. 6 This question is same as that of Q. 4. Students are advised to refer to solution of Q. 4. **Ans. (C)**

Sol. 7 Moment of inertia of a rod about an axis passing through its end and perpendicular to its length is given as

$$I = \frac{ml^2}{3}$$

The situation described in question is shown in figure below.

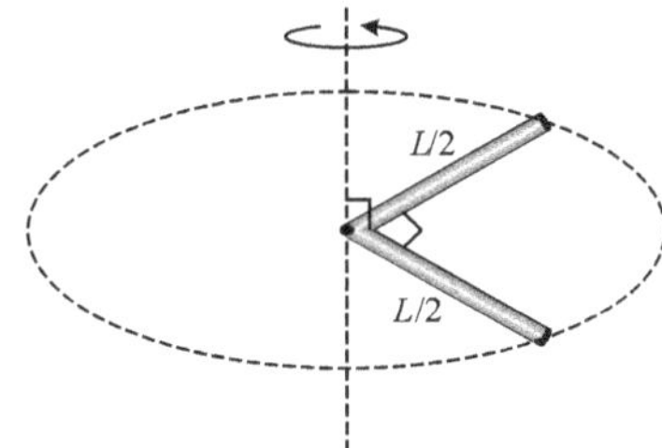

Moment of inertia of this system can be given as

$$I = \frac{M(L/2)^2}{3} + \frac{M(L/2)^2}{3}$$

$$\Rightarrow \qquad I = \frac{ML^2}{13} + \frac{ML^2}{12} = \frac{ML^2}{6} \qquad \textbf{Ans. (D)}$$

Sol. 8 Radius of gyration of a ring and disc are given as

$$K_{\text{Ring}} = R$$

$$K_{\text{Disc}} = \frac{R}{\sqrt{2}}$$

$$\Rightarrow \qquad \frac{K_{\text{Disc}}}{K_{\text{Ring}}} = \frac{1}{\sqrt{2}} \qquad\qquad \textbf{Ans. (D)}$$

Sol. 9 Figure below shows the situation described in question.

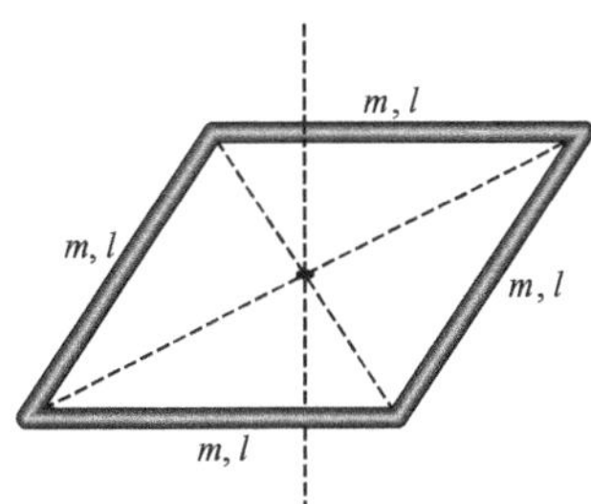

Moment of inertia of each rod about an axis passing through the centre of square frame and perpendicular to the plane of square is given by parallel axes theorem and it is given as

$$I = \frac{Ml^2}{12} + \frac{Ml^2}{4}$$

Total moment of inertia of four rods of square frame is given as

$$I_{\text{Total}} = 4I = \frac{4Ml^2}{3} \qquad\qquad \textbf{Ans. (B)}$$

Sol. 10 Using parallel axis theorem, we have

$$I = I_0 + \frac{ML^2}{4} \qquad\qquad \textbf{Ans. (B)}$$

Sol. 11 By parallel axis theorem, moment of inertia of a disc about a parallel axis is given as

$$I = I_{\text{cm}} + md^2$$

We can see that d is maximum for point B in above cases.
Ans. (D)

Sol. 12 Figure below shows the disc described in the question.

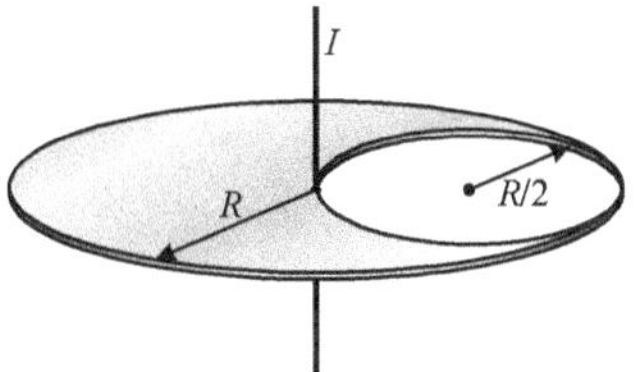

Moment of inertia of complete disc is the sum of MI of remaining object and the disc of radius $R/2$ which is removed from the full disc, given as

$$I = I_{\text{remaining}} + I_{(R/2)}$$

$$\Rightarrow \qquad I_{\text{remaining}} = I - I_{(R/2)}$$

$$\Rightarrow \qquad I_{\text{remaining}} = \frac{MR^2}{2} - \left[\frac{\dfrac{M}{4}(R/2)^2}{2} + \frac{M}{4}\left(\frac{R}{2}\right)^2 \right]$$

$$\Rightarrow \qquad I_{\text{remaining}} = \frac{MR^2}{2} - \left[\frac{MR^2}{32} + \frac{MR^2}{16} \right]$$

$$\Rightarrow \qquad I_{\text{remaining}} = \frac{MR^2}{2} - \left[\frac{MR^2 + 2MR^2}{32} \right]$$

$$\Rightarrow \qquad I_{\text{remaining}} = \frac{MR^2}{2} - \frac{3MR^2}{32} = \frac{16MR^2 - 3MR^2}{32}$$

$$\Rightarrow \qquad I_{\text{remaining}} = \frac{13MR^2}{32} \qquad\qquad \textbf{Ans. (B)}$$

Sol. 13 Figure below shows the situation described in the question

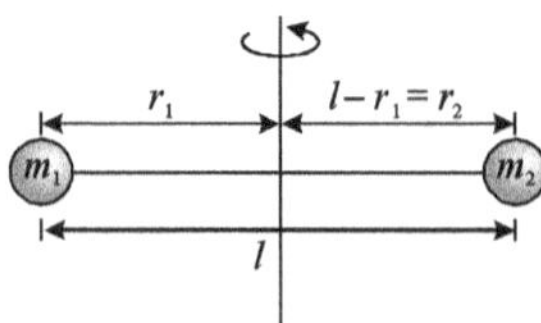

Distance of center of mass (axis of rotation) from mass m_1 is given as

$$r_1 = \frac{m_2 l}{m_1 + m_2}$$

and

$$r_2 = l - r_1 = l - \frac{m_2 l}{m_1 + m_2} = \frac{m_1 l}{m_1 + m_2}$$

The moment of inertia of the two masses is given as

$$I = I_1 + I_2$$
$$\Rightarrow \quad I = m_1 r_1^2 + m_2 r_2^2$$
$$\Rightarrow \quad I = m_1 \left(\frac{m_2 l}{m_1 + m_2} \right)^2 + m_2 \left(\frac{m_1 l}{m_1 + m_2} \right)^2$$
$$\Rightarrow \quad I = \frac{m_1 m_2}{m_1 + m_2} l^2 \qquad \textbf{Ans. (A)}$$

Sol. 14 Remaining mass of ring is given as

$$M_{\text{remain}} = \frac{3}{4} M$$

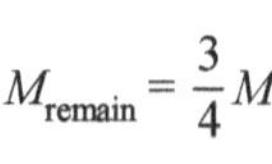

Moment of inertial of ring remaining is given as

$$I = M_{\text{remain}} R^2 = \frac{3}{4} M R^2 \qquad \textbf{Ans. (A)}$$

Sol. 15 Figure below shows the two axis of rotations as described in the question.

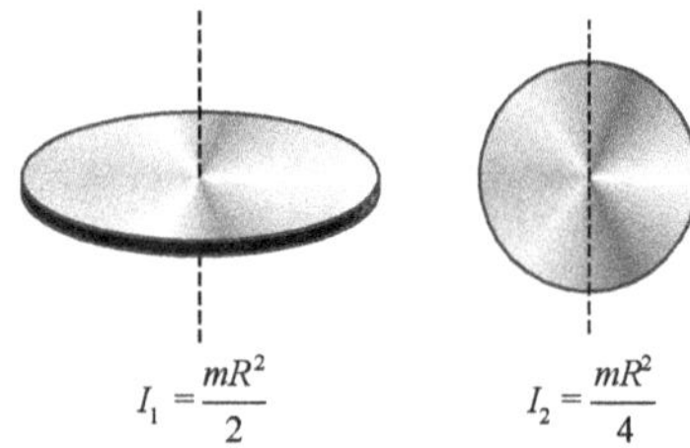

$$I_1 = \frac{mR^2}{2} \qquad I_2 = \frac{mR^2}{4}$$

The radius of gyration is given as

$$k = \sqrt{\frac{I}{m}}$$

Thus for the two cases ratio is calculated as

$$\frac{k_1}{k_2} = \sqrt{\frac{I_1}{I_2}} = \sqrt{\frac{mR^2 / 2}{mR^2 / 4}} = \sqrt{2} : 1 \qquad \textbf{Ans. (A)}$$

6.4 Torque & Angular Acceleration

Sol. 1 If α is the angular retardation of the wheel, we use

$$\omega_f = \omega_i - \alpha t$$
$$\Rightarrow \quad 0 = \omega - \alpha t$$
$$\Rightarrow \quad \alpha = \omega / t$$

The torque on the wheel is given as

$$\tau = I\alpha = \frac{I\omega}{t} = \frac{I \cdot 2\pi \upsilon}{t} = \frac{2 \times 2 \times \pi \times 60}{60 \times 60} = \frac{\pi}{15} \text{ Nm} \qquad \textbf{Ans. (C)}$$

Sol. 2 Moment of inertia of rod about an axis passing through its end and perpendicular to length is given as

$$I = \frac{ml^2}{3}$$

From horizontal position when rod is released as shown in figure below, torque on it causes angular acceleration. Writing equation of rotational motion of this rod, we have

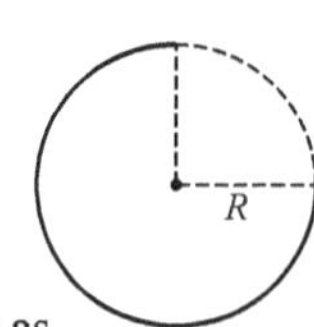

$$(mg)\left(\frac{l}{2} \right) = \left(\frac{ml^2}{3} \right)(\alpha)$$
$$\Rightarrow \quad \alpha = \frac{3g}{2l} \qquad \textbf{Ans. (A)}$$

Sol. 3 For uniformly accelerated rotational motion, we use

$$\theta = \omega_0 t + \frac{1}{2} \alpha t^2$$

Where α is angular acceleration and ω_0 is the initial angular speed. At $t = 2\text{s}$, we use

$$\theta = 2 \times 2 + \frac{1}{2} \times 3(2)^2 = 4 + 6 = 10 \text{ rad} \qquad \textbf{Ans. (A)}$$

Sol. 4 This question is same as that of Q. 2. Students are advised to refer solution of Q. 2. **Ans. (C)**

Sol. 5 Torque of a force about a given point from which position vector of point of application of force is given can be written as

$$\vec{\tau} = \vec{r} \times \vec{F}$$

As $\vec{\tau}$ is perpendicular to $\vec{r}$ and $\vec{F}$
So we have

$$\vec{r} \cdot \vec{\tau} = 0$$

and

$$\vec{F} \cdot \vec{\tau} = 0 \qquad \textbf{Ans. (D)}$$

Sol. 6 The angular velocity and angular acceleration of the given wheel can be obtained by differentiating the angular position as

$$\theta(t) = 2t^3 - 6t^2$$

$$\omega = 6t^2 - 12t$$

$$\alpha = 12t - 12$$

Torque becomes zero when $\alpha = 0$, it happens when

$$\alpha = 12t - 12 = 0 \qquad \textbf{Ans. (A)}$$

$$\Rightarrow \qquad t = 1 \text{ s}$$

Sol. 7 Torque about point 'O' can be calculated from the figure shown below.

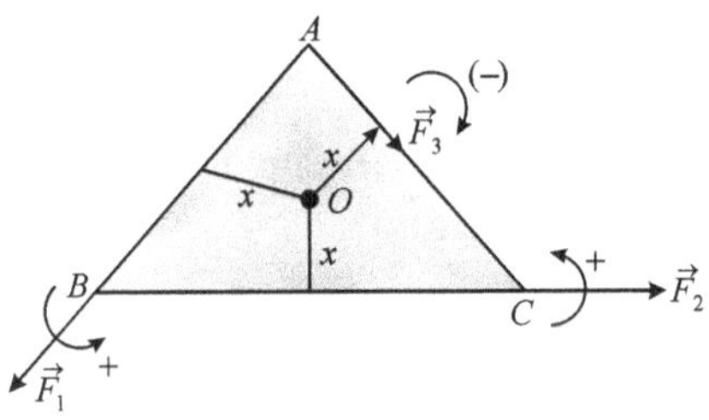

As torque of F_3 is in opposite sense than that of other two forces, for net zero torque, we use

$$F_1 x + F_2 x = F_3 x$$

$$F_3 = F_1 + F_2 \qquad \textbf{Ans. (A)}$$

Sol. 8 Just after string is cut, torque of weight acting on the rod is given as

$$\tau = mg\frac{L}{2} = I\alpha$$

$$\Rightarrow \qquad \frac{L}{2} Mg = \frac{ML^2}{3}\alpha$$

$$\Rightarrow \qquad \alpha = \frac{3g}{2L} \qquad \textbf{Ans. (A)}$$

Sol. 9 Figure below shows the given situation described in question

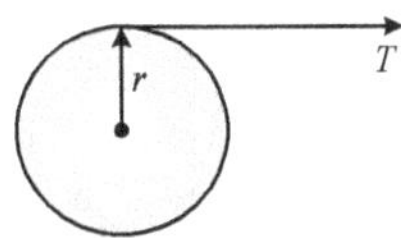

Torque due to tension in string is Tr so we use

$$Tr = I\alpha$$

$$\Rightarrow \qquad T = \frac{I\alpha}{r} = \frac{mr^2}{2}\times\frac{\alpha}{r} = \frac{mr\alpha}{2}$$

$$\Rightarrow \qquad T = \frac{50\times0.5\times2\times2\pi}{2} N = 157\,\text{N} \qquad \textbf{Ans. (D)}$$

Sol. 10 Speed of wheels in m/s is given as

$$v = 54 \text{ kph} = 15 \text{ m/s}$$

Thus angular speed of wheels is given as

$$\omega_0 = \frac{v}{r} = \frac{15}{.45} = 100/3 \text{ rad/s}$$

For uniformly retarded rotational motion, we use

$$\omega = \omega_0 + \alpha t$$

$$\Rightarrow \qquad 0 = \frac{15}{.45} - \alpha(15)$$

$$\Rightarrow \qquad \alpha = -\frac{15}{.45\times15} = -\frac{1}{.45} \text{ rad/s}^2$$

$$\Rightarrow \qquad \tau = I\alpha = -\frac{3}{.45} = -\frac{300}{45} = -6.66 \text{ kgm}^2/\text{s}^2$$

$$\textbf{Ans. (B)}$$

Sol. 11 Moment of inertia about the axis passing through P is given as

$$I = m_1 x^2 + m_2(L-x)^2$$

$$\Rightarrow \qquad I = m_1 x^2 + m_2 L^2 + m_2 x^2 - 2m_2 Lx$$

Work required to rotate the system at angular speed ω_0 is given as

$$W = \frac{1}{2} I \omega_0^2$$

This work will be minimum when

$$\frac{dI}{dx} = 2m_1 x + 0 + 2m_2 x - 2m_2 L = 0$$

$$\Rightarrow \qquad x(2m_1 + 2m_2) = 2m_2 L$$

$$\Rightarrow \qquad x = \frac{m_2 L}{m_1 + m_2}$$

When I is minimum, work done

$$W = \frac{1}{2} I \omega_0^2$$

Will also be minimum. $\qquad \textbf{Ans. (B)}$

Sol. 12 Angular momentum remain conserved when net torque about origin is zero so we use

Torque $\qquad\qquad \vec{\tau} = 0$

$$\Rightarrow \qquad \vec{r}\times\vec{F} = 0$$

$$\Rightarrow \qquad \begin{vmatrix} \hat{i} & \hat{j} & \hat{k} \\ 2 & -6 & -12 \\ \alpha & 3 & 6 \end{vmatrix} = 0$$

$$\Rightarrow \qquad (-36+36)\hat{i} - (12+12\alpha)\hat{j} + (6+6\alpha)\hat{k} = 0$$

$$\Rightarrow \qquad 0\hat{i} - 12(1+\alpha)\hat{j} + 6(1+\alpha)\hat{k} = 0$$

$$-12(1+\alpha) = 0$$

$$\alpha = -1$$

$$\textbf{Ans. (B)}$$

Sol. 13 Angular speed of disc after time t is given as

$$\omega = \alpha t = 4 \text{ rad s}^{-1}$$

Centripetal acceleration of a point on circumference of disc is given as

$$a_c = r\omega^2 = 0.5 \times 16 = 8 \text{ m/s}^2$$

Tangential acceleration of this point is given as

$$a_t = \alpha r = 1 \text{ rad/s}$$

Total acceleration of this point is given as

$$a = \sqrt{a_c^2 + a_t^2} = \sqrt{8^2 + 1^2} = 8 \text{ m/s}^2 \quad \textbf{Ans. (A)}$$

Sol. 14 Figure below shows the situation described in the question

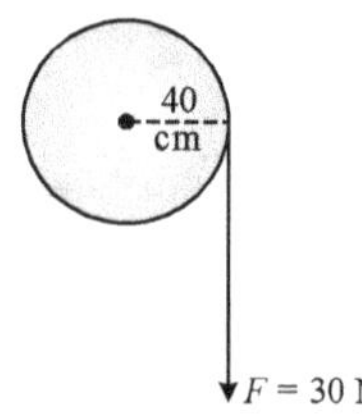

Torque of force acting on the cylinder is given as

$$\tau = F \cdot R$$

As moment of inertia of hollow cylinder is taken as MR^2, the angular acceleration of the cylinder can be calculated as

$$\tau = I\alpha$$

$$\Rightarrow \qquad F \times R = MR^2 \alpha$$

$$\Rightarrow \qquad 30 \times 0.4 = 3 \times (0.4)^2 \alpha$$

$$\Rightarrow \qquad 12 = 3 \times 0.16\alpha$$

$$\Rightarrow \qquad \alpha = 25 \text{ rad/s}^2 \qquad \textbf{Ans. (C)}$$

Sol. 15 Figure below shows the application of force at the given point P of which torque is to be calculated about point $A(2,-2,-2)$.

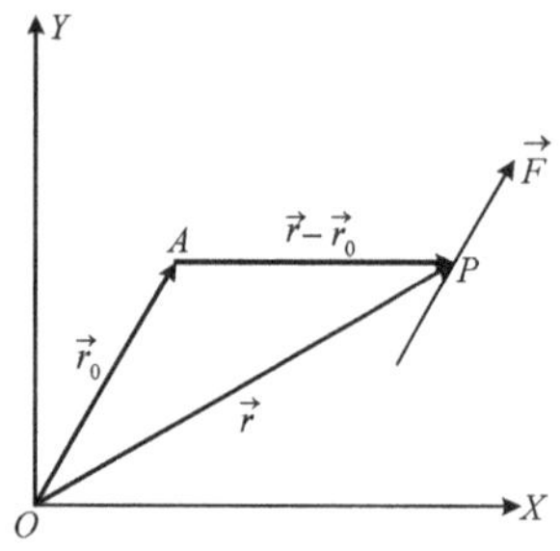

Torque is given as

$$\vec{\tau} = (\vec{r} - \vec{r_0}) \times \vec{F} \qquad \ldots(1)$$

Here vector $\vec{r} - \vec{r_0}$ is calculated as

$$\vec{r} - \vec{r_0} = (2\hat{i} + 0\hat{j} - 3\hat{k}) - (2\hat{i} - 2\hat{j} - 2\hat{k})$$

$$= 0\hat{i} + 2\hat{j} - \hat{k}$$

Torque value now can be given as

$$\vec{\tau} = \begin{vmatrix} \hat{i} & \hat{j} & \hat{k} \\ 0 & 2 & -1 \\ 4 & 5 & -6 \end{vmatrix} = -7\hat{i} - 4\hat{j} - 8\hat{k} \quad \textbf{Ans. (D)}$$

Sol. 16 Work need to stop the rolling disc is equal to its initial kinetic energy, given as

$$K = \frac{1}{2}mv^2 + \frac{1}{2}I\omega^2 = \frac{3}{4}mv^2$$

$$= \frac{3}{4} \times 100 \times (20 \times 10^{-2})^2 = 3\text{J} \qquad \textbf{Ans. (A)}$$

Sol. 17 Kinetic energy of the solid cylinder is given as

$$W = \frac{1}{2}I\omega^2 = \frac{1}{2}\left(\frac{1}{2}mr^2\right)(\omega^2)$$

Total angle after which cylinder stops is given as

$$\theta = 2\pi \text{ revolution} = 2\pi \times 2\pi = 4\pi^2 \text{ rad}$$

Work done in stopping the cylinder is equal to the loss in its kinetic energy so we use

$$\tau\theta = \frac{1}{2} \times \frac{1}{2}mr^2(\omega^2)$$

$$\Rightarrow \qquad \tau = \frac{\frac{1}{2} \times \frac{1}{2} \times 2 \times (4 \times 10^{-2})^2 \left(3 \times \frac{2\pi}{60}\right)^2}{4\pi^2}$$

$$\Rightarrow \qquad \tau = 2 \times 10^{-6} \text{ Nm} \qquad \textbf{Ans. (A)}$$

Sol. 18 Torque of the given force is calculated as

$$\vec{\tau} = \vec{r} \times \vec{F} = 2\hat{k} \times 3\hat{j} = 6(\hat{k} \times \hat{j}) = 6(-\hat{i}) = -6\hat{i} \text{ Nm} \quad \textbf{Ans. (D)}$$

Sol. 19 For the rod to be in equilibrium, net torque due to gravity forces acting on the rod about pivot must be zero.

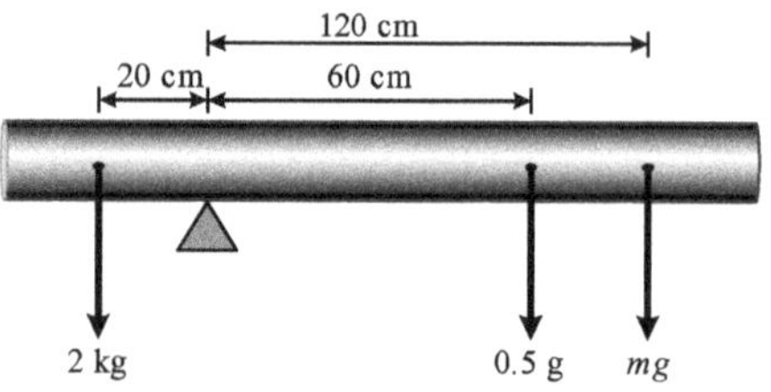

Balancing torque about pivot, we have

$$2g \times 20 = 0.5\,g \times 60 + mg \times 120$$

$$\Rightarrow \qquad m = \frac{0.5}{6} \text{ kg} = \frac{1}{12} \text{ kg} \qquad \textbf{Ans. (D)}$$

6.5 Angular Momentum & Conservation

Sol. 1 When a child sits on the disc, in this process no external torque is acted upon the system so the angular momentum of the system remain conserved. **Ans. (B)**

Sol. 2 By conservation of angular momentum we use

$$I_2\omega_2 = I_1\omega_1$$

$$\Rightarrow \qquad \omega_2 = \frac{I_1\omega_1}{I_2} = \frac{Mr^2\omega}{(M+4m)r^2}$$

$$\Rightarrow \qquad \omega_2 = \frac{M\omega}{M+4m} \qquad \textbf{Ans. (B)}$$

Sol. 3 Using conservation of angular momentum in this case, we have

$$I_1\omega = (I_1 + I_2)\omega_1$$

$$\Rightarrow \qquad \omega_1 = \frac{I_1}{(I_1 + I_2)}\omega \qquad \textbf{Ans. (C)}$$

Sol. 4 For a particle moving in a straight line angular momentum is given as moment of its linear momentum about the point and it can be expressed as

Angular momentum = Linear momentum

$$\times \text{ distance of line of action of}$$
$$\text{linear momentum about the origin}$$

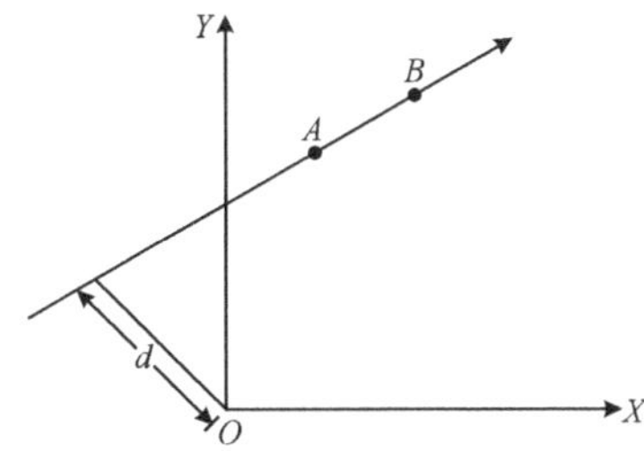

From the figure shown above, we use

$$L_A = P_A \times d,$$
$$L_B = P_B \times d$$

As linear momenta are equal at points A and B, we have

$$L_A = L_B \qquad \textbf{Ans. (A)}$$

Sol. 5 In this case while masses are added to the ring, no external torque is present so angular momentum of the ring system will remain conserved. So we will use

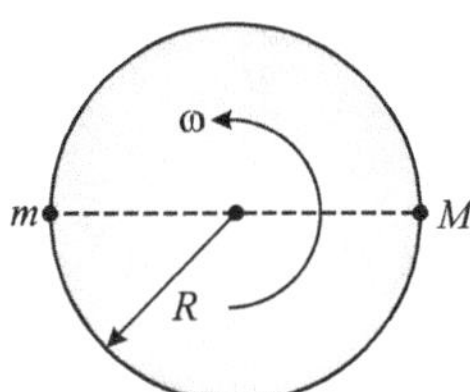

$$I\omega = I'\omega'$$

$$\Rightarrow \qquad MR^2\omega = (M + 2m)\,R^2\omega'$$

$$\Rightarrow \qquad \omega' = \frac{M\omega}{M+2m} \qquad \textbf{Ans. (C)}$$

Sol. 6 In the process of dropping of another disc, angular momentum of system remain conserved so we use

$$I_t\omega_i = (I_t + I_b)\,\omega_f$$

$$\Rightarrow \qquad \omega_f = \frac{I_t\omega_i}{I_t + I_b}$$

Loss of energy in the process can be given as

$$\Delta E = \frac{1}{2}I_t\omega_i^2 - \frac{I_t^2\omega_i^2}{2(I_t + I_b)}$$

$$\Rightarrow \qquad \Delta E = \frac{I_b I_t \omega_i^2}{2(I_t + I_b)} \qquad \textbf{Ans. (A)}$$

Sol. 7 For a mass rotating in a plane, always its angular momentum is in axial direction perpendicular to the plane in which it is rotating. **Ans. (A)**

Sol. 8 By conservation of angular momentum for the man and platform system, we use

$$I_1\omega_1 + I_2\omega_2 = 0$$

$$\Rightarrow \qquad 200\left(\frac{1}{2}\right) + 200\,\omega_2 = 0$$

$$\Rightarrow \qquad \omega_2 = -\frac{1}{2}$$

In frame of platform, relative angular speed of man can be given as

$$\omega_R = \omega_1 - \omega_2 = 1 \text{ rad/s}$$

Time period can be given as

$$T = \frac{2\pi}{\omega_R} = 2\pi \text{ second} \qquad \textbf{Ans. (B)}$$

Sol. 9 Rotational kinetic energy of a body is given as

$$K.E = \frac{1}{2}I\omega^2$$

$$\frac{K.E_{\text{sphere}}}{K.E_{\text{cylinder}}} = \frac{I_{\text{sphere}}}{I_{\text{cylinder}}}\left(\frac{\omega_{\text{sphere}}}{\omega_{\text{cylinder}}}\right)^2$$

$$= \frac{\dfrac{2}{5}MR^2}{\dfrac{MR^2}{2}}\left(\frac{\omega}{2\omega}\right)^2 \qquad \left\{ \begin{array}{l} I_{\text{sphere}} = \dfrac{2}{5}MR^2 \\[2mm] I_{\text{cylinder}} = \dfrac{MR^2}{2} \end{array} \right\}$$

$$= \frac{4}{5} \times \frac{1}{4} = 1 : 5 \qquad \textbf{Ans. (B)}$$

Sol. 10 Given that kinetic energies of both are same so we use

$$K.E_A = K.E_B$$

$$\Rightarrow \qquad \frac{1}{2}I_A\omega_A^2 = \frac{1}{2}I_B\omega_B^2$$

$$\Rightarrow \qquad \frac{\omega_A}{\omega_B} = \sqrt{\frac{I_B}{I_A}} \qquad \qquad \dots(1)$$

As $I_B > I_A \Rightarrow \dfrac{I_A}{I_B} < 1$, the angular momentum ratio of the two bodies are given as

$$\frac{L_A}{L_B} = \frac{I_A}{I_B} \times \frac{\omega_A}{\omega_B} = \frac{I_A}{I_B} \times \sqrt{\frac{I_A}{I_B}}$$

$$\Rightarrow \qquad \frac{L_A}{L_B} = \sqrt{\frac{I_A}{I_B}} < 1$$

$$\Rightarrow \qquad L_A < L_B \qquad \text{Ans. (C)}$$

Sol. 11 If final angular velocity of combination is ω then by conservation of angular momentum, we have

$$I\omega_1 + I\omega_2 = (I + I)\omega$$

$$\Rightarrow \qquad \omega = \frac{1}{2}(\omega_1 + \omega_2)$$

Initial kinetic energy of system is given as

$$K_i = \frac{1}{2} I\omega_1^2 + \frac{1}{2} I\omega_2^2$$

Final kinetic energy of system is given as

$$K_f = \frac{1}{2}(2I)\omega^2$$

$$\Rightarrow \qquad K_f = \frac{1}{4} I(\omega_1 + \omega_2)^2$$

Loss in energy can be calculated as

$$\Delta K = K_i - K_f$$

$$\Rightarrow \qquad \Delta K = \frac{1}{2} I(\omega_1^2 + \omega_2^2) - \frac{1}{4} I(\omega_1 + \omega_2)^2$$

$$\Rightarrow \qquad \Delta K = \frac{I}{4}[\omega_1^2 + \omega_2^2 - 2\omega_1\omega_2]$$

$$\Rightarrow \qquad \Delta K = \frac{I}{4}(\omega_1 - \omega_2)^2 \qquad \text{Ans. (B)}$$

Sol. 12 Work done required to bring these *tp* rest is equal to the change in kinetic energies of these objects, so we use

$$\Delta W = \Delta KE$$

$$\Rightarrow \qquad \Delta W = \frac{1}{2} I\omega^2$$

$$\Rightarrow \qquad \Delta W \propto I \text{ for identical values of } \omega$$

$$\Rightarrow \qquad W_A : W_B : W_C = \frac{2}{5} MR^2 : \frac{1}{2} MR^2 : MR^2$$

$$\Rightarrow \qquad W_A : W_B : W_C = \frac{2}{5} : \frac{1}{2} : 1$$

$$\Rightarrow \qquad W_A : W_B : W_C = 4 : 5 : 10$$

$$\Rightarrow \qquad W_C > W_B > W_A \qquad \text{Ans. (C)}$$

Sol. 13 As no external torque is acting on the sphere so its angular momentum will remain conserved. **Ans. (D)**

6.6 Rolling

Sol. 1 In case of pure rolling the respective velocities of different points on the disc are shown in figure below. For the given options, option (A) is correct.

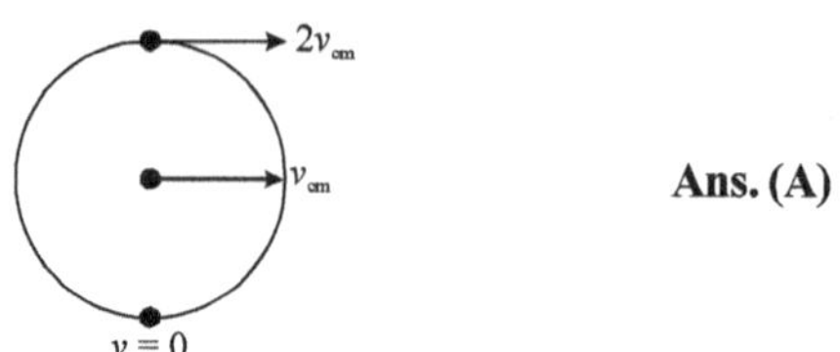

Ans. (A)

Sol. 2 When wheel completes half rotation the displacement of point P can be calculated by figure shown below.

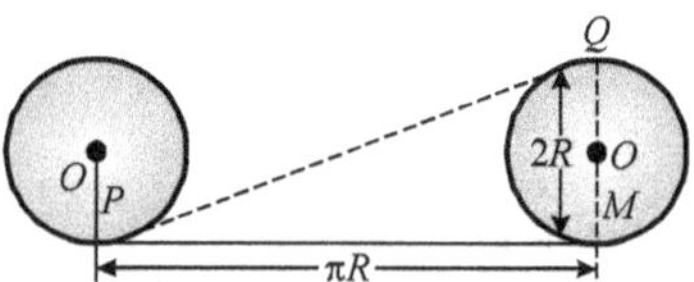

In half rotation point P has moved horizontal distance given as

$$\frac{\pi d}{2} = \pi r = \pi \times 1\,\text{m} = \pi\,\text{m}$$

In the same time, it has moved vertical distance which is equal to its diameter $= 2$ m

Thus displacement of point P is given as

$$P = \sqrt{\pi^2 + 2^2} = \sqrt{\pi^2 + 4}\,\text{m} \qquad \text{Ans. (B)}$$

Sol. 3 Since there is no friction at the contact surface (smooth horizontal surface) there will be no rolling. Hence, the acceleration of the centre of mass of the sphere will be independent of the position of the applied force F. Therefore, there is no relation between h and R. **Ans. (D)**

Sol. 4 For pure rolling on inclined plane the velocity attained by the body at the bottom of in-line plane is given as

$$v = \sqrt{\frac{2gh}{(1 + K^2 / R^2)}}$$

For a cylinder we use $K = R / \sqrt{2}$ thus the velocity is given as

$$v = \sqrt{\frac{2gh}{1 + \dfrac{1}{2}}} = \sqrt{\frac{4gh}{3}} \qquad \text{Ans. (C)}$$

Sol. 5 Total energy of ball is given as

$$E = \frac{1}{2} I\omega^2 + \frac{1}{2} mv^2$$

$$E = \frac{1}{2} mv^2(1 + K^2/R^2)$$

Fraction of Total energy which gives the rotational energy of ball is given as

$$f = \frac{Mv^2(K^2/R^2)}{Mv^2(1+K^2/R^2)}$$

$$\Rightarrow \qquad f = \frac{K^2/R^2}{1+K^2/R^2}$$

$$\Rightarrow \qquad f = \frac{K^2}{R^2+K^2} \qquad \textbf{Ans. (C)}$$

Sol. 6 When a body rolls down without slipping on an inclined plane, component of weight along the incline plane provides translational motion to the body and friction acting at the bottom contact point opposes it as well as torque due to friction provides the rotational motion to body so that it starts rolling. Thus friction reduces translational motion and imparts rotational motion to the body hence option (D) is most appropriate out of given options. **Ans. (D)**

Sol. 7 At maximum compression the kinetic energy of solid cylinder will be converted into potential energy of spring, given as

$$\frac{1}{2}mv^2 + \frac{1}{2}I\omega^2 = \frac{1}{2}kx^2$$

$$\Rightarrow \quad \frac{1}{2}mv^2 + \frac{1}{2}\frac{mR^2}{2}\left(\frac{V}{R}\right)^2 = \frac{1}{2}kx^2$$

$$\Rightarrow \qquad \frac{3}{4}mv^2 = \frac{1}{2}kx^2$$

$$\Rightarrow \qquad \frac{3}{4}\times 3\times (4)^2 = \frac{1}{2}\times 200\,x^2$$

$$\Rightarrow \qquad \frac{36}{100} = x^2$$

$$\Rightarrow \qquad x = 0.6\,\text{m} \qquad \textbf{Ans. (B)}$$

Sol. 8 Figure below shows the situation described in the question.

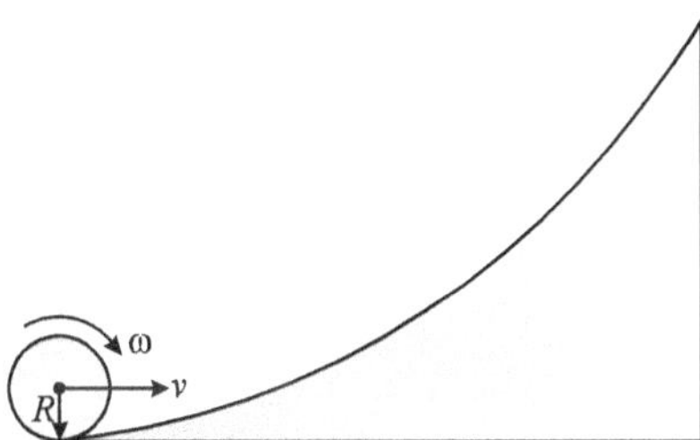

By conservation of energy, we can write

$$\frac{1}{2}mv^2 + \frac{1}{2}I\omega^2 = mgh$$

As for pure rolling we can use $\omega = \dfrac{v}{R}$

$$\Rightarrow \qquad \frac{1}{2}mv^2 + \frac{1}{2}I\left(\frac{v}{R}\right)^2 = mg\left(\frac{3v^2}{4g}\right)$$

$$\Rightarrow \qquad \frac{1}{2}mv^2 + \frac{1}{2}I\frac{v^2}{R^2} = \frac{3}{4}mv^2$$

$$\Rightarrow \qquad \frac{1}{2}I\frac{v^2}{R^2} = \frac{3}{4}mv^2 - \frac{1}{2}mv^2$$

$$\Rightarrow \qquad \frac{1}{2}I\frac{v^2}{R^2} = \frac{1}{4}mv^2$$

$$\Rightarrow \qquad I = \frac{mR^2}{2}$$

Thus the object used is a disc. **Ans. (D)**

Sol. 9 Acceleration without rolling on inclined plane is given as

$$a_{\text{slipping}} = g\sin\theta$$

Acceleration in state of pure rolling of body on inclined plane is given as

$$a_{\text{rolling}} = \frac{g\sin\theta}{1+\dfrac{K^2}{r^2}} = \frac{5}{7}g\,\sin\theta$$

As for sphere in above expression we used $mK^2 = \dfrac{2}{5}mR^2$

$$\Rightarrow \qquad \frac{a_{\text{rolling}}}{a_{\text{slipping}}} = \frac{5}{7} \qquad \textbf{Ans. (A)}$$

Sol. 10 Acceleration of a rolling body on incline plane is given as

$$a = \frac{g\sin\theta}{1+K^2/r^2}$$

As for sphere K^2/R^2 is less its acceleration will be more so

$$a_{\text{sphere}} > a_{\text{disc}}$$

Thus sphere will reach the bottom of plane earlier. **Ans. (B)**

Sol. 11 Coefficient of sliding friction has no dimension so option (D) is incorrect. Rest all other options are correct.
Ans. (D)

Sol. 12 Translational kinetic energy of sphere is given as

$$K_t = \frac{1}{2}mv^2$$

Total kinetic energy of sphere is given as

$$K_t + K_r = \frac{1}{2}mv^2 + \frac{1}{2}I\omega^2$$

$$= \frac{1}{2}mv^2 + \frac{1}{2}\left(\frac{2}{5}mr^2\right)\left(\frac{v}{r}\right)^2 = \frac{7}{10}mv^2$$

The required ratio of translational kinetic energy to the total kinetic energy is given as

$$\frac{K_t}{K_t + K_r} = \frac{5}{7}$$ **Ans. (B)**

Ch-7 Gravitation

7.1 Gravitational Field & Force

Sol. 1 The gravitational force does not depend upon the medium in which objects are placed so force will remain same.
Ans. (B)

Sol. 2 The initial velocity of the mass on both the planets is same so we use

$$\sqrt{2g'h'} = \sqrt{2gh}$$

$$\Rightarrow \quad \sqrt{2 \times g' \times h'} = \sqrt{2 \times 9g \times 2}$$

$$\Rightarrow \quad 2h' = 36$$

$$\Rightarrow \quad h' = 18\,\text{m}$$ **Ans. (B)**

Sol. 3 Acceleration due to gravity on surface of earth is given as

$$g_e = \frac{GM_e}{R_e^2} = \frac{G(4/3)\pi R_e^3}{R_e^2}\rho_e$$

$$g_e \propto R_e \rho_e$$

Acceleration due to gravity of planet can be written as

$$g_p \propto R_p \rho_p$$

$$R_e \rho_e = R_p \rho_p$$

$$\Rightarrow \quad R_e \rho_e = R_p 2\rho_e$$

$$\Rightarrow \quad R_p = \frac{1}{2}R_e = \frac{1}{2}R$$ **Ans. (D)**

Sol. 4 Gravity at surface of a planet is given as

$$g = \frac{GM}{R^2} = \frac{G\dfrac{4}{3}\pi R^3 \rho}{R^2} = \frac{4}{3}\pi G\rho R$$

Thus value of g is directly proportional to R for same density hence value of g becomes 3 times.   **Ans. (A)**

Sol. 5 Acceleration due to gravity at a height h is given as

$$g' = \frac{g}{\left(1+\dfrac{h}{R}\right)^2}$$

For $g' = \dfrac{g}{16}$, we use

$$\frac{g}{16} = \frac{g}{\left(1+\dfrac{h}{R}\right)^2}$$

$$\Rightarrow \quad \left(1+\frac{h}{R}\right)^2 = 16$$

$$\Rightarrow \quad 1+\frac{h}{R} = 4$$

$$\Rightarrow \quad \frac{h}{R} = 3$$

$$\Rightarrow \quad h = 3R$$ **Ans. (C)**

Sol. 6 Gravitational attraction force on particle

$$F_g = \frac{GM_p m}{(D_p / 2)^2}$$

Acceleration of particle due to gravity is given as

$$a = \frac{F_g}{m} = \frac{4GM_p}{D_p^2}$$ **Ans. (A)**

Sol. 7 Variation of gravitational field with distance r from center of a thin spherical shell is given as

$$g_{\text{in}} = 0 \quad (r < R)$$

$$g_{\text{out}} = \frac{GM}{r^2} \quad (r \geq R)$$

The variation is shown in below figure

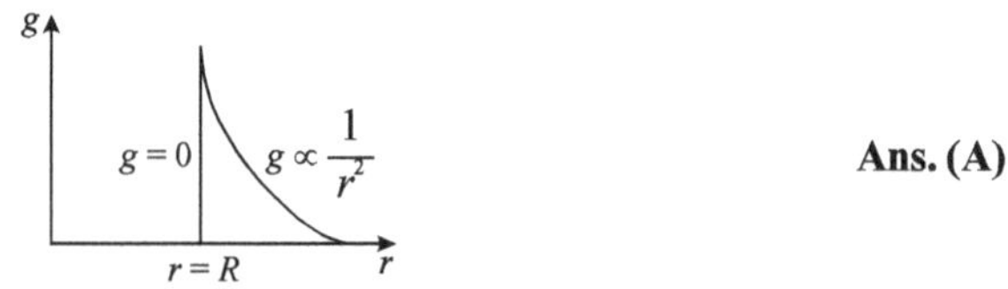

Ans. (A)

Sol. 8 For a point inside earth ($r < R$), gravitational field is given as

$$E_{\text{in}} = -\frac{GMr}{R^3}$$

For a point on the surface or outside of earth ($r \geq R$) is given as

$$E_{\text{out}} = -\frac{GM}{r^2}$$

For above values appropriate option among given options is option-(A).   **Ans. (A)**

Sol. 9 This question is same as that of Q. 8. Students are advised to refer solution of Q. 8.   **Ans. (B)**

Sol. 10 Above earth surface at a height h, acceleration due to gravity is given as

$$g_h = g\left(1 - \frac{2h}{R_e}\right)$$

Below earth surface at a depth d, acceleration due to gravity is given as

$$g_d = g\left(1 - \frac{d}{R_e}\right)$$

For the given condition, we use $g_h = g_d$, this gives

$$g\left(1 - \frac{2h}{R_e}\right) = g\left(1 - \frac{d}{R_e}\right)$$

$$\Rightarrow \qquad d = 2h$$

$$\Rightarrow \qquad d = 2 \times 1 = 2 \text{ km} \qquad \textbf{Ans. (D)}$$

Sol. 11 Both the astronauts are in state of weightlessness and due to mutual gravitational force between them they will attract each other and start moving towards each other. **Ans. (B)**

Sol. 12 Acceleration due to gravity at a depth d from surface of earth is given as

$$g_d = g\left(1 - \frac{d}{R}\right)$$

Multiplying by mass m on both sides of above equation gives

$$mg_d = mg\left(1 - \frac{d}{R}\right)$$

$$\Rightarrow \qquad mg_d = 200\left(1 - \frac{R}{2R}\right) = \frac{200}{2} = 100 \text{ N} \qquad \textbf{Ans. (D)}$$

Sol. 13 Weight of body on earth surface is given as

$$W_s = mg_s = 72 \text{ N}$$

At a height $h = R/2$ above the earth surface weight is given as

$$W_h = mg_h$$

$$\Rightarrow \qquad W_h = \frac{mg_s}{\left(1 + \dfrac{h}{R}\right)^2} = \frac{72N}{\left(1 + \dfrac{R/2}{R}\right)^2} \quad \left\{ g_n = \frac{g_s}{\left(1 + \dfrac{h}{R}\right)^2} \right\}$$

$$\Rightarrow \qquad W_h = \frac{72}{9/4} = 32 \text{ N} \qquad \textbf{Ans. (C)}$$

Sol. 14 Gravitational field intensity at a point is given as

$$g = \frac{F}{m}$$

$$\Rightarrow \qquad g = \frac{3}{60 \times 10^{-3}} = 50 \text{ N/kg} \qquad \textbf{Ans. (A)}$$

7.2 Gravitational Energy & Gravitational Potential

Sol. 1 By energy conservation projection velocity of a particle and maximum height attained can be given by the relation

$$v^2 = \frac{2gh}{1 + \dfrac{h}{R}}$$

It is given that $h = R$, so we have

$$v = \sqrt{gR} = \sqrt{\frac{GM}{R}} \qquad \textbf{Ans. (A)}$$

Sol. 2 Gravitational potential energy of body on earth's surface is given as

$$U = -\frac{GMm}{R}$$

Here M and R are the mass and radius of the earth respectively, m is the mass of the body and G is the universal gravitational constant.

Gravitational potential energy at a height $h = 3R$ is given as

$$U_{3R} = -\frac{GMm}{R + h} = -\frac{GMm}{R + 3R} = -\frac{GMm}{4R}$$

Change in potential energy of body is given as

$$\Delta U = -\frac{GMm}{4R} - \left(-\frac{GMm}{R}\right)$$

$$\Rightarrow \qquad \Delta U = -\frac{GMm}{4R} + \frac{GMm}{R}$$

$$\Rightarrow \qquad \Delta U = \frac{3}{4}\frac{GMm}{R} = \frac{3}{4}mgR \qquad \textbf{Ans. (C)}$$

Sol. 3 According to question and by using conservation of energy, we have

$$-\frac{GMm}{R + R} + \frac{1}{2}m(fv)^2 = 0 + 0$$

$$\Rightarrow \qquad fv = \sqrt{\frac{GM}{R}}$$

Escape velocity from the surface of earth is given as

$$v = \sqrt{\frac{2GM}{R}}$$

Therefore $\qquad f\sqrt{\dfrac{2GM}{R}} = \sqrt{\dfrac{GM}{R}}$

$$\Rightarrow \qquad f = \frac{1}{\sqrt{2}} \qquad \textbf{Ans. (B)}$$

Sol. 4 Gravitational potential due to both masses will be added up at the point, which is given as

$$V_g = -\frac{Gm}{r_1} - \frac{Gm}{r_2}$$

$$\Rightarrow \qquad V_g = \frac{-GM}{a} - \frac{GM}{\dfrac{a}{2}}$$

$$\Rightarrow \qquad V_g = \frac{-3GM}{a} \qquad \textbf{Ans. (B)}$$

Sol. 5 Power exerted by gravitational force can be given as

$$P = Fv$$

Velocity is maximum at instant just after projected so at the projection instant only the power will be maximum. **Ans. (D)**

Sol. 6 Escape velocity for a satellite on the earth surface is given as

$$v_{escape} = \sqrt{\frac{2GM}{R}}$$

Orbital velocity of satellite is given as

$$v_{orbital} = \sqrt{\frac{GM}{R}}$$

$$\Rightarrow \qquad v_{escape} = \sqrt{2}\, v_0 \qquad\qquad \textbf{Ans. (C)}$$

Sol. 7 Gravitation potential energy at any point at a distance r from the centre of earth is given as

$$U = \frac{-GMm}{r}$$

Where M and m are masses of earth and body. At the surface of earth we use $r = R$, so we have

$$U_i = \frac{-GMm}{R}$$

At a height h from surface of earth we use

$$r = R + h = R + 2R = 3R$$

Thus final potential energy is given as

$$U_f = \frac{-GMm}{3R}$$

Change in potential energy is given as

$$\Delta U = U_F - U_i$$

$$\Rightarrow \qquad \Delta U = \frac{GMm}{R}\left(1 - \frac{1}{3}\right) = \frac{2}{3}\frac{GMm}{R}$$

$$\Rightarrow \qquad \Delta U = \frac{2}{3}mgR \qquad\qquad \textbf{Ans. (B)}$$

Sol. 8 The gravitational potential at origin O due to all the masses as shown in figure below can be given as

$$
\begin{array}{ccccc}
\text{2kg} & \text{2kg} & \text{2kg} & \text{2kg} \\
\bullet\!\!-\!\!\!\!-\!\!\bullet & \bullet & \bullet & \bullet \\
x=0 \quad \text{1m} & \text{2m} & \text{4m} & \text{8m} \dots \infty
\end{array}
$$

$$V_g = -\frac{G(2)}{1} - \frac{G(2)}{2} - \frac{G(2)}{4} - \frac{G(2)}{8} \dots \infty$$

$$\Rightarrow \qquad V_g = -2G\left[1 + \frac{1}{2} + \frac{1}{4} + \frac{1}{8} + \cdots \infty\right]$$

$$\Rightarrow \qquad V_g = -2G\left[\frac{1}{1 - \frac{1}{2}}\right] = -2G(2) = -4G \qquad \textbf{Ans. (D)}$$

Sol. 9 As light cannot escape from a black hole so we can consider the escape velocity to be equal to speed of light, thus we use

$$V_e = \sqrt{\frac{2GM}{R}} = c$$

$$\Rightarrow \qquad R = \frac{2GM}{c^2} = \frac{2 \times 6.67 \times 10^{-11} \times 5.98 \times 10^{24}}{(3 \times 10^8)^2}$$

$$\Rightarrow \qquad R = \frac{2 \times 6.67 \times 5.98}{9} \times 10^{-3}\,\text{m}$$

$$\Rightarrow \qquad R = 8.86 \times 10^{-3}\,\text{m} \approx 10^{-2}\,\text{m} \qquad \textbf{Ans. (C)}$$

Sol. 10 Gravitational potential at a height h from the surface of earth is given as

$$V = -\frac{GM}{(R + h)}$$

At the same point acceleration due to gravity is given as

$$g' = \frac{GM}{(R + h)^2}$$

$$\Rightarrow \qquad \frac{|V|}{g'} = R + h$$

$$\Rightarrow \qquad \frac{5.4 \times 10^7}{6.0} = R + h$$

$$\Rightarrow \qquad 9 \times 10^6 = R + h$$

$$\Rightarrow \qquad h = (9 - 6.4) \times 10^6$$

$$= 2.6 \times 10^6 = 2600\,\text{km} \qquad \textbf{Ans. (A)}$$

Sol. 11 Escape velocity from the surface of a planet is given as

$$v_e = \sqrt{2gR} = R\sqrt{\frac{8}{3}\pi G\rho}$$

$$\Rightarrow \qquad \frac{v_e}{v_p} = \frac{R\sqrt{\rho_e}}{R_p\sqrt{\rho_p}} = \frac{1}{2} \times \sqrt{\frac{1}{2}}$$

$$\Rightarrow \qquad \frac{v_e}{v_p} = \frac{1}{2\sqrt{2}} \qquad\qquad \textbf{Ans. (B)}$$

Sol. 12 Initial potential energy of mass at earth surface is given as

$$U_i = \frac{-GMm}{R}$$

Final potential energy at a height $h = R$ can be given as

$$U_f = \frac{-GMm}{2R}$$

As required work is given by change in potential energy, we use

$$W = U_f - U_i$$

$$\Rightarrow \quad W = \frac{GMm}{2R} = \frac{gR^2 m}{2R} = \frac{mgR}{2} \qquad (\text{As } GM = gR^2)$$

Ans. (C)

Sol. 13 The escape velocity from the surface of a planet is given as

$$v_e = \sqrt{\frac{2GM}{R}} = \sqrt{\frac{2G}{R} \times \frac{4}{3}\pi R^3 \rho} = \sqrt{\frac{8\pi G \rho}{3}} R^2$$

As $v_e \propto R$, the escape velocity from the surface of another planet of radius four times that of earth is given as

$$\frac{v_e}{v} = \frac{4R}{R}$$

$$\Rightarrow \quad v_e = 4v$$

Ans. (D)

Sol. 14 The maximum height to which the particle may rise can be calculated by energy conservation, as

$$\frac{1}{2}mv^2 = \frac{GMm}{(R+h)}$$

$$\Rightarrow \quad \frac{1}{2}mk^2 V_e^2 - \frac{GMm}{R} = \frac{GMm}{(R+h)}$$

$$\Rightarrow \quad \frac{1}{2}mk^2 \left(\frac{2GM}{R}\right) - \frac{GMm}{R} = -\frac{GMm}{(R+h)}$$

$$\Rightarrow \quad \frac{k^2}{R} - \frac{1}{R} = -\frac{1}{R+h}$$

$$\Rightarrow \quad h = \frac{Rk^2}{1-k^2}$$

Ans. (D)

7.3 Satellite & Planetary Motion

Sol. 1 For a satellite moving in an orbit around the earth, its kinetic and potential energies are given as

$$K = \frac{GM}{2R} \text{ and } U = \frac{-GMm}{R}$$

$$\Rightarrow \quad K = \frac{|U|}{2}$$

$$\Rightarrow \quad \left|\frac{K}{U}\right| = \frac{1}{2}$$

Ans. (D)

Sol. 2 Satellite of mass m is moving in a circular orbit of radius r, the kinetic and potential energies of the satellites are given as

$$K = \frac{GMm}{2r} \text{ and } U = \frac{-GMm}{r}$$

Orbital speed of the satellite in orbit of radius r is given as

$$v = \sqrt{\frac{GM}{r}}$$

Time period of satellite is given as

$$T = \left[\left(\frac{4\pi^2}{Gm}\right)r^3\right]^{1/2}$$

In question, it is given that

$$m_{S_1} = m_{S_2}$$

From above values we can see that orbital speed of satellite is independent of mass of satellite so orbital speed is same for both satellites S_1 and S_2 thus only option (B) is correct.

Ans. (B)

Sol. 3 From Kepler's second law, we use

$$\frac{A_1}{t_1} = \frac{A_2}{t_2}$$

$$\Rightarrow \quad \frac{2A}{t_1} = \frac{A}{t_2}$$

$$\Rightarrow \quad t_1 = 2t_2$$

Ans. (D)

Sol. 4 Orbital speed of satellite around the earth is given as

$$V = \sqrt{\frac{GM}{r}} \qquad \ldots(1)$$

For satellite A, $r_A = 4R$ and $V_A = 3V$, we use

$$V_A = \sqrt{\frac{GM}{r_A}} \qquad \ldots(2)$$

For satellite B, $r_B = R$, we use

From equation-(1) & (2), we have

$$\frac{V_B}{V_A} = \sqrt{\frac{r_A}{r_B}}$$

$$\Rightarrow \quad V_B = V_A \sqrt{\frac{r_A}{r_B}}$$

$$\Rightarrow \quad V_B = 3V\sqrt{\frac{4R}{R}}$$

$$\Rightarrow \quad V_B = 6V$$

Ans. (C)

Sol. 5 By the law of conservation of angular momentum, we use

$$mv_1 r_1 = mv_2 r_2$$

$$\Rightarrow \quad \frac{v_1}{v_2} = \frac{r_2}{r_1}$$

Ans. (B)

Sol. 6 By Kepler's third law we have

$$T^2 \propto R^3$$

$$\Rightarrow \quad \frac{T_1^2}{T_2^2} = \frac{R_1^3}{R_2^3} = \frac{(6R)^3}{(3R)^3} = 8$$

$$\Rightarrow \qquad \frac{24 \times 24}{T_2^2} = 8$$

$$\Rightarrow \qquad T_2^2 = \frac{24 \times 24}{8} = 72$$

$$\Rightarrow \qquad T_2 = 6\sqrt{2} \qquad \qquad \textbf{Ans. (C)}$$

Sol. 7 Force on satellite is only gravitational force, which is always be acting towards the centre of earth. **Ans. (A)**

Sol. 8 Orbital speed of satellite is given as

$$v = \sqrt{\frac{GM}{r}} = \sqrt{\frac{GMR^2}{R^2 r}} = \sqrt{\frac{g}{r}} R$$

$$\Rightarrow \qquad v = \left(\sqrt{\frac{9.8}{.25 \times 10^6 + 6.38 \times 10^6}} \right) \times 6.38 \times 10^6$$

$$\Rightarrow \qquad v = \sqrt{\frac{1.47}{10^6}} \times 6.38 \times 10^6$$

$$\Rightarrow \qquad v = 7.76 \times 10^3 \text{ m/s} = 7.76 \text{ km/s} \qquad \textbf{Ans. (B)}$$

Sol. 9 Total energy of the satellite is given as

$$E = -\frac{GMm}{2r}$$

Gravity at the surface of earth is given as

$$g_0 = g_{\text{surface}} = \frac{GM}{R^2}$$

$$\Rightarrow \qquad GM = g_0 R^2$$

$$\Rightarrow \qquad E = -\frac{g_0 R^2 m}{2(R+h)} \qquad \qquad \textbf{Ans. (B)}$$

Sol. 10 In the figure shown below point A is perihelion and C is aphelion so for the points shown in figure, we can use

$$V_A > V_B > V_C$$

$$\Rightarrow \qquad K_A > K_B > K_C$$

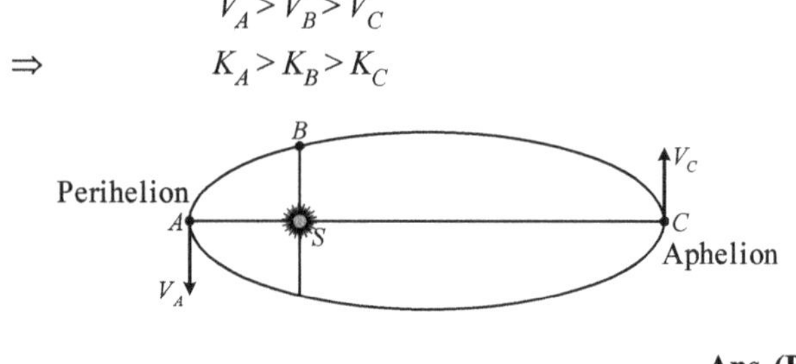

$$\textbf{Ans. (B)}$$

Sol. 11 If Universal Gravitational constant becomes ten times, then $G_{\text{new}} = 10G$, thus acceleration due to gravity increases. **Ans. (D)**

Sol. 12 The dimensions of the given physical quantities are listed below

Gravitational constant $= [\text{M}^{-1}\text{L}^3\text{T}^{-2}]$

Gravitational potential energy $= [\text{ML}^2\text{T}^{-2}]$

Gravitational potential $= [\text{L}^2\text{T}^{-2}]$

Gravitational intensity $= [\text{LT}^{-2}]$ **Ans. (A)**

Ch-8 Mechanical Properties of Solids

8.1 Elasticity

Sol. 1 Young's modulus of the wire material is given as

$$Y = \frac{FL}{A\Delta L} = \frac{4FL}{\pi D^2 \Delta L}$$

$$\Rightarrow \qquad \Delta L = \frac{4FL}{\pi D^2 Y}$$

As each wire is made up of same material so Young's modulus is same for each material for all the four wires so we have

$$\Delta L \propto \frac{L}{D^2}$$

checking these values for all above cases given in four options, we have

(A) $\dfrac{L}{D^2} = \dfrac{50\text{cm}}{(005\text{cm})^2} = 20 \times 10^3 \text{ cm}^{-1}$

(B) $\dfrac{L}{D^2} = \dfrac{100\text{cm}}{(0.1\text{cm})^2} = 10 \times 10^3 \text{ cm}^{-1}$

(C) $\dfrac{L}{D^2} = \dfrac{200}{(0.2)^2} = 5 \times 10^3 \text{ cm}^{-1}$

(D) $\dfrac{L}{D^2} = \dfrac{300}{(0.3)^2} = 3.3 \times 10^3 \text{ cm}^{-1}$

Thus ΔL is maximum for the case mentioned in option (A). **Ans. (A)**

Sol. 2 Volume of wire is taken as

$$V = Al$$

Where A is its cross section area and l is its length. Young's modulus of wire material is given as

$$Y = \frac{(F/A)}{(\Delta l / l)}$$

$$\Rightarrow \qquad Y = \frac{Fl}{A\Delta l}$$

$$\Rightarrow \qquad \Delta l = \frac{Fl}{AY} = \frac{Fl^2}{VY}$$

$$\Rightarrow \qquad \Delta l \propto l^2$$

Thus Δl versus l^2 will be a straight line curve. **Ans. (B)**

Sol. 3 As per condition given in question, we use

$$Y_{steel} = 2Y_{brass}$$

Given that $L_s = L_b$, $A_s = A_b$ and after loading these wires with weights they should have equal extensions so we also have

$$\Delta L_s = \Delta L_b$$

Situation described in question is shown in figure below.

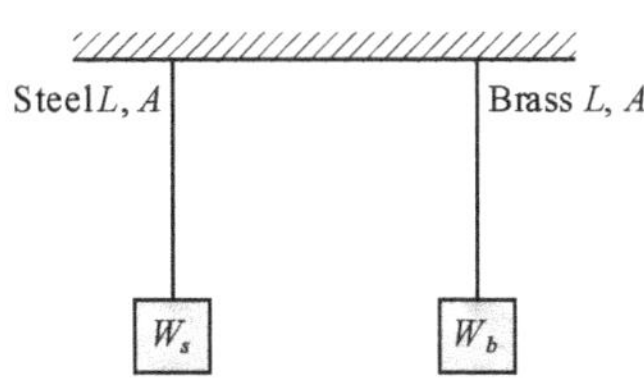

Young's modulus of wire is given as

$$Y = \frac{\text{stress}}{\text{strain}} = \frac{\dfrac{F}{A}}{\dfrac{\Delta L}{L}} = \frac{WL}{A\Delta L}$$

$$\Rightarrow \qquad \Delta L = \frac{WL}{Ar}$$

Using $\Delta L_s = \Delta L_b$, we have

$$\frac{W_s L}{r_s A} = \frac{W_b L}{r_b A}$$

$$\Rightarrow \qquad W = \frac{YA\Delta L}{L} \propto Y$$

$$\Rightarrow \qquad \frac{W_s}{W_b} = \frac{Y_s}{Y_b} = 2 : 1 \qquad\qquad \text{Ans. (C)}$$

Sol. 4 Bulk modulus of object B is given as

$$B = \frac{p}{\left(\dfrac{\Delta V}{V}\right)}$$

$$\Rightarrow \qquad \frac{\Delta V}{V} = \frac{p}{B}$$

Volume of sphere is given as

$$V = \frac{4}{3}\pi r^3$$

$$\Rightarrow \qquad \Delta V = \frac{4}{3}\pi(3r^2 \Delta r)$$

$$\Rightarrow \qquad -\frac{V}{\Delta V} = -\frac{r}{3\Delta r}$$

$$\Rightarrow \qquad 3\frac{\Delta r}{r} = \frac{p}{B}$$

$$\Rightarrow \qquad \frac{\Delta r}{r} = \frac{p}{3B} \qquad\qquad \text{Ans. (D)}$$

Sol. 5 Figure below shows the two wires extended by applying the external forces.

Wire-1 : $\qquad\qquad\qquad\qquad\qquad\; \rightarrow F$
$\qquad\qquad\qquad\qquad\qquad\qquad A, 3l$

Wire-2 : $\qquad\qquad\qquad\qquad\qquad\; \rightarrow F'$
$\qquad\qquad\qquad\qquad\qquad\qquad 3A, l$

Young's modulus of wires is given as

$$Y = \frac{(F/A)}{(\Delta\mu l)} = \frac{Fl}{A\Delta l}$$

For wire-1, we have

$$\Delta l = \left(\frac{F}{AY}\right)3l \qquad\qquad \dots(1)$$

For wire-2, we have

$$\frac{F'}{3A} = Y\frac{\Delta l}{l}$$

$$\Rightarrow \qquad \Delta l = \left(\frac{F'}{3AY}\right)l \qquad\qquad \dots(2)$$

From equation-(1) & (2), we have

$$\Delta l = \left(\frac{F}{AY}\right)3l = \left(\frac{F'}{3AY}\right)l$$

$$\Rightarrow \qquad F' = 9F \qquad\qquad \text{Ans. (C)}$$

Sol. 6 Due to loaded block stress in wire is given as

$$\text{Stress} = \frac{F}{A} = \frac{mg}{A}$$

Due to extension in wire, strain in it is given as

$$\text{Strain} = \frac{\Delta l}{l} = \frac{L + l - L}{L} = \frac{l}{L}$$

Elastic potential energy stored in the wire is given as

$$U = \frac{1}{2}\,(\text{work done by gravity})$$

$$\Rightarrow \qquad U = \frac{1}{2} \times \text{stress} \times \text{strain} \times \text{volume}$$

$$\Rightarrow \qquad U = \frac{1}{2}Mgl \qquad\qquad \text{Ans. (C)}$$

Sol. 7 Young's modulus of the material of wire is given as

$$Y = \frac{\text{Stress}}{\text{Strain}} = \frac{F/A}{\Delta L/L}$$

$$\Rightarrow \qquad Y = \frac{FL}{A\Delta L} = \frac{MgL}{A(L_1 - L)} \qquad \text{Ans. (A)}$$

Sol. 8 In stretching of a spring shape of spring changes so shear modulus is used to determine the force constant of the spring hence assertion (A) is true. For the copper Young's modulus is less than that of steel so reason (R) is false.

$$\text{Ans. (B)}$$

Ch-9 Mechanical Properties of Fluids

9.1 Fluid Statics

Sol. 1 Situation described in question is shown in figure below.

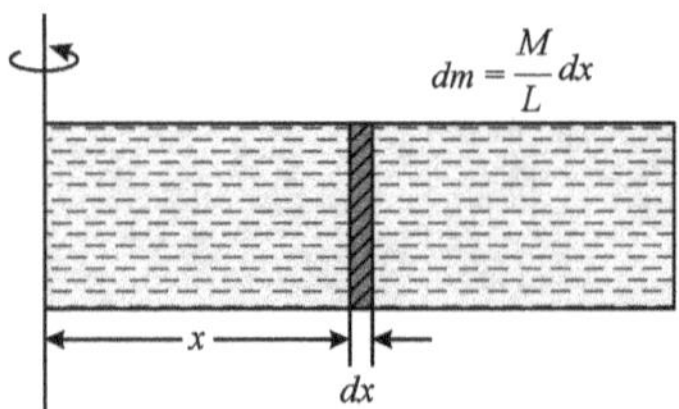

We consider a small elemental mass dm at distance x from the axis of rotation of the tube. The force acting on whole liquid can be calculated by integration of the centripetal force acting on this elemental mass dm. So we have

$$F = \int dF = \int (dm)(\omega^2)(x)$$

$$\Rightarrow \qquad F = \int_0^L \frac{M}{L}\omega^2 x\, dx = \frac{M\omega^2 L}{2}$$

As tube is of uniform cross sectional area and force is a linear function of distance so above result can also be obtained by considering force at center of mass of the liquid. **Ans. (A)**

Sol. 2 The situation described in question is shown in figure below. For floatation of cylinder its weight is to be balanced by the buoyant forces acting on it due to the two liquids.

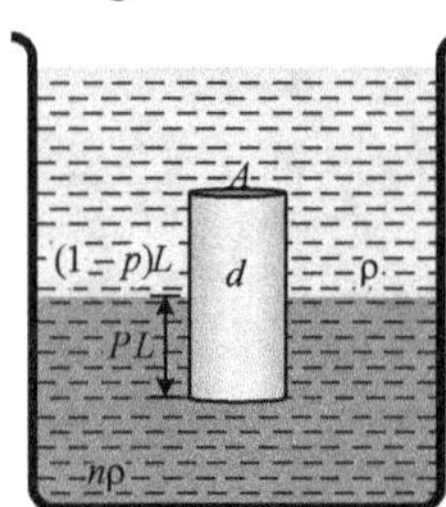

For floatation, we use

Weight of cylinder $= F_{b1} + F_{b2}$

$$ALdg = (1-p)\, LA\rho g + (pLA)n\rho g$$

$$\Rightarrow \qquad d = (1-p)\rho + pn\rho$$

$$\Rightarrow \qquad d = \rho - p\rho + np\rho = \rho[1 + (n-1)p] \quad \textbf{Ans. (D)}$$

Sol. 3 In question shown U tube, pressure at point C can be given as

$$P_c = P_a + \rho_{\text{water}}\, gh_{\text{water}}$$

Here height of water level can be given as

$$h_{\text{water}} = CE = (65 + 55)\,\text{mm} = 130\,\text{mm}$$

Pressure at point B is given as

$$P_B = P_a + \rho_{\text{oil}} gh_{\text{oil}}$$

$$h_{\text{oil}} = AB = (65 + 65 + 10)\,\text{mm} = 140\,\text{mm}$$

In liquid pressure is same at same liquid level, so $P_B = P_C$

$$\Rightarrow \qquad \rho_{\text{oil}} gh_{\text{oil}} = \rho_{\text{water}} \times g \times h_{\text{water}}$$

$$140 \times \rho_{\text{oil}} = 130 \times \rho_{\text{water}}$$

$$\Rightarrow \qquad \rho_{\text{oil}} = \frac{13}{14} \times 1000\,\text{kg/m}^3 = 928\,\text{kg m}^{-3}\ \textbf{Ans. (D)}$$

9.2 Fluid Dynamics

Sol. 1 If the speed of ejection of the liquid through the holes be V_2, then according to the equation of continuity, we use

$$A_1 V_1 = A_2 V_2$$

$$\Rightarrow \qquad V_2 = \frac{A_1 V_1}{A_2} = \frac{\pi R^2 \times V}{n(\pi r^2)}$$

$$\Rightarrow \qquad V_2 = \frac{R^2}{nr^2} V \qquad\qquad \textbf{Ans. (C)}$$

Sol. 2 Figure below shows the situation described in the question.

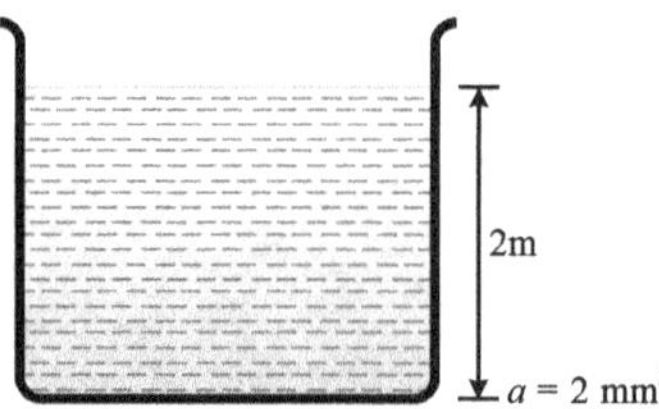

According to torricelli theorem, the efflux velocity of water is given as

$$v = \sqrt{2gh}$$

Volume flow rate of water coming out of hole is given as

$$Q = av = a\sqrt{2gh}$$

$$\Rightarrow \qquad Q = 2 \times 10^{-6}\, m^2 \times \sqrt{2 \times 10 \times 2}\ \text{m/s}$$

$$\Rightarrow \qquad Q = 2 \times 2 \times 3.14 \times 10^{-6}\ \text{m}^2/\text{s} = 12.56 \times 10^{-6}\ \text{m}^3/\text{s}$$

$$\textbf{Ans. (A)}$$

9.3 Surface Tension

Sol. 1 The wettability of a surface by a liquid depends on angle of contact between the surface and the liquid. If it is an acute angle then it wets the surface in contact and for obtuse angle it doesn't wet the surface. **Ans. (D)**

Sol. 2 When drops coalesce to form a single drop then Energy released is given by the difference in initial and final surface energies. Final and initial surface area of the liquid drop(s) is/are given as

$$A_f = 4\pi R^2 = \frac{3}{4}\, 4\pi \frac{R^3}{R} = \frac{3V}{R}$$

and
$$A_i = n \times 4\pi r^2 = \frac{V}{\frac{4}{3}\pi r^3} 4\pi r^2 = \frac{3V}{r}$$

Thus Energy released can be given as
$$E = (A_f - A_i)T$$
$$= 3VT\left[\frac{1}{r} - \frac{1}{R}\right] \qquad \textbf{Ans. (C)}$$

Sol. 3 As height of water column is more than the capillary height above the water level so in this case liquid rises to the top and then its curvature changes till pressure balances and liquid stays upto that point only. **Ans. (C)**

Sol. 4 Work done can be given by change in surface energy of the film, calculated as
$$W = 2(T\,\Delta A)$$
$$\Rightarrow \quad \Delta A = A_2 - A_1$$
$$\Rightarrow \quad \Delta A = (20 - 8) \times 10^{-4}\ \text{m}^2 = 12 \times 10^{-4}\ \text{m}^2$$
$$\Rightarrow \quad T = \frac{W}{2\Delta A} = \frac{3 \times 10^{-4}}{2 \times 12 \times 10^{-4}} = 0.125\ \text{N/m} \qquad \textbf{Ans. (B)}$$

Sol. 5 Height in capillary tube is given as
$$h = \frac{2T\cos\theta_c}{r\rho g}$$
As capillary height is same for all three, we can use
$$\cos\theta_c \propto \rho$$
As $\rho_1 > \rho_2 > \rho_3$, we have
$$\cos\theta_{c_1} > \cos\theta_{c_2} > \cos\theta_{c_3}$$
$$\Rightarrow \quad 0 \le \theta_1 < \theta_2 < \theta_3 < \frac{\pi}{2} \qquad \textbf{Ans. (B)}$$

Sol. 6 Pressure at a point Z_0 below the surface of water is given as
$$P_{Z_0} = P_0 + \rho g Z_0$$
Pressure inside a soap bubble is given as
$$P = P_0 + \frac{4T}{R}$$
$$\Rightarrow \quad P_0 + \frac{4T}{R} = P_0 + \rho g Z_0$$
$$\Rightarrow \quad Z_0 = \frac{4T}{R \times \rho g}$$
$$\Rightarrow \quad Z_0 = \frac{4 \times 2.5 \times 10^{-2}}{10^{-3} \times 1000 \times 10}\ \text{m} = 1\ \text{cm} \qquad \textbf{Ans. (C)}$$

Sol. 7 Mass of water in capillary tube can be given as
$$m = \rho \times (\pi r^2 h)$$

For different capillary radii, we use
$$rh = \text{constant}$$
$$\Rightarrow \quad \frac{h_2}{h_1} = \frac{r_1}{r_2}$$
Ratio of masses of water in the two capillary tubes is given as
$$\frac{m_2}{m_1} = \left(\frac{r_2}{r_1}\right)^2 \times \frac{h_2}{h_1}$$
$$\Rightarrow \quad \frac{m_2}{m_1} = \frac{r_2}{r_1}$$
$$\Rightarrow \quad \frac{m_2}{5} = \frac{2r}{r}$$
$$\Rightarrow \quad m_2 = 10\ \text{g} \qquad \textbf{Ans. (D)}$$

Sol. 8 Pressure inside the bubble is given as
$$P = P_0 + \frac{4T}{R}$$
As R increases, pressure P decreases. **Ans. (D)**

9.4 Viscosity

Sol. 1 Viscous drag force at terminal speed v is given as
$$F = 6\pi\eta r v$$
Rate of heat produced can be given as
$$P_T = F v$$
Terminal velocity of falling sphere is given as
$$v_T = \frac{2r^2(\rho - \sigma)g}{9\eta}$$
Thus thermal power produced can be written as
$$P_T = 6\pi\eta r V_T \cdot V_T = 6\pi\eta r V_T^2$$
As $V_T \propto r^2$, thermal power can be written as
$$P_T \propto r^5 \qquad \textbf{Ans. (A)}$$

Sol. 2 As after sometime velocity of ball becomes constant, means net force on ball becomes zero. The viscous force acts in direction opposite to motion of ball in liquid, as shown in figure. Net buoyant force on ball is given as

$$F_B = V_s \rho_l g = V \frac{d}{2} g$$
For constant velocity of ball, we use
$$F_B + F_v = Mg$$
$$\Rightarrow \quad F_v = Mg - F_B = Vdg - \frac{Vdg}{2} = \frac{Mg}{2} \qquad \textbf{Ans. (A)}$$

Sol. 3 Initially speed is zero, it gradually increases & after some time it attains terminal speed and becomes constant. Hence acceleration (slope of v/t curve) of ball first decreases and after some time it becomes zero. **Ans. (B)**

Ch-10 Thermal Properties of Matter

10.1 Thermal Expansion

Sol. 1 If W is the temperature reading on new scale corresponding to 39°C on °C scale then we use

$$\frac{C-0}{100-0} = \frac{W-39}{239-39}$$

$$\Rightarrow \qquad \frac{C}{100} = \frac{W-39}{200}$$

$$\Rightarrow \qquad W = \frac{C}{100} \times 200 + 39$$

$$\Rightarrow \qquad W = \frac{39}{100} \times 200 + 39 = 78 + 39 = 117°W \qquad \textbf{Ans. (D)}$$

Sol. 2 If ρ and ρ_0 are the densities of glycerine at 0°C and 40°C then we use

$$\rho = \rho_0(1 + y\Delta T)$$

$$\Rightarrow \qquad \rho - \rho_0 = \rho_0 \gamma \Delta T$$

Fractional change in density of glycerine is given as

$$\frac{\rho - \rho_0}{\rho_0} = \gamma \Delta T = 5 \times 10^{-4} \times 40$$

$$= 200 \times 10^{-4} = 0.020 \qquad \textbf{Ans. (C)}$$

Sol. 3 As change in lengths is maintained same at all temperatures, we use

$$l'_2 - l'_1 = l_2 - l_1$$

$$\Rightarrow \qquad l_2(1 + \alpha_2 \Delta t) - l_1(1 + \alpha_1 \Delta t) = l_2 - l_1$$

$$\Rightarrow \qquad l_2 \alpha_2 = l_1 \alpha_1 \qquad \textbf{Ans. (D)}$$

Sol. 4 It is given that change in length of aluminium rod and that of copper rod is same at all temperatures, so we use

$$\Delta l_{cm} = \Delta l_{Al}$$

$$\Rightarrow \qquad \alpha_{Cu} L_{Cu} = \alpha_{Al} L_{Al}$$

$$\Rightarrow \qquad 1.7 \times 10^{-5} \times 88\,cm = 2.2 \times 10^{-5} \times L_{Al}$$

$$\Rightarrow \qquad L_{Al} = \frac{1.7 \times 88}{2.2} = 68\,cm \qquad \textbf{Ans. (D)}$$

10.2 Calorimetry

Sol. 1 Heat required to boil 1 kg of water in electric kettle is given as

$$Q = ms\Delta T$$

$$\Rightarrow \qquad Q = 1000 \times 1 \times (100 - 20) = 80\,kcal$$

Heat supplied by electric current is given as

$$H = Vit = 220 \times 4 \times t$$

As $H = Q$, we use

$$220 \times 4 \times t = 80,000 \times 4.2$$

$$\Rightarrow \qquad t = \frac{80,000 \times 4.2}{220 \times 4}\,s$$

$$\Rightarrow \qquad t = \frac{4200}{11}\,s$$

$$\Rightarrow \qquad t = \frac{4200}{11 \times 60} = 6.36\,min \qquad \textbf{Ans. (C)}$$

Sol. 2 By energy conservation, we use

Heat gain by water = Heat lost by steam

$$20 \times 1 \times (80 - 10) = m \times 540 + m \times 1 \times (100 - 80)$$

$$\Rightarrow \qquad 1400 = 560\,m$$

$$\Rightarrow \qquad m = 2.5\,g$$

Thus total mass of water present is given as

$$m_T = 20 + 2.5 = 22.5\,g \qquad \textbf{Ans. (D)}$$

Sol. 3 One quarter of the potential energy released by falling is used in melting the ice, so we use

$$\frac{mgh}{4} = mL_f$$

$$\Rightarrow \qquad h = \frac{4L_f}{g} = \frac{4 \times 3.4 \times 10^5}{10}$$

$$\Rightarrow \qquad h = 136\,km \qquad \textbf{Ans. (C)}$$

Sol. 4 As with temperature heat capacity increase so heat capacity of second body is higher than that of first body. Let average heat capacities of the two bodies are c_1 & c_2 and common equilibrium temperature is T so, we use

$$mc_1(T - 0) = mc_2(100 - T)$$

$$\Rightarrow \qquad \frac{T}{100 - T} = \frac{c_2}{c_1} > 1 \qquad [c_2 > c_1]$$

$$\Rightarrow \qquad T > 50°C \qquad \textbf{Ans. (B)}$$

Sol. 5 Heat supplied to copper spheres can be given as

$$\Delta Q = Ms\Delta T$$

For same material, we use

$$\Delta Q \propto M$$

and

$$M = \frac{4}{3}\pi r^3 \rho$$

$$\Rightarrow \qquad \Delta Q \propto r^3$$

$$\Rightarrow \qquad \frac{\Delta Q_1}{\Delta Q_2} = \left(\frac{r_1}{r_2}\right)^3 = \left(\frac{1.5}{1}\right)^3 = \frac{27}{8} \qquad \textbf{Ans. (B)}$$

10.3 Conduction of Heat

Sol. 1 We consider steady state in above case so heat flow rate is given as

$$\frac{dQ}{dt} = \frac{KA(T_1 - T_2)}{L} = Q_1$$

As linear dimensions are doubled we use $A_2 = 4A_1$ & $L_2 = 2L_1$

$$\Rightarrow \qquad Q_2 = 2Q_1 \qquad\qquad \textbf{Ans. (B)}$$

Sol. 2 Considering steady state of heat conduction, we have

Rate of heat loss in rod 1 $= Q_1 = \dfrac{K_1 A_1 (T_1 - T_2)}{l_1}$

Rate of heat loss in rod 2 $= Q_2 = \dfrac{K_2 A_2 (T_1 - T_2)}{l_2}$

As specified in the question, we use $Q_1 = Q_2$

$$\Rightarrow \quad \dfrac{K_1 A_1 (T_1 - T_2)}{l_2} = \dfrac{K_2 A_2 (T_1 - T_2)}{l_2}$$

$$\Rightarrow \qquad K_1 A_1 = K_2 A_2 \qquad\qquad \textbf{Ans. (A)}$$

Sol. 3 We can consider the slabs described in questions in series. So total thermal resistance can be given as

$$R_{Th} = R_1 + R_2$$

$$\Rightarrow \quad \dfrac{l}{AK_{\text{effective}}} = \dfrac{l}{A.K} + \dfrac{l}{A2K}$$

$$\Rightarrow \quad \dfrac{1}{K_{\text{effective}}} = \dfrac{1}{K} + \dfrac{1}{2K} = \dfrac{3}{2K}$$

$$\Rightarrow \qquad K_{\text{effective}} = \dfrac{2K}{3} \qquad\qquad \textbf{Ans. (A)}$$

Sol. 4 In steady state of conduction, rate of heat flow is given as

$$Q = \dfrac{kA(T_1 - T_2)t}{l} = \dfrac{k\pi r^2 (T_1 - T_2)t}{l}$$

From above expression we can see that the rod with maximum

ratio of $\dfrac{r^2}{l}$ will conduct most heat thus from the given options

the rod with $r = 2r_0$ and $l = l_0$ will conduct most. **Ans. (B)**

Sol. 5 For steady state rate of heat conduction is given as

$$\dfrac{dQ}{dt} = \dfrac{kA(T_1 - T_2)}{L} \qquad\qquad \textbf{Ans. (A)}$$

Sol. 6 The amount of heat conduction in time t through a cylindrical metallic rod of length L and uniform cross sectional area $A = \pi R^2$ with its ends maintained at temperature T_1 and T_2 in steady state is given as

$$Q = \dfrac{kA(T_1 - T_2)t}{L}$$

Area of cross-section of new rod is given as

$$A' = \pi\left(\dfrac{R}{2}\right)^2 = \dfrac{\pi R^2}{4} = \dfrac{A}{4}$$

As volume of rod remains unchanged, so new length becomes

$$AL = A'L'$$

$$\Rightarrow \qquad L' = \dfrac{LA}{A'} = 4L$$

Now heat conduction in same time t in new rod, with its ends maintained at same temperature T_1 and T_2 is given as

$$Q' = \dfrac{kA'(T_1 - T_2)t}{L'}$$

$$\Rightarrow \qquad Q' = \dfrac{k\left(\dfrac{A}{4}\right)(T_1 - T_2)t}{4L}$$

$$\Rightarrow \qquad Q' = \dfrac{1}{16}\dfrac{kA(T_1 - T_2)t}{L} = \dfrac{Q}{16} \qquad \textbf{Ans. (C)}$$

Sol. 7 Heat conduction rate in steady state through the slab is given as

$$\dfrac{dQ}{dt} = \dfrac{KA}{L}(T_1 - T_2)$$

$$\Rightarrow \qquad Q = \dfrac{KA}{L}(T_1 - T_2)t$$

Heat required to melt the ice which is supplied through condition, is given as

$$Q = mL_f$$

$$\Rightarrow \quad \dfrac{KA}{L}(T_1 - T_2)t = mL_f$$

$$\Rightarrow \qquad K = \dfrac{mL_f(L)}{A(T_1 - T_2)t}$$

$$\Rightarrow \qquad K = \dfrac{4.8 \times 3.36 \times 10^5 \times 0.1}{0.36 \times 100 \times 3600}\ \text{J/m/s/}^\circ\text{C}$$

$$\Rightarrow \qquad K = \dfrac{4.8 \times 3.36}{0.36 \times 36}$$

$$\Rightarrow \qquad K = 1.24\ \text{J/m/s/}^\circ\text{C} \qquad\qquad \textbf{Ans. (D)}$$

Sol. 8 The shown rods are considered in parallel combination so thermal current through the combination is given as

$$H = H_1 + H_2$$

$$\Rightarrow \qquad H = \dfrac{K_1 A(T_1 - T_2)}{d} + \dfrac{K_2 A(T_1 - T_2)}{d}$$

$$\Rightarrow \quad \dfrac{K_{\text{eff}} 2A(T_1 - T_2)}{d} = \dfrac{A(T_1 - T_2)}{d}[K_1 + K_2]$$

$$\Rightarrow \qquad K_{\text{eff}} = \left[\dfrac{K_1 + K_2}{2}\right] \qquad\qquad \textbf{Ans. (A)}$$

10.4 Radiation of Heat

Sol. 1 For black body radiation, using Wein's Displacement Law gives

$$\lambda T = \text{constant}$$

$$\Rightarrow \qquad \lambda_1 T_1 = \lambda_2 T_2$$
$$\Rightarrow \qquad \lambda_m \times 2000 = \lambda \times 3000$$
$$\Rightarrow \qquad \lambda = \frac{2}{3}\lambda_m \qquad \text{Ans. (B)}$$

Sol. 2 From electromagnetic spectrum, range of wavelengths of given options above are

$$\text{Cosmic wave} = 10^{-14}\,\text{m to } 10^{-12}\,\text{m}$$
$$\gamma\text{-ray} = 10^{-12}\,\text{m to } 10^{-10}\,\text{m}$$
$$X\text{-ray} = 10^{-10}\,\text{m to } 10^{-9}\,\text{m}$$
$$uv\text{-rays} = 10^{-7}\,\text{m to } 4 \times 10^{-7}\,\text{m}$$

Thus cosmic wave have minimum wavelength out of the given options in question. **Ans. (D)**

Sol. 3 Radiating power of a black body placed in a surrounding of given temperature is given as

$$E_0 = \sigma(T^4 - T_0^4)A$$

Here σ is the Stefan-Boltzmann constant, A is the surface area of a black body, T is the temperature of the black body and T_0 is the temperature of the surrounding. From the available data in question, we have

$$60 = \sigma\,(1000^4 - 500^4) \qquad \ldots(1)$$

In the second case, $T = 1227°C = 1500$ K and if radiation power is changed to E', we have

$$\Rightarrow \qquad E' = \sigma\,(1500^4 - 500^4) \qquad \ldots(2)$$

From (1) and (2) we have

$$\frac{E'}{60} = \frac{1500^4 - 500^4}{1000^4 - 500^4}$$
$$\Rightarrow \qquad \frac{E'}{60} = \frac{15^4 - 5^4}{10^4 - 5^4} = \frac{50000}{9375}$$
$$\Rightarrow \qquad E' = \frac{50000}{9375} \times 60$$
$$\Rightarrow \qquad E' = 320\text{ W} \qquad \text{Ans. (B)}$$

Sol. 4 Out of the given options a cavity with a rough interior surface and a small hole can be considered as a black body with absorptivity close to unity (ideal black body). In such a cavity when through small hole some radiation enters, due to continuous internal reflections from the interior surface of cavity its eventually gets absorbed. So out of the given options, most appropriate option is option (B). **Ans. (B)**

Sol. 5 Wien's displacement law states that the product of absolute temperature of black body and the wavelength of emitted radiation at which the emissive power is maximum is constant, given as

$$\lambda_{\text{max}} T = b \;(\text{Wien's Constant}) \qquad \text{Ans. (A)}$$

Sol. 6 According to Wein's displacement law, we have

$$\lambda_m T = \text{constant}$$
$$\Rightarrow \qquad \lambda_m \propto T^{-1} \qquad \text{Ans. (D)}$$

Sol. 7 By using Wien's displacement law in the two situations, we have

$$\lambda_{m_1} T_1 = \lambda_{m_2} T_2$$
$$\Rightarrow \qquad (5000)(1500) = (\lambda_m')(1500 + 1000)$$
$$\Rightarrow \qquad \lambda_m' = \frac{(5000)(1500)}{(2500)} = 3000\text{ Å} \qquad \text{Ans. (D)}$$

Sol. 8 For energy emission from a black body, according to Stefan's law, we have

$$E \propto T^4$$
$$\Rightarrow \qquad E \propto (727 + 273)^4 K$$
$$\Rightarrow \qquad E \propto (1000)^4 K \qquad \text{Ans. (A)}$$

Sol. 9 Thermal power emitted by Sun at $t°$C is given as

$$E = \sigma(t + 273)^4\, 4\pi r^2$$

Power received per unit surface area at a distance R from Sun is given as

$$E = \frac{\sigma(t + 273)^4\, 4\pi r^2}{4\pi R^2} = \frac{r^2 \sigma(t + 273)^4}{R^2} \qquad \text{Ans. (C)}$$

Sol. 10 For black body radiation by Stefan's law, we have

$$P \propto T^4$$
$$\Rightarrow \qquad \frac{P_2}{P_1} = \left(\frac{1000}{500}\right)^4$$
$$\Rightarrow \qquad P_2 = 16 P_1 = 112\text{ cal/cm}^2\text{-s} \qquad \text{Ans. (D)}$$

Sol. 11 According to Stefan's law, power emitted by the star whose outer surface radiates as a block body at temperature TK is given by

$$P = \sigma(\pi r^2)T^4$$
$$r = \text{radius of star;}$$
$$\sigma = \text{stefan's constant}$$

Radiant power per unit area received at a distance R from the centre of a star is

$$\sigma = \frac{P}{4\pi R^2} = \frac{\sigma 4\pi r^2 T^4}{4\pi R^2} = \frac{\sigma r^2 T^4}{R^2} \qquad \text{Ans. (B)}$$

Sol. 12 By Stefan's law, the energy radiation from star is given as

$$Q = \sigma A T^4$$
$$\Rightarrow \qquad T = \left[\frac{Q}{\sigma(4\pi R^2)}\right]^{1/4} \qquad \text{Ans. (D)}$$

Sol. 13 The colours are observed at different temperatures because of the wavelength radiated corresponding to the peak radiation intensity which is given by Wien's displacement law, states as

$$\lambda_m \propto \frac{1}{T}$$ **Ans. (B)**

Sol. 14 By Newtons law of cooling, we use

$$\frac{\theta_1 - \theta_2}{\Delta t} = K\left[\frac{\theta_1 + \theta_2}{2} - \theta_0\right]$$

For first 5 min, we use

$$\Rightarrow \qquad \frac{70 - 60}{5} = K[65 - \theta_0]$$

$$\Rightarrow \qquad 2 = K[65 - \theta_0] \qquad \ldots(1)$$

For next 5 min, we use

$$\frac{60 - 54}{5} = K[57 - \theta_0] \qquad \ldots(2)$$

Dividing equation-(1) by (2), gives

$$\frac{5}{3} = \frac{65 - \theta_0}{57 - \theta_0}$$

$$\Rightarrow \qquad 285 - 5\theta_0 = 195 - 3\theta_0$$

$$\Rightarrow \qquad 2\theta_0 = 90$$

$$\Rightarrow \qquad \theta_0 = 45°$$ **Ans. (A)**

Sol. 15 According to Wien's Displacement law, we use

$$\lambda_m T = 2.88 \times 10^6 \text{ nmK}$$

$$\Rightarrow \qquad \lambda_m = \frac{2.88 \times 10^6 \text{ nmK}}{5760\text{K}} = 500 \text{ nm}$$

Thus at 500 nm, radiation energy is maximum, thus U_2 is highest compared to U_1 and U_3.   **Ans. (D)**

Sol. 16 Figure below shows the cooling process of the body

$$3T \xrightarrow{\ t_1 = 10\,\text{min}\ } 2T \xrightarrow{\ t_2 = 10\,\text{min}\ } T_f$$

By Newton's law of cooling we use for the two bodies

$$T_0 = T$$

$$\left(\frac{3T - 2T}{10}\right) = c_1\left(\frac{3T + 2T}{2} - T\right) \qquad \ldots(1)$$

and $$\left(\frac{2T - T_f}{10}\right) = c_1\left(\frac{2T + T_f}{2} - T\right) \qquad \ldots(2)$$

$$\Rightarrow \qquad \frac{\text{Eq.(1)}}{\text{Eq.(2)}} = \frac{T/10}{\dfrac{2T - T_f}{10}} = \frac{\dfrac{5T - 2T}{2}}{\dfrac{T_f}{2}}$$

$$\Rightarrow \qquad \frac{T}{2T - T_f} = \frac{3T}{T_f}$$

$$\Rightarrow \qquad T_f = 6T - 3T_f$$

$$\Rightarrow \qquad 4T_f = 6T$$

$$\Rightarrow \qquad T_f = \frac{3}{2}T$$ **Ans. (B)**

Sol. 17 Using Stefan's law the rate of thermal energy radiated by a black body is given as

$$E = \sigma A T^4 = \sigma \pi R^2 T^4$$

For two situations with change in radius and temperature, we use the ratio of power radiated is given as

$$\frac{E_1}{E_2} = \frac{R_1^2 T_1^4}{R_2^2 T_2^4}$$

$$\Rightarrow \qquad \frac{E_1}{E_2} = 4 \times \frac{1}{16}$$

$$\Rightarrow \qquad \frac{450}{E_2} = \frac{1}{4}$$

$$\Rightarrow \qquad E_2 = 1800 \text{ W}$$ **Ans. (D)**

Sol. 18 By Wien's Displacement law, we use

$$\lambda_{max} T = \text{constant}$$

$$\Rightarrow \qquad \lambda_{max_1} T_1 = \lambda_{max_2} T_2$$

$$\Rightarrow \qquad \lambda_0 T = \frac{3\lambda_0}{4} T'$$

$$\Rightarrow \qquad T' = \frac{4}{3} T$$

By Stefan's law for black body radiation power, we have

$$\frac{P_2}{P_1} = \left(\frac{T'}{T}\right)^4 = \left(\frac{4}{3}\right)^4 = \frac{256}{81}$$ **Ans. (A)**

Sol. 19 According to Newton's law of cooling, the temperature of ball drops from T_1 to T_2 in time t is related as

$$\frac{T_1 - T_2}{t} = K\left[\frac{T_1 + T_2}{2} - T_0\right]$$

For 1st cup of coffee, we use

$$\Rightarrow \qquad \frac{90 - 80}{t} = K\left[\frac{90 + 80}{2} - 20\right] \qquad \ldots(1)$$

For 2nd cup of coffee, we use

$$\Rightarrow \qquad \frac{80 - 60}{t'} = K\left[\frac{80 + 60}{2} - 20\right] \qquad \ldots(2)$$

Dividing equation (1) by (2) gives

$$\frac{t'}{2t} = \frac{65}{50}$$

$$\Rightarrow \qquad t' = \frac{13}{5} t$$ **Ans. (B)**

Ch-11 Thermodynamics

11.1 First Law of Thermodynamics

Sol. 1 In adiabatic process work done by the gas is given as

$$W = \frac{-1}{\gamma - 1}(P_f V_f - P_i V_i)$$

$$\Rightarrow \qquad 6R = \frac{-1}{5/3 - 1} R(T_f - T_i)$$

$$\Rightarrow \qquad T_f - T_i = -4$$

$$\Rightarrow \qquad T_f = (T - 4)\,\text{K} \qquad\qquad \textbf{Ans. (D)}$$

Sol. 2 Ideally only Isothermal process out of above is the only reversible process. **Ans. (C)**

Sol. 3 Specific heat of gas at constant volume is given as

$$C_V = C_P - R = \frac{5}{2}R$$

$$\Rightarrow \qquad \gamma = \frac{C_P}{C_V} = \frac{7}{5} \qquad\qquad \textbf{Ans. (A)}$$

Sol. 4 In isochoric pressure volume is constant thus option (C) is not true. **Ans. (C)**

Sol. 5 By first law of thermodynamics, heat absorbed by gas is given as

$$dQ = dU + dW$$

Here dU is change in internal energy and dW is work done. The values of heat supplied and work done given as

$$dQ = 2\,\text{kcal} = 2000 \times 4.2\,\text{J}$$

$$dW = 500\,\text{J}$$

$$\Rightarrow \qquad 2000 \times 4.2 = dU + 500$$

$$\Rightarrow \qquad dU = 7900\,\text{J} \qquad\qquad \textbf{Ans. (A)}$$

Sol. 6 By first law of thermodynamics, we have

$$\Delta Q = \Delta U + \Delta W$$

In adiabatic process as there is no heat exchange with surrounding, we have

$$\Delta Q = 0$$

$$\Rightarrow \qquad \Delta U + \Delta W = 0$$

$$\Rightarrow \qquad \Delta U = -\Delta W$$

For isothermal process, we have $\Delta U = 0$ so we use

$$\Delta Q = \Delta U + \Delta W$$

$$\Rightarrow \qquad \Delta Q = \Delta W$$

Thus option (B) is correct. **Ans. (B)**

Sol. 7 In isothermal explanation by first law of thermodynamics heat supplied by gas is completely used in doing work against surrounding as there is no change in internal energy of gas. It implies that 150 J of heat has been removed from the gas.

Ans. (A)

Sol. 8 Heat absorbed in changing phase from ice to water, the amount of heat used is given as

$$\Delta Q = mL$$

$$\Rightarrow \qquad \Delta Q = 1000 \times 80 = 8 \times 10^4\,\text{cal}$$

The change in entropy is given as

$$\Delta S = \frac{\Delta Q}{T}$$

$$\Rightarrow \qquad \Delta S = \frac{8 \times 10^4}{273} = 293\,\text{cal/K} \qquad \textbf{Ans. (D)}$$

Sol. 9 Given that gas first undergoes isothermal expansion from volume V to $3V$ so for isothermal expansion we use

$$T = \text{constant}$$

$$\Rightarrow \qquad PV = \text{constant}$$

Thus curve will be hyperbolic for first part.

Now in second part gas undergoes isobaric compression, so we use

$$P = \text{constant}$$

Thus second part of curve will be a horizontal straight line hence option (D) is correct. **Ans. (D)**

Sol. 10 As internal energy is a state function so in above case from state A to B, we use $\Delta U_1 = \Delta U_2 = \Delta U_3$. In the given graph in path 1 work is more compared to path 2 and in path 3 work is least. As internal energy change is same, heat absorbed by the gas will be in same order of work so we have

$$Q_1 > Q_2 > Q_3 \qquad\qquad \textbf{Ans. (D)}$$

Sol. 11 For and ideal gas, we use

$$C_p - C_v = R$$

$$\Rightarrow \qquad \frac{C_p}{C_v} - \frac{C_v}{C_v} = \frac{R}{C_v}$$

$$\Rightarrow \qquad \gamma - 1 = \frac{R}{C_v}$$

$$\Rightarrow \qquad C_v = \frac{R}{\gamma - 1} \qquad\qquad \textbf{Ans. (B)}$$

Sol. 12 In the given adiabatic process, it is given that

$$P \propto T^3$$

Using ideal gas equation $PV = nRT$, we have

$$P \propto (PV)^3$$

$\Rightarrow \qquad P^2 V^3 = \text{constant}$

$\Rightarrow \qquad PV^{3/2} = \text{constant}$

$\Rightarrow \qquad \gamma = \dfrac{3}{2}$ **Ans. (D)**

Sol. 13 From ideal gas equation $PV = nRT$ we use

$$\frac{V}{T} \propto \frac{1}{P}$$

From the above graph we can see that slope of the curve is given as

$$\frac{V}{T} = \tan\theta$$

$\Rightarrow \qquad \dfrac{1}{P} \propto \tan\theta$

$\Rightarrow \qquad P_1 > P_2$ **Ans. (C)**

Sol. 14 Internal energy of gas is given as

$$E = \frac{f}{2} nRT = \frac{f}{2} NkT$$

Where N are the total number of molecules of the gas given as

$$N = nN_A$$

$\Rightarrow \qquad E = \dfrac{3}{2} nN_a k_B T$

In 1g He, number of moles are $n = 1/4$, thus energy is given as

$$E = \frac{3}{8} N_a k_B T$$

Thus amount of energy required to raise temperature from T_1 to T_2 is given as

$$\theta = E_2 - E_1 = \frac{3}{8} N_a k_B (T_2 - T_1) \quad \textbf{Ans. (A)}$$

Sol. 15 First gas undergoes isothermal expansion from volume V to $2V$, so we use

$$PV = P_2(2V)$$

$\Rightarrow \qquad P_2 = \dfrac{P}{2}$

Secondly gas undergoes adiabatic expansion from volume $2V$ to $16V$ so we use

$$P_2 V_2^\gamma = P_3 V_3^\gamma$$

$\Rightarrow \quad \dfrac{P}{2}(2V)^{5/3} = P_3(16V)^{5/3}$

$\Rightarrow \quad P_3 = \dfrac{P}{2}\left(\dfrac{2V}{16V}\right)^{5/3} = \dfrac{P}{2}\times\left(\dfrac{1}{8}\right)^{5/3} = \dfrac{P}{64}$ **Ans. (C)**

Sol. 16 For all the above processes, indicator diagrams are shown in below figure.

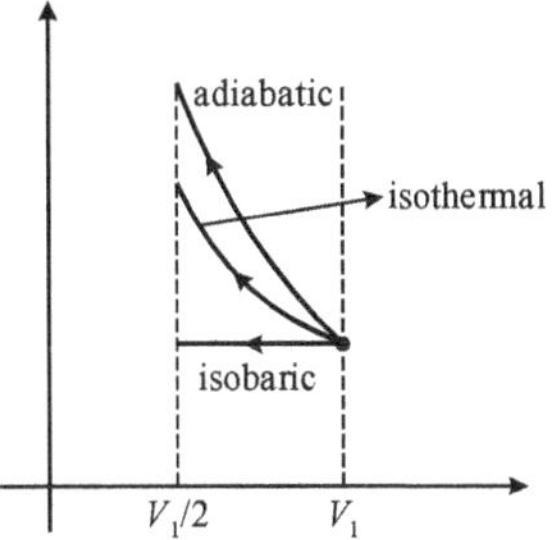

Work done can be estimated by the area under indicator diagram above volume axis so in above cases we have

$$W_{\text{adiabatic}} > W_{\text{isothermal}} > W_{\text{isobaric}} \qquad \textbf{Ans. (B)}$$

Sol. 17 The corresponding PV curves are shown in indicator diagrams in below figure.

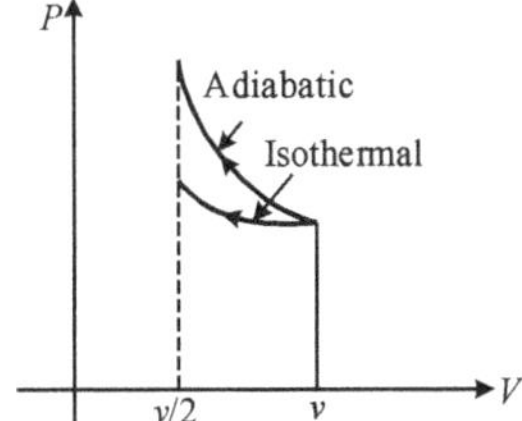

So slope of adiabatic is more than isothermal so by graph adiabatic will be more stepper so from graph we can see that area under adiabatic curve is more than that of isothermal curve so work done will be more in case of adiabatic process. **Ans. (B)**

Sol. 18 For the given polytropic process the process equation given as

$$PV^3 = C$$

Here polytropic constant is $n = 3$ so in terms of n molar specific heat of gas is given as

$$C = C_v + \frac{R}{1-n} = \frac{3}{2}R + \frac{R}{1-3} = R \quad \textbf{Ans. (D)}$$

Sol. 19 Internal energy for all gases in a mixture is given as

$$U = n_1 \frac{f_1}{2} RT + n_2 \frac{f_2}{2} RT$$

$\Rightarrow \qquad U = 2\times\dfrac{5}{2}RT + 4\times\dfrac{3}{2}RT$

$\Rightarrow \qquad U = 5RT + 6RT = 11RT$ **Ans. (D)**

Sol. 20 From the indicator diagrams we can identify that

Process-I = Isochoric as volume is constant

Process-II = Adiabatic as it is steeper than isothermal curve

Process-III = Isothermal as it is along isothermal curve

Process-IV = Isobaric as pressure is constant. **Ans. (B)**

Sol. 21 As VT curve is a straight line and passing through origin, this indicates that given process is isobaric so heat supplied to gas can be given as

$$dQ = n\, C_p\, dT$$

$$\Rightarrow \qquad dQ = n\left(\frac{5}{2}R\right)dT$$

In isobaric process work done can be given as

$$dW = P\, dV = n\, RdT$$

Ratio of work done to heat supplied can be given as

$$\frac{dW}{dQ} = \frac{nRdT}{n\left(\frac{5}{2}R\right)dT} = \frac{2}{5} \qquad \textbf{Ans. (C)}$$

Sol. 22 From first law of thermodynamics, we have

$$\Delta Q = \Delta U + \Delta W$$

$$\Rightarrow \qquad 54 \times 4.18 = \Delta U + 1.013 \times 10^5 (167.1 \times 10^{-6} - 0)$$

$$\Rightarrow \qquad \Delta U = 208.7\,\text{J} \qquad \textbf{Ans. (B)}$$

Sol. 23 Internal energy of gas is directly proportional to the temperature of gas at any instant and internal energy is a measure of kinetic energy of gas molecules. **Ans. (B)**

Sol. 24 In adiabatic process, no exchange of heat takes place hence option (B) is correct. **Ans. (B)**

Sol. 25 When a gas expands against vacuum, no work is done by the gas so no change in internal energy takes. Thus final temperature is equal to initial temperature for ideal gases. But in this case we cannot consider the process to be isothermal as no work is done by the gas so process will be considered as adiabatic in which $\Delta W = \Delta U = 0$ **Ans. (C)**

Sol. 26 For the four given processes shown in the figure given, based on slope of the curves, we can identify the process as listed below

1 : Isochoric

2 : Adiabatic

3 : Isothermal

4 : Isobaric **Ans. (A)**

11.2 Cyclic Process, Heat Engine and Refrigerator

Sol. 1 For an heat engine, efficiency is maximum in Carnot cycle which is an ideal cycle used for a heat engine. Thus efficiency for the given source and sink temperature is given as

$$\eta = \frac{400 - 300}{400} \times 100\,\% = 25\,\%$$

Thus efficiency of 26 % is impossible for this heat engine.

Ans. (A)

Sol. 2 Efficiency of a carnot engine is given as

$$\eta = 1 - \frac{T_2}{T_1}$$

Here T_1 is the temperature of the source and T_2 is the temperature of the sink. For the given data in question, we have

$$0.5 = 1 - \frac{500}{T_1}$$

$$\Rightarrow \qquad T_1 = 1000\,\text{K}$$

For 60% efficiency of the engine, and if new temperature of the sink is T_2' then we have

$$\eta = 0.6 = 1 - \frac{T_2'}{1000}$$

$$\Rightarrow \qquad T_2' = 400\,\text{K} \qquad \textbf{Ans. (C)}$$

Sol. 3 Efficiency of Carnot engine is given as

$$\eta = \frac{W}{Q_1} = 1 - \frac{T_2}{T_1}$$

$$\Rightarrow \qquad \frac{W}{6} = 1 - \frac{400}{500} = \frac{1}{5}$$

$$\Rightarrow \qquad W = \frac{6}{5} = 1.2\,\text{kcal} \qquad \textbf{Ans. (D)}$$

Sol. 4 Efficiency of Carnot cycle is given as

$$\eta = \frac{W}{Q} = 1 - \frac{T_2}{T_1}$$

Net heat converted into work in the cycle is given as

$$W = Q\left(1 - \frac{T_2}{T_1}\right)$$

$$\Rightarrow \qquad W = 1.2 \times 10^4\,\text{cals} \qquad \textbf{Ans. (C)}$$

Sol. 5 Efficiency of engine based on Carnot cycle is given as

$$\eta = 1 - \frac{T_2}{T_1}$$

$$\Rightarrow \qquad 1 - \frac{300}{T_1} = 0.4$$

$$\Rightarrow \qquad T_1 = 500\,\text{K}$$

Efficiency is to be increased by 50% of 40% so new efficiency will become 60% $(40 + 40 \times 0.5 = 60)$. If temperature is increased for this by ΔT, we use

$$0.6 = 1 - \frac{300}{500 + \Delta T}$$

$$\Rightarrow \qquad 500 + \Delta T = 750$$

$$\Rightarrow \qquad \Delta T = 250\,\text{K} \qquad \textbf{Ans. (C)}$$

Sol. 6 Efficiency of Carnot engine is given as

$$\eta = 1 - \frac{T_2}{T_1}$$

Here T_2 is the temperature of sink and T_1 is the source temperature. Initially efficiency is given as

$$\frac{1}{6} = 1 - \frac{T_2}{T_1} \qquad \ldots(1)$$

$$\Rightarrow \qquad T_2 = \frac{5}{6}T_1$$

After decreasing the temperature of sink by 62°C, efficiency is doubled, so we use

$$\frac{2}{6} = 1 - \frac{T_2 - 62}{T_1} \qquad \ldots(2)$$

$$\Rightarrow \qquad \frac{2}{3} = \frac{T_2 - 62}{T_1}$$

$$\Rightarrow \qquad 2T_1 = 3T_2 - 186$$

$$\Rightarrow \qquad 2T_1 = 3\left[\frac{5}{6}\right]T_1 - 186$$

$$\Rightarrow \qquad \left[\frac{5}{2} - 2\right]T_1 = 186$$

$$\Rightarrow \qquad \frac{T_1}{2} = 186$$

$$\Rightarrow \qquad T_1 = 372\,\text{K} = 99°\text{C} \qquad \textbf{Ans. (C)}$$

Sol. 7 In cycle process we use $\Delta U = 0$. Thus heat absorbed by gas is given as

$$\Delta Q = W = \text{Area enclosed by the } PV \text{ curve}$$

$$\Rightarrow \qquad \Delta Q = -(2V)(P) = -2PV$$

Thus total heat rejected by gas is $2PV$. **Ans. (A)**

Sol. 8 Total work done by the gas in a cyclic process is given by the area enclosed by the indicator diagram. In this case it is given as

$$W = \frac{1}{2} \times 4 \times 10^5 \times 5 \times 10^{-3}$$

$$\Rightarrow \qquad W = 10 \times 10^5 \times 10^{-3} = 1000\,\text{J} \qquad \textbf{Ans. (B)}$$

Sol. 9 For cyclic process work done can be calculated by area enclosed by the indicator diagram. In the diagram shown in question, work done can be given as

$$W = \text{Area of } BCE + \text{Area of } ADE$$

$$\Rightarrow \qquad W = -W_0 + W_0 = 0 \qquad \textbf{Ans. (D)}$$

Sol. 10 Coefficient of performance of refrigerator is given in terms of temperature of freezer T_2 and that of surrounding T_1 is

given as

$$\alpha = \frac{\text{Heat}}{\text{workdone}} = \frac{T_2}{T_1 - T_2}$$

$$\Rightarrow \qquad 5 = \frac{253}{T_1 - 253}$$

$$\Rightarrow \qquad 5T_1 - 1265 = 253$$

$$\Rightarrow \qquad T_1 = \frac{1518}{5} = 303.6\,\text{K} = 30.6°\text{C} \approx 31°\text{C} \qquad \textbf{Ans. (B)}$$

Sol. 11 Coefficient of performance of refrigerator is given as

$$\alpha = \frac{T_2}{T_1 - T_2} = \frac{Q_{out}}{W}$$

$$\Rightarrow \qquad \frac{277}{303 - 277} = \frac{277}{26}$$

Thus power required which is work to be done per unit time can be calculated as

$$W = \frac{26}{277} \times 600 \times 4.2\,\text{J/s} = 236.5\,\text{W} \qquad \textbf{Ans. (C)}$$

Sol. 12 Coefficient of performance of refrigerator is given as

$$\beta = \frac{1 - \eta}{\eta} = \frac{Q_2}{W}$$

$$\Rightarrow \qquad \beta = \frac{1 - \dfrac{1}{10}}{\dfrac{1}{10}} = \frac{\dfrac{9}{10}}{\dfrac{1}{10}} \qquad \left\{\eta = \frac{1}{10}\right\}$$

$$\Rightarrow \qquad \beta = 9 = \frac{Q_2}{W}$$

$$\Rightarrow \qquad Q_2 = 9 \times 10 = 90\,\text{J} \qquad \textbf{Ans. (B)}$$

Sol. 13 Efficiency of ideal heat engine based on Carnot cycle is given as

$$\eta = \left(1 - \frac{T_2}{T_1}\right) \times 100\,\%$$

$$\Rightarrow \qquad \eta = \left(1 - \frac{273}{373}\right) \times 100$$

$$\Rightarrow \qquad \eta = \left(\frac{100}{373}\right) \times 100 = 26.8\% \qquad \textbf{Ans. (C)}$$

11.3 Thermocouple

Sol. 1 Thermocouple emf is given as

$$e = \alpha(\theta - \theta_C) + \beta(\theta^2 - \theta_C^2)$$

At inversion temperature $e = 0$

$$\Rightarrow \qquad \theta_i = -\theta_C - \frac{\alpha}{\beta}$$

At neutral temperature $\dfrac{de}{d\theta} = 0$

$$\Rightarrow \quad \theta_n = -\frac{\alpha}{2\beta}$$

$$\Rightarrow \quad \theta_i = -\frac{\alpha}{\beta} - \theta_C = 2\theta_n - \theta_C$$

$$\Rightarrow \quad \theta_n = \frac{\theta_i + \theta_C}{2}$$

$$\Rightarrow \quad 300 = \frac{320 + \theta_C}{2}$$

$$\Rightarrow \quad \theta_C = -20°C \qquad \text{Ans. (D)}$$

Ch-12 Kinetic Theory

12.1 Kinetic Theory of Gases

Sol. 1 In ideal gas equation for 5 g of oxygen number of moles are taken as

$$n = \frac{m}{\text{molecular mass}} = \frac{5}{32}$$

As gas equation is written as

$$PV = nRT$$

$$\Rightarrow \quad PV = \left(\frac{5}{32}\right)RT \qquad \text{Ans. (A)}$$

Sol. 2 Ideal gas equation in density form is written as

$$\frac{P}{\rho} = \frac{RT}{M_0}$$

$$\Rightarrow \quad \frac{\rho}{P} \propto \frac{1}{T}$$

$$\Rightarrow \quad \frac{\rho_1}{P_1} \bigg/ \frac{\rho_2}{P_2} = \frac{T_2}{T_1}$$

$$\Rightarrow \quad \frac{x}{\rho_2 / P_2} = \frac{383}{283}$$

$$\Rightarrow \quad \frac{\rho_2}{P_2} = \frac{283}{383}x \qquad \text{Ans. (B)}$$

Sol. 3 Initially liquid oxygen will absorb heat and its temperature linearly rises upto its boiling point then it change its phase from liquid to gas. After this again its temperature increases. Out of given options, option-(A) is most appropriate for this situation. **Ans. (A)**

Sol. 4 Mean free path of molecules in a gas is given as

$$\lambda = \frac{1}{\pi d^2 n\sqrt{2}} = \frac{1}{4\pi r^2 n\sqrt{2}}$$

$$\Rightarrow \quad \lambda \propto \frac{1}{r^2} \qquad \text{Ans. (B)}$$

Sol. 5 Given that $P_A = 2P_B$ and $\rho_A = 1.5\rho_B$

From ideal gas equation, we have

$$\frac{P}{\rho} = \frac{RT}{M_0}$$

$$\Rightarrow \quad M_0 = \frac{\rho RT}{P}$$

$$\Rightarrow \quad M_0 \propto \frac{\rho}{P}$$

$$\Rightarrow \quad \frac{M_A}{M_B} = \frac{\rho_A}{\rho_B} \times \frac{P_B}{P_A} = 1.5 \times \frac{1}{2} = 0.75 = 3/4 \qquad \text{Ans. (C)}$$

Sol. 6 Speed of sound in gas is given as

$$v_{\text{sound}} = \sqrt{\frac{\gamma PV}{M}}$$

$$\Rightarrow \quad \gamma = \frac{M}{PV}v_{\text{sound}}^2 = \frac{C_P}{C_V}$$

$$\Rightarrow \quad C_P = C_V\left(\frac{M}{PV}\right)v_{\text{sound}}^2$$

$$\Rightarrow \quad C_P = 5\left[\frac{4 \times 10^{-3}}{10^5 \times 22.4 \times 10^{-3}}\right](952)^2$$

$$\Rightarrow \quad C_P = \frac{20}{22.4} \times (952)^2 \times 10^{-5} = 8.09 \text{ J/moles K} \quad \text{Ans. (B)}$$

Sol. 7 RMS velocity of gas molecules is given as

$$v_{\text{rms}} = \sqrt{\frac{3RT}{M}}$$

$$\frac{(v_{rms})}{(v_{rms})_2} = \sqrt{\frac{T_1}{T_2}}$$

$$\Rightarrow \quad \frac{v_2}{v_1} = \sqrt{\frac{T_2}{T_1}}$$

$$\Rightarrow \quad v_2 = \sqrt{\frac{400}{300}} \times 200 = \frac{400}{\sqrt{3}} \text{ m/s} \qquad \text{Ans. (B)}$$

Sol. 8 By ideal gas equation

$$PV = nRT$$

Using Boltzman's constant value $\left(k = \dfrac{R}{N_A}\right)$, gives

$$\frac{n}{V} = \frac{P}{kN_A T}$$

$$\Rightarrow \quad \frac{nN_A}{V} = \frac{P}{kT}$$

$$\Rightarrow \quad \frac{mnN_A}{V} = \frac{mP}{kT}$$

$$\Rightarrow \quad \rho = \frac{mP}{kT} \qquad \text{Ans. (B)}$$

Sol. 9 Figure below shows the block diagram of refrigerator mentioned in the question.

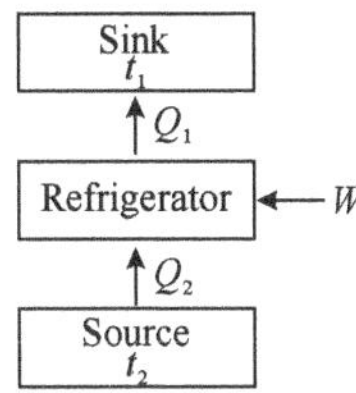

Ratio of heat rejected by the refrigerator to the electrical work done in the engine cycle which is same as heat delivered to room per unit of electrical energy consumed.

$$\frac{Q_1}{W} = \frac{Q_1}{Q_1 - Q_2}$$

$$\Rightarrow \qquad \frac{Q_1}{W} = \frac{t_1 + 273}{t_1 - t_2} \qquad \textbf{Ans. (B)}$$

Sol. 10 Escape velocity at earth surface is given as

$$v_{esc} = 11200 \text{ m/s}$$

If at temperature T oxygen molecules attains it then we use

$$\sqrt{\frac{3k_B T}{m_{O_2}}} = 11200 \text{ m/s}$$

$$\Rightarrow \qquad T = 8.360 \times 10^4 \text{ K} \qquad \textbf{Ans. (B)}$$

Sol. 11 Mean free path for a gas is given as

$$\lambda_m = \frac{1}{\sqrt{2}\,\pi d^2 n}$$

Here d is the diameter of a gas molecule and n is the molecular density. **Ans. (C)**

Sol. 12 A monoatomic gas has 3 degrees of freedom so by law of equipartition of energy, its total energy is given as

$$E = \frac{3}{2}k_B T \qquad \textbf{Ans. (C)}$$

Sol. 13 For an ideal gas by gas law we have

$$\frac{P}{\rho} = \frac{RT}{M_w}$$

$$\Rightarrow \qquad \rho = \frac{PM_w}{RT} = \frac{249 \times 10^3 \times 2 \times 10^{-3}}{8.314 \times 300} = 0.199 \text{ kg/m}^3$$

$$\textbf{Ans. (C)}$$

Sol. 14 In a gas at temperature T, root mean square speed of gas molecules is given as

$$v_{rms} = \sqrt{\frac{3RT}{M}}$$

Pressure exerted by ideal gas on container wall is given as

$$P = \frac{1}{3}\rho v_{rms}^2 = \frac{1}{3}mnv^2$$

Average kinetic energy of a molecule is given as

$$K = \frac{3}{2}kT$$

Total internal energy of 1 mole of a diatomic gas is given as

$$U = \frac{f}{2}nRT = \frac{5}{2}RT \qquad \textbf{Ans. (C)}$$

Sol. 15 At STP volume occupied by a gas can be calculated as

$$V = (\text{number of moles}) \times (22.4 \text{ litre})$$

$$\Rightarrow \qquad V = \frac{\text{mass}}{\text{molar mass}} (22.4 \times 10^{-3} \text{ m}^3)$$

$$\Rightarrow \qquad V = \frac{4.5 \times 10^3}{18} \times 22.4 \times 10^{-3} \text{ m}^3$$

$$\Rightarrow \qquad V = 5.6 \text{ m}^3 \qquad \textbf{Ans. (C)}$$

Ch-13 Oscillations

13.1 Simple Harmonic Motion

Sol. 1 Total energy of a particle in SHM is given as

$$E = \frac{1}{2}m\omega^2 a^2 = \frac{1}{2}ka^2 \qquad \textbf{Ans. (B)}$$

Sol. 2 In SHM, between extreme positions, with O as the mean position, maximum kinetic energy of the particle executing SHM will be at O and maximum potential energy will occur at extreme position. **Ans. (C)**

Sol. 3 As springs are connected in parallel, equivalent force constant of the system is given as $k_1 + k_2$

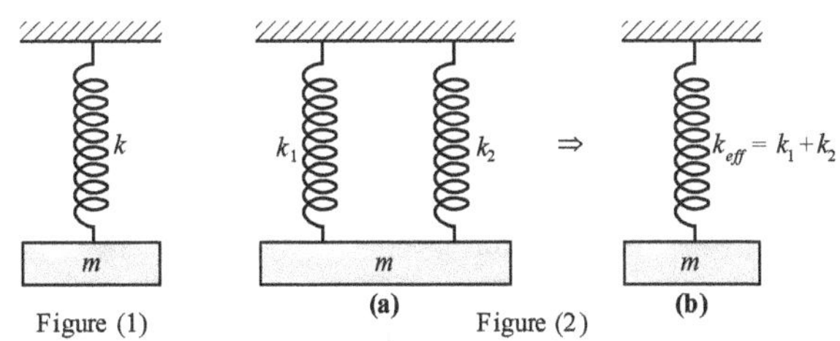

The oscillation period of a spring mass system with mass m and spring constants k is given as

$$T = 2\pi\sqrt{m/k},$$

$$\Rightarrow \qquad t_1 = 2\pi\sqrt{m/k_1} \qquad \dots(1)$$

and $\qquad t_2 = 2\pi\sqrt{m/k_2} \qquad \dots(2)$

Now, when they are connected in parallel as shown in

figure-2 (a), the system can be replaced by a single spring of spring constant, $k_{eff} = k_1 + k_2$, as shown in figure-2 (b). Since $mg = k_1 x + k_2 x = k_{eff} x$

$$t_0 = 2\pi\sqrt{m/k_{eff}}$$

$$t_0 = 2\pi\sqrt{m/(k_1 + k_2)} \qquad \ldots(3)$$

From (1), $\qquad \dfrac{1}{t_1^2} = \dfrac{1}{4\pi^2} \times \dfrac{k_1}{m} \qquad \ldots(4)$

From (2), $\qquad \dfrac{1}{t_2^2} = \dfrac{1}{4\pi^2} \times \dfrac{k_2}{m} \qquad \ldots(5)$

From (3), $\qquad \dfrac{1}{t_0^2} = \dfrac{1}{4\pi^2} \times \dfrac{k_1 + k_2}{m} \qquad \ldots(6)$

From equations-(4), (5) and (6)

$$\dfrac{1}{t_1^2} + \dfrac{1}{t_2^2} = \dfrac{1}{t_0^2}$$

$\Rightarrow \qquad\qquad t_0^{-2} = t_1^{-2} + t_2^{-2} \qquad$ **Ans. (B)**

Sol. 4 This is a case of damped oscillation the amplitude of oscillation decreases with time. Amplitude of oscillations at any instant t is given as

$$a = a_0 e^{-bt}$$

In above expression a_0 is the initial amplitude of oscillations and b is the damping constant. If T is the oscillation period and when $t = 100T$ and $a = a_0/3$, we use

$$a = a_0/3 = a_0 e^{-100Tb} \qquad \ldots(1)$$

$\Rightarrow \qquad\qquad \dfrac{1}{3} = e^{-100Tb}$

and $\qquad\qquad a' = a_0 e^{-200Tb} \qquad \ldots(2)$

$\Rightarrow \qquad\qquad e^{-200Tb} = \dfrac{1}{9}$

$\Rightarrow \qquad\qquad a' = a_0 \times \dfrac{1}{9} = \dfrac{a_0}{9}$

Thus amplitude will be reduced to 1/9 of initial value. **Ans. (D)**

Sol. 5 In SHM at mean position speed of particle is maximum and acceleration is zero and at extreme position speed is zero and acceleration is maximum. **Ans. (D)**

Sol. 6 Potential energy of simple harmonic oscillator is given as

$$U = \dfrac{1}{2}m\omega^2 y^2$$

At $y = a/2$, potential energy in terms of total energy E of the oscillator is given as

$$U = \dfrac{1}{2}m\omega^2 \dfrac{a^2}{4} = \dfrac{E}{4} \qquad \textbf{Ans. (C)}$$

Sol. 7 Potential energy of particle executing SHM varies parabolically with position such that at mean position it becomes zero and maximum at extreme position. **Ans. (A)**

Sol. 8 Let k be the force constant of spring. If k' is the force constant of each part after cutting, then we have

$$k' = 4k$$

Time period of oscillation if one part is used is given as

$\Rightarrow \qquad\qquad T' = 2\pi\sqrt{\dfrac{m}{4k}}$

$\Rightarrow \qquad T' = \dfrac{1}{2} \times 2\pi\sqrt{\dfrac{m}{k}} = \dfrac{T}{2} \qquad \textbf{Ans. (C)}$

Sol. 9 Smaller damping gives a taller and narrower resonance peak hence option-(A) is correct. **Ans. (A)**

Sol. 10 When the spring joined in series, the effective force constant of combination is given as

$$\dfrac{1}{k_{eff}} = \dfrac{1}{k_1} + \dfrac{1}{k_2}$$

$\Rightarrow \qquad\qquad k = \dfrac{k_1 k_2}{k_1 + k_2} \qquad \textbf{Ans. (D)}$

Sol. 11 Maximum speed of particle in SHM is given as

$$V_{max} = a\omega$$

$\Rightarrow \qquad f = \dfrac{\omega}{2\pi} = \dfrac{V_{max}}{2\pi a} = \dfrac{31.4}{2\pi \times 5}$

$\Rightarrow \qquad f = \dfrac{31.4}{10\pi} = 1\,\text{Hz} \qquad \textbf{Ans. (A)}$

Sol. 12 When the floating block in liquid is depressed by an extra depth x in liquid, restoring force on it upward can be calculated by excess buoyant force on it, given as

$$F = -Ax\rho g$$

Acceleration of block due to restring force is given as

$$a = -\dfrac{A\rho g}{m}x$$

For SHM $\qquad a = -\omega^2 x$

$\Rightarrow \qquad\qquad \omega^2 = \dfrac{A\rho g}{m}$

$\Rightarrow \qquad\qquad T = 2\pi\sqrt{\dfrac{m}{A\rho g}} \qquad \textbf{Ans. (B)}$

Sol. 13 Position of particle in SHM can be given by equation

$$y = A\sin\omega t$$

Velocity of particle is given as

$$v_{\text{inst}} = \frac{dy}{dt} = A\omega \cos \omega t = A\omega \sin (\omega t + \pi/2)$$

Acceleration of particle is given

$$a = -A\omega^2 \sin \omega t$$

$$\Rightarrow \qquad \frac{d^2 y}{dt^2} = A\omega^2 \sin (\pi + \omega t)$$

So phase difference between velocity and acceleration is given as

$$\Rightarrow \qquad \phi = \frac{\pi}{2} = 0.5\pi \qquad \textbf{Ans. (D)}$$

Sol. 14 Considering minimum potential energy at mean position of oscillation to be zero, maximum potential energy and maximum total energy will be equal to maximum kinetic energy so we have

$$U_{\text{max}} = K_0$$

and $\qquad E = K_0 \qquad \textbf{Ans. (C)}$

Sol. 15 Displacement equation of particle in SHM from the mean position can be given by equation

$$y = a \sin \left(\frac{2\pi}{T} \right) t$$

At $y = a/2$, we use

$$a/2 = a \sin \left(\frac{2\pi}{T} \right) t$$

$$\Rightarrow \qquad \frac{\pi}{6} = \left(\frac{2\pi}{T} \right) t$$

$$\Rightarrow \qquad t = T/12 \qquad \textbf{Ans. (B)}$$

Sol. 16 During SHM, maximum acceleration is at extreme positions so in this case mass gets detached at the upper extreme position. During SHM below figure shows the free body diagram of the block at upper extreme position in which pseudo force is considered on block in upward direction when pan is going down with maximum acceleration a.

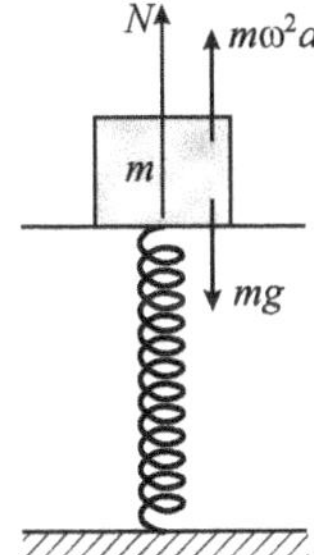

At topmost point if mass gets detached, we use normal reaction to be zero, so we have

$$N = mg - m\omega^2 a = 0$$

$$\Rightarrow \qquad g = \omega^2 a$$

$$\Rightarrow \qquad a = g/\omega^2 = mg/K \qquad \left[\text{As } = \omega^2 = \frac{K}{m} \right]$$

$$\Rightarrow \qquad a = \frac{2 \times 10}{200} \text{ m}$$

$$\Rightarrow \qquad a = 1/10 \text{ m} = 10 \text{ cm} \qquad \textbf{Ans. (A)}$$

Sol. 17 Maximum acceleration of particle in SHM is given as

$$a = -\omega^2 A$$

$$\Rightarrow \qquad \frac{a_1}{a_2} = \frac{\omega_1^2 A}{\omega_2^2 A} = \frac{(100)^2}{(1000)^2} = \frac{1}{10^2} \qquad \textbf{Ans. (D)}$$

Sol. 18 Equation of SHM for the point can be taken as

$$x = a \sin \left(\omega t + \frac{\pi}{6} \right)$$

Velocity equation is given as

$$v = \frac{dx}{dt} = a\omega \cos \left(\omega t + \frac{\pi}{6} \right)$$

After time t if velocity becomes half of its maximum then we use

$$\frac{a\omega}{2} = a\omega \cos \left(\omega t + \frac{\pi}{6} \right)$$

$$\Rightarrow \qquad \omega t + \frac{\pi}{6} = \frac{\pi}{3}$$

$$\Rightarrow \qquad \omega t = \frac{\pi}{6}$$

$$\Rightarrow \qquad t = \frac{\pi}{6\omega} = \frac{\pi \times T}{6 \times 2\pi} = \frac{T}{12} \qquad \textbf{Ans. (B)}$$

Sol. 19 Velocity of pendulum bob in terms of position is taken as

$$v = \omega \sqrt{A^2 - x^2}$$

At $x = a/2$, we have

$$v = \frac{2\pi}{T} \sqrt{a^2 - \frac{a^2}{4}} = \frac{\pi a \sqrt{3}}{T} \qquad \textbf{Ans. (A)}$$

Sol. 20 In SHM as acceleration is directly or linearly proportional to the displacement of particle from mean position and in opposite direction so out of given options (C) is most appropriate which represents SHM. $\qquad$ **Ans. (C)**

Sol. 21 We can express $\sin^2 \omega t$ using half angle formula as

$$\sin^2 \omega t = \frac{1 - \cos 2\omega t}{2}$$

Thus given equation can be re-written as

$$x = \frac{a}{2} (1 - \cos 2 \omega t)$$

Above equation is representing SHM with mean position at

$x = a/2$ and angular frequency 2ω. Thus SHM frequency is given as

$$f = \frac{2\omega}{2\pi} = \frac{\omega}{\pi} \qquad \textbf{Ans. (B)}$$

Sol. 22 Time period of oscillation of a spring-mass system is given as

$$T = 2\pi\sqrt{\frac{m}{k}}$$

$$\Rightarrow \qquad T \propto \sqrt{M}$$

$$\Rightarrow \qquad \frac{T_2}{T_1} = \sqrt{\frac{M + M}{M}}$$

$$\Rightarrow \qquad T_2 = \sqrt{2}\, T_1 \qquad \textbf{Ans. (A)}$$

Sol. 23 (a) is linear sum of two SHMs of same frequency so this represents SHM, (b) is not harmonic being the third power of $\sin \omega t$. This is sum of oscillations of different frequencies so it does not represent SHM. (c) is clearly SHM and (d) is an algebraic function so not SHM. Hence (a) and (c) represent SHM. $\qquad$ **Ans. (C)**

Sol. 24 It is given that damping force on oscillator F

$$F \propto v$$

$$\Rightarrow \qquad F = kv$$

$$\Rightarrow \qquad k = \frac{F}{v}$$

Thus units of this proportionality constant can be given as

$$[k] = \frac{[\text{kg ms}^{-2}]}{[\text{ms}^{-1}]} = \text{kg s}^{-1} \qquad \textbf{Ans. (C)}$$

Sol. 25 All options shown are sinusoidal graphs have difference in initial phase. For the given equation, graph can be drawn as shown in figure below

$$x = A \cos \omega t$$

Velocity of particle is given as

$$v = \frac{dx}{dt} = -A\omega \sin \omega t$$

Acceleration can be given as

$$a = \frac{d^2 x}{dt^2} = -A\omega^2 \cos \omega t$$

Thus graph shape should be inverse of the graph of x. Hence option (C) is correct. $\qquad$ **Ans. (C)**

Sol. 26 Maximum acceleration & maximum velocity in SHM are given as

$$\alpha = A\omega^2 \qquad \ldots(1)$$

$$\text{and} \qquad \beta = A\omega \qquad \ldots(2)$$

$$\Rightarrow \qquad \frac{\alpha}{\beta} = \omega = \frac{2\pi}{T}$$

$$\Rightarrow \qquad T = 2\pi\frac{\beta}{\alpha} \qquad \textbf{Ans. (A)}$$

Sol. 27 Time period of a spring mass system is given as

$$T = 2\pi\sqrt{\frac{m}{k}}$$

$$\Rightarrow \qquad 3 = 2\pi\sqrt{\frac{m}{k}} \qquad \ldots(1)$$

Now as mass m is increased by 1 kg, we have

$$5 = 2\pi\sqrt{\frac{m+1}{k}} \qquad \ldots(2)$$

From equations-(1) and (2), we have

$$\Rightarrow \qquad \frac{3}{5} = \sqrt{\frac{m}{m+1}}$$

$$\Rightarrow \qquad \frac{9}{25} = \frac{m}{m+1}$$

$$\Rightarrow \qquad 9m + 9 = 25m$$

$$\Rightarrow \qquad 16m = 9$$

$$\Rightarrow \qquad m = \frac{9}{16}\,\text{kg} \qquad \textbf{Ans. (D)}$$

Sol. 28 Velocity and acceleration of particle in SHM in terms of its position is given as

$$v = \omega\sqrt{A^2 - x^2}$$

$$\text{and} \qquad a = x\omega^2$$

As stated in question at $x = 2$ cm, $v = a$ and $A = 3$ cm

$$\omega\sqrt{A^2 - x^2} = x\omega^2$$

$$\Rightarrow \qquad \sqrt{(3)^2 - (2)^2} = 2\left(\frac{2\pi}{T}\right)$$

$$\Rightarrow \qquad \sqrt{5} = \frac{4\pi}{T}$$

$$\Rightarrow \qquad T = \frac{4\pi}{\sqrt{5}} \qquad \textbf{Ans. (C)}$$

Sol. 29 Acceleration of bob of pendulum in terms of its position is given as

$$|a| = \omega^2 x$$

$$\Rightarrow \qquad 20 = \omega^2(5)$$

$$\Rightarrow \qquad \omega = 2 \text{ rad/s}$$

Time period of pendulum is given as

$$T = \frac{2\pi}{\omega} = \frac{2\pi}{2} = \pi \text{ s} \qquad \textbf{Ans. (B)}$$

Sol. 30 SHM equation is given as

$$y = A_0 + A \sin \omega t + B \sin \omega t$$

In this equation mean position of particle is A_0, so we can rewrite the equation as

$$y' = y - A_0 = A \sin \omega t + B \cos \omega t$$

Thus resultant amplitude of oscillation is given as

$$R = \sqrt{A^2 + B^2 + 2AB \cos 90°}$$

$$\Rightarrow \qquad R = \sqrt{A^2 + B^2} \qquad \textbf{Ans. (B)}$$

Sol. 31 In one complete vibration, total displacement of particle is zero. Thus average velocity in one complete vibration is also zero. **Ans. (D)**

Sol. 32 Displacement equation of a particle in SHM is given as

$$x = A\sin(\omega t + \phi) \qquad \ldots(1)$$

Velocity of particle is given as

$$\frac{dx}{dt} = A\omega\cos(\omega t + \phi)$$

Acceleration of particle is given as

$$a = \frac{d^2x}{dt^2} = -\omega^2 A\sin(\omega t + \phi)$$

$$\Rightarrow \qquad a = \omega^2 A\sin(\omega t + \phi + \pi) \qquad \ldots(2)$$

From equations-(1) & (2), we can see that the phase difference between displacement and acceleration is π. **Ans. (B)**

Sol. 33 If displacement equation of SHM for body is given as

$$x = A \sin(\omega t) = A \sin(2\pi nt)$$

The potential energy of body as a function of time is given as

$$U = \frac{1}{2}kx^2 = \frac{1}{2}KA^2 \sin^2(2\pi nt)$$

$$= \frac{1}{2}kA^2 \left[\frac{1 - \cos(2\pi(2n)t)}{2}\right]$$

Above function is a sinusoidal function of frequency '$2n$'. **Ans. (B)**

Sol. 34 At equilibrium of applied force, extension in spring is related as

$$F = kx$$

$$\Rightarrow \qquad 10 = k(5 \times 10^{-2})$$

$$\Rightarrow \qquad k = \frac{10}{5 \times 10^{-2}} = 2 \times 10^2 = 200 \text{ N/m}$$

Time period of oscillations of a spring block system is given as

$$T = 2\pi\sqrt{\frac{m}{k}} = 2\pi\sqrt{\frac{2}{200}} = \frac{2\pi}{10} = 0.628 \text{ s} \qquad \textbf{Ans. (D)}$$

Sol. 35 The two pendulums will be in exactly same phase again when one will complete one oscillation more than other in same time. For this condition, we use

$$(n)T_l = (n+1)T_s$$

$$\Rightarrow \qquad (n)2\pi\sqrt{\frac{1.21}{g}} = (n+1)\,2\pi\sqrt{\frac{1}{g}}$$

$$\Rightarrow \qquad (n)(1.1) = 1$$

$$\Rightarrow \qquad n = 10$$

Number of oscillation of smaller one will be one more as it is faster so we have

$$n' = n + 1$$

$$\Rightarrow \qquad n' = 10 + 1 = 11 \qquad \textbf{Ans. (D)}$$

Ch-14 Waves

14.1 Wave Motion

Sol. 1 Comparing the given equation with general equation of simple harmonic propagating wave, we have

$$y = a\sin 2\pi\left(\frac{t}{T} - \frac{x}{\lambda}\right)$$

$$\Rightarrow \qquad T = \frac{2\pi}{100} \text{ and } \lambda = 20\pi$$

$$\Rightarrow \qquad v = \upsilon\lambda = \frac{100}{2\pi} \times 20\pi = 1000 \text{ m/s} \qquad \textbf{Ans. (C)}$$

Sol. 2 The general equation of progressive wave travelling in positive x-direction is given as

$$y = a \sin\frac{2\pi}{\lambda}(vt - x)$$

$$\Rightarrow \qquad y = 0.2 \sin\frac{2\pi}{60}(360\,t - x)$$

$$\Rightarrow \qquad y = 0.2 \sin\left[2\pi\left(6t - \frac{x}{60}\right)\right] \qquad \textbf{Ans. (C)}$$

Sol. 3 Second wave equation can be modified as given below, we have

$$y_2 = 10^{-6}\cos[100t + (x/50)]$$

$$\Rightarrow \qquad y_2 = 10^{-6}\sin[100t + (x/50) + \pi/2]$$

$$\Rightarrow \qquad y_2 = 10^{-6}\sin[100t + (x/50) + 1.57]$$

Thus phase difference between y_1 and y_2 is given as

$$\phi = 1.57 - 0.5 = 1.07 \text{ rad} \qquad \textbf{Ans. (A)}$$

Sol. 4 Intensity of sound produced by spherical wave sources or point sources is given as

$$I = \frac{P}{4\pi r^2}$$

$$\Rightarrow \quad I \propto \frac{1}{r^2}$$

$$\Rightarrow \quad \frac{I_1}{I_2} = \left(\frac{r_2}{r_1}\right)^2 = \left(\frac{3}{2}\right)^2 = \frac{9}{4} \qquad \textbf{Ans. (C)}$$

Sol. 5 Comparing the wave with general wave equation of propagating wave, we have

$$y = A \sin(kx - \omega t + \phi)$$

$$k = \frac{2\pi}{\lambda} = 0.5\pi, \omega = \frac{2\pi}{T} = 4\pi$$

Thus wave speed is given as

$$v = \frac{\omega}{k} = \frac{4\pi}{0.5\pi} = 8 \qquad \textbf{Ans. (D)}$$

Sol. 6 Reverberation time of a room can be given by Sabine's Formula, in terms of room volume V and room carpet area A, as

$$T_r \propto \frac{V}{A}$$

Area of new room becomes 4 times volume becomes 8 time as dimensions are double that of initial room. So time of reverberation will be 2 second. **Ans. (A)**

Sol. 7 Comparing the given equation with general equation of propagating simple harmonic wave, we have

$$y = A \sin(kx - \omega t)$$

$$\Rightarrow \quad A = 0.25, k = 10\pi, \omega = 2\pi$$

$$\Rightarrow \quad f = 1\,\text{Hz} \text{ and } \lambda = \frac{1}{5} = 0.2\,\text{m}$$

When sign of coefficient of t and x are opposite so wave is propagating in the direction of growing x. **Ans. (A)**

Sol. 8 Path difference between the two points is given as

$$\Delta x = x_1 - x_2 = 15 - 10 = 5\,\text{m}$$

Wavelength of wave is given as

$$\lambda = \upsilon T = 300 \times 0.05 = 15\,\text{m}$$

Thus phase difference between the given points can be given as

$$\phi = \frac{2\pi}{\lambda} \cdot \Delta x = \frac{2\pi}{15} \times 5 = \frac{2\pi}{3} \qquad \textbf{Ans. (D)}$$

Sol. 9 For the situation described in question about the given wave we have

$$5\lambda = 4; A = 2\,\text{cm} = 0.02\,\text{m}$$

$$\Rightarrow \quad \lambda = \frac{4}{5} \text{ and } k = \frac{2\pi}{\lambda} = \frac{10\pi}{4} = 7.85$$

Wave speed can be written as

$$v = \frac{\omega}{k} = 128\,\text{m/s}$$

$$\Rightarrow \quad \omega = vk = 128 \times 7.85 = 1005\,\text{rad/s}$$

As wave moves along positive x direction, its equation can be written as

$$y = A \sin(kx - \omega t)$$

$$y = 0.02 \sin(7.85x - 1005t) \qquad \textbf{Ans. (A)}$$

Sol. 10 Maximum particle velocity in a propagating wave is given as

$$v_p = A\omega$$

Wave velocity in medium is given as

$$v = \frac{\omega}{k}$$

As per given condition in question, $v = v_P$

$$\frac{\omega}{k} = A\omega$$

$$\Rightarrow \quad \frac{\lambda}{2\pi} = A$$

$$\Rightarrow \quad \lambda = 2\pi A \qquad \textbf{Ans. (D)}$$

Sol. 11 This question is same as Q. 3, students are advised to refer solution of Q. 3. **Ans. (A)**

Sol. 12 Wave velocity in a medium is given as

$$v = n\lambda$$

On changing medium, wave frequency n remain unchanged, so we use

$$\frac{v_1}{v_2} = \frac{\lambda_1}{\lambda_2}$$

$$\Rightarrow \quad \lambda_2 = \lambda_1 \cdot \frac{v_2}{v_1} = \lambda_1 \times 10 \qquad \textbf{Ans. (C)}$$

Sol. 13 Maximum particle velocity in propagating harmonic wave is given as

$$v_{max} = a\omega$$

Wave velocity in medium is given as

$$v = n\lambda$$

$$\Rightarrow \quad \frac{v_{max}}{v} = \frac{a\omega}{n\lambda}$$

$$\Rightarrow \quad \frac{v_{max}}{v} = \frac{a(2\pi n)}{n\lambda} = \frac{2\pi a}{\lambda}$$

$$\Rightarrow \quad \frac{v_{max}}{v} = \frac{2\pi a}{\frac{2\pi}{K}} = Ka = \frac{\pi}{2} \times 3 = \frac{3\pi}{2} \qquad \textbf{Ans. (A)}$$

Sol. 14 General equation of a simple harmonic propagating wave is given as

$$y = a \sin (kx - \omega t)$$

From the data given in the question, we have

$$k = \frac{2\pi}{\lambda} = \frac{2\pi}{2\pi} = 1 \text{ m}^{-1}$$

and

$$\omega = 2\pi \cdot \nu = 2\pi \cdot \frac{1}{\pi} = 2 \text{ rad/s}$$

and

$$a = 1 \text{ m}$$

Thus the equation of wave can be given as

$$y = \sin (x - 2t) \qquad \textbf{Ans. (A)}$$

Sol. 15 Wave velocity in rope is given as

$$v = \frac{\lambda}{T} = f\lambda$$

As wave velocity $\left(v = \sqrt{\dfrac{T}{\mu}} \right)$ depends on string tension and linear mass density, we use

$$\frac{\lambda_2}{\lambda_1} = \frac{v_2}{v_1} = \sqrt{\frac{T_2}{T_1}}$$

String tension at bottom end of rope is $m_2 g$ and at the top end of rope is $(m_1 + m_2)g$, substituting the values of tension in above equation, we get

$$\frac{\lambda_2}{\lambda_1} = \sqrt{\frac{(m_1 + m_2)}{m_2}} \qquad \textbf{Ans. (B)}$$

14.2 Stationary Waves

Sol. 1 Resultant amplitude is given as

$$R = 2a(1 + \cos\phi) = a$$

$$\Rightarrow \qquad (1 + \cos\phi) = 1/2$$

$$\Rightarrow \qquad \cos\phi = -\frac{1}{2}$$

$$\Rightarrow \qquad \phi = \frac{2\pi}{3} \qquad \textbf{Ans. (B)}$$

Sol. 2 Fundamental frequency of sonometer wire is given as

$$n = \frac{1}{2l} \sqrt{\frac{T}{\mu}}$$

$$\Rightarrow \qquad n = \frac{1}{2l} \sqrt{\frac{T}{\pi r^2 \rho}}$$

Linear mass density of sonometer wire is given as

$$\mu = \rho \pi r^2$$

If tension and diameter are doubled and density is halved, then new fundamental frequency becomes

$$n' = \frac{1}{2l} \sqrt{\frac{2T}{\pi (2r)^2 \dfrac{\rho}{2}}} = \frac{1}{2l} \sqrt{\frac{T}{\pi r^2 \rho}} = n \quad \textbf{Ans. (C)}$$

Sol. 3 The fundamental frequency of string is given as

$$v = \frac{1}{2l} \sqrt{\frac{T}{\mu}}$$

$$\Rightarrow \qquad v \propto \frac{1}{l}$$

For the three segments, we use

$$l = l_1 + l_2 + l_3$$

$$\Rightarrow \qquad \frac{1}{v} = \frac{1}{v_1} + \frac{1}{v_2} + \frac{1}{v_3} \qquad \textbf{Ans. (C)}$$

Sol. 4 When pipe is open at both ends then all the odd and even harmonics will be present in oscillations of the pipe with open end as displacement antinode thus option (A), (B) and (C) are correct. At displacement antinode, node of pressure variation is present so at open ends, pressure variation will be minimum hence option (D) is not correct.   **Ans. (D)**

Sol. 5 This question is same as that of Q. 3. Students are advised to refer solution of Q. 3.   **Ans. (A)**

Sol. 6 For a closed organ pipe, fundamental oscillation frequency is given as

$$f_0 = \frac{v}{4l_c} = \frac{340 \text{ms}^{-1}}{4 \times 0.85 \text{m}} = 100 \text{ Hz}$$

For closed pipe, only odd harmonic frequencies are present for resonance so available frequencies are

$$f_n = (2n+1)f_0 = f_0, 3f_0, 5f_0, 7f_0, 9f_0, 11f_0, 13f_0$$

$$\Rightarrow \qquad f_n = 100 \text{ Hz}, 300 \text{ Hz}, 500 \text{ Hz}, 700 \text{ Hz}, 900 \text{ Hz}, 1100 \text{ Hz}.$$

$$\textbf{Ans. (D)}$$

Sol. 7 From the given frequencies we have

$$315 : 420 = 3 : 4$$

Thus 315 Hz is 3rd harmonic of string and 420 Hz is 4th harmonic of string. Thus fundamental frequency is given as

$$3n_f = 315$$

$$\Rightarrow \qquad n_f = \frac{315}{3} = 105 \text{ Hz} \qquad \textbf{Ans. (A)}$$

Sol. 8 In case of an air column closed at one end, minimum length of air column for resonance is $\lambda/4$. So we have

$$L_{\min} = 50 \text{ cm} = \lambda/4$$

At all odd multiples of this length resonance occurs, so other lengths for resonance are $3L_{\min}, 5L_{\min}, 7L_{\min} \ldots$ which are given as 150 cm, 250 cm, 350 cm.....   **Ans. (C)**

Sol. 9 Second overtone frequency of an open organ pipe is given as

$$f_1 = \frac{3v}{2l_0}$$

First overtone frequency for closed organ pipe of length L is given as

$$f_2 = \frac{3v}{4L}$$

Given that $f_1 = f_2$, this gives

$$\frac{3v}{2l_0} = \frac{3v}{4L}$$

$$\Rightarrow \qquad 2l_0 = 4L$$

$$\Rightarrow \qquad l_0 = 2L \qquad\qquad \textbf{Ans. (B)}$$

Sol. 10 Two successive resonant frequencies of closed pipe are given as

$$\frac{nv}{4l} = 220 \text{ and } \frac{(n+2)v}{4l} = 260$$

In above values n is an odd integer. Now from above values we have

$$\frac{n+2}{n} = \frac{260}{220} = \frac{13}{11}$$

$$\Rightarrow \qquad 11n + 22 = 13n$$

$$\Rightarrow \qquad n = 11$$

$$\Rightarrow \qquad 11\frac{v}{4l} = 220$$

$$\Rightarrow \qquad \frac{v}{4l} = 20 \text{ Hz}$$

Thus fundamental frequency of pipe is 20 Hz. **Ans. (B)**

Sol. 11 Third harmonic frequency of a closed organ pipe is given as

$$n_{13} = \frac{3v}{4l}$$

Fundamental frequency of an open organ pipe is given as

$$n_{00} = \frac{v}{2l'}$$

Given that $n_{03} = n_{00}$, so we have

$$\frac{3v}{4l} = \frac{v}{2l'}$$

$$\Rightarrow \qquad l' = \frac{4l}{3 \times 2} = \frac{2l}{3}$$

$$\Rightarrow \qquad l' = \frac{2 \times 20}{3} = 13.33 \text{ cm} \qquad \textbf{Ans. (C)}$$

Sol. 12 Two successive resonance are produced at 20 cm and 73 cm of column length so we use

$$\frac{\lambda}{2} = (73 - 20) \times 10^{-2} \text{ m}$$

Sound velocity is given as

$$v = n\lambda$$

$$\Rightarrow \qquad v = 2 \times 320 \, [73 - 20] \times 10^{-2} = 339.2 \text{ m/s} \qquad \textbf{Ans. (B)}$$

Sol. 13 For a stretched string, velocity of wave is given as

$$v \propto \sqrt{\frac{T}{\mu}}$$

$$\Rightarrow \qquad \frac{v_i}{v_f} = \sqrt{\frac{T_i}{T_f}}$$

$$\Rightarrow \qquad \frac{v_i}{v_f} = \sqrt{\frac{T}{2T}}$$

$$\Rightarrow \qquad \frac{v_i}{v_f} = \sqrt{\frac{1}{2}} = \frac{1}{\sqrt{2}} \qquad \textbf{Ans. (B)}$$

14.3 Beats

Sol. 1 Number of beats produced per second are given as

$$f_b = n_2 - n_1 = 3 \text{ beats/s}$$

Thus number of beats produced per minute are given as

$$f_b = 3 \times 60 = 180 \text{ beats/min} \qquad \textbf{Ans. (C)}$$

Sol. 2 Number of beats per second are given as

$$f_b = n_1 - n_2$$

$$\Rightarrow \qquad f_b = \frac{v}{\lambda_1} - \frac{v}{\lambda_2} = 330\left(\frac{1}{5} - \frac{1}{5.5}\right)$$

$$\Rightarrow \qquad f_b = 66 - 60 = 6 \text{ beats/s} \qquad \textbf{Ans. (D)}$$

Sol. 3 Number of beats per second produced are calculated by the difference in fundamental frequencies of the two strings, given as

$$\Delta f = \frac{V}{2l_1} - \frac{V}{2l_2} = \frac{V}{2}\left[\frac{1}{l_1} - \frac{1}{l_2}\right]$$

$$\Rightarrow \qquad \Delta f = \frac{1}{2}\sqrt{\frac{T}{\mu}}\left\{\frac{1}{l_1} - \frac{1}{l_2}\right\}$$

$$\Rightarrow \qquad \Delta f = \frac{1}{2}\sqrt{\frac{20}{10^{-3}}}\left[\frac{1}{51.6 \times 10^{-2}} - \frac{1}{49.1 \times 10^{-2}}\right]$$

$$\Rightarrow \qquad \Delta f = 144 - 137 = 7 \text{ beats/s} \qquad \textbf{Ans. (C)}$$

Sol. 4 Number of beats decreases so frequency of piano string is given as

$$f = 512 - 4 = 508 \text{ Hz} \qquad \textbf{Ans. (A)}$$

Sol. 5 For waves y_1 and y_2 frequencies are given as

$$f_1 = 300 \text{ Hz and } f_2 = 304 \text{ Hz}$$

So beat frequency is given as

$$\Delta f = |f_1 - f_2| = 4 \text{ beats/s}$$

Ratio of maximum to minimum intensities due to superposition of the two waves is given as

$$\frac{I_{max}}{I_{min}} = \frac{(A_1 + A_2)^2}{(A_1 + A_2)^2} = \frac{(5+4)^2}{(5-4)^2} = \frac{81}{1} \qquad \textbf{Ans. (D)}$$

Sol. 6 The unknown frequency must be either 246 Hz or 254 Hz. It is also specified that the second harmonic of this i.e. 292 Hz or 308 Hz will give 5 beats per second with 513 Hz. This indicates the unknown frequency has to be 254 Hz. **Ans. (A)**

Sol. 7 For a guitar string, we use

$$\text{Frequency} \propto \sqrt{\text{Tension}}$$

If tension in string B is slightly decreased then frequency of B decreases. If frequency of B is 536 Hz, as the frequency decreases, beat frequency produced with A also decreases. Thus original frequency of B would be 524 Hz. **Ans. (C)**

14.4 Doppler's Effect

Sol. 1 As whistle is revolving in a circle of radius 50 cm and the observer is fixed. The minimum frequency will be heard by the observer when the whistle (source) will be moving away from the stationary source along the tangent to the circle drawn from the position of observer. Thus the apparent frequency heard by the observer is then given by

$$n_{ap} = n_0 \left(\frac{v}{C+v} \right)$$

Whistle velocity is given as

$$v = r\omega = 0.5 \times 20 = 10 \text{ m/s}$$

$$\Rightarrow \qquad n_{ap} = 385 \times \frac{340}{340+10} = 374 \text{ Hz} \qquad \textbf{Ans. (B)}$$

Sol. 2 Apparent frequency in the situation described in question is given as

$$f_{ap} = \frac{v+v_0}{v} f$$

$$\Rightarrow \qquad f_{ap} = \frac{v+(1/5)v}{v} f = 1.2 f$$

As wavelength does not change by motion of observer, it remains the same. **Ans. (B)**

Sol. 3 The car is source of sound and at the cliff, we can consider the observed frequency is f' which is given as

$$f' = \frac{v}{v-v_s} f$$

Now for reflected sound cliff is considered as source. It emits

frequency f' and the observer is now the driver who observes frequency f'', given as

$$f'' = \left[\frac{v+v_0}{v} \right] f'$$

$$\Rightarrow \qquad 2f = \left[\frac{v+v_0}{v-v_s} \right] f$$

$$\Rightarrow \qquad 2v - 2v_0 = v + v_0$$

$$\Rightarrow \qquad v_0 = v/3 \qquad \textbf{Ans. (B)}$$

Sol. 4 Apparent frequency for the situation described in question is given as

$$n' = v \left(\frac{c+u}{c-u} \right)$$

$$\Rightarrow \qquad n' = 600 \left(\frac{330+30}{330-30} \right) = 720 \text{ Hz} \qquad \textbf{Ans. (D)}$$

Sol. 5 Apparent frequency received by driver of train can be directly given below from the explanation described in solution of Q.3 as

$$n' = n \left(\frac{v+v_s}{v-v_s} \right)$$

$$\Rightarrow \qquad n' = 1000 \left(\frac{330+220}{330-220} \right)$$

$$\Rightarrow \qquad n' = 1000 \left(\frac{550}{110} \right) = 5000 \text{ Hz} \qquad \textbf{Ans. (B)}$$

Sol. 6 Velocities of motorcyclist and that of car in m/s are given as

$$v_0 = 36 \text{ km/h} = 10 \text{ m/s}$$

$$v_s = 18 \text{ km/h} = 5 \text{ m/s}$$

Apparent frequency heard by the motorcyclist is

$$\Rightarrow \qquad f' = f \left[\frac{v+v_0}{v+v_s} \right] = 1392 \times \left(\frac{343+10}{343+5} \right) \text{Hz}$$

$$\Rightarrow \qquad f' = 1392 \times \frac{353}{348} \text{ Hz} = 1412 \text{ Hz} \qquad \textbf{Ans. (C)}$$

Sol. 7 The apparent frequency observed by the observer is calculated by considering source velocity component along the line joining source and observer as shown in figure below.

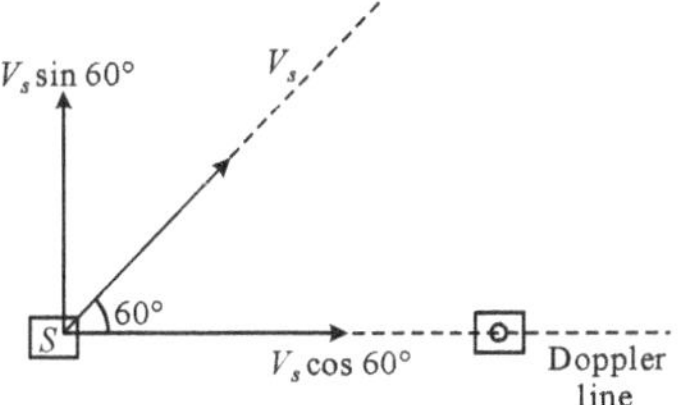

The apparent frequency is now given as

$$n_{ap} = n\left(\frac{v}{v - v_s \cos 60°}\right)$$

$$\Rightarrow \qquad n_{ap} = 100\left(\frac{330}{330 - 19.4 \times \dfrac{1}{2}}\right)$$

$$\Rightarrow \qquad n_{ap} = 100\left(\frac{330}{330 - 9.7}\right)$$

$$\Rightarrow \qquad n_{ap} = 100\left(\frac{330}{320.3}\right) = 103.02\,\text{Hz} \qquad \textbf{Ans. (C)}$$

Sol. 8 Figure below shows the situation described in the question. Here we can consider image of source considering cliff as a mirror which is moving toward the observer. So the reflected sound from cliff will appear to be coming from the image of source as shown.

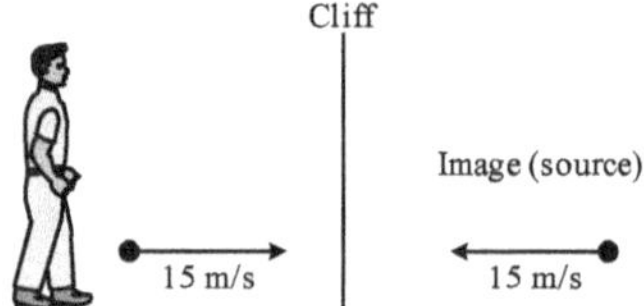

Thus apparent frequency is given as

$$\Rightarrow \qquad f' = \left(\frac{v}{v - v_s}\right)f = \left(\frac{330}{330 - 15}\right)800$$

$$\Rightarrow \qquad f' = 838\,\text{Hz} \qquad \textbf{Ans. (C)}$$

Sol. 9 Apparent frequency for the situation described is given as

$$f_A = f\left[\frac{v + v_0}{v - v_s}\right] = 400\left[\frac{340 + 16.5}{340 - 22}\right] = 448\,\text{Hz} \qquad \textbf{Ans. (D)}$$

Ch-15 Electric Charges and Fields

15.1 Electric Force and Electric Field

Sol. 1 In a uniform electrical field $\vec{E}$, the torque on the dipole is given by $\vec{\tau} = \vec{p} \times \vec{E}$. **Ans. (B)**

Sol. 2 The net electric field due to the uniformly charged ring is zero at its centre O. Thus electric field due to AKB section is equal and opposite to electric field due to $ACDB$, so if $\vec{E}$ is field strength at O due to AKB along $\overrightarrow{KO}$ then electric field strength due to $ACDB$ will be along $\overrightarrow{OK}$ and it is also equal to E.

Ans. (D)

Sol. 3 By Coulomb's law, the force is given as

$$F = \frac{1}{4\pi\varepsilon_0} \times \frac{e^2 n^2}{d^2}$$

$$\Rightarrow \qquad n = \sqrt{\frac{4\pi\varepsilon_0 F d^2}{e^2}} \qquad \textbf{Ans. (D)}$$

Sol. 4 Figure below shows the forces acting on each of the balls.

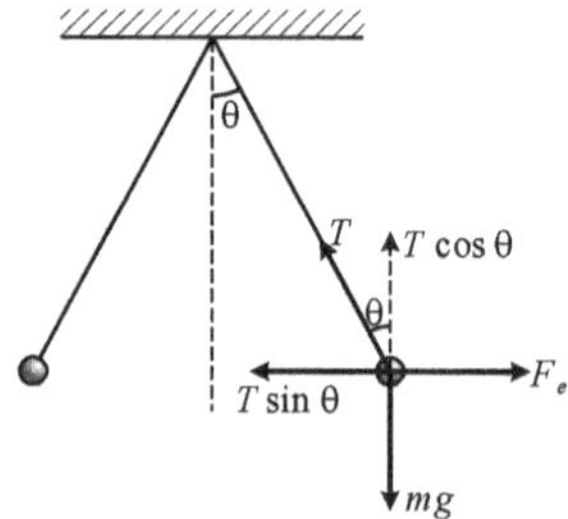

At equilibrium position of ball, we use

$$T \cos \theta = mg$$

$$T \sin \theta = F_e = \frac{Kq^2}{r^2}$$

$$\Rightarrow \qquad \tan \theta = \frac{Kq^2}{r^2 mg} = \frac{r/2}{y}$$

$$\Rightarrow \qquad y = \frac{mgr^3}{2kq^2} \qquad \qquad \ldots(1)$$

$$\Rightarrow \qquad y \propto r^3$$

$$\Rightarrow \qquad r \propto y^{1/3}$$

In second situation, we use

$$r' \propto (y/2)^{1/3} \propto \frac{r}{2^{1/3}} \qquad \textbf{Ans. (B)}$$

Sol. 5 Figure below shows the forces acting on each of the spheres in the situation described in question.

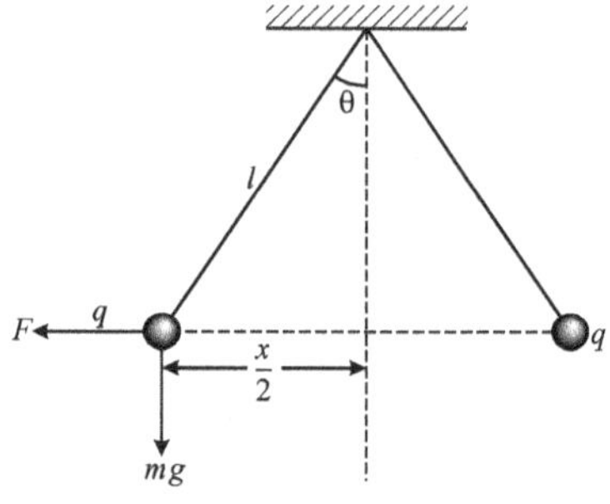

At equilibrium position, we use

$$\frac{F}{mg} = \tan \theta$$

$$\Rightarrow \qquad \frac{Kq^2}{x^2 mg} = \frac{\dfrac{x}{2}}{\sqrt{l^2 - \dfrac{x^2}{4}}}$$

$$\Rightarrow \qquad \frac{Kq^2}{x^2 mg} = \frac{x}{2l} \quad (\text{As } x \ll l)$$

$$\Rightarrow \qquad q^2 \propto x^3$$

$$\Rightarrow \qquad q \propto x^{3/2}$$

$$\Rightarrow \qquad \frac{dq}{dt} \propto \frac{d(x^{3/2})}{dx}\frac{dx}{dt}$$

$$\Rightarrow \qquad \frac{dq}{dt} \propto x^{1/2} v$$

$$\Rightarrow \qquad v \propto \frac{1}{\sqrt{x}} \qquad\qquad \textbf{Ans. (C)}$$

Sol. 6 For the situation given in question, we use

$$F_e = F_g$$

$$\Rightarrow \qquad \frac{1}{4\pi\varepsilon_0}\frac{\Delta e^2}{d^2} = \frac{Gm^2}{d^2}$$

$$\Rightarrow \quad 9 \times 10^9 (\Delta e^2) = 6.67 \times 10^{-11} \times 1.67 \times 10^{-27} \times 1.67 \times 10^{-27}$$

$$\Rightarrow \qquad \Delta e^2 = \frac{6.67 \times 1.67 \times 1.67}{9} \times 10^{-74}$$

$$\Rightarrow \qquad \Delta e = 10^{-37} \qquad\qquad \textbf{Ans. (C)}$$

Sol. 7 For uniformly accelerated motion of electron and proton, we can use

$$s = \frac{1}{2}at^2 \quad (\text{As } u = 0)$$

Acceleration of particles we use $a = \dfrac{F}{m} = \dfrac{eE}{m}$

$$\Rightarrow \qquad h = \frac{1}{2}\frac{eE}{m}t^2$$

$$\Rightarrow \qquad t = \sqrt{\frac{2hm}{eE}}$$

$$\Rightarrow \qquad t \propto \sqrt{m} \quad (\text{As charge of } e \text{ and } p \text{ is same})$$

Thus electron has smaller mass so it will take smaller time.

$$\textbf{Ans. (C)}$$

Sol. 8 The acceleration of car can be calculated as

$$a = \frac{6-0}{1} = 6 \text{ ms}^{-2}$$

For $t = 0$ to $t = 1$ s, distance travelled by car is given as

$$s_1 = \frac{1}{2} \times 6 (1)^2 = 3\text{m} \qquad\qquad \ldots(1)$$

For $t = 1$ s to $t = 2$ s,

$$s_2 = 6.1 - \frac{1}{2} \times 6(1)^2 = 3 \text{ m} \qquad\qquad \ldots(2)$$

For $t = 2$ s to $t = 3$ s,

$$s_3 = 0 - \frac{1}{2} \times 6(1)^2 = -3 \text{ m} \qquad\qquad \ldots(3)$$

Total displacement of car is given as

$$s_T = s_1 + s_2 + s_3 = 3 \text{ m}$$

Average velocity of car is given as

$$<v_{av}> = \frac{3}{3} = 1 \text{ m/s}$$

In this case total distance travelled by car is 9 m, so average speed of car can be given as

$$v_{av} = \frac{9}{3} = 3 \text{ ms}^{-1} \qquad\qquad \textbf{Ans. (B)}$$

Sol. 9 For a metal sphere of radius R, the electric field at a distance r from its center at different values of r is given as

(i) For $r < R$ (inside)

$$E_{in} = 0$$

(ii) For $r \geq R$ (outside and on surface)

$$\Rightarrow \qquad E_0 \propto \frac{1}{r^2} \qquad\qquad \textbf{Ans. (B)}$$

Sol. 10 Figure below shows the situation described in question.

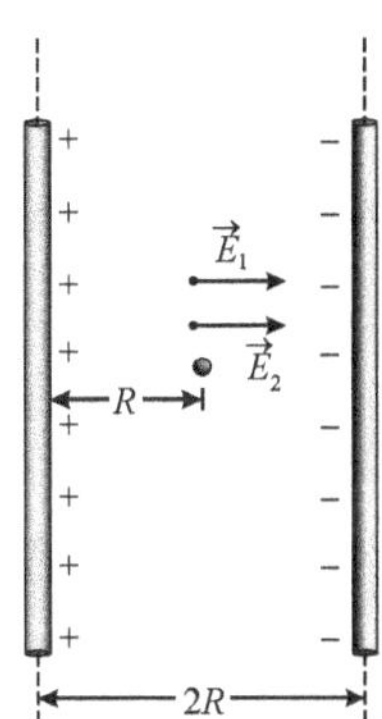

Electric field due to line charges at mid point are given as

$$\vec{E}_1 = \frac{\lambda}{2\pi\varepsilon_0 R}\hat{i} \text{ N/C}$$

and

$$\vec{E}_2 = \frac{\lambda}{2\pi\varepsilon_0 R}\hat{i} \text{ N/C}$$

Net electric field at mid point is given as

$$\vec{E}_{net} = \vec{E}_1 + \vec{E}_2$$

$$\Rightarrow \qquad \vec{E}_{net} = \frac{\lambda}{2\pi\varepsilon_0 R}\hat{i} + \frac{\lambda}{2\pi\varepsilon_0 R}\hat{i}$$

$$\Rightarrow \qquad \vec{E}_{net} = \frac{\lambda}{\pi\varepsilon_0 R}\hat{i} \text{ N/C} \qquad\qquad \textbf{Ans. (C)}$$

Sol. 11 By Coulomb's law the force between the two charges is given as

$$F = \frac{KQ^2}{r^2}$$

If 25% of charge of A transferred to B then final charges of A and B will be

$$q_A = Q - \frac{Q}{4} = \frac{3Q}{4}$$

and

$$q_B = -Q + \frac{Q}{4} = \frac{-3Q}{4}$$

New force between the two charges is given as

$$F_1 = \frac{K q_A q_B}{r^2}$$

$$\Rightarrow \qquad F_1 = \frac{K\left(\dfrac{3Q}{4}\right)^2}{r^2} = \frac{9}{16}\frac{KQ}{r^2} = \frac{9F}{16} \qquad \textbf{Ans. (B)}$$

Sol. 12 Electric field at a point located at a distance r from the centre of sphere is given as

$$E = \frac{kQ}{r^2}$$

$$\Rightarrow \qquad E = \frac{9\times10^9 \times 3.2\times10^{-7}}{(15\times10^{-2})^2} = 1.28 \times 10^5 \text{ N/C} \qquad \textbf{Ans. (C)}$$

15.2 Electric Flux and Gauss Law

Sol. 1 Total electric flux coming out from all faces of the cube is given as

$$\phi = \frac{Q}{\varepsilon_0} \times 10^{-6}\,\text{V-m}$$

Flux from each face can be given as one sixth of the total flux as all faces are symmetric, so we have

$$\phi_{\text{face}} = \frac{1}{6}\frac{Q}{\varepsilon_0} \times 10^{-6}\,\text{V-m} \qquad \textbf{Ans. (A)}$$

Sol. 2 This is same questions as that of Q.1. Students are advised to refer solution of Q.1. **Ans. (B)**

Sol. 3 As the surface is placed parallel to electric field vector, no flux is passing through the area of surface. **Ans. (C)**

Sol. 4 As charge enclosed in the cylindrical surface is q, the total flux coming out from complete surface of cylinder is given as

$$\phi_{\text{total}} = \phi_A + \phi_B + \phi_C = \frac{q}{\varepsilon_0} \qquad \ldots(1)$$

As shown in the figure given in question, flux associated with the curved surface B is given as $\phi = \phi_B$. In this case flux linked with the plane surfaces A and C are equal so we use

$$\phi_A = \phi_C = \phi'$$

Thus from equation-(1), we have

$$\frac{q}{\varepsilon_0} = 2\phi' + \phi_B = 2\phi' + \phi$$

$$\Rightarrow \qquad \phi' = \frac{1}{2}\left(\frac{q}{\varepsilon_0} - \phi\right) \qquad \textbf{Ans. (D)}$$

Sol. 5 As area of surface is in the plane of electric field, the flux linked through the surface will be zero. Same can also be mathematically proves as explained below.

$$\phi = \int \vec{E} \cdot d\vec{s}$$

$$\Rightarrow \qquad \phi = \vec{E} \cdot \vec{S} \quad (\text{As } \vec{E} \text{ is uniform here})$$

$$\Rightarrow \qquad \phi = 0 \quad (\text{As } \vec{E} \perp \vec{S}) \qquad \textbf{Ans. (A)}$$

Sol. 6 As the charge Q is still enclosed by the surface after doubling the radius, total flux remain same which is given by Gauss's law, stated as

$$\phi = \frac{Q}{\varepsilon_0} \qquad \textbf{Ans. (C)}$$

Sol. 7 To understand the situation described in question, let us consider eight identical cubes each of dimension half of the original and arranged so that this charge is at centre of the original cube as shown in figure below.

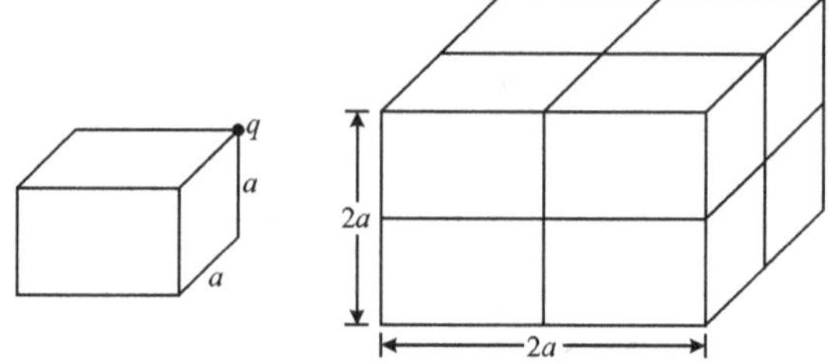

From above explained situation, we can state that total flux of charge q will equally divide among the surfaces of all eight cubes thus, flux from one such cube surface is given as

$$\phi = \frac{q/\varepsilon_0}{8} = \frac{q}{8\varepsilon_0} \qquad \textbf{Ans. (B)}$$

Sol. 8 Electric field is always perpendicular to equipotential surfaces in space. **Ans. (B)**

Ch-16 Electric Potential and Capacitance

16.1 Electric Potential and Energy

Sol. 1 There are eight corners of a cube and in each corner there is a charge of $(-q)$. At the centre of the corner there is a charge of $(+q)$. Distance of each of charge at vertex from the central charge is given as

Cube-Diagonal of the cube $= \sqrt{b^2 + b^2 + b^2} = \sqrt{3}\,b$

$$\Rightarrow \qquad d = \sqrt{3}\,b/2$$

The electric potential energy of the charge $(+q)$ due to a charge $(-q)$ at one corner is given as U

$$U = \frac{q_1 q_2}{4\pi\varepsilon_0 r} = \frac{(+q)\times(-q)}{4\pi\varepsilon_0(\sqrt{3}b/2)}$$

$$\Rightarrow \qquad U = -\frac{q^2}{2\pi\varepsilon_0(\sqrt{3}b)}$$

Total electric potential energy due to all the eight identical charges is given as

$$U_T = 8U = -\frac{8q^2}{2\pi\varepsilon_0\sqrt{3}b}$$

$$\Rightarrow \qquad U_T = \frac{-4q^2}{\sqrt{3}\pi\varepsilon_0 b} \qquad \textbf{Ans. (C)}$$

Sol. 2 Inside a conductor throughout its substance electric field intensity E is zero within a conductor due to charge given to it. Due to a conductor charges exist outside the inner body of conductor. Thus electric potential is uniform throughout the body of conductor. **Ans. (C)**

Sol. 3 For an accelerating potential difference V, kinetic energy gained by the charge is given as

$$\Rightarrow \qquad \frac{1}{2}mv^2 = qV$$

$$\Rightarrow \qquad V = \frac{1}{2}\times\frac{2\times10^{-3}\times10\times10}{2\times10^{-6}} = 50\,\text{kV} \qquad \textbf{Ans. (B)}$$

Sol. 4 Potential energy of two charge system is given as

$$U = \frac{Kq_1 q_2}{r_{12}}$$

When charge $-Q$ is at point A, potential energy is given as

$$U_A = \frac{-KqQ}{(OA)} = \frac{-Qq}{4\pi\varepsilon_0 a}$$

When charge $-Q$ at point B, potential energy is given as

$$U_B = \frac{-KQq}{(OB)} = \frac{-Qq}{4\pi\varepsilon_0 a}$$

Work done is given as

$$W_{AB} = -Q(V_B - V_A) = V_B - V_A$$

$$\Rightarrow \qquad W_{AB} = 0 \qquad \textbf{Ans. (B)}$$

Sol. 5 Below figure shows the actual path

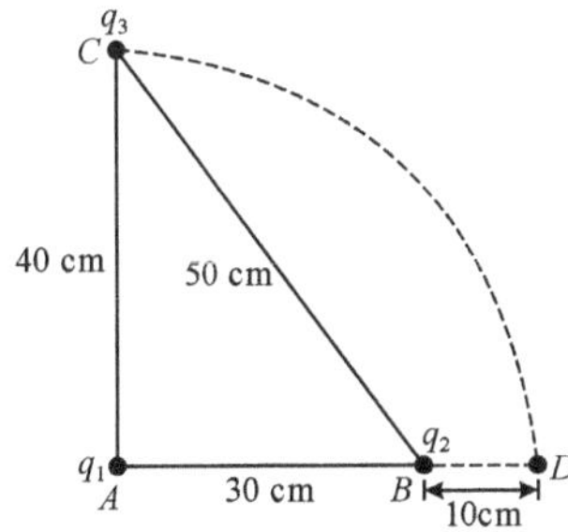

Initial Potential Energy of the system of changes is given as

$$U_i = \frac{1}{4\pi\in_0}\left[\frac{q_1 q_3}{(0.4)} + \frac{q_1 q_2}{(0.3)} + \frac{q_2 q_3}{(0.5)}\right]$$

Final Potential Energy of system of changes is given as

$$U_f = \frac{1}{4\pi\in_0}\left[\frac{q_1 q_3}{(0.4)} + \frac{q_1 q_2}{(0.3)} + \frac{q_2 q_3}{(0.1)}\right]$$

Change in potential energy is given as

$$\Delta U = U_f - U_i = \frac{1}{4\pi\in_0}q_2 q_3\left(\frac{1}{0.1} - \frac{1}{0.5}\right)$$

$$\Delta U = \frac{q_2 q_3}{\pi\in_0}(10^{-2}) = \frac{q_3}{4\pi\in_0}(8q_2)$$

$$\Rightarrow \qquad k = 8q_2 \qquad \textbf{Ans. (A)}$$

Sol. 6 In situation shown in below figure distances are clearly mentioned.

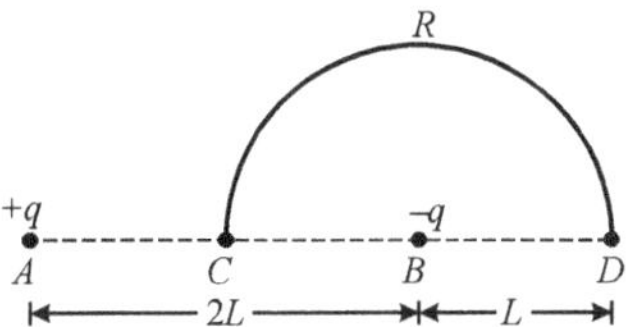

Potential at C is given as, $V_C = 0$

Potential at D is given as

$$V_D = K\left(\frac{-q}{L}\right) + \frac{Kq}{3L} = -\frac{2}{3}\frac{Kq}{L}$$

Potential difference between points C and D are given as

$$V_D - V_C = \frac{-2}{3}\frac{Kq}{L} = \frac{1}{4\pi\in_0}\left(-\frac{2}{3}\cdot\frac{q}{L}\right)$$

Work done can now be calculated as

$$W = Q(V_D - V_C)$$

$$\Rightarrow \qquad W = -\frac{2}{3}\times\frac{1}{4\pi\varepsilon_0}\frac{qQ}{L} = \frac{-qQ}{6\pi\varepsilon_0 L} \qquad \textbf{Ans. (C)}$$

Sol. 7 Electric potential at a point due to point charge is given as

$$V = \frac{Q}{4\pi\varepsilon_0 r}$$

$$\Rightarrow \qquad V = Q\times10^{11} = \frac{Q}{4\pi\varepsilon_0 r}$$

$$\Rightarrow \qquad r = \frac{1}{4\pi\varepsilon_0\times10^{11}}$$

At the same point electric field is given as

$$E = \frac{Q}{4\pi\varepsilon_0 r^2}$$

$$\Rightarrow \qquad E = \frac{V}{r}$$

$$\Rightarrow \qquad E = Q \times 10^{11} \times 4\pi\varepsilon_0 \times 10^{11}$$

$$\Rightarrow \qquad E = 4\pi\varepsilon_0 Q \times 10^{22} \text{ volt/m} \qquad \textbf{Ans. (C)}$$

Sol. 8 The electric field at a point in three dimensional space is given as

$$\vec{E} = -\frac{\delta V}{\delta x}\hat{i} - \frac{\delta V}{\delta y}\hat{j} - \frac{\delta V}{\delta z}\hat{k}$$

Here potential gradients along three dimensions are given as

$$\frac{\delta V}{\delta x} = -2xy - z^3$$

and

$$\frac{\delta V}{\delta y} = -x^2$$

and

$$\frac{\delta V}{\delta z} = -3xz^2$$

$$\Rightarrow \qquad \vec{E} = (2xy + z^3)\hat{i} + x^2\hat{j} + 3xz^2\hat{k} \qquad \textbf{Ans. (B)}$$

Sol. 9 Charge on 3 shells are given as

$$q_A = 4\pi a^2 \sigma$$

$$q_B = -4\pi b^2 \sigma$$

$$q_C = 4\pi c^2 \sigma, c = a + b$$

Using above charges potential at shell A is given as

$$V_A = \frac{1}{4\pi\in_0}\left(\frac{q_A}{a} + \frac{q_B}{b} + \frac{q_C}{c}\right) = \frac{2\sigma a}{\in_0}$$

Potential at shell B is given as

$$V_B = \frac{1}{4\pi\in_0}\left(\frac{q_A}{a} + \frac{q_B}{b} + \frac{q_C}{c}\right)$$

$$= \frac{\sigma}{\in_0}\left(\frac{a^2}{b} - b + c\right) = \frac{\sigma}{\in_0}\left(a + \frac{a^2}{b}\right)$$

Potential at shell C is given as

$$V_C = \frac{1}{4\pi\in_0}\left(\frac{q_A}{a} + \frac{q_B}{b} + \frac{q_C}{c}\right)$$

$$= \frac{\sigma}{\in_0}\left(\frac{a^2 - b}{c} + c\right) = \frac{2\sigma a}{\in_0}$$

$$\Rightarrow \qquad V_C = V_A \neq V_B \qquad \textbf{Ans. (B)}$$

Sol. 10 The distance of charges $+q$ and $+q$ from point A is equal to L and distance of charges $-q$ and $-q$ from point A is given as $\sqrt{L^2 + (2L)^2} = \sqrt{5}L$. Now potential at point A is given as

$$V_A = \frac{1}{4\pi\varepsilon_0}\left[\frac{q}{L} + \frac{q}{L} - \frac{q}{\sqrt{5}L} - \frac{q}{\sqrt{5}L}\right]$$

$$\Rightarrow \qquad V_A = \frac{1}{4\pi\varepsilon_0}\frac{2q}{L}\left[1 - \frac{1}{\sqrt{5}}\right] \qquad \textbf{Ans. (C)}$$

Sol. 11 Figure below shows the situation described in the question. If the side length of square be a then potential at centre O is given as

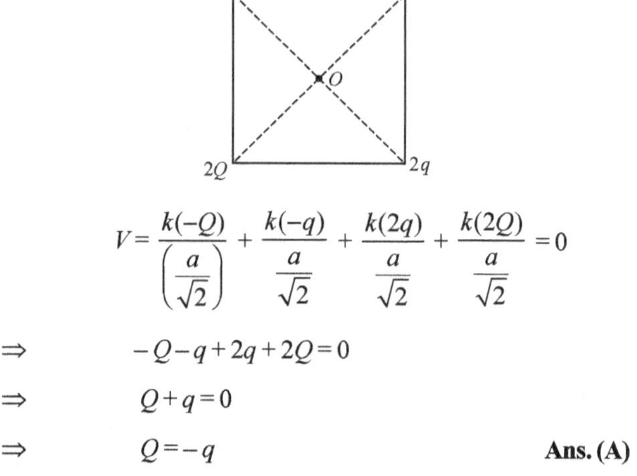

$$V = \frac{k(-Q)}{\left(\dfrac{a}{\sqrt{2}}\right)} + \frac{k(-q)}{\dfrac{a}{\sqrt{2}}} + \frac{k(2q)}{\dfrac{a}{\sqrt{2}}} + \frac{k(2Q)}{\dfrac{a}{\sqrt{2}}} = 0$$

$$\Rightarrow \qquad -Q - q + 2q + 2Q = 0$$

$$\Rightarrow \qquad Q + q = 0$$

$$\Rightarrow \qquad Q = -q \qquad \textbf{Ans. (A)}$$

Sol. 12 Electric field in space exist always in direction from high potential to low potential. Thus in the situation shown in figure below, potential is maximum at B.

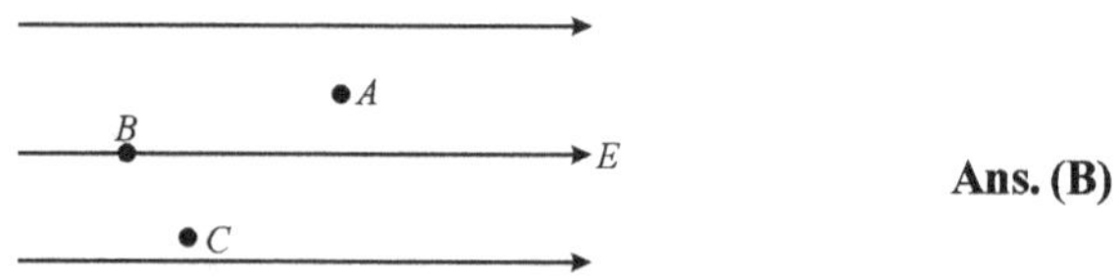

$$\textbf{Ans. (B)}$$

Sol. 13 Inside a conducting charged sphere, electric potential at every interior point is equal to that on its surface, so at center of sphere potential is given as

$$V = \frac{Q}{4\pi\varepsilon_0 R}$$

Inside a conducting body at every interior point electric field is equal to zero. $\qquad \textbf{Ans. (B)}$

Sol. 14 Electric field at a point in three dimensional space is given by potential gradient as

$$\vec{E} = -\frac{\delta V}{\delta x}\hat{i} - \frac{\delta V}{\delta y}\hat{j} - \frac{\delta V}{\delta z}\hat{k}$$

Gradient of potential along each direction is given as

$$E_x = -\frac{\partial V}{\partial x} = -(6 - 8y) = 2 \text{ V/m}$$

$$E_y = -\frac{\partial V}{\partial y} = -(-8x - 8 + 6z) = 10 \text{ V/m}$$

$$E_z = -\frac{\partial V}{\partial z} = -6y = -6 \text{ V/m}$$

Thus magnitude of electric field at the given point is calculated as

$$E = \sqrt{E_x^2 + E_y^2 + E_z^2} = \sqrt{4 + 100 + 36} = \sqrt{140}$$

$$\Rightarrow \qquad E = 2\sqrt{35} \text{ N/C}$$

Force on charge at this point is given as

$$F = qE = 4\sqrt{35} \text{ N} \qquad\qquad \textbf{Ans. (D)}$$

Sol. 15 Electric field at a point in three dimensional space is given by potential gradient as

$$\vec{E} = -\frac{\delta V}{\delta x}\hat{i} - \frac{\delta V}{\delta y}\hat{j} - \frac{\delta V}{\delta z}\hat{k}$$

Gradient of potential along each direction is given as

$$E = -6y\hat{i} - (6x-1)\hat{j} - 2y\hat{k}$$

At $(1, 1, 0)$, electric field is given as

$$E = -6\hat{i} - 5\hat{j} - 2\hat{k}$$

$$\Rightarrow \qquad E = -(6\hat{i} + 5\hat{j} + 2\hat{k}) \qquad\qquad \textbf{Ans. (C)}$$

Sol. 16 Work done in displacing a charge from one point to another is given as

$$W = q\Delta V$$

In all the four cases shown, ΔV is same, thus work done will be same in all the cases. **Ans. (B)**

Sol. 17 Potential is constant throughout the volume, thus at every point of this region electric field is zero. **Ans. (B)**

Sol. 18 For a conducting sphere, electric potential on its surface is given as

$$V = \frac{\sigma R}{\in_0}$$

After two spheres are connected by a wire, both spheres have same potential, so we use

$$V_1 = V_2$$

$$\Rightarrow \qquad \sigma_1 R_1 = \sigma_2 R_2$$

$$\Rightarrow \qquad \frac{\sigma_1}{\sigma_2} = \frac{R_2}{R_1} \qquad\qquad \textbf{Ans. (B)}$$

Sol. 19 The radius R of bigger drop is given as

$$\frac{4}{3}\pi R^3 = 27\left(\frac{4}{3}\pi r^3\right)$$

$$\Rightarrow \qquad R = 3r \qquad\qquad \ldots(1)$$

The potential of bigger drop can be given as

$$V = \frac{K(27q)}{R} = \frac{K(27q)}{3r} = \frac{9Kq}{r}$$

$$\Rightarrow \qquad V_2 = 9 \times 220 = 1980 \text{ V} \qquad \textbf{Ans. (D)}$$

Sol. 20 Potential on a conducting sphere of radius R and charge Q is given as

$$V = \frac{1}{4\pi \in_0} \cdot \frac{Q}{R}$$

As charge is same on the spheres, we have

$$V \propto \frac{1}{R}$$

Thus potential is more on smaller sphere. **Ans. (A)**

16.2 Electric Dipole

Sol. 1 The total force on dipole is always zero in uniform electric field because $F = qE$ is applied on each charge but in opposite direction. The potential energy is $U = \vec{p} \cdot \vec{E}$, which is minimum when $\vec{p}$ and $\vec{E}$ are parallel. **Ans. (C)**

Sol. 2 Work done in rotating a dipole from θ_1 and θ_2 is given as

$$W = pE(\cos\theta_1 - \cos\theta_2)$$

Here $\theta_1 = 0°$ and $\theta_2 = 90°$ so it gives workdone $W = pE$.

Ans. (D)

Sol. 3 The system of point charges described in question consists of two dipole moment vectors due to $(+q$ and $-q)$ and again due to $(+q$ and $-q)$ charges having equal magnitudes qa units, one along $\overrightarrow{OA}$ and other along $\overrightarrow{OB}$ as shown in figure below. Hence, net dipole moment here is given as

$$p_{\text{net}} = \sqrt{(qa)^2 + (qa)^2} = \sqrt{2}qa$$

Along $\overrightarrow{OP}$ at an angle $45°$ with positive x-axis.

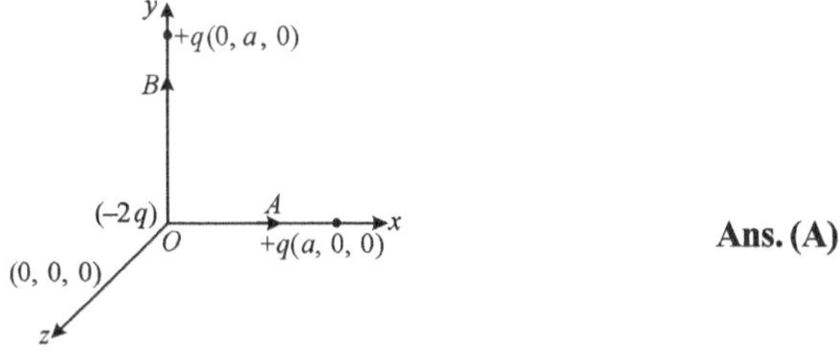

Ans. (A)

Sol. 4 The potential energy of dipole placed in uniform electric field is given as

$$U = -PE\cos\theta$$

The torque on dipole due to electric field is given as

$$\tau = PE\sin\theta \qquad\qquad \textbf{Ans. (A)}$$

Sol. 5 Torque on dipole in electric field is given as

$$\tau = pE\sin\theta$$

$$\Rightarrow \qquad q = \frac{\tau}{lE\sin\theta}$$

$$\Rightarrow \qquad q = \frac{4}{2\times10^{-2} \times 2\times10^5 \times \frac{1}{2}} = 2 \times 10^{-3} \text{ C} = 2 \text{ mC} \quad \textbf{Ans. (B)}$$

Sol. 6 Electric potential due to dipole at any point at an angle θ from the axis of dipole is given as

$$V = \frac{kP\cos\theta}{r^2}$$

$$\Rightarrow \quad V = \frac{9\times10^9 \times 16\times10^{-9}(1/2)}{(0.6)^2} = 200 \text{ V} \quad \textbf{Ans. (C)}$$

Sol. 7 As field lines are closer at charge $+q$, so net force on the dipole acts towards right side and along the direction of electric field electric potential decreases so total potential energy of dipole will decrease toward right so it moves rightward.

Ans. (B)

Sol. 8 Polar molecules have positive and negative charges separated by some distance due to which they have a permanent dipole moment.   **Ans. (D)**

Sol. 9 Due to electric dipole electric field intensity at a large distance is given as

$$E = \frac{KP}{R^3}\sqrt{1+3\cos^2\theta}$$

$$\Rightarrow \quad E \propto \frac{1}{R^3} \quad\quad\quad \textbf{Ans. (A)}$$

16.3 Capacitance

Sol. 1 Energy density in the region of electric field can be directly given as

$$u_e = \frac{1}{2}\varepsilon_0 \frac{V^2}{d^2} \quad (\text{As } E = \frac{V}{d}) \quad \textbf{Ans. (A)}$$

Sol. 2 When capacitors are connected in parallel total charge on combination is given as

$$q = q_1 + q_2$$

$$\Rightarrow \quad q = C_1 V + 0$$

Total combination capacitance in parallel combination is given as

$$C = C_1 + C_2$$

If V' is the common potential difference across the combination, we have

$$V' = \frac{q}{C} = \frac{C_1}{C_1+C_2}V \quad\quad \textbf{Ans. (B)}$$

Sol. 3 The required capacitance can be achieved by connection of capacitors in combination as shown in figure below.

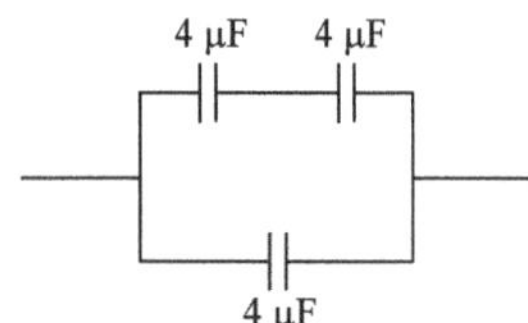

$$C_{eq} = \frac{4\times4}{4+4} + 4 = 2 + 4 = 6 \text{ µF} \quad\quad \textbf{Ans. (C)}$$

Sol. 4 Figure below shows the equivalent reduction of circuit by using combination of three capacitors in series as calculated below

$$\frac{1}{C'} = \frac{1}{3C} + \frac{1}{2C} + \frac{1}{C}$$

$$\frac{1}{C'} = \frac{11}{6C}$$

$$\Rightarrow \quad C' = \frac{6C}{11}$$

Charges across C_4 is given as

$$Q_4 = 4CV$$

Charge across the combination of three capacitors in series which is same on each of the three capacitors is given as

$$Q_2 = \left(\frac{6}{11}C\right)V = \frac{6CV}{11}$$

The ratio of charges on C_2 and C_4 is now given as

$$\Rightarrow \quad \frac{Q_2}{Q_4} = \frac{6CV}{11}\times\frac{1}{4CV} = \frac{3}{22} \quad\quad \textbf{Ans. (C)}$$

Sol. 5 As charging battery is disconnected, charge on capacitor will now become constant that means the electric field between plates will also become constant as it is proportional to the charge on plates, given as

$$E = \frac{q}{A\,\epsilon_0}$$

If the plate separation is increased, the potential difference between the plates also increases because $V = Ed$. **Ans. (D)**

Sol. 6 Work done in full charging of the two capacitors is equal to the change in their energy given as

$$U = \frac{1}{2}\left(C+\frac{C}{2}\right)V^2 = \frac{1}{2}\left(\frac{3C}{2}\right)V^2 = \frac{3CV^2}{4}$$

Thus correct answer here is option (B). In this question it is asking to calculate the work done on condensers but if it asked the total work done by battery then the result will be double that of the above result because in charging capacitor same amount of energy is also dissipated as heat. Students should keep this concept in mind for any future such questions.

Ans. (B)

Sol. 7 Energy stored in capacitor as field energy of electric field is given as

$$U = \frac{1}{2}CV^2$$

$$\Rightarrow \qquad U = \frac{1}{2}\left(\frac{\varepsilon_0 A}{d}\right)(E \cdot d)^2 = \frac{1}{2}\varepsilon_0 A E^2 d$$

Total energy required to charge a capacitor can be given as work done by the battery which includes the amount of energy dissipated in wires due to joule heating effect while charging the capacitors (As described in solution of previous question also). This energy is equal to the energy stored in capacitor. Total energy required in charging process is given as

$$W = 2 \times \text{Energy stored in capacitor}$$

$$\Rightarrow \qquad W = \varepsilon_0 E^2 A d \qquad \textbf{Ans. (A)}$$

Sol. 8 In series combination, equivalent capacitance of the combination is given as

$$C_{eq} = \frac{C}{3}$$

When a potential difference is applied across the series combination of equal capacitances then voltage will be equally divided among all capacitors so the breakdown voltage of combination can be given as

$$V_b = 3V \qquad \textbf{Ans. (D)}$$

Sol. 9 Energy stored in capacitor combination of first case mentioned in question is given as

$$U_1 = \frac{1}{2}CV^2$$

$$\Rightarrow \qquad U_1 = \frac{1}{2}\left(\frac{C_1}{n_1}\right)(4V)^2 = \frac{8C_1 V^2}{n_1}$$

In second case when n_2 capacitors of capacitance C_2 are connected in parallel, energy stored in combination is given as

$$U_2 = \frac{1}{2}(n_2 C_2)V^2$$

As mentioned in question $U_1 = U_2$, we use

$$\frac{8C_1 V^2}{n_1} = \frac{n_2 C_2 V^2}{2}$$

$$\Rightarrow \qquad \frac{8C_1}{n_1} = \frac{n_2 C_2}{2}$$

$$\Rightarrow \qquad C_2 = \frac{16C_1}{n_1 n_2} \qquad \textbf{Ans. (A)}$$

Sol. 10 Energy stored in capacitor is given as

$$U = \frac{1}{2}CV^2$$

$$\Rightarrow \qquad U = \frac{1}{2}\left(\frac{\varepsilon_0 A}{d}\right)(Ed)^2 = \frac{1}{2}\varepsilon_0 A E^2 d \qquad \textbf{Ans. (D)}$$

Sol. 11 This question is same as Q. 10. Students are advised to refer to the solution of Q. 10. **Ans. (B)**

Sol. 12 Total charge on the combination of the two sphere is given as

$$Q_{total} = 4 \times 10^{-2}\,C$$

As the spheres are connected by a conducting wire, their potentials must be same so we use

$$\frac{Q_{big}}{Q_{small}} = \frac{r_{big}}{r_{small}} = \frac{3}{1}$$

$$\Rightarrow \qquad Q_{big} = \frac{3}{4} \times (Q_{big} + Q_{small})$$

$$\Rightarrow \qquad Q_{big} = \frac{3}{4} \times 4 \times 10^{-2} = 3 \times 10^{-2}\,C \qquad \textbf{Ans. (A)}$$

Sol. 13 Between capacitor plates, the electric field in the region where dielectric slab is not there, is given as

$$E_1 = \frac{Q}{A\varepsilon_0}$$

The points inside the dielectric slab, electric field is given as

$$E_2 = \frac{Q}{KA\varepsilon_0}$$

Here $E_2 < E_1$ and E_2 will be different for the two slabs of dielectric. Thus most appropriate option is (C). **Ans. (C)**

Sol. 14 Force of attraction between the plates of a capacitor is given as

$$F = \frac{q^2}{2A\varepsilon_0}$$

Using charge on capacitor as $q = CV$, we have

$$F = \frac{C^2 V^2}{2A\varepsilon_0} = \frac{\left(\frac{A\varepsilon_0}{d}\right)CV^2}{2A\varepsilon_0} \quad F = \frac{CV^2}{2d} \qquad \textbf{Ans. (C)}$$

Sol. 15 Initial energy stored in 2 μF capacitor is given as

$$U = \frac{1}{2}(2\mu F)V^2$$

Energy dissipated on connection across 8 μF in parallel to 2 μF capacitor is given as

$$H = \frac{1}{2}\frac{C_1 C_2}{C_1 + C_2}V^2$$

$$\Rightarrow \qquad H = \frac{1}{2} \times \frac{2\mu F \times 8\mu F}{10\mu F} \times V^2 = \frac{1}{2}(1.6\mu F)V^2$$

Thus percentage energy loss is given as

$$\% \text{ Loss} = \frac{H}{U} \times 100\% = \frac{1.6}{2} \times 100 = 80\% \quad \textbf{Ans. (D)}$$

Sol. 16 According to the question we can consider each of top three dielectrics in series with one third of lower dielectric slab and such three capacitors made are connected in parallel so the resulting capacitance is given as C_{eq}
For equivalent capacitance we use

$$C_{eq} = \frac{\epsilon_0\,(A/3)}{\dfrac{d}{2k_1} + \dfrac{d}{2k_4}} + \frac{\epsilon_0\,(A/3)}{\dfrac{d}{2k_2} + \dfrac{d}{2k_4}} + \frac{\epsilon_0\,(A/3)}{\dfrac{d}{2k_3} + \dfrac{d}{2k_4}}$$

$$\Rightarrow \quad C_{eq} = \frac{\epsilon_0\,A}{3d}\left(\frac{k_1 k_4}{k_1 + k_4} + \frac{k_2 k_4}{k_2 + k_4} + \frac{k_3 k_4}{k_3 + k_4}\right)$$

If we consider a single dielectric of constant k, replaces the combination shown in question figure then we have

$$\frac{d}{kA\,\epsilon_0} = \frac{\epsilon_0\,A}{3d}\left(\frac{k_1 k_4}{k_1 + k_4} + \frac{k_2 k_4}{k_2 + k_4} + \frac{k_3 k_4}{k_3 + k_4}\right)$$

$$\Rightarrow \qquad \frac{1}{k} = \frac{1}{3}\left(\frac{k_1 k_4}{k_1 + k_4} + \frac{k_2 k_4}{k_2 + k_4} + \frac{k_3 k_4}{k_3 + k_4}\right)$$

None of given option matches with above so no answer option is correct in this question.   **Ans. (None)**

__IMPORTANT__: *If the above question is solved by considering top three dielectric slabs in parallel and their combination is taken in series with the bottom big slab then by calculating the resulting capacitance, option (C) matches with the result but the process is wrong as we cannot consider top three dielectrics in parallel because electric field in these three dielectrics are different so their edges are not at same potential difference.*

Sol. 17 Initial charge on capacitor after battery is removed is given as

$$q = CV$$

The energy stored in capacitor is given as

$$U = \frac{1}{2}CV^2$$

After it is connected with another uncharged capacitor, the heat loss due to parallel connection is given as

$$H = \frac{1}{2}\frac{C_1 C_2}{C_1 + C_2}V^2$$

$$\Rightarrow \qquad H = \frac{CV^2}{4}$$

Thus total energy stored in system decreases by a factor of 2.
                                                          Ans. (B)

Sol. 18 For an isolated parallel plate capacitor, force of attraction between its plats is given as

$$F_{\text{plate}} = \frac{Q^2}{2A\varepsilon_0}$$

Out of given options only option (C) is correct.   **Ans. (C)**

Sol. 19 Capacitance of capacitor

$$C = 20\,\mu F = 20 \times 10^{-6}\,F$$

Rate of change of potential difference across the plates of capacitor is given as

$$\left(\frac{dV}{dt}\right) = 3\ \text{V/s}$$

Instantaneous charge on capacitor can be considered as

$$q = CV$$

Differentiating above expression with respect to time, gives

$$\frac{dq}{dt} = C\frac{dV}{dt}$$

$$\Rightarrow \qquad i_C = 20 \times 10^{-6} \times 3 = 60 \times 10^{-6}\,A = 60\,\mu A$$

For a capacitor conduction current in lead wires is equal to the displacement current between capacitor plates, so we have

$$i_d = i_c = 60\,\mu A \qquad\qquad \textbf{Ans. (B)}$$

Sol. 20 Capacitance with dielectric medium is given as

$$C_m = \epsilon_r C$$

Thus relative permittivity of medium is given as

$$\epsilon_r = \frac{30}{6} = 5$$

Permittivity of medium is now given as

$$\epsilon = \epsilon_0 \epsilon_r = 8.85 \times 10^{-12} \times 5 = 0.44 \times 10^{-10}\ \text{N}^{-1}\ \text{m}^{-2}$$

                                                          Ans. (D)

Sol. 21 Figure below shows the reduced circuit of the given circuit as the capacitance connected in vertical branch is short circuited so it can be removed.

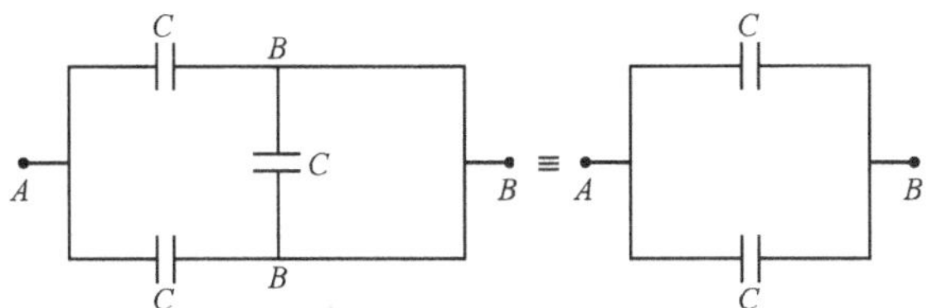

In this state the capacitors are connected in parallel so combination equivalent is given as

$$\Rightarrow \qquad C_{eq} = C_1 + C_2 = C + C = 2C \qquad \textbf{Ans. (B)}$$

Sol. 22 Energy stored in capacitor is given as

$$E = \frac{1}{2}CV^2 = \frac{1}{2}\left(\frac{\varepsilon_0 A}{d}\right)(Ed)^2 = \frac{1}{2}\varepsilon_0 E^2 A d$$

$$\textbf{Ans. (C)}$$

Sol. 23 Figure below shows the situation given in question

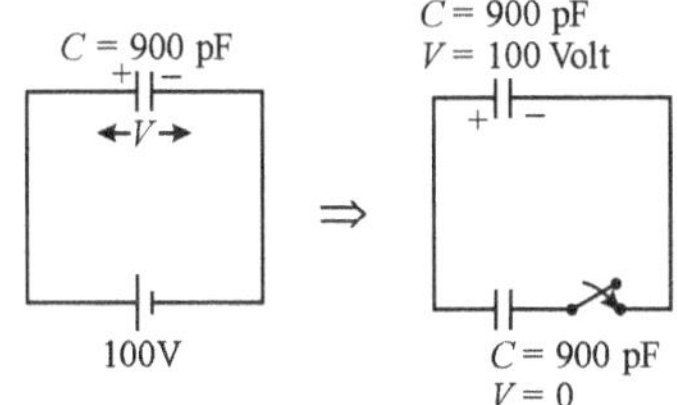

After closing the switch common potential across the two capacitors is given as

$$V_C = \frac{C_1 V_1 + C_2 V_2}{C_1 + C_2}$$

$$\Rightarrow \qquad V_C = \frac{C \times 100 + C \times 0}{C + C} = 50 \text{ Volt}$$

Electrostatic energy stored in the two capacitors is given as

$$U = 2 \times \frac{1}{2}CV^2 = CV^2$$

$$\Rightarrow \qquad U = 900 \times 10^{-12} \times 50 \times 50$$

$$\Rightarrow \qquad U = 225 \times 10^{-8} \text{ J}$$

$$\Rightarrow \qquad U = 2.25 \times 10^{-6} \text{ J} \qquad \textbf{Ans. (B)}$$

Ch-17 Current Electricity

17.1 Resistance and Ohm's Law

Sol. 1 Figure below shows the situation described in the question.

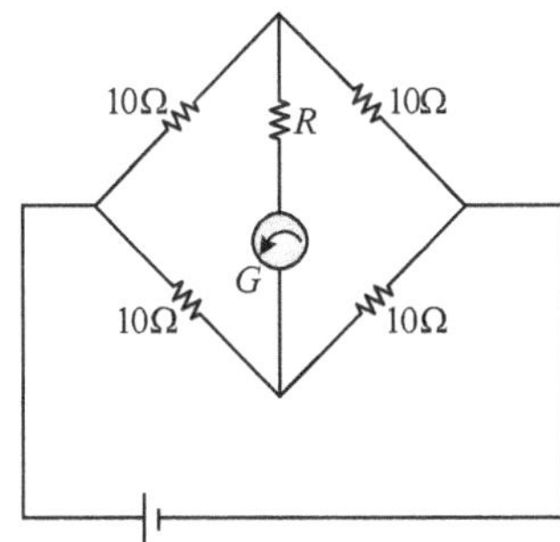

As the given Wheatstone bridge is balanced, we can remove the resistance R, thus final equivalent circuit across battery will be as shown in below figure.

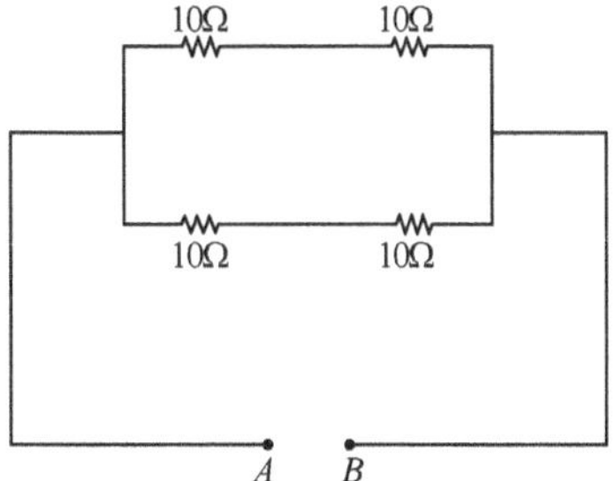

Equivalent resistance of above circuit across terminals A and B is given as

$$R_{AB} = 10 \ \Omega \qquad \textbf{Ans. (A)}$$

Sol. 2 The given circuit is a balanced Wheatstone bridge. The equivalent circuit of given circuit is shown in below figure.

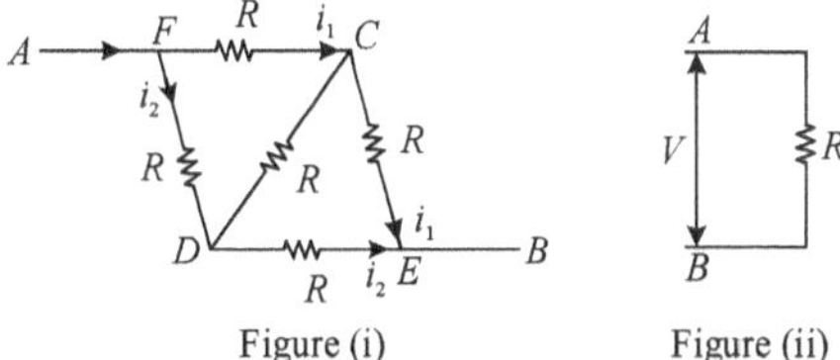

Figure (i)   Figure (ii)

As points C and D are at same potential, no current will flow in this resistance across C and D, therefore this resistance can be removed from circuit. Thus equivalent resistance of this remaining circuit shown in figure (ii) is R. Now potential difference across terminals F and E is V and resistance of branch $AFCEB$ is $2R$ so current in this branch is given as

$$i_1 = \frac{V}{2R} \qquad \textbf{Ans. (C)}$$

Sol. 3 When n resistance of r ohm connected in parallel then their equivalent resistance is given as r/n ohm, thus we have

$$r = nR$$

When these resistances are connected in series then equivalent resistance becomes $nr = n^2 R$ $\qquad \textbf{Ans. (A)}$

Sol. 4 Resistance of a wire is given as

$$R = \rho \frac{l}{A}$$

$$\Rightarrow \qquad R \propto \frac{l}{A} = \frac{l}{\pi r^2}$$

As length and radius are both doubled, new resistance can be given as

$$R_1 \propto \frac{2l}{\pi (2r)^2}$$

$$\Rightarrow \qquad R_1 \propto \frac{1}{2}R \qquad \textbf{Ans. (B)}$$

Sol. 5 The resistance of wire is given as

$$R = \rho \frac{l}{A}$$

$$\Rightarrow \quad 100\,\Omega = \rho \frac{3}{A}$$

$$\Rightarrow \quad \frac{\rho}{A} = \frac{100}{3}$$

Total resistance of 50 cm wire is given as

$$R_1 = \frac{\rho}{A} l = \frac{100}{3} \times 0.5 = \frac{50}{3}\,\Omega$$

Current in the wire can be given as

$$I = \frac{6}{100}\,\text{A}$$

Thus potential difference across the two points on the wire separated by a distance of 50 m is given as

$$V = IR_1 = \frac{50}{3} \times \frac{6}{100} = 1\,\text{V} \qquad \textbf{Ans. (C)}$$

Sol. 6 Specific resistance or resistivity of a wire is a material property and it increases with the increase of temperature, but it does not vary with the dimensions of the conductor.

$$\textbf{Ans. (A)}$$

Sol. 7 For metals specific resistance decreases with decrease in temperature whereas for semiconductors like silicon specific resistance increases with decrease in temperature. **Ans. (A)**

Sol. 8 Resistance of wire bent in form of circular ring is R. The diametric ends A and B of the ring divides the ring into 2 parts each with a resistance $R/2$ and across these diametric ends, these two can be considered to be in parallel combination. Thus total resistance across A and B is given as

$$R_{AB} = \left(\frac{R/2}{2}\right) = \frac{R}{4} \qquad \textbf{Ans. (B)}$$

Sol. 9 Resistance of a conductor is given as

$$R = \frac{\rho l}{A}$$

After the wire length is stretched by 10%, its new length will become

$$l' = l + \frac{l}{10} = \frac{11l}{10}$$

As volume of wire material is constant, its new cross sectional area will become

$$A' = \frac{10A}{11}$$

Thus new resistance will be given as

$$R' = \frac{P \times \left(\frac{11l}{10}\right)}{\left(\frac{10A}{11}\right)} = \frac{\rho l}{A} \times \frac{(11)^2}{(10)^2} = 1.21R$$

Specific resistance of a wire is material property so it will remain same. **Ans. (D)**

Sol. 10 The potential difference across the cell is given as

$$V = \epsilon - Ir$$

Comparing above relation with $y = mx + c$ gives slope of line as '$-r$' and intercept as 'ϵ'. **Ans. (C)**

Sol. 11 Workdone on charge is given as

$$W = qV$$

$$qV = 2\,\text{eV}$$

$$\Rightarrow \quad 1.6 \times 10^{-19}\,V = 2 \times 1.6 \times 10^{-19}$$

$$\Rightarrow \quad V = 2\,\text{V}$$

Electric field can be given as

$$E = \frac{V}{d}$$

$$\Rightarrow \quad E = \frac{2}{4 \times 10^{-8}} = 5 \times 10^7\,\text{V/m} \qquad \textbf{Ans. (A)}$$

Sol. 12 Total resistance of wire of complete circle is given as

$$R = 12\,\Omega \times 2\pi \times 10^{-1}$$

$$\Rightarrow \quad R = 2.4\pi$$

Resistance of each half of circle will be

$$R_1 = \frac{2.4\pi}{2} = 1.2\pi$$

Across points A and B, both parts are taken in parallel combination so equivalent resistance is given as

$$R_{AB} = \frac{1.2\pi}{2} = 0.6\,\pi\Omega \qquad \textbf{Ans. (B)}$$

Sol. 13 When length of wire is increased n times $l_2 = nl_1$ as volume remains constant, new area of cross section of wire is given as

$$A_2 = \frac{A_1}{n}$$

New resistance of stretched wire can be given as

$$R_2 = \frac{\rho(nl_1)}{\left(\frac{A_1}{n}\right)} = \frac{n^2 \rho l_1}{A_1} = n^2 R$$

$$\Rightarrow \quad R_2 = 4 \times 4 = 16\,\Omega \qquad \textbf{Ans. (D)}$$

Sol. 14 As two metal wires are connected in series, their equivalent resistance is given as

$$R_{eq} = R_1 + R_2$$

$$\Rightarrow \quad \rho\frac{2L}{A} = \rho_1\frac{L}{A} + \rho_2\frac{L}{A}$$

$$\Rightarrow \quad 2\rho = \rho_1 + \rho_2$$

$$\Rightarrow \quad \frac{2}{\sigma} = \frac{1}{\sigma_1} + \frac{1}{\sigma_2}$$

$$\Rightarrow \quad \frac{2}{\sigma} = \frac{\sigma_1 + \sigma_2}{\sigma_1\sigma_2}$$

$$\Rightarrow \quad \sigma = \frac{2\sigma_1\sigma_2}{\sigma_1 + \sigma_2} \qquad \textbf{Ans. (B)}$$

Sol. 15 Students can refer to the solution of Q. 13 to understand this. Final resistance of stretched wire is given as n^2R. **Ans. (C)**

Sol. 16 Given resistance is $(47 \pm 4.7)\,k\Omega = 47 \times 10^3 \pm 10\%$ Thus the colour code representing this value is written as

Yellow – Violet – Orange – Silver   **Ans. (B)**

Sol. 17 Mobility of charged particle in a conductor is given as

$$\mu = \frac{v_d}{E}$$

$$\Rightarrow \quad \mu = \frac{7.5 \times 10^{-4}}{3 \times 10^{-10}}$$

$$\Rightarrow \quad \mu = 2.5 \times 10^6 \qquad \textbf{Ans. (C)}$$

Sol. 18 For metals like copper, resistivity is linearly proportional to temperature for small range of temperature variations but for large range of variation in temperature, non linear relation exists. Thus option (D) is more appropriate.   **Ans. (D)**

Sol. 19 By colour coding, the resistance value is given as

$$R = ab \times 10^C \pm d\%$$

Codes of respective colors here are

yellow = 4

violet = 7

brown = 1

gold = 5%

$$\Rightarrow \quad R = 47 \times 10^1 \pm 5\% \qquad \textbf{Ans. (A)}$$

Sol. 20 (a) Drift speed of free electrons is given as

$$v_d = \left(\frac{eE}{m}\right)\tau$$

(b) Current density in a current carrying conductor is given as

$$J = \sigma E = E/\rho$$

$$\Rightarrow \quad \rho = E/J$$

(c) Drift speed in terms of electric field is given as

$$v_d = \frac{E}{ne\rho}$$

$$\Rightarrow \quad \frac{eE}{m}\tau = \frac{E}{ne\rho}$$

$$\Rightarrow \quad \tau = \frac{m}{ne^2\rho}$$

(d) Current in terms of drift speed in a conductor is given as

$$i = neAv_d$$

$$\Rightarrow \quad \frac{i}{A} = nev_d$$

$$\Rightarrow \quad J = nev_d \qquad \textbf{Ans. (A)}$$

Sol. 21 For conductors α is (+) ve and for semiconductors α is (−) ve.   **Ans. (B)**

Sol. 22 The cross sectional area of copper wire is given as

$$A = \pi r^2 = 10^{-4}\,m^2$$

Current density in wire is given as

$$J = \frac{i}{A} = \left(\frac{V}{R}\right)\cdot\frac{1}{A} = \frac{El}{RA}$$

$$\Rightarrow \quad J = \frac{10 \times 10}{10 \times 10^{-4}} = 10^5\,A/m^2 \qquad \textbf{Ans. (C)}$$

17.2 Kirchhoff's Law & Electric Circuits

Sol. 1 Terminal potential difference of cell is given as 2.2 V when circuit is open so this is the EMF of the cell. When the cell is connected to the external resistance, current in the circuit is given as

$$I = \frac{E}{R+r} = \frac{2.2}{5+r}\,A$$

Potential difference across the cell is equal to that of the potential difference across external resistance, given as

$$\frac{2.2}{5+r} \times 5 = 1.8$$

$$\Rightarrow \quad 5+r = \frac{11}{1.8}$$

$$\Rightarrow \quad r = \frac{11}{1.8} - 5 = \frac{110-90}{18} = \frac{10}{9}\,\Omega \qquad \textbf{Ans. (A)}$$

Sol. 2 In this case the given Wheatstone bridge is balanced so middle resistance can be ignored. So equivalent resistance across battery is given as

$$R_{AB} = \frac{6 \times 9}{6 + 9} = \frac{54}{15} = \frac{18\,\Omega}{5}$$

Thus current i is given as

$$i = \frac{5V}{18} \qquad\qquad \textbf{Ans. (D)}$$

Sol. 3 Circuit shown below describes the situation explained in question.

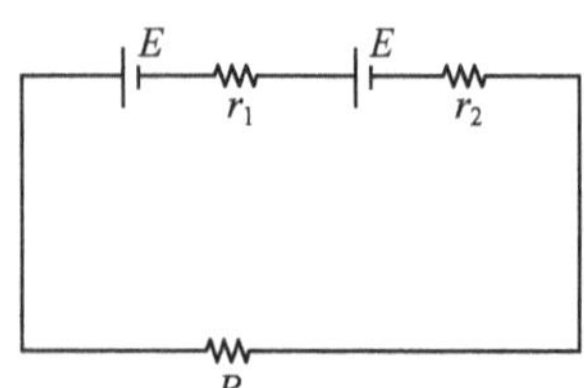

As stated in question as potential difference across first cell is zero, we use

$$E - Ir_1 = 0$$

Circuit current is given as

$$I = \frac{E + E}{r_1 + r_2 + R}$$

$$\Rightarrow \qquad \frac{E}{r_1} = \frac{2E}{r_1 + r_2 + R}$$

$$\Rightarrow \qquad r_1 + r_2 + R = 2r_1$$

$$\Rightarrow \qquad R = r_1 - r_2 \qquad\qquad \textbf{Ans. (A)}$$

Sol. 4 In a discharge tube electrons get accelerated to very high speed and with high kinetic energy due to applied voltage when these collide with other neutral atoms or molecules, these get ionized. **Ans. (B)**

Sol. 5 Kirchhoff's first law is based on conservation of charge. Kirchhoff's second law is based on conservation of energy.

Ans. (B)

Sol. 6 The currents in different parts of circuit are shown in figure below. As potential is same across 4Ω and 3Ω resistance, this potential difference across PM is given as

$$V_{PM} = 1\,A \times 4\,\Omega = 4\,V$$

Thus current through lower part of circuit can be given as

$$I_4 = \frac{4}{5/4}\,A = 3.2\,A$$

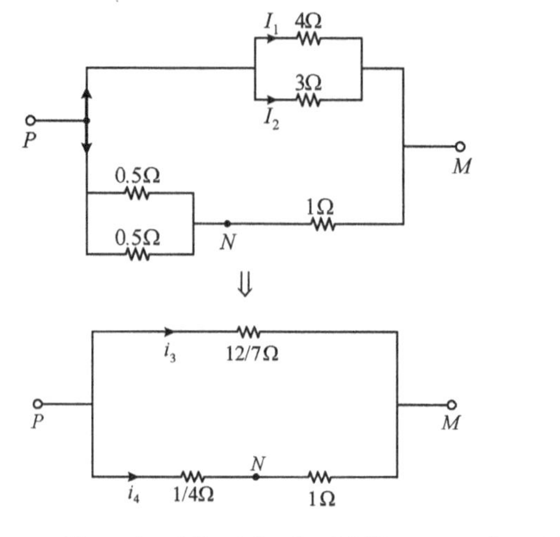

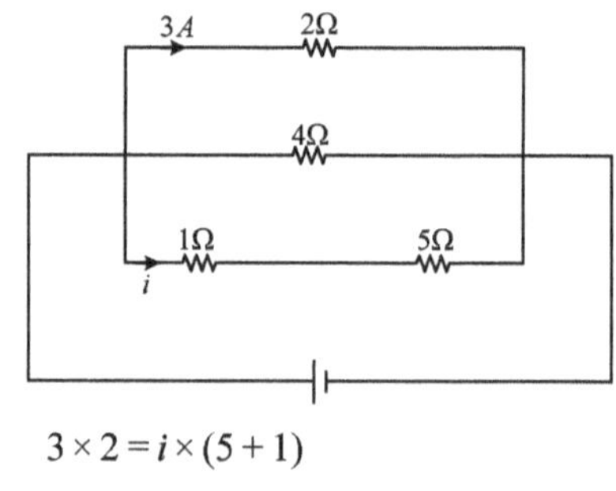

$$\Rightarrow \qquad V_{NM} = I_4 \times 1\,\Omega = 3.2 \times 1 = 3.2\,V \qquad\qquad \textbf{Ans. (B)}$$

Sol. 7 As the three branches of circuit are in parallel, the voltage across all three branches are same, so we use

$$3 \times 2 = i \times (5 + 1)$$

$$\Rightarrow \qquad i = 1A$$

Power dissipated in $5\ \Omega$ can be given as

$$P = i^2 R$$

$$\Rightarrow \qquad P = (1)^2 \times 5 = 5\ \text{watt} \qquad\qquad \textbf{Ans. (B)}$$

Sol. 8 This question is same as Q. 5. Students are advised to refer solution of Q. 5. **Ans. (A)**

Sol. 9 If internal resistance of battery is taken as r. By Ohm's law, we use

$$\frac{E}{r + 2} = 2$$

In second case, we use

$$\frac{E}{r + 9} = \frac{1}{2}$$

$$\Rightarrow \qquad 2(r + 2) = \frac{(r + 9)}{2}$$

$$\Rightarrow \qquad 4(r + 2) = r + 9$$

$$\Rightarrow \qquad 4r + 8 = r + 9$$

$$\Rightarrow \qquad 3r = 1$$

$$\Rightarrow \qquad r = \frac{1}{3}\,\Omega \qquad\qquad \textbf{Ans. (B)}$$

Sol. 10 Power dissipated across 7 Ω resistance is given as

$$I^2R = 36 \text{ W}$$

$$\Rightarrow \quad I^2 \times 9 = 36$$

$$\Rightarrow \quad I = 2 \text{ A}$$

Thus current through 6 Ω resistance is given as

$$I_{6\Omega} = \frac{18}{6} = 3 \text{A}$$

Thus total current through batter is $2\,A + 3\,A = 5\,A$ so potential difference across $2\,\Omega = 5 \times 2 = 10$ V   **Ans. (C)**

Sol. 11 Let x is the resistance per unit length of the across terminals A and B equivalent circuit is written as

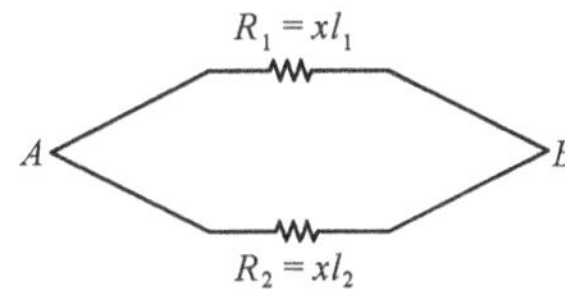

Equivalent resistance of this circuit is given as

$$R = \frac{R_1 R_2}{R_1 + R_2} = \frac{(x_1 l_1)(x_2 l_2)}{x l_1 + x l_2}$$

$$\Rightarrow \quad \frac{8}{3} = x \frac{l_1 l_2}{l_1 + l_2} \qquad \qquad \ldots(1)$$

Total resistance is given as 12 ohm, so we have

$$12 = x(l_1 + l_2) \qquad \qquad \ldots(2)$$

From equations-(1) and (2), we have

$$x^2 l_1 l_2 = 32 \qquad \qquad \ldots(3)$$

Solving equations-(2) and (3), we get

$$\Rightarrow \quad \frac{l_1}{l_2} = \frac{1}{2} \ \text{ or } \ 2 \qquad \qquad \textbf{Ans. (D)}$$

Sol. 12 By Ohm's law, terminal potential difference of cell is given as

$$V = E - \frac{E}{R+r} \times r$$

If above function is plotted on V-R axis, the equation in X and Y axis can be compared with

$$y = C_1 - \frac{C_2}{x}$$

Out of the given options, most appropriate is option (B).
          Ans. (B)

Sol. 13 By Ohm's law, current through the cell is given as

$$I = \frac{E}{R+r}$$

$$\Rightarrow \quad 0.2 = \frac{2.1}{10+r}$$

$$\Rightarrow \quad 2 + 0.2r = 2.1$$

$$\Rightarrow \quad 0.2r = 0.1$$

$$\Rightarrow \quad r = 0.5\,\Omega \qquad \qquad \textbf{Ans. (B)}$$

Sol. 14 The given Wheatstone's bridge is balanced, so here equivalent resistance of bridge is given as

$$R_{eq} = \frac{40 \times 120}{40 + 120} = 30\,\Omega$$

As internal resistance of cell is 5 Ω. Current through battery is given as

$$I_{\text{battery}} = \frac{7}{30+5} = 0.2\,\text{A} \qquad \qquad \textbf{Ans. (B)}$$

Sol. 15 The potentials at different parts of circuit are shown in figure below.

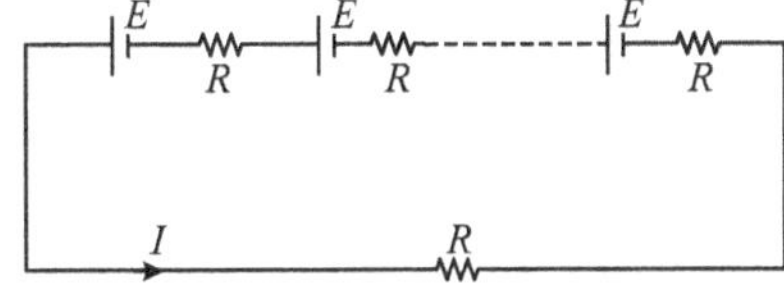

From Kirchhoff's voltage law, we have

$$V_B = V_A - 9$$

$$V_A - V_B = 9 \text{ V} \qquad \qquad \textbf{Ans. (D)}$$

Sol. 16 Figures below shows the two situation described in the question.

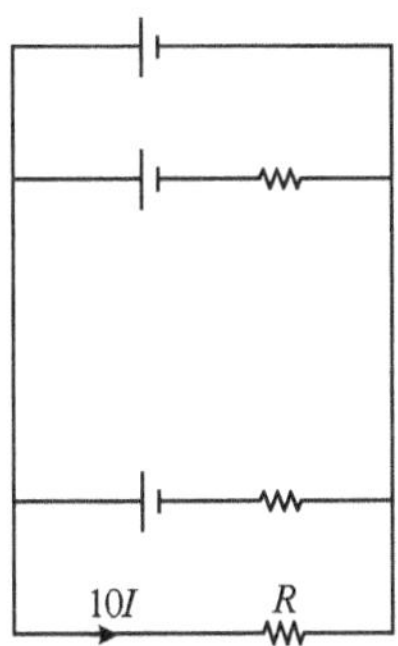

By Ohm's law, we have current in first circuit given as

$$I = \frac{E}{nR + R} \qquad \qquad \ldots(1)$$

Similarly by Ohm's law, current in second circuit is given as

$$10I = \frac{E}{\dfrac{R}{n} + R} \qquad \ldots(2)$$

Dividing equation-(2) by (1), we have

$$10 = \frac{(n+1)R}{\left(\dfrac{1}{n}+1\right)R}$$

$$\Rightarrow \quad 10\left(\frac{1}{n}+1\right) = n+1$$

$$\Rightarrow \quad \frac{10}{n}+10 = n+1$$

$$\Rightarrow \quad n-\frac{10}{n} = 9$$

$$\Rightarrow \quad n^2 - 9n - 10 = 0$$

$$\Rightarrow \quad n = 10 \qquad\qquad \textbf{Ans. (C)}$$

Sol. 17 The current due to n batteries in the loop is given as

$$I = \frac{n\varepsilon}{nr} = \frac{\varepsilon}{r}$$

Thus current I is independent of n hence it remain constant.

$$\textbf{Ans. (C)}$$

Sol. 18 Equivalent resistance of four identical resistances in parallel is given as

$$R_p = \frac{R}{4} = 0.25\,\Omega$$

$$\Rightarrow \qquad\qquad R = 1\Omega$$

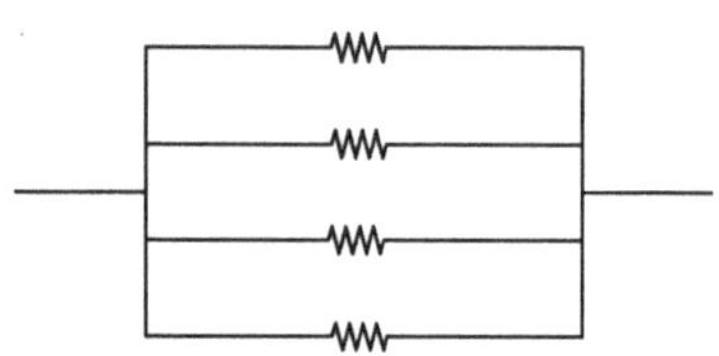

When these resistance are connected in series, equivalent resistance is given as

$$R_{\text{series}} = 4R = 4(1) = 4\Omega \qquad \textbf{Ans. (D)}$$

Sol. 19 For parallel combination of resistances, current is divided in inverse ratio of resistances so we have

$$\frac{i_2}{i_3} = \frac{r_3}{r_2}$$

$$\Rightarrow \qquad i_3 = \frac{r_2}{r_2+r_3}i_1 \quad \text{and} \quad i_2 = \frac{r_3}{r_2+r_3}i_1$$

$$\Rightarrow \qquad \frac{i_3}{i_1} = \frac{r_2}{r_2+r_3} \qquad\qquad \textbf{Ans. (B)}$$

17.3 Thermal Effects of Current

Sol. 1 The resistance of the bulbs is given as

$$R = \frac{V^2}{P} = \frac{220\times220}{100} = 484\,\Omega$$

In series combination, resistance will become

$$R_{\text{eq}} = 484 + 484 = 968\,\Omega$$

Thus the power drawn in series combination will be

$$P_{\text{eq}} = \frac{V^2}{968}$$

$$\Rightarrow \qquad P_{\text{eq}} = \frac{220\times220}{968} = 50\,\text{watt}$$

In parallel combination resistance will be reduced to half

$$R_{\text{eq}} = 242\,\Omega$$

Thus the power drawn in parallel combination will be

$$P_{\text{eq}} = \frac{V^2}{242}$$

$$\Rightarrow \qquad P_{\text{eq}} = \frac{220\times220}{242} = 200\,\text{watt} \qquad \textbf{Ans. (D)}$$

Sol. 2 If R_1 and R_2 are the resistance of the two coils and V be the voltage supplied then effective resistance of two coils in parallel is given as

$$R_{\text{eq}} = \frac{R_1 R_2}{R_1 + R_2}$$

If H be the heat required to start boiling water in kettle, we use

$$H = \frac{V^2 t_1}{R_1} = \frac{V^2 t_2}{R_2}$$

For parallel combination, we if time required to boil is t_p, we use

$$H = \frac{V^2(R_1 + R_2)t_p}{R_1 R_2}$$

$$\Rightarrow \qquad \frac{1}{t_p} = \left(\frac{t_2 + t_1}{t_2 t_1}\right)$$

$$\Rightarrow \qquad t_p = \frac{t_1 t_2}{t_1 + t_2} = \frac{10\times40}{10+40} = 8\,\text{min} \qquad \textbf{Ans. (A)}$$

Sol. 3 Fuse wire should have high resistance and low melting point. $\qquad\qquad\qquad\qquad$ **Ans. (B)**

Sol. 4 In India, power consumption of a bulb of resistance R is given as

$$P_I = \frac{(220)^2}{R}$$

In USA same is given as

$$P_U = \frac{(110)^2}{R_U}$$

For 60 W bulb to consume same power in India & USA, we use

$$P_I = P_U$$

$$\Rightarrow \quad \frac{(200)^2}{R} = \frac{(110)^2}{R_U}$$

$$\Rightarrow \quad R_U = \frac{R}{4} \qquad \textbf{Ans. (C)}$$

Sol. 5 For the given battery percentage watt hour efficiency is given as

$$\eta = \frac{E_{\text{out}}}{E_{\text{in}}} \times 100$$

$$\Rightarrow \quad \eta = \frac{(14)(5)(15)}{(15)(10)(8)} \times 100$$

$$\Rightarrow \quad \eta = 87.5\% \qquad \textbf{Ans. (C)}$$

Sol. 6 The resistance of each of the three bulbs is given as

$$R = \frac{V^2}{P} = \frac{(200)^2}{60} \, \Omega$$

When three bulbs are connected in series their equivalent resistance is given as

$$R_s = \frac{3 \times (200)^2}{60} \, \Omega$$

Thus power drawn by bulb when connected across 200 V supply is given as

$$P = \frac{V^2}{R_{re}} = \frac{(200)^2}{3 \times (200)^2 / 60}$$

$$\Rightarrow \quad P = 20 \text{ W} \qquad \textbf{Ans. (D)}$$

Sol. 7 Power dissipated in fuse wire is given as

$$P = I^2 R$$

$$\Rightarrow \quad R = \frac{P}{I^2} = \frac{1}{25} = 0.04 \, \Omega \qquad \textbf{Ans. (B)}$$

Sol. 8 Voltage drop across 8 Ω resistance is given as

$$V = \sqrt{PR} = \sqrt{2 \times 8} = 4V$$

Thus voltage drop across 3 Ω is equal to $3V$ and power dissipated in 3 Ω resistance can now be given as

$$P = \frac{(3)^2}{3} = 3 \text{ watt} \qquad \textbf{Ans. (D)}$$

Sol. 9 Mass of substance deposited or liberated at an electrode is directly proportional to the quantity of charge passed through the electrolyte. Power consumed in electrolysis is given as

$$P = 100 \text{ W}$$

Voltage applied is $V = 125$ V, thus current in circuit is

$$I = \frac{P}{V} = \frac{180}{125} = 0.8\text{A}$$

The mass liberated on electrode is directly proportional to charge passed through electrolyte so we use

$$m \propto Q$$

$$\Rightarrow \quad m = ZQ$$

$$\Rightarrow \quad m = ZIt$$

$$\Rightarrow \quad m = ZIt = (Z)\left(\frac{P}{V}\right)(t)$$

$$\Rightarrow \quad m = (0.367 \times 10^{-6})\left(\frac{100}{125}\right)(60)$$

$$\Rightarrow \quad m = 1.76 \times 10^{-5} \text{ kg} = 17.6 \text{ mg} \qquad \textbf{Ans. (A)}$$

Sol. 10 Equivalent resistance of the circuit across battery is 6 ohm so power dissipated is given as

$$P = \frac{V^2}{R} = \frac{(18)^2}{6} = 54 \text{ W} \qquad \textbf{Ans. (B)}$$

Sol. 11 Mass deposited is given as

$$m = ZIt$$

$$\Rightarrow \quad m = 30 \times 10^{-5} \times 1.5 \times 10 \times 60 \text{ gm}$$

$$\Rightarrow \quad m = 0.27 \text{ gm} \qquad \textbf{Ans. (C)}$$

Sol. 12 Neutral temperature is given as

$$T_n = \frac{T_i + T_c}{2}$$

$$\Rightarrow \quad T_n = \frac{T_i + 0}{2} = \frac{T_i}{2} \qquad \textbf{Ans. (D)}$$

Sol. 13 Writing equations of KVL for the loops in given circuit, we have

For upper loop $\in_1 - (i_1 + i_2)R - i_1 r_1 = 0$

For lower loop $\in_1 + i_1 r_1 - i_2 r_2 + E_2 = 0$

For outer loop $\in_2 - (i_1 + i_2)R - i_2 r_2 = 0$ $\qquad \textbf{Ans. (B)}$

Sol. 14 At neutral temperature as we know $\dfrac{de}{dt} = 0$. **Ans. (B)**

Sol. 15 As resistance of bulb is constant and power rating of bulb is given as

$$P = \frac{V^2}{R}$$

$$\Rightarrow \qquad \frac{\Delta p}{p} = \frac{2\Delta V}{V} + \frac{\Delta R}{R}$$

Percentage decreased in power can now be given as

$$\frac{\Delta p}{p} = 2 \times 2.5 + 0 = 5\% \qquad \textbf{Ans. (C)}$$

Sol. 16 Power dissipated in circuit is given as

$$P = \frac{V^2}{R_{eq}}$$

$$\Rightarrow \qquad 30 = \frac{(10)^2}{\left(\dfrac{5R}{R+5}\right)}$$

$$\Rightarrow \qquad \frac{5R}{R+5} = \frac{10}{3}$$

$$\Rightarrow \qquad 3R = 2R + 10$$

$$\Rightarrow \qquad R = 10\ \Omega \qquad \textbf{Ans. (B)}$$

Sol. 17 The resistance of wire between two cities is given as

$$R = 150 \times 0.5 = 75\ \Omega$$

Current in the wire is given as

$$I = \frac{\Delta V}{\Delta R} = \frac{8}{0.5} = 16\ \text{A}$$

Total power loss in wire between cities is given as

$$P = I^2 R = (16)^2 \times 75 = 19200 = 19.2\ \text{kW} \qquad \textbf{Ans. (B)}$$

Sol. 18 Current in resistance is given as

$$I = \frac{dQ}{dt} = a - 2bt$$

Current becomes zero at $t = \dfrac{a}{2b}$ so heat produced upto this instant is calculated as

$$P = \int_0^t I^2 R\,dt = \int_0^{\frac{a}{2b}} (a - 2bt)^2 R\,dt$$

$$\Rightarrow \qquad P = \int_0^{\frac{a}{2b}} (a^2 + 4b^2 t^2 - 4abt) R\,dt$$

$$\Rightarrow \qquad P = \left[a^2 t + 4b^2 \frac{t^3}{3} - 4ab\frac{t^2}{2} \right]_0^{\frac{a}{2b}} R = \frac{a^3 R}{6b}$$

$$\textbf{Ans. (A)}$$

Sol. 19 Resistance of bulb is calculated as

$$R_b = \frac{V^2}{P} = \frac{10000}{500} = 20\ \Omega$$

Across 230 V supply current is given as

$$i = \frac{230}{R + 20} = \frac{100}{20}$$

$$\Rightarrow \qquad R = 26\ \Omega \qquad \textbf{Ans. (C)}$$

Sol. 20 As all bulbs are glowing, equivalent circuit is shown in figure below.

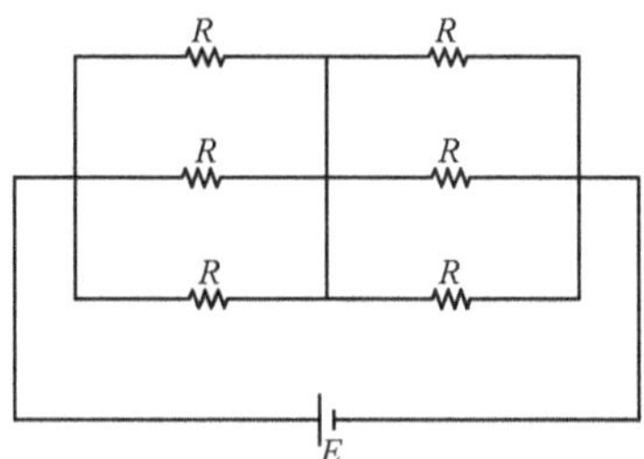

The equivalent resistance of circuit in this state is given as

$$R_{eq} = \frac{R}{3} + \frac{R}{3} = \frac{2R}{3}$$

Power consumed in this state is given as

$$P_i = \frac{E^2}{R_{eq}} = \frac{3E^2}{2R} \qquad \ldots(1)$$

In second situation when two from section A and one from section B are glowing, the equivalent circuit is shown in figure below

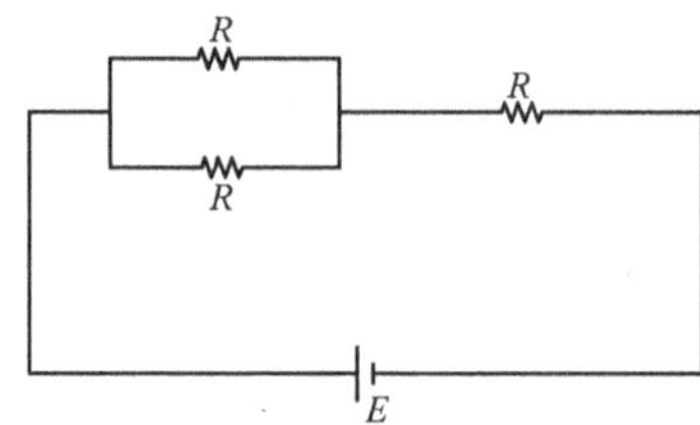

Equivalent resistance in this state is given as

$$R_{eq} = \frac{R}{2} + R = \frac{3R}{2}$$

Power consumption in this state is given as

$$P_f = \frac{3E^2}{3R} \qquad \ldots(2)$$

$$\Rightarrow \qquad \frac{P_i}{P_f} = \frac{3E^2}{2R} \frac{3R}{2E^2} = 9 : 4 \qquad \textbf{Ans. (B)}$$

Sol. 21 Fuse wire has lower melting point so when excess current flows, due to heat produced in it, it melts and can act as circuit protecting device. $\qquad$ **Ans. (D)**

Sol. 22 Figure below shows the situation described in the question

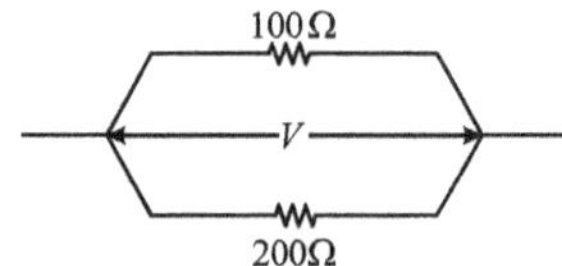

As both resistors are in parallel combination so potential difference across both will be same. The power dissipation across the two resistances is given as

$$P = \frac{V^2}{R}$$

$$\Rightarrow \quad P \propto \frac{1}{R}$$

$$\Rightarrow \quad \frac{P_1}{P_2} = \frac{R_2}{R_1} = \frac{200}{100} = \frac{2}{1} \qquad \textbf{Ans. (A)}$$

17.4 Electrical Measurements

Sol. 1 Potential gradient of potentiometer wire is given as

$$\lambda = \frac{V}{l} = \frac{IR}{l}$$

$$\Rightarrow \quad \lambda = \frac{I\rho l}{Al} = \frac{0.1 \times 10^{-7}}{10^{-6}}$$

$$\Rightarrow \quad \lambda = 0.01 = 10^{-2}\,\text{V/m} \qquad \textbf{Ans. (A)}$$

Sol. 2 For conversion of a galvanometer into a voltmeter, high resistance is needed to be put in series to reduce the current in circuit when a given range of voltage is applied across the combination. The current thus measured by galvanometer indicates the applied potential difference on a pre-calibrated scale. **Ans. (A)**

Sol. 3 In the balance Wheatstone bridge, galvanometer arm can be neglected so in this case equivalent resistance can be calculated from the figure shown below

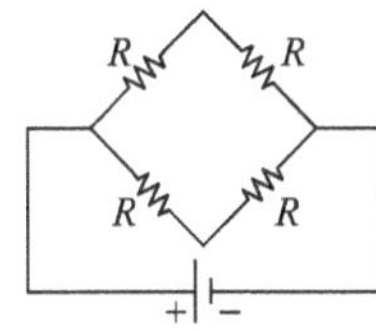

$$R_{\text{eq}} = \frac{2R \times 2R}{2R + 2R} = \frac{4R^2}{4R} = R \qquad \textbf{Ans. (C)}$$

Sol. 4 The total current shown in galvanometer is given as

$$I_g = 25 \times 4 \times 10^{-4}\,\text{A} = 10^{-2}\,\text{A}$$

The high resistance connected in series to convert galvanometer into voltmeter of 25 V is given as

$$R = \frac{V}{I_g} - G$$

$$\Rightarrow \quad R = \frac{25}{10^{-2}} - 50$$

$$\Rightarrow \quad R = 2450\,\Omega \qquad \textbf{Ans. (D)}$$

Sol. 5 In the given question circuit we can consider the two batteries in parallel combination so the voltmeter reading can be given as

$$V = \frac{\dfrac{E_1}{r_1} + \dfrac{E_2}{r_2}}{\dfrac{1}{r_1} + \dfrac{1}{r_2}} = \frac{E_1 r_2 + E_2 r_1}{r_1 + r_2}$$

$$\Rightarrow \quad V = 14\,\text{V} \qquad \textbf{Ans. (C)}$$

Sol. 6 In absence of wire connection, potential difference across A & B can be given as

$$V_A - V_B = \left[V - \left(\frac{V}{8} \times 4\right)\right] - \left[V - \left(\frac{V}{4} \times 1\right)\right]$$

$$\Rightarrow \quad V_A - V_B = -\frac{V}{2} + \frac{V}{4} = -\frac{V}{4}$$

$$\Rightarrow \quad V_B > V_A$$

Thus on connecting the wire between A and B, current flows from high potential end to low potential end i.e. from B to A. **Ans. (D)**

Sol. 7 For the given bridge to be balanced final resistance of arm S should also be 2 Ω. A resistance of 6 Ω is connected in parallel with initial value of S so we use

$$\Rightarrow \quad \frac{1}{R} = \frac{1}{R_1} + \frac{1}{R_2}$$

$$\Rightarrow \quad \frac{1}{2} = \frac{1}{6} + \frac{1}{S}$$

$$\Rightarrow \quad S = 3\,\Omega \qquad \textbf{Ans. (A)}$$

Sol. 8 The situation described in question is shown in figure below. If a shunt resistance R_S is connected in parallel to the given value of ammeter resistance $R_A = 13$ Ω. Out of 750 A current 100 A will pass through R_A and remaining 650 A will pass through the shunt resistance, so we use

$$I_2 \times R_S = I_1 \times R_A$$

$$\Rightarrow \quad 650 \times R_S = 100 \times 13$$

$$\Rightarrow \quad R_S = 2\,\Omega$$

Ans. (A)

Sol. 9 Current through galvanometer for 3 V batter is given as

$$I = \frac{3V}{50\Omega + 2950\Omega} = 10^{-3} A$$

Current for 30 division deflection (full scale) is

$$I = 10^{-3} A$$

Current required for 20 division deflection is given as

$$I_1 = \frac{20}{30} \times 10^{-3}$$

If this deflection is to be produced by same 3 V battery then we use

$$I_1 = \frac{2}{3} \times 10^{-3} A = \frac{3}{50 + R}$$

$$\Rightarrow \qquad R = 4450\,\Omega \qquad\qquad \textbf{Ans. (B)}$$

Sol. 10 For measurement of internal resistance of a cell if balancing lengths are l_1 and l_2 for cell without and with external resistance then internal resistance is given as

$$r = R\left(\frac{l_1 - l_2}{l_2}\right) = 10\left(\frac{110 - 100}{100}\right) = 1\,\Omega \qquad \textbf{Ans. (C)}$$

Sol. 11 To convert galvanometer into an ammeter a shunt resistance is connected in parallel such that the full deflection current passes through galvanometer when current equal to range of ammeter is supplied. In this state we have

$$(I_R - I_g)R_s = I_g R_g$$

$$\Rightarrow \qquad (5 - 1)R_s = 60 \times 1$$

$$\Rightarrow \qquad R_s = \frac{60}{4} = 15\Omega \qquad\qquad \textbf{Ans. (A)}$$

Sol. 12 When key is in 1-2 state, resistance R is balanced on wire, so we use

$$IR = kl_1$$

When key is in 1-3 state resistance $(R + X)$ is balanced on wire, so we use

$$I(R + X) = kl_2$$

$$\Rightarrow \qquad IX = k(l_2 - l_1)$$

As $I = 1$ A, option (C) is correct. $\qquad\qquad \textbf{Ans. (C)}$

Sol. 13 If we consider millivoltmeter to be ideal, it does not draw any current. So for application of 25 mV potential difference, 25 A current should flow through shunt resistance only. Thus we have

$$R_s = \frac{V_g}{I} = \frac{25 \times 10^{-3}}{25} = 1\,\text{m}\Omega = 0.001\,\Omega \qquad \textbf{Ans. (A)}$$

Sol. 14 As there is no deflection in galvanometer, this indicates the EMF of second batter is equal to the potential difference across the resistance R in vertical branch. Current in left loop of circuit is given as

$$I = \frac{V_A}{R_1 + R}$$

$$\Rightarrow \qquad I = \frac{12}{500 + 100} = \frac{12}{600}\,\text{A}$$

As per condition stated above, we use

$$V_B = IR$$

$$\Rightarrow \qquad V_B = \frac{12}{600} \times 100 = 2\,V \qquad\qquad \textbf{Ans. (B)}$$

Sol. 15 When the bridge is balanced, initially condition will be given as

$$\frac{5}{l_1} = \frac{R}{100 - l_1} \qquad\qquad \ldots(1)$$

After adding shunt resistance, resistance of this branch becomes half, so we use

$$\frac{5}{1.6l_1} = \frac{R}{2(100 - 1.6l_1)} \qquad\qquad \ldots(2)$$

$$\Rightarrow \qquad \frac{R}{1.6(100 - l_1)} = \frac{R}{2(100 - 1.6l_1)} \qquad\qquad \ldots(3)$$

$$\Rightarrow \qquad 160 - 1.6l_1 = 200 - 3.2l_1$$

$$\Rightarrow \qquad 1.6l_1 = 40$$

$$\Rightarrow \qquad l_1 = 25$$

From equation-(1), we use

$$\frac{5}{25} = \frac{R}{75}$$

$$\Rightarrow \qquad R = 15\Omega \qquad\qquad \textbf{Ans. (B)}$$

Sol. 16 As already discussed and explained in theory, the internal resistance for two balancing lengths under normal and with external resistance connected across battery can be given as

$$r = \left(\frac{l_1}{l_2} - 1\right)R$$

$$\Rightarrow \qquad r = \left(\frac{3}{2.85} - 1\right)9.5\Omega$$

$$\Rightarrow \qquad r = \frac{0.15}{2.85} \times 9.5 = 0.5\Omega \qquad\qquad \textbf{Ans. (C)}$$

Sol. 17 Current through galvanometer is given as $I_g = 0.002\, I_R$ so we use for galvanometer and shunt in parallel

$$I_G G = I_S S$$

$$\Rightarrow \quad \left(\frac{1}{500}\right)\cdot G = \left(\frac{499}{500}\right)\cdot S$$

$$\Rightarrow \quad S = \frac{G}{499}$$

Resistance of ammeter R_A can now be given by parallel combination of shunt resistance and galvanometer, given as

$$\frac{1}{R_A} = \frac{1}{G}+\frac{1}{S} = \frac{1}{G}+\frac{1}{\left(\dfrac{G}{499}\right)} = \frac{500}{G}$$

$$\Rightarrow \quad R_A = \frac{1}{500}G \qquad \textbf{Ans. (C)}$$

Sol. 18 For the given potentiometer wire, current in wire is given as

$$I_{AB} = \frac{E_0}{r_1 + r}$$

Potential gradient on wire can be given as

$$\lambda = \left(\frac{E_0}{r_1 + r}\right)\cdot\frac{r}{L}$$

Thus e.m.f. of the cell can be given as

$$\Rightarrow \quad E = \lambda l = \left(\frac{E_0}{r_1 + r}\right)\frac{r}{L}\times l \qquad \textbf{Ans. (C)}$$

Sol. 19 Figure below shows the situation described in the question.

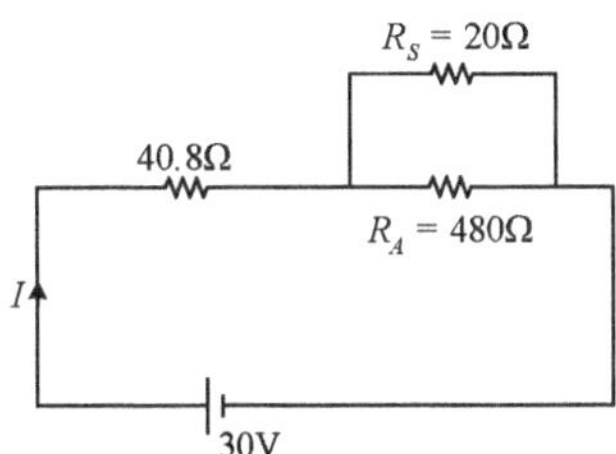

Equivalent resistance across battery can be given as

$$R_{eq} = 40.8 + \frac{480\times 20}{500}$$

$$\Rightarrow \quad R_{eq} = 40.8 + 19.2$$

$$\Rightarrow \quad R_{eq} = 60\ \Omega$$

Ammeter reading can be given as

$$I = \frac{30}{60} = 0.5\,\text{A} \qquad \textbf{Ans. (B)}$$

Sol. 20 If potential gradient on wire is l, then for the two situations of cells in supportive and opposing sense, we use

$$E_1 + E_2 = \lambda l_1$$
$$\text{and} \quad E_1 - E_2 = \lambda l_1$$

$$\Rightarrow \quad \frac{E_1 + E_2}{E_1 - E_2} = \frac{50}{10} = \frac{5}{1}$$

$$\Rightarrow \quad \frac{E_1}{E_2} = \frac{5+1}{5-1} = \frac{6}{4} = \frac{3}{2} \qquad \textbf{Ans. (D)}$$

Sol. 21 Potentiometer measurement is accurate because while taking the readings it does not draw any current from the circuit.

$$\textbf{Ans. (C)}$$

Sol. 22 Current sensitivity of a galvanometer is given as

$$I_S = \frac{NBA}{C}$$

Voltage sensitivity of galvanometer is given as

$$V_S = \frac{NBA}{CR_G}$$

Thus, resistance of galvanometer can be given as

$$R_G = \frac{I_S}{V_S} = \frac{5\times 1}{20\times 10^{-3}} = \frac{5000}{20} = 250\Omega$$

$$\textbf{Ans. (A)}$$

Sol. 23 For ideal voltmeter, resistance is infinite and for the ideal ammeter, resistance is zero. Thus in above case, we use

$$V_1 = i_1 \times 10 = \frac{10}{10}\times 10 = 10\,\text{V}$$

$$V_2 = i_2 \times 10 = \frac{10}{10}\times 10 = 10\,\text{V}$$

$$\Rightarrow \quad V_1 = V_2$$

$$\Rightarrow \quad i_1 = i_2 = \frac{10V}{10\Omega} = 1\,\text{A} \qquad \textbf{Ans. (C)}$$

Sol. 24 Figure below shows the situation described in the question.

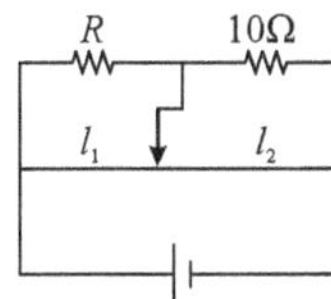

For balanced meter bridge, we use

$$\frac{R}{10} = \frac{l_1}{l_2} = \frac{3}{2}$$

$$\Rightarrow \quad R = 15\ \Omega$$

Length of 15 Ω resistance wire is 1.5 m thus length of 1 Ω resistance wire is given as

$$l = \frac{1.5}{15} = 0.1\ \text{m} \qquad \textbf{Ans. (C)}$$

Sol. 25 In a potentiometer if l_1 and l_2 are the balancing lengths for the cells of EMF E_1 and E_2 then for a potential gradient λ on the potentiometer wire, we have

$$\frac{E_1}{E_2} = \frac{\lambda l_1}{\lambda l_2}$$

$$\Rightarrow \quad \frac{1.5}{2.5} = \frac{36}{l_2}$$

$$\Rightarrow \quad l_2 = 36 \times \frac{5}{3} = 60 \text{ cm} \qquad \textbf{Ans. (A)}$$

Sol. 26 Error in measurement will be least when resistance P & Q are equal. **Ans. (A)**

Ch-18. Moving Charges & Magnetism

18.1 Magnetic Effects of Current

Sol. 1 The magnetic field B produced at the centre of a circular coil due to current I flowing through this is given by

$$B = \frac{\mu_0 NI}{2r}$$

For $N = 1$, we have

$$B = \frac{\mu_0 I}{2r}$$

If same wire is used in making a 2 turn coil, we have

$$2 \times 2\pi r' = 2\pi r$$

$$\Rightarrow \quad r' = r/2$$

Thus new magnetic field at the centre for two turns ($N = 2$) is given by

$$B' = \frac{\mu_0 \times 2I}{2r'} = \frac{\mu_0 \times 2I}{2r/2} = \frac{4\mu_0 I}{2r} = 4\,B \quad \textbf{Ans. (C)}$$

Sol. 2 Magnetic field induction at interior points of a long solenoid, having n turns per unit length and carrying a current i is given as

$$B = \mu_0 ni$$

As current is doubled and n is halved so B remains same.

Ans. (B)

Sol. 3 For the two coils if r_1 and r_2 are their radii and if B_1 and B_2 are magnetic induction at their centres, then we have

$$B_1 = \frac{\mu_0 I_1}{2r_1} \text{ and } B_2 = \frac{\mu_0 I_2}{2r_2}$$

Given that $B_1 = B_2$ and $r_1 = 2r_2$ so it gives $I_1 = 2I_2$.

As length of wire of coil 1 is double that of coil 2 and if R_1 and R_2 are resistance of the two coils then $R_1 = 2R_2$. If V_1 and V_2 are the potential difference applied across the two coils such that

magnetic fields at centre are same, then we use

$$\frac{V_1}{V_2} = \frac{I_1 R_1}{I_2 R_2} = \frac{(2I_2)(2R_2)}{I_2 R_2} = 4 \qquad \textbf{Ans. (B)}$$

Sol. 4 Energy density and Young's modulus have same dimensions and equal to $[ML^{-1}T^{-2}]$. In above list Dielectric constant and refractive index are dimensionless. **Ans. (A)**

Sol. 5 Due to continuous rotation of charge, electric current is given in terms of charge and frequency as

$$I = qf$$

Thus magnetic field intensity at center of ring can be calculated by considering as an equivalent current carrying coil, given as

$$B = \frac{\mu_0 I}{2R} = \frac{\mu_0 qf}{2R} \qquad \textbf{Ans. (A)}$$

Sol. 6 Figure below shows the situation described in figure.

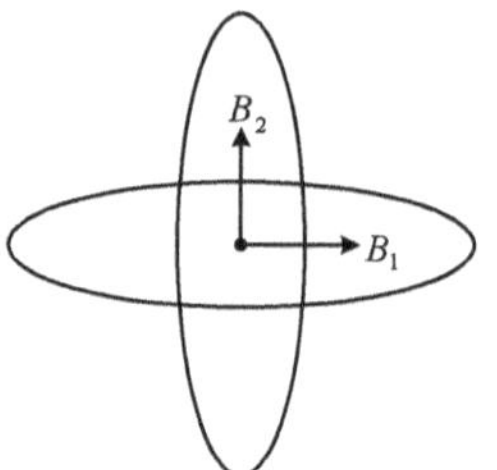

As both coils are mutually perpendicular to each other, at the centre both magnetic fields are also perpendicular with magnitudes given as

$$B_1 = \frac{\mu_0 I}{2R} \text{ and } B_2 = \frac{\mu_0 (2I)}{2R}$$

Net magnetic field at common center is given as

$$B_{net} = \sqrt{B_1^2 + B_2^2} = \frac{\mu_0 (2I)}{2R}\sqrt{1+4} = \frac{\sqrt{5}\mu_0 I}{2R} \qquad \textbf{Ans. (A)}$$

Sol. 7 At point O the magnetic field due to the two wires will be perpendicular to each other with values, given as

$$B_1 = \frac{\mu_0 I_1}{2\pi d} \text{ and } B_2 = \frac{\mu_0 I_2}{2\pi d}$$

At the point P, net magnetic field is given as

$$B = \sqrt{B_1^2 + B_2^2}$$

$$\Rightarrow \quad B = \frac{\mu_0}{2\pi d}(I_1^2 + I_2^2)^{1/2} \qquad \textbf{Ans. (D)}$$

Sol. 8 At interior point of wire at a distance $a/2$ from the axis magnetic induction is given as

$$B_1 = \frac{\mu_0 I(a/2)}{2\pi a^2} = \frac{\mu_0 I}{4\pi a} \qquad \ldots(1)$$

Magnetic induction outside the wire at a distance $2a$ from axis is given as

$$B_2 = \frac{\mu_0 I}{4\pi a} \qquad \ldots(2)$$

From equations-(1) and (2), we have

$$\frac{B_1}{B_2} = 1 \qquad \textbf{Ans. (C)}$$

Sol. 9 For a single turn circular loop, magnetic field at the centre of loop is given as

$$B = \frac{\mu_0 i}{2R}$$

For n turn loop made from same length of wire, its radius will become

$$r = \frac{R}{n}$$

Now magnetic field at centre of the loop of n turns, is given as

$$B' = \frac{\mu_0 n i}{2(R/n)} = \frac{\mu_0 n^2 i}{2R} = n^2 B \qquad \textbf{Ans. (B)}$$

Sol. 10 For a solid cylindrical conductor magnetic field at interior points at a distance x $(x < R)$ from the axis is given as

$$B = \frac{\mu_0 i x}{2\pi R^2} \qquad \ldots(1)$$

At the surface of conductor, magnetic field is given as

$$B = \frac{\mu_0 i}{2\pi R} \qquad \ldots(2)$$

At exterior points of conductor at a distance x $(x > R)$ from the axis of conductor, magnetic field is given as

$$B = \frac{\mu_0 i}{2\pi x} \qquad \ldots(3)$$

From equations-(1), (2) and (3), we can see that the most appropriate curve is shown in option (C). **Ans. (C)**

Sol. 11 Magnetic field at the centre of a long solenoid is given as

$$B = \mu_0 \left(\frac{N}{l}\right) I = 4\pi \times 10^{-7} \times \frac{100}{(0.5)} \times 25 = 6.28 \times 10^{-4}\,\text{T}$$

$$\textbf{Ans. (B)}$$

Sol. 12 Inside a current carrying cylindrical conductor, the magnetic induction at a distance r from the axis of conductor is given as

$$B = \frac{\mu_0 I}{2\pi R^2} r$$

$$\Rightarrow \qquad B \propto r$$

And outside the conductor magnetic induction at a distance r

from the axis of conductor is given as

$$B = \frac{\mu_0 I}{2\pi r}$$

$$\Rightarrow \qquad B \propto \frac{1}{r}$$

Thus from above relations the variation curve of magnetic induction as a function of distance for a current carrying conductor is plotted as shown below.

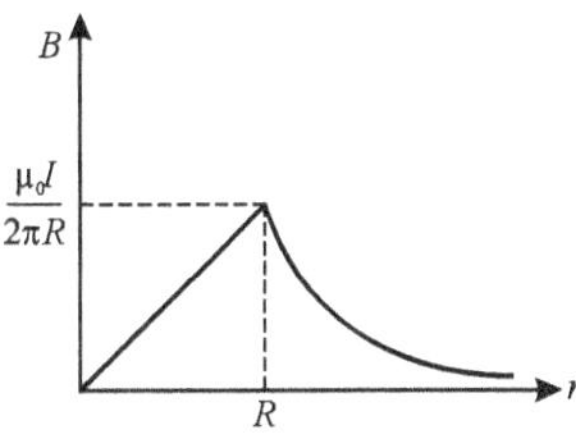

$$\textbf{Ans. (C)}$$

Sol. 13 Magnetic field strength due to a long solenoid at interior points including centre is given as

$$B = \mu_0 n i = \mu_0 \frac{N}{l} i$$

$$\Rightarrow \qquad B = 4\pi \times 10^{-7} \times \frac{100}{10^{-3}} \times 1$$

$$\Rightarrow \qquad B = 12.56 \times 10^{-2}\,\text{T} \qquad \textbf{Ans. (A)}$$

Sol. 14 Magnetic field due to a current element in surrounding space is vectorially given as

$$d\vec{B} = \frac{\mu_0 (I d\vec{l} \times \vec{r})}{4\pi r^3}$$

Hence statement-I is correct. Statement-II is incorrect because the magnetic field configuration due to current element Idl, is not similar to the radial electric field configuration produced by a point charge. **Ans. (B)**

Sol. 15 The magnetic field due to a current carrying long straight wire inside and outside the wire at a distance r from its axis is given as

$$B_{\text{in}} = \frac{\mu_0 I r}{2\pi R^2} \quad \text{and} \quad B_{\text{out}} = \frac{\mu_0 I}{2\pi r}$$

For this magnetic field variation curve is plotted as

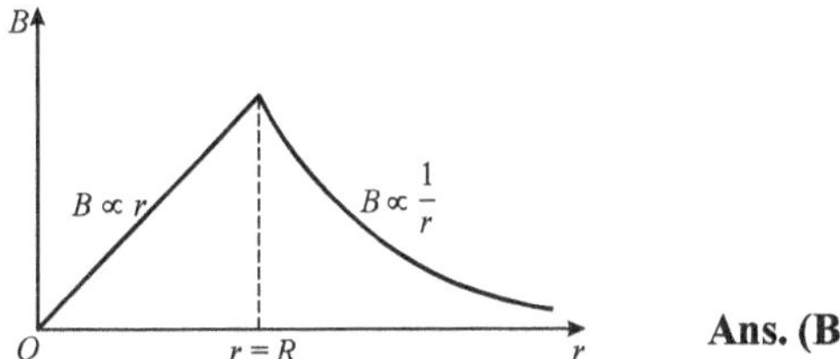

$$\textbf{Ans. (B)}$$

18.2 Magnetic Force on Moving Charges

Sol. 1 The frequency of revolution of a charged particle in a uniform perpendicular magnetic field is given as

$$\upsilon = \frac{\omega}{2\pi} = \frac{eB}{2\pi m}$$ **Ans. (C)**

Sol. 2 In the spectrograph mentioned, charge particles travel in straight line so we use

Force due to electric field = Force due to magnetic field

$$\Rightarrow \qquad eE = evB$$

$$\Rightarrow \qquad v = \frac{|\vec{E}|}{|\vec{B}|}$$ **Ans. (A)**

Sol. 3 The net electromagnetic force on the charge mentioned in question is given by Lorentz force equation which is stated in option (B).   **Ans. (B)**

Sol. 4 In perpendicular uniform magnetic field motion of a charge particle is uniform circular motion hence out of given option (A) is correct.   **Ans. (A)**

Sol. 5 Equivalent electric current due to revolution of electron is given as

$$I = \frac{e\omega}{2\pi} = \frac{ev}{2\pi R}$$

Due to this current magnetic field at the centre O is given as

$$B = \frac{\mu_0 I}{2R} = \frac{\mu_0}{2R}\left(\frac{e}{T}\right) = \frac{\mu_0}{2R}\left(\frac{ev}{2\pi R}\right)$$

$$\Rightarrow \qquad R^2 = \frac{\mu_0 ev}{4\pi B}$$

$$\Rightarrow \qquad R \propto \sqrt{\frac{v}{B}}$$ **Ans. (A)**

Sol. 6 Force on moving charge in magnetic field is given as

$$\vec{F} = q(\vec{v}\times\vec{B}) = qvB(\hat{i}\times(-\hat{k})) = qvB\hat{j}$$

Thus force on the charge is acting along direction OY.   **Ans. (C)**

Sol. 7 The magnetic force vector on a moving charge in magnetic field is given as

$$\vec{F} = q(\vec{V}\times\vec{B}) = qvB\sin\theta\,\hat{n}$$

Thus at $\theta = 0°$ or $\theta = 180°$, $F = 0$.   **Ans. (C)**

Sol. 8 When electric field is switched off, under the same magnetic field, electrons move in a circular orbit as only magnetic force would be acting on these perpendicular to their velocity.   **Ans. (A)**

Sol. 9 In mass spectrometer, when ions are accelerated through potential V, the kinetic energy gain is given as

$$\frac{1}{2}mv^2 = qV \qquad \ldots(1)$$

Due to magnetic field the path of the ions becomes semicircular, so we use

$$qvB = \frac{mv^2}{R}$$

$$\Rightarrow \qquad v = \frac{BqR}{m} \qquad \ldots(2)$$

From equation-(1) and (2), we have

$$\frac{1}{2}m\left[\frac{BqR}{m}\right]^2 = qV$$

$$\Rightarrow \qquad \frac{q}{m} = \frac{2V}{B^2 R^2}$$

Since V and B are constants, we use

$$\Rightarrow \qquad \frac{q}{m} \propto \frac{1}{R^2}$$ **Ans. (A)**

Sol. 10 Magnetic moment due to a circulating charge can be calculated by considering equivalent current due to charge's motion in circular path and it is given as

$$m = IA$$

$$\Rightarrow \qquad m = \frac{qv}{2\pi R}(\pi R^2) = \frac{qvR}{2}$$ **Ans. (D)**

Sol. 11 Time period of circular motion of charge can be directly given as

$$T = \frac{2\pi R}{v}$$

Centripetal force on charge is provided by the magnetic force on the particle, given as

$$\frac{mv^2}{R} = qvB$$

$$\Rightarrow \qquad v = \frac{qBR}{m}$$

$$\Rightarrow \qquad T = \frac{2\pi R}{\left(\dfrac{qBR}{m}\right)} = \frac{2\pi m}{qB}$$ **Ans. (D)**

Sol. 12 As magnetic force always acts in direction perpendicular to the velocity or motion of charge particle, it never does any work on particle so its kinetic energy cannot change. Thus final kinetic energy will remain T.   **Ans. (A)**

Sol. 13 Force on the moving charge in given magnetic field is given as

$$\vec{F} = q(\vec{v} \times \vec{B})$$

$$\Rightarrow \qquad \vec{F} = -2 \times 10^{-6}[(2\hat{i} + 3\hat{j}) \times 10^6 \times 2\hat{j}]$$

$$\Rightarrow \qquad \vec{F} = -(8\text{N})\,\hat{k} \qquad \qquad \textbf{Ans. (B)}$$

Sol. 14 As mentioned in the question that the beam is not deflected thus electric field force balances the force due to magnetic field. So we use

$$qE = qVB$$

$$\Rightarrow \qquad v = \frac{E}{B}$$

As beam is accelerated by the potential difference V, the kinetic energy of particles is given as

$$qV = \frac{1}{2}mv^2$$

$$\Rightarrow \qquad \frac{q}{m} = \frac{v^2}{2V}$$

$$\Rightarrow \qquad \frac{q}{m} = \frac{E^2}{2VB^2} \qquad \qquad \textbf{Ans. (A)}$$

Sol. 15 As electric field $\vec{E}$, velocity $\vec{v}$ and magnetic field $\vec{B}$ are all parallel so magnetic force $\vec{F} = q(\vec{v} \times \vec{B})$ acting on electron will be zero and only electric force is acting on it opposite to direction of velocity so its velocity will decrease. **Ans. (B)**

Sol. 16 Time period of electron revolution in cyclotron is given as

$$T = \frac{2\pi m}{eB} = \frac{1}{v}$$

$$\Rightarrow \qquad B = \frac{2\pi mv}{e}$$

Radius of revolving electrons is given as

$$R = \frac{mv}{eB} = \frac{p}{eB}$$

Momentum $\qquad P = eBR = e\left(\frac{2\pi mv}{e}\right)R$

Kinetic energy of electrons is given as

$$K = \frac{p^2}{2m} = \frac{(2\pi mvR)^2}{2m} = 2\pi^2 mv^2 R^2 \quad \textbf{Ans. (C)}$$

Sol. 17 Radius of moving charge in uniform magnetic field is given as

$$r = \frac{mv}{qB}$$

$$\Rightarrow \qquad r = \frac{\sqrt{2m(KE)}}{qB}$$

For same magnetic field and radius of circle, we use

$$q \propto \sqrt{m(KE)}$$

$$\Rightarrow \qquad \frac{e}{2e} = \sqrt{\frac{(m_p)(1MeV)}{(4m_p)(KE_\alpha)}}$$

$$\Rightarrow \qquad \frac{1}{4} = \frac{1}{4(KE_\alpha)}$$

$$\Rightarrow \qquad KE_\alpha = 1\,\text{MeV} \qquad \qquad \textbf{Ans. (A)}$$

Sol. 18 Initially at rest, no magnetic force acts on proton, so it moves only under the influence of electric force so its initial acceleration can be given as

$$a_0 = \frac{qE}{m}$$

$$\Rightarrow \qquad E = \frac{ma_0}{q}$$

Thus electric field direction is also along its acceleration i.e toward west.

When particle is projected toward north, its acceleration is $3a_0$ toward west out of which a_0 is due to electric force as stated above and remaining $2a_0$ is due to magnetic force, so we use

$$\frac{qvB}{m} = 2ma_0$$

$$\Rightarrow \qquad B = \frac{2ma_0}{qv}$$

For the direction of magnetic force acting along west, direction of magnetic field should be along vertically downward direction.

Ans. (B)

Sol. 19 This question is same as that of Q. 17. Students are advised to refer solution to Q. 17. **Ans. (A)**

Sol. 20 Frequency of revolution of electron in magnetic field is given as

$$f = \frac{qB}{2\pi m}$$

$$\Rightarrow \qquad f = \left(\frac{q}{m}\right) \cdot \frac{B}{2\pi}$$

$$\Rightarrow \qquad f = \frac{1.76 \times 10^{11} \times 3.57 \times 10^{-2}}{2 \times 3.14} = 1\,\text{GHz} \quad \textbf{Ans. (A)}$$

Sol. 21 In uniform magnetic field radius of circular path of moving charge is given as

$$R = \frac{mv}{qB} = \frac{p}{eB}$$

$$\Rightarrow \qquad r_H = \frac{p}{eB} \quad \text{and} \quad r_\alpha = \frac{p}{2eB}$$

$$\Rightarrow \qquad \frac{r_H}{r_\alpha} = \frac{\dfrac{p}{eB}}{\dfrac{p}{2eB}} = \frac{2}{1} \qquad \qquad \textbf{Ans. (A)}$$

Sol. 22 Magnetic force on electron due to magnetic field of current carrying wire is given as

$$F = ev\left(\frac{\mu_0 i}{2\pi r}\right)$$

$$\Rightarrow \qquad F = \frac{1.6 \times 10^{-19} \times 10^5 \times 2 \times 10^{-7} \times 5}{0.2}$$

$$\Rightarrow \qquad F = 8 \times 10^{-20}\,\text{N} \qquad \qquad \textbf{Ans. (D)}$$

Sol. 23 Substituting the vector expressions of magnetic force and velocity in product gives

$$\vec{F} = q(\vec{v} \times \vec{B})$$

$$4i - 20j + 12\,\hat{k} = 1\begin{vmatrix} i & j & \hat{k} \\ 2 & 4 & 6 \\ B & B & B_0 \end{vmatrix}$$

Comparing LHS and RHS coefficient of unit vectors, gives

$$4 = 4B_0 - 6B$$

$$-20 = -2B_0 + 6B$$

$$12 = 2B - 4B$$

Solving above equations, gives $B = -6$ and $B_0 = -8$

$$\Rightarrow \qquad \vec{B} = -6\,\hat{i} - 6\,\hat{j} - 8\,\hat{k} \qquad \qquad \textbf{Ans. (B)}$$

18.3 Magnetic Force on Current

Sol. 1 Torque on the coil with magnetic moment vector perpendicular to the magnetic field direction is given as

$$\tau = MB = (IA)B = 1\frac{\sqrt{3}}{4}\lambda^2 B$$

$$\Rightarrow \qquad l = 2\left(\frac{\tau}{\sqrt{3}BI}\right)^{1/2} \qquad \qquad \textbf{Ans. (C)}$$

Sol. 2 In uniform magnetic field always total force acting on a current carrying closed loop is equal to zero. Thus magnetic force on segment PQ must be equal and opposite to the resultant of all the forces acting on rest three segments, which is given as

$$F_{\text{horizontal}} = (F_3 - F_1)$$

$$F_{\text{vertical}} = F_2$$

Thus resultant of above two forces is given as

$$F = \sqrt{(F_3 - F_1)^2 + F_2^2} \qquad \qquad \textbf{Ans. (D)}$$

Sol. 3 In uniform magnetic field the net force on a current

carrying loop is always zero so force on remaining 3 arms of loop will be opposite to that of the given arm i.e. $-\vec{F}$. **Ans. (C)**

Sol. 4 As the net magnetic force on a current carrying loop in uniform magnetic field is always zero, in this case as arm AB is along the magnetic field direction so it will not experience any force and force on arm AC will be opposite to that of arm BC hence force on arm AC is equal to $-\vec{F}$. **Ans. (B)**

Sol. 5 When a current carrying loop is placed in magnetic field it experiences a torque, given as

$$\vec{\tau} = \vec{M} \times \vec{B} = MB\sin\theta$$

In this state as already discussed in theory that loop can be in equilibrium for two angles between magnetic moment and magnetic field, stated as

$\theta = 0°$ for stable equilibrium

$\theta = 180°$ for unstable equilibrium. **Ans. (D)**

Sol. 6 External torque required to keep the coil stable has to be equal in magnitude of magnetic torque and opposite in direction. Torque on the coil due to magnetic field is given as

$$\vec{\tau} = \vec{M} \times \vec{B}$$

$$\tau = MB\sin\theta = BINA\sin\theta$$

$$\tau = 50 \times .012 \times 2 \times 0.2 \times \sin 60° = 0.20\,\text{Nm} \qquad \textbf{Ans. (C)}$$

Sol. 7 The magnetic force will be exerted only on parallel sides AB and CD and the force on AD and BC will be equal and in opposite direction so that will get cancelled out. The magnetic field at distance r from long wire XY is given as

$$B = \frac{\mu_0 I}{2\pi r}$$

The force on the current in loop along AB and CD due to magnetic field of wire XY is given as

$$F = BiL$$

Thus force on AB is given as

$$F_1 = \frac{\mu_0 I}{\left(2\pi\dfrac{L}{2}\right)}[iL] = \frac{\mu_0 i I}{\pi}$$

Thus force on CD is given as

$$F_2 = \frac{\mu_0 I}{2\pi\left(L + \dfrac{L}{2}\right)}[iL] = \frac{\mu_0 I i}{3\pi}$$

As the current direction on AB and CD are opposite so force acting on these will also be opposite, thus net force is given as

$$F = F_1 - F_2 = \frac{2\mu_0 I i}{3\pi} \qquad \qquad \textbf{Ans. (A)}$$

Sol. 8 Work done in rotating a coil of magnetic moment M in magnetic field B from angle θ_1 to θ_2 against magnetic torque is given as

$$W = MB\,(\cos\theta_1 - \cos\theta_2)$$

When it is rotated by angle $180°$ then, we use

$$W = 2MB$$

$$\Rightarrow \quad W = 2(NIA)B$$

$$\Rightarrow \quad W = 2 \times 250 \times 85 \times 10^{-6}\,(1.25 \times 2.1 \times 10^{-4}) \times 85 \times 10^{-2}$$

$$\Rightarrow \quad W = 9.4\,\mu J \qquad \textbf{Ans. (A)}$$

Sol. 9 Force due to wires C and A on B will be equal in magnitude but perpendicular in direction as shown in figure below. All wires carrying current in same directions so force exerted will be attractive in nature.

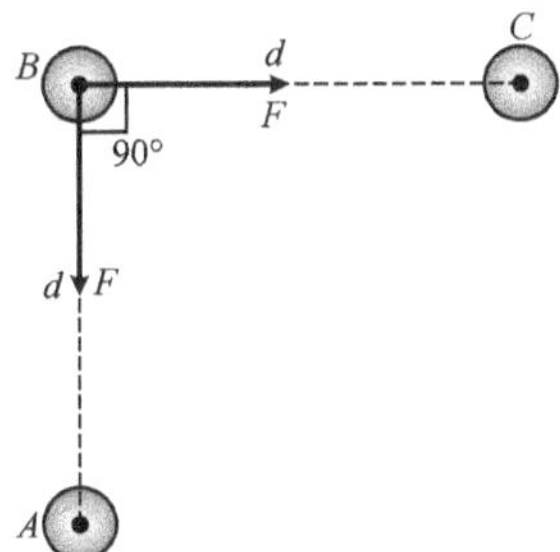

Magnitude of force due to wires A and C on B are given as

$$F_{BC} = F_{BA} = \frac{\mu_0 I^2}{2\pi d}$$

As these forces are perpendicular, resulting force is given as

$$F = \sqrt{2}\,F_{BC} = \sqrt{2}\,\frac{\mu_0}{2\pi}\,\frac{I^2}{d} \qquad \textbf{Ans. (D)}$$

Sol. 10 For equilibrium of rod along the inclined plane upward and downward forces on it must be balanced as shown in *FBD* of rod in figure below.

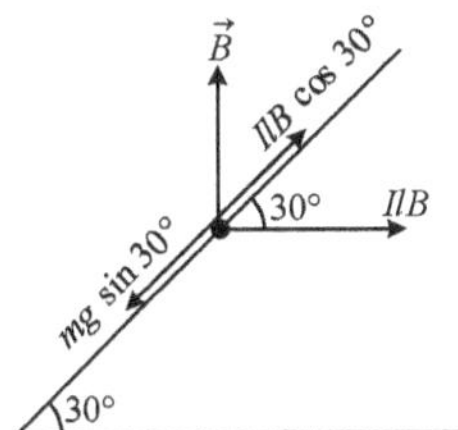

For equilibrium, we use

$$mg\sin 30° = IlB\cos 30°$$

$$\Rightarrow \quad I = \frac{mg}{lB}\tan 30°$$

$$\Rightarrow \quad I = \frac{0.5 \times 9.8}{0.25 \times \sqrt{3}} = 11.32\,\text{A} \qquad \textbf{Ans. (D)}$$

Ch-19 Magnetism and Matter

19.1 Magnetism of a Bar Magnet

Sol. 1 When magnetic poles of the two magnets are on same side, the resulting dipole moment of the two magnets is given by sum of the two, given as

$$M = M_1 + M_2$$

When opposite poles are placed at the same side then the resulting dipole moment is given by the difference of the two, given as

$$M = M_1 - M_2$$

If I_1 and I_2 are the moments of inertia of the two magnets then for their combined oscillatory motion, the moment of inertia of the combination is given as

$$I = I_1 + I_2$$

As specified in question we are given that $M_1 = M$ and $M_2 = 2M$, and for same geometry and shape of magnets (made up of same material) we consider $I_1 = I_2 = I$ (say). The time period of oscillation of a magnet in magnetic field is given as

$$T = 2\pi\sqrt{\frac{I_{Total}}{MB}}$$

For first case it is given as

$$T_1 = 2\pi\sqrt{\frac{I_1 + I_2}{(M_1 + M_2)B}} = 2\pi\sqrt{\frac{2I}{3MB}}$$

For second case it is given as

$$T_2 = 2\pi\sqrt{\frac{I_1 + I_2}{(M_2 - M_1)B}} = 2\pi\sqrt{\frac{2I}{MB}}$$

$$\Rightarrow \quad \frac{T_1}{T_2} = \sqrt{\frac{M}{3M}} = \frac{1}{\sqrt{3}}$$

$$\Rightarrow \quad T_1 < T_2 \qquad \textbf{Ans. (A)}$$

Sol. 2 Time period of small oscillations of a bar magnet in magnetic field is given as

$$T = 2\pi\sqrt{\frac{I}{MB}}$$

Here moment of inertia is directly proportional to mass of magnet, so we use $I \propto$ mass. If mass is quadrupled then moment of inertia will also become four times, so new time period of oscillations is given as

$$T' = 2\pi\sqrt{\frac{4I}{MB}} = 2T \qquad \textbf{Ans. (B)}$$

Sol. 3 We have studied in basic theory that materials without any unpaired electrons are considered diamagnetic. Diamagnetic substances do not have magnetic dipole moments and have negative susceptibilities. Thus diamagnetic materials atoms have zero magnetic dipole moments. Materials having unpaired electrons are called paramagnetic. These substances atoms have magnetic dipole moments and positive susceptibilities and Ferromagnetic materials have domains which are the aligned dipole moment of atoms in same directions in small pockets called domains. Thus atoms of ferromagnetic materials also have dipole moments and very high positive susceptibilities.

Ans. (D)

Sol. 4 Work done in rotating a bar magnet of magnetic moment M *in* magnetic field B from angle θ_1 to θ_2 against magnetic torque is given as

$$W = MB(\cos\theta_1 - \cos\theta_2)$$

$$\Rightarrow \quad W = 2\times 10^4 \times 6 \times 10^{-4}\,(\cos\theta - \cos 60°)$$

$$\Rightarrow \quad W = 12 \times \frac{1}{2} = 6\,\text{J} \qquad\qquad \textbf{Ans. (D)}$$

Sol. 5 In the magnet shown in figure of question the distance between magnetic poles is also equal to r, so length of magnet is given as

$$l = \frac{\pi}{3}\, r$$

$$\Rightarrow \qquad\qquad r = \frac{3l}{\pi}$$

The new magnetic dipole moment of magnet can be given as

$$M' = m(r) = m\left(\frac{3l}{\pi}\right) = \frac{3M}{\pi} \qquad \textbf{Ans. (B)}$$

Sol. 6 Magnetic dipole moment of combination is given by vector sum of both the magnetic dipole moments. For the four cases shown in figure of question this value is calculated as

For option (a), it is given as

$$M_\text{a} = \sqrt{m^2 + m^2 + 2m^2 \cos 90°} = \sqrt{2}\,m$$

For option (b), it is given as

$$M_\text{b} = m - m = 0$$

For option (c), it is given as

$$M_\text{c} = m\sqrt{(1+\cos 30°)2} = m\sqrt{\left(1+\frac{\sqrt{3}}{2}\right)2}$$

$$\Rightarrow \qquad M_\text{c} = m\sqrt{2+\sqrt{3}}$$

For option (d), it is given as

$$M_\text{d} = 2m\cos 30° = m\sqrt{3}$$

Thus highest magnetic moment is for the configuration given in option (c).   **Ans. (C)**

Sol. 7 Work done in rotating the bar magnet in uniform magnetic field in above case mentioned in question is given as

$$W = MB\,(\cos 0° - \cos 60°)$$

$$\Rightarrow \qquad W = MB(1 - 1/2) = \frac{MB}{2}$$

Required torque for this position is given as

$$\tau = MB\sin\theta$$

$$\Rightarrow \qquad \tau = MB\sin 60° = \frac{\sqrt{3}}{2}MB = \sqrt{3}W \quad \textbf{Ans. (B)}$$

Sol. 8 In case (i) as length of wire is $12a$, for an equilateral triangle of side a, there will be 4 turns so magnetic moment of this coil is given as

$$M_1 = \left(\frac{\sqrt{3}}{4}a^2\right)I \times 4 = \sqrt{3}\,Ia^2$$

In case (ii) for a square of side a, there will be 3 turns so magnetic moment of the coil is given as

$$M_2 = a^2 I \times 3 = 3Ia^2 \qquad\qquad \textbf{Ans. (A)}$$

19.2 Earth's Magnetism

Sol. 1 Tangent galvanometer uses the magnetic properties of current and by comparing/balancing it with earth's magnetic field, it is used to measure the current or horizontal earth's magnetic field components hence out of given options, option (B) is most appropriate.   **Ans. (B)**

Sol. 2 Time period of small oscillations of a bar magnet in magnetic field is given as

$$T = 2\pi\sqrt{\frac{I}{MB}}$$

$$\Rightarrow \qquad T \propto \frac{1}{\sqrt{B}}$$

$$\Rightarrow \qquad \frac{T_2}{T_1} = \sqrt{\frac{B_1}{B_2}} = \sqrt{\frac{24}{6}} = 2$$

$$\Rightarrow \qquad T_2 = 2T_1 = 2\times 2 = 4\,\text{s} \qquad \textbf{Ans. (A)}$$

Sol. 3 At geographic north or south poles, magnetic field is in vertical direction and Needle is free to rotate in horizontal plane only so magnetic field at any geomagnetic pole can not exert a torque in horizontal direction to rotate the needle in horizontal plane so needle can stay in any position. **Ans. (B)**

Sol. 4 Work done in rotating a bar magnet of magnetic moment M in magnetic field B from angle θ_1 to θ_2 against magnetic torque is given as

$$W = MB(\cos\theta_1 - \cos\theta_2)$$

$$\Rightarrow \qquad \sqrt{3} = MB(\cos0° - \cos60°)$$

$$\Rightarrow \qquad \sqrt{3} = \frac{MB}{2} \qquad \qquad ...(1)$$

Magnetic torque on needle is given as

$$\tau = MB\sin\theta$$

$$\Rightarrow \qquad \tau = MB\sin60° = \sqrt{3}\,\frac{MB}{2} \qquad \qquad ...(2)$$

$$\Rightarrow \qquad \tau = (\sqrt{3})(\sqrt{3}) = 3 \text{ J} \qquad \qquad \textbf{Ans. (A)}$$

Sol. 5 For dip angle θ at a position we use

$$\tan\theta = \frac{B_V}{B_H} \qquad \qquad ...(1)$$

If at a point on earth surface we consider two vertical planes at an angle α and $90° - \alpha$ from the direction of horizontal component of earth's magnetic field then for the two apparent angles of dip θ_1 and θ_2 in these two planes, we use

$$\tan\theta_1 = \frac{B_V}{B_H \cos\alpha} \qquad \qquad ...(2)$$

and $$\qquad \tan\theta_2 = \frac{B_V}{B_H \sin\alpha} \qquad \qquad ...(3)$$

$$\Rightarrow \qquad \cot^2\theta_1 + \cot^2\theta_2 = \frac{B_H^2}{B_V^2}(\cos^2\alpha + \sin^2\alpha)$$

$$\Rightarrow \qquad \cot^2\theta_1 + \cot^2\theta_2 = \cot^2\theta \qquad \qquad \textbf{Ans. (A)}$$

Sol. 6 At any point on earth's surface angle of dip is the angle between earth's total magnetic field and horizontal. Dip angle is zero at equator positive in northern hemisphere and negative in southern hemisphere. **Ans. (C)**

19.3 Magnetic Properties of Materials

Sol. 1 Susceptibility of Diamagnetism is negative and the atoms of diamagnetic material have zero dipole moment so temperature does not have any impact on diamagnetic materials. **Ans. (A)**

Sol. 2 Magnetic moment of a coil is given as

$$M = niA \qquad \qquad \textbf{Ans. (A)}$$

Sol. 3 Diamagnetic material have negative intensity of magnetisation and have a tendency to feebly repel the magnetic field so it moves from stronger to weaker field. **Ans. (A)**

Sol. 4 According to Curie's law magnetic susceptibility of a material is inversely proportional to the absolute temperature of the material. **Ans. (A)**

Sol. 5 It is observed that above curie temperature ferromagnetic materials behave like paramagnetic materials. **Ans. (A)**

Sol. 6 This question is same as Q. 5. Students are advised to refer solution to Q. 5. **Ans. (D)**

Sol. 7 This question is same as Q. 5. Students are advised to refer solution to Q. 5. **Ans. (C)**

Sol. 8 Diamagnetic material have negative intensity of magnetisation and have a tendency to feebly repel the magnetic field so it moves from stronger to weaker field. **Ans. (B)**

Sol. 9 Magnetic retentivity indicates the magnetism left in the material after the magnetizing-field has been removed or switched off. So for electromagnets retentivity should be low. Susceptibility indicates, upto what maximum value material respond to applied field. So material of electromagnet should have high susceptibility for it to be quickly magnetised. Thus soft iron is a material with low retentivity and high susceptibility. **Ans. (D)**

Sol. 10 Susceptibility of diamagnetic substance is negative. Susceptibility of para and ferromagnetic substance is positive. **Ans. (A)**

Sol. 11 Diamagnetic materials when placed in magnetic field will be feebly repelled. Paramagnetic materials will be feebly attracted when placed in external magnetic field and ferromagnetic materials will be strongly attracted. So A is made up of diamagnetic material, B is made up of paramagnetic material and C is made up of ferromagnetic material. Here D is made up of a non magnetic material. **Ans. (A)**

Sol. 12 Energy of current source produces magnetic field and magnetic force pushes the rod up thus eventually energy to increase the potential energy of the rod comes from the current source. **Ans. (C)**

Sol. 13 Relative permeability of iron rod is given as

$$\mu_r = \chi_m + 1$$

$$\Rightarrow \qquad \mu_r = 599 + 1 = 600$$

Permeability of material is given as

$$\mu = \mu_0\mu_r$$

$$\Rightarrow \qquad \mu = 4\pi \times 10^{-7} \times 600$$

$$\Rightarrow \qquad \mu = 2.4\pi \times 10^{-4} \text{ T m/A} \qquad \qquad \textbf{Ans. (B)}$$

Ch-20 Electromagnetic Induction

20.1 Faraday's Law of EMI

Sol. 1 Induced emf in circuit is given as

$$V = \frac{\Delta\phi}{\Delta t}$$

Current in circuit is given as

$$i = \frac{Q}{\Delta t}$$

$$\Rightarrow \qquad \frac{\Delta\phi}{\Delta t} \times \frac{1}{R} = \frac{Q}{\Delta t}$$

$$\Rightarrow \qquad Q = \frac{\Delta\phi}{R} \qquad \textbf{Ans. (B)}$$

Sol. 2 Work done in moving a test charge Q around the loop with total loop emf V can be given directly as QV. **Ans. (A)**

Sol. 3 In the situation described in question, the magnetic flux linked with the disc is given as

$$\phi = BA \cos\theta$$

$$\Rightarrow \qquad \phi = \frac{1}{\pi} \times 0.04\,\pi \times \cos 60° = 0.02 \text{ Wb } \textbf{Ans. (C)}$$

Sol. 4 Induced emf in the loop is given as

$$e = \frac{d\phi}{dt} = \frac{d}{dt}(B\pi r^2)$$

$$\Rightarrow \qquad e = 2\pi r B \frac{dr}{dt}$$

$$\Rightarrow \qquad e = 2 \times \pi \times 2 \times 10^{-2} \times 4 \times 10^{-2} \times 2 \times 10^{-3}$$

$$\Rightarrow \qquad e = 3.2 \times 10^{-6}\pi\,V = 3.2\,\pi\,\mu V \qquad \textbf{Ans. (B)}$$

Sol. 5 Flux linked with the loop is given as

$$\phi = B\pi r^2$$

Emf induced in the loop is given as

$$e = \frac{d\phi}{dt} = B\pi 2\rho\frac{dr}{dt}$$

$$\Rightarrow \qquad e = 0.025 \times \pi \times 2 \times 10^{-2} \times 1 \times 10^{-3} = \pi\,\mu V \ \textbf{Ans. (C)}$$

Sol. 6 From the given graph, induced *emf* is given in different time intervals is calculated as below

From $t = 0$ to $\dfrac{T}{4}$ *emf* is constant as $-\dfrac{di}{dt} = $ Constant (–ve)

From $t = \dfrac{T}{4}$ to $\dfrac{T}{2}$ *emf* is 0 as $\dfrac{di}{dt} = 0$

From $t = \dfrac{T}{2}$ to $\dfrac{3T}{4}$ *emf* constant as $-\left(-\dfrac{di}{dt}\right) = $ Constant (+ve)

From $t = \dfrac{3T}{4}$ to T *emf* is 0 as $\dfrac{di}{dt} = 0$ **Ans. (A)**

Sol. 7 Induced *emf* in coil is given as

$$\varepsilon = -\frac{d\phi}{dt} = -(100t)$$

Induced current i at $t = 2$ s can be given as

$$i = \left|\frac{\varepsilon}{R}\right| = +\frac{100 \times 2}{400} = +0.5\,A \qquad \textbf{Ans. (A)}$$

Sol. 8 Induced current in coil can be given as

$$I = \left|\frac{1}{R}\frac{d\phi}{dt}\right|$$

Induced *emf* in coil is given as

$$\varepsilon = -\frac{\Delta\phi}{Dt}$$

$$\Rightarrow \qquad |d\phi| = |IRdt|$$

$$\Rightarrow \qquad d\phi = (\text{Area of triangle}) \times R$$

$$\Rightarrow \qquad d\phi = \left(\frac{1}{2} \times 4 \times 0.1\right) \times 10 = 2 \text{ Wb} \qquad \textbf{Ans. (A)}$$

Sol. 9 Due to rotation of a wire loop in magnetic field, the *emf* induced in loop is given as

$$e = N\omega AB \sin\omega t$$

This is a sinusoidal *emf* so direction of emf changed two times. **Ans. (B)**

Sol. 10 Motional *emf* induced in the semicircular ring will be same which is induced in the straight conductor of length equal to PR and by right hand palm rule or Fleming's left hand rule we can check that end R is at higher potential. The motional *emf* in PR is given as

$$\varepsilon = VBl_{eq} = VB(2r) \qquad \textbf{Ans. (D)}$$

Sol. 11 When e^- is moving toward the loop, magnetic flux increases through the loop and when going away same magnetic flux decreases so induced current while approaching and receding away will be opposite to each other. **Ans. (D)**

Sol. 12 Figure below shows the two loops as described in question.

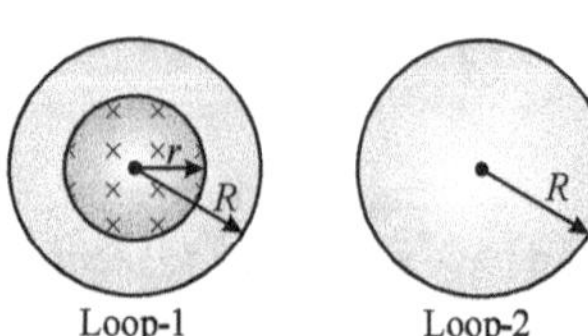

Induced *emf* in loop (1) is given as

$$e = -\frac{d\phi}{dt} = -\frac{AdB}{dt} = \pi r^2 \frac{dB}{dt}$$

As Loop (2) is not in magnetic field so no flux change thus induced *emf* in it will be zero.   **Ans. (D)**

Sol. 13 Total charge flowing through the coil can be directly given as

$$\Delta Q = \frac{N(\Delta\phi)}{R} = \frac{(NBA)}{R} = \frac{\mu_0 ni\pi r^2}{R}$$

$$\Rightarrow \qquad \Delta Q = \frac{4\pi \times 10^{-7} \times 100 \times 4 \times \pi \times (0.01)^2}{10\pi^2} = 32\ \mu C$$

Ans. (C)

Sol. 14 Change in magnetic flux due to rotation of coil is given as

$$\Delta\phi = NBA \cos 90^\circ - BA \cos 0^\circ = -NBA$$

$$\Rightarrow \qquad \Delta\phi = -800 \times 5 \times 10^{-5} \times 0.05 = -2 \times 10^{-3}\ Wb$$

Induced *emf* in the coil can be given as

$$e = -\frac{\Delta\phi}{\Delta t} = \frac{-(-)2 \times 10^{-3}\ Wb}{0.1 s} = 0.02\ V \qquad \textbf{Ans. (D)}$$

Sol. 15 Figure below shows the square loop mentioned in question with its area vector in normal direction

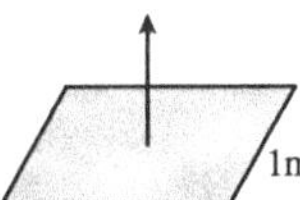

As angle between $\vec{B}$ & $\vec{A}$ is zero, flux is given as

$$\phi = B.A.\cos 0$$

$$\Rightarrow \qquad \phi = 0.5 \times (1) \times 1$$

$$\Rightarrow \qquad \phi = 0.5\ Wb \qquad\qquad \textbf{Ans. (A)}$$

Sol. 16 The maximum induced current in coil is given as

$$i_{max} = \frac{E_{max}}{R} = \frac{NBA\omega}{R}$$

$$\Rightarrow \qquad i_{max} = \frac{1000 \times 2 \times 10^{-5} \times \pi (10^2) \times 2}{12.56}$$

$$\Rightarrow \qquad i_{max} = 1\ A \qquad\qquad \textbf{Ans. (B)}$$

20.2 Self & Mutual Induction

Sol. 1 For the given coil, potential across coil is given as

$$|e| = L\frac{dI}{dt}$$

Emf is zero when $\frac{dI}{dt} = 0$

$$\Rightarrow \qquad \frac{dI}{dt} = 2te^{-t} - t^2 e^{-t} = 0$$

$$\Rightarrow \qquad 2te^{-t} = t^2 e^{-t}$$

$$\Rightarrow \qquad te^{-t}(t-2) = 0$$

Thus $t \neq \infty$ and $t \neq 0$, so we have

$$t = 2\ s \qquad\qquad \textbf{Ans. (A)}$$

Sol. 2 Time constant of LR circuit is $\tau = L/R$

$$\Rightarrow \qquad \tau = \frac{40}{8} = 5\ s \qquad\qquad \textbf{Ans. (A)}$$

Sol. 3 The core of the transformer is laminated to reduce the eddy currents and prevent the copper losses of transformer.

Ans. (A)

Sol. 4 For complete flux linkage in coils the coupling factor of mutual induction will be $K = 1$. Thus mutual induction is given as

$$M = K\sqrt{L_1 L_2}$$

$$\Rightarrow \qquad M = \sqrt{16} = 4\ mH \qquad\qquad \textbf{Ans. (C)}$$

Sol. 5 For a transformer coil, from transformer equation, we have

$$\frac{V_s}{V_p} = \frac{N_s}{N_p}$$

Voltage in primary coil is given as

$$V_p = \frac{d\phi}{dt} = \frac{d}{dt}(\phi_0 + 4t) = 4\ V$$

Thus from transformer equation, secondary coil voltage is given as

$$V_s = \frac{1500}{50} \times 4 = 120\ V \qquad\qquad \textbf{Ans. (A)}$$

Sol. 6 Efficiency of the transformer is given as

$$\eta = \frac{P_{output}}{P_{input}} \times 100 = \frac{100}{220 \times 0.5} \times 100$$

$$\Rightarrow \qquad \eta = 90.9\% \qquad\qquad \textbf{Ans. (B)}$$

Sol. 7 Total Flux linkage with a coil is given by product of Flux through each turn and total number of turns

$$\phi = 500 \times 4 \times 10^{-3} = 2\ Wb$$

As $\qquad \phi = Li$

$$\Rightarrow \qquad L = \frac{\phi}{i} = \frac{2}{2} = 1\ H \qquad\qquad \textbf{Ans. (A)}$$

Sol. 8 Out of the four loops mentioned in question, only in case of square and rectangular loops if their two edges are parallel to the boundary of the magnetic field then while coming out of magnetic field the motional emf induced in these two loops will remain constant due to one of the moving edge inside the magnetic field but when the circular and elliptical loops come out from the field, motional emf continuously changes. So emf induced in circular and elliptical loops does not remain constant while coming out of magnetic field. **Ans. (C)**

Sol. 9 Efficiency of transformer is given as

$$\eta = \frac{P_{\text{out}}}{P_{\text{in}}} = \frac{E_2 I_2}{E_1 I_1}$$

$$\Rightarrow \qquad I_1 = \frac{E_2 I_2}{\eta E_1}$$

$$\Rightarrow \qquad I_1 = \frac{440 \times 2}{220} \times \frac{100}{80} = 5\,\text{A} \qquad \textbf{Ans. (A)}$$

Sol. 10 Potential across inductance

$$V = -L\frac{di}{dt}$$

For the variation curve of current in terms of time which is linear with time so for this slope di/dt will be constant and we can also see that here di/dt is positive for time $t = 0$ to $T/2$ and for time $t = T/2$ to T it is negative hence option (D) is correct. **Ans. (D)**

Sol. 11 At 90% efficiency, power output of the transformer is given as

$$P_{\text{out}} = 3\,\text{kW} \times \frac{90}{100} = 2.7\,\text{kW}$$

As current in secondary coil is $I_S = 6$ A, voltage across it is given as

$$V_S = \frac{2.7\,\text{kW}}{6\text{A}} = 450\,\text{V}$$

Current in primary coil is given as

$$I_P = \frac{3\text{kW}}{200\text{V}} = 15\,\text{A} \qquad \textbf{Ans. (B)}$$

Sol. 12 Self inductance of solenoid is given as

$$L = \frac{\phi N}{I} = \frac{4 \times 10^{-3} \times 1000}{4} = 1\,\text{H} \qquad \textbf{Ans. (D)}$$

Sol. 13 Just after closing the switch all inductors in circuit behaves as open circuit so no current flows through the branches in which inductors are connected, thus equivalent circuit just after closing the switch is down as shown in figure below

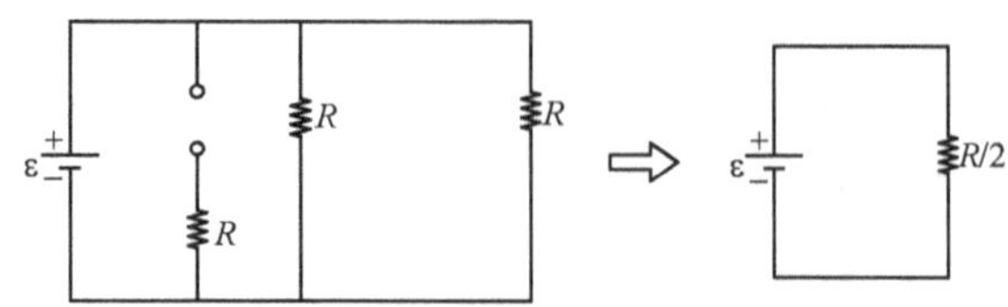

Thus current through battery is given as

$$i = \frac{\varepsilon}{R/2} = \frac{18}{4.5} = 4\,\text{A}$$

This result does not match with any of the given option in question. **Ans. (None)**

Sol. 14 Energy stored in inductor carrying a current I is given as

$$U = \frac{1}{2}LI^2$$

$$\Rightarrow \qquad 25 \times 10^{-3} = \frac{1}{2} \times L \times (60 \times 10^{-3})^2$$

$$\Rightarrow \qquad L = \frac{25 \times 2 \times 10^6 \times 10^{-3}}{3600} = \frac{500}{36} = 13.89\,\text{H}$$

Ans. (D)

Sol. 15 Electric heater is based on Joule heating effect and it does not involve Eddy currents. **Ans. (D)**

Sol. 16 Given current amplitude is $I_0 = 10\sqrt{2}\,$A, thus RMS value of current is given as

$$I_{\text{RMS}} = \frac{I_0}{\sqrt{2}} = 10\,\text{A}$$

As the RMS values of potential differences across the three components are shown in circuit, the source EMF is calculated by phasor sum of these values, given as

$$V_{\text{RMS}} = \sqrt{V_R^2 + (V_L - V_C)^2}$$

$$\Rightarrow \qquad V_{\text{RMS}} = \sqrt{(40)^2 + (40-10)^2} = 50\,\text{V}$$

Circuit impedance can now be given as

$$Z = \frac{V_{\text{RMS}}}{I_{\text{RMS}}} = \frac{50V}{10V} = 5\,\Omega \qquad \textbf{Ans. (D)}$$

Sol. 17 If current in primary circuit is i_p then for the total power 44 W in both coils (as no power losses), we use

$$V_p \times i_p = P$$

$$220 \times i_p = 44$$

$$\Rightarrow \qquad i_p = \frac{44}{220} = \frac{1}{5} = 0.2\ \text{A} \qquad \textbf{Ans. (A)}$$

Sol. 18 The magnetic induction due to large coil at the center (at the location of smaller coil) is given as

$$B_1 = \frac{\mu_0 I}{2R_1}$$

The magnetic flux linked due to above magnetic induction from the area of smaller coil is given as

$$\phi_2 = B_1 \times \pi R_2^2 = \frac{\mu_0 I}{2R_1} \times \pi R_2^2$$

The mutual induction between the coils can be given as

$$M = \frac{\phi_2}{I_1} = \frac{B_1 A_2}{I_1} = \frac{\left(\dfrac{\mu_0 I_1}{2R_1}\right)(\pi R_2^2)}{I_1}$$

$$\Rightarrow \qquad M = \frac{\mu_0 \pi R_2^2}{2R_1}$$

$$\Rightarrow \qquad M \propto \frac{R_2^2}{R_1} \qquad \textbf{Ans. (D)}$$

Ch-21 Alternating Current

21.1 AC emf, Current, Impedance and Power

Sol. 1 In an AC circuit capacitive reactance of a capacitor is given as

$$X_C = \frac{1}{C\omega}$$

Now capacitance and frequency are doubled, so we use

$$C' = 2C;\ \omega' = 2\omega$$

Thus new capacitive reactance becomes

$$X' = \frac{1}{4C\omega} = \frac{X}{4} \qquad \textbf{Ans. (C)}$$

Sol. 2 Average power in AC circuit is given as

$$P_{av.} = E_{\text{rms}} \cdot I_{\text{rms}} \cdot \cos\phi$$

$$\Rightarrow \qquad P_{av.} = \frac{E_0}{\sqrt{2}} \cdot \frac{I_0}{\sqrt{2}} \cdot \cos\phi = \frac{E_0 I_0}{2}\cos\phi \qquad \textbf{Ans. (A)}$$

Sol. 3 In the given RL circuit phase difference is given as

$$\phi = \tan^{-1}\left(\frac{\omega L}{R}\right) = \tan^{-1}\left(\frac{3}{3}\right) = 45^\circ = \frac{\pi}{4} \qquad \textbf{Ans. (B)}$$

Sol. 4 In the given circuit, the rms value of current is given as

$$I_{\text{rms}} = \frac{E_{\text{rms}}}{Z}$$

$$\Rightarrow \qquad I_{\text{rms}} = \frac{\left(\dfrac{E_0}{\sqrt{2}}\right)}{X_C} = \frac{\left(\dfrac{200\sqrt{2}}{\sqrt{2}}\right)}{\dfrac{1}{100\times 1\times 10^{-6}}}$$

$$\Rightarrow \qquad I_{\text{rms}} = 200 \times 100 \times 10^{-6} = 2 \times 10^{-2}\,\text{A} = 20\ \text{mA} \qquad \textbf{Ans. (D)}$$

Sol. 5 Average power in an AC circuit is given as

$$P = V_{\text{rms}}\, I_{\text{rms}}\, \cos\phi$$

$$\Rightarrow \qquad P = \left(\frac{1}{2}\right)\left(\frac{1}{2}\right)\cos\left(\frac{\pi}{3}\right)$$

$$\Rightarrow \qquad P = \frac{1}{8} \qquad \textbf{Ans. (C)}$$

Sol. 6 Figure below shows the situation described in the question.

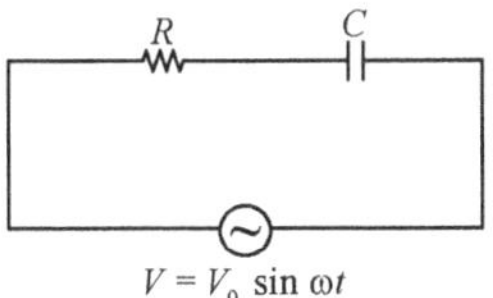

Capacitive reactance is given as

$$X_C = \frac{1}{2\pi f C}$$

Current in circuit can be given as

$$I = \frac{V}{Z} = \frac{V}{\sqrt{R^2 + \left(\dfrac{1}{2\pi f C}\right)^2}}$$

$$\Rightarrow \qquad I = \frac{2\pi f C}{\sqrt{4\pi^2 f^2 C^2 R^2 + 1}} \times V$$

Across capacitor, potential difference is given as

$$V_C = I \times X_C$$

$$\Rightarrow \qquad V_C = \frac{2\pi f C \times V}{\sqrt{4\pi^2 f^2 C^2 R^2 + 1}} \times \frac{1}{2\pi f C}$$

$$\Rightarrow \qquad V_C = \frac{V}{\sqrt{4\pi^2 f^2 C^2 R^2 + 1}}$$

When mica is introduced between plates of capacitor, its capacitance will increase, so voltage across capacitor decreases.

$$\textbf{Ans. (C)}$$

Sol. 7 For an AC voltage applied across a pure capacitor, current always leads voltage by phase $\pi/2$ and at this phase difference power factor becomes zero and no average power is consumed by the voltage source in one complete cycle or over a large period of time.   **Ans. (B)**

Sol. 8 In a series RC circuit as described in question, the circuit impedance is given as

$$Z = \sqrt{(100)^2 + (100)^2} = 100\sqrt{2}\,\Omega$$

Current in circuit is given as

$$I = \frac{E}{Z} = \frac{220}{100\sqrt{2}} = \frac{2.2}{\sqrt{2}}\,A$$

Peak value of current in circuit is given as

$$I_0 = \frac{2.2}{\sqrt{2}} \times \sqrt{2} = 2.2\,A \qquad \textbf{Ans. (A)}$$

Sol. 9 The *rms* value of current in the given circuit with only capacitor is given as

$$I = \frac{V}{X_C} = \frac{V}{1/C\omega} = VC\omega$$

$$\Rightarrow \qquad I = 200 \times 40 \times 10^{-6} \times 2\pi \times 50 = 2.5\,A \qquad \textbf{Ans. (D)}$$

Sol. 10 Peak voltage is $\sqrt{2}$ times rms voltages in ac.

$$\textbf{Ans. (B)}$$

21.2 RLC Circuit and Resonance

Sol. 1 The impedance of a series LCR circuit is given as

$$Z = \sqrt{R^2 + (X_L - X_C)^2}$$

Here $X_L = \omega L$ and $X_C = \dfrac{1}{\omega C}$ and ω is the angular frequency.

At resonance, $X_L = X_C$ and impedance becomes purely resistive, given as

$$Z = R$$

$$\Rightarrow \qquad V_R = V$$

At resonance rms current in circuit is given as

$$\Rightarrow \qquad I = \frac{V_R}{R} = \frac{V}{R}$$

At resonance power loss is given as

$$P_L = I^2 R = V^2/R \qquad \textbf{Ans. (C)}$$

Sol. 2 It is given that current leads the voltage by 45° that means the phase angle of circuit impedance is $-45°$ as shown in phasor diagram below so we use

$$X_C - X_L = R$$

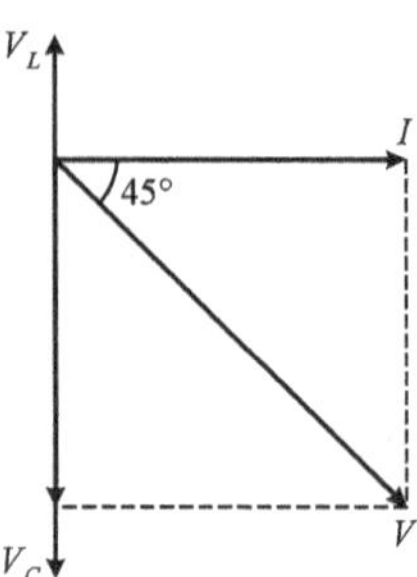

$$\Rightarrow \qquad \frac{1}{2\pi fC} = (R + 2\pi fL)$$

$$\Rightarrow \qquad C = \frac{1}{2\pi f(2\pi fL + R)} \qquad \textbf{Ans. (B)}$$

Sol. 3 Power factor of AC circuit is given as

$$\cos\phi = \frac{R}{|Z|} = \frac{8}{\sqrt{8^2 + (31-25)^2}} = \frac{8}{\sqrt{8^2 + 6^2}} = \frac{8}{10} = 0.8$$

$$\textbf{Ans. (C)}$$

Sol. 4 In LCR series circuit current becomes maximum at resonance when source frequency becomes

$$\omega = \frac{1}{\sqrt{LC}}$$

$$\Rightarrow \qquad 1000 = \frac{1}{\sqrt{L(10\times 10^{-6})}}$$

$$\Rightarrow \qquad L = 100\,\text{mH} \qquad \textbf{Ans. (D)}$$

Sol. 5 In AC Circuit power dissipated in LCR circuit is given as

$$P_{av} = E_{rms} \cdot I_{rms} \cos\phi$$

$$\Rightarrow \qquad P_{av} = \varepsilon \cdot \frac{\varepsilon}{z} \cdot \frac{R}{z} = \frac{\varepsilon^2 R}{z^2}$$

$$\Rightarrow \qquad P_{av} = \frac{\varepsilon^2 R}{R^2 + \left(\omega L - \dfrac{1}{\omega C}\right)^2} \qquad \textbf{Ans. (B)}$$

Sol. 6 For the above given LCR series circuit, voltage applied can be written as

$$V = \sqrt{V_R^2 + (V_L - V_C)^2}$$

Here we have $V_L = V_C = 300$ V, so we can use

$$X_L = X_C$$

Thus given circuit is at resonance so we use

$$V_3 = V_R = 220\text{V}$$

$$\Rightarrow \qquad I = \frac{V_3}{Z} = \frac{220}{R} \qquad \{\because\ X_L = X_C\}$$

$$\Rightarrow \qquad I = \frac{220}{100} = 2.2\,A \qquad \textbf{Ans. (C)}$$

Sol. 7 According to given situation the inductive reactant and capacitive reactance of the circuit are equal so overall impedance of the circuit will be purely resistive hence power factor of the circuit is unity. **Ans. (C)**

Sol. 8 Situation described in question is shown in figure below

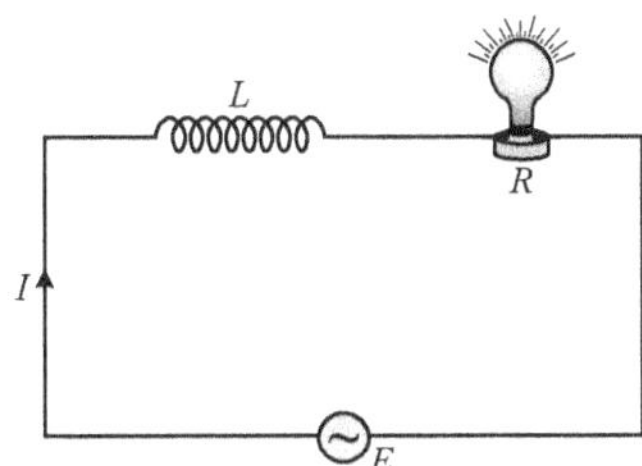

Current in above circuit is given as

$$I = \frac{E}{\sqrt{\omega^2 L^2 + R^2}}$$

The self inductance of the coil is given as

$$L = \frac{\mu_0 \mu_r N^2 A}{l}$$

$$L \propto \mu_r$$

Thus L is increased when iron rod inserted due to which current decreases and hence brightness of bulb decreases. **Ans. (D)**

Sol. 9 Average power loss in AC circuit is given as

$$P_{av} = I_v^2 R = \left(\frac{E_v}{Z}\right)^2 R$$

$$\Rightarrow \quad P_{av} = \left(\frac{E_v}{\sqrt{R^2 + \left(\omega L - \frac{1}{\omega C}\right)^2}}\right)^2 R$$

$$\Rightarrow \quad P_{av} = \left(\frac{10/\sqrt{2}}{\sqrt{40^2 + \left(340 \times 20 \times 10^{-3} - \frac{1}{340 \times 50 \times 10^{-6}}\right)}}\right)^2 \times 40$$

$$\Rightarrow \quad P_{av} = \frac{100}{2} \times 40 \, \frac{1}{1600 + [6.8 - 58.8]^2}$$

$$\Rightarrow \quad P_{av} = \frac{2000}{1600 + 2704} = 0.46W = 051W \qquad \textbf{Ans. (A)}$$

Sol. 10 For good tuning of a circuit in communication systems, quality factor of LCR circuit should be high, given as

$$Q = \frac{1}{R}\sqrt{\frac{L}{C}}$$

Out of the given options below values of R, L and C, it results in highest value of Q-factor of circuit.

$$R = 15 \, \Omega, L = 3.5 \text{ H}, C = 30 \, \mu F \qquad \textbf{Ans. (C)}$$

Sol. 11 For the given circuit, power factor can be given as

$$\cos \phi = \frac{R}{Z} = \frac{V_R}{V_{net}}$$

$$\Rightarrow \quad \cos\phi = \frac{V_R}{V_{net}} = \frac{V_R}{\sqrt{(V_L - V_C)^2 + V_R^2}}$$

$$\Rightarrow \quad \cos\phi = \frac{80}{\sqrt{(100 - 40)^2 + 80^2}} = \frac{80}{100} = 0.8 \qquad \textbf{Ans. (C)}$$

Sol. 12 The circuit impedance is given as

$$Z = \sqrt{R^2 + \left(\omega L - \frac{1}{\omega C}\right)^2} = 56 \, \Omega$$

Power loss in a series LCR circuit across AC source is given as

$$P_{av} = \left(\frac{V_{RMS}}{Z}\right)^2 R$$

$$\Rightarrow \quad P_{av} = \left(\frac{10}{(\sqrt{2})56}\right)^2 \times 50 = 0.79 \text{ W} \qquad \textbf{Ans. (C)}$$

Sol. 13 This question is same as Q. 7. Students are advised to see the solution of Q. 7. **Ans. (D)**

Sol. 14 Resonance frequency of the series LCR circuit is given as

$$\omega_0 = \frac{1}{\sqrt{LC}} = \frac{1}{\sqrt{5 \times 80 \times 10^{-6}}} = 50 \text{ rad/sec}$$

Quality factor of a series LCR circuit is given as

$$Q = \frac{\omega}{\Delta\omega} = \frac{\omega L}{R} \quad \text{(where } \Delta\omega \text{ is the bandwidth)}$$

$$\Rightarrow \Delta\omega = R/L = \frac{50}{4} = 8 \text{ rad/sec}$$

Thus half power frequencies on the two sides of resonant frequency are given as

$$\omega_{min} = \omega_0 - \frac{\Delta\omega}{2} = 46 \text{ rad/sec}$$

$$\omega_{max} = \omega_0 - \frac{\Delta\omega}{2} = 54 \text{ rad/sec} \qquad \textbf{Ans. (C)}$$

Sol. 15 Angular frequency of the source is given as

$$\omega = 100 \text{ rad/s}$$

$$\Rightarrow \qquad v = \frac{\omega}{2\pi} = \frac{100}{2\pi} = \frac{50}{\pi}\,\text{Hz}$$

Resonant frequency of the given circuit is calculated as

$$v_0 = \frac{1}{2\pi\sqrt{LC}} = \frac{1}{2\pi}\sqrt{\frac{1}{10\times10\times10^{-6}}}$$

$$\Rightarrow \qquad v_0 = \frac{50}{\pi}\,\text{Hz} \qquad\qquad \textbf{Ans. (A)}$$

Ch-22 Electromagnetic Waves

22.1 Electromagnetic Spectrum

Sol. 1 The ozone layer absorbs ultraviolet rays coming from sun and protects the environment under it. **Ans. (A)**

Sol. 2 When the electromagnetic radiations coming from Sun enters earth's atmosphere, some of these are absorbed by atmosphere and rest enters and reaches the earth. The range of wavelength of radiation which reaches earth in infrared region gets trapped due to greenhouse gases and due to it earth's surface temperature increases. Because other radiation emitted from the earth being of longer wavelength can escape through atmospheric layers containing greenhouse gases. **Ans. (A)**

Sol. 3 Radiation emitted by human body mostly lies in Infrared region. **Ans. (A)**

Sol. 4 β rays are fast moving electrons not electromagnetic wave. **Ans. (C)**

Sol. 5 By microwaves water molecule oscillates at the frequency of microwaves and large heat is developed due to such eddy currents internally in the food itself. **Ans. (A)**

Sol. 6 The wavelength of given electromagnetic wave can be given as

$$\lambda = \frac{12400}{E(\text{in }eV)}\,\text{Å}$$

$$\Rightarrow \qquad \lambda = \frac{12400}{15\times10^3}\,\text{Å} = .826\,\text{Å}$$

$\lambda < 0.01$ Å is the part of X-ray spectrum. **Ans. (B)**

Sol. 7 According to Maxwell's theory, accelerated charge particle produces electromagnetic wave. **Ans. (D)**

Sol. 8 The wavelength of the given electromagnetic waves in List-I are approximately matched with the electromagnetic spectrum as

(a) Radio wave (ii) $\approx 10^2$ m (ii)

(b) Microwave $\approx$ (iii) 10^{-2} m (iii)

(c) Infrared radiations $\approx$ (iv) 10^{-4} m (iv)

(d) X-ray (i) $\approx$ Å $= 10^{-10}$ m (i)

(a) $\rightarrow$ (ii), (b) $\rightarrow$ (iii), (c) $\rightarrow$ (iv), (d) $\rightarrow$ (i) **Ans. (C)**

22.2 $\vec{E}, \vec{B}$ and $\vec{C}$ of Electromagnetic Wave

Sol. 1 The electromagnetic wave propagates in direction along Poynting vector which is proportional to $\vec{E}\times\vec{B}$. **Ans. (B)**

Sol. 2 Variation in magnetic field causes induction of electric field and vice versa in normal direction to the source field. In electromagnetic waves, $\vec{E} \perp \vec{B}$ and both $\vec{E}$ and $\vec{B}$ are in the same phase. **Ans. (C)**

Sol. 3 Speed of electromagnetic waves is given as

$$C = \frac{1}{\sqrt{\mu_0\varepsilon_0}} \qquad\qquad \textbf{Ans. (A)}$$

Sol. 4 In the expression of y-component of electric field, the coefficient of x is negative thus it is moving along positive x-axis and by comparing it with general equation of wave given as $y = A\cos(\omega t - kx)$, we get

$$\omega = 2\pi \times 10^6\,\text{rad/s}$$

$$\Rightarrow \qquad f = \frac{\omega}{2\pi} = 10^6\,\text{Hz}$$

and $\qquad k = \pi \times 10^{-2}\,\text{m}^{-1}$

$$\Rightarrow \qquad \lambda = \frac{2\pi}{k} = \frac{2\pi}{\pi\times10^{-2}} = 200\,\text{m} \qquad \textbf{Ans. (D)}$$

Sol. 5 As the direction of propagation of electromagnetic wave is along $\vec{E}\times\vec{B}$ vector, which is along $+z$ direction. Thus $\vec{E}$ is along $+x$-axis $(\hat{i})$ and $\vec{B}$ along $+y$-axis $(+\hat{j})$. **Ans. (A)**

Sol. 6 From the given equation, comparing it with standard equation of wave, we have

$$\omega = 6 \times 10^8\,\text{rad/s}$$

$$\Rightarrow \qquad k = \frac{\omega}{v} = \frac{6\times10^8}{3\times10^8} = 2\,\text{m}^{-1} \qquad \textbf{Ans. (A)}$$

Sol. 7 Ratio of electric field to magnetic field gives speed of light

$$c = \frac{E_0}{B_0}$$

$$\Rightarrow \qquad \frac{B_0}{E_0} = \frac{1}{c} \qquad\qquad \textbf{Ans. (A)}$$

Sol. 8 For an electromagnetic wave ratio of electric and magnetic field is given as

$$\frac{E_{rms}}{B_{rms}} = c$$

$$\Rightarrow \quad B_{rms} = \frac{6}{3 \times 10^8} = 2 \times 10^{-8}\,T$$

The *rms* value of magnetic field is related to peak value of magnetic field as

$$\Rightarrow \quad B_{rms} = \frac{B_0}{\sqrt{2}}$$

$$\Rightarrow \quad B_0 = \sqrt{2} \times B_{rms}$$

$$\Rightarrow \quad B_0 = \sqrt{2} \times 2 \times 10^{-8} = 2.83 \times 10^{-8}\,T \quad \textbf{Ans. (B)}$$

Sol. 9 The direction of propagation of electromagnetic wave (direction of wave velocity) is along the vector $\vec{E} \times \vec{B}$ and it is given along positive x-direction. As electric field is given along y-direction so by the cross product of electric and magnetic field, the direction of magnetic field must be along $+z$-axis.

$$\textbf{Ans. (B)}$$

Sol. 10 In an electromagnetic wave, electric and magnetic field have same energy density in space thus have same energy contribution in total intensity of the electromagnetic wave.

$$\textbf{Ans. (C)}$$

Sol. 11 Instantaneous charge on capacitor plates is given as

$$q = CV$$

Displacement current between plates of capacitor is given as

$$\Rightarrow \quad \frac{dq}{dt} = \frac{CdV}{dt}$$

$$\Rightarrow \quad I_d = C\,(V_0\omega \cos \omega t) = V_0 \omega C \cos \omega t \quad \textbf{Ans. (A)}$$

Sol. 12 Direction of electromagnetic wave is along the vector $\vec{E} \times \vec{B}$ which should be along $\hat{i}$ as specified so we can check for the given options

Option (A) $\vec{E} \times \vec{B} = \vec{0} \Rightarrow \vec{E}$ is parallel to $\vec{B}$

Option (B) $\vec{E} \times \vec{B} = 2\hat{i} \Rightarrow$ Wave is travelling along $\hat{i}$

Option (C) $\vec{E} \times \vec{B} = \vec{0} \Rightarrow \vec{E}$ is opposite to $\vec{B}$

Option (D) $\vec{E} \times \vec{B} = \vec{0} \Rightarrow \vec{E}$ is parallel to $\vec{B}$ **Ans. (B)**

Sol. 13 Refractive index of medium is given as

$$n = \sqrt{\epsilon_r\,\mu_r}$$

$$n = \frac{c}{v}$$

$$\Rightarrow \quad v = \frac{c}{n}$$

$$\Rightarrow \quad v = \left(\frac{c}{\sqrt{\epsilon_r\,\mu_r}} \right) \qquad \textbf{Ans. (C)}$$

Ch-23 Ray Optics and Optical Instruments

23.1 Geometrical Optics I - Reflection of Light

Sol. 1 Figure below shows the situation described in the question. Here AB is the rod mentioned in question and $A'B'$ is its image.

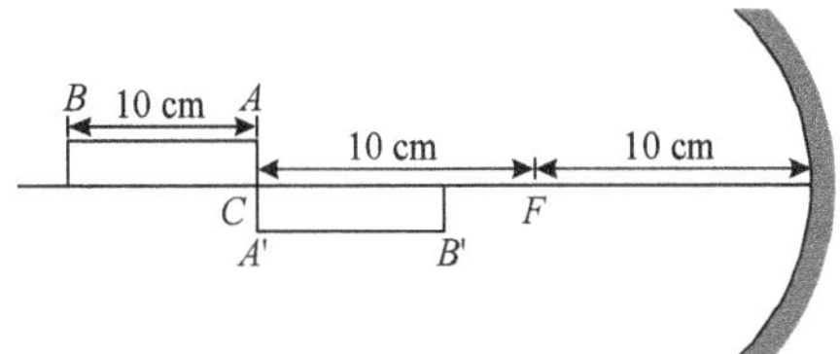

As end A is located at focal point of mirror so its image A' will be produced at the same point. Image position of the end B is calculated by mirror formula as given below.

$$\frac{1}{v_B} + \frac{1}{-30} = \frac{1}{-10}$$

$$\Rightarrow \quad \frac{1}{v_B} = \frac{1}{-15}$$

$$\Rightarrow \quad v_B = -15\,cm$$

Length of the image is given as

$$L_{A'B'} = |v_A| - |v_B| = 20 - 15 = 5\,cm \qquad \textbf{Ans. (C)}$$

Sol. 2 Magnification for a spherical mirror is given as

$$m = \frac{-v}{u} = \frac{h_I}{h_0} = \frac{\text{height of image}}{\text{height of object}}$$

Here if m is negative, image is real and if m is positive, image in virtual and for $|m| > 1$, image is enlarged, $|m| = 1$, image is equal in size and for $|m| < 1$, image is smaller then object.   **Ans. (A)**

Sol. 3 On rotation of mirror by angle θ, the reflected ray rotates by and angle 2θ, as shown in figure below.

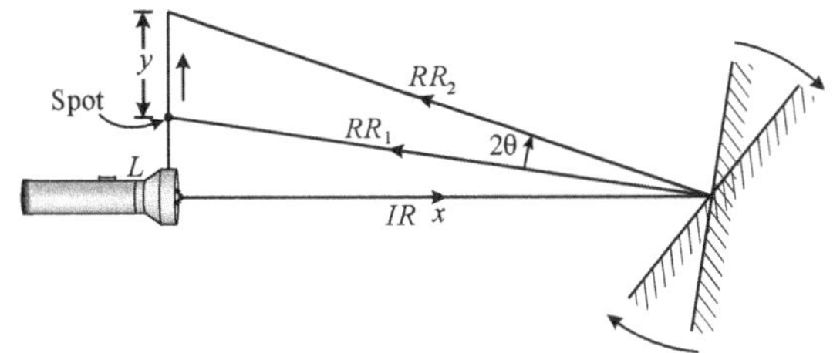

For small angle, from above figure, we use

$$\frac{y}{x} = 2\theta$$

$$\Rightarrow \quad \theta = \frac{y}{2x} \qquad \textbf{Ans. (A)}$$

Sol. 4 Image position can be obtained by mirror formula as

$$\frac{1}{f} = \frac{1}{v_1} + \frac{1}{u}$$

$$\Rightarrow \quad -\frac{1}{15} = \frac{1}{v_1} - \frac{1}{40}$$

$$\Rightarrow \quad \frac{1}{v_1} = \frac{1}{-15} + \frac{1}{40}$$

$$\Rightarrow \quad v_1 = -24\,\text{cm}$$

After object is displaced by 20 cm toward mirror, new position of image can be obtained by mirror formula again with object distance equal to 20 cm from the mirror, given as

$$\frac{1}{f} = \frac{1}{v_2} + \frac{1}{u_2}$$

$$\Rightarrow \quad \frac{1}{-15} = \frac{1}{v_2} - \frac{1}{20}$$

$$\Rightarrow \quad \frac{1}{v_2} = \frac{1}{20} - \frac{1}{15}$$

$$\Rightarrow \quad v_2 = -60\,\text{cm}$$

Thus, image gets shifted away from mirror by a distance

$$\Delta v = 60 - 24 = 36\,\text{cm} \qquad \textbf{Ans. (B)}$$

23.2 Geometrical Optics II - Refraction of Light

Sol. 1 In refraction of light frequency remains same. **Ans. (B)**

Sol. 2 In optical fibres light propagates by successive internal reflections from the inner surface of the fiber as shown in figure below thus optical fibres are based on total internal reflection.

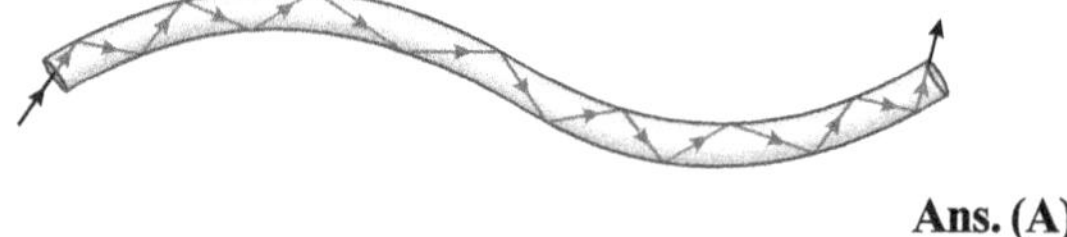

Ans. (A)

Sol. 3 Disc radius is such that the light rays directly going from source to the edges of disc will get internally reflected and no light will come out from the pond as shown in figure below.

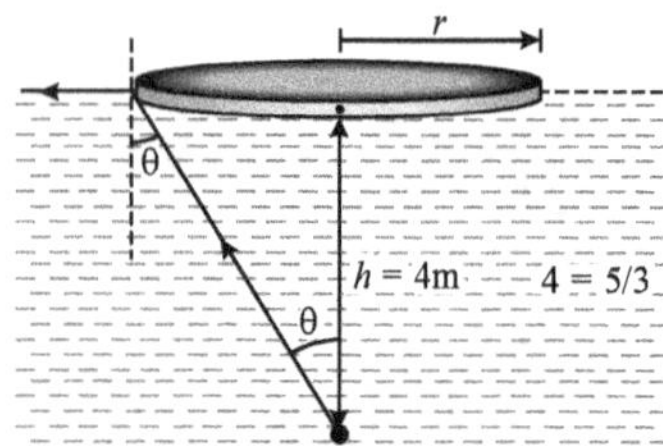

For the light to be internally reflected at the edge of the disc, angle θ shown in figure should be the critical angle, so we use

$$\theta = \sin^{-1}(1/\mu) = \sin^{-1}(3/5)$$

$$\Rightarrow \quad \sin\theta = 3/5$$

$$\Rightarrow \quad \tan\theta = 3/4 = r/4$$

$$\Rightarrow \quad r = 3\,\text{m} \qquad \textbf{Ans. (B)}$$

Sol. 4 Below figure shows the angle made by the refracted ray with the respective normal to the surfaces of the tetrahedral prism (glass slab).

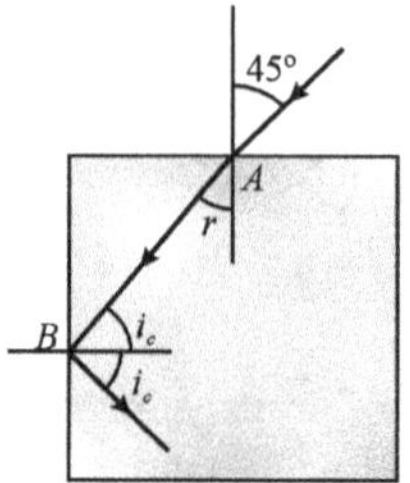

Using Snell's law at point A, we have

$$\mu = \frac{\sin i}{\sin r} = \frac{\sin 45^\circ}{\sin r}$$

$$\Rightarrow \quad \sin r = 1/\sqrt{2}\mu$$

$$\Rightarrow \quad r = \sin^{-1}\left(\frac{1}{\sqrt{2}\mu}\right) \qquad \ldots(1)$$

For total internal reflection to occur at point B on vertical face, we have

$$i_c = \sin^{-1}(1/\mu)$$

Where i_c is the critical angle, so we use

$$r + i_c = 90^\circ = \pi/2$$

$$\Rightarrow \quad \sin^{-1}\frac{1}{\sqrt{2}\mu} = \frac{\pi}{2} - \sin^{-1}\frac{1}{\mu}$$

$$\Rightarrow \quad \sin^{-1}\frac{1}{\sqrt{2}\mu} = \cos^{-1}\frac{1}{\mu}$$

$$\Rightarrow \quad \frac{1}{\sqrt{2}\mu} = \frac{\sqrt{\mu^2 - 1}}{\mu}$$

or

$$\frac{1}{2} = \mu^2 - 1$$

$$\Rightarrow \quad \mu = \sqrt{3/2} \qquad \textbf{Ans. (C)}$$

Sol. 5 Figure below shows the situation described in the question.

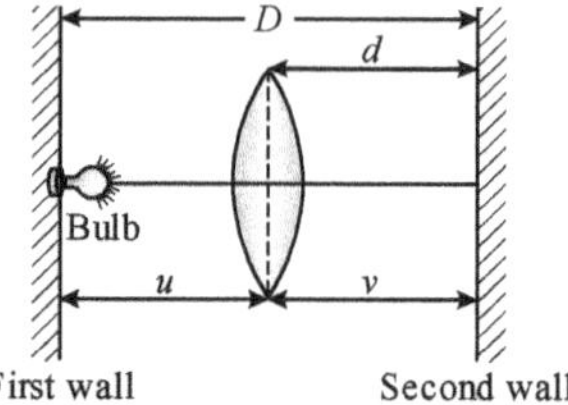

In the displacement method experiment we have studied that for real image is to be produced on the 2nd wall by the convex lens, the distance between the two walls must be more than or equal to four times the focal length of the lens so we use

$$D \geq 4f$$

$$\Rightarrow \quad f \leq D/4$$

If image size is taken same as that of object size then by lens formula we have

$$u = v = d = D/2$$

For same image size we use $f \leq D/4 = d/2$. However this condition is not specified in the question but considering this condition option (B) is the correct answer otherwise no answer can be chosen so most appropriate option is (B). **Ans. (B)**

Sol. 6 As the lens is equiconvex, the radius of curvature of both surface are same. From Lens maker's formula, we use

$$\frac{1}{f} = (\mu - 1)\left(\frac{1}{R_1} - \frac{1}{R_2}\right)$$

In above case for full lens, we use $R_1 = R$, $R_2 = -R$, it gives

$$\Rightarrow \quad \frac{1}{f} = (\mu - 1)\frac{2}{R}$$

$$\Rightarrow \quad f = \frac{R}{2(\mu - 1)} \qquad ...(1)$$

When the lens is cut along YOY' axis, then for each half one surface has radius R and other flat ($R = \infty$) so focal length of each half can be given by lens maker's formula with

$$R_1 = R \text{ but } R_2 = \infty$$

$$\Rightarrow \quad \frac{1}{f''} = (\mu - 1)\left(\frac{1}{R} - \frac{1}{\infty}\right)$$

$$\Rightarrow \quad \frac{1}{f''} = (\mu - 1)\frac{1}{R} = \frac{1}{2f}$$

$$\Rightarrow \quad f'' = 2f$$

If we cut the lens along XOX' then the two halves of the lens will be having the same radii of curvature, thus focal length will remain same, so we use

$$f' = f \qquad \qquad \textbf{Ans. (A)}$$

Sol. 7 If refractive index of lens is same as that of the refractive index of liquid, from lens maker's formula the focal length of the lens becomes infinity. **Ans. (B)**

Sol. 8 Figure below shows the situation described in the question.

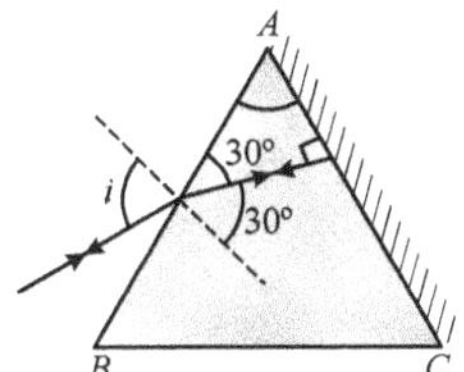

By Snell's law at the surface AB of prism, we have

$$\sin i = \mu \sin 30°$$

$$\Rightarrow \quad \sin i = \sqrt{2} \times \frac{1}{2} = \frac{1}{\sqrt{2}}$$

$$\Rightarrow \quad i = 45° \qquad \qquad \textbf{Ans. (D)}$$

Sol. 9 Speed of light in the given material is given as

$$v = n\lambda$$

$$\Rightarrow \quad v = 2 \times 10^{14} \times 5000 \times 10^{-10} = 10^8 \text{ m/s}$$

Refractive index of the material is given by the ratio of speed of lights, given as

$$\mu = \frac{c}{v} = \frac{3 \times 10^8}{10^8} = 3 \qquad \qquad \textbf{Ans. (B)}$$

Sol. 10 The length of given light ray from coin to the surface of liquid is equal to 5 cm. By Snell's law of refraction, we use

$$\frac{1}{\mu} = \frac{\sin i}{\sin 90°}$$

$$\Rightarrow \quad \mu = \frac{1}{\sin i} = \frac{5}{3}$$

$$\Rightarrow \quad v = \frac{c}{\mu} = \frac{3 \times 10^8}{5/3} = 1.8 \times 10^8 \text{ m/s} \qquad \textbf{Ans. (D)}$$

Sol. 11 For total internal reflection to take place at angle of incidence $i = 45°$, we use

$$i > \sin^{-1}\left(\frac{1}{\mu}\right)$$

$$\Rightarrow \quad \sin i > \frac{1}{\mu}$$

$$\Rightarrow \quad \mu > \frac{1}{\sin i}$$

$$\Rightarrow \quad \mu > \sqrt{2} \qquad \qquad \textbf{Ans. (D)}$$

Sol. 12 Phenomenon mentioned in options (A), (B) and (C) are based on total internal refraction but the concept of apparent and real depth of pond as mentioned in option (B) is due to refraction of light. **Ans (B)**

Sol. 13 For normal emergence of light from the opposite face, we use angle of emergence $e = 0°$ thus refracting angle at this surface is also $r_2 = 0°$ hence the refracting angle at first surface will be given as $r_1 = A$ as shown in figure below.

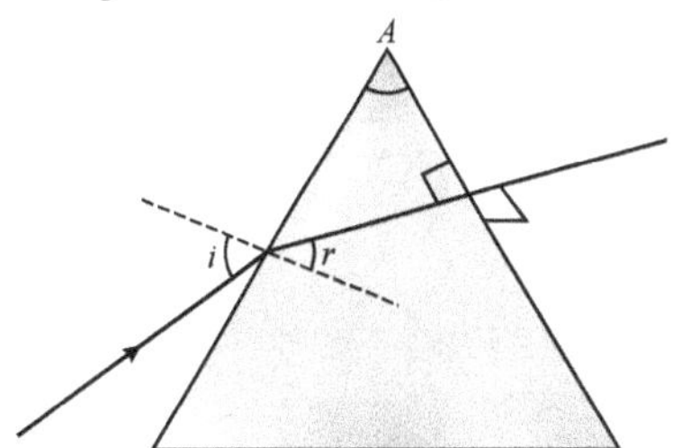

Using Snell's law of refraction for incident ray, we have

$$1 \sin i = \mu \sin r_1 = \mu \sin A$$

For small angle of incidence we can use $i = \mu A$.　　　　**Ans. (A)**

Sol. 14 Figure below shows the situation described in question.

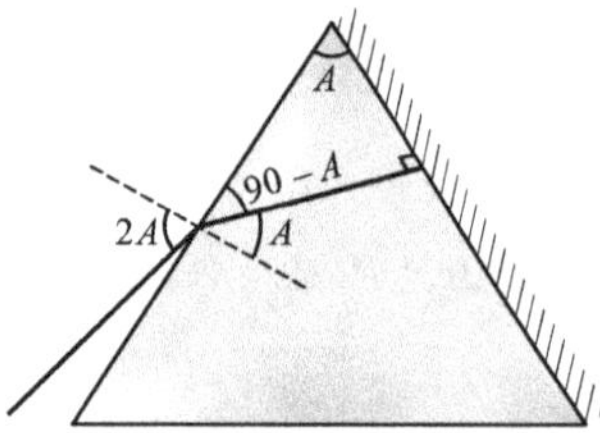

Using Snell's law at first surface where light ray incidents, it gives

$$\mu = \frac{\sin i}{\sin r} = \frac{\sin 2A}{\sin A} = \frac{2 \sin A \cos A}{\sin A} = 2 \cos A \quad \textbf{Ans. (B)}$$

Sol. 15 Figure below shows the situation described in the question. For minimum deviation of the light through the prism here $r_1 = r_2 = 30°$

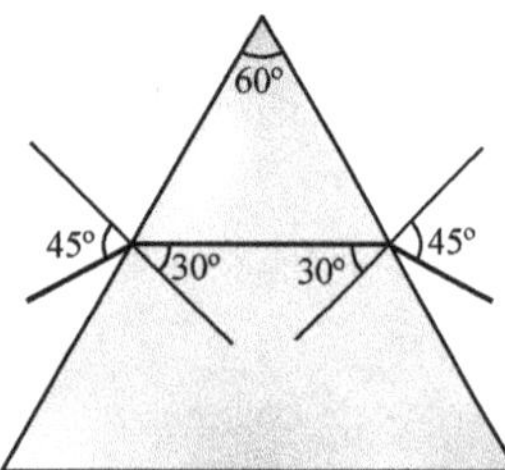

Minimum deviation of the light is given as

$$\delta_{min} = (i + e) - A = 30°$$

Thus refractive index of the material is given as

$$\mu = \frac{\sin\left(\dfrac{A + \delta_m}{2}\right)}{\sin\dfrac{A}{2}}$$

$$\Rightarrow \quad \mu = \frac{\sin\dfrac{(60° + 30°)}{2}}{\sin\dfrac{60}{2}} = \frac{\sin 45°}{\sin 30°} = \sqrt{2} \quad \textbf{Ans. (B)}$$

Sol. 16 The apparent depth of the air bubble from the face it is being looked can be written as

$$\text{Apparent depth} = \frac{\text{Actual depth}}{\text{Refractive index}}$$

From first surface the real depth of air bubble is given as

$$d_1 = 5 \times 1.5 = 7.5 \text{ cm}$$

From second surface the real depth of air bubble is given as

$$d_2 = 3 \times 1.5 = 4.5 \text{ cm}$$

The actual thickness of glass slab is given as

$$d_{ac} = 7.5 + 4.5 = 12 \text{ cm} \quad \textbf{Ans. (C)}$$

Sol. 17 Figure below shows the situation described in the question.

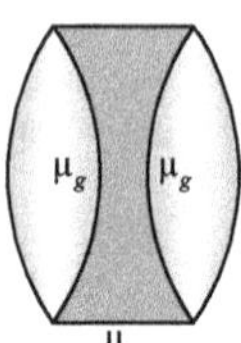

For equiconvex lenses, the focal length can be calculated by lens makers formula, given as

$$\frac{1}{f} = \left(\frac{3}{2} - 1\right)\left(\frac{1}{R} - \frac{1}{-R}\right)$$

$$\Rightarrow \quad \frac{1}{f} = \frac{1}{2} \cdot \frac{2}{R}$$

$$\Rightarrow \quad R = f$$

For lens made up of liquid filled between the two lenses, the focal length is given as

$$\frac{1}{f_2} = \left(\frac{4}{3} - 1\right)\left(\frac{1}{-f} - \frac{1}{f}\right)$$

$$\Rightarrow \quad \frac{1}{f_2} = \frac{1}{3} \times \frac{2}{-f}$$

$$\Rightarrow \quad f_2 = \frac{-3f}{2}$$

For the given combination, we use equivalent focal length is given as

$$\frac{1}{f'} = \frac{1}{f_1} + \frac{1}{f_2} + \frac{1}{f_3}$$

$$\Rightarrow \quad \frac{1}{f'} = \frac{1}{f} + \frac{2}{-3f} + \frac{1}{f}$$

$$\Rightarrow \quad \frac{1}{f'} = \frac{3 - 1 + 3}{3f} = \frac{4}{3f}$$

$$\Rightarrow \quad f' = \frac{3f}{4} \quad \textbf{Ans. (D)}$$

Sol. 18 For retracing the path of light ray, it must incident normally on the mirrored face as shown in figure below

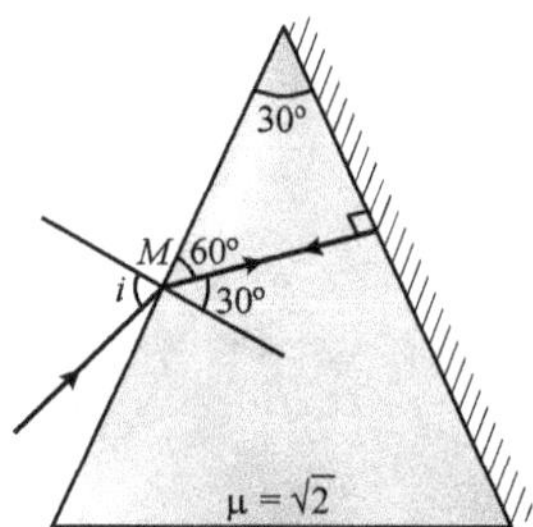

Applying Snell's law at point M, it gives

$$\frac{\sin i}{\sin 30°} = \frac{\sqrt{2}}{1}$$

$\Rightarrow \qquad \sin i = \sqrt{2} \times \frac{1}{2}$

$\Rightarrow \qquad \sin i = \frac{1}{\sqrt{2}}$

$\Rightarrow \qquad i = 45°$ **Ans. (B)**

Sol. 19 Figure below shows the situation described in question for total internal reflection at the given surface

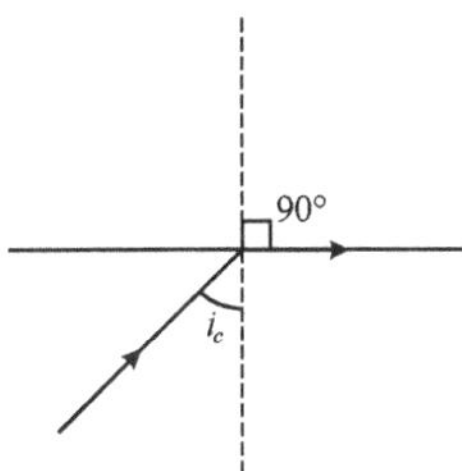

At incidence angle $i = i_c$, the refracted ray grazes along the surface. Thus angle of refraction is $90°$. **Ans. (D)**

Sol. 20 This question is same as that of Q. 13. Students are advised to refer solution of Q. 13. **Ans. (D)**

Sol. 21 In the given figure light ray incident at an angle $30°$ on the vertical face of prism as shown below.

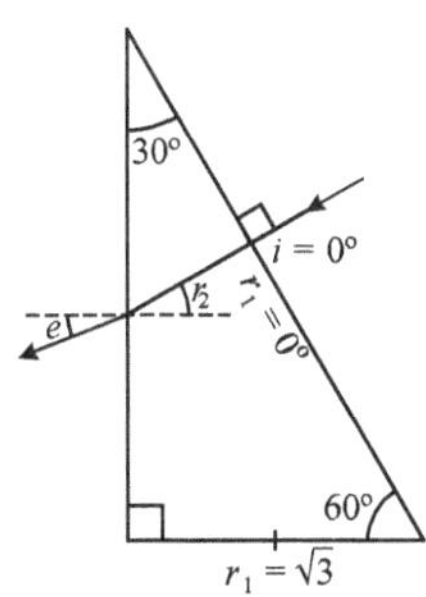

From Snell's law, we use at vertical face of prism

$\qquad \sqrt{3} \sin r_2 = 1 \times \sin e$

$\Rightarrow \qquad \sqrt{3} \sin 30° = \sin e$

$\Rightarrow \qquad e = 60°$ **Ans. (A)**

Sol. 22 Figure below shows the situation described in question

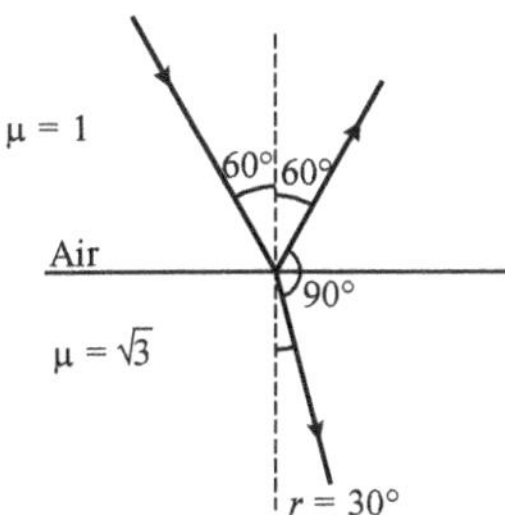

Using Snell's law, we have

$$1 \sin 60° = \sqrt{3} \sin r$$

$$\frac{\sqrt{3}}{2} = \sqrt{3} \sin r$$

$$\sin r = \frac{1}{2}$$

$$r = 30°$$

Thus angle between refracted and reflected ray is $90°$. **Ans. (B)**

Sol. 23 Refractive index of a medium is given as

$$\mu = \frac{c}{v}$$

$\Rightarrow \qquad \mu \propto \frac{1}{v}$

Critical angle of the given interface of transparent media is given as

$$\sin i_c = \frac{\mu_A}{\mu_B} = \frac{v_B}{v_A} = \frac{1.5}{2} = \frac{3}{2}$$

$\Rightarrow \qquad i_c = \sin^{-1}\left(\frac{3}{4}\right)$ **Ans. (A)**

23.3 Geometrical Optics III - Thin Lenses

Sol. 1 Effective power of combination of a system of thin lenses is given as

$$P = P_1 + P_2 = \frac{1}{f_1} + \frac{1}{f_2} = \frac{1}{25} + \frac{1}{(-25)} = 0 \qquad \textbf{Ans. (D)}$$

Sol. 2 Angular width of Sun at the surface of earth can be calculated as

$$\theta = \frac{1.39 \times 10^9}{1.5 \times 10^{11}} \text{ rad}$$

Diameter of Sun's image in focal plane of lens is given as

$\Rightarrow \qquad D_i = f\theta = 0.1 \times \frac{1.39 \times 10^8}{1.5 \times 10^{11}} = 9.2 \times 10^{-4} \text{ m}$ **Ans. (C)**

Sol. 3 Effective power of combination of thin lenses is given as

$$P = P_1 + P_2 = \frac{1}{f_1} + \frac{1}{f_2}$$

$\Rightarrow \qquad P = \frac{f_1 + f_2}{f_1 f_2}$ **Ans. (B)**

Sol. 4 Focal length of every part of lens remain same but intensity of image formed by lens is proportional to area of lens exposed to incident light from object, thus we have

$$\frac{I_2}{I_1} = \frac{A_2}{A_1}$$

Initial area through which light is passing through lens before putting black paper is

$$A_1 = \pi\left(\frac{d}{2}\right)^2 = \frac{\pi d^2}{4}$$

After blocking exposed area, as described in question, remaining area through which light will pass through lens is given as

$$A_2 = \frac{\pi d^2}{4} - \frac{\pi\left(\frac{d}{2}\right)^2}{4} = \frac{3\pi d^2}{16}$$

$$\Rightarrow \qquad \frac{I_2}{I_1} = \frac{A_2}{A_1} = \frac{\dfrac{3\pi d^2}{16}}{\dfrac{\pi d^2}{4}} = \frac{3}{4}$$

$$\Rightarrow \qquad I_2 = \frac{3}{4}I_1 = \frac{3}{4}I \qquad\qquad \textbf{Ans. (D)}$$

Sol. 5 Magnitude of magnification produced due to a thin lens is given as

$$|m| = \frac{v}{u}$$

From Lens maker's formula we have

$$\frac{1}{f} = (\mu - 1)\left(\frac{1}{R_1} - \frac{1}{R_2}\right)$$

With $\mu = 1.5$, focal length of lens is given as

$$\frac{1}{f} = \frac{1}{2} \cdot \frac{2}{R} = \frac{1}{R}$$

$$\Rightarrow \qquad f = 20\,\text{cm}$$

From lens formula we have

$$\frac{1}{v} = \frac{1}{f} + \frac{1}{u} = \frac{1}{20} - \frac{1}{30} = \frac{1}{60}$$

$$\Rightarrow \qquad v = 60\,\text{cm}$$

$$\Rightarrow \qquad m = \frac{60}{30} = 2 \qquad\qquad \textbf{Ans. (C)}$$

Sol. 6 When a lens is placed in a medium of same refractive index as that of its material, it behaves like a glass slab. **Ans. (A)**

Sol. 7 Figure shown below describes the situation explained in question. The light rays will retrace their own path when rays incident normally to the mirror as shown below.

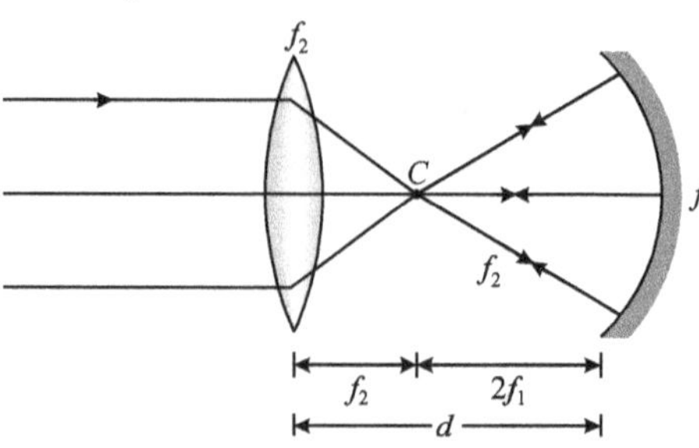

For this the image produced by lens must be located at the center of curvature of the mirror, thus distance d can be given as

$$d = 2f_1 + f_2 \qquad\qquad \textbf{Ans. (C)}$$

Sol. 8 Figure below shows the situation described in the question. Focal lengths of lenses can be calculated by Lens maker's formula.

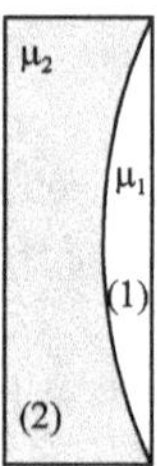

Focal length of first lens is given as

$$\frac{1}{f_1} = (\mu_1 - 1)\left(\frac{1}{\infty} - \frac{1}{-R}\right) = \frac{\mu_1 - 1}{R}$$

Focal length of second lens is given as

$$\frac{1}{f_2} = (\mu_2 - 1)\left(\frac{1}{-R} - \frac{1}{\infty}\right) = -\frac{(\mu_2 - 1)}{R}$$

Focal length of the combination is given as

$$\frac{1}{f} = \frac{1}{f_1} + \frac{1}{f_2} = \frac{\mu_1 - 1}{R} - \frac{(\mu_2 - 1)}{R}$$

$$\Rightarrow \qquad \frac{1}{f} = \frac{\mu_1 - \mu_2}{R}$$

$$\Rightarrow \qquad f = \frac{R}{\mu_1 - \mu_2} \qquad\qquad \textbf{Ans. (C)}$$

Sol. 9 Initially when there is no glycerine, the focal length of the combination is given as

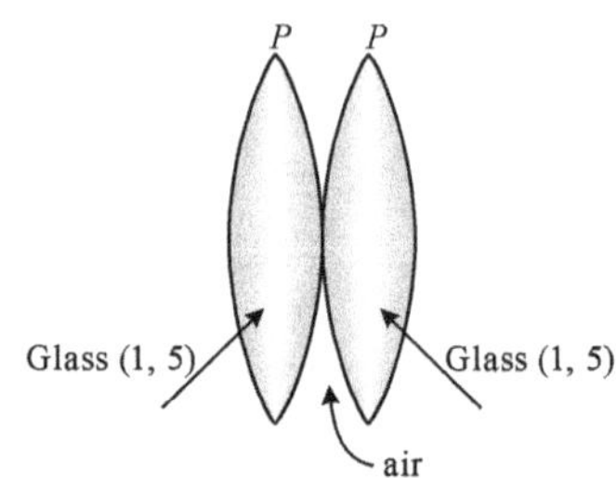

$$\frac{1}{F_1} = \frac{1}{f} + \frac{1}{f} = \frac{2}{f}$$

When in the gap, glycerine is filled, the middle lens will be a diverging lens of same focal length $-f$, so the new focal length of combination now is given as

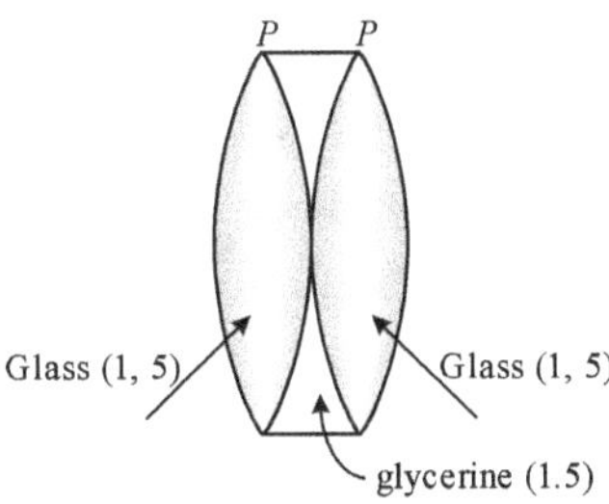

$$\frac{1}{F_2} = \frac{1}{f} + \frac{1}{f} - \frac{1}{f} = \frac{1}{f}$$

$\Rightarrow \qquad \dfrac{F_1}{F_2} = \dfrac{1}{2}$ **Ans. (B)**

Sol. 10 After refraction through the convex lens the parallel light rays converge at a distance 20 cm from the lens. If the concave lens is places such that the converging light rays are toward focal point of this lens then after refraction these rays will emerge as a parallel beam of light as shown in figure below.

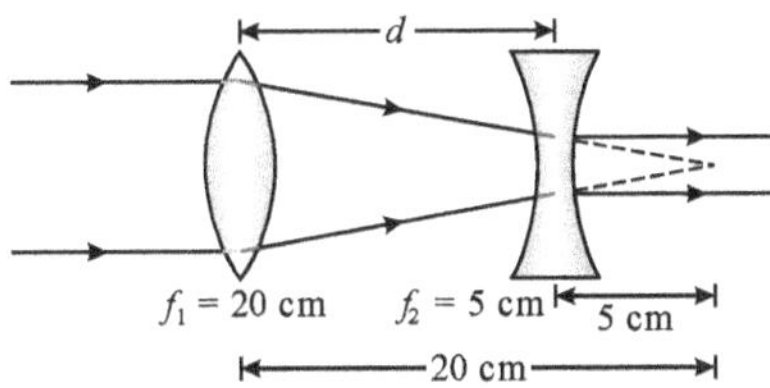

Thus for the given setup the separation between the two lenses can be given as

$$d = f_1 - f_2 = 20 - 5 = 15 \text{ cm} \qquad \textbf{Ans. (B)}$$

Sol. 11 For image formation from lens, using lens formula, we have

$$u = -60 \text{ cm}$$

$$f = +30 \text{ cm}$$

$$\Rightarrow \qquad v = \frac{uf}{u+f} = \frac{-60 \times 30}{-60+30} = 60 \text{ cm}$$

This real image formed by lens acts as virtual object for mirror so mirror produces image at the same distance in front of it as shown in the ray diagram below.

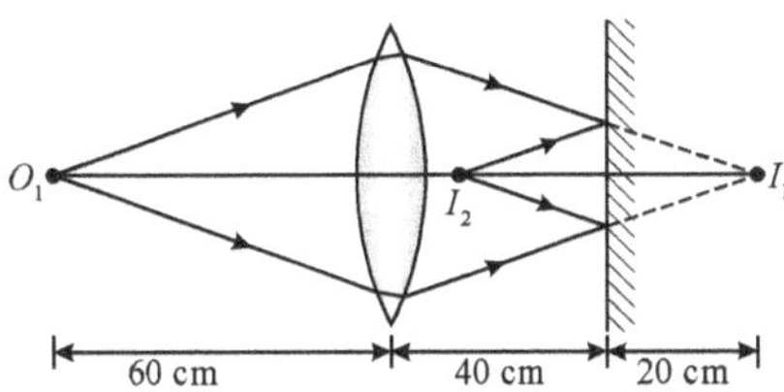

Now this real image produced by plane mirror at 20 cm in front of mirror which is also at 20 cm distance from lens and it will act as a real object for lens.

Now, for second refraction from lens, using lens formula again, we have

$$u = -20 \text{ cm}$$

$$f = +30 \text{ cm}$$

$$\Rightarrow \qquad v = \frac{uf}{u+f} = \frac{-20 \times 30}{-20+30} = -60 \text{ cm}$$

Thus final image produced is virtual and located at a distance of 60 cm from the lens, as shown in the ray diagram given below and at a distance 20 cm behind the mirror.

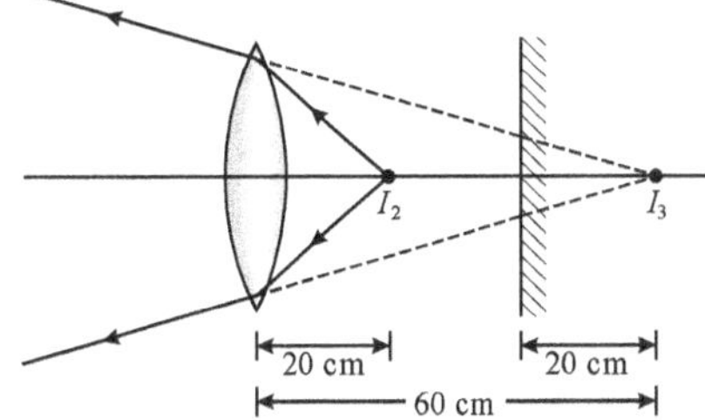

Ans. (D)

Sol. 12 Using lens maker's formula, the power of given lens is calculated as

$$P = \frac{1}{f}(\mu - 1)\left(\frac{1}{R_1} - \frac{1}{R_2}\right)$$

$$\Rightarrow \qquad P = \left(\frac{3}{2} - 1\right)\left(\frac{1}{0.2} + \frac{1}{0.2}\right)$$

$$\Rightarrow \qquad P = \frac{1}{2}\left(\frac{2}{0.2}\right) = \frac{10}{2} = +5 \text{ D} \qquad \textbf{Ans. (B)}$$

23.4 Dispersion of Light

Sol. 1 The refraction of light beam through the slab is shown in the figure below as described in question.

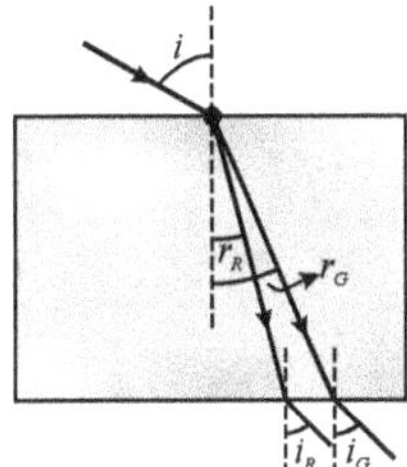

Considering the two rays independently, the refractive indices of the two colours will be different due to which they will refract in different directions at the point light beam enters the glass slab but at the point of emergence both lights are coming out in same medium so emergence angle will be same as incidence angle as shown. Thus most appropriate answer is option (B).

Ans. (B)

Sol. 2 Minimum deviation of a prism can be related to refractive index of prism and its prism angle, given as

$$\mu = \frac{\sin\left(\dfrac{\delta_m + A}{2}\right)}{\sin\left(\dfrac{A}{2}\right)} = \frac{\sin(A)}{\sin\left(\dfrac{A}{2}\right)}$$

$$\mu = \frac{2\sin(A/2)\cos(A/2)}{\sin(A/2)}$$

$$\mu = 2\cos(A/2)$$

When minimum deviation angle is set equal to the prism angle, we use

$$\delta_m = i + e - A$$

For $\delta_{min} = A$, and for minimum deviation, we use $i = e$, so we have

$$A = i + e - A$$
$$\Rightarrow \quad 2A = i + e$$
$$\Rightarrow \quad 2A = 2i$$
$$\Rightarrow \quad A = i$$

For a very small angled prism $A_{min} = 0$ thus for minimum deviation, we use

$$i_{min} = 0 = A_{min}$$
$$\Rightarrow \quad \mu_{min} = 2$$

Maximum value of incidence angle can be 90° thus for maximum value, we use

$$i_{max} = \pi/2 = A_{max}$$
$$\Rightarrow \quad \mu_{max} = \sqrt{2}$$

Range of μ between $\sqrt{2} < \mu < 2$ **Ans. (A)**

Sol. 3 If a light incident normally on the vertical face of prism as shown in figure below internally reflects from the diagonal face, we use

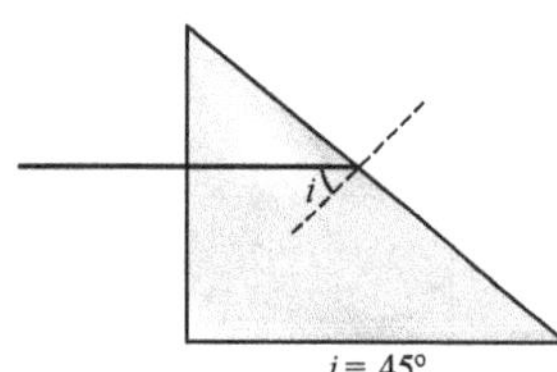

$$i > C$$
$$\Rightarrow \quad \sin i > \sin C$$

$$\Rightarrow \quad \sin i > \frac{1}{\mu}$$

$$\Rightarrow \quad \frac{1}{\sqrt{2}} > \frac{1}{\mu}$$

$$\Rightarrow \quad \mu > \sqrt{2} \qquad \textbf{Ans. (A)}$$

Sol. 4 Total deviation of a prism combination is set to zero, so we have

$$(\mu - 1)A + (\mu' - 1)A' = 0$$
$$\Rightarrow \quad |(\mu - 1)A| = |(\mu' - 1)A'|$$
$$\Rightarrow \quad (1.42 - 1) \times 10° = (1.7 - 1)A'$$
$$\Rightarrow \quad 4.2 = 0.7A'$$
$$\Rightarrow \quad A' = 6° \qquad \textbf{Ans. (B)}$$

Sol. 5 Red has the longest wavelength among the given options. **Ans. (A)**

Sol. 6 Rainbow is produced by dispersion of sunlight through suspended water droplets in atmosphere after total internal reflection from inner surface of these drops. As rainbow is seen via reflected light, it cannot be seen by an observer who is facing toward sun. **Ans. (C)**

23.5 Optical Instruments

Sol. 1 Resolving power of eye lens is given as

$$\frac{1}{\theta} = \frac{d}{\lambda} = \frac{2 \times 10^{-1}}{5000 \times 10^{-8}} \text{ rad}^{-1}$$

If S be the minimum distance between two points so that these may be resolved by eye then we have

$$S = r\theta$$
$$\Rightarrow \quad S = 5000 \times \frac{5000 \times 10^{-8}}{2 \times 10^{-1}} = 1.25 \text{ cm} \quad \textbf{Ans. (C)}$$

Sol. 2 Resolution limit of telescope is given as

$$\theta = 1.22\frac{\lambda}{D} = 1.22 \times \frac{5000 \times 10^{-8}}{10}$$

The distance between objects which can be resolved by this telescope is given as

$$x = d\theta \times d = \frac{1.22 \times 5000 \times 10^{-8} \times 10^5}{10}$$
$$\Rightarrow \quad x = 6.1 \times 10^{-1} \text{ cm} \simeq 5 \text{ mm} \qquad \textbf{Ans. (C)}$$

Sol. 3 Angular resolution of the given telescope is given as

$$\theta = 1.22\frac{\lambda}{D} \sim 10^{-6} \text{ rad} \qquad \textbf{Ans. (B)}$$

Sol. 4 Due to placement of the glass slab, image of mark shifts upward due to its apparent depth. By the same distance microscope is to be shifted upward, given as

$$s = t\left(t - \frac{1}{\mu}\right) = 3\left(1 - \frac{1}{1.5}\right) = 1 \text{ cm} \qquad \textbf{Ans. (A)}$$

Sol. 5 Magnifying power of telescope for parallel rays, is given as

$$m = 9 = \frac{f_0}{f_e} \qquad \qquad \dots(1)$$

Tube length of telescope in such condition is given as

$$f_0 + f_e = 20 \qquad \qquad \dots(2)$$

Solving equation-(1) and (2), we get

$$f_0 = 18 \text{ cm}$$

$$f_e = 2 \text{ cm} \qquad \textbf{Ans. (C)}$$

Sol. 6 Combination of eye lens and cornea forms the image of distant object at retina so total converging power can be given as

$$P_T = 40 + 20 = 60 D$$

Distance between retina and cornea eye lens is equal to the effective focal length, given as

$$f = \frac{1}{P_T} = \frac{5}{3} \text{ cm} = 1.67 \text{ cm} \qquad \textbf{Ans. (C)}$$

Sol. 7 Magnifying power of microscope is given as

$$m_M = \frac{L}{f_0}\left[1 + \frac{P}{f_e}\right]$$

MP of telescope is given as

$$m_T = \frac{f_0}{f_e}\left[1 + \frac{f_e}{D}\right]$$

From above expressions of magnifying powers, we can see that on increasing focal length of objective lens, it increases for telescope and decreases for microscope. **Ans. (D)**

Sol. 8 In normal adjustment the tube length of telescope is given as $f_o + f_e$

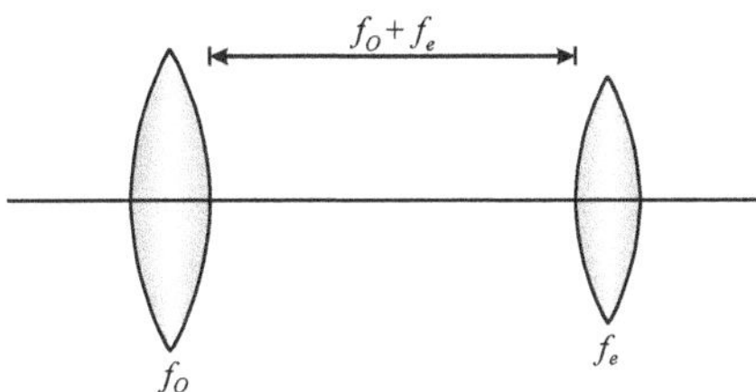

For eyepiece lens, magnification is given as

$$m = \frac{f}{f + u} = \frac{h_I}{h_O} = \frac{l}{L}$$

$$\Rightarrow \quad \frac{f_e}{f_e + [-(f_o + f_e)]} = \frac{l}{L}$$

$$\Rightarrow \quad -\frac{f_e}{f_o} = \frac{l}{L}$$

Magnifying power of telescope is given as

$$m = \left|\frac{f_o}{f_e}\right| = \frac{L}{l} \qquad \textbf{Ans. (A)}$$

Sol. 9

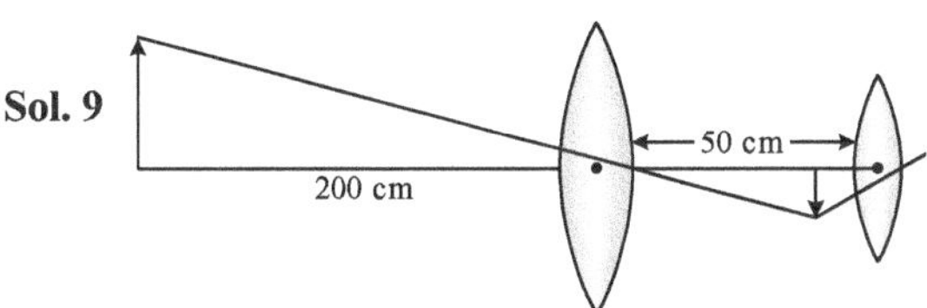

For objective lens, by lens formula we have

$$\frac{1}{v} - \frac{1}{u} = \frac{1}{f}$$

$$\Rightarrow \quad \frac{1}{v} - \frac{1}{-200} = \frac{1}{40}$$

$$\Rightarrow \quad \frac{1}{v} = \frac{1}{40} - \frac{1}{200} = \frac{5-1}{200} = \frac{1}{50}$$

$$\Rightarrow \quad v = 50$$

For normal adjustment tube length is given as

$$L = v + f_e = 54 \text{ cm} \qquad \textbf{Ans. (D)}$$

Sol. 10 Using lens formula, we have

$$\frac{1}{v} - \frac{1}{u} = P = \frac{1}{f}$$

$$\Rightarrow \quad \frac{1}{-4} - \frac{1}{\infty} = P$$

$$\Rightarrow \quad P = -0.25 \text{ D}$$

Negative sign indicates that lens is diverging (Concave).

Ans. (B)

Sol. 11 Resolving power is inversely proportional to the wavelength of light used so we have

$$\frac{R_1}{R_2} = \frac{\lambda_2}{\lambda_1} = \frac{6000\text{Å}}{4000\text{Å}} = \frac{3}{2} \qquad \textbf{Ans. (C)}$$

Sol. 12 For an astronomical telescope, angular magnification is given as

$$m = \frac{f_0}{f_E}$$

To have high angular magnification, focal length of objective lens should be large. Resolving power of telescope is given as

$$R = \frac{1}{\theta} = \frac{D}{1.22\lambda}$$

For higher angular resolution means at lower angles telescope will be able to resolve the objects for which its resolving power should be high. Thus D should be large. **Ans. (A)**

Sol. 13 Limit of resolution for a telescope is given as

$$\theta = \frac{1.22\lambda}{a} = \frac{1.22 \times 6 \times 10^{-7}}{2} = 3.66 \times 10^{-7} \text{ rad} \quad \textbf{Ans. (B)}$$

Sol. 14 Magnifying power of telescope is given as

$$M = \frac{f_0}{f_e}$$

Thus large focal length of objective lens provides good magnification and resolving power of a telescope objective is given as

$$\text{R.P.} = \frac{a}{1.22\lambda}$$

Large aperture of the objective lens provides better resolution so quality of image produced is high and large aperture allows more light gathering in telescope so image is brighter and clear.

Ans. (D)

Ch-24 Wave Optics

24.1 Interference

Sol. 1 Fringe width for first wave length 12000 Å is given as

$$\beta_1 = \frac{\lambda_1 D}{d} = \frac{12000 \times 10^{-10}}{2 \times 10^{-3}} = 1.2 \times 10^{-3} \text{ m} = 1.2 \text{ mm}$$

For second wave length, fringe width is given as

$$\beta_2 = \frac{\lambda_2 D}{d} = \frac{10000 \times 10^{-10} \times 2}{2 \times 10^{-3}} = 1 \text{ mm}$$

With above values of fringe widths, we can analyze that at 6 mm distance from center 5th bright fringe of first wavelength coincides with the 6th bright fringe of second wavelength.

Ans. (B)

Sol. 2 Path difference λ indicates constructive interference and it will result in maximum intensity, given as

$$I_{max} = K$$

For a phase difference ϕ, the path difference Δ is related as

$$\phi = \frac{2\pi}{\lambda} \times \Delta$$

The point on YDSE screen where phase difference is ϕ, intensity of light is given as

$$I = K \cos^2 \frac{\phi}{2} = K \cos^2 \left[\frac{2\pi}{\lambda} \times \frac{\lambda}{4} \times \frac{1}{2} \right]$$

$$\Rightarrow \qquad I = K \cos^2 \frac{\pi}{4} = \frac{K}{2} \qquad \textbf{Ans. (C)}$$

Sol. 3 Ratio of maximum to minimum intensity on screen of YDSE setup is given as

$$\frac{I_{max}}{I_{min}} = \left(\frac{\sqrt{I_1} + \sqrt{I_2}}{\sqrt{I_1} - \sqrt{I_2}} \right)^2 = \left(\frac{\sqrt{\frac{I_1}{I_2}} + 1}{\sqrt{\frac{I_1}{I_2}} - 1} \right)^2$$

$$\Rightarrow \qquad \frac{I_{max}}{I_{min}} = \left(\frac{\sqrt{\frac{1}{25}} + 1}{\sqrt{\frac{1}{25}} - 1} \right)^2 = \frac{36}{16} = \frac{9}{4} \qquad \textbf{Ans. (B)}$$

Sol. 4 Path difference in the two waves from slits to the point directly in front of one of the slit can be calculated from the below figure, is given as

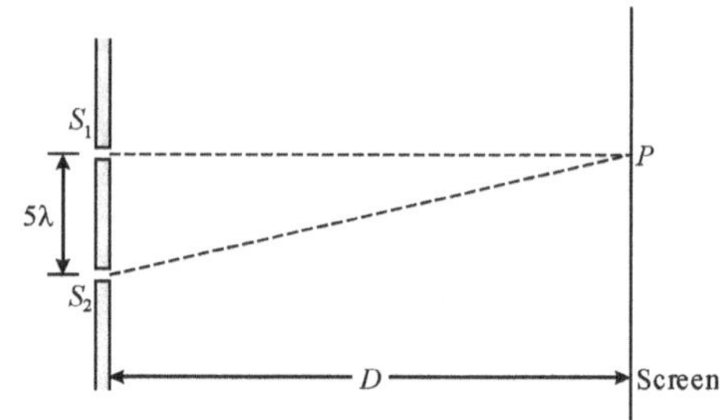

$$\Delta = S_2 P - S_1 P$$

$$\Rightarrow \qquad \Delta = \sqrt{D^2 + d^2} - D$$

$$\Rightarrow \qquad \Delta = D \left(1 + \frac{1}{2} \frac{d^2}{D^2} \right) - D$$

$$\Rightarrow \qquad \Delta = D \left[\frac{1}{2} \frac{d^2}{D^2} \right] = \frac{d^2}{2D} = \frac{(5\lambda)^2}{2 \times 1 \cdot d}$$

$$\Rightarrow \qquad \Delta = \frac{25\lambda^2}{20 \times 5\lambda} = \frac{\lambda}{4}$$

The phase difference in the path of waves at this point is given as

$$\phi = \frac{2\pi}{\lambda} \Delta = \frac{2\pi}{\lambda} \cdot \frac{\lambda}{4} = \frac{\pi}{2}$$

The maximum intensity in Young's double slit experiment is given as

$$I_{max} = I_1 + I_2 + 2I_1 I_2$$

$$I_0 = 4I \qquad \text{(As } I_1 = I_2 = I)$$

Thus intensity on screen due to each source is given as

$$I = \frac{I_0}{4}$$

Intensity at point P, directly in front of one of the slit is given as

$$I_P = I_1 + I_2 + 2I_1 I_2 \cos \frac{\pi}{2}$$

$$\Rightarrow \qquad I_P = 2I = \frac{I_0}{2} \qquad \textbf{Ans. (D)}$$

Sol. 5 It is specified in question that $I_2 = nI_1$, thus maximum and minimum intensity of light produced on YDSE screen are given as

$$I_{max} = (\sqrt{I} + \sqrt{nI})^2$$

and $$I_{min} = (\sqrt{I} - \sqrt{nI})^2$$

Thus required ratio can be calculated as

$$\frac{I_{max} - I_{min}}{I_{max} + I_{min}} = \frac{(\sqrt{I} + \sqrt{nI})^2 - (\sqrt{I} - \sqrt{nI})^2}{(\sqrt{I} + \sqrt{nI})^2 + (\sqrt{I} - \sqrt{nI})^2}$$

$$\Rightarrow \quad \frac{I_{max} - I_{min}}{I_{max} + I_{min}} = \frac{1 + n + 2\sqrt{n} - 1 - n + 2\sqrt{n}}{1 + n + 2\sqrt{n} + 1 + n - 2\sqrt{n}}$$

$$\Rightarrow \quad \frac{I_{max} - I_{min}}{I_{max} + I_{min}} = \frac{4\sqrt{n}}{2 + 2n} = \frac{2\sqrt{n}}{1 + n} \qquad \textbf{Ans. (B)}$$

Sol. 6 Distance of 5th dark fringe in Young's double slit experiment from screen center is given as

$$x_1 = x_{5th\,dark} = (2 \times 5 - 1)\frac{\lambda D}{2d}$$

Position of 3rd bright fringe in Young's double slit experiment submerged in a medium is given as

$$x_2 = \frac{n\lambda' D}{d} = \frac{nD}{d} \times \frac{\lambda}{\mu}$$

For the given situation described in question, we use

$$x_1 = x_2$$

$$\Rightarrow \qquad \frac{9}{2}\frac{\lambda D}{d} = 8\frac{\lambda D}{\mu d}$$

$$\Rightarrow \qquad \mu = \frac{16}{9} = 1.78 \qquad \textbf{Ans. (D)}$$

Sol. 7 Angular width of fringes obtained on screen are given as

$$\text{as} \qquad \alpha = \frac{\lambda}{d}$$

$$0.20° = \frac{\lambda}{2\,mm} \qquad \qquad ...(1)$$

When angular width is increase, we use

$$0.21° = \frac{\lambda}{d_1} \qquad \qquad ...(2)$$

Dividing above two equations, we get

$$\frac{0.20}{0.21} = \frac{d}{2\,mm}$$

$$\Rightarrow \qquad d = 1.9\,mm \qquad \textbf{Ans. (B)}$$

Sol. 8 When YDSE is performed in air the angular fringe width is given as

$$\theta_0 = \frac{\beta}{D} = \frac{\lambda}{d}$$

When the YDSE setup is submerged in water, light wavelength changes to λ/μ so angular fringe width in water becomes

$$\theta_w = \frac{\beta}{\mu D} = \frac{\theta_0}{\mu}$$

$$\Rightarrow \qquad \theta_w = \frac{0.2°}{\left(\dfrac{4}{3}\right)} = 0.15° \qquad \textbf{Ans. (B)}$$

Sol. 9 Fringe width in YDSE setup is given as

Initially $$\beta = \frac{\lambda D}{d}$$

Finally $$\beta' = \frac{\lambda D'}{d'}$$

As stated in given question, we use

$$D' = 2D, \; d' = \frac{d}{2}$$

$$\Rightarrow \qquad \beta' = \frac{\lambda \times 2D}{d/2} = \frac{4\lambda D}{d}$$

$$\Rightarrow \qquad \beta' = 4\beta$$

Thus new fringe width becomes 4 times. $\qquad$ **Ans. (D)**

Sol. 10 The region of screen in which n fringes are observed is given as

$$y = (n\lambda)\left(\frac{D}{d}\right)$$

Thus in same region if n_1 and n_2 fringes are seen for wavelengths λ_1 and λ_2 then we have

$$n_1 \lambda_1 = n_2 \lambda_2$$

$$\Rightarrow \qquad (8)(600\,nm) = n_2 (400)$$

$$\Rightarrow \qquad n_2 = 12 \qquad \textbf{Ans. (C)}$$

24.2 Diffraction

Sol. 1 Distance between 1st order dark fringes is equal to the width of principal maxima in diffraction pattern, which is given as

$$x = \frac{2\lambda D}{d}$$

$$\Rightarrow \quad x = \frac{2 \times 600 \times 10^{-9} \times 2}{10^{-3}} = 2400 \times 10^{-6} = 2.4 \times 10^{-3}\,\text{m} = 2.4\,\text{mm}$$

Ans. (D)

Sol. 2 Figure below shows the slit AC and variation in intensity on screen in diffraction pattern produced.

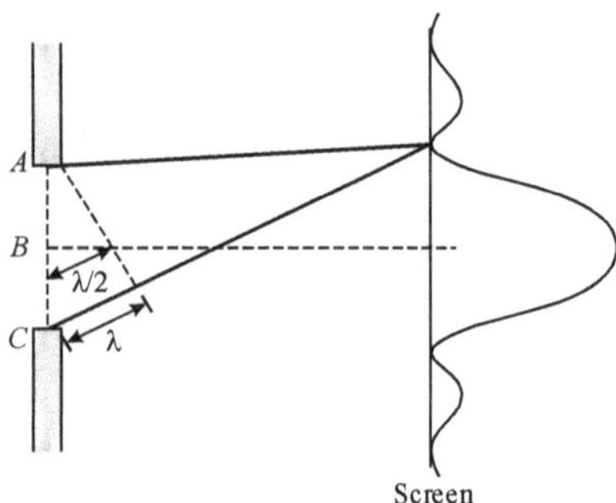

For first minima on screen, the path difference between A and C is λ so path difference between A and B (mid point of slit) should be $\lambda/2$ so corresponding phase difference is π. **Ans. (D)**

Sol. 3 In single slit diffraction pattern, for minima location, we use

$$a \sin \theta = n\lambda$$

For first minima, we use $n = 1$, it gives

$$a \sin 30° = \lambda$$

$$\Rightarrow \quad a = 2\lambda$$

First secondary maxima is obtained at approximately

$$a \sin \theta_1 = (2n+1)\frac{\lambda}{2} = \frac{3\lambda}{2} \quad \text{(For } n = 1\text{)}$$

$$\Rightarrow \quad \sin \theta_1 = \frac{3\lambda}{2a} = \frac{3}{4}$$

$$\Rightarrow \quad \theta = \sin^{-1}\frac{3}{4}$$

Ans. (D)

Sol. 4 Location of first dark band on the diffraction pattern screen is given as

$$x = \frac{\lambda D}{b}$$

$$\Rightarrow \quad x = \frac{5 \times 10^{-5} \times 60}{0.02} = \frac{300 \times 10^{-5}}{0.02} = 0.15\,\text{cm}$$

Ans. (D)

24.3 Polarization of Light

Sol. 1 Sound waves are longitudinal waves in all media and being electromagnetic in nature, light waves are transverse wave in all media. **Ans. (B)**

Sol. 2 Situation described in question is shown in figure below

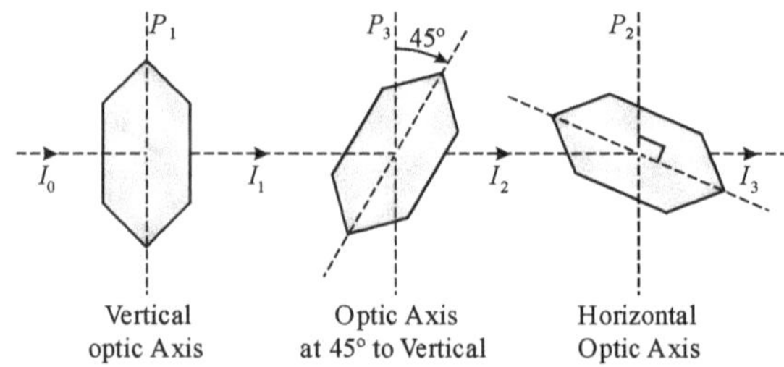

In above case the intensity of transmitted light through Polaroid P_1 is given as

$$I_1 = \frac{I_0}{2}$$

Intensity of transmitted light through P_3 is given as

$$I_2 = \frac{I_0}{2}\cos^2 45° = \frac{I_0}{2} \times \frac{1}{2} = \frac{I_0}{4}$$

Thus angle between P_3 and P_2 is given as

$$P_2 = 90 - 45° = 45°$$

Intensity of transmitted light through P_2

$$I_3 = \frac{I_0}{4}\cos^2 45° = \frac{I_0}{8}$$

Ans. (C)

Sol. 3 According to Brewster's law when a light ray incident on a boundary of two media at such an angle so that reflected and refracted rays are perpendicular then reflected ray is plane polarized with electric field vector perpendicular to the plane of incidence and parallel to the surface on which light incidents as shown in figure below. In this case the incidence angle is called Brewster's angle given as

$$i = \tan^{-1}(\mu)$$

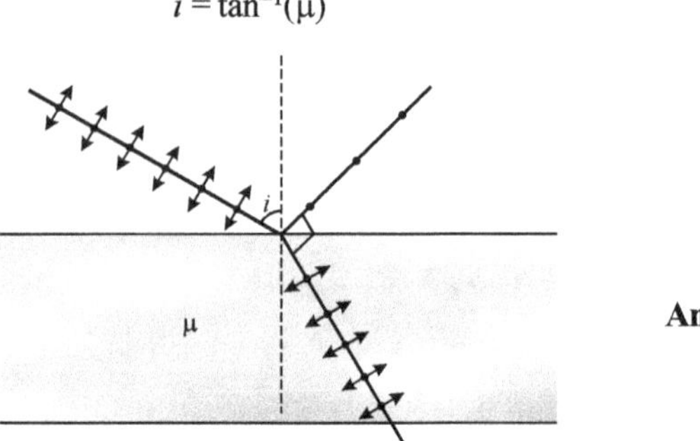

Ans. (B)

Sol. 4 For an interface of two different media, Brewster's angle i_b is given as

$$\tan i_b = \mu$$

As $\mu > 1$, we use

$\Rightarrow \qquad \tan i_b > 1$

$\Rightarrow \qquad 90° > i_b > 45°$ $\qquad\qquad$ **Ans. (D)**

Ch-25 Dual Nature of Radiation, Matter & X-Ray

25.1 Photoelectric Effect

Sol. 1 Intensity of light due to a point source of power P at a distance r from the source is given as

$$I = \frac{P}{4\pi r^2}$$

$$\Rightarrow \qquad \frac{I_2}{I_1} = \frac{r_1^2}{r_2^2} = \frac{r_1^2}{\left(\frac{r_1}{2}\right)^2} = 4$$

$$\Rightarrow \qquad I_2 = 4I_1$$

Thus on decreasing distance from d to $d/2$, intensity becomes 4 times so number of photons in light also becomes four times and as one photon ejects one electron from a surface, number of ejected electrons also become four times. **Ans. (B)**

Sol. 2 Phenomenon of Interference Refraction and polarization of light are wave nature phenomenon and photoelectric effect is based on particle nature of light. **Ans. (A)**

Sol. 3 Ultraviolet rays are not able to start photoelectric effect that indicates its wavelength is more than the threshold wavelength for metal so energy higher than ultraviolet rays are needed for this purpose. In given options only X-rays have lower wavelength or higher energy than ultraviolet rays.

Ans. (B)

Sol. 4 Planck's constant is a universal constant with numerical value 6.63×10^{-34} J s. **Ans. (D)**

Sol. 5 Intensity of light due to a point source of power P at a distance r from the source is given as

$$I = \frac{P}{4\pi r^2}$$

Thus on increasing the distance of cell from source to twice the value, intensity of light becomes one fourth thus number of ejected electrons from surface will become one quarter of the initial value. **Ans. (D)**

Sol. 6 The maximum kinetic energy of photoelectron ejected is given as

$$K = h\upsilon - \phi = h\upsilon - h\upsilon_0$$

The work function of metal depends on the material and its surface. If the frequency of incident radiation is greater than υ_0

then only the ejection of photoelectrons start and at frequency higher than threshold frequency kinetic energy varies linearly with frequency. **Ans. (D)**

Sol. 7 Photoelectrons are emitted for a radiation which has photon energy more than work function of the metal. For the radiation of 4100Å, photon energy is given as

$$w = \frac{hc}{\lambda} = \frac{12400}{4100\text{Å}} = 3\,\text{eV}$$

For the given metals we can see that metals A and B have work functions less than the photon energy of above radiation hence both metals A and B will emit photoelectrons. **Ans. (C)**

Sol. 8 When photons of energy $2h\upsilon_0$ are incident on the metal surface then maximum kinetic energy of ejected photoelectrons is given as

$$\frac{1}{2}mv_1^2 = 2h\upsilon_0 - h\upsilon_0$$

$$\Rightarrow \qquad \frac{1}{2}mv_1^2 = h\upsilon_0 \qquad\qquad\qquad \dots(1)$$

When photons of energy $5h\upsilon_0$ are incident on metal surface, the kinetic energy of ejected photoelectrons is given as

$$\frac{1}{2}mv_2^2 = 5h\upsilon_0 - h\upsilon_0 = 4h\upsilon_0 \qquad\qquad \dots(2)$$

Dividing equation-(2) by equation-(1) gives

$$v_2^2 = 4v_1^2$$

$$\Rightarrow \qquad v_2 = 2v_1 = 2 \times 4 \times 10^6 = 8 \times 10^6\,\text{m/s} \quad \textbf{Ans. (D)}$$

Sol. 9 When intensity of incident light changes then the photon flux changes and photoelectric current in experiment is directly proportional to the photon flux or intensity of illumination. Thus change in intensity of incident light will result into change the photo current. **Ans. (B)**

Sol. 10 From photoelectric effect equation, we use

$$h\upsilon = E_0 + K$$

and $\qquad 2h\upsilon = E_0 + K'$

From above equations, we have

$$K' = K + h\upsilon \qquad\qquad\qquad\qquad \textbf{Ans. (D)}$$

Sol. 11 From a source of light power P and number of photons emitted per second n from the source are related as

$$P = nh\upsilon$$

$$\Rightarrow \qquad n = \frac{P}{h\upsilon} = \frac{2 \times 10^{-3}}{6.6 \times 10^{-34} \times 6 \times 10^{14}} = 5 \times 10^{15}$$

Ans. (D)

Sol. 12 Intensity of light due to a point source of power P at a distance r from the source is given as

$$I = \frac{P}{4\pi r^2}$$

Thus on increasing the distance of cell from source to twice the value, intensity of light becomes one fourth thus number of ejected electrons from surface will become one quarter of the initial value. **Ans. (D)**

Sol. 13 In discharge tube high speed electrons ejected from cathode collides with the gas atoms due to which these atoms gets excited and when these atoms de-excite to lower energy levels different radiations are emitted and some of these are in visible range due to which the coloured glow appears in the tube. Thus it is a result of collisions between the charged particles emitted from cathode and the atoms of the gas.

Ans. (C)

Sol. 14 Incident energy of radiation is used in form of work function and maximum kinetic energy imparted to electrons, so we have

$$hv = \phi + K_{max}$$

$$\Rightarrow \qquad hv = hv_0 + eV_0$$

$$\Rightarrow \qquad \frac{hc}{\lambda} = 6.2e + 5e$$

$$\Rightarrow \qquad \lambda = \frac{h \times c}{11.2 \times 1.6 \times 10^{-19}} = \frac{6.63 \times 10^{-34} \times 3 \times 10^8}{11.2 \times 1.6 \times 10^{-19}}$$

$$\Rightarrow \qquad \lambda = 1.1 \times 10^{-7}\,\text{m} = 1100\,\text{Å}$$

This wavelength lies in ultraviolet region. **Ans. (C)**

Sol. 15 Number of photoelectrons emitted in photoelectric effect depends on the intensity of incident light and it independent of frequency. **Ans. (D)**

Sol. 16 From the curves, we can analyze that stopping potential is same for radiations a and b and that of c is more than that of these two. Saturation photocurrent produced due to the radiations b and c are same and that of a is less than these two. The stopping potential depends on frequency and photo current depends on the intensity of light so out of all the given options (C) is correct. **Ans. (C)**

Sol. 17 Stopping potential is given as

$$V_0 = \frac{hc}{e\lambda} - \frac{\phi}{e}$$

$$V_0 = \left(\frac{12400}{2000} - 5.01\right)\text{eV}$$

$$V_0 = 6.2 - 5.01 = 1.2\,\text{V} \qquad \textbf{Ans. (C)}$$

Sol. 18 The photoelectric emission starts only when the incident light has frequency more than a minimum frequency called threshold frequency of the metal surface. **Ans. (D)**

Sol. 19 For maximum speed of the photo electrons, we use

$$\frac{1}{2}mv^2 = E_{ph} - \phi$$

Work function of metal surface is given as $\phi = 0.5$ eV and for first light of $E_{ph} = 1$ eV, we have

$$\frac{1}{2}mv_1^2 = 1.0 - 0.5 = 0.5\,\text{eV} \qquad \ldots(1)$$

For second light of photon energy $E_{ph} = 2.5$ eV, we have

$$\frac{1}{2}mv_2^2 = 2.5 - 0.5 = 2\,\text{eV} \qquad \ldots(2)$$

From equation-(1) and (2), we have

$$\frac{v_1^2}{v_2^2} = \frac{0.5}{2} = \frac{1}{4}$$

$$\Rightarrow \qquad \frac{v_1}{v_2} = \frac{1}{2} \qquad \textbf{Ans. (B)}$$

Sol. 20 In photoelectric effect the stopping potential is given as

$$V_0 = \frac{K_{max}}{e} = 0.5\,\text{V} \qquad \textbf{Ans. (C)}$$

Sol. 21 De-Broglie wavelength for a moving electron is given as

$$\lambda = \frac{h}{p}$$

$$\Rightarrow \qquad p = \frac{h}{\lambda}$$

$$\Rightarrow \qquad \left|\frac{\Delta p}{p}\right| = \frac{\Delta \lambda}{\lambda}$$

$$\Rightarrow \qquad p = \frac{P}{\dfrac{0.5}{100}}$$

Initial momentum of electron is given as

$$p = \frac{1000}{5}P = 200P \qquad \textbf{Ans. (D)}$$

Sol. 22 This question is same as that of Q. 19. Students are advised to refer solution to Q. 19. **Ans. (A)**

Sol. 23 Wavelength of corresponding light is given as

$$\lambda = \frac{C}{v} = \frac{3 \times 10^{17}}{6 \times 10^{15}} = 50\,\text{nm} \qquad \textbf{Ans. (C)}$$

Sol. 24 By using photoelectric equation, we have

$$E_{ph} = h\nu - \phi$$

Before and after increasing the energy, we have

$$0.5 = h\nu - \phi \qquad \ldots(1)$$

Again $\qquad 0.8 = 1.2h\nu - \phi \qquad \ldots(2)$

Solving $(2) - (1) \times 1.2$ gives

$$\Rightarrow \qquad 0.2 = 0.2\phi$$

$$\Rightarrow \qquad \phi = 1\,eV \qquad \qquad \textbf{Ans. (B)}$$

Sol. 25 From photoelectric effect equation, we have

$$K_{max} = E - \phi$$

For the two cases given in question, we use

$$K_{max} = \frac{hc}{\lambda} - \phi \qquad \ldots(1)$$

$$3K_{max} = \frac{hc}{(\lambda/2)} - \phi \qquad \ldots(2)$$

Solving equation-(1) and (2) gives

$$\phi = \frac{hc}{2\lambda} \qquad \qquad \textbf{Ans. (B)}$$

Sol. 26 Writing photoelectric effect equation for the two cases given in question, we have

$$eV = \frac{hc}{\lambda} - \frac{hc}{\lambda_0} \qquad \ldots(1)$$

and $\qquad \dfrac{eV}{4} = \dfrac{hc}{2\lambda} - \dfrac{hc}{\lambda_0}$

$$\Rightarrow \qquad eV = \frac{4hc}{2\lambda} - \frac{4hc}{\lambda_0} \qquad \ldots(2)$$

Equation-(1) - (2) gives

$$\frac{hc}{\lambda} - \frac{2hc}{\lambda} = \frac{4hc}{\lambda_0} + \frac{hc}{\lambda_0}$$

$$\Rightarrow \qquad -\frac{hc}{\lambda} = -\frac{3hc}{\lambda_0}$$

$$\Rightarrow \qquad \lambda_0 = 3\lambda \qquad \qquad \textbf{Ans. (D)}$$

Sol. 27 Work function of surface is given as

$$\phi = 5 - 2 = 3\,eV$$

When incident energy is changed to 6 eV, maximum kinetic energy of ejected photoelectrons is given as

$$KE_{max} = 6 - 3 = 3\,eV$$

Stopping potential in this case can be given as

$$V_0 = \frac{KE_{max}}{e} = 3\,V$$

Stopping potential is the high potential of Cathode relative to Anode so potential of A relative to C will be -3 V. **Ans. (D)**

Sol. 28 Using threshold wavelength we can calculate the work function of metal surface as

$$\phi = \frac{1243.1}{325} = 3.82\,eV$$

Photon energy of incident ultraviolet light is given as

$$h\nu = \frac{1243.1}{253.6} = 4.89\,eV$$

Maximum kinetic energy of photoelectrons can be calculated as

$$KE_{max} = (4.89 - 3.82)\,eV = 1.007\,eV$$

$$\Rightarrow \qquad \frac{1}{2}mv^2 = 1.077 \times 1.6 \times 10^{-19}$$

$$\Rightarrow \qquad v = \sqrt{\frac{2 \times 1.077 \times 1.6 \times 10^{-19}}{9.1 \times 10^{-31}}} = 0.6 \times 10^6\,m/s$$

Result matches with both answer options (A) and (B).

Ans. (A & B)

Sol. 29 Using photoelectric effect equation, we have

$$E_{ph} = \phi + KE_{max}$$

In first case when light of frequency $2\nu_0$ incident on the metal, we use

$$h(2\nu_0) = h\nu_0 + \frac{1}{2}mv_1^2$$

$$\Rightarrow \qquad h\nu_0 = \frac{1}{2}mv_1^2 \qquad \ldots(1)$$

In second case when light of frequency $5\nu_0$ incident on the metal, we use

$$h(5\nu_0) = h\nu_0 + \frac{1}{2}mv_2^2$$

$$\Rightarrow \qquad 4h\nu_0 = \frac{1}{2}mv_2^2 \qquad \ldots(2)$$

Dividing equation-(1) by (2) gives

$$\frac{1}{4} = \frac{v_1^2}{v_2^2}$$

$$\Rightarrow \qquad \frac{v_1}{v_2} = \frac{1}{2} \qquad \qquad \textbf{Ans. (C)}$$

Sol. 30 When frequency of incident radiation is halved it becomes 0.75 times the threshold frequency and as the incident frequency is less than threshold frequency so no emission of electron take place therefore no current will exist in circuit.

Ans. (A)

Sol. 31 Due to the incident illumination flux with intensity I, total energy received by the surface of area A in time t is given as

$$E = IAt$$

$$\Rightarrow \quad E = \frac{20}{10^{-4}} \times 20 \times 10^{-4} \times 60 \text{ J}$$

$$\Rightarrow \quad E = 24 \times 10^3 \text{ J} \qquad \textbf{Ans. (D)}$$

Sol. 32 As work function of surface is negligible, complete photon energy gets converted to the kinetic energy of emitted photoelectron, so we use

$$\frac{hc}{\lambda} = K_{max}$$

deBroglie wavelength of electron of given kinetic energy is given as

$$\lambda_d = \frac{h}{\sqrt{2m\,K_{max}}}$$

$$\Rightarrow \quad K_{max} = \frac{h^2}{2m\lambda_d^2}$$

$$\Rightarrow \quad \left(\frac{hc}{\lambda}\right) = \frac{h^2}{2m\lambda_d^2}$$

$$\Rightarrow \quad \lambda = \left(\frac{2mc}{h}\right)\lambda_d^2 \qquad \textbf{Ans. (C)}$$

Sol. 33 If n photons are emitted per second then average power produced by the light source is given as

$$P = \frac{nhc}{\lambda}$$

$$\Rightarrow \quad n = \frac{p\lambda}{hc}$$

$$\Rightarrow \quad n = \frac{3.3 \times 10^{-3} \times 600 \times 10^{-9}}{6.6 \times 10^{-34} \times 3 \times 10^8} = 10^{16} \qquad \textbf{Ans. (C)}$$

Sol. 34 Using the photoelectric effect equation for the two given frequencies, we have

$$\frac{eV_s}{2} = \frac{h\upsilon}{2} - h\upsilon_{th} \qquad \ldots (1)$$

and $\qquad eV_s = h\upsilon - h\upsilon_{th} \qquad \ldots (2)$

Solving equations (1) and (2), we have

$$\upsilon_{th} = 0$$

This is not possible. Thus data given in question is incorrect.

NOTE: This question was awarded with Bonus marks in exam.

$$\textbf{Ans. (Bonus)}$$

25.2 Matter Waves and X-Rays

Sol. 1 Using Bragg's law of diffraction, we have

$$2d\sin\phi = n\lambda$$

For maximum wavelength we use $\phi = 90°$, so for $n = 1$ this gives

$$\Rightarrow \quad \lambda_{max} = 2d$$

$$\Rightarrow \quad \lambda_{max} = 2 \times 2.8 \times 10^{-8} = 5.6 \times 10^{-8} \text{ m} \qquad \textbf{Ans. (B)}$$

Sol. 2 For a moving particle, de-Broglie wavelength is given as

$$\lambda = \frac{h}{p} = \frac{h}{mv}$$

Here m, v and p are the mass, velocity and momentum of the particle respectively and h is Planck's constant. As speed of all particles is same, de-Broglie wavelength will be maximum for least mass which is that of β-particles among all options as these are fast moving electrons. $\qquad \textbf{Ans. (D)}$

Sol. 3 Cathode rays are negatively charged electrons and all charged particles are deflected in electric field so option (B) is not the property of cathode rays. $\qquad \textbf{Ans. (B)}$

Sol. 4 Thomson's experiment was used to calculate the charge to mass ratio of a moving charge particle. With that it can be demonstrated that mass of proton is more than mass of electron as these are having same charge. Thus option (C) is correct.

$$\textbf{Ans. (C)}$$

Sol. 5 Below is the different radiation shown in electromagnetic spectrum arranged in decreasing order of wavelengths. Matching with the given radiation, option (D) is correct.

G & T waves	10^3 m $- 10^{-6}$ m & Higher
Radio Wave	10^{-2} m $- 10^3$ m
Microwaves	10^{-5} m $- 10^{-2}$ m
Infrared Rays	8000 Å $- 10^{-5}$ m
Visible light	4000 Å $-$ 8000 Å
Ultraviolet Rays	100 Å $-$ 4000 Å
X-Rays	0.1 A $-$ 100 Å
γ-Rays	10^{-11} m or Lower $\qquad$ **Ans. (D)**

Sol. 6 For a photon, its energy is given as

$$E = pc$$

$$\Rightarrow \quad p = \frac{E}{c} = \frac{10^6 \times 1.6 \times 10^{-19}}{3 \times 10^8}$$

$$= 5.33 \times 10^{-22} \text{ kg ms}^{-1} \qquad \textbf{Ans. (D)}$$

Sol. 7 de-Broglie wavelength associated with the electron moving with velocity v is given as

$$\lambda_\varepsilon = \frac{h}{mv} = \frac{h}{9.1\times10^{-31}\times3\times10^6}$$

Wavelength of particle of mass 1 mg moving with velocity v, its de-Broglie wavelength is given as

$$\lambda_p = \frac{h}{10^{-3}\times v}$$

As specified in question, we use

$$\lambda_e = \lambda_p$$

$$\Rightarrow \qquad \frac{h}{10^{-3}\times v} = \frac{h}{9.1\times10^{-31}\times3\times10^6}$$

$$\Rightarrow \qquad v = \frac{27.3\times10^{-25}}{10^{-3}}\ \text{m/s} = 2.73\times10^{-21}\ \text{m/s}$$

Ans. (B)

Sol. 8 Number of photons emitted per second from a power source is given as

$$n = \frac{P\lambda}{hc}$$

$$\Rightarrow \qquad n = \frac{9\times10^{-3}\times6.67\times10^{-7}}{6.6\times10^{-34}\times3\times10^8} = 3\times10^{16}\ \textbf{Ans. (C)}$$

Sol. 9 Number of photons emitted per second from a power source is given as

$$n = \frac{P\lambda}{hc}$$

$$\Rightarrow \qquad P = n\frac{hc}{\lambda}$$

Thus ratio of powers of the two sources is given as

$$\frac{P_1}{P_2} = \frac{n_1\dfrac{hc}{\lambda_1}}{n_2\dfrac{hc}{\lambda_2}}$$

$$\Rightarrow \qquad \frac{P_2}{P_1} = \frac{n_2\lambda_1}{n_1\lambda_2}$$

$$\Rightarrow \qquad \frac{P_2}{P_1} = \frac{1.02\times10^{15}\times5000\text{Å}}{10^{15}\times5100\text{Å}} = 1 \qquad \textbf{Ans. (B)}$$

Sol. 10 de-Broglie wavelength associated with the moving electron which is accelerated by a potential difference V is given as

$$\lambda = \frac{1.227}{\sqrt{V}}\ \text{nm}$$

$$\Rightarrow \qquad \lambda \propto \frac{1}{\sqrt{V}}$$

Thus ratio of de-Broglie wavelengths of electron for the two given accelerating voltages is given as

$$\frac{\lambda_1}{\lambda_2} = \sqrt{\frac{V_2}{V_1}} = 2$$

$$\Rightarrow \qquad \lambda_2 = \frac{\lambda_1}{2} \qquad \textbf{Ans. (B)}$$

Sol. 11 When the potential difference across the tube increases, the acceleration of charge particle will be high so emitted charged particles will come out with higher magnitude of velocity. **Ans. (A)**

Sol. 12 Students are advised to refer solution to Q. 4 for understanding radiation order in electromagnetic spectrum.

Ans. (A)

Sol. 13 Number of photons emitted per second from a power source is given as

$$n = \frac{P\lambda}{hc}\times0.25$$

$$\Rightarrow \qquad n = \frac{200\times25}{100}\times\frac{\lambda}{hc}$$

$$\Rightarrow \qquad n = \frac{200\times25\times0.6\times10^{-6}}{100\times6.2\times10^{-34}\times3\times10^8} = 1.5\times10^{20}$$

Ans. (A)

Sol. 14 de-Broglie wavelength associated with the α-particle is given as

$$\lambda = \frac{h}{p} = \frac{h}{mv} \qquad \qquad \ldots(1)$$

Radius of circular motion in uniform magnetic field is given as

$$r = \frac{mv}{qB}$$

$$\Rightarrow \qquad mv = qrB$$

From equation-(1), we have

$$\lambda = \frac{h}{qrB} = \frac{6.6\times10^{-34}\times4}{2\times1.6\times10^{-19}\times0.83\times10^{-12}} = 0.01\text{Å}\ \textbf{Ans. (D)}$$

Sol. 15 de-Broglie wavelength an electron moving with energy E is given as

$$\lambda_e = \frac{h}{\sqrt{2mE}}$$

$$\Rightarrow \qquad \lambda_e \propto \frac{1}{\sqrt{E}}$$

$$\Rightarrow \qquad \lambda_e^2 \propto \frac{1}{E} \qquad \ldots(1)$$

Wavelength of a photon is given as

$$\lambda_p = \frac{hc}{E}$$

$$\Rightarrow \qquad \lambda_p \propto \frac{1}{E} \qquad \ldots(2)$$

From equation-(1) and (2), we have

$$\lambda_e^2 \propto \lambda_p \qquad \textbf{Ans. (A)}$$

Sol. 16 As electron speed increases, its de-Broglie wavelength decreases as it is given as

$$\lambda = \frac{h}{mv}$$

The angular width for central maxima of diffraction pattern is given as

$$\theta = \frac{2\lambda}{d}$$

Thus on increasing the speed of electrons, angular width of central maxima in diffraction pattern obtained decreases.

$$\textbf{Ans. (C)}$$

Sol. 17 The average force exerted on a perfectly reflecting surface for normal incidence is given as

$$F_{av} = \frac{2IA}{c}$$

$$\Rightarrow \qquad F_{av} = \frac{2 \times 25 \times 10^4 \times 15 \times 10^{-4}}{3 \times 10^8} \text{N}$$

$$\Rightarrow \qquad F_{av} = 250 \times 10^{-8} \text{N} = 2.5 \times 10^{-6} \text{N} \qquad \textbf{Ans. (B)}$$

Sol. 18 de-Broglie wavelength of a moving particle with kinetic energy E is given as

$$\lambda = \frac{h}{p} = \frac{h}{\sqrt{2mE}}$$

If energy is made 16 times, new de-Broglie wavelength is given as

$$\lambda' = \frac{h}{\sqrt{2m(16E)}} = \frac{\lambda}{4} = 0.25\lambda$$

Thus percentage change in wavelength is -75%. $\qquad \textbf{Ans. (B)}$

Sol. 19 Energy of photon having wavelength 500 nm is given as

$$E_{\text{Ph}} = \frac{1243.1}{500} \text{eV} = 2.48 \text{eV}$$

By photoelectric effect equation, we have

$$K_{\max} = E_{\text{Ph}} - \phi = 2.48 - 2.28 = 0.2 \text{ eV}$$

$$\Rightarrow \qquad \lambda_{e\min} = \frac{12.27}{\sqrt{K_{\max}(in\,eV)}} \text{Å} = \frac{12.27}{\sqrt{0.2}} \text{Å} = 27.436 \text{ Å}$$

$$\Rightarrow \qquad \lambda_{\min} = 2.7436 \times 10^{-9} \text{ m}$$

As all electrons have kinetic energy less than or equal to the maximum kinetic energy thus the de-Broglie wavelength of all electrons emitted will be equal to or more than the minimum wavelength calculated above corresponding to the maximum energy electrons. $\qquad \textbf{Ans. (D)}$

Sol. 20 de-Broglie wavelength of an electron moving with energy E is given as

$$\lambda_e = \frac{h}{\sqrt{2mE}}$$

The wavelength of photon is given as

$$\lambda_p = \frac{hc}{E}$$

$$\Rightarrow \qquad \frac{\lambda_e}{\lambda_p} = \frac{h}{\sqrt{2mE}} \frac{E}{hc} = \frac{1}{c}\sqrt{\frac{E}{2m}} \qquad \textbf{Ans. (A)}$$

Sol. 21 de-Broglie wavelength of a moving electron is related to its kinetic energy as

$$\lambda = \frac{h}{\sqrt{2mE}}$$

$$\Rightarrow \qquad E = \frac{h^2}{2m\lambda^2}$$

Cut of wavelength of X-ray is corresponding to the energy of incident electron, given as

$$\lambda_0 = \frac{hc}{E}$$

$$\Rightarrow \qquad \lambda_0 = \frac{2mc}{h}\lambda^2 \qquad \textbf{Ans. (A)}$$

Sol. 22 de-Broglie wavelength of a neutron with energy E is given as

$$\lambda = \frac{h}{\sqrt{2mE}}$$

Thermal energy of neutron at temperature T is given as

$$E = \frac{3}{2}kT$$

Thus de-Broglie wavelength of this neutron is given as

$$\lambda = \frac{h}{\sqrt{2m\left(\frac{3}{2}kT\right)}} = \frac{h}{\sqrt{3mkT}} \qquad \textbf{Ans. (B)}$$

Sol. 23 Initial de-Broglie wavelength of the electron can be given as

$$\lambda_0 = \frac{h}{mV_0} \qquad \ldots(1)$$

In electric field, acceleration of electron is given as

$$a = \frac{eE_0}{m}$$

After time t, the velocity of electron is given as

$$V = \left(V_0 + \frac{eE_0}{m}t\right)$$

Thus after time t, the de-Broglie wavelength of electron is given as

$$\lambda = \frac{h}{mV} = \frac{h}{m\left(v_0 + \dfrac{eE_0}{m}t\right)}$$

$$\Rightarrow \qquad \lambda = \frac{h}{mV_0\left[1 + \dfrac{eE_0}{mV_0}t\right]} \qquad \ldots(2)$$

Dividing equation-(2) by (1) gives

$$\lambda = \frac{\lambda_0}{\left[1 + \dfrac{eE_0}{mV_0}t\right]} \qquad \textbf{Ans. (C)}$$

Sol. 24 For an electron accelerated through a potential V, is given as

$$\lambda = \frac{12.27}{\sqrt{V}}\,\text{Å} = \frac{12.27 \times 10^{-10}}{\sqrt{10000}} = 12.27 \times 10^{-12}\,\text{m} \quad \textbf{Ans. (B)}$$

Sol. 25 For an electron accelerated through a potential difference V, its de-Broglie wavelength is given as

$$\lambda = \frac{12.27}{\sqrt{V}}\,\text{Å}$$

$$\Rightarrow \qquad 0.1227 = \frac{12.27}{\sqrt{V}}\,\text{Å}$$

$$\Rightarrow \qquad \sqrt{V} = 10^2$$

$$\Rightarrow \qquad V = 10^4\,\text{V} \qquad \textbf{Ans. (A)}$$

Sol. 26 de-Broglie wavelength of a particle having momentum p is given as

$$\lambda = \frac{h}{p}$$

Thus for $\lambda \propto \dfrac{1}{p}$, graph will be rectangular hyperbolic curve, which is drawn as

Ans. (C)

Ch-26 Atoms

26.1 Properties of Electron in Bohr Model

Sol. 1 Energy in n^{th} orbit of a hydrogenic ion is given as

$$E_n \propto \frac{Z^2}{n^2}$$

In same orbit for $Z = 2$ (Helium) the energy will become 4 times.

Ans. (A)

Sol. 2 As radius of orbit in Bohr model is inversely proportional to atomic number out of given options for doubly ionized lithium $Z\,(=3)$ is maximum, hence for doubly ionized lithium, r will be minimum. **Ans. (A)**

Sol. 3 The Coulombic force on electron due to nucleus of hydrogen atom is given as

$$F = K\frac{q_1 q_2}{r^2} = K\frac{(+e)(e)}{r^2}$$

As force is attractive in nature, we choose negative sign here, so vectorially it is given as

$$\vec{F} = -\frac{Ke^2}{r^2}\hat{r} = -\frac{Ke^2}{r^3}\vec{r} \qquad \textbf{Ans. (D)}$$

Sol. 4 Bohr's second postulate states that those electron orbits are stable in which angular momentum of electron is quantized i.e. it is given as integral multiple of a constant factor $h/2\pi$, given as

$$mvr = \frac{nh}{2\pi} \qquad \textbf{Ans. (A)}$$

Sol. 5 Kinetic energy of electron in any orbit of hydrogen atom is equal in magnitude of total energy and opposite in sign, given as

$$K_n = -E_n = +3.4\,\text{eV} \qquad \textbf{Ans. (B)}$$

Sol. 6 Total energy of electron in the first excited state is given as

$$E_2 = \frac{-13.6}{n^2} = \frac{-13.6}{2^2} = -3.4\,\text{eV}$$

Kinetic energy of electron in any orbit of hydrogen atom is equal in magnitude of total energy and opposite in sign, given as

$$K_n = -E_n = +3.4\,\text{eV} \qquad \textbf{Ans. (D)}$$

Sol. 7 Total energy of electron in the first excited state is given as

$$E_2 = -\frac{13.6}{n^2} = \frac{-13.6}{4} = -3.4 \, \text{eV}$$

Thus excitation energy of electron in first excited state is the energy required to raise the electron from ground state to first excited state. It is given as

$$\Delta E = -3.4 + 13.6 = 10.2 \, \text{eV} \qquad \textbf{Ans. (A)}$$

Sol. 8 Energy of hydrogenic ions in n^{th} orbit is given as

$$E_n = -13.6 \frac{Z^2}{n^2} \, \text{eV}$$

For helium ion $Z = 2$ and $n = 2$, we have

$$E_2 = \frac{4}{4}(-13.6 \, \text{eV}) = -13.6 \, \text{eV} \qquad \textbf{Ans. (B)}$$

Sol. 9 For $n = 3$, $l = 1$ and $m = -1$, the orbital must be corresponding to $3p_x$ or $3p_y$ and in each orbital maximum number of electrons can be 2. **Ans. (D)**

Sol. 10 In Bohr model kinetic energy of electron in an orbit is equal to the magnitude of total energy of electron and opposite in sign, so we have

$$K_n = -E_n$$

$$\Rightarrow \qquad K_n : E_n = 1 : -1 \qquad \textbf{Ans. (B)}$$

Sol. 11 In Bohr's model in an orbit kinetic energy, total energy and potential energy of an electron are related as

$$\Rightarrow \qquad K_n = -E_n = -\frac{1}{2} U_n$$

As total energy of electron is given as -3.4 eV. In same orbit potential energy is given as

$$U = -2K = -6.8 \, \text{eV}$$

and kinetic energy is given as

$$K = 3.4 \, \text{eV} \qquad \textbf{Ans. (C)}$$

Sol. 12 Bohr model is applicable only for single electron system or hydrogenic ions. **Ans. (A)**

Sol. 13 For first excited state, we use $n = 2$ for which energy of electron is given as

$$E_1 = -13.6 \frac{z^2}{n^2} = -\frac{13.6}{4} \, \text{eV}$$

For second excited state $n = 3$ for which energy of electron is given as

$$E_2 = -13.6 \frac{z^2}{n^2} = -\frac{13.6}{9} \, \text{eV}$$

$$\Rightarrow \qquad E_1 : E_2 = \frac{1}{4} : \frac{1}{9} = 9 : 4 \qquad \textbf{Ans. (C)}$$

26.2 Electron Transition & Hydrogen Spectrum

Sol. 1 Energy of photon for a transition from $n = 3$ to $n = 2$ state is given as

$$\Delta E = E_3 - E_2$$

$$\Delta E = \frac{-13.6}{9} - \left(\frac{-13.6}{4}\right) = \frac{5}{36} \times 13.6 = 1.9 \, \text{eV} \qquad \textbf{Ans. (C)}$$

Sol. 2 Figure below shows the energy level diagram for the three energy levels and the respective transitions described in question.

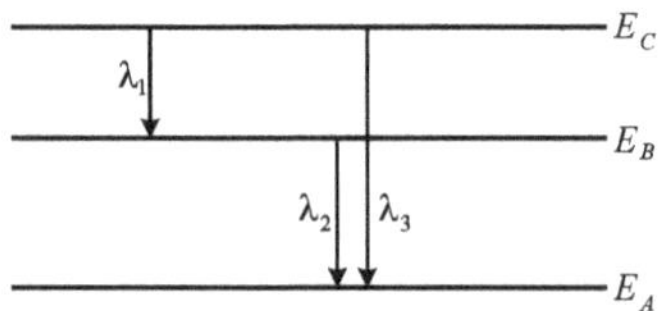

From above diagram we can write

$$\Rightarrow \qquad (E_C - E_B) + (E_B - E_A) = (E_C - E_A)$$

$$\Rightarrow \qquad \frac{hc}{\lambda_3} = \frac{hc}{\lambda_1} + \frac{hc}{\lambda_2}$$

$$\Rightarrow \qquad \frac{1}{\lambda_3} = \frac{1}{\lambda_1} + \frac{1}{\lambda_2}$$

$$\Rightarrow \qquad \lambda_3 = \left(\frac{\lambda_1 \lambda_2}{\lambda_1 + \lambda_2}\right) \qquad \textbf{Ans. (D)}$$

Sol. 3 12.1 eV is the transition energy corresponding to a transition from $n = 1$ to $n = 3$. Thus after excitation of atoms to the excited state $n = 3$, number of spectral lines emitted are given as

$$^nC_2 = \frac{n(n-1)}{2} = \frac{(3)(2)}{2} = 3 \qquad \textbf{Ans. (B)}$$

Sol. 4 Number of spectral lines emitted in hydrogen spectrum are given as

$$^nC_2 = \frac{n(n-1)}{2} = 6$$

$$\Rightarrow \qquad n = 4$$

Thus in above question, atom is excited to $n = 4$ energy level and out of 6 spectral lines emitted, wavelength will be maximum for the transition in which difference in energy levels is minimum and that will be corresponding to transition between two successive highest energy levels as difference between energy of orbit decreases as we go to higher levels so in this case it will be corresponding to the transition of electron from the energy level $n = 4$ to $n = 3$. **Ans. (A)**

Sol. 5 Wavelength of first line of Lyman series for hydrogen atom ($Z = 1$) can be calculated by Rydberg's formula, given as

$$\frac{1}{\lambda_L} = R\,(1)^2 \left[\frac{1}{1^2} - \frac{1}{2^2} \right]$$

Wavelength of second line of Balmer series for a hydrogen like ion (Z) is given as

$$\frac{1}{\lambda_B} = RZ^2$$

It is specified that $\lambda_L = \lambda_B$, this gives

$$\frac{3}{4} R = \frac{3}{16} RZ^2$$

$$\Rightarrow \qquad Z^2 = 4$$

$$\Rightarrow \qquad Z = 2 \qquad\qquad \textbf{Ans. (D)}$$

Sol. 6 Figure below shows the energy level diagram and corresponding transition of electron as described in question.

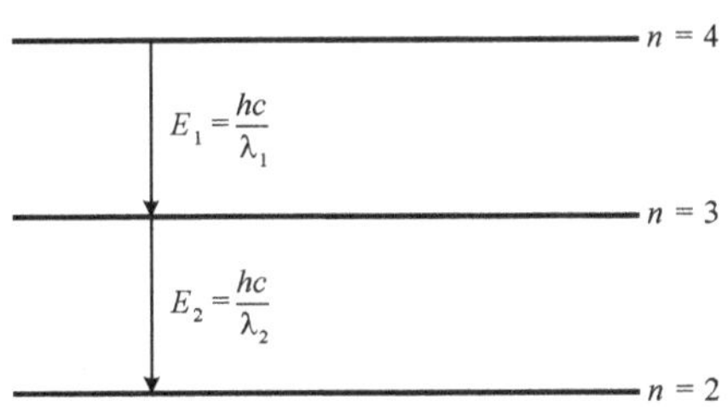

Energy emitted when electron jumps from $n = 4$ to $n = 3$ is given as

$$E_1 = \frac{hc}{\lambda_1} = 13.6 \left[\frac{1}{(3)^2} - \frac{1}{(4)^2} \right] \qquad \ldots(1)$$

Energy emitted when electron jumps from $n = 3$ to $n = 2$ is given as

$$E_2 = \frac{hc}{\lambda_2}\, 13.6 \left[\frac{1}{(2)^2} - \frac{1}{(3)^2} \right] \qquad \ldots(2)$$

Dividing equation-(2) by equation (1) gives

$$\frac{\lambda_1}{\lambda_2} = \frac{\dfrac{1}{4} - \dfrac{1}{9}}{\dfrac{1}{9} - \dfrac{1}{16}} = \frac{20}{7} \qquad\qquad \textbf{Ans. (D)}$$

Sol. 7 Infrared radiation has energy less compared to ultraviolet. In hydrogen atom infrared radiation is emitted when any transition from higher level to $n = 3, 4, 5$ so for hydrogen like atoms ($Z \geq 2$), energy difference for the energy level must be less compared to $n = 3$ to $n = 1$ level which is for transitions given in options (B) and (C) but option (C) is even lesser so this is most appropriate answer. **Ans. (C)**

Sol. 8 Energy of emitted photon when an electron in hydrogen atom jumps from first excited state to ground state is given as

$$h\nu = E_2 - E_1 = [-3.4 - (-13.6)]\,\text{eV} = 10.2\,\text{eV}$$

From photoelectric effect equation, we have

$$K_{\max} = h\nu - \phi$$

Here ϕ is work function and $h\nu$ is the incident energy

$$\phi = h\nu - K_{\max}$$

$$\Rightarrow \qquad \phi = 10.2\,\text{eV} - 3.57\,\text{eV} = 6.63\,\text{eV}$$

Threshold frequency for the metal is given as

$$\nu_0 = \frac{\phi_0}{h} = \frac{6.63 \times 1.6 \times 10^{-19}}{6.67 \times 10^{-34}} = 1.6 \times 10^{15}\,\text{Hz} \;\; \textbf{Ans. (C)}$$

Sol. 9 For emission of electron due to transition from $n = 5$ to $n = 4$ energy level can be calculated by Rydberg's formula, given as

$$\frac{1}{\lambda} = Rz^2 \left(\frac{1}{n_1^2} - \frac{1}{n_2^2} \right)$$

$$\Rightarrow \qquad \frac{1}{\lambda} = R \left(\frac{1}{1^2} - \frac{1}{5^2} \right) = R\left(1 - \frac{1}{25} \right) = R\left(\frac{24}{25} \right)$$

For this emitted photon of wavelength λ, its linear momentum is given as

$$p = \frac{h}{\lambda} = hR\left(\frac{24}{25} \right)$$

When photon is emitted to conserve momentum, atom recoils back with speed v, which is given by conserving momentum of the system of atom and emitted photon as initially system was at rest so final momentum of photon and atom must be equal, given as

$$mv = \frac{24hR}{25}$$

$$\Rightarrow \qquad v = \frac{24hR}{25m} \qquad\qquad \textbf{Ans. (A)}$$

Sol. 10 Figure below shows the energy level diagram of hydrogen atom and corresponding transition lines of maximum wavelength of Lyman and Blamer series (First line of each spectral series has minimum energy in that series).

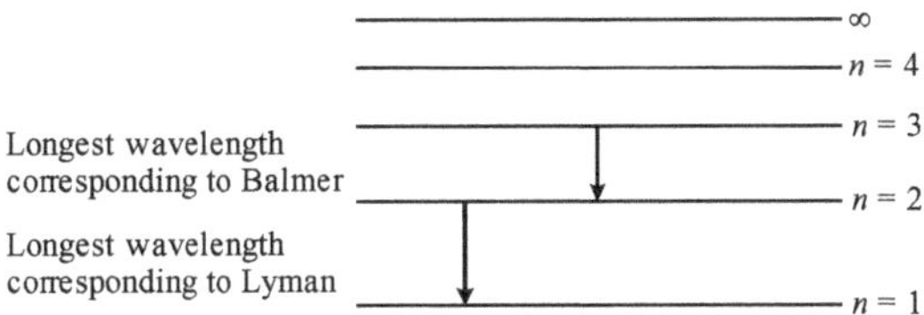

Wavelength corresponding to first line of Lyman series is given by Rydberg's formula as

$$\frac{1}{\lambda_L} = R(1)^2 \left[\frac{1}{1^2} - \frac{1}{2^2}\right] = \frac{3R}{4}$$

$$\Rightarrow \qquad \lambda_L = \frac{4}{3R} \qquad \ldots(1)$$

Wavelength corresponding to first line of Balmer series is also given by Rydberg's formula as

$$\frac{1}{\lambda_B} = R(1)^2 \left[\frac{1}{2^2} - \frac{1}{3^2}\right] = \frac{5R}{36}$$

$$\Rightarrow \qquad \lambda_B = \frac{36}{5R} \qquad \ldots(2)$$

Dividing equation-(2) by equation-(1) gives

$$\frac{\lambda_L}{\lambda_B} = \frac{4}{3R} \times \frac{5R}{36} = \frac{5}{3 \times 9} = \frac{5}{27} \qquad \textbf{Ans. (A)}$$

Sol. 11 Energy of incident radiation photon can be given as

$$\Delta E = \frac{hc}{\lambda} = \frac{6.63 \times 10^{-34} \times 3 \times 10^8}{975 \times 10^{-10} \times 1.6 \times 10^{-19}} \text{ eV}$$

$$\Delta E = \frac{12431}{975} = 12.75 \text{ eV}$$

Above the energy difference between $n = 1$ and $n = 4$ so hydrogen atom in this case is excited to $n = 4$. Thus number of spectral lines emitted are given as

$$^nC_2 = \frac{n(n-1)}{2} = \frac{4(4-1)}{2} = 6 \qquad \textbf{Ans. (C)}$$

Sol. 12 Last line of Balmer series is corresponding to the transition $n_2 = \infty$ to $n_1 = 2$. The wave number for this transition is given as

$$\bar{v} = \frac{1}{\lambda} = RZ^2 \left(\frac{1}{n_1^2} - \frac{1}{n_2^2}\right)$$

$$\Rightarrow \qquad \bar{v} = \frac{1}{\lambda} = 10^7 \left(\frac{1}{2^2} - \frac{1}{\infty^2}\right) = 0.25 \times 10^7 \qquad \textbf{Ans. (C)}$$

Sol. 13 For transition of electron from $n = 3$ to $n = 2$, the wavelength emitted is given by Rydberg's formula as

$$\frac{1}{\lambda} = R(1)^2 \left(\frac{1}{2^2} - \frac{1}{3^2}\right) \qquad \ldots(1)$$

For the transition of electron from $n = 4$ to $n = 3$, the wavelength is given as

$$\frac{1}{\lambda_2} = R(1)^2 \left(\frac{1}{3^2} - \frac{1}{4^2}\right) \qquad \ldots(2)$$

Dividing equation-(1) by (2) gives

$$\frac{\dfrac{1}{\lambda}}{\dfrac{1}{\lambda_2}} = \frac{\dfrac{1}{4} - \dfrac{1}{9}}{\dfrac{1}{9} - \dfrac{1}{16}} = \frac{\dfrac{5}{4 \times 9}}{\dfrac{16-9}{9 \times 16}}$$

$$\Rightarrow \qquad \frac{\lambda_2}{\lambda} = \frac{5}{4 \times 9} \times \frac{9 \times 16}{7} = \frac{20}{7}$$

$$\Rightarrow \qquad \lambda_2 = \frac{20}{7}\lambda \qquad \textbf{Ans. (C)}$$

Sol. 14 Wavelength of last line of Balmer series is given as

$$\frac{1}{\lambda_b} = R\left[\frac{1}{2^2} - \frac{1}{\infty^2}\right]$$

$$\Rightarrow \qquad \lambda_b = \frac{4}{R}$$

Wavelength of last line of Lyman series is given as

$$\frac{1}{\lambda_l} = R\left[\frac{1}{1^2} - \frac{1}{\infty^2}\right]$$

$$\Rightarrow \qquad \lambda_l = \frac{1}{R}$$

$$\Rightarrow \qquad \frac{\lambda_b}{\lambda_l} = \frac{\dfrac{4}{R}}{\dfrac{1}{R}} = 4 \qquad \textbf{Ans. (C)}$$

Ch-27 Nuclei

27.1 Radioactivity

Sol. 1 By radioactive decay law if m is the mass left after time t and m_0 was the mass at $t = 0$ then we have

$$\frac{N}{N_0} = 2^{-t/T}$$

$$\Rightarrow \qquad \frac{1}{256} = \left(\frac{1}{2}\right)^8 = \left(\frac{1}{2}\right)^{t/T}$$

$$\Rightarrow \qquad t = 8T = 8 \times 12.5 = 100 \text{ hours} \qquad \textbf{Ans. (B)}$$

Sol. 2 Number of nuclei left after 30 days (three half life) will be given as

$$N = N_0 \left(\frac{1}{2}\right)^n = 4 \times 10^{16} \times \left(\frac{1}{2}\right)^3 = 0.5 \times 10^{16}$$

Thus, number of decayed nuclei after 30 days will be given as

$$N_0 - N = 4 \times 10^{16} - 0.5 \times 10^{16} = 3.5 \times 10^{16} \textbf{ Ans. (C)}$$

Sol. 3 After two mean lives, time is

$$t = 2\tau = 2\left(\frac{1}{\lambda}\right)$$

By radioactive decay law, we use

$$m = m_0 e^{-\lambda t} = 10\, e^{-\lambda(2/\lambda)}$$

$$\Rightarrow \qquad m = 10\left(\frac{1}{e}\right)^2 = 10\left(\frac{1}{2.718}\right)^2 = 1.35\,\text{g} \quad \textbf{Ans. (A)}$$

Sol. 4 After n half lives element remain unchanged is given as

$$m = m_0\left(\frac{1}{2}\right)^n$$

$$\Rightarrow \qquad \frac{25}{100} = \left(\frac{1}{2}\right)^n$$

$$\Rightarrow \qquad n = 2$$

Thus after 2 half lives radium left will change from 100 g to 25 g, thus the time is given as

$$t = 2 \times 1600 = 3200 \text{ yrs} \qquad \textbf{Ans. (D)}$$

Sol. 5 The activity R of a radioactive material after time t is given by radioactive decay law, given as

$$R = R_0 e^{-\lambda t}$$

$$\Rightarrow \qquad \frac{R_1}{R_2} = \frac{e^{-\lambda t_1}}{e^{-\lambda t_2}} = e^{-\lambda(t_1 - t_2)}$$

$$\Rightarrow \qquad R_1 = R_2\, e^{-\lambda(t_1 - t_2)} \qquad \textbf{Ans. (A)}$$

Sol. 6 At $t = 0$, it is specified in question that total number of nuclei are same for both substances A and B, so we have

$$N_{0A} = N_{0B}$$

If after time t, the ratio of left over nuclei of A and B are $(1/e)^2$, we have

$$\frac{N_A}{N_B} = \left(\frac{1}{e}\right)^2$$

Using radioactive decay law we have

$$N = N_0\, e^{-\lambda t}$$

$$\Rightarrow \qquad N_A = N_{0A}\, e^{-\lambda_A t} \qquad \ldots(1)$$

and $\qquad N_B = N_{0B}\, e^{-\lambda_B t} \qquad \ldots(2)$

Dividing equation-(1) by (2) gives

$$\frac{N_A}{N_B} = e^{-(5\lambda - \lambda)t}$$

$$\Rightarrow \qquad \left(\frac{1}{e}\right)^2 = e^{-4\lambda t} = \left(\frac{1}{e}\right)^{4\lambda t}$$

$$\Rightarrow \qquad 4\lambda t = 2$$

$$\Rightarrow \qquad t = \frac{1}{2\lambda} \qquad \textbf{Ans. (C)}$$

Sol. 7 In beta minus decay (β^-), a neutron is transformed into a proton, and an electron. This electron is emitted from the nucleus along with antineutrino according to the reaction given below.

$$n = p + e^- + \overline{v} \qquad \textbf{Ans. (A)}$$

Sol. 8 At $t = 0$, it is specified in question that total number of nuclei are same for both substances A and B, so we have

$$N_{0X_1} = N_{0X_2}$$

If after time t, the ratio of left over nuclei of A and B are $(1/e)$, we have

$$\frac{N_{X_1}}{N_{X_2}} = \frac{1}{e}$$

Using radioactive decay law we have

$$N = N_0\, e^{-\lambda t}$$

$$\Rightarrow \qquad N_{X_1} = N_{0X_1}\, e^{-\lambda_1 t} \qquad \ldots(1)$$

and $\qquad N_{X_2} = N_{0X_2}\, e^{-\lambda_2 t} \qquad \ldots(2)$

Dividing equation-(1) by (2) gives

$$\frac{N_{X_1}}{N_{X_2}} = e^{-(5\lambda - \lambda)t}$$

$$\Rightarrow \qquad \frac{1}{e} = e^{-4\lambda t} = \left(\frac{1}{e}\right)^{4\lambda t}$$

$$\Rightarrow \qquad 4\lambda t = 1$$

$$\Rightarrow \qquad t = \frac{1}{4\lambda} \qquad \textbf{Ans. (A)}$$

Sol. 9 Activity of a radioactive sample reduces to $1/e$ times in its mean life time so for given sample mean life time is given as 5 min, thus we use

$$\lambda = \frac{1}{5}\,\text{minute}^{-1}$$

Thus half life time of element is given as

$$T_{1/2} = \frac{\log_e 2}{\lambda} = 5\log_e 2 \text{ min} \qquad \textbf{Ans. (A)}$$

Sol. 10 If at the time of formation of rock all nuclei were of element X and total number were N_0 then after time t (today) the number of nuclei are N then from the given ratio we have

$$\frac{N_X}{N_Y} = \frac{N}{N_0 - N} = \frac{1}{15}$$

$$\Rightarrow \qquad N = \frac{1}{16} N_0$$

From radioactive decay law, we have

$$N = N_0 (2)^{-t/T}$$

$$\Rightarrow \qquad (2)^{-4} = (2)^{-t/T}$$

$$\Rightarrow \qquad t = 4T = 200 \text{ years} \qquad \textbf{Ans. (B)}$$

Sol. 11 After t seconds if amount of A_1 and A_2 become equal in mixture then by radioactive decay law we use

$$N_1 = N_{01}\,(2)^{-t/20} = \frac{N_{01}}{(2)^{t/20}}$$

$$N_2 = N_{02}\,(2)^{-t/10} = \frac{N_{02}}{(2)^{t/10}}$$

As $N_1 = N_2$ from above relations we have

$$\frac{40}{(2)^{t/20}} = \frac{160}{(2)^{t/10}}$$

$$\Rightarrow \qquad 2^{t/20} = 2^{\left(\frac{t}{10}-2\right)}$$

$$\Rightarrow \qquad \frac{t}{20} = \frac{t}{10} - 2$$

$$\Rightarrow \qquad \frac{t}{20} - \frac{t}{10} = 2$$

$$\Rightarrow \qquad \frac{t}{20} = 2$$

$$\Rightarrow \qquad t = 40 \text{ s} \qquad\qquad \textbf{Ans. (D)}$$

Sol. 12 By radioactive decay law, we have

$$N = N_0 e^{-\lambda t}$$

As specified in the question that t_2 is the time after which two third of it has decayed means one third is left, so we use

$$N = \frac{1}{3}N_0 = N_0 e^{-\lambda t_2} \qquad\qquad \dots(1)$$

As also specified in the question that t_1 is the time after which one third of it has decayed means two third is left, so we use

$$N = \frac{2}{3}N_0 = N_0 e^{-\lambda t_1} \qquad\qquad \dots(2)$$

Dividing equation-(2) by (1) gives

$$e^{-\lambda(t_2 - t_1)} = 2$$

$$\Rightarrow \qquad (t_2 - t_1) = \frac{\ln 2}{\lambda} = T_{1/2}$$

$$\Rightarrow \qquad t_2 - t_1 = 50 \text{ days} \qquad\qquad \textbf{Ans. (A)}$$

Sol. 13 If at the time of formation of rock all nuclei were of element X and total number were N_0 then after time t (today) the number of nuclei are N then from the given ratio we have

$$\frac{N_X}{N_Y} = \frac{N}{N_0 - N} = \frac{1}{7}$$

$$\Rightarrow \qquad N = \frac{1}{8}N_0$$

From radioactive decay law, we have

$$N = N_0(2)^{-t/T}$$

$$\Rightarrow \qquad (2)^{-3} = (2)^{-t/T}$$

$$\Rightarrow \qquad t = 3T = 60 \text{ years} \qquad\qquad \textbf{Ans. (B)}$$

Sol. 14 This question is same as that of Q. 13. Students are advised to refer solution to Q. 13. According to that solution age of rock can be given as

$$t = 3T = 4.20 \times 10^9 \text{ years} \qquad\qquad \textbf{Ans. (C)}$$

Sol. 15 If initially at $t = 0$, there were N_0 nuclei of the substance and N_1 are remaining nuclei after 40% decay and N_2 are remaining nuclei after 85% decay then we have

$$N_1 = (1 - 0.4)\,N_0 = 0.6\,N_0$$

and $$N_2 = (1 - 0.85)\,N_0 = 0.15\,N_0$$

By radioactive decay law from the time of no of nuclei were N_1 to N_2, we have

$$N_2 = N_1\,(2)^{-t/T}$$

$$\Rightarrow \qquad \frac{N_2}{N_1} = \frac{0.15 N_0}{0.6 N_0} = \frac{1}{4} = \left(\frac{1}{2}\right)^2 = (2)^{-t/T}$$

$$\Rightarrow \qquad t = 2T = 2 \times 30 = 60 \text{ min} \qquad\qquad \textbf{Ans. (D)}$$

Sol. 16 At $t = 0$, it is specified in question that total number of nuclei are same for both substances A and B, so we have

$$N_{0A} = N_{0B}$$

If after time t, the ratio of left over nuclei of A and B are $(1/e)$, we have

$$\frac{N_A}{N_B} = \frac{1}{e}$$

Using radioactive decay law we have

$$N = N_0\,e^{-\lambda t}$$

$$\Rightarrow \qquad N_A = N_{0A}\,e^{-\lambda_1 t} \qquad\qquad \dots(1)$$

and $$N_B = N_{0B}\,e^{-\lambda_2 t} \qquad\qquad \dots(2)$$

Dividing equation-(1) by (2) gives

$$\frac{N_A}{N_B} = e^{-(8\lambda - \lambda)t}$$

$$\Rightarrow \qquad \frac{1}{e} = e^{-7\lambda t} = \left(\frac{1}{e}\right)^{7\lambda t}$$

$$\Rightarrow \qquad 7\lambda t = 1$$

$$\Rightarrow \qquad t = \frac{1}{7\lambda} \qquad\qquad \textbf{Ans. (B)}$$

Sol. 17 If after time t, 450 nuclei are disintegrated then number of nuclei remaining are given as

$$N = 600 - 450 = 150$$

By radioactive decay law, we have

$$N = N_0 (2)^{-t/T}$$

$$\Rightarrow \quad \frac{150}{600} = \left(\frac{1}{2}\right)^{\frac{t}{T}}$$

$$\Rightarrow \quad \left(\frac{1}{2}\right)^2 = \left(\frac{1}{2}\right)^{\frac{t}{T}}$$

$$\Rightarrow \quad t = 2T = 2 \times 10 = 20 \text{ min} \qquad \textbf{Ans. (C)}$$

Sol. 18 Based on the changes in atomic number of intermediate nuclei of the given reaction the possible emissions are shown in the reaction below

$$_Z^A X \xrightarrow{\ \beta^+\ } {}_{z-1} B \xrightarrow{\ \alpha\ } {}_{z-3} C \xrightarrow{\ \beta^-\ } {}_{z-2} D$$

In above reaction emission of β^+ decreases atomic number by 1, emission of α decreases atomic number by 2 and emission of β^- increases atomic number by 1. **Ans. (C)**

Sol. 19 If initial activity of a radioactive substance is A_0 then after time t, activity A is given by radioactive decay equation, stated as

$$\frac{A}{A_0} = \left(\frac{1}{2}\right)^{t/T_H}$$

$$\Rightarrow \quad \frac{A}{A_0} = \left(\frac{1}{2}\right)^{150/100} = \frac{1}{2\sqrt{2}} \qquad \textbf{Ans. (B)}$$

27.2 Nuclear Physics

Sol. 1 In all types of nuclear reactions even in nuclear fission when some energy is released, some mass defect is converted into energy. **Ans. (A)**

Sol. 2 For any stable nucleus it atomic mass is always less than sum of masses of constituents due to mass defect.

Ans. (A)

Sol. 3 α-rays are doubly ionized helium nuclei so these are positively charged particles. **Ans. (A)**

Sol. 4 In the given reaction conserving charge and mass number gives

$$_5^{10}B + {}_0^1 n \rightarrow {}_2^4 He + {}^7 Li \qquad \textbf{Ans. (A)}$$

Sol. 5 Light nuclei are more useful for nuclear fusion as the nuclei of light elements have a lower binding energy than that for the elements of intermediate mass due to this the fusion of the light elements results in more stable nucleus. **Ans. (A)**

Sol. 6 The nuclear reaction for the case described in question is given as

$$_8 O^{16} + {}_1 H^2 \rightarrow {}_7 N^{14} + {}_2 He^4$$

Thus when a deuteron is bombarded on $_8 O^{16}$ nucleus then an α-particle ($_2 He^4$) is emitted and the product nucleus is $_7 N^{14}$.

Ans. (D)

Sol. 7 The mass defect for helium nuclei is given as

$$\Delta m = 2M_P + 2M_N - M_{He}$$

$$\Rightarrow \quad \Delta m = 2 \times 1.0073 + 2 \times 1.0087 - 4.0015 = 0.0305$$

Binding energy of helium nucleus is given as

$$\Delta E = 931 \times 0.0305 \text{ MeV} = 28.4 \text{ MeV} \qquad \textbf{Ans. (C)}$$

Sol. 8 Mass number of an element is the total number of nucleons in the nucleus of that element. For hydrogen atom its mass number is same as that of its atomic number so mass number is sometimes equal to atomic number and in most cases it is higher than atomic number. **Ans. (C)**

Sol. 9 Radius of an atom is of the order of 10^{-10} m and that of the nucleus is of the order of 10^{-15} m. Thus the ratio of volumes of the two is given as

$$\frac{V_{Atom}}{V_{Nucleus}} = \frac{\frac{4}{3}\pi(10^{-10})^3}{\frac{4}{3}\pi(10^{-15})^3} = 10^{15} \qquad \textbf{Ans. (D)}$$

Sol. 10 Energy in sun is produced by nuclear fusion reaction.

Ans. (C)

Sol. 11 In the reaction given one β minus particle ($_{-1}e^0$) is emitted so this is a β-decay reaction. **Ans. (A)**

Sol. 12 For a stable nucleus always mass of nucleus is slightly less than sum of masses of its constituents and the mass defect of the nucleus is related to its binding energy as

$$\Rightarrow \quad \Delta m = \frac{B}{c^2} = (ZM_P + NM_n) - M(N, Z)$$

$$\Rightarrow \quad M(N, Z) = NM_n + ZM_P - \frac{B}{c^2} \qquad \textbf{Ans. (B)}$$

Sol. 13 In all nuclear reactions in which energy is liberated, including nuclear fusion reaction, the mass of end product or is always less than the sum of initial product. The difference of mass is released in form of energy. **Ans. (C)**

Sol. 14 In the symbol of an element Z is atomic number which is number of protons and A is the mass number or total number of protons and neutrons. **Ans. (B)**

Sol. 15 Energy released in given reaction can be given by the difference in binding energies of the products and that of reactants, here it is given as

$$\Delta E = c - (a + b) = c - a - b \qquad \textbf{Ans. (C)}$$

Sol. 16 Isotones are the elements having same number of neutrons in their nuclei. **Ans. (A)**

Sol. 17 In every nuclear reaction in which energy is liberated, including fission process, when a nucleus splits into two or more middle weight fragments, then some mass is lost in the form of energy as Q value of the fission reaction. Thus mass of fission products is always less than mass of parent nucleus, so we have

$$\frac{\text{mass of fission products}}{\text{mass of parent nucleus}} < 1 \qquad \textbf{Ans. (D)}$$

Sol. 18 In fission process when a heavy weight element nucleus splits into middle weight fragments then energy is released because middle weight elements are more stable as they have higher binding energy per nucleon. Heavy nuclei are relatively less stable and have higher binding energy per nucleon. **Ans. (C)**

Sol. 19 Energy released in the fusion process described in question is given as

$$\Delta E = 28 - 2 \times 2.2 = 28 - 4.4 = 23.6 \, \text{MeV} \qquad \textbf{Ans. (B)}$$

Sol. 20 Radius of nucleus is given by the formula of fermi radius, given as

$$R = R_0 A^{1/3}$$

$$\Rightarrow \qquad \frac{A_{Ge}}{A_{Be}} = \left(\frac{R_{Ge}}{R_{Be}}\right)^3$$

$$\Rightarrow \qquad A_{Ge} = \left(\frac{R_{Ge}}{R_{Be}}\right)^3 (A_{Be}) = (2)^3 (9) = 8 \times 9 = 72 \qquad \textbf{Ans. (D)}$$

Sol. 21 Mass defect Δm for the given element is given as

$$\Delta m = [ZM_p + (A - Z)M_n] - M(A, Z)$$

Binding energy of the nucleus is given as

$$\Delta E = \Delta mc^2$$

$$\Rightarrow \qquad \Delta E = [\{ZM_p + (A - Z)M_n\} - M(A, Z)]c^2 \, \textbf{Ans. (A)}$$

Sol. 22 Radius of a nucleus of mass number A is given by formula of fermi radius, given as

$$R = R_0 A^{1/3}$$

In case of $_{13}^{27}Al$, if its nuclear radius is R_1 and for $_{32}^{125}Te$, nuclear

radius is R_2 then we use

$$R_1 = R_0 (27)^{1/3} = 3R_0$$

and

$$R_2 = R_0 (125)^{1/3} = 5R_0$$

$$\Rightarrow \qquad \frac{R_2}{R_1} = \frac{5R_0}{3R_0} = \frac{5}{3} R_1 = \frac{5}{3} \times 3.6 = 6 \, \text{fm} \qquad \textbf{Ans. (D)}$$

Sol. 23 Nuclear density of elements is independent of mass number of elements. **Ans. (B)**

Sol. 24 This question is same as that of Q. 12. Students are advised to refer solution of Q. 12. **Ans. (C)**

Sol. 25 Below nuclear reaction shows the radioactive series as described in the question.

$$_z X^A \xrightarrow{\ \alpha\ } {}_{Z-2}Y^{A-4} \xrightarrow{\ 2\beta\ } {}_Z P^{A-4}$$

We can see that the resulting daughter and parent nucleus has same atomic number. So they are isotopes. **Ans. (A)**

Sol. 26 The particles and radiations emitted in the given radioactive series are shown in the below reaction.

$$_Z X^A \xrightarrow{\ \beta\ } {}_{Z+1}Y^A \xrightarrow{\ \alpha\ } {}_{Z-1}B^{A-4} \xrightarrow{\ \gamma\ } {}_{Z-1}B^{A-4} \qquad \textbf{Ans. (B)}$$

Sol. 27 At the point of closest approach, the total energy of projectile becomes the potential energy which is given as

$$P = \frac{1}{4\pi \in_0} \frac{(Z_1 e)(Z_2 e)}{r_0}$$

$$\Rightarrow \qquad E \propto Z_1 Z_2 \qquad \textbf{Ans. (C)}$$

Sol. 28 Binding energy of the nucleus is given as

$$\Delta E = \Delta Mc^2 = 0.042 \times 931 \, \text{MeV}$$

Binding energy per nucleon of nucleus is given as

$$\frac{\Delta E}{A} = \frac{0.042 \times 931}{7} \, \text{MeV} = 5.6 \, \text{MeV} \qquad \textbf{Ans. (C)}$$

Sol. 29 At the distance of closest approach kinetic energy of bombarding particle transforms into the potential energy of system. If r is the distance of closest approach in the case described in question, we use

$$\frac{1}{2}mv^2 = \frac{K(Ze)(2e)}{r} = \frac{2KZe^2}{r}$$

$$\Rightarrow \qquad r = \frac{K 4 Ze^2}{mv^2} \propto \frac{1}{m} \qquad \textbf{Ans. (B)}$$

Sol. 30 Power produced by reactor in joule per hour is given as

$$P = 1000 \, \text{kW} = 10^6 \times 60 \times 60 \, \text{J/hr}$$

Mass of uranium required per hour for this energy output is given as

$$m = \frac{10^8 \times 36}{9 \times 10^{16}} = \frac{36}{9} \times 10^{-8} = 4 \times 10^{-8}\,\text{kg} = 40\,\mu\text{g}$$ **Ans. (C)**

Sol. 31 The nuclear reaction corresponding to the situation described in question is written below

$$_n^m X \longrightarrow {}_{n}^{m-4} X + {}_2\text{He}^4 + 2\,{}_{-1}e^0$$ **Ans. (C)**

Sol. 32 Nuclear fusion starts when lighter nuclei get close to each other upto such an extent when nuclear attraction overcomes coulombic repulsion between the nuclei and then they fuse into each other due to nuclear attraction and combine to form heavier nucleus. Fusion reaction takes place at high temperature because at high temperature kinetic energy of particles is high enough to overcome repulsion between nuclei.

  Ans. (C)

Sol. 33 The released energy $h\nu$ comes from mass defect so the total energy left with recoil nucleus is given as

$$E_{\text{recoil}} = Mc^2 - h\nu$$ **Ans. (A)**

Sol. 34 Nuclear radius is given by the formula of fermi radii, given as

$$R = R_0(A)^{1/3}$$

For two nuclei of Al and Cu, we use

$$\frac{R_2}{R_1} = \left(\frac{A_2}{A_1}\right)^{1/3} = \left(\frac{64}{27}\right)^{1/3} = \frac{4}{3}$$

$$\Rightarrow \quad R_2 = 3.6 \times \frac{4}{3} = 4.8\,\text{fm}$$ **Ans. (C)**

Sol. 35 Nuclear fusion reaction described in question can be written as

$$_1\text{H}^2 + {}_1\text{H}^2 \rightarrow {}_2\text{He}^4$$

Mass defect of this reaction is given as

$$\Delta m = 0.02866\,u$$

Thus energy liberated can be given as

$$E = \Delta mc^2 = 0.02866 \times 931\,\text{MeV} = 26.68\,\text{MeV}$$

Energy liberated per nucleon is given as

$$E_n = \frac{E}{A} = \frac{26.68}{4} = 6.678\,\text{MeV}$$ **Ans. (C)**

Sol. 36 Q-value of the energy released in above given reaction is given as

$$Q = 2(BE\ of\ He) - (BE\ of\ Li)$$

$$\Rightarrow \quad Q = 2 \times (4 \times 7.06) - (7 \times 5.60)\,\text{MeV}$$

$$\Rightarrow \quad Q = 56.48 - 39.2 = 17.3\,\text{MeV}$$ **Ans. (D)**

Sol. 37 The nuclear reaction of the given case in question is written below

$$_{92}\text{U}^{238} \rightarrow {}_{90}\text{Th}^{234} + {}_2\text{He}^4$$

As uranium nucleus was at rest, its momentum was zero and due to internal nuclear forces it splits into two nuclei so total momentum after split will also remain zero. Thus by conservation of momentum, we have

$$|\vec{p}_{\text{Th}}| = |\vec{p}_{\text{He}}| = p$$

Kinetic energy of helium and thorium can be given as

$$K = \frac{p^2}{2m}$$

$$\Rightarrow \quad K \propto \frac{1}{m}$$

As $m_{\text{He}} < m_{\text{Th}}$, so kinetic energy of the two are related as

$$K_{\text{He}} > K_{\text{Th}}$$ **Ans. (B)**

Sol. 38 This question is same as that of Q. 29. Students are advised to refer solution of Q. 29.   **Ans. (A)**

Sol. 39 An α-particle is nucleus of Helium which has two protons and two neutrons.   **Ans. (A)**

Sol. 40 Energy required to break one bond in eV is given as

$$E = \frac{10^{-20}}{1.6 \times 10^{-19}}\,\text{eV} = 0.0625\,\text{eV}$$ **Ans. (D)**

Sol. 41 The nuclear reaction for the fission of $^{235}_{92}\text{U}$ is given below

$$_{92}^{235}\text{U} + {}_0^1\text{n} \rightarrow {}_{36}^{89}\text{Kr} + {}_{56}^{144}\text{Ba} + 3{}_0^1\text{n} + Q$$ **Ans. (B)**

Sol. 42 By Einstein's mass-energy equivalence principle, we have

$$E = mc^2$$

$$\Rightarrow \quad E = 0.5 \times 10^{-3} \times 9 \times 10^{16} = 4.5 \times 10^{13}\,\text{J}$$ **Ans. (C)**

Sol. 43 The explained fission reaction can be written as

$$X^{240} \rightarrow Y^{120} + Z^{120}$$

Given binding energy per nucleon of X, Y & Z are 7.6 MeV, 8.5 MeV & 8.5 MeV respectively.

Gain in binding energy in above reaction or Q value of reaction is given as

Q = Binding Energy of products

      − Binding energy of reactants

$$= (120 \times 8.5 \times 2) - (240 \times 7.6)\,\text{MeV} = 216\,\text{MeV} \qquad \textbf{Ans. (D)}$$

Sol. 44 The given nuclear reaction is

$$^{22}_{11}\text{Na} \longrightarrow X + e^+ + \nu$$

This is the reaction of β^+ decay hence by conservation of charge the reaction with element X can be written as

$$^{22}_{11}\text{Na} \longrightarrow {}^{22}_{10}\text{Ne} + e^+ + \nu \qquad \textbf{Ans. (B)}$$

Sol. 45 Nuclear Radius of a nucleus is given as

$$R = R_0(A)^{1/3}$$

$$\Rightarrow \qquad \frac{R(125)}{R(64)} = \frac{R_0(125)^{1/3}}{R_0(64)^{1/3}} = \frac{5}{4} \qquad \textbf{Ans. (B)}$$

Ch-28 Semiconductors Electronics

28.1 Semiconductor

Sol. 1 In a pn junction on p-side there are negatively charged impurity ions and on n-side there are positively charged impurity ions which develops an electric field from n-side to p-side due to which n-side is at high potential and p-side is at low potential.

      Ans. (A)

Sol. 2 In semiconductors at room temperature the electrons get enough energy so that they are able to transit to conduction band. Thus at room temperature the valence band is partially empty and conduction band is partially filled.   **Ans. (A)**

Sol. 3 Resistivity of a semiconductor decreases with increase in the temperature.   **Ans. (A)**

Sol. 4 For given elements, the energy band gap of carbon is 7 eV, that of Silicon is 1.14 eV and that of germanium is 0.71 eV.

      Ans. (B)

Sol. 5 In the diagram it is seen that in valance band holes are in excess compared to electrons thus it is a p-type semiconductor.

      Ans. (D)

Sol. 6 Majority carriers in n-type semiconductors are electrons.

      Ans. (C)

Sol. 7 The electronic configuration of Carbon and Silicon are given below

$$^6C = 1s^2, 2s^2\, 2p^2$$

$$^{14}Si = 1s^2\, 2p^6, 3s^2\, 3p^2$$

As in Silicon valance electrons are away from Nucleus, so nucleus attraction is low and less gap is there in valance band and conduction band for Si.   **Ans. (C)**

Sol. 8 An intrinsic semiconductor when doped with trivalent impurities, it reduces electrons in valance band called holes which are majority charge carriers.   **Ans. (B)**

Sol. 9 Native temperature coefficient indicates more charge carriers in substance at higher temperature. In semiconductors, number of charge carries per unit volume increases with an increase in temperature so α is negative for semiconductors. Even for insulators, at some temperature breakdown occurs and free charge carriers are developed in it. In this state as temperature increases number of carriers increased due to excitation of electrons in it so most appropriate option is (A).

      Ans. (A)

28.2 PN Junction and Diodes

Sol. 1 For the given circuit diode D_2 is forward biased and D_1 is reverse biased so in upper branch no current flows. Thus current in circuit is given as

$$I = \frac{5V}{(30 + 20)\Omega} = \frac{5}{50}\,\text{A} \qquad \textbf{Ans. (B)}$$

Sol. 2 In forward biased state, the resistance of p-n junction is very low. So across the given resistance R, voltage can be taken as V. In reverse biased state, the resistance of p-n junction is very high so the voltage drop across R can be taken as zero.

      Ans. (A)

Sol. 3 In case of reverse biasing high potential terminal of battery is connected to n-side and low potential terminal of battery is connected to p-side due to which electric field inside the junction is in the same direction of internal electric field of the junction due to which size of depletion region (potential barrier) rises.   **Ans. (B)**

Sol. 4 Across depletion layer barrier potential depends upon temperature, doping density and biasing.   **Ans. (A)**

Sol. 5 The fundamental ripple frequency in full wave rectifier is double that of input frequency because in each cycle there are two ripples produced.   **Ans. (D)**

Sol. 6 The *emf* produced across p-n junction due to incident light is proportional to the current produced due to e-h pairs produced in depletion layer by incident photons and it increases with intensity of incident light. **Ans. (A)**

Sol. 7 A diode reverse biased if its n-type is at high potential with respect to p-side of the junction. Thus correct option is (C).
Ans. (C)

Sol. 8 Figure below shows the input and output waveforms of a half wave rectifier.

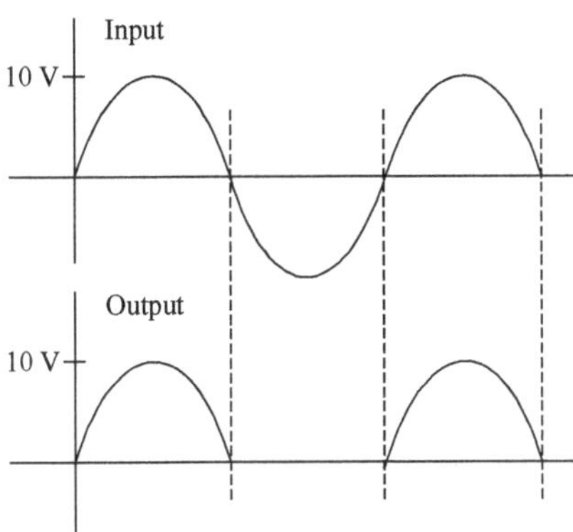

The dc component of the output is given as
$$V_{dc} = \frac{V_m}{\pi} = \frac{10}{\pi}\text{V}$$ **Ans. (B)**

Sol. 9 Zener diode operates in reverse bias conditions with out getting damaged under breakdown conditions and maintains breakdown voltage. In breakdown condition the current in zener diode can change but the voltage across the p-n junction remains unaffected so this feature makes it useful for voltage stabilisation. **Ans. (B)**

Sol. 10 Options (A), (C) and (D) are wrong for forward biasing and in forward bias conditions current starts flowing by the external power supply which decreases the width of depletion layer due to which on both sides of junction impurity atoms increases. **Ans. (B)**

Sol. 11 A diode is forward biased if its n-type is at low potential with respect to p-side of the junction. Thus correct option is (D). **Ans. (D)**

Sol. 12 Frequency corresponding to 2 eV energy photon is given as
$$E = h\nu$$
$$\Rightarrow \quad 2 \times 1.6 \times 10^{-19} = 66 \times 10^{-34} \times \nu$$
$$\Rightarrow \quad \nu = \frac{3.2 \times 10^{-19}}{6.6 \times 10^{-34}} = 5 \times 10^{14}\,\text{Hz} \quad \textbf{Ans. (D)}$$

Sol. 13 Wavelength corresponding to 2.5 eV energy photon is given as

$$\lambda_{max} = \frac{hc}{eV} = \frac{12431}{E(in\,eV)}$$

$$\Rightarrow \quad \lambda_{max} = \frac{12431}{2.5}\,\text{Å} = 497.2\,\text{Å} \qquad \textbf{Ans. (A)}$$

Sol. 14 Complete electronic circuit fabricated using semiconductors is called integrated circuit. **Ans. (C)**

Sol. 15 A diode is forward biased if its n-type is at low potential with respect to p-side of the junction. Thus correct option is (D). **Ans. (D)**

Sol. 16 Antimony (Sb) is a fifth group donor impurity material so when added to germanium it becomes n-types semiconductor. So these will be more free electrons than holes in semiconductor.
Ans. (C)

Sol. 17 In the circuit shown in figure in the question, diode D_1 is forward biased and D_2 is reverses biased so no current flows in middle branch of circuit hence current supplied by battery is given as
$$I = \frac{V}{R} = \frac{5}{10} = \frac{1}{2}\text{A} \qquad \textbf{Ans. (D)}$$

Sol. 18 In n-type semiconductors minority charge carriers are hole and doping impurity is pentavalent. **Ans. (C)**

Sol. 19 The shown curve is of a solar cell as in a solar cell open circuit current is zero at point A and the maximum emf is V and for short circuit current I at point B the emf reduces to zero.
Ans. (A)

Sol. 20 Across depletion layer barrier potential difference depends on width of depletion layer and width of depletion layer depends on type of semiconducting material, amount of doping and temperature. **Ans. (D)**

Sol. 21 The potential drop across diode opposes the battery due to its knee point voltage when it starts conducting so the circuit current is given as
$$i = \frac{V - V_K}{R} = \frac{3.5 - 0.5}{100} = \frac{3}{100} = 30\,\text{mA} \qquad \textbf{Ans. (B)}$$

Sol. 22 As the diode is given ideal, its resistance can be taken as zero as it is forward biased. Thus current in circuit can be given as
$$I = \frac{V_A - V_B}{R} = \frac{10}{10^3} = 10^{-2}\,\text{A} \qquad \textbf{Ans. (B)}$$

Sol. 23 In the circuit shown in figure, diode D_2 is forward biased and D_1 is reverses biased so no current flows in middle branch of circuit hence equivalent circuit is given as shown in figure below.

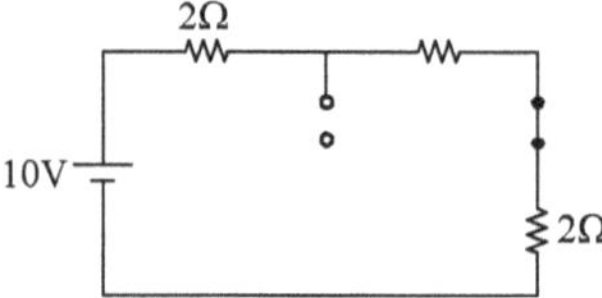

Thus current flowing through resistance through battery is given as

$$I = \frac{10}{2+2} = 2.5 \text{ A}$$ **Ans. (A)**

Sol. 24 This question is same as that of Q. 11. Students are advised to refer solution of Q. 11.   **Ans. (A)**

Sol. 25 Temperature rises due to heating and with increase in temperature number of electron-hole pairs will increase. It changes the electron and hole concentration in semiconductor due to which the conductivity and resistance of semiconductor changes and it affects both forward and reverse biasing characteristics.   **Ans. (D)**

Sol. 26 When a diode is reverse biased, the electric field in the junction due to external battery is in the same direction as that of the internal electric field and this increases the width of depletion layer.   **Ans. (C)**

Sol. 27 In N-type semiconductor majority charge carriers e^- have higher mobility compared to majority charge carriers holes of P-type semiconductor. The current due to each majority carriers in substrate is given as

$$I = neAv_d = neA\,(\mu E)$$

As $\mu_e > \mu_h$

$\Rightarrow$ $I_e > I_h$ **Ans. (C)**

Sol. 28 When a Zener diode is connected in reverse bias connections then at the breakdown voltage or higher voltage it maintains the potential difference in state of breakdown and acts as a voltage regulator hence statement-(A) is correct. Potential barrier of Germanium diode is 0.3V and that for a Silicon diode is 0.7V hence statement-(B) is incorrect.   **Ans. (C)**

Sol. 29 In circuit (a) both the junctions are forward biased in series so these two junctions offer equal resistances to circuit so equal potential drops will be there across the two junctions. In circuit (c), both the junctions reverse biased in series so these two junctions offers equal resistances to circuit so equal potential drops will be there across the two junctions.

                                                                 Ans. (C)

Sol. 30 In half wave rectification the output frequency is equal to the input frequency.

$$f_{out} = 60 \text{ Hz}$$ **Ans. (B)**

28.3 Transistors

Sol. 1 Common base current gain α is given as

$$\frac{I_C}{I_E} = \alpha = 0.98$$

So common emitter current gain can be given as

$$\frac{I_C}{I_B} = \beta = \frac{\alpha}{1-\alpha} = 49$$ **Ans. (A)**

Sol. 2 This question is same as that of Q. 1. Students are advised to refer solution of Q. 1.   **Ans. (D)**

Sol. 3 In normal operating conditions, a n-p-n transistor conducts when emitter-base junction is forward biased while collector-base junction is reverse biased.   **Ans. (B)**

Sol. 4 Resonant frequency of an oscillator is given as

$$f = \frac{1}{2\pi\sqrt{LC}}$$

After changing inductor to $2L$ and capacitor to $4C$, new resonant frequency is given as

$$f' = \frac{1}{2\pi\sqrt{2L(4C)}}$$

$\Rightarrow$ $$f' = \left(\frac{1}{2\sqrt{2}}\right)\frac{1}{2\pi\sqrt{LC}} = \frac{f}{2\sqrt{2}}$$ **Ans. (C)**

Sol. 5 Current gain in common emitter configuration is given as

$$\beta = \frac{\Delta I_C}{\Delta I_B} = \frac{(10-5)\times10^{-3}}{(150-100)\times10^{-6}} = 100$$ **Ans. (C)**

Sol. 6 For common emitter amplifier voltage gain is given as

Voltage gain = $\beta \times$ Impedance gain

$\Rightarrow$ $$50 = \beta \times \frac{200}{100}$$

$\Rightarrow$ $$\beta = 25$$

Power gain of amplifier is given as

$$\text{Power gain} = \beta^2 \times \frac{200}{100} = 1250$$ **Ans. (B)**

Sol. 7 Voltage gain of an amplifier with feedback is given as

$$G = \frac{A_V}{1 + \beta \cdot A_V}$$

Here feedback ratio $\beta = \dfrac{9}{100} = 0.09$, thus we have

$$10 = \frac{A_V}{1 + \dfrac{9}{100} \cdot A_V}$$

$\Rightarrow \qquad A_V = \dfrac{10}{0.1} = 100$ **Ans. (B)**

Sol. 8 This question is same as that of Q. 5. Students are advised to refer solution of Q. 5.   **Ans. (A)**

Sol. 9 This question is same as that of Q. 6. Students are advised to refer solution of Q. 6.   **Ans. (D)**

Sol. 10 This question is same as that of Q. 5. Students are advised to refer solution of Q. 5.   **Ans. (A)**

Sol. 11 Figure below shows the corresponding circuit of common emitter amplifier as described in the question.

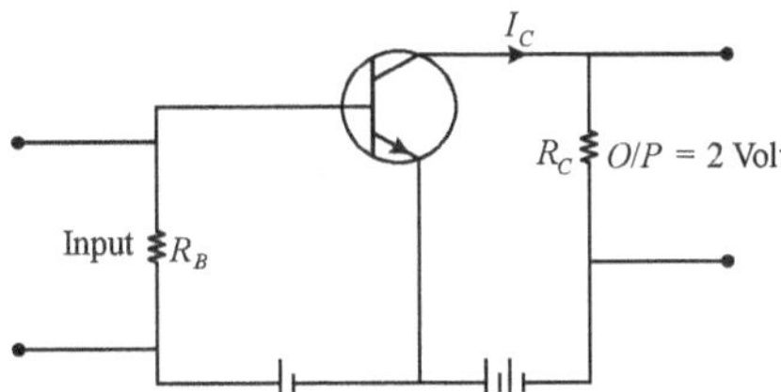

Collector current in above circuit is given as

$$I_C = \frac{2}{2 \times 10^3} = 10^{-3}\,A$$

Current gain of circuit is given as

$$\beta = \frac{I_C}{I_B} = 100$$

$\Rightarrow \qquad I_B = \dfrac{I_C}{100} = \dfrac{10^{-3}}{100} = 10^{-5}\,A$

Input voltage of the circuit is given as

$$V_i = I_B R_B = 10^{-5} \times 1 \times 10^3 = 10^{-2}\,V = 10\,mV$$

     Ans. (D)

Sol. 12 In region-I, transistor is in ON state and in region-III, transistor is in OFF state so it is to be used in region I and III for operating as a switch. In region-II it can be used as an amplifier in its active region.   **Ans. (B)**

Sol. 13 In common emitter amplifier current gain is given as

$$\beta = \frac{\Delta I_c}{\Delta I_B} = \frac{2 \times 10^{-3}}{40 \times 10^{-6}} = 50$$

Voltage gain of amplifier is given as

$$A_V = \beta \left(\frac{R_{out}}{R_{in}} \right) = 50 \left(\frac{4 \times 10^3}{100} \right) = 2000 \qquad \textbf{Ans. (D)}$$

Sol. 14 Voltage gain of a common emitter amplifier is given as

$$G = \frac{V_0}{V_i} = \frac{I_0 R_0}{V_i} = g_m R_0$$

$\Rightarrow \qquad G \propto g_m$

$\Rightarrow \qquad \dfrac{G}{G'} = \dfrac{g_{m_1}}{g_{m_2}}$

$\Rightarrow \qquad G' = \dfrac{2}{3} G$ **Ans. (A)**

Sol. 15 Output signal will be legging in phase by a phase angle 180° with output voltage given as

$$V_{Opeak} = A_v \times V_{Ipeak} = 300$$

$\Rightarrow \qquad V_{out} = 300 \cos(18t + \pi/3 + \pi)$

$\Rightarrow \qquad V_{out} = 300 \cos(15t + 4\pi/3)$ **Ans. (A)**

Sol. 16 As current amplification factor $\beta = 0.96$, voltage gain is given as

$$A_v = \beta^2 \frac{R_{out}}{R_{in}} = (0.96)^2 \times \frac{800}{192} = 4$$

Power gain of amplifier is given as

$$A_P = \beta^2 \frac{R_{out}}{R_{in}} = (0.96)^2 \times \frac{800}{192} = 3.84 \qquad \textbf{Ans. (A)}$$

Sol. 17 This question is same as that of Q. 11. Students are advised to refer solution of Q. 11.   **Ans. (B)**

Sol. 18 Voltage gain of amplifier is given as

$$A_V = \beta \frac{R_c}{R_b} = 100 \left(\frac{3}{2} \right) = 150$$

Power gain of amplifier is given as

$$A_P = \beta^2 \frac{R_c}{R_b} = (100)^2 \left(\frac{3}{2} \right) = 15000 \qquad \textbf{Ans. (C)}$$

Sol. 19 Figure below shows the direction of currents in the transistor terminals.

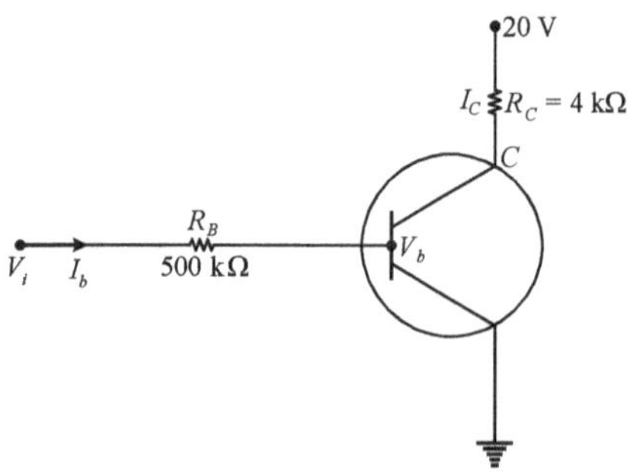

Collector current can be given as

$$I_C = \frac{(20-0)}{4\times10^3} = 5 \times 10^{-3} = 5 \text{ mA}$$

Input voltage in the circuit can be given as

$$V_i = V_{BE} + I_B R_B = 0 + I_B R_B$$
$$\Rightarrow \qquad 20 = I_B \times 500 \times 10^3$$
$$\Rightarrow \qquad I_B = \frac{20}{500\times10^3} = 40 \ \mu A$$

Common emitter current gain is given as

$$\beta = \frac{I_C}{I_b} = \frac{25\times10^{-3}}{40\times10^{-6}} = 125 \qquad \textbf{Ans. (D)}$$

Sol. 20 In transistor construction base region is made very thin and lightly doped so that it can allow maximum of majority charge carriers of emitter to pass through it to collector.

Ans. (A)

28.4 Logic Gates

Sol. 1 Given truth table is that of NAND gate.   **Ans. (C)**

Sol. 2 First gate is NAND gate followed by a an inverter (equivalent to NOT gate), The output of above logic circuit is given as
$$Y = \overline{X}$$
$$\Rightarrow \qquad Y = \overline{\overline{A.B}} \qquad\qquad [\text{As } X = \overline{A.B}\,]$$
$$\Rightarrow \qquad Y = A \cdot B$$
Thus final output corresponds to a AND gate.   **Ans. (A)**

Sol. 3 The truth table of OR gate is given as

A	B	Y
0	0	0
0	1	1
1	0	1
1	1	1

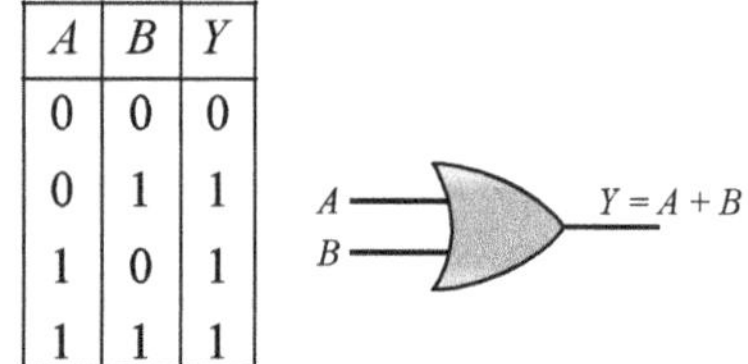

Thus for an OR gate, output is 1 if either input is one. Also if both the inputs are one then also output is one.   **Ans. (B)**

Sol. 4 In given waveforms we can see that output is high when both inputs A and B are high so the given logic circuit represents an AND gate.   **Ans. (A)**

Sol. 5 In the given logic circuit first gate is NOR gate and it is followed by an inverter (equivalent to NOT gate) so final output Y is given as

$$Y = \overline{\overline{A+B}} = A + B$$

This is equivalent to OR gate for which truth table is given as

A	B	Y
0	0	0
0	1	1
1	0	1
1	1	1

Ans. (C)

Sol. 6 In above circuit NOR gate is followed by an inverter and again a NOT gate so last two gates nullify the effect of each other so the circuit will act like NOR gate only. Intermediate outputs in above circuit are shown in below figure.

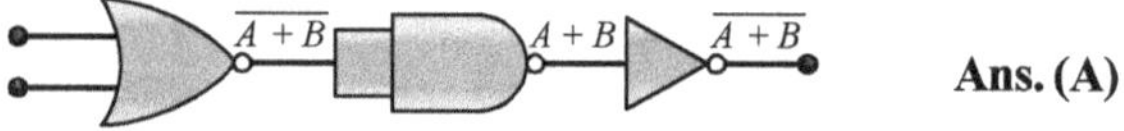

Ans. (A)

Sol. 7 The respective symbols of OR, NOT and NAND gates are shown below.

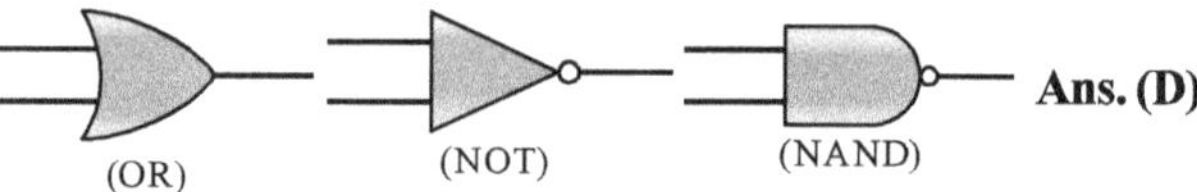

Ans. (D)

Sol. 8 To get output Y to be equal to 1 both inputs of the AND gate must be 1 for this C must be equal to 1 and output of OR gate can be 1 if either of A and B are equal to 1. Out of given options, only in option (D) it can happen.   **Ans. (D)**

Sol. 9 The respective symbols of AND, NAND and NOT gates are shown below.

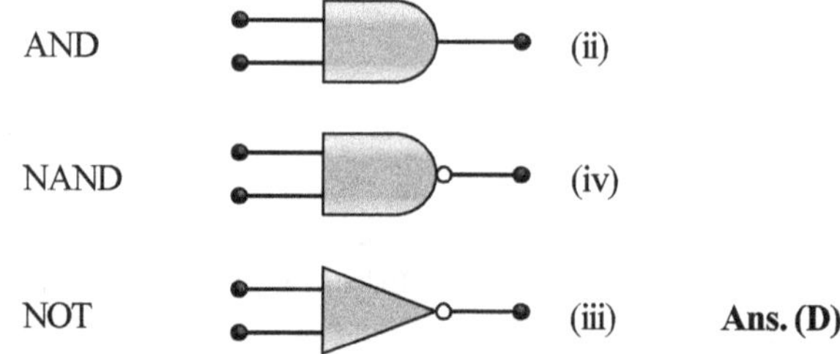

Ans. (D)

Sol. 10 In given waveforms we can see that output is high when either or both of inputs A and B are high so the given logic circuit represents an OR gate.   **Ans. (A)**

Sol. 11 To get the output $Y = 1$, both inputs of second NAND gate must not be 1. That means if $C = 0$ then A/B can have any values and output $Y = 1$. If $C = 1$ then A/B must both be equal to 1 to get $Y = 1$. Thus $Y = 0$ possible only for values of A, B and C given in option (A).   **Ans. (A)**

Sol. 12 Given logic circuit is a NAND gate followed by an inverter (NOT) gate which makes it equivalent to AND gate.   **Ans. (C)**

Sol. 13 For the output of above gate to be equal to 1, C must be equal to 1 and A/B must not be both 1. Thus out of given options, only option (D) is correct.   **Ans. (D)**

Sol. 14 Figures below shows the final outputs for the given conditional inputs. Figures also shows the intermediate output from the first gate.

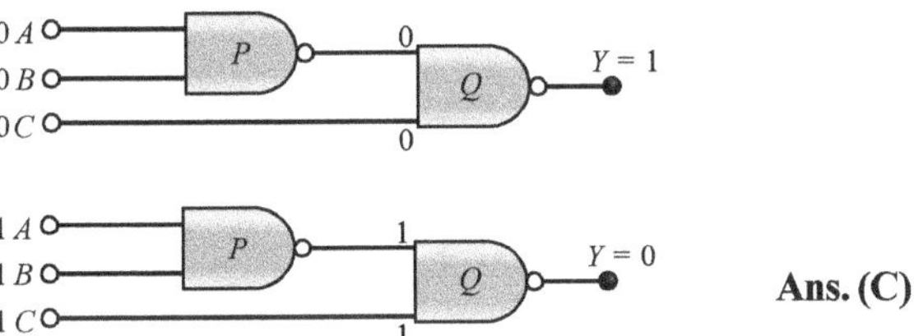

                    Ans. (C)

Sol. 15 In above circuit NOR gate is followed by an inverter and again a NOT gate so last two gates nullify the effect of each other so the circuit will act like NOR gate only. This question is also similar to Q. 6. Students are also advised to refer solution of Q. 6.   **Ans. (C)**

Sol. 16 Figure below shows the given logic circuit with intermediate outputs shown from these boolean expression of final output is given as

$$Y = (A \cdot \overline{B} + \overline{A} \cdot B)$$

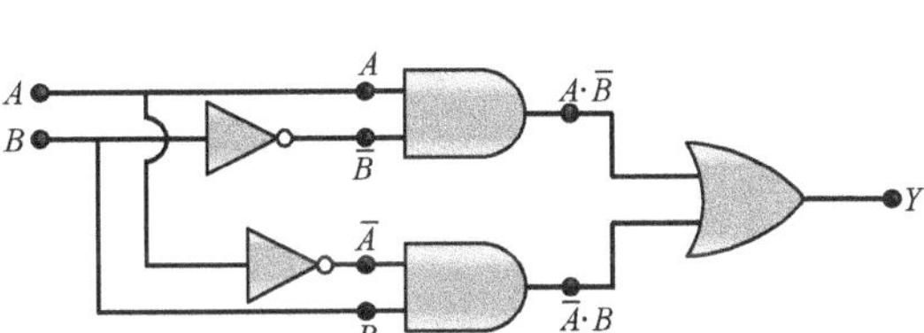

                    Ans. (B)

Sol. 17 From the given logic circuit LED will glow, when voltage across LED is high and this happens when either or both of switches are open. In case of both closed current will bypass through the shunt branch and LED will be short circuited.

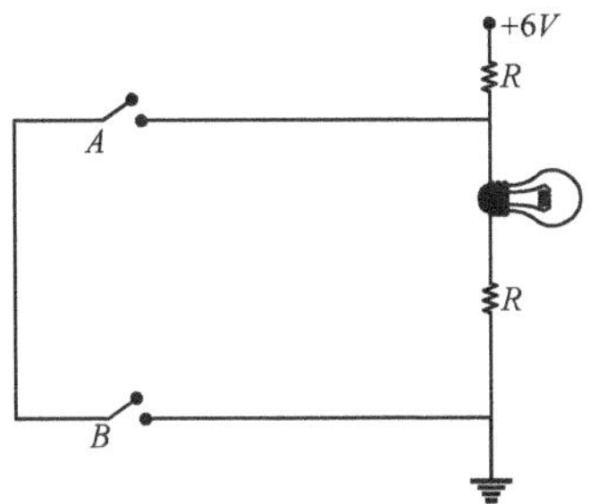

The truth table of this circuit can be written as

A	B	Y
0	0	1
0	1	1
1	0	1
1	1	0

This truth table is of NAND gate.   **Ans. (C)**

Sol. 18 The two inputs to NOR gate given in logic circuit are also inverted so boolean expression of final output is given as

$$Y = \overline{\overline{A} + \overline{B}} = \overline{\overline{A}} . \overline{\overline{B}} = A.B$$

Thus the final output represents AND gate. For this truth table is given as

A	B	Y
0	0	0
0	1	0
1	0	0
1	1	1

                    Ans. (B)

Sol. 19 For the given circuit the boolean expression for the output Y is given as

$$Y = A \cdot B + \overline{B \cdot C}$$

For the three time zones - 0 to t_1, t_1 to t_2 and t_2 to t_3 we analyze the output value Y for the inputs A, B and C as given in question, so we get

(i)   0 to t_1 $A = 0, B = 0, C = 1$

$Y = 0 \cdot 0 + \overline{0 \cdot 1} = 0 + 1 = 1$

(ii) t_1 to t_2 $A = 1, B = 0, C = 1$

$Y = 1 \cdot 0 + \overline{0 \cdot 1} = 0 + 1 = 1$

(iii) t_2 to t_3 $A = 0, B = 1, C = 0$

$Y = 0 \cdot 1 + \overline{1 \cdot 0} = 0 + 1 = 1$

Thus for all time zones output remains in high state (5V) so correct answer is option-(C).   **Ans. (C)**

Sol. 20 For the given logic circuit in question the boolean expression of output is given as

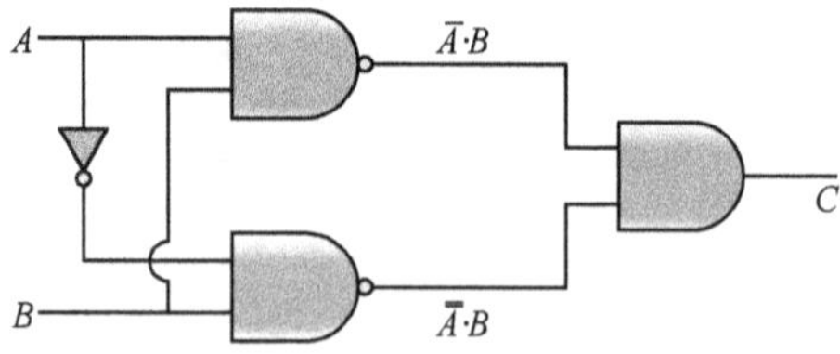

$$C = \overline{\overline{A \cdot B}} \cdot \overline{\overline{A} \cdot B}$$

Using De-Morgan Theorem, we have

$$C = \overline{A \cdot B + \overline{A} \cdot B}$$

$\Rightarrow \qquad C = \overline{B(A + \overline{A})} = \overline{B}$

Thus truth table of the given logic circuit is written as

A	B	C
0	0	1
0	1	0
1	0	1
1	1	0

Ans. (B)

* * * * *